Baroque and Rococo   Gauvin Alexander Bailey

ART&IDEAS

Baroque and Rococo   Gauvin Alexander Bailey

Φ

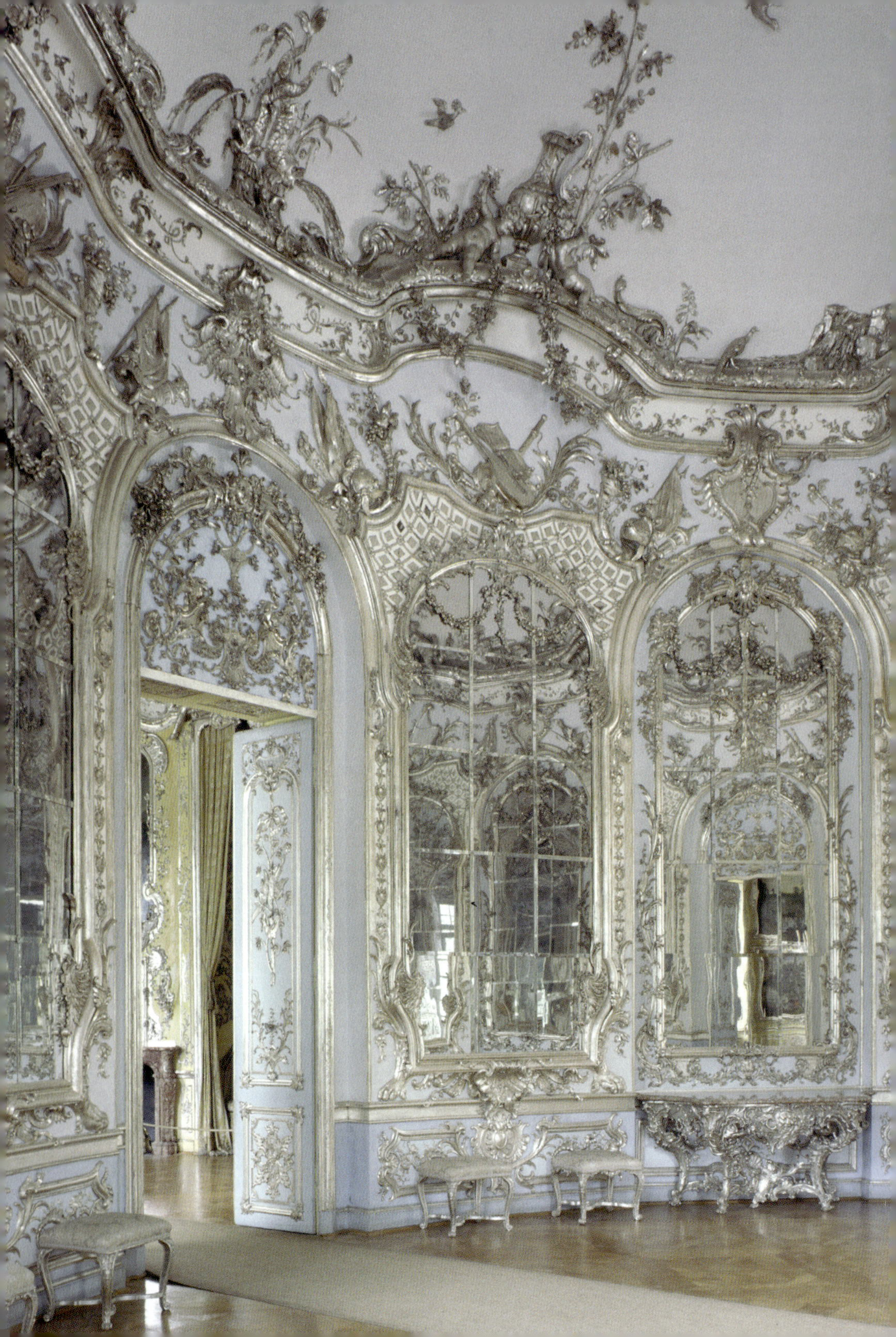

Introduction

The Baroque and its late variant the Rococo were the first truly global styles in the arts. Dominating more than two centuries of art and architecture in Europe, Latin America and beyond from c.1580 to c.1800, they were the first to focus so intensely on their impact on the viewer, and they owed much of their popularity and global scope to this visual allure. Born in the painting studios of Bologna and Rome in the 1580s and 1590s, and in Roman sculptural and architectural ateliers in the second and third decades of the seventeenth century, the Baroque spread swiftly throughout Italy and to Spain and Portugal, Flanders, France, Holland, England and Scandinavia, as well as to central and eastern European centres from Munich to Vilnius. The Rococo, a more refined, prosaic and capricious version of Baroque that originated in French domestic interiors in the first decades of the eighteenth century, followed a similar trajectory: eastward to Dresden, Vienna and St Petersburg, and westward to Valencia and Lisbon. Both styles also expanded – via the Iberian and French empires and the Dutch trading network – into the Americas and colonial Africa and Asia: to places such as Lima, Mozambique and Goa. In fact, Baroque and Rococo art and architecture cannot be fully appreciated without considering these Latin American, African and Asian variants, which will be treated in Chapter Seven.

Baroque (c.1580–c.1700) grew out of the Catholic Reformation, and is a powerfully persuasive style based on rhetoric and drama, whereas Rococo (c.1700–c.1800) began as décor, a whimsical, more intimate style that values ornamentation over structure and is more concerned with pastoral and exotic forms than with weighty theological or historical themes. Both styles are theatrical in spirit and inspiration. Adopting the dramatics, gesture and illusionistic perspective of the stage, they seek to engage and employ the human passions, from the mystical and ecstatic to the violent and erotic. They also favour action over stasis, so that sculptures no longer stand placidly within their niches – as they continued to do despite Michelangelo's experiments with having his figures push forwards from the wall (see 87) –

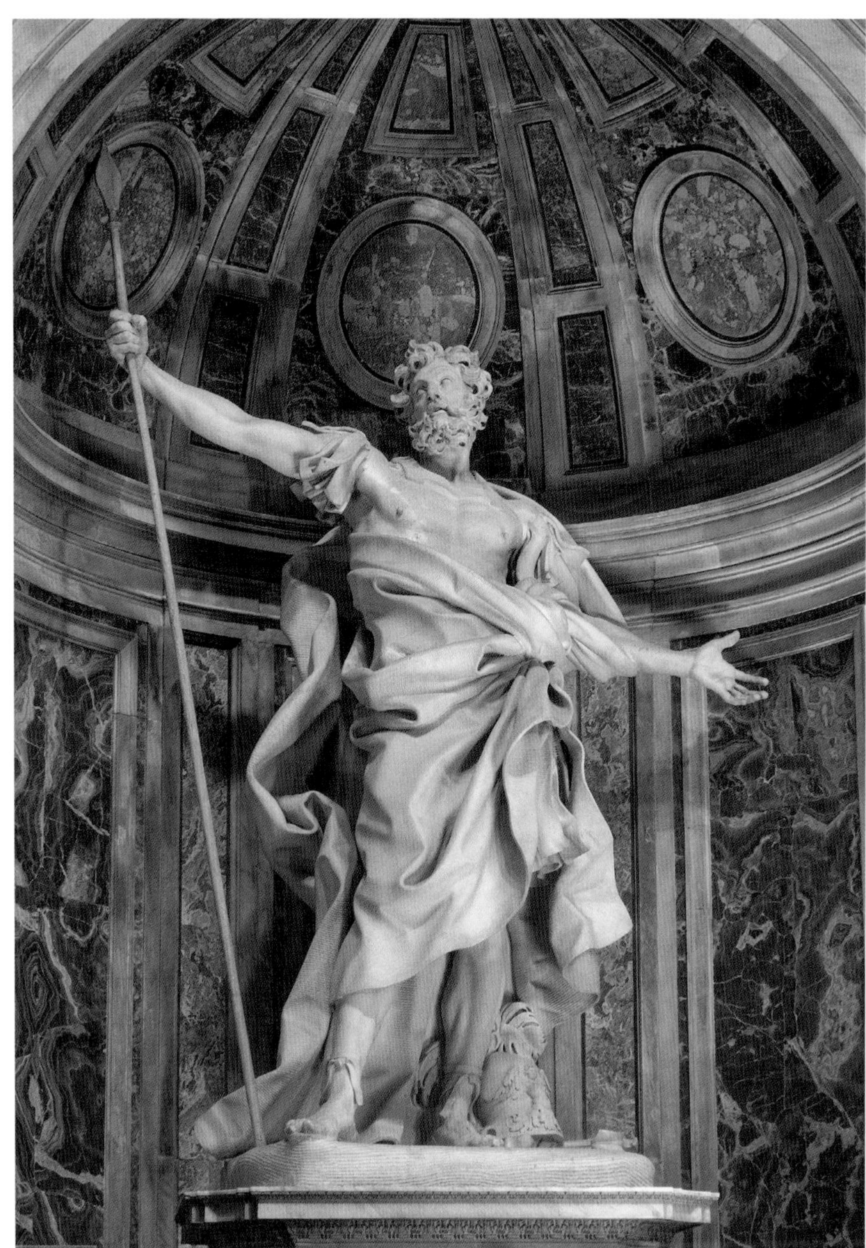

1.
Gianlorenzo Bernini,
Saint Longinus,
1629–38.
Marble; 4.5 m
(14 ft 9 in).
St Peter's
Basilica, Rome

but reach into the area beyond. This radical new concept of space is most dramatically demonstrated by Gianlorenzo Bernini's *Saint Longinus* in St Peter's Basilica in Rome (1). Carved of four massive blocks of marble, the Roman soldier who pierced Christ's side at the Cross suddenly throws his arms open to receive Christianity, thrusting his spear into the crossing of the basilica in response to a vision in the dome above. He is caught in mid-motion like a snapshot and at a moment of transformation, both favourite motifs of a style infatuated with the illusion of movement. Architecture also takes bold liberties with classical tradition. In the Baroque and Rococo, walls that in the Renaissance would have been flat and solid begin to bend, at times expanding and receding beyond the columns that frame them, like a giant lung. The counteracting concave and convex surfaces of the façade of Francesco Borromini's S. Carlo alle Quattro Fontane (3) give the walls the fluency of waves, opening up a variety of viewpoints and encouraging viewers to linger over individual carved details. Baroque and Rococo challenge our expectations about architecture's very stability.

In fact, the concealment of distinctions between tradition and innovation, reality and fantasy, lies at the very heart of Baroque and Rococo. Artists pushed materials to their limits, as when Bernini and his assistants transformed marble into windswept hair, supple flesh and lacelike leaves and twigs in the mythological sculpture *Apollo and Daphne* (2) – a quintessentially Baroque subject as it depicts both a transformation (the nymph metamorphoses into a tree to avoid the advances of the Greek god) and a dramatic capture of a single moment. The Dutch still-life painter Rachel Ruysch made lissome roses and glistening grapes so lifelike that we can almost smell them. In *Still Life with Roses* (4) her bouquet even attracts painted moths in a nod to the ancient Greek painter Zeuxis (fifth century BC), whose naturalistic depictions of fruit captivated real-life birds. This deliberate confusion between art and nature finds its ultimate expression in the Baroque garden, where grottos and hillocks are constructed of marble and plaster while the straight-edged, architectural topiaries and box-hedges are crafted of living plants. Such confusion enhances Ottaviano Diodati's gardens at the Villa Garzoni at Collodi (5), where well-tended yews in the parterres (formal gardens on level surfaces edged with hedges or gravel) of

**2.
Gianlorenzo
Bernini**, *Apollo
and Daphne*,
1622–5.
Marble;
2.43 m (8 ft)
Galleria
Borghese,
Rome

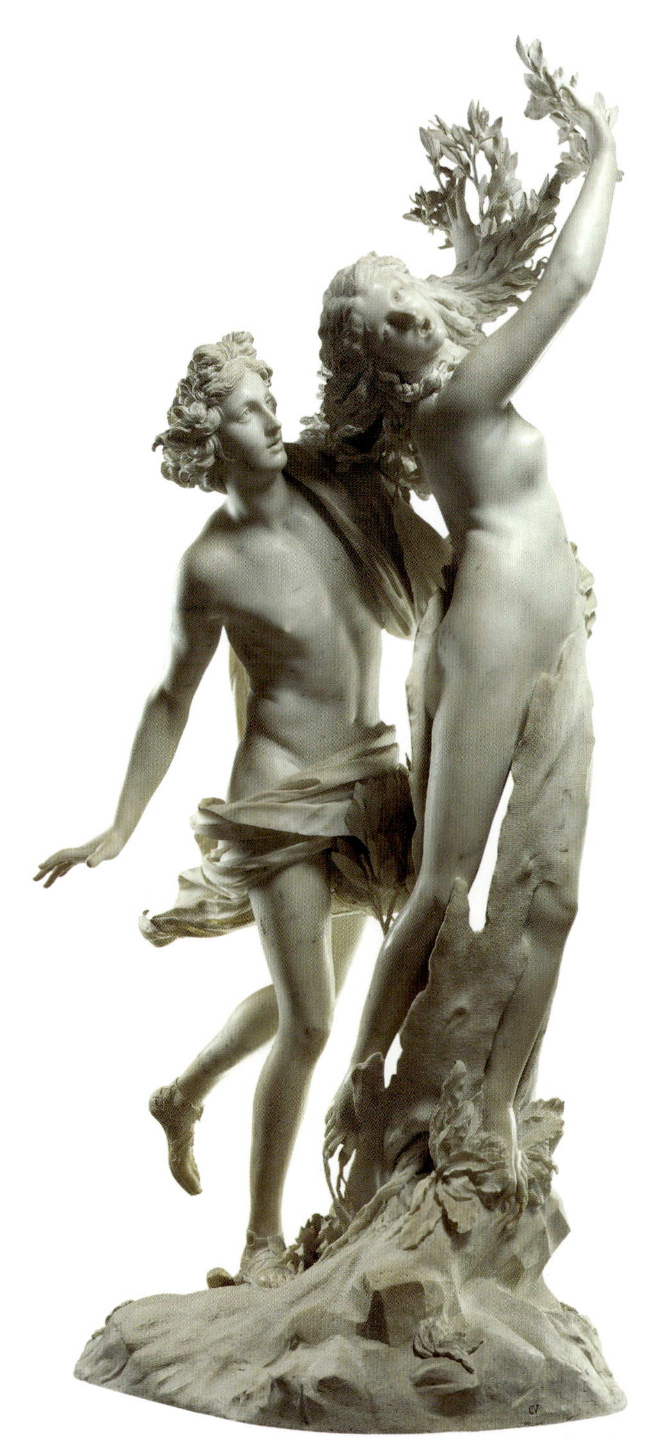

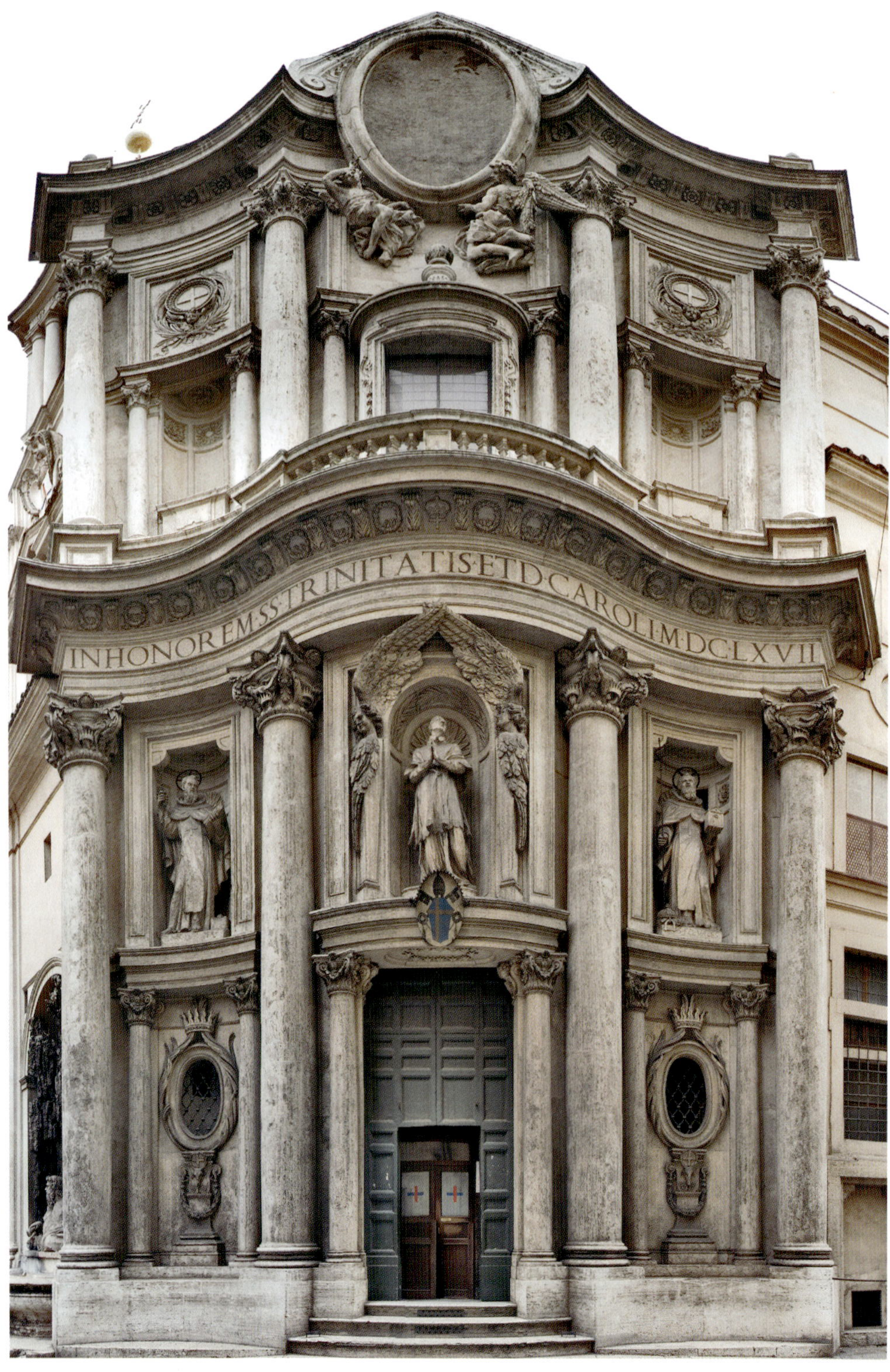

INHONOREM·SS·TRINITATISEID·CAROLI·M·DCLXVII

the lower garden contrast with artificial caves, rock faces and mosses in the cascading upper garden – all carved by hand.

Like the opera, a genre invented in the Baroque period, Baroque and Rococo visual arts unite a variety of media, with the principal designer at times more an impresario than a hands-on craftsman. During the Renaissance, painting, sculpture and architecture were divided not only by technique but also by function. This concept was celebrated in a literary debate called the *paragone* in which painting and sculpture (and to a degree architecture) were each championed as superior to – and therefore distinct from – the others. By

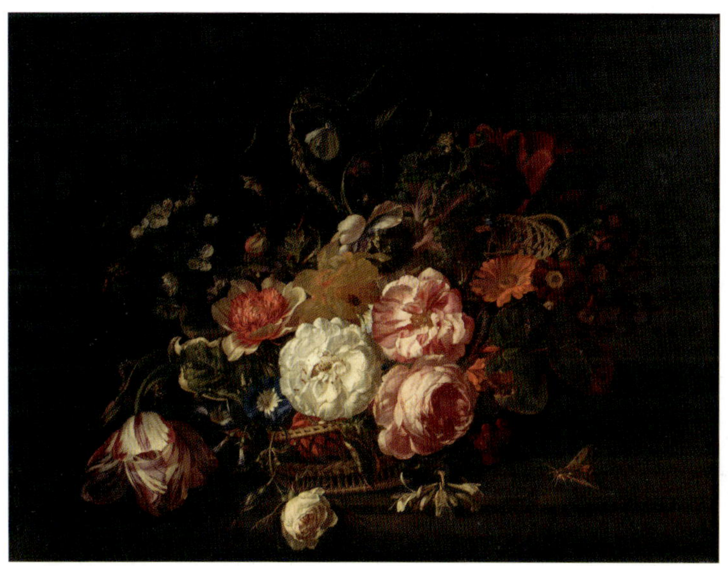

3.
Francesco Borromini, façade of S. Carlo alle Quattro Fontane, begun 1665, Rome

4.
Rachel Ruysch, *Still Life with Roses*, 1711. Galleria degli Uffizi, Florence

contrast, Baroque and Rococo arts joined forces to form a single, unified experience characterized by Filippo Baldinucci (1625–97) as a '*bel composto*' ('beautiful whole'), the subject of Chapter Three. Frescos, canvas paintings, stuccos and sculptures inside monuments like the Benedictine monastery at Einsiedeln renovated by Brother Caspar Moosbrugger and others (6) invade each other's space, crawling over frames and partitions to create a single integrated experience both literally and – through shared themes and mutual references – metaphorically. In architecture columns, pediments and friezes no longer merely connect but interconnect, as with the soaring façade of the pilgrimage cathedral of Santiago de Compostela by Fernando de Casos y

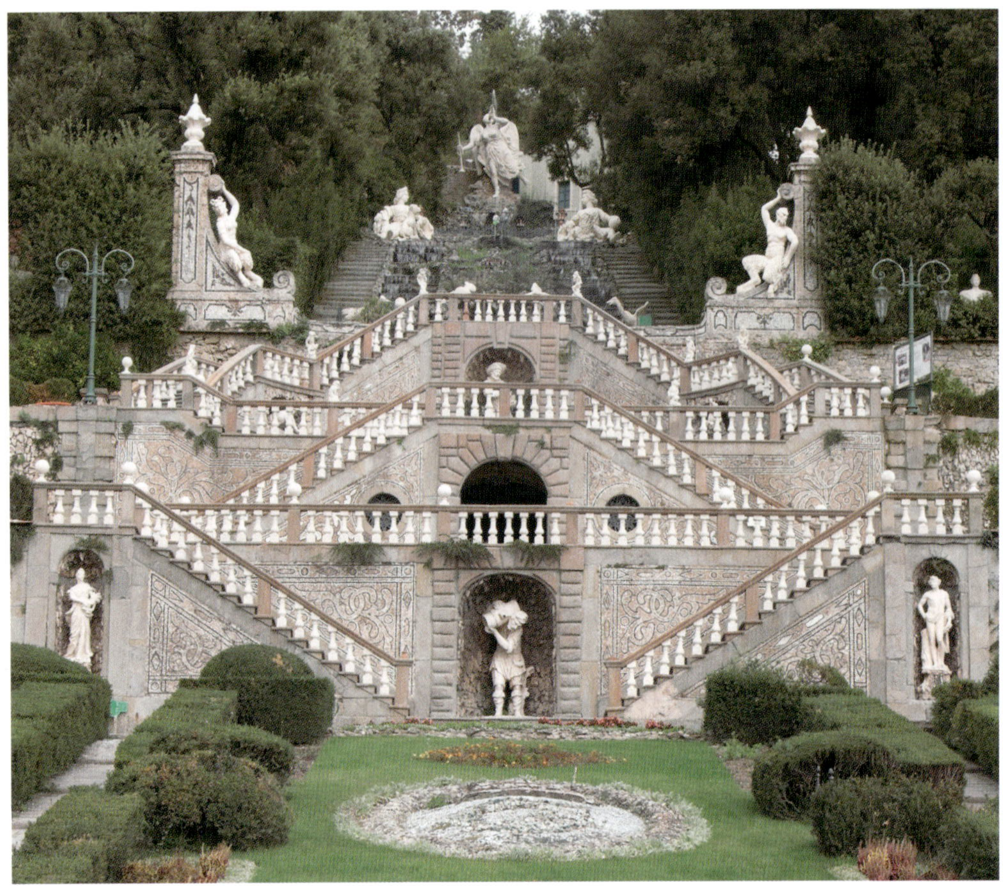

5.
**Ottaviano
Diodati**,
Villa Garzoni
gardens,
c.1650–1786,
Collodi (Italy)

6.
**Brother
Caspar
Moosbrugger**
and others,
Einsiedeln
Monastery,
after 1719
(Switzerland)

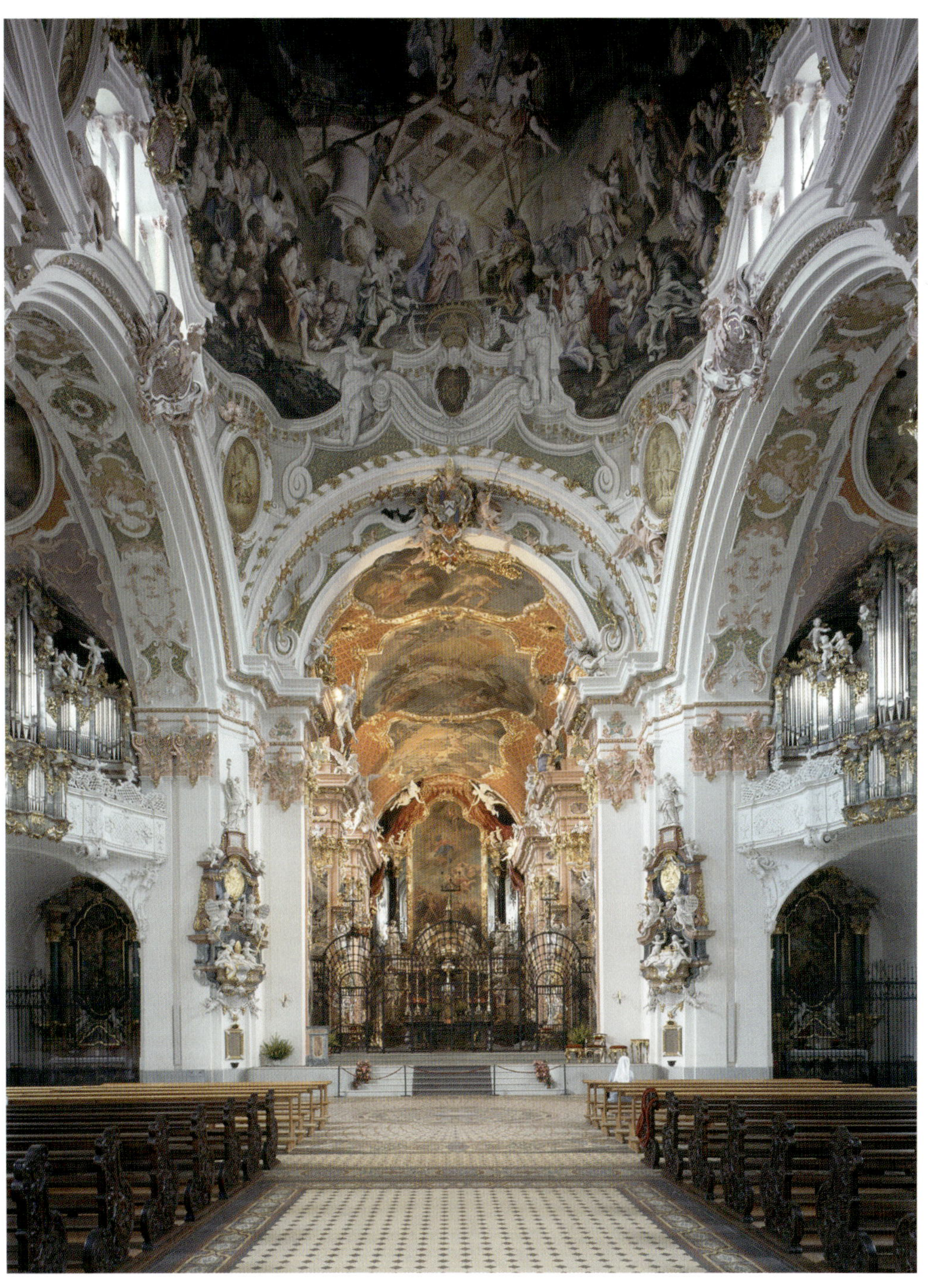

Novoa (8), in which the lines of the central window frame thrust past the upper part of the façade, breaking through the pediment and ending in a pavilion-like structure called an aedicule. The result – also underscored by the vertical linkage between the columns of the two lower storeys – emphasizes height, a Baroque concern that recalls Gothic cathedrals. The *bel composto* was by no means relegated to the visual arts: in its fullest manifestation it could encompass music and dance, as well as ephemeral forms such as waterworks and fireworks, the subject of Chapter Six. The media borrowed techniques from each other in a way that would have appalled the artists of the Renaissance, as when Bernini crafted flames and smoke from marble in his *Martyrdom of Saint Lawrence* (7), effects that the *paragone* debates had made the exclusive domain of painters. The aim was to surround, dazzle and astonish the viewer.

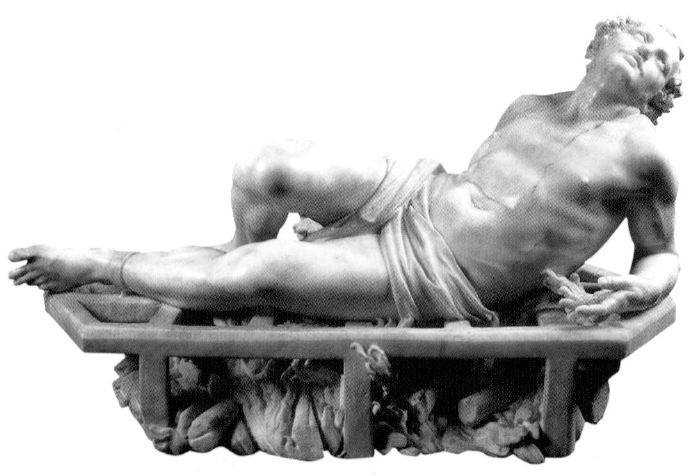

7.
Gianlorenzo Bernini, *Martyrdom of Saint Lawrence*, c.1618. Marble; 66 × 108 cm (26 × 43 in). Galleria degli Uffizi, Florence

8.
Fernando de Casos y Novoa, façade of the cathedral of Santiago de Compostela, 1738 (Spain)

Baroque and Rococo are notoriously difficult to define as styles, as they encompass more variety and contradiction than any before them. They embrace saturated decoration such as Francesco La Barbera's nave interior at the Gesù in Palermo (9), a paroxysm of multicoloured marble mosaics and three-dimensional reliefs called *marmi mischi* (mixed marble), or the portal of the palace of the Marquis de Dos Aguas in Valencia (10), which erupts into an organic mass of vegetal, animal and human figures, and anticipates Art Nouveau by 150 years. Yet the Baroque also encompasses the hushed despair of Caravaggio's *Flagellation of Christ* (see 38), a threnody over the tortured body of Christ, emerging twisted and broken from the blackness,

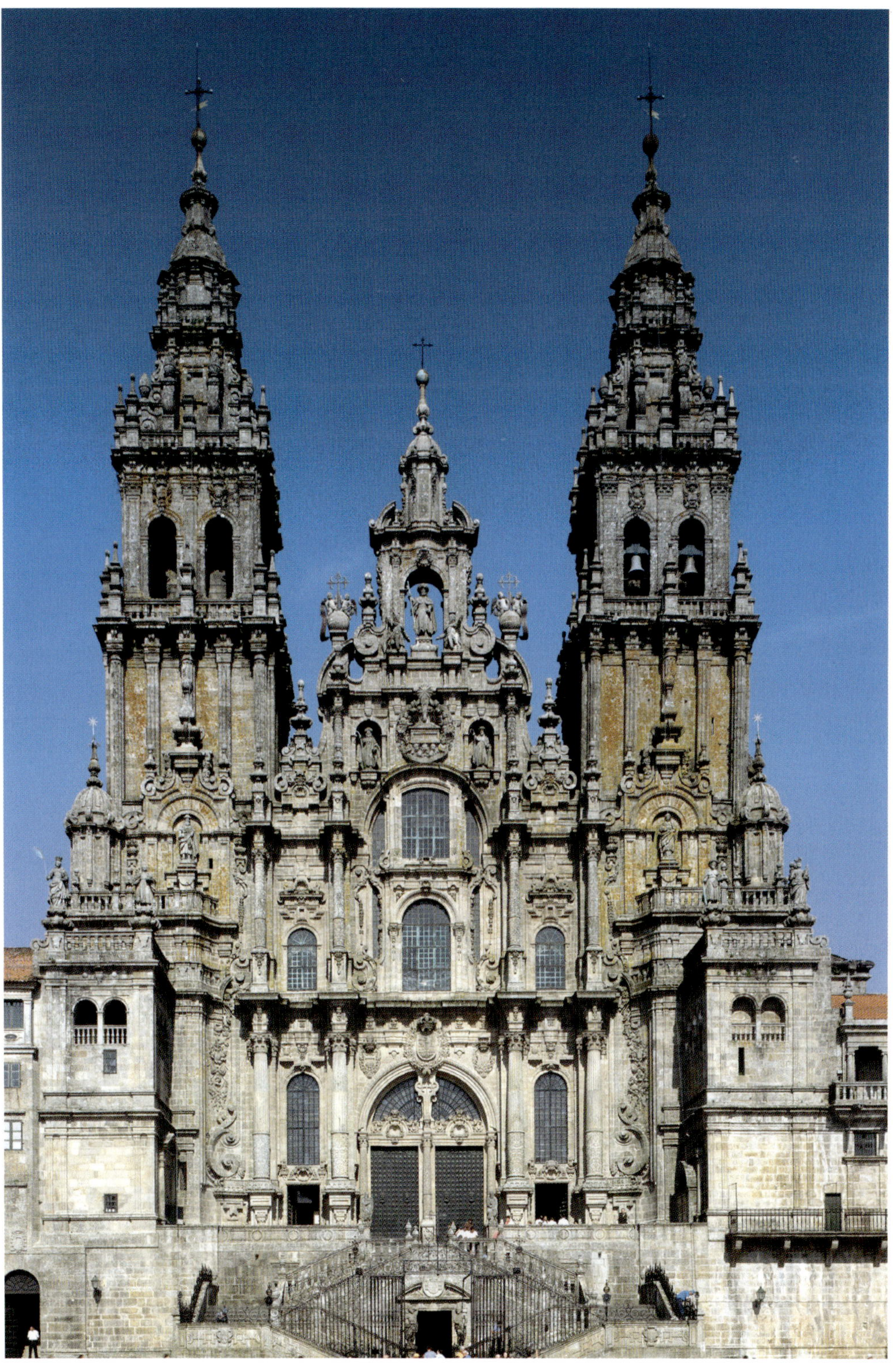

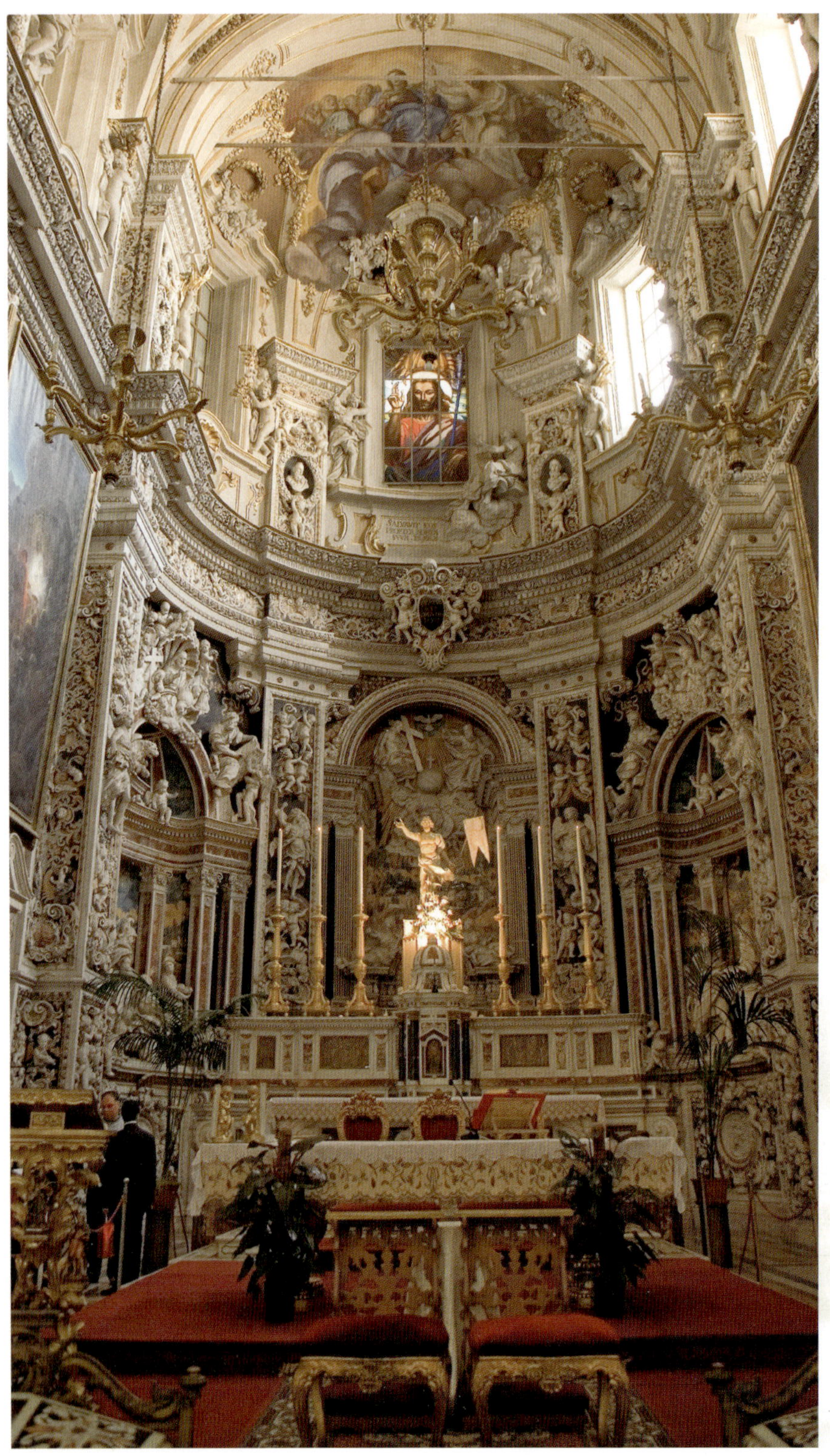

**9.
Francesco
La Barbera,**
interior of
the Gesù in
Palermo,
1622–1767
(Italy)

**10.
Hipólito
Rovira y
Brocandel,**
Palace of the
Marquis de
Dos Aguas,
1740–4,
Valencia
(Spain)

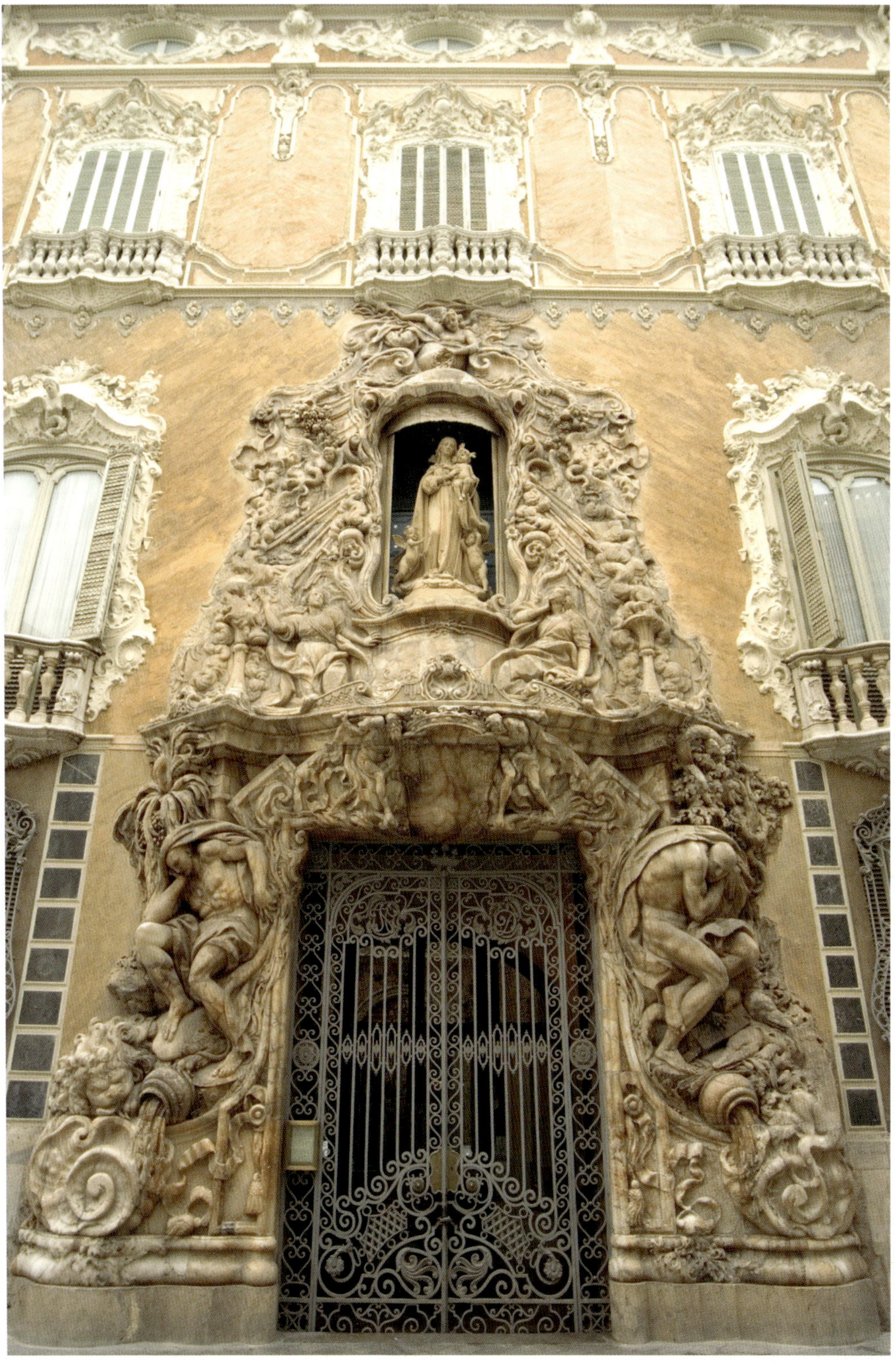

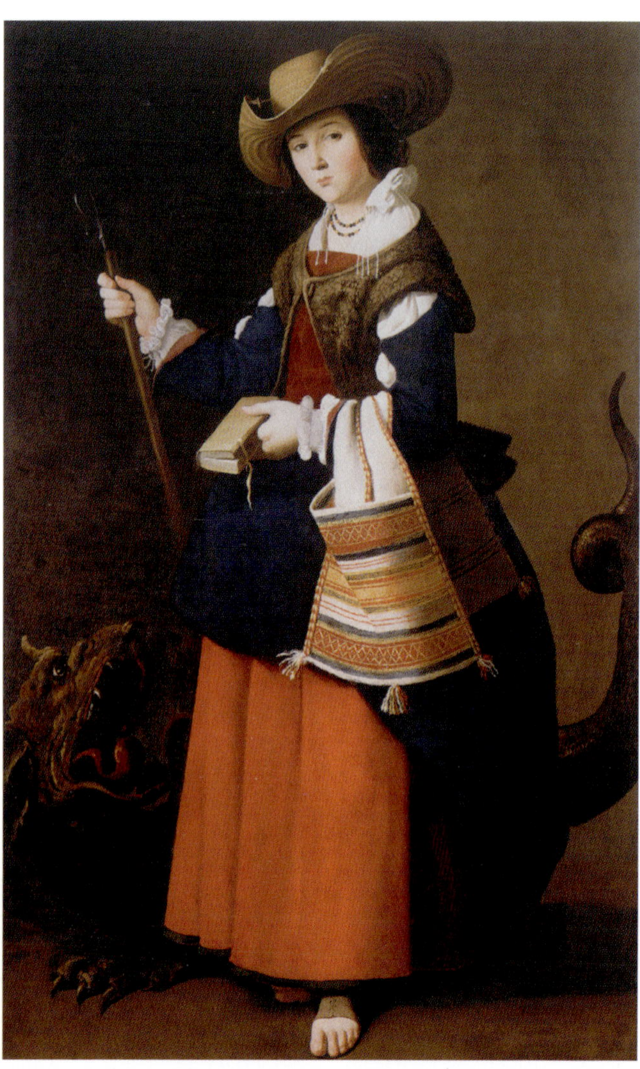

11.
Francisco de Zurbarán,
Saint Margaret,
c.1631. Oil
on canvas;
163 × 105 cm
(64 × 41 in).
National
Gallery,
London

or *Saint Margaret* (11) by the Spanish master Francisco de Zurbarán, in which a poised virgin martyr gazes resolutely at the viewer despite having being burnt, boiled, beheaded and swallowed by a dragon. Artworks from this period range from the mystical and transcendent, as in the gossamer stucco *Assumption of the Virgin* (see 103) by German sculptor Egid Quirin Asam in the apse of the pilgrimage church at Rohr, to the earthy and erotic, characterized by the lascivious glances and bared breast in the Dutch painter Matthias Stom's *Sarah Presenting Hagar to Abraham* (12). The latter demonstrates that sensuous skin and falling necklines were not limited to profane subjects, but were used to attract viewers to biblical scenes such as this episode from the Old Testament in which the heroine presents her handmaiden to the Prophet Abraham in hopes that she will bear him a son.

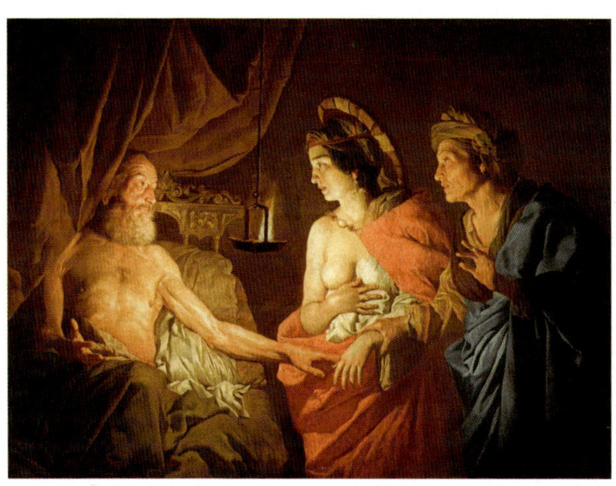

12.
Matthias Stom, *Sarah Presenting Hagar to Abraham*, c.1637. Oil on canvas; 150 × 204 cm (59 × 80 in). Musée Condé, Chantilly

Baroque and Rococo art appealed to many different audiences, whether urban mobs in large public squares or solitary pilgrims meditating in a lonely wayside chapel. Some works were aimed at intellectuals, such as the mythological frescos that adorned the ballrooms of the aristocracy or the challengingly erudite emblems and allegories that decorated Jesuit colleges and papal audience halls. One of the former is Annibale Carracci's ceiling fresco depicting the loves of the gods at the Palazzo Farnese in Rome, painted for Cardinal Odoardo Farnese (13). Based on an interpretation of Ovid's *Metamorphoses* by the Farnese family librarian Fulvio Orsini, its classical theme also complemented the family's collection of antique sculpture and championed their wealth and erudition. Considered the greatest fresco since Michelangelo's Sistine Ceiling (1508–12), Annibale's massive work traps its complex subject in an intricate web of feigned architecture, combining Michelangelo's *quadratura* (illusionistic architecture) with a conceit called *quadri riportati* (false frames painted around frescoed images to make them look like easel paintings). The result is a three-dimensional overlapping of frames, false stuccos, flesh-coloured nudes and bronze medallions that nevertheless preserves the fresco's unity as it builds up towards the central panel of the *Triumph of Bacchus and Ariadne*. Other works of art appealed to more popular audiences. The polychrome wooden crucifixion carved by Francesco Brunelli for the sacristy of the Gesù in Rome (15) belongs to a tradition of hyper-realistic sculpture more common in Spain and Latin America, and is meant to provoke and shock the viewer (see 94, 219). Even today the contrast between the suppleness of the flesh and the tortured pose and bloodied wounds in this dying Christ induces a visceral sense of pathos and sorrow.

Paradoxically, Baroque and Rococo's mass appeal helped destroy their reputations in the centuries that followed. The very terms 'Baroque' and 'Rococo' were originally derogatory, coined in the eighteenth and nineteenth centuries by critics who scoffed at their supposed aberrations and complexity, their lowbrow appeal, and – especially – the reckless ways in which they broke the rules of art. The term 'Baroque' first came to denote a period style in nineteenth-century Germanic literature, although it was certainly used earlier. It is not entirely clear where the word comes from, although theories include a Spanish term for an uncultured pearl or a memory device used in the Middle Ages to tackle a particularly abstruse kind of deductive reasoning – neither of them particularly flattering analogies. The celebrated nineteenth-century Swiss historian Jacob Burckhardt, who also helped coin the term 'Renaissance', used the term 'Baroque' to refer to the decomposition of Renaissance classicism. His countryman and pupil Heinrich Wölfflin was the first to make a clear historical distinction between the two styles in a book published in 1888. Less polemical, the term 'Rococo' can be traced to the French term *rocaille*, a kind of ornamental pebble or shell work found in aristocratic gardens, as seen in this fanciful grotto at the Palácio de Queluz, a country palace begun in 1747 outside Lisbon by the Infante Dom Pedro (later Dom Pedro III), formed of shells, leaves, scrolls, flowers and even birds (14).

**13.
Annibale Carracci**,
The Loves of the Gods,
1597–1602.
Fresco; Palazzo Farnese, Rome

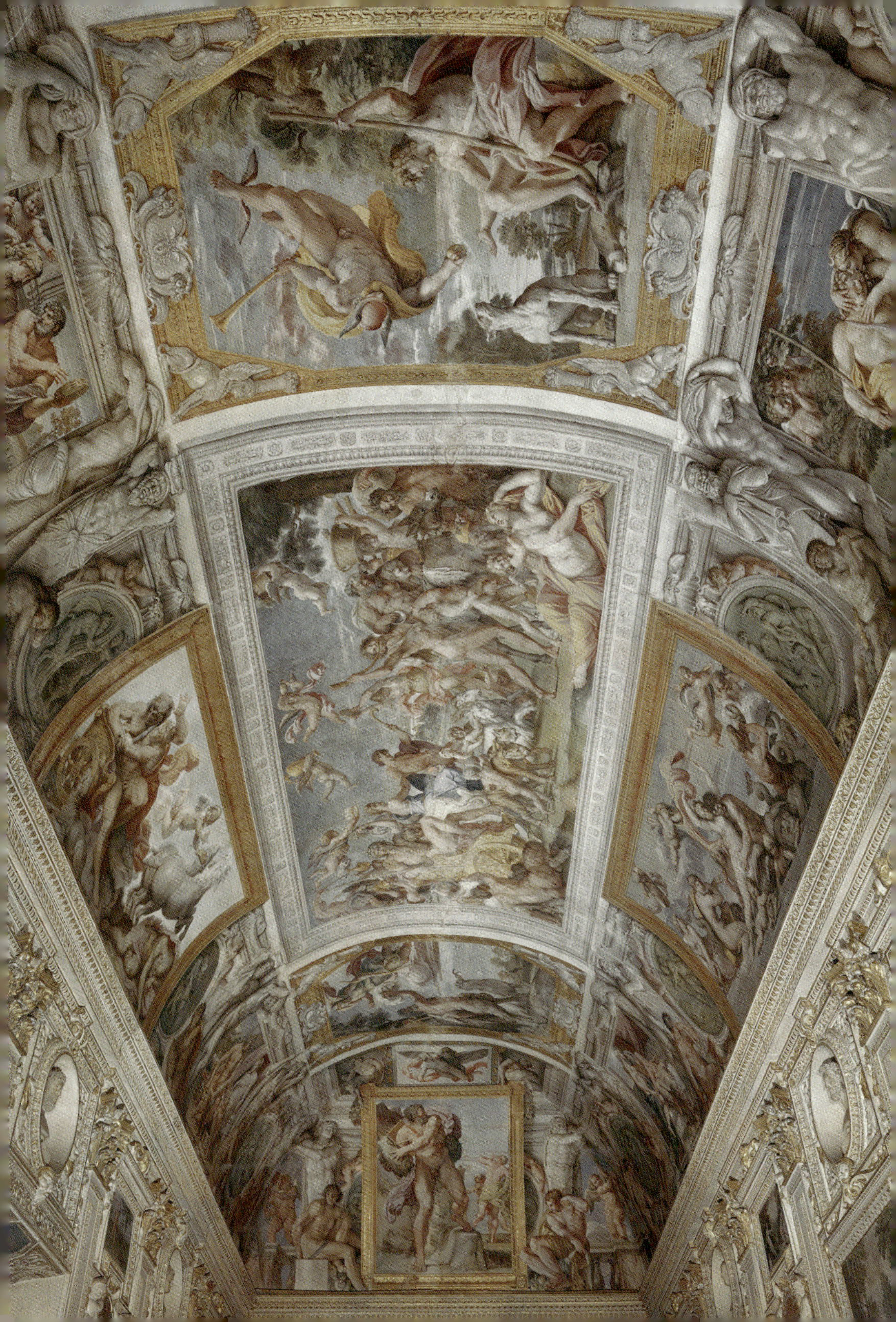

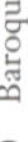

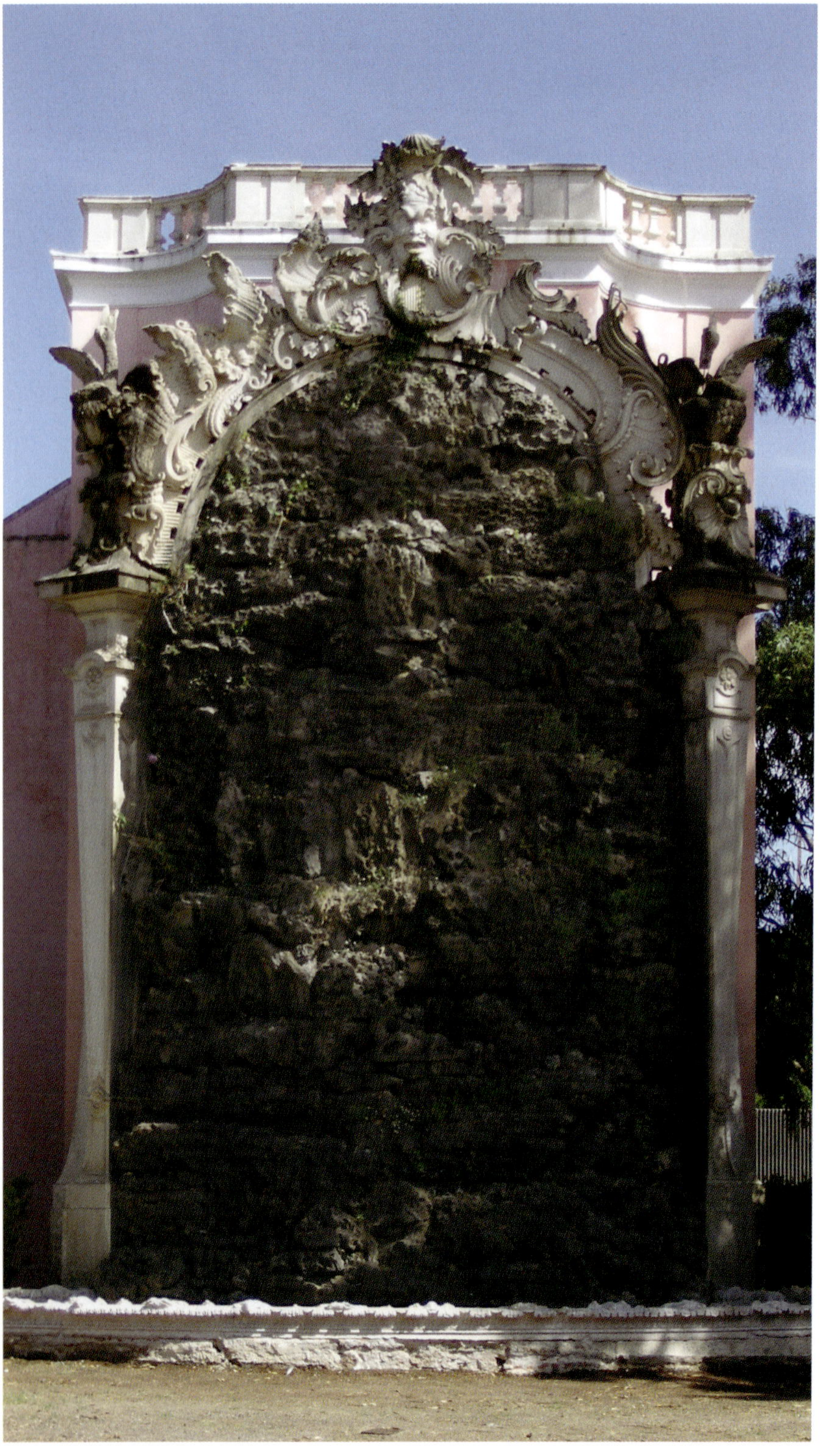

**14.
Jean-Baptiste
Robillon,**
grotto at
Palácio de
Queluz,
begun 1747
(Portugal)

Although no longer pejorative, the terms 'Baroque' and 'Rococo' are far from perfect today. To begin with, neither was contemporary – none of the artists treated in this book knew that they were 'Baroque' or 'Rococo' artists. Second, the terms insinuate a monolithic, institutional sameness that obscures the variety and originality that make these styles so fascinating in the first place (at the beginning of the twentieth century the Baroque was known as the 'eclectic style'). Some art historians would be happy to abandon period labels altogether, opting for something more neutral such as 'seventeenth- and eighteenth-century art' or 'the art of the early Modern era' – the latter confusing to most people, who might reasonably suppose an 'early Modern' artist to be Picasso or Magritte, not Bernini or Caravaggio. But despite their limitations the terms 'Baroque' and 'Rococo' are deeply ingrained in the popular imagination and art-historical discipline, and they give us a convenient way to categorize a wide spectrum of artworks created in a particular time and in specific parts of the world that share stylistic and ideological commonalities. Another use of the terms can be abandoned without a second thought. Using the lower case, 'baroque' and 'rococo' were employed to describe stages in any art tradition in which a highly regulated and austere 'classical' episode gave way to styles that were more decorative, inventive and rebellious. Such are the 'baroque' stage of the sculpture of Tang Dynasty China (AD 618–907) or the late Classic Maya (ninth century AD), or the better-known 'baroque' phase of Hellenistic sculpture in Greece and Asia Minor (c.330–30 BC). These types of labels are based on coincidental similarities only, a correspondingly profuse kind of ornamentation or a taste for the bizarre and exotic. Not only is their use in this context anachronistic, but it can be misleading: in one notorious incident they inspired scholars to trace the origins of European Baroque to Hindu temple architecture, as imported via Lisbon by Portuguese explorers.

Baroque and Rococo art and architecture provoke passionate responses even today. Since the best-known proponents of the styles were major institutions, whether the papacy, powerful Catholic religious orders such as the Jesuits, or absolutist monarchs like Louis XIV of France, the styles have traditionally been equated with dogmatism, tyranny, decadence and political manipulation – especially in the twentieth century, when Baroque became associated anachronistically with the much more nefarious term 'propaganda'. As scholars learn more about the period, we recognize that much of the driving force behind Baroque and Rococo came from other quarters, not least from the artists themselves, and that they represent the goals of a much wider spectrum of humanity than previously acknowledged, including lay religious groups called confraternities, merchants and tradesmen, widows and nuns, pilgrims and even the urban poor.

The dubious reputations of Baroque and Rococo today also owe something to the epoch that created them – one of the most turbulent in European history and a far cry from the pretty scrolls, lively colours and optimism of much of its art and architecture. The seventeenth century was a time of economic, military, religious and social crisis, worsened by natural disaster. Despite having survived the Renaissance largely intact, the medieval feudal system, with its long-entrenched reciprocity between peasant, aristocracy and monarch, unravelled completely. Under that system the monarch granted land, or fiefs, to the nobility, who in turn offered military service to the monarch in the form of vassals who were given smaller concessions of land. The vassals then protected the peasants working their lands in exchange for produce and coinage. In the seventeenth century the gentry, no longer constrained by that sense of responsibility, increasingly avoided military service, leaving the burden of enlistment to the heavily taxed peasants themselves. The gentry also forced the peasantry out of the economic equation at every turn, buying up huge tracts of land to be farmed on a large scale and at a profit, monopolizing their produce and selling it at inflated prices to commoners, operating as absentee landlords with little concern for their tenants, and embracing the glittering world of the urban courts instead of their social responsibilities.

The ultimate affront to the feudal system was absolutism, a uniquely seventeenth-century political institution. Best illustrated by France and Spain, an absolutist state is one in which the monarch holds unconditional power over his or her subjects through a self-proclaimed divine right to rule. Such monarchs supported themselves by limiting the power of the nobility, while – paradoxically – relying on the increasing supremacy of aristocratic

land ownership and revenue. Instead of expecting the nobility to provide
military service (which ran the danger of influencing military decisions), the
monarchs created professional standing armies loyal only to themselves, and
in France King Louis XIV went so far as to require the landed gentry to leave
their estates and live at court in his city-sized palace of Versailles (see 135),
where they could be better observed – and controlled – in a manipulative
system of court ceremonial. Many smaller monarchies copied the French, as
when the Bourbon king Charles III of Naples began his gargantuan palace
at Caserta in 1752 (it was largely completed by Ferdinand I in 1774 from

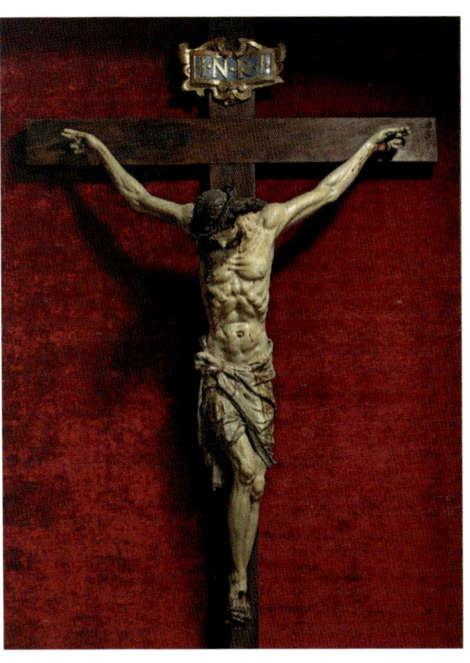

15.
Francesco
Brunelli,
Crucifixion,
c.1600. Wood;
life sized.
Church of the
Gesù, Rome

plans by Luigi Vanvitelli), a 1,200-room monstrosity with façades 247 metres
(810 ft) long and 36 metres (118 ft) high, built with the help of 2,861
workers, including convicts and galley slaves as well as camels and elephants
(16). Charles did not have to worry about moving the landed gentry to
Naples – a former Spanish colony – as the Spanish viceroys had already done
the job for him. Absolutism gave birth to modern notions such as the nation
state and the capital city, and it created a highly centralized network of power
and information that increasingly restricted individual freedom and benefited
the few. The landless masses had no alternative but to join the ranks of the

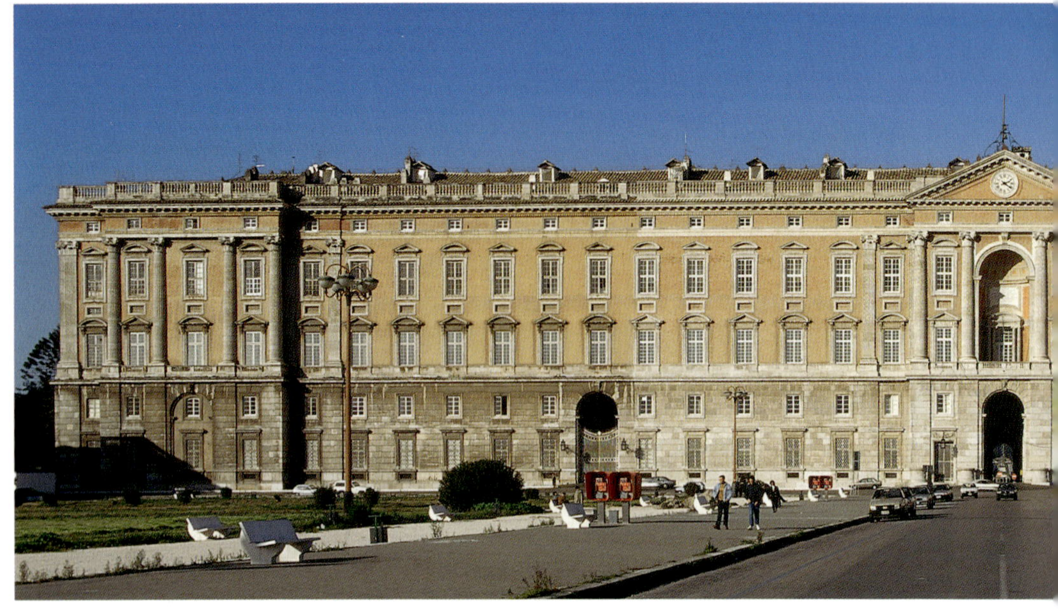

urban poor in the increasingly choked cities. Absolutism also allowed the monarchies to indulge in crippling fiscal irresponsibility, so that both France and Spain nearly bankrupted themselves by the later seventeenth century.

People faced many other crises during the seventeenth and eighteenth centuries, some physical and others spiritual. One of the most devastating was the Bubonic Plague. Although the Black Death of 1347–50 was the most famous pestilence in Western history, this scourge reappeared with unpredictable and fatal regularity, striking somewhere in Europe – especially Italy – every year until 1670 and less frequently well into the eighteenth century, and it had a profound impact on the arts (see Chapter One). The beginning of modern science, particularly advances in astronomy and theories of infinity and planetary motion, was also seen as a calamity by the Catholic and Protestant faithful, because these new discoveries challenged some of the most fundamental bases of Church doctrine. The first salvo came from the Polish astronomer Nicholas Copernicus, who in 1543 challenged the Church belief that the sun revolved around Earth, a position later championed by the Italian astronomer Galileo Galilei in a 1613 study on sunspots, which eventually brought him up before the Inquisition and subjected him to house arrest from 1633. Giordano Bruno

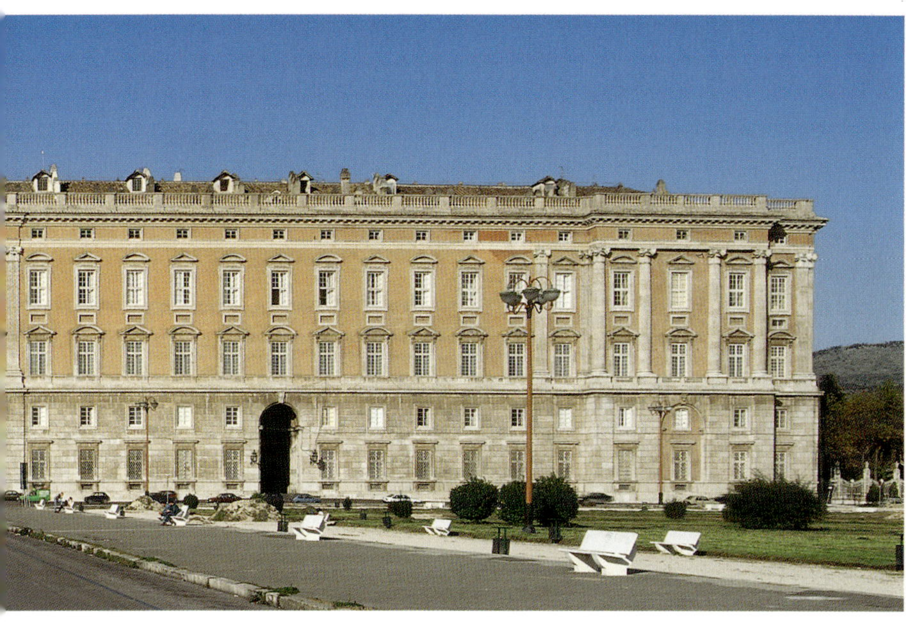

16.
Luigi Vanvitelli, Caserta Palace, 1752–74 (Italy)

– burnt at the stake in 1600 for his then heretical beliefs – went further by proposing the idea of infinity and a multiplicity of worlds, and Johann Kepler developed the laws of planetary motion. The impact of these discoveries on the Catholic Church in particular can be gauged by the severity of its punishments. For the people at large, however, it created yet another alternative to Church teachings, one that would lead to even greater social dissent and existential introspection.

But the greatest crisis of all was war. The Baroque period witnessed nearly constant warfare and rioting, often as a direct result of the struggle between Catholics and Protestants (see Chapter One). At the dawn of the era in 1572, a Catholic mob slaughtered about 3,000 Huguenot Protestants during a wedding in Paris in what became known as the St Bartholomew's Day Massacre. The worst conflict of the seventeenth century – its devastation of central Europe is comparable to the World Wars of the twentieth century – was the Thirty Years War (1618–48), in which religious fighting in the Germanic principalities of the Holy Roman Empire ignited a regional battle that pitted Habsburg Austria and Spain against France, and Catholic powers against Protestant Sweden, Denmark and Holland. The war's interacting political and religious agendas were epitomized by Count-Bishop Christoph

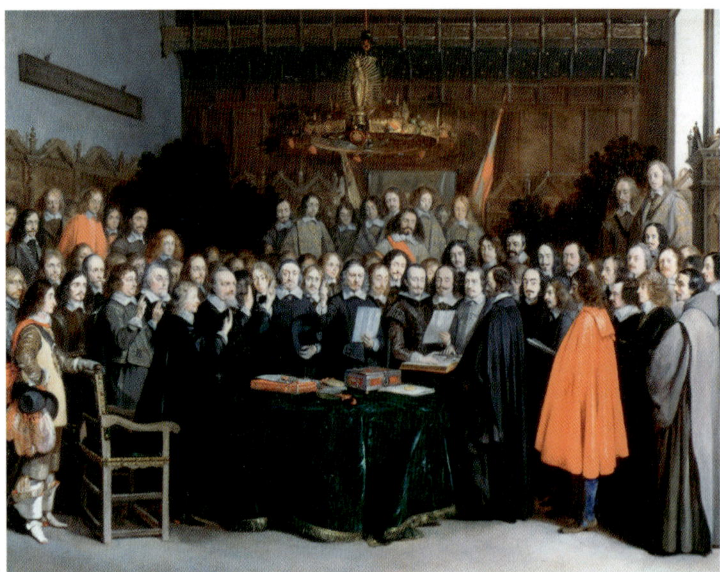

Bernhard von Galen of Münster – a religious leader and defender of Catholicism whose fondness for artillery earned him the nickname 'Bombing Bernhard'. The Thirty Years War had a direct impact on the arts, as the destruction and famine left in its wake ensured that major architectural projects would not resume until the end of the century, most of them in the next. The Peace of Westphalia of 1648, signed in Bernhard's home town, granted private religious freedom in the German principalities, and government bodies became non-sectarian. In a contemporary painting of the peace, an example of a Dutch group portrait called a *doelenstuk* (see Chapter Two), Gerard Terborch evokes – through elegant postures, calm facial expressions and a rigidly symmetrical composition – a sense of order a world apart from the actual bickering and infighting that took place when eighty contentious officials swarmed the claustrophobic Münster council chamber (17). The Dutch officials (on the left) and the Spanish (on the right) swear the oath, the former with their right hand raised and the latter touching the cross and Bible – as a witness Terborch places himself at the far left in the foreground.

One of the most significant results of the crises of the seventeenth century was the mass migration of the disenfranchised into cities, causing crowding and widespread urban homelessness on a scale not seen since the Roman Empire. Fuelled by the availability of printed broadsheets and pamphlets,

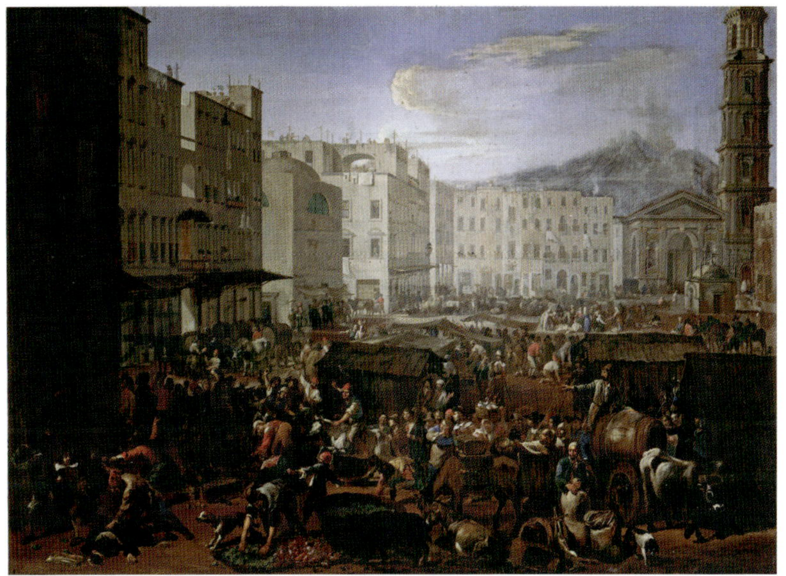

urban mobs became increasingly politicized and critical of the rulers and nobility: the seventeenth century was punctuated by organized riots and rebellions and the first popular execution of a monarch (the English king Charles I in 1649). The turbulent atmosphere of Baroque cities is vividly captured in *The Revolt of Masaniello* by Michelangelo Cerquozzi, the only Italian member of the *Bamboccianti*, a group of northern European painters working in Italy who specialized in scenes of everyday life, full of beggars and bandits (18). A fisherman, Masaniello (Tommaso Aniello) led a rebellion in 1647 against Naples' Spanish rulers in reaction to oppressive taxes on fruit, a staple of the urban poor. In this animated scene, Masaniello on his white horse leads a group of armed fruit vendors and bystanders in an attack on the customs officers in the Piazza del Mercato, while assailants in the left foreground butcher two customs officers. As it happened, even Masaniello could not tame the mob, who beheaded him a few months later. Baroque Rome, Naples and Toledo (as dangerous as the New York Bronx in the 1970s or Rio de Janeiro today) featured public lynching, armed children, rampant banditry – some bandits even posed as pilgrims – and widespread prostitution and gambling. Consequently, these cities were also the scene of frequent and gruesome public executions, which served as models for the biblical murders and martyrdoms depicted with a keen eye for detail by such artists as Caravaggio or Jusepe Ribera (see 33, 37).

In this restless age, when people across Europe were at once fearful and sceptical, the arts provided a sense of peace and order through their rhetoric of humanity and divine justice, as well as by using perspective and other theatrical or optical effects to manipulate viewers' visual and emotional experiences. The chapters that follow will explore the manifold ways the arts accomplished these goals. But first I would like briefly to note an event that occurred at the dawn of the Baroque that can be seen as the prototype for the Baroque's exploitation of peoples' surroundings. Pope Sixtus V, frustrated by the crowded, irrational medieval city that Rome had become, launched an immense urban renewal project in 1585 that forever changed the face of the city and inspired urban restructurings throughout Europe in the seventeenth and eighteenth centuries (see Chapter Four). He levelled neighbourhoods to build palaces, restored dilapidated churches and erected an extensive system of aqueducts to supply drinking water to his subjects. But more significant are the wide avenues his architect Domenico Fontana sliced through the fabric of the city to unite the early Christian basilicas – popular pilgrimage sites and a major source of Rome's revenue – into a network of straight lines. These avenues extended outwards from the church of S. Maria Maggiore towards the other principal basilicas of the city, allowing for easy access by crowds during Lent, Holy Week and Jubilee years, and imposing a new rationality onto peoples' experience of the city by directing their attentions towards specific foci. The ideological foundations of Sixtus' urban renewal were most conspicuous in his decision to raise Egyptian obelisks as focal points in the city's principal squares, such as the one in the Piazza del Popolo (19). The Roman emperors had transported the obelisks into the city as a symbol of Rome's imperial might, and Sixtus incorporated them into his urban renewal as a proclamation of Christian triumph – but not before the pope performed a ceremony in which each was exorcised from its pagan past and crowned with a bronze cross. Although imposed from above, Sixtus' plan gave the inhabitants of one of Europe's most turbulent cities an illusion of safety and a faith in the power of its rulers, an effect sought in later centuries by democracies and dictators alike, whether in Pierre L'Enfant's utopian plan for Washington, DC in 1791, Baron Haussmann's introduction of gracious boulevards into Napoleon III's Paris in 1852, or Albert Speer's unfulfilled plans for Adolf Hitler's Berlin in 1937–9.

**19.
Piazza del
Popolo**, Rome

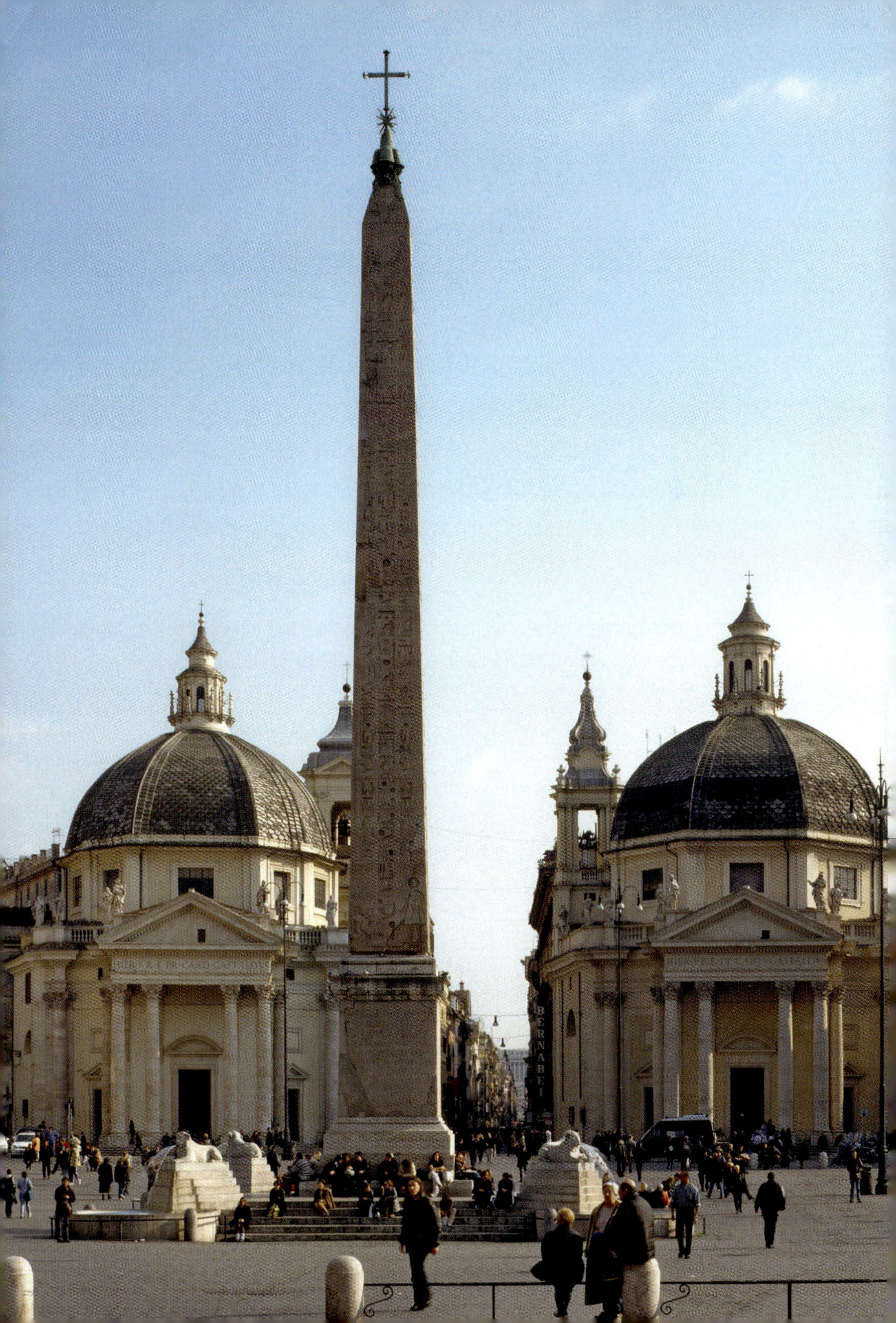

Pictures at War   Painting and the Catholic Reformation

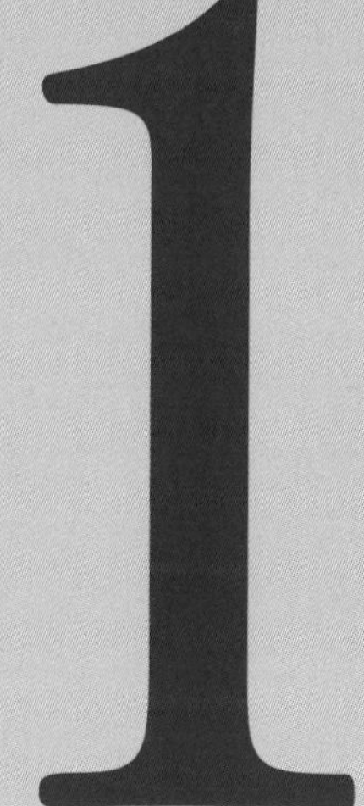

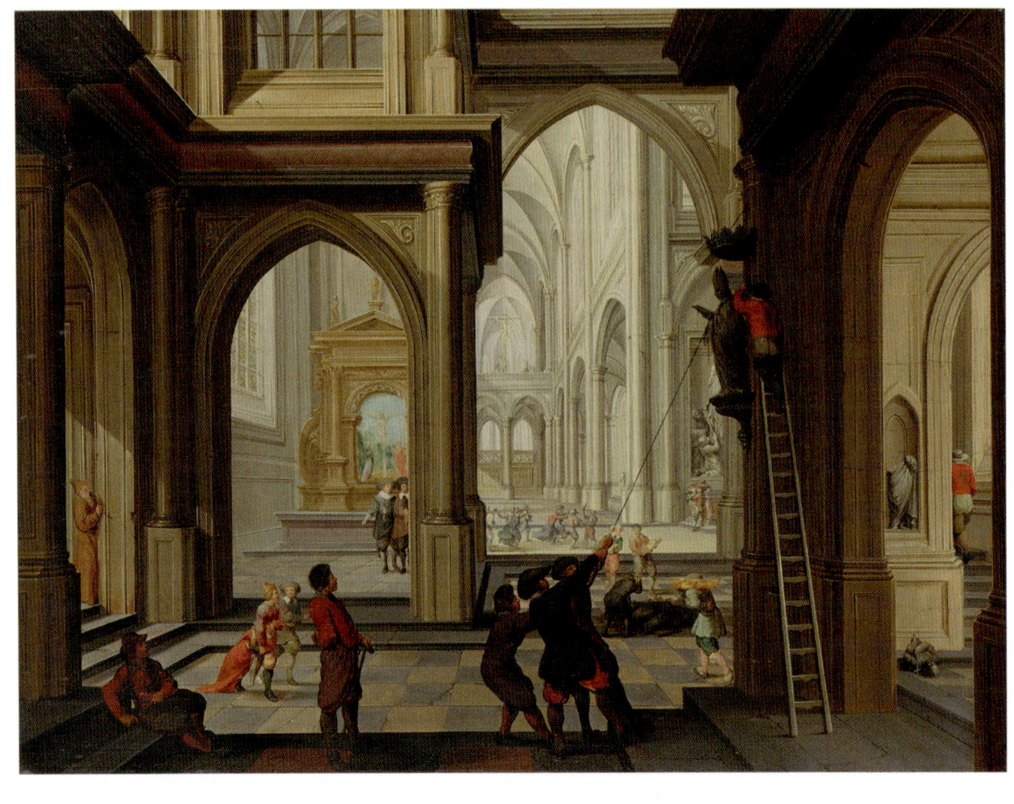

Baroque art was born out of calamity. Some of the catastrophes of the age were social and physical, such as the violence, disease and warfare discussed in the Introduction. But the most significant changes shaping Baroque culture – those with the greatest repercussions in the centuries to come – were spiritual. From the second decade of the sixteenth century ordinary Europeans faced the most wrenching crises of faith in well over a millennium, involving radical new interpretations of Scripture and the natural world; harsh, often violent challenges to existing customs and dogma; and a general sense of religious unease. These battles of faith, fought between Catholics and those who called themselves Protestants (from the verb 'to protest') left their most palpable mark in the visual arts. Protestantism was opposed to the cult of images and therefore removed images of the saints, the Virgin Mary and Christ from their churches, sometimes desecrating and destroying those artworks. The Catholic Church responded by reforming sacred imagery and promoting it as never before. Without this emphatic new endorsement of holy pictures, Baroque art as we know it would never have happened.

The beginnings of the Protestant Reformation are easy to trace, although the movement's roots run deep and are connected with events such as the Great Schism (in which the Catholic Church was divided between 1378 and 1416) and the work of early reformist theologians like John Wycliffe (c.1330–1384) and Jan Huss (c.1372–1415). In 1517 an Augustinian monk named Martin Luther (1483–1546), nailed ninety-five theses to the door of the castle church in Wittenberg, attacking papal abuses such as the sale of indulgences (remissions from punishment for sins) – largely undertaken to finance the construction of the new Saint Peter's Basilica in Rome – and challenging the pope's hegemony. Aided by the printing press, which allowed new ideas to spread quickly across Europe, Luther's challenge opened a permanent rift with Catholicism. Other Protestant groups followed, led by figures such as Frenchman John Calvin (1509–1564) and the Swiss Ulrich Zwingli (1484–1531), and within a very short time much of the population

20.
Dirck van Delen,
Iconoclasts in a Church, 1630.
Oil on wood;
50 × 67 cm
(20 × 26 in).
Rijksmuseum, Amsterdam

of central and northern Europe had embraced Protestantism, including Henry VIII of England (r. 1509–47) and the future King Henry IV of France (r. 1589–1610), who only reconverted to Catholicism so that he could take the throne. The main Protestant groups included the Lutherans, the Reformed Churches (derived from Zwingli and Calvin) and the Anabaptists (precursors of modern-day Mennonites and Quakers). Protestantism was not merely a secession from the papacy but a fundamental departure from the tenets of the Catholic Church. Maintaining that Scripture was the only legitimate text, Protestants believed in salvation by faith alone – not through good works as in Catholicism – and Luther and Calvin promoted the doctrine of predestination, whereby God has already determined who will be saved before Creation. Luther and Zwingli reduced the number of sacraments (visible signs of God's grace) from Catholicism's seven (Baptism, Confirmation, the Eucharist, Penance, Extreme Unction, Ordination and Matrimony) to two (Baptism and the Eucharist), although they disagreed profoundly about their nature.

Iconoclasm played a central role in the Protestant Reformation, particularly at the behest of Calvin, Zwingli and the Wittenberg theologian Andreas Karlstadt (1486–1541), who were opposed to sacred imagery (Luther believed that some images should be permitted and spoke out against their destruction). Although their views varied in the details, the main thrust of the anti-imagery argument held that Scripture was the only allowable 'image' of the invisible God. The veneration of painted or sculpted images was tantamount to idolatry, and went against the Second Commandment proscription 'Thou shalt not make thee any graven image' (Deuteronomy 5:8). Some leaders, including Calvin, did not deny the valuable role images could play as didactic tools – but only in their narrative, not iconic, function, and only in a domestic setting. Iconoclasm sometimes manifested itself more gently, as in 1524 when Zwingli allowed citizens and parishes to remove paintings and sculptures from the churches of Zürich instead of having them destroyed. Often images were merely subjected to defamations, mock trials and mock martyrdoms to demonstrate that God would not come to their aid. But other iconoclasts reacted violently, especially the more radical members of the Reformed Church.

The storm broke quickly. Echoing events that shook the Byzantine
Church to its foundations in the eighth and ninth centuries, angry mobs
of Protestants burst into churches and monasteries, smashing stained-
glass windows and statues, hurling paintings and carved altarpieces to the
ground, and carting them off to be burnt. Some of the most violent of
these iconoclastic riots took place in central and northern Europe, in places
such as Switzerland (St Gallen in 1529 and Geneva in 1535), Germany
(Wittenberg in 1522, Münster in 1534 and Augsburg in 1537), and
Scandinavia (Copenhagen in 1530). The British Isles and the Netherlands
were particularly hard hit. In England in 1535–40 Henry VIII initiated the
Dissolution of the Monasteries, the largest land grab in early modern British
history, when monasteries and pilgrimage sites were seized by the state,
and statues, stained glass and paintings were destroyed en masse. Henry's
iconoclastic policy continued under his son, the boy king Edward VI
(r. 1547–53), who ordered that churches be cleansed of all imagery and
chantry chapels (private family chapels, the object of lavish artistic patronage)
be shut down. In 1559 total iconoclasm raged further north. During this
uprising and one a century later led by the English Civil War leader Oliver
Cromwell, Scotland's great cathedrals and churches were stripped of religious
imagery, whitewashed and often abandoned. No other country was as
reckless with its architectural and artistic heritage: today skeletal abbeys and
cathedrals crumble in the towns and roofless churches waste away in the
graveyards of countless villages. But the worst was yet to come, elsewhere.

In the summer of 1566 the Low Countries (including both modern-day
Holland and Belgium) were the scene of the *Beeldenstorm*, a massive wave
of iconoclastic attacks on monastic buildings and priest lynching inspired
by fiery sermons that brought Calvinism to the Netherlands. The general
fury that characterized the event – it was probably inspired more by social
and political tensions than actual hatred for artworks – is vividly portrayed
in a painting of 1630 by the Dutch artist Dirck van Delen (c.1605–1671) of
the stripping of a fictitious church in the Netherlands, with people climbing
ladders to get at sculptures and altarpieces and heaving them to the ground
(20). A storm indeed, the *Beeldenstorm* had an immeasurable impact on
that region's artistic heritage and set off a civil war between Catholics and

Protestants that eventually bought the Dutch their independence. England

suffered a further iconoclastic revolt under the Puritan regime in 1643, when

Cromwell's troops and restless mobs further destroyed church imagery,

organs and vestments, burning them in giant bonfires in town squares. Sad

reminders of these attacks can still be seen across the country, as in the

Lady Chapel and chantry chapels in the Cathedral at Ely – a town in which

Cromwell owned property – where Puritans long ago hacked off the heads

and hands of the delicately carved late Gothic statues and other figural

ornamentation (21).

The Catholic Church responded immediately to this attack on images. The

German humanist preacher Hieronymus Emser (1477–1527) launched a

salvo against Karlstadt as early as 1522, defending Catholicism's use of sacred

images as part of a tradition going back to the time of the early Church, and

he supported his arguments with an impressive array of sources, including

John of Damascus, the eighth-century monk who led the struggle on behalf

of images during the Byzantine Iconoclast controversy, and the resolutions of

the Second Nicene Council (AD 787), the Church council that officially – if

not decisively – defeated the Iconoclasts. Others followed, including a similar

diatribe by Luther's arch-rival Johann Eck (1486–1543), which criticized

the removal of images from churches, and the issue became such a key part

of the Protestant–Catholic debate that an entire session was devoted to

the cult of the saints and the veneration of relics and images (the two went

hand-in-hand) at the Council of Trent in 1563. Set in the northern Italian

town of Trent in the futile hope of attracting northern European Protestants,

the Council of Trent (1545–63) was convened to reform the abuses of

the Church and strengthen its foundation, mostly by calling for a more

centralized system of control and by increasing the power of the papacy and

the bishops. The anxiety and tension that marked this often confrontational

event is carefully concealed in this triumphalist fresco by Italian painter

Pasquale Cati da Iesi in the Roman church of S. Maria in Trastevere (22). In

this congested scene in Trent's cathedral, a row of cardinals preside over the

deliberations of bishops and other clerics in the background while female

allegories in the foreground represent Faith, the Eucharist, Charity and –

most importantly – the victory of the Church over Heresy (the recumbent

21.
Lady Chapel,
Ely Cathedral,
completed
1349 (England)

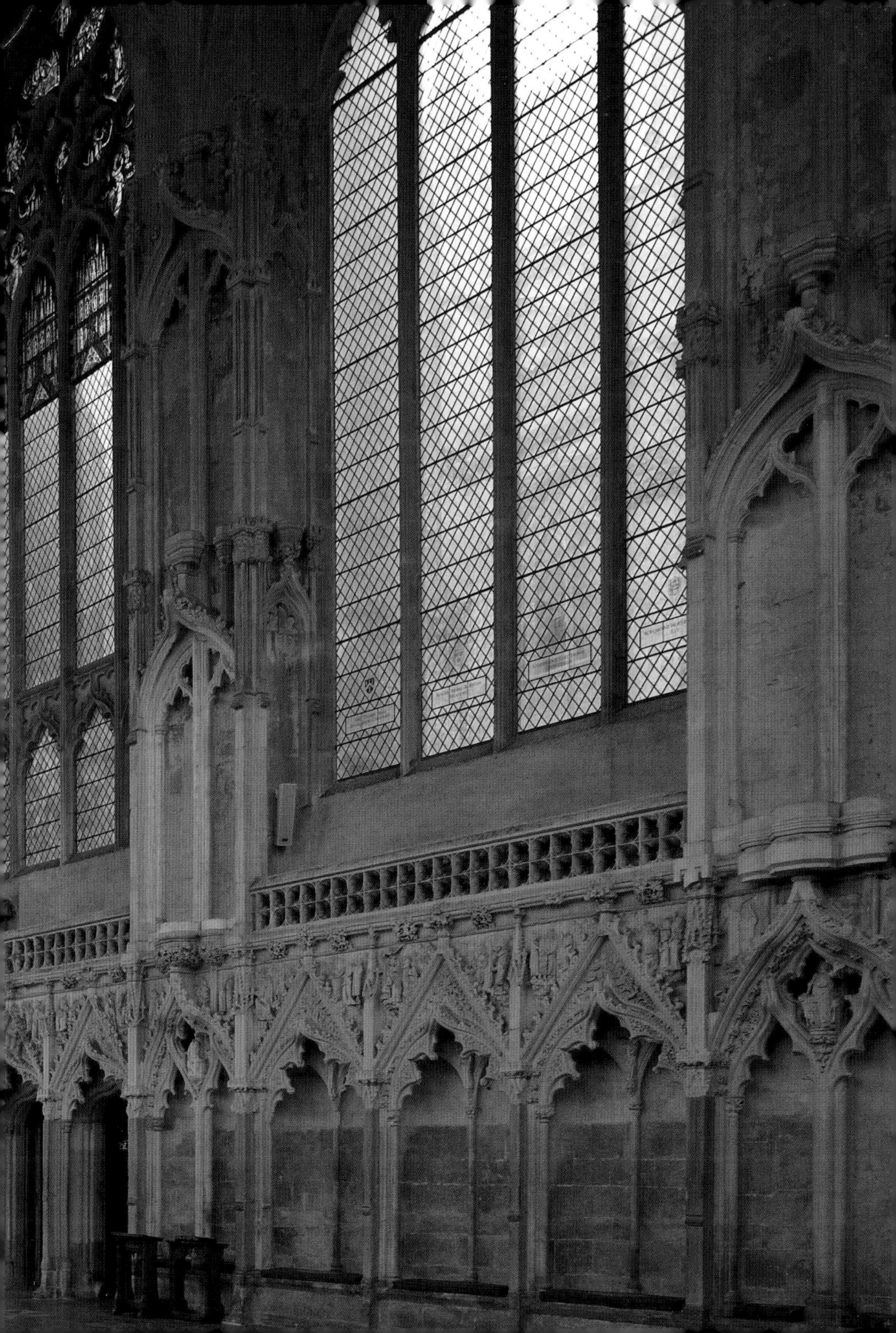

in mid-century painting, a style frequently referred to today as 'Maniera', in which content often yielded to style and aesthetics, and many artists were less concerned with devoutness than with virtuosity. Sebastiano's sombre and muted colours contrast conspicuously with Bassano's shimmering lavender and iridescent reds and greens, and his decision to restrict his painting to a single figure against an obscure background instead of providing a narrative – Bassano's canvas shows Christ's encounter with Saint Veronica – gives

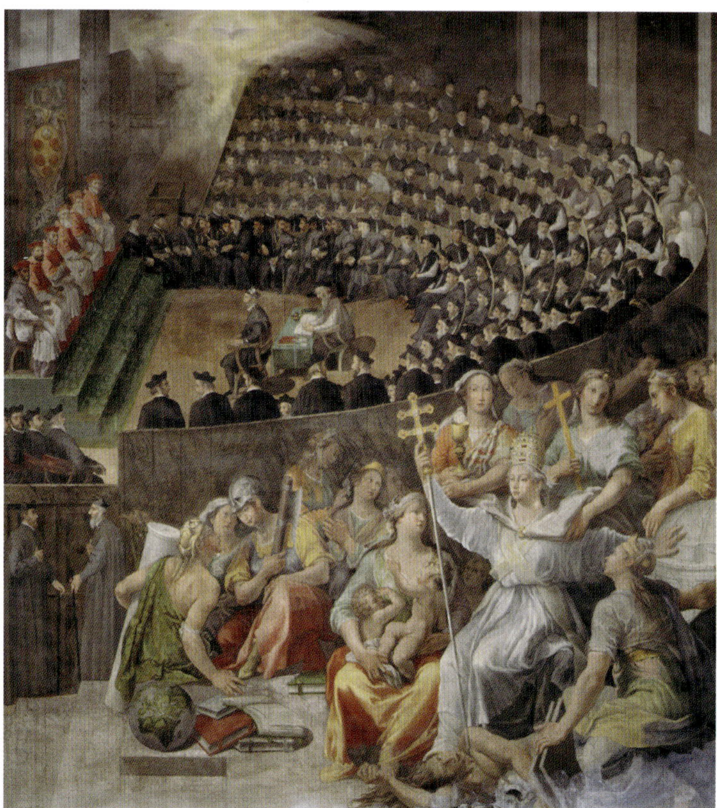

it greater immediacy. By comparison, the luxurious clothing, sparkling armour, and artfully windswept capes and sashes of Bassano's crowd evoke the pageantry of a Venetian procession. Equally significant is the two artists' approach to Christ's facial expression, Bassano's melancholy contrasting with Sebastiano's agony and terror. Bassano delights in artificial postures and anatomical details, like the unnaturally serpentine stance and rippling muscles of a soldier in the upper central part of the painting, and his figures

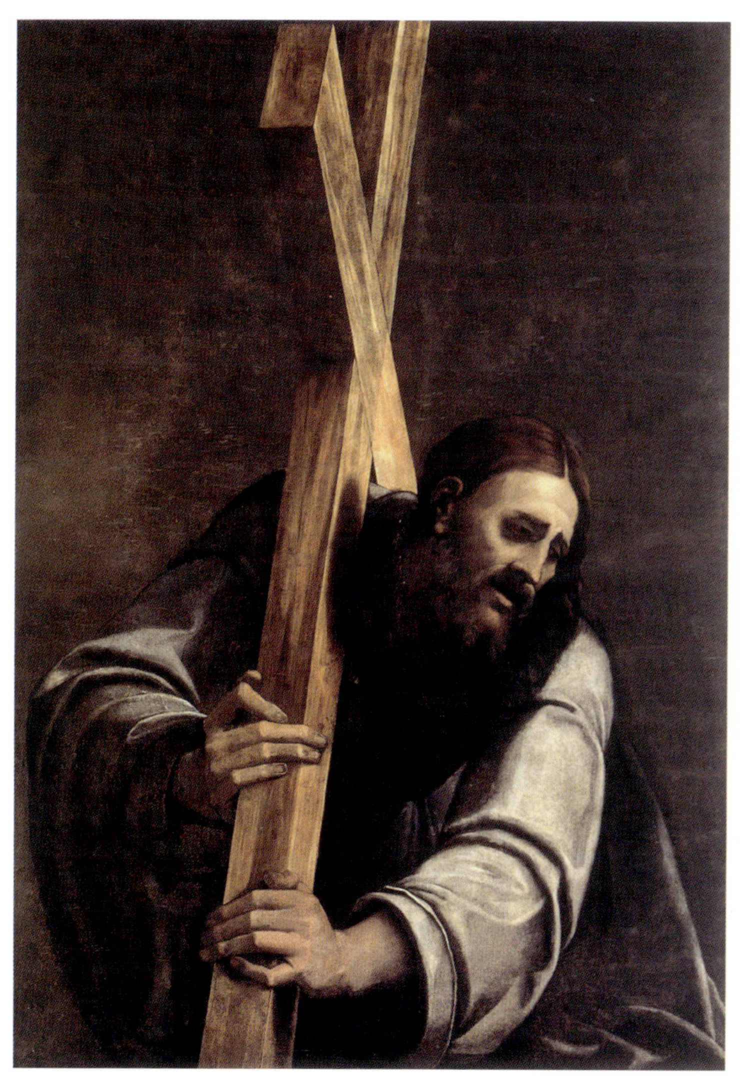

crowd so tightly against the picture plane that they block the viewer's gaze and restrict the painting's sense of depth. Sebastiano also offers a more realistic sense of mass and weight – in fact the crippling heaviness of the cross is the main theme of the painting. Sebastiano's monumental figure of Christ emerges dramatically from the gloom and – through the powerful foreshortening of his arms and the Cross – into our space, evoking Kempis's opening line: 'He that followeth me shall not walk in darkness, saith the Lord.' Sebastiano's painting is a kind of image called the *Andachtsbild* (devotional picture), which derives from northern Europe and is meant to interact directly with the worshipper.

Although they rarely appear in art-survey books, several Italian reformist painters followed Sebastiano's example in the last decades of the sixteenth century: artists such as Girolamo Muziano (1528–1592), Taddeo Zuccaro (1529–1566) and Santi di Tito (1536–1602), the founder of a group of painters subsequently called the Florentine reformers. Santi's *The Dead Christ with the Virgin, Saint John the Baptist, Saint Catherine of Alexandria and Baldassare Suarez* (25) – another meditation on the Passion and death of Christ – anticipates trends in early Baroque painting with its larger figures, muted colours, convincing sense of sorrow and elimination of unnecessary detail. Rather than being crowded into the foreground as in the Bassano painting, the figures around the dead Christ form a semicircle to give the scene depth, and the dark background recalls Sebastiano (see 23). Yet even Santi's best work is not Baroque: the biblical figures on the left still have idealized, generic facial features, and the body of Christ seems weightless, his body disposed in an elegant diagonal across the foreground. By contrast, those on the right side are solider and more naturalistic, particularly the donor, Suarez – wearing the cross of the Florentine Order of Santo Spirito, of which he was head – whose representation is a carefully observed portrait. The earliest truly Baroque response to the post-Tridentine reforms was a bold and risky debut by the young Annibale Carracci (1560–1609), one of a stupendously successful group of Bolognese painters who would take Rome and central Italy by storm in the first decades of the seventeenth century. When Annibale unveiled his *Crucifixion with Saints* (26) in the Bolognese church of S. Niccolò, he was treated to the scorn and contempt of his rivals.

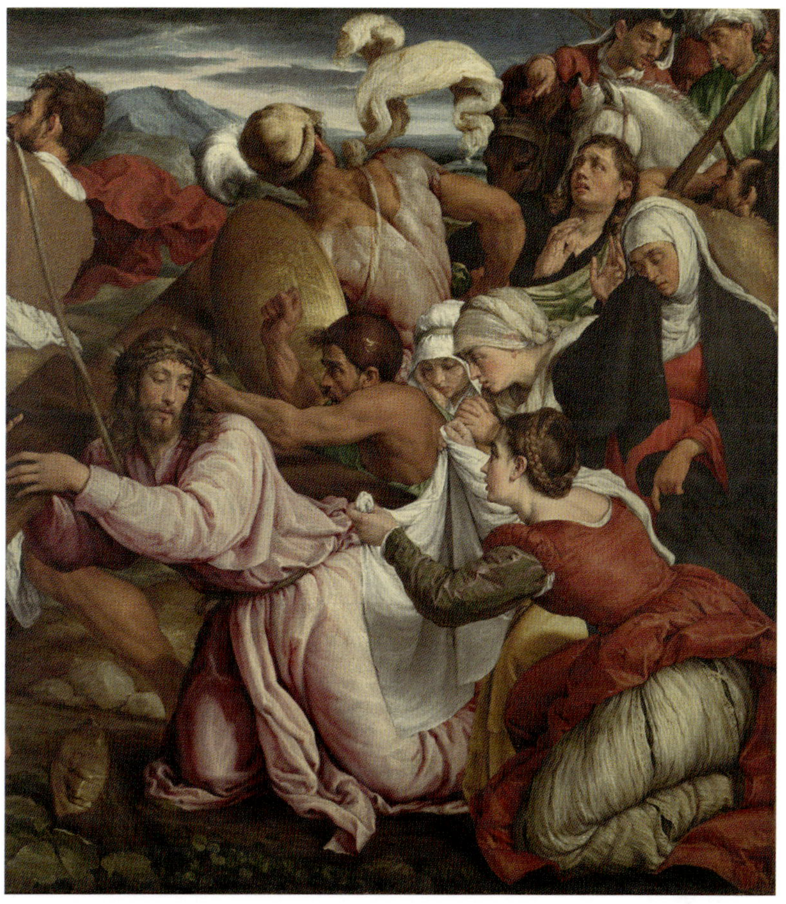

Instead of distant aristocratic figures he portrayed ordinary people who might have walked in off the street. In place of dance-like postures and weightlessness he introduced naturalistic stances and bulkiness: his men and women plausibly occupy real space. And instead of shimmering surfaces (the bishop's robe is an exception) and uniform brightness, Annibale drenched the foreground with a natural golden light from a single source. This diffuse light, enhanced by a subtle loosening of the brushstrokes, was inspired by the Venetian Renaissance – particularly Titian (c.1488–1576) – and would remain a key element of much Baroque and Rococo painting for the next 200 years. The painting's clarity and frank realism was accessible to people from all walks of life and its logical composition – the figures are all close to the picture plane yet allow a glimpse into a distant stormy landscape – drives home its message of salvation through Christ's sacrifice.

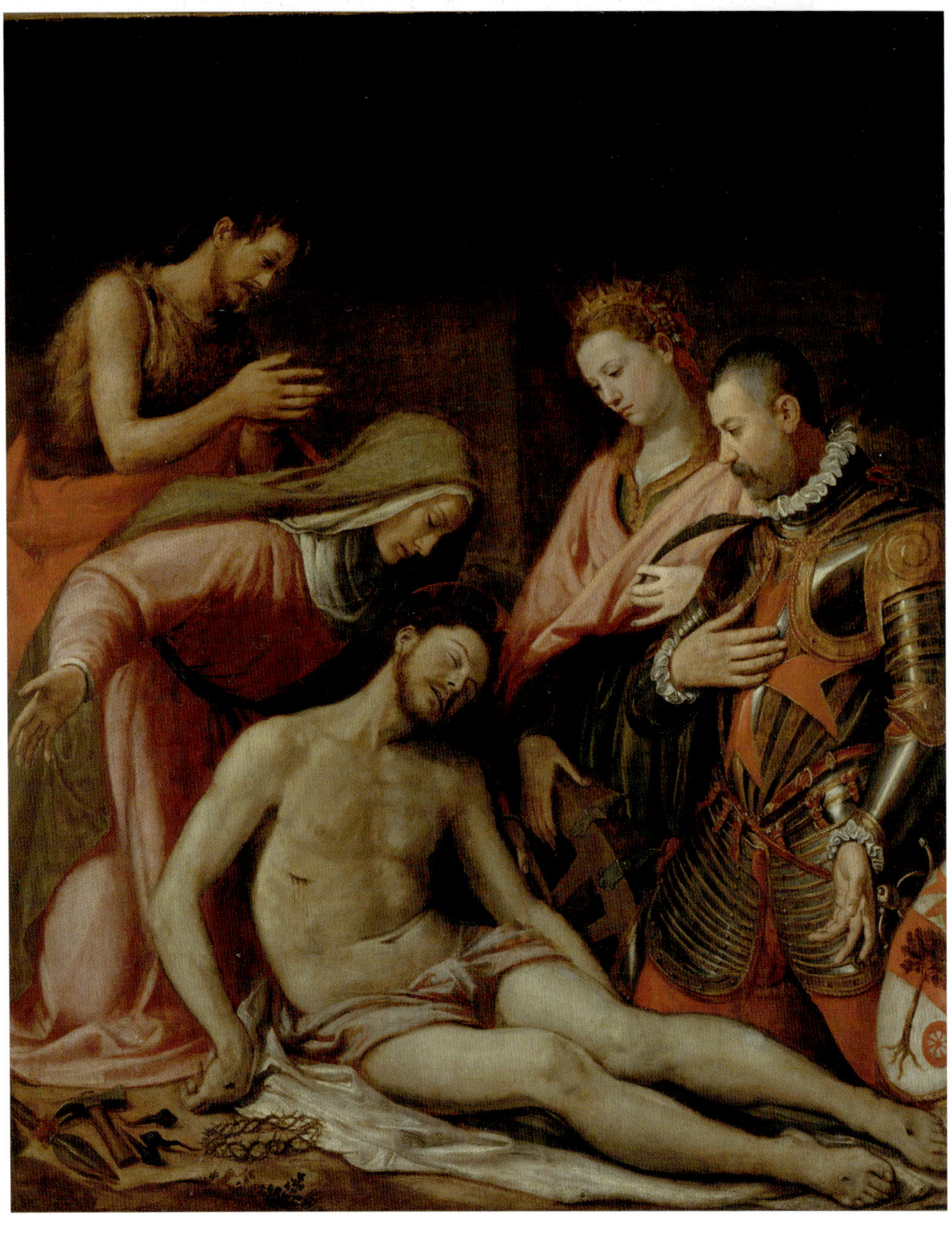

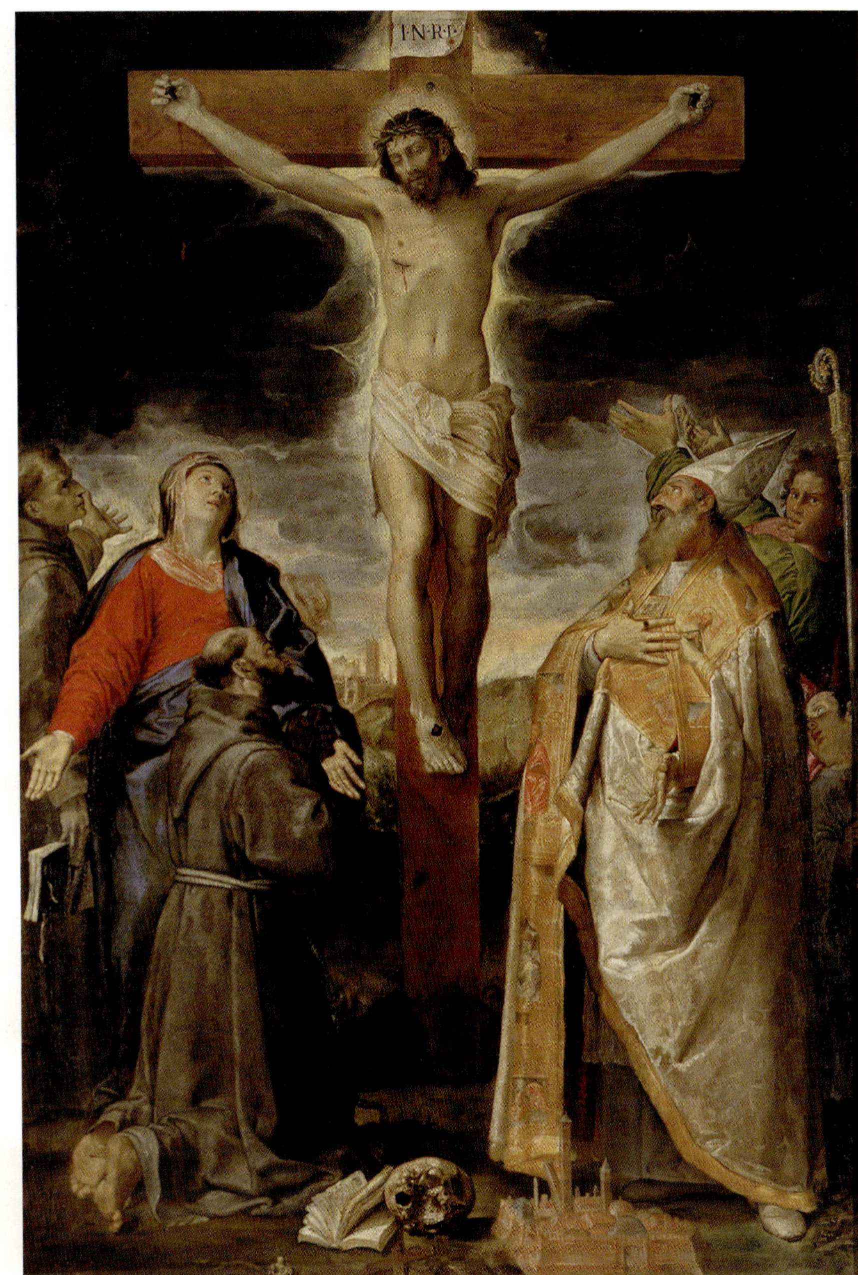

25.
Santi di Tito,
*The Dead
Christ with the
Virgin, Saint
John the Baptist,
Saint Catherine
of Alexandria
and Baldassare
Suarez*, c.1590.
Oil on panel;
2 × 1.68 m
(6 ft 7 in ×
5 ft 6 in).
Accademia,
Florence

26.
**Annibale
Carracci**,
*Crucifixion with
Saints*, 1583.
Oil on canvas;
3.05 × 2.1 m
(10 ft × 6 ft
10½ in).
Santa Maria
della Carità,
Bologna (Italy)

 Baroque and Rococo

Annibale belonged to an informal, family-run art school in Bologna called the Accademia degli Incamminati (Academy of the Progressives, founded around 1582), which included his older cousin Lodovico Carracci (1555–1619) and his older brother Agostino (1557–1602). Owing to a providential political climate at the papal court in the last decade of the sixteenth century – Monsignor Giovanni Battista Agucchi, the secretary to the papal nephew Cardinal Pietro Aldobrandini, was from Bologna and shared the ideals of these young artists from his home city – and to the early enthusiasm of key Roman art collectors Vincenzo Giustiniani (1564–1637) and Odoardo Farnese (1573–1626), Annibale and Agostino were invited to Rome in 1595 and 1597. They established theirs as the favoured style of the papacy and central Italy for decades to come (although Agostino left for Parma in 1600). One of the reasons for their lasting success was the young talent they were able to promote from their home city. Lodovico, who remained in Bologna, trained such luminaries as Guido Reni (1575–1642), Domenichino (1581–1641), Giovanni Lanfranco (1582–1647), Alessandro Algardi (1598–1654) and – indirectly – Guercino (Giovanni Francesco Barbieri, 1591–1666), all of whom had a decisive impact on Italian Baroque art. But the Incamminati and their descendants did not succeed on talent and connections alone. Their public altarpieces and private devotional pictures provided a brand of sacred imagery that met the needs of the reformed Catholic Church, but they also reintroduced a less devout element – and not only in private commissions – for which the sophisticated cardinals and monsignors of Rome had been hungering throughout the bleak decades of reform: classicism.

Annibale's classical strain became more pronounced the longer he spent in Rome, where he sought inspiration in the works of antiquity, Raphael (1483–1520) and Michelangelo (1475–1564). Although its clearest manifestation was in such pagan subjects as the Farnese ceiling with its sculptural nudes and mythological subject matter (see 13), a staid, disciplined classicism tamed his later religious paintings as well, working out a balance with the naturalistic tendencies of his early work. A supreme example of Annibale's classicism is his small *Domine Quo Vadis* – made for Cardinal Aldobrandini – a depiction of the moment the resurrected Christ encounters Peter outside the city of Rome and beckons him to return to meet his fate (27). At first glance, the panel's classicism dominates: the balance and corporeality of the figures, the restrained emotions, and the antique costume and setting all contribute to this impression, as does the bold but simple harmony of light and colours (especially the red, blue, gold and white of the draperies) that derive from a close study of Raphael. In fact, Christ's pose is a quotation in reverse from a Graeco-Roman sculpture known as the *Borghese Warrior*, and it also recalls Michelangelo's *Risen Christ* at S. Maria sopra Minerva (1521). Yet Annibale also gives us something more forceful and expressive – and Baroque. Christ is dramatically foreshortened and appears to stride out of the painting into the viewer's space, while Peter recoils from the divine presence, awkwardly retreating into the lower right-hand corner of the panel. Peter's startled expression and humiliated gesture humanize the moment, as do his and Christ's non-idealized, slightly stocky bodies. Christ's realism is so striking – Annibale and the Incamminati made the use of live models and the scientific study of human emotions the foundation of their practice – that he has the tanned legs and forearms of a Roman labourer.

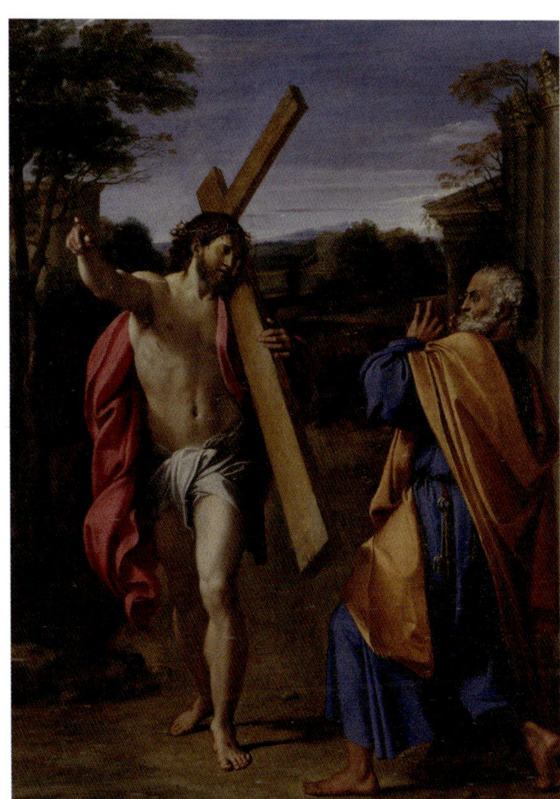

27.
Annibale Carracci, *Domine Quo Vadis*, 1601–2. Oil on wood; 77.4 × 66.3 cm (30½ × 26 in). National Gallery, London

Annibale's mediated classicism, championed by clerical treatise writers and art critics alike, was characterized as 'nature perfected'. Giovanni Battista Agucchi – a personal friend of Annibale's – wrote a *Treatise on Painting* between 1607 and 1615 that revived an idea from antiquity in which nature is imperfect and artists must improve on it by selecting only the most beautiful parts of what they observe. According to the theory of 'nature perfected', exclusive dependency either on nature studies or on the idealized fantasies of the inner mind (*disegno interno*, or 'internal design', was a key component of late Renaissance art theory) were equally misguided. Loosely based on a school of thought known as Neoplatonism – a third-century AD reinterpretation of the teachings of the Greek philosopher Plato (c.429–c.347 BC) that influenced Christian image theory from the days of the early Church – the doctrine of 'nature perfected' became the standard for official Church art in central Italy and also France in the seventeenth century. It was explored further in *The Ideal of the Painter, Sculptor and Architect* (1664; published 1672) by the celebrated art critic Giovanni Pietro Bellori (1613–1696). Aside from his emphasis on classicism, Bellori also echoed Trent and the treatise writers by insisting that art must instruct the viewer. In fact, painting was widely seen as a form of visual rhetoric, and clerics related it to the oratorical style of the Roman philosopher and statesman Cicero (106–43 BC), who used three main modes in his speeches characterized by the verbs *delectare* (to delight), *docere* (to teach) and *movere* (to move). *Delectare* was an entertaining style, much embellished with imagery and anecdote, meant to capture the attention of the listener; *docere* took the intellectual route, trying to persuade the audience through narrative and argumentation; finally, *movere* sought to make a psychological impact on the listeners, inspiring them to join the orator's cause. Catholic preachers revived these techniques during the Catholic Reformation, and before long they were being applied to painting, a medium exposed to similar ideas since the publication in 1435 of the most important art treatise of the Renaissance, *On Painting* by Leon Battista Alberti (1404–1472).

To demonstrate how this rhetorical device works, let us look at a typical High Baroque painting inspired by the Bolognese school: the *Madonna and Child in Glory Flanked by Saint John the Baptist and Saint Rosalie*, by Sicily's

undeservedly unfamiliar Baroque master, Pietro Novelli (1603–1647; 28).
We will begin with *delectare*. In the visual arts, that meant using spectacular
light effects, bright colours and rich ornamentation aimed at capturing
viewers' attentions. Novelli's canvas makes a commanding impression
through its monumental size and large, noble figures rendered in bold relief.
The figures are also beautiful, Rosalie (on the lower left) with her rosy cheeks
and golden tresses, the Virgin with her graceful, long neck, and the Child
with his pink skin and healthy tousle of flaxen hair. The picture's grandeur
is enhanced by colours traditionally associated with wealth, such as the lapis
blue of the Virgin's gown or the shock of red in John the Baptist's cloak –
not to mention a shimmering gold background that recalls Byzantine icons.
Novelli accentuates the drama through light and dark effects (*chiaroscuro*
in Italian) that cast the lower part of the painting in shadow, heightening
the contrast with the golden light above. The angels add anecdotal delight
through their playful interaction and joyful response to the main figures.
Once we are drawn to this painting, we now begin to appreciate its ability
to instruct: *docere*. Here the artist focuses on a picture's ability to tell a story
and provide a model for good behaviour. Novelli's canvas does both. Viewers
recognize the saints through symbols such as John's staff and Rosalie's habit,
and are reminded of their stories – both saints abandoned worldly things
for a life of poverty and solitude in their devotion to God – prompting
meditations on living a good Christian life. Rosalie further reminds viewers
that saints can cause miracles, as she is believed to have stopped the
devastating plague of 1624 in Palermo, an event all too familiar to its Sicilian
audience. The position of the figures – the more earthly saints are below and
the Madonna and Child above – guides viewers' prayers by demonstrating
that saints can intercede for us only through the Virgin Mary and Christ, and
Novelli highlights their divine status by surrounding the mother and child
with angels and cloudbursts. We are now ready for *movere*, or emotional
transformation. In Novelli's picture viewers are startled by the skull in the
lower part of the canvas – the area closest to their gaze – a *memento mori*
(reminder of death) and further remembrance of the plague. The fear this
image provokes is transformed into empathy by the lamb on the right, a
symbol of Christ's sacrifice that lessens viewers' fear of death and inspires
them to follow Christ's example. Finally, the golden glow and presence of

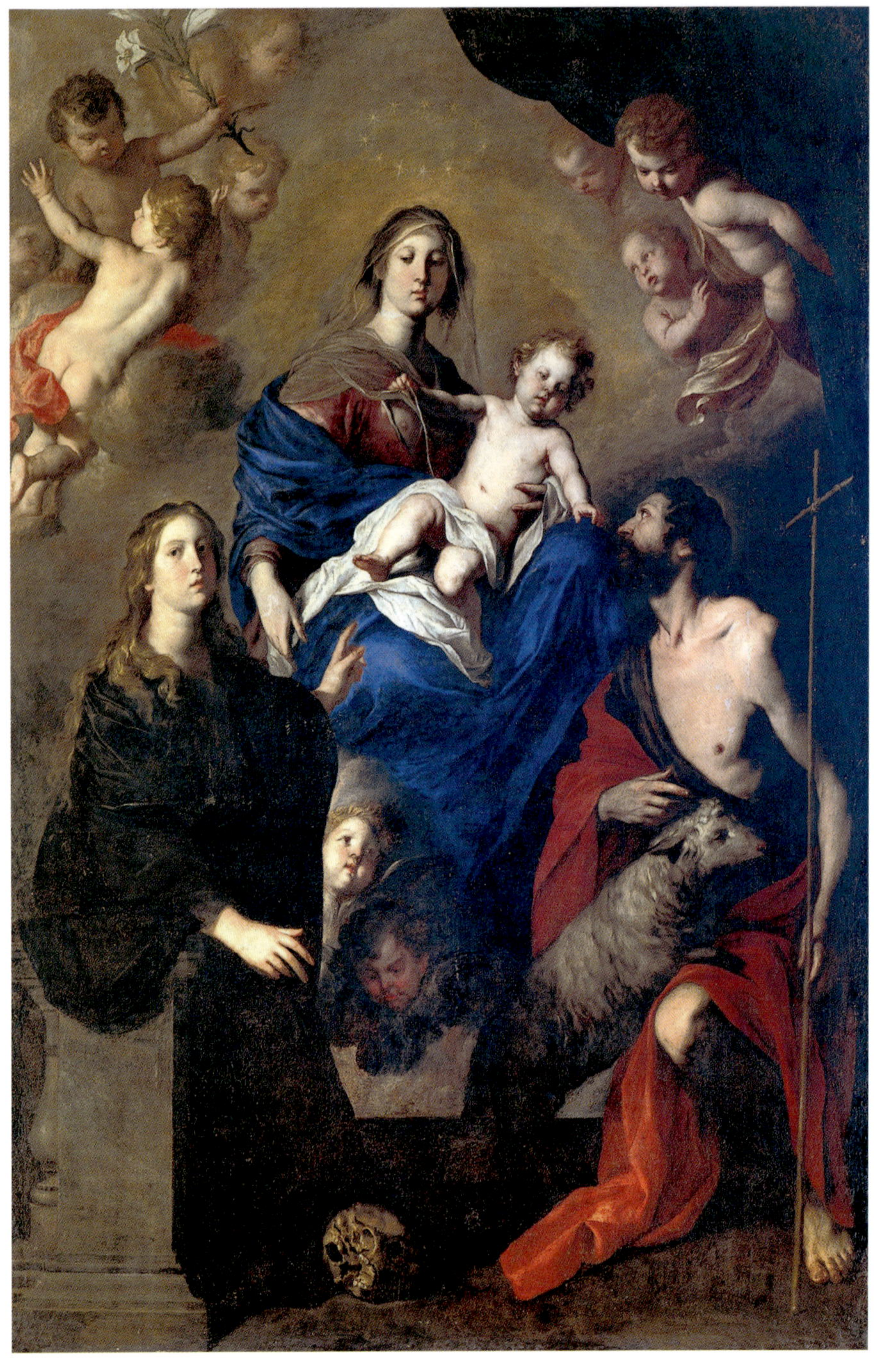

angels above make the central part of the painting resemble a religious vision, as if the viewer were experiencing it personally while standing in front of the canvas. The literature of the day is full of stories of visions inspired by paintings and worshippers (including celebrities such as popes and monarchs) being so moved that they burst into tears in ecstasy, and the theme of visions, ecstasies and conversion is treated quite openly in Baroque art.

This conversion experience was achieved in part by allowing viewers to become participants in the work of art, often through a deliberate sense of incompleteness that compels them to finish the work in their minds: Novelli leaves a suggestive glimpse of Heaven at the top of the painting as the angels peel back the curtain, revealing God's light but not allowing a view of the Almighty. This use of the imagination to invoke or complete sacred images during meditation was extremely widespread and it derives from sources such as the popular devotional manual *Spiritual Exercises* (1548) by Jesuit founder Ignatius of Loyola (1491–1556), who called the process the 'composition of place'. In the 'composition of place' a participant is encouraged to recreate sacred tableaux (such as the Flight into Egypt or the Nativity) in their minds, and the *Exercises* are deliberately vague about the details so that people can tailor their vision to fit their own needs. Men and women from all walks of life made the Exercises – itself a descendant of Kempis's *Imitation of Christ* – including artists as varied as Gianlorenzo Bernini (1598–1680) and Luis de Morales (c.1510–1586).

Annibale and his followers – indeed most of the artists in this book – were not merely painters, but prolific and brilliant draughtsmen and often printmakers. Our view of Baroque art, derived from museum exhibitions and art books that privilege bright colours over monochromes, tends to overlook these media even though they were as valued as paintings in their time – some of them, like Annibale's massive lifesize study for the Silenus panel in the Farnese Ceiling now in Urbino (compare 29 and 13), were even of a comparable scale. In fact, it is hard to underestimate the importance of drawing (*disegno*) in Renaissance and Baroque Italy, not only as a first or final step in making a painting, sculpture or building but as a metaphor for artistic genius (the concept derives from the Greek philosopher Aristotle,

**28.
Pietro
Novelli**,
*Madonna and
Child in Glory
Flanked by
Saint John the
Baptist and
Saint Rosalie*,
c.1630s. Oil
on canvas;
2.6 × 1.74 m
(8 ft 6 in × 5 ft
9 in). Galleria
Regionale della
Sicilia Palazzo
Abatellis, Sicily

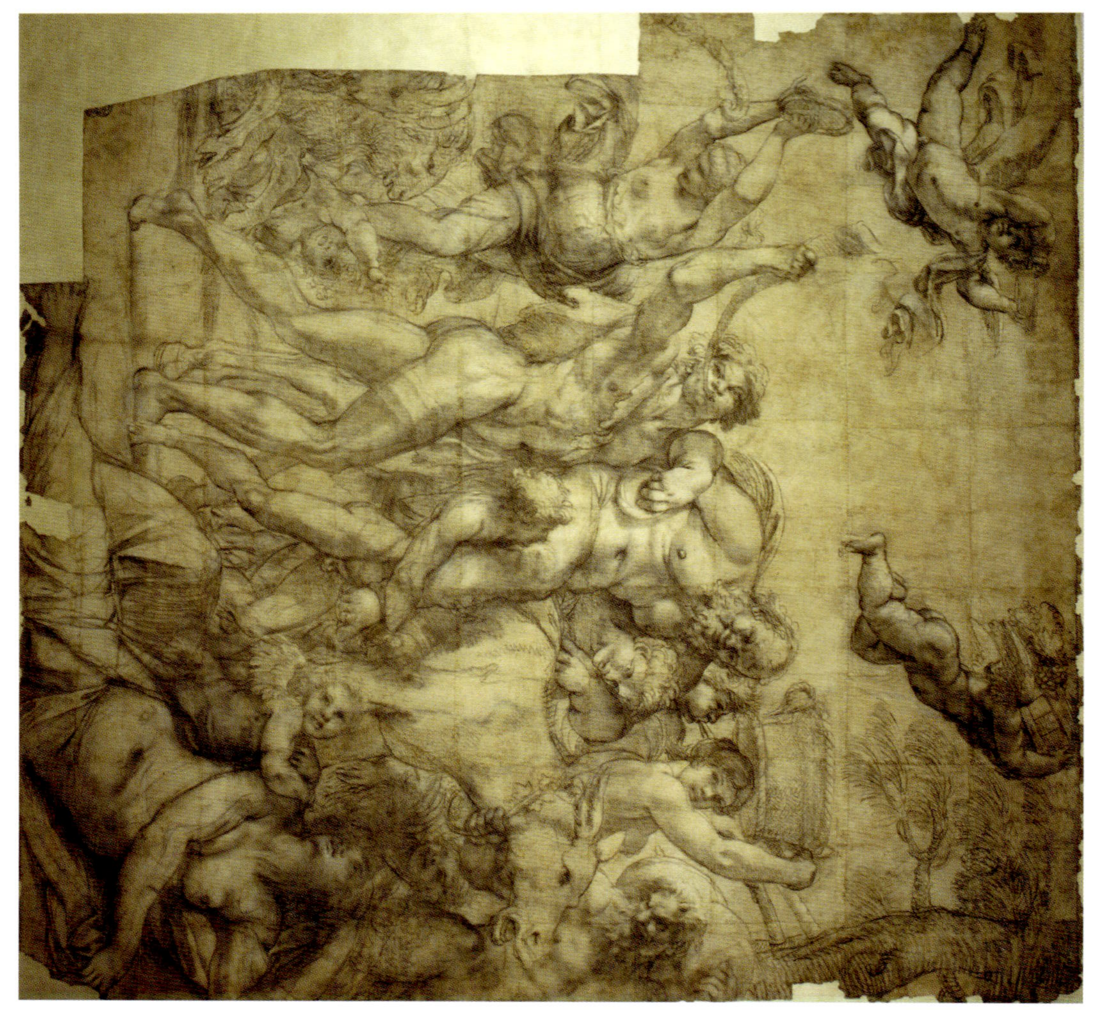

384–322 BC, and was at the foundation of Florentine Renaissance art).
The Carracci and their followers executed some of the most accomplished
drawings of the seventeenth century. The giant *Silenus* cartoon, likely the
largest surviving drawing of the Baroque – it is only half the original and
is still comparable to Raphael's Sistine cartoons in London – is particularly
fascinating because it represents the ultimate stage of a laborious process of
sketching from life and classical sculpture, refining initial studies, and playing
with compositions and poses that involved hundreds of drawings. Executed
on over fifty sheets of paper glued together, it is meant as a lifesize guide

29.
Annibale Carracci,
A Bacchic Procession with Silenus, c.1598. Black chalk heightened with white on more than fifty joined sheets of brown paper, partially pricked for transfer; 3.45 × 3.32 m (11 ft 3¾ in x 10 ft 10¾ in). Galleria Nazionale delle Marche, Urbino (Italy)

30.
Guercino,
Saint William Kneeling Before a Bishop. c.1620. Ink and wash; 34 × 27 cm (13½ × 10½ in). Louvre, Paris

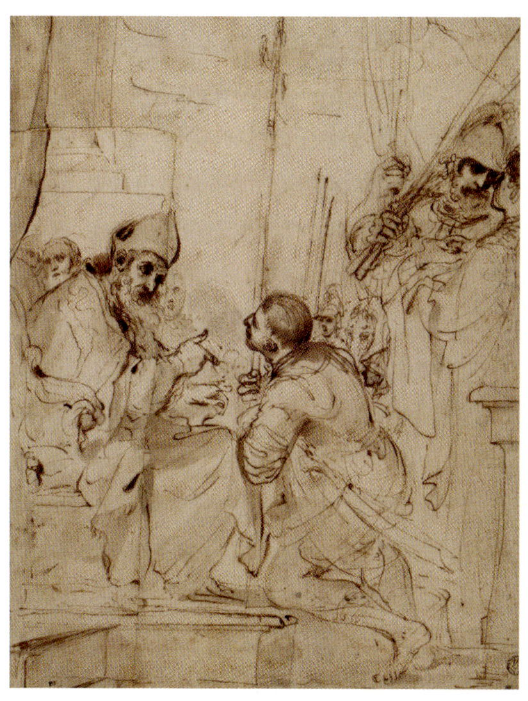

for painting the fresco (its contours are pricked allowing a light dusting of
charcoal to reproduce them onto the ceiling or – as scholars believe was
the case here – a second sheet itself used for the ceiling). Yet Annibale still
made adjustments not seen in this 'final' cartoon, keeping drawings of the
individual figures on hand to assist him in completing his fresco. Guercino's
industriousness as a draughtsman invited comparisons with Rembrandt (see
below). Guercino's *Saint William Kneeling Before a Bishop* (30) one of four
large-scale studies for his celebrated altarpiece *Saint William of Aquitaine
Receiving the Cowl* (31) for S. Gregorio in Bologna, demonstrates how

different a preparatory drawing can be from the final product and how it stands on its own as a work of art.

The main distinction is one of immediacy. As they often reveal the artist's first thoughts as he or she worked out the composition of a setting or placement of figures – including alterations made directly on the paper called *pentimenti* – preparatory drawings have a freshness and energy that sometimes become muted in the painted version. Guercino's sketches are especially lively as he favoured pens made from goose feathers, which allowed for rapid application of ink highlighted later by wash. Guercino's working method differed from many of his contemporaries. Rather than devising a scheme from multiple drawings on the same sheet, he used the whole page to work out versions of the entire composition, later testing out individual expressions and gestures on separate sheets in black ink or chalk, in this case roughly fifteen of them. The subject is the moment when the soldier William renounces his military career for monastic life before his bishop, and the drawing and painting feature similar compositions, with prominent soldiers on the right and a large throne and vertical lines framing the upper part of the picture, although the classical column on the left in the drawing appears on the right in the painting. In the drawing Guercino places the protagonist closer to us than the bishop so that we see his back and the bishop's face, whereas in the painting the order is reversed so that William's face is clearly revealed and the bishop has turned away from the viewer. Guercino probably chose this solution so that William's moment of conversion (*movere*) – the main point of the painting – would be clearer to the audience. Guercino also left out the giant cross in William's hands, possibly because it looked too militant, and he included at the top two saints calling for the Madonna's intercession, a much more conspicuous representation of Divine approbation. Although not as finished as the faces, which are highlighted with wash, the drapery in the sketch flows smoothly, energized in places – the saint's sash and bishop's robe – by staccato diagonals, whereas in the painting it appears stiffer, almost starched.

It may come as a surprise that the most revolutionary painter of the early Baroque, Annibale's stylistic antithesis and a man known for violent crime,

31.
Guercino, *Saint William of Aquitaine Receiving the Cowl*, 1620. Oil on canvas; 3.48 × 2.31 m (11 ft 5 in × 7 ft 6 in). Pinacoteca Nazionale di Bologna (Italy)

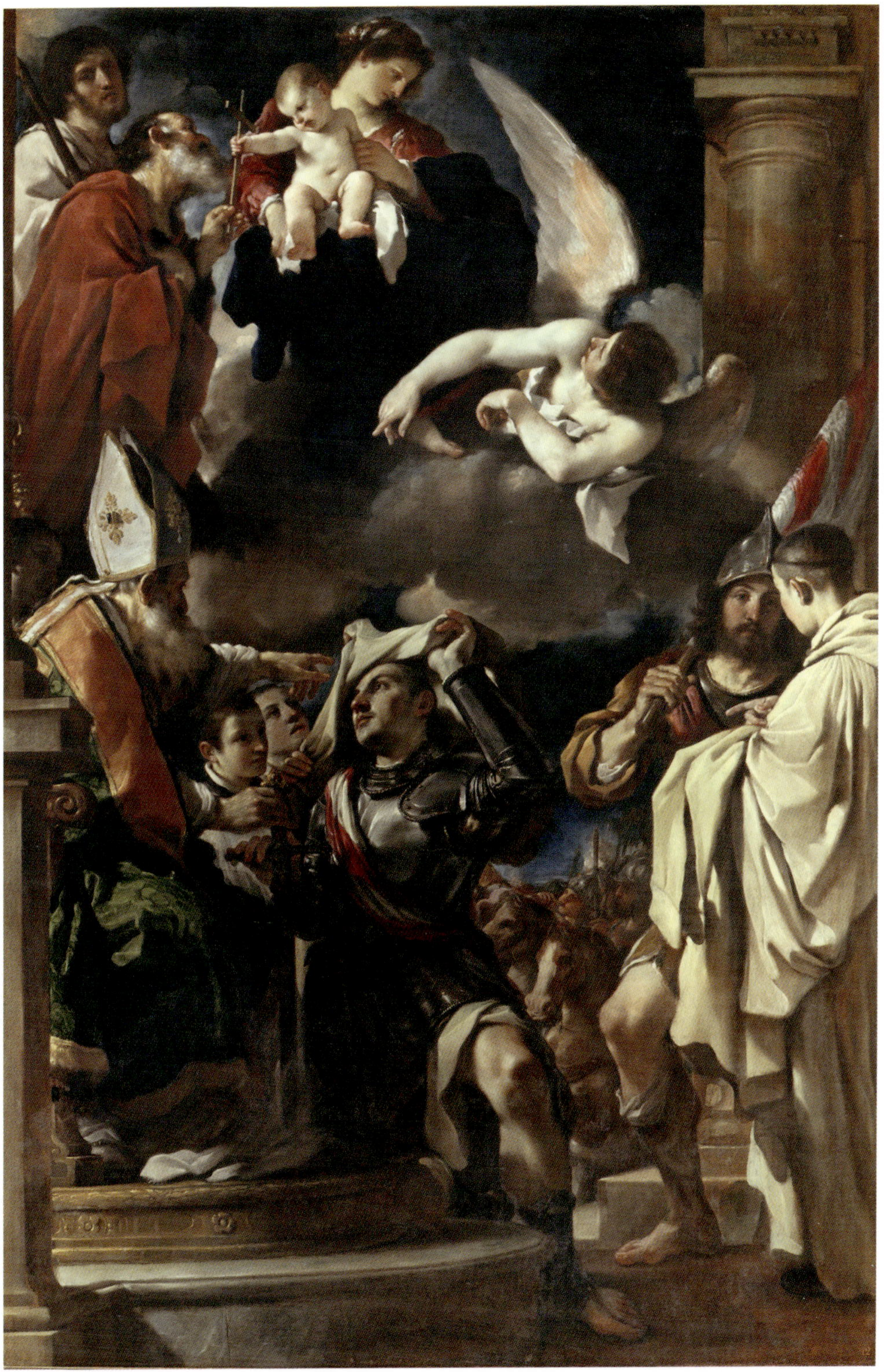

alleged bisexual liaisons and frankly erotic paintings (see 84), could also create works of profound devotion. Michelangelo Merisi da Caravaggio (1571–1610) was a man of such staggering originality that his legacy to Baroque sacred painting in large parts of Europe equalled that of the entire Bolognese school. Although he is a superstar today, with an ever-increasing number of films, novels, biographies and art-historical studies to his name, he struggled against the most crushing criticism during his years in Rome – a career that ended abruptly in 1606 when he killed a hooligan named Ranuccio Tomassoni and was forced to flee the city. Although much has been made of his violence and other character traits, such as his fondness for wearing a sword, Caravaggio managed to produce in the few years between c.1595 and 1610 a body of sacred paintings that may have been Italy's most radical response to the Catholic Reformation. Far more than

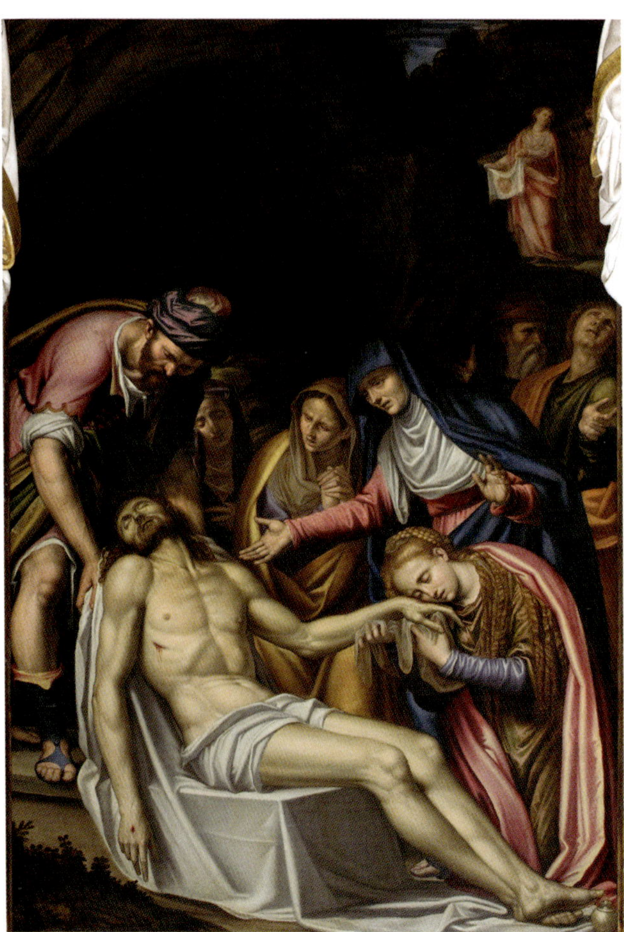

32.
Simone Peterzano, *Entombment*, 1573–8. Oil on canvas; 2.9 × 1.85 m (9 ft 5 in × 6 ft). S. Fedele, Milan

the Incamminati and their followers, Caravaggio was an artist of the people, and his celebrations of poverty, austerity and simple piety cut to the bone, not only by honouring a class of people considered unworthy by the official Church but also exposing some of Rome's most critical social problems. This was the reason – together with his blunt, proletarian style that made use of a startling naturalism and penetrating light effects – that gained him the enmity of the champions of 'nature perfected'.

Caravaggio came by his realism naturally. He grew up in the northern Italian region of Lombardy, where artists had emphasized the observation of the natural world since the days when Leonardo da Vinci (1452–1519) sketched mountain landscapes. Northern Italian painters also brought a reformist solemnity to their work as in the paintings of Caravaggio's first teacher, the Milanese painter Simone Peterzano (c.1540–c.1596), whose gloomy *Entombment* anticipates Caravaggio's intense chiaroscuro (called tenebrism), yet whose stiff, idealized figures are a world apart from his realism and pathos (32). But in Rome, where Caravaggio first struggled to make ends meet selling his paintings on the open market and then by working in the private service of patrons, most notably Cardinal Francesco del Monte, his Lombard brand of earthy naturalism did not generally appeal to highbrow taste. Critics from Agucchi to Bellori and fellow artists from Giovanni Baglione (1566–1643) to Francesco Albani (1578–1660) went on the attack, dismissing the vulgarity of his artistic style and lifestyle alike. Not surprisingly, the main criticism from the 'nature perfected' camp was that Caravaggio's subjects are not ennobled by a sense of beauty or expedient selection and that they are too reliant on life models. But one of Caravaggio's greatest shortcomings in these men's eyes was his choice not to paint frescos (an artist's main route to choice papal and aristocratic commissions) and to abandon the all-important preparatory drawing. Like the late Titian, Caravaggio painted directly onto the canvas, working out his ideas as he went along.

Caravaggio's sacred paintings were as provocative as his profane ones. Unfortunately, Caravaggio's critics and the scant surviving documents about his life give us few clues about his religious beliefs. Some contemporaries simply threw up their hands when trying to explain the two sides to his work:

Cardinal Ottavio Paravicino famously remarked in 1603 that Caravaggio existed somewhere 'between the devout and the profane'. Scholars have experienced similar difficulties. Some have proposed that Caravaggio's close attention to nature comes from the *Spiritual Exercises*, others saw his affinity for the poor as a product of Oratorian devotions – the Oratorians are an Italian Order founded in 1575 that encouraged direct contact with God and simplicity of faith – while still others have seen Caravaggio as a crypto-Protestant. More recently, scholars have emphasized Caravaggio's ties with the Augustinian Order. Some of his most celebrated religious pictures were lateral altarpieces in Augustinian churches (S. Maria del Popolo and S. Agostino) and the Order had strong ties with Lombardy. Augustinian writers of the early seventeenth century promoted a climate of what scholars call 'pauperism', a concern for the poor and a desire to live humbly that is evoked in Caravaggio's work. Caravaggio painted substantially more religious paintings than anything else: two-thirds of his total output was devoted to New Testament subjects alone, and he painted many Old Testament scenes and episodes from the lives of the saints. Some are marked by the same violence that plagued Caravaggio's life, while others seek a kind of humility and piety quite antithetical to what we know about the artist's behaviour.

Caravaggio's brutal side dominates in his *Martyrdom of Saint Matthew* (33), one of two altarpieces he painted for the Contarelli Chapel in the Roman church of S. Luigi dei Francesi, his first public commission and one of the first large-scale paintings he attempted. Few of his religious scenes contain such turbulence and rage, and at first glance it recalls the street fights that punctuated Caravaggio's life. Loosely following an outline written by his patron Mattieu Cointrel (Contarelli) and based in part on a 1528–30 altarpiece by Titian, Caravaggio's canvas features a semi-nude assassin who fatally stabs the Evangelist during Mass on the orders of the Ethiopian king Hirtacus, whose marriage with a Christian woman Matthew had tried to stop. Instead of the imposing classical architecture requested by his patron, which dominated the artist's first version of the scene (revealed underneath by X-radiograph), Caravaggio places the action on an almost empty stage, with only the merest hints of columns, steps and an altar. Onlookers, including three more semi-nude figures in the foreground (the nudes are either pagans

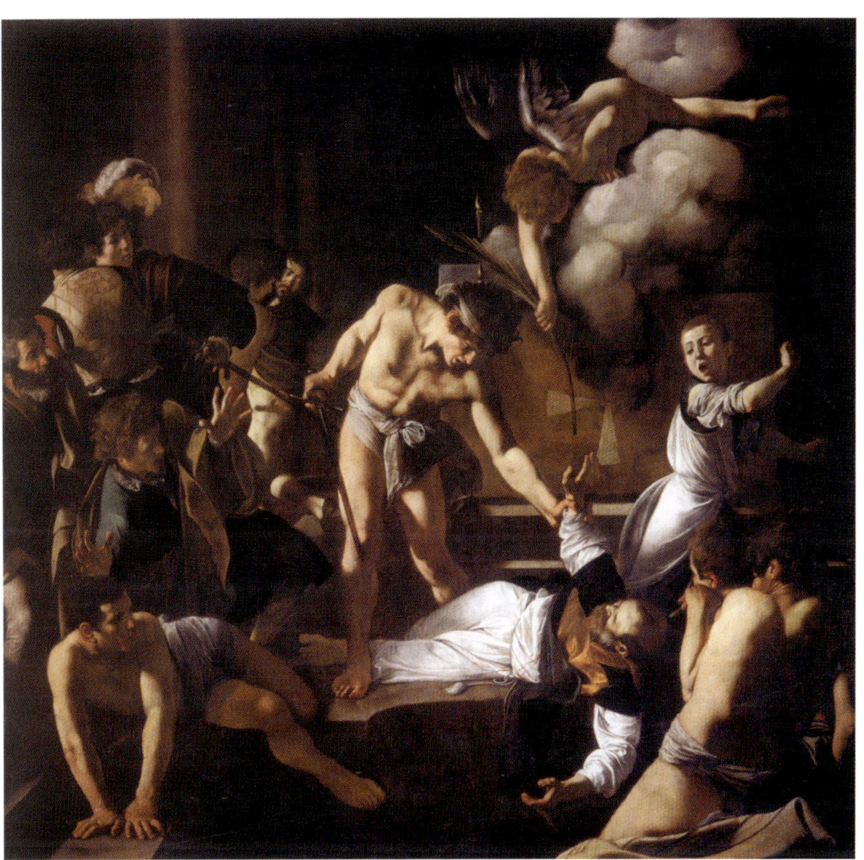

or Christian neophytes), men in contemporary dress and – famously – a self-portrait of Caravaggio (immediately to the left of the assassin), flee in all directions in an explosive, centrifugal retreat.

By including people in contemporary dress – a novelty in historical paintings at the time – Caravaggio brought the biblical past vividly into the present and gave viewers a sense that they were witnessing the event in real time. This conceit recalls popular devotional practices inspired by *Devotio Moderna* in which practitioners allowed an event in their own lives to prompt contemplations upon similar episodes in the lives of Christ or the saints. Thus, the bystanders in Caravaggio's altarpiece could be Roman citizens watching a street murder, who turn the horror of what they see into a pious exercise, reflecting upon the martyr's death and the fleetingness of life. Caravaggio places his self-portrait among them as an authentic 'witness' of the sacred scene, attesting both to its immediacy and historical accuracy. The faces and gestures of the bystanders reflect a subtle range of human emotions, from fear to remorse – Caravaggio shares his interest in emotions with the Incamminati – providing the viewer with a variety of possible responses to the scene. Here Caravaggio's trademark tenebrism serves two purposes. It exposes the harsh cruelty of the central action but also serves as a metaphor for the divine reward Matthew receives from God as the light gently caresses the arm of the angel who hands him his martyr's palm. The parallel juxtaposition of this delicate palm branch with the executioner's steel sword at the centre of the canvas is one of the most arresting passages in the painting.

Caravaggio's *Madonna of Loreto* (34), painted for the Cavaletti Chapel of the Augustinian church of S. Agostino, represents the artist's other side: the man of faith who felt a personal connection with God and gave the poor and displaced a dignity they rarely received in life. This painting was commissioned by the heirs to Ermete Cavalletti, a member of the Arch-Confraternity of the Most Holy Trinity of the Pilgrims and Convalescents, a lay religious group set up to care for destitute pilgrims who came to Rome by the thousands, especially during the years when the pope declared a papal jubilee (a year of universal pardon typically celebrated every twenty-five or fifty years). By the time Caravaggio painted this altarpiece he had already become a polemical figure and had received substantial criticism for his work – particularly for his open sympathy for the poor with their tattered clothes and dirty feet – and two of his altarpieces for Roman churches had been rejected. Therefore, the Cavalletti knew precisely what they were getting into when they hired Caravaggio, and they must have been drawn to his pauperistic tendencies – tendencies that would also have been shared by the Augustinian caretakers of the church. And despite the scathing criticism this painting received from Roman connoisseurs (led by his arch-rival Baglione) almost immediately upon its unveiling, the patrons and Augustinian fathers refused to part with it.

The uniqueness of Caravaggio's canvas becomes clear when we compare it to a more mainstream painting of the same scene, in this case an anonymous early seventeenth-century canvas of the *Madonna of Loreto with Saint John the Baptist and Saint George* (35) from the church of S. Maria Nuova in

34.
Caravaggio, *Madonna of Loreto*, c.1603–6. Oil on canvas, 2.6 × 1.5 m (8 ft 5 in × 4 ft 11 in). S. Agostino, Rome

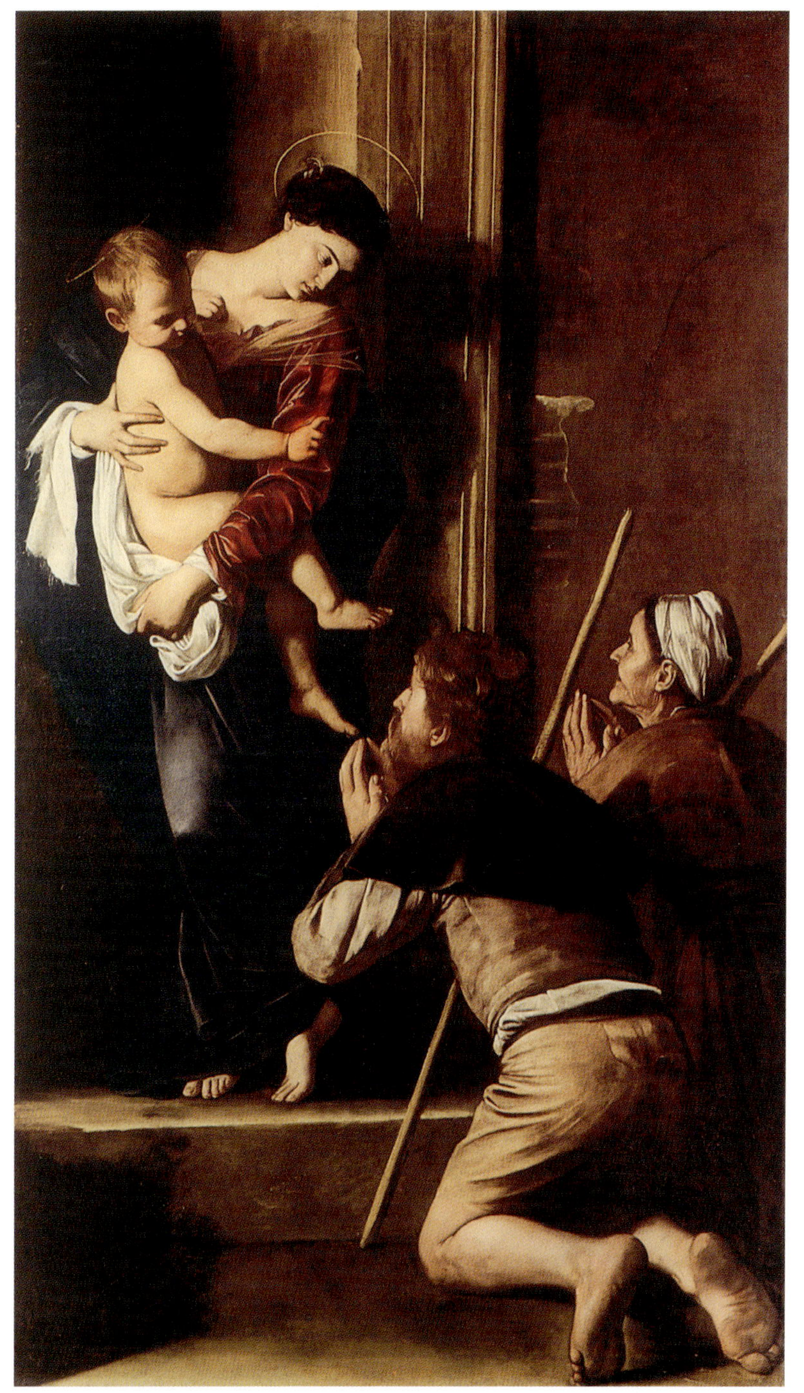

Abbiategrasso, a Lombard town about as far to the southwest of Milan as the town of Caravaggio was to the east. The Madonna of Loreto, housed in an extremely popular pilgrimage site in the Marches that also contains what is believed to be Mary's house (the Holy House), is a blackened cedar statue, probably from the fifteenth century but allegedly carved by Saint Luke. In the Abbiategrasso altarpiece, the artist underscores the statue's identity as a cult image. Wooden and mute, it stands on a ledge behind two flanking saints, one of them invoking it directly and the other beckoning us to do so. This painting leaves no doubt that the statue is an object, and its stiff, frontal appearance shows that the artist even made an effort to paint it in an older, archaic style – a method of making copies of cult images look more authentic that dates back to the early Middle Ages.

By contrast, Caravaggio brings the Madonna of Loreto alive, transforming her from a cold work of sculpture into a warm, loving figure of compassion – and one of the most beautiful women in his oeuvre. Like a working-class Roman girl who had been called unexpectedly to the door, Mary steps barefoot out of a crumbling building, her child hastily gathered in her arms. Unlike the cult image, which wears a golden crown and is draped with golden and bejewelled chains, Caravaggio's Madonna lacks all finery – save the barest hint of a halo – and her dress is artless and unpretentious. In place of the stiff flanking saints of the Abbiategrasso painting, Caravaggio gives us two pilgrims, a man and woman, who kneel barefoot and prostrate before the image – they are even shown humbly from behind. Instead of festive reds, pinks and gold, Caravaggio restricts himself to muted colours such as dark purples, browns and greys, and casts his scene in shadow. Indeed the simplicity and humility of the painting – and particularly the frankness of the pilgrims' poverty – would seem at first to belittle the Virgin by reducing her to the squalor of the Roman streets. This certainly was the impression Caravaggio gave Baglione, who sneered, 'he painted a Madonna of Loreto portrayed from life, with two pilgrims, one of them with muddy feet, and the other wearing a torn and soiled bonnet; and … the populace made a great fuss over it'. It was precisely the immense popularity this painting had with the lower classes that inspired the ire of the aristocratic art community. But there is much more to this painting than meets the eye.

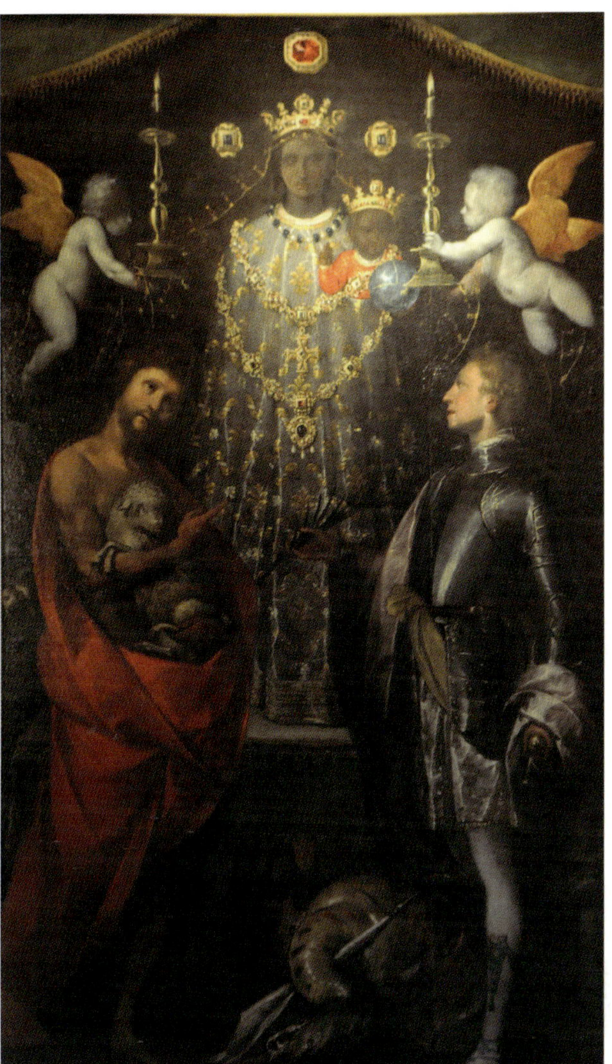

**35.
Anonymous
Italian**,
*Madonna of
Loreto with
Saint John the
Baptist and
Saint George*,
17th century.
Oil on canvas;
2.43 × 1.53 m
(8 ft × 5 ft).
S. Maria
Nuova,
Abbiategrasso
(Italy)

Scholars are increasingly recognizing how misleadingly ingenuous
Caravaggio's naturalism can be. In fact, the *Madonna of Loreto* is saturated
with scriptural and liturgical meaning, including specific references to
the Loreto pilgrimage, such as the pilgrims' gestures and attire (kneeling
and barefoot, his head uncovered), which are traditional when visiting the
shrine, and iconographic clues, such as the crumbling plaster revealing a
brick structure like that of the Holy House itself. The key to the painting
is in the pilgrims. Possibly portraits of the chapel's donors, these tattered
figures serve not only as a symbol of pilgrimage, but also of humility and

piety. Their devotions bring the cult image to life and compel viewers to participate in their vision and join them in their prayers. The pose of the Madonna and Child enhances the scene's visionary quality: they seem to float on the threshold (note that her feet never quite rest on the step and her heavy child never strains her frail arms), and they emerge from the darkness as if into the viewer's space. The heavenly pair mirror the earthly pair below, not only because both consist of a male and female but also because their heads are posed along parallel diagonal lines, elevating the humble pilgrims to the dignity of the sacred figures. Similarly, the male pilgrim's dirty feet (a symbol of the earthly, world-bound status of humanity) are contrasted with those of Christ, which are pure and unsullied. These contrasts reflect popular treatises of the day that focused on the contradiction between the Holy House's humble appearance and its divine status.

Despite the disarming naturalism of the mother and child, Caravaggio never deviates from the iconography of the Loreto image, a standing Madonna with a child holding up his right hand in benediction. Many other seemingly artless details link the painting with the *Litany of Loreto*, a popular meditative prayer made up of a series of invocations of the Virgin Mary under different

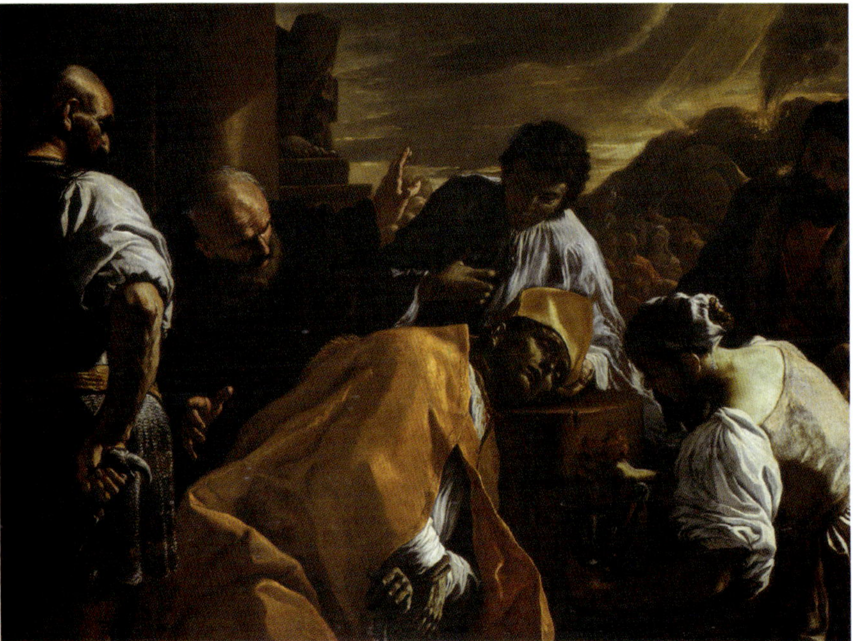

36.
Mattia Preti,
*The Martyrdom
of Saint
Januarius*,
c.1685. Oil on
canvas; 1.54
× 2 m (5 ft ×
6 ft 6¾ in).
National
Gallery,
Washington,
DC

honorific names that had just been re-approved by Pope Clement VIII in 1601. Among the many appellations given to the Virgin in the Litany – the prayer may have originated in Loreto in c.1558 – are 'Tower of Ivory', which Caravaggio intimates through the Virgin's upright bearing and white skin, and 'Gate of Heaven', evoked by the marble doorway, which Caravaggio subtly accents with light. The *Madonna of Loreto* operates on two levels. Through its directness and candor it offers consolation and humanity, but through deliberate iconographic references it can serve as a deeper meditative tool, allowing the viewer to undertake a virtual pilgrimage of the soul.

Caravaggio's reputation in Rome precluded him from leaving much of an artistic legacy in that city. After his exile, he worked in Naples, Malta and Sicily, where his style found fertile ground, spreading to Spain, Flanders and France. The most important centre was Naples, where he revolutionized local tastes in painting after his arrival in 1606. If Rome was the leader of the Catholic reform movement in the arts, Naples was one of its most ardent acolytes. The second largest city in Europe after Paris and one of the most cosmopolitan thanks to centuries of French and Spanish rule, its thriving port and its role as a haven for displaced northern Italians, Naples was also a profoundly devout city. Its most prized relics, the head and liquefying blood of the martyr Saint Januarius, inspired several public processions each year, and they were invoked during the city's frequent plagues. In *The Martyrdom of Saint Januarius* by the Calabrian painter Mattia Preti (1613–1699; 36) – still paying homage to Caravaggio seventy-five years after his death – these relics serve as the painting's focus. The saint's severed head rests on the executioner's block while his blood trickles into a cup held by Eusebia, the woman credited with preserving this precious relic. Although Preti uses purples and blues never employed by Caravaggio, the muddy browns of the background, the tenebrism, the large-scale figures and the bluntness of the violence reflect his legacy. Neapolitans were firm believers in the supernatural power of images, as when the same Preti was hired in 1656 to paint monumental ex-voto frescos of the Virgin Immaculate and saints on the seven city gates in a last-ditch attempt to put an end to a devastating plague. The passing of that pestilence shortly after the commission began turned Preti's frescos into miracle workers.

A Neapolitan painter of Spanish origin, Jusepe de Ribera (c.1591–1652) was among the first in the city to embrace Caravaggio's populist style and he also stimulated enthusiasm for it in his native country. Ribera's earliest Neapolitan paintings, such as *The Martyrdom of Saint Bartholomew* (37), evoke works such as Caravaggio's *Flagellation* (38), itself a Neapolitan commission. Both paintings employ vivid tenebrism to heighten their sense of intimacy and to focus unmercifully on the protagonists' suffering: they linger over the subtlest anatomical details, from the strained, awkward musculature to the unidealized skin textures, and stress the cruelty of the executioners, in Caravaggio's case through the mechanical, workmanlike way they fulfil their task and in Ribera's through their mocking jeers, implicating us by association in their crime. But Ribera also makes some noteworthy innovations. His Bartholomew, on the verge of being skinned alive, combines inner fervour with outer frailty in a way that invites the viewer to meditate on mortality and the urgency of salvation. Ribera also places more emphasis on skin tone than Caravaggio in an ingenious method all his own. Using a brush thick with paint, he precisely follows every line or blemish of the old man's skin, so that the wrinkles catch the light and enhance the illusion of the third dimension (using a technique called impasto). Ribera provided exactly the kind of sombre meditative image that Spanish patrons were looking for, and he enjoyed generous patronage from the viceroys (stand-ins for the Spanish king who governed Naples for multiples of three years), and from the aristocracy at home. By 1666, no fewer than sixty-four of Ribera's works were hanging in the three principal Spanish palaces of the Alcázar, Buen Retiro and Escorial.

The Spanish monarchy and gentry were receptive to Caravaggio's and Ribera's styles because they had been enthusiastic about reformist trends in sacred painting before either artist came on the scene. With their vast empire in Europe, the Americas and the Philippines, Spain saw itself as the global guardian of Catholic orthodoxy, challenging Protestants and non-Christians alike. Spanish spirituality was unusually austere and patrons wanted scenes of Christ's Passion, martyrdom and death, as well as such Spanish saints as Ignatius of Loyola or Teresa of Ávila. Unsurprisingly, the Spanish had been one of the main markets for Sebastiano del Piombo's paintings (see 23),

37.
Jusepe de Ribera, *The Martyrdom of Saint Bartholomew*, c.1628–30. Oil on canvas; 1.45 × 2.16 m (4 ft 9 in × 7 ft 1 in). Palazzo Pitti, Florence

which inspired works such as Luis de Morales's *Christ Carrying the Cross* (39).
Active during the era of the Council of Trent and its aftermath, the
Extremadura painter was so profoundly moved by the *Spiritual Exercises*
and the *Imitation of Christ* that he gained the epithet '*el divino*' (the divine).
Morales favoured small devotional paintings with few figures that could be
installed in private oratories to aid in the practice of the 'composition of
place' and other meditative exercises. His *Christ Carrying the Cross* achieves
greater tension than Sebastiano's version. Christ is so large that he almost
bursts from the panel, forcing his Cross, bloodied face and gnarled crown on

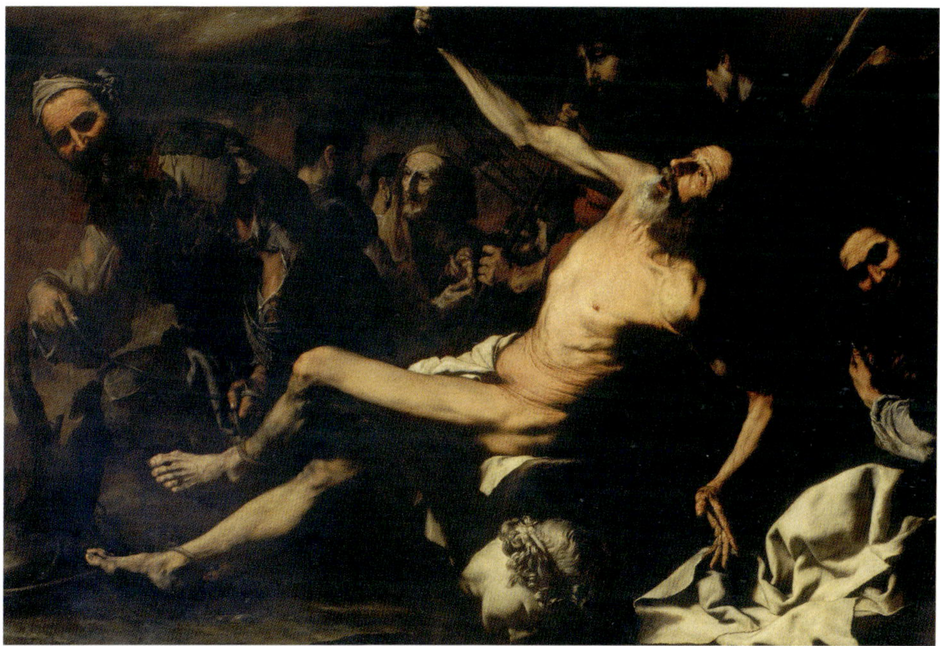

thorns directly into our gaze, and the painting's obscure tones (deepened by
an extremely limited palette) enhance Christ's nearness. Morales's ethereal
style enjoyed a long legacy in Spain, finding an echo in the work of fellow
Extremaduran Francisco de Zurbarán (see 11).

As in Italy, Spanish clerical art theorists tried to dictate style in painting,
particularly in Seville, the empire's leading artistic centre. Francisco Pacheco
(1564–1654) was a modestly talented painter and became governor of the
painter's guild and prestigious Seville Academy (an association of writers,

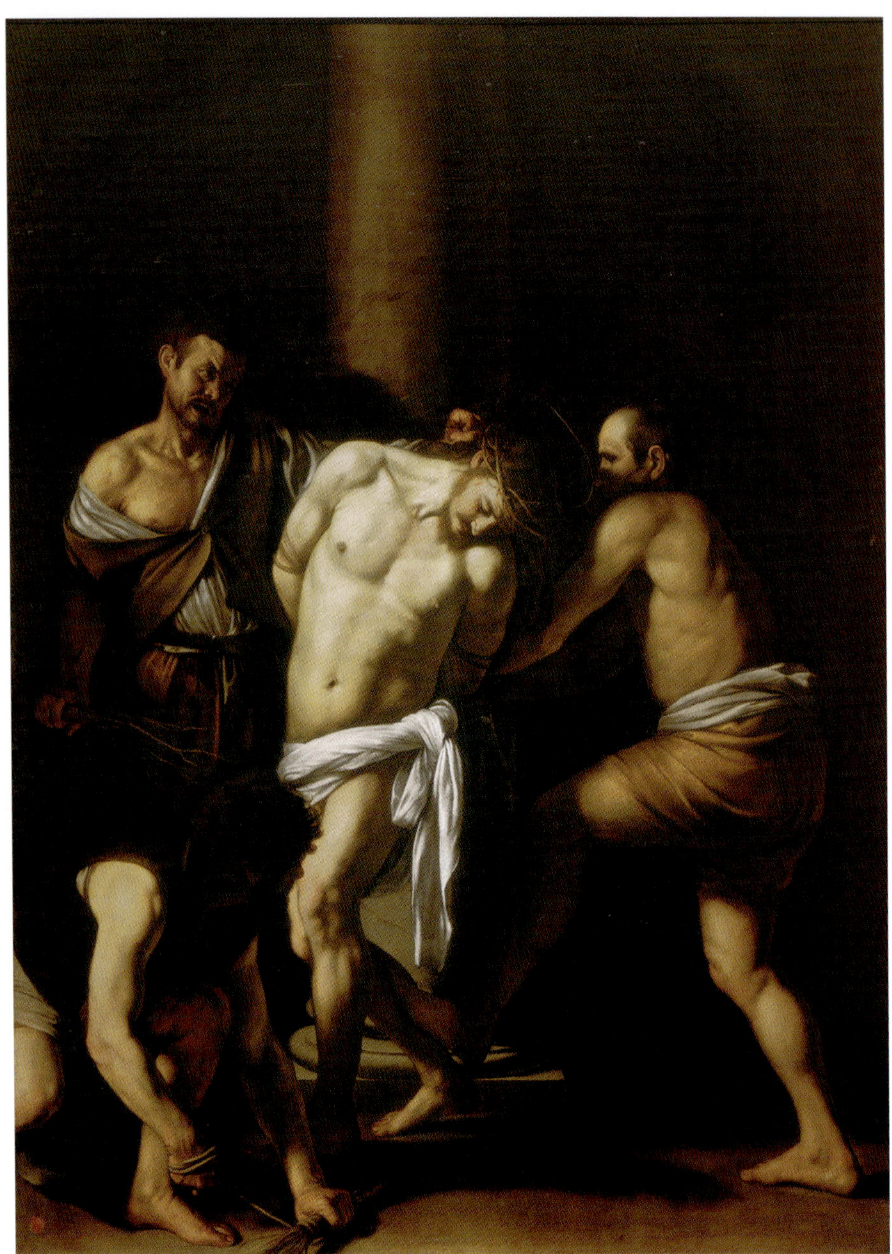

38.
Caravaggio,
*Flagellation of
Christ*, c.1607.
Oil on canvas,
2.66 × 2.13 m
(8 ft 8¾ in ×
7 ft). Museo
Nazionale di
Capodimonte,
Naples

antiquarians and theologians) in 1599. During his tenure at the Academy,
he wrote *The Art of Painting* (published in 1649), which attempted both to
ennoble the medium through a concept of 'nature perfected' similar to that
of Agucchi and Bellori and to defend the Catholic faith. Although intended
to be more practical than Italian treatises – he was a painter, unlike Gilio
or Gabriele Paleotti – the book established almost obsessively orthodox
guidelines for sacred painting, some echoing Trent almost verbatim, and
Pacheco called upon a legion of Seville theologians to support the minutest
points of doctrine. As he wrote: 'it is a great fault in good painters that they

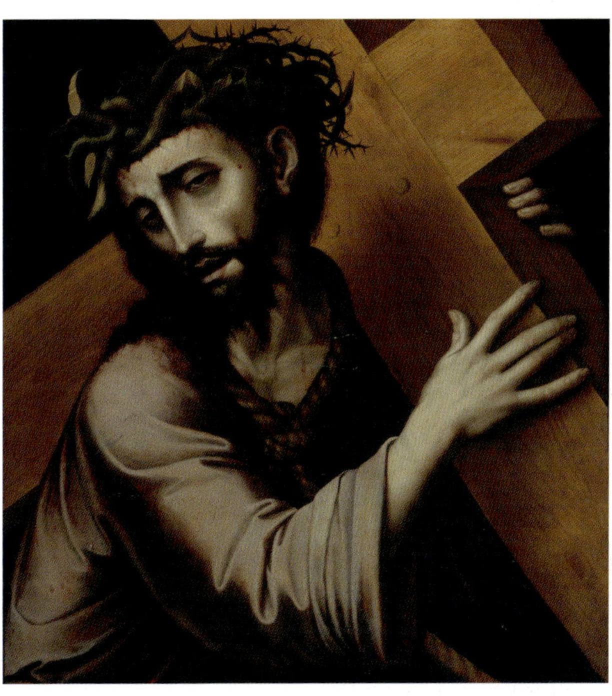

39.
Luis de
Morales,
*Christ Carrying
the Cross*, 1566.
Oil on panel;
59 × 56 cm
(23 × 22¼ in)
Galleria
degli Uffizi,
Florence

do not follow the authority of books and the judgement of the studious and
well informed …'. Pacheco was rewarded for his efforts by being elevated in
1618 to the office of overseer of sacred images by the Seville branch of the
Spanish Inquisition. But as luck would have it, he had to sit by and watch as
his star pupil and son-in-law Diego Velázquez (1599–1660) was appointed
at the tender age of twenty-four as royal painter – a position Pacheco had
considered his right – and went on to become Spain's greatest master of the
Baroque. Ironically, Velázquez was a champion of naturalism (like Caravaggio
in Italy), not the idealism promoted in his teacher's book.

We can distinguish the two artists' styles by examining two versions of
the *Virgin Immaculate*, an image of the Virgin Mary based on the Book of
Revelation (12:1–4; 14) that depicts her standing on the moon and wearing
a crown of stars. The cult of the Immaculate Conception, in which the
Virgin Mary was born without the stain of original sin, was extraordinarily
popular in Spain and her colonies, including Latin America, Sicily and
Naples – Preti's lost frescos for the city gates are an example – but above all
in Seville. Pacheco's Virgin is a stiff, formal and iconic type, her face idealized
by an aquiline nose, arched eyebrows and puckered lips, and her drapery
with sharp, starched folds is inspired by Flemish models (40). By contrast,
Velázquez's version – possibly a portrait of his nineteen-year-old wife Juana
(Pacheco's daughter) – is an ordinary young woman (41). Demurely lowering
her eyes, she assumes a natural and relaxed pose, her hair draped casually
over her right shoulder, and her shimmering drapery subtly revealing the
form of her legs beneath. Pacheco has given his Virgin a crown like those
worn by holy statues in Spanish churches, making her look even more like a
cult image. By eliminating that motif, Velázquez humanizes her in the same
way Caravaggio brought his Virgin of Loreto to life (see 34). In Pacheco's
painting more light appears behind the figure than on it – illuminating the
landscape and clouds at the expense of the Virgin, especially her lower body.
With Velázquez the light is more dominant and focused: although Mary
still lights up the clouds behind her, she is also bathed by a single shaft of
divine light that contrasts sharply with the background. Despite this hint of
Caravaggio's tenebrism, Velázquez's brushstrokes are a departure from his
Italian predecessor. They are less precise and demonstrate a suppleness and
fluidity that increased as his style matured.

The most celebrated paintings of the Immaculate Conception came decades
later, after a 1661 papal ruling that declared Mary immune from original sin
(the cult would not become dogma until 1854) ushered in a wave of more
triumphalist Marian imagery in Spain and its colonies. The most prolific painter
of Marian imagery was Bartolomé Esteban Murillo (c.1617–1682), Zurbarán's
rival and successor in Seville, who revived the principle of 'nature perfected'.
Like the second generation of Bolognese painters (Guido Reni, Guercino,
see 31) who helped to inspire his work, Murillo championed idealized,

emotionally appealing figures and equated physical beauty with spiritual purity. These same Bolognese painters, along with Peter Paul Rubens (1577–1640) and Anthony van Dyck (1599–1641), also provided Murillo with a taste for the looser, flowing brushwork, heavier impasto and less intense contrasts of the international High Baroque. Murillo's hazy golden light, gentle expressions and soft moods had a special appeal to the middle classes, and his decision to paint in this style was no coincidence. After a series of economic crises in the 1670s sharply reduced institutional patronage, the artist was compelled to seek commissions from the growing population of foreign merchants resident in Seville, and these men with their luxurious surroundings and sentimental tastes preferred pretty pictures to dour reminders of death.

Murillo's *The Infant Jesus Distributing the Bread to Pilgrims* (42) provides a particularly instructive contrast with Caravaggio's *Madonna of Loreto* (see 34). Where Caravaggio gives us strong, focused light and precise brushwork, Murillo's looser handling softens the edges, particularly in the heavenly background with its clouds and trademark cherubs, which in itself departs significantly from Caravaggio since the latter avoided glimpses into the hereafter. Murillo's palette is warmer and more colourful with a balance of reds, yellows, blues and greens that evokes Raphael. Instead of Caravaggio's girl from the tenements, Murillo gives us an idealized Mary with high cheekbones and aquiline nose, and the infant Jesus, performing the charity of giving bread to the pilgrims, is the very picture of tow-headed youth. But the pilgrims are the most significant contrast between the two paintings, even though both groups are likely portraits and executed with keen realism. (Murillo's naturalism is partly inspired by his study of Dutch realist paintings, provoked by his desire to attract his Dutch and Flemish expatriate patrons.) Murillo has replaced Caravaggio's ragged devotees with three well-dressed, older gentlemen who approach the sacred vision with much more decorum. With Murillo, Spanish and Spanish-American painting moved from darkened scenes of reproachful martyrs to playful and increasingly sentimental paintings of the Madonna and infant Christ.

Unlike Italy or Spain, France was directly on the front lines in the battle

against Protestantism, and had just barely escaped becoming Protestant
itself. The last decades of the sixteenth century witnessed repeated riots, civil
wars and massacres that pitted the Calvinist Huguenots against the French
Catholic establishment. The violence ended only in 1598 with the Edict
of Nantes, a treaty of religious tolerance that was to last until Louis XIV
revoked it in 1685, sending half a million Huguenots into exile. Although
France grew dramatically in power and prestige throughout the seventeenth
century under Henry IV, Louis XIII and Louis XIV, it remained a divided

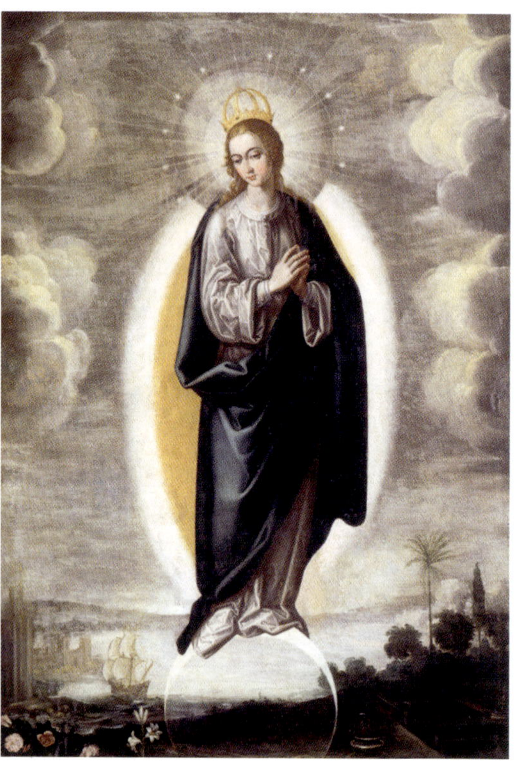

40.
**Francisco
Pacheco**,
*Virgin
Immaculate*,
c.1621–35.
Oil on canvas;
1.44 × 1 m
(4 ft 9 in × 3 ft
3 in). Palacio
Arzobispal,
Seville (Spain)

41.
**Diego
Velázquez**,
*Virgin
Immaculate*,
1618. Oil on
canvas; 1.35 ×
1 m (4 ft 5 in
× 3 ft 3 in).
National
Gallery,
London

country, with limited Huguenot freedom of worship, a Huguenot political
party and – until 1628 when the king besieged and overthrew the Huguenots
at La Rochelle – fortified Huguenot strongholds. Catholicism was divided
as well, in a theological battle between the establishment, led by the Jesuits,
and Jansenism, a fundamentally pessimistic Catholic philosophy based
on the writings of Dutch theologian Cornelius Otto Jansen (1585–1638).
Jansenism stressed the corrupt and depraved nature of humankind, proposing

that men and women were passive creatures unable to resist evil unless guided by the more powerful force of God's grace. As a result the movement stressed moral rigour, asceticism and piety. Although condemned by Pope Innocent X in 1653, Jansenist doctrine continued to thrive in France well into the eighteenth century, and the Jansenist faction counted many leading intellectuals among its adherents, including the playwright Jean Racine (1639–1699), the mathematician and philosopher Blaise Pascal (1623–1662), and the painter Philippe de Champaigne (1602–1674).

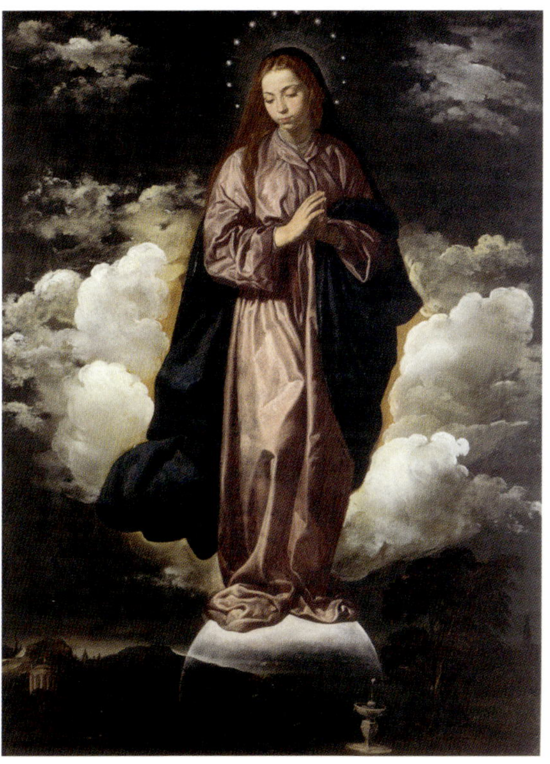

Two contemporary paintings of the *Penitent Magdalene*, by Georges de La Tour (1593–1652) and Philippe de Champaigne, accentuate the diversity of religious life in seventeenth-century France (see 43, 45). Baroque painting came relatively late to France, which still favoured sixteenth-century courtly styles as late as the 1620s. It was thus something of a shock when La Tour, a small-town painter from Lunéville in the northeastern region of Lorraine, introduced one of the most original interpretations of Caravaggio's populist style ever conceived (although he experienced it second-hand via Dutch artists). La Tour is best known for his religious paintings, which he executed mainly for the local bourgeoisie and the government in nearby Nancy – he was never very popular with the aristocracy, despite being named 'Painter to the King' in 1639. These works satisfied a hunger for intimate images of private devotion in the tradition of the *Devotio Moderna* and the thirteenth-century Franciscan manual *Meditations on the Life of Christ*, both of which continued to enjoy popularity in the provinces. In fact, a Franciscan grass-roots religious revival in Lorraine specifically inspired La Tour's populism, and its influence left a mark in his *Penitent Magdalene* (43).

For much of his career, Flemish-born Philippe de Champaigne represented a very different world. A metropolitan artist based in Paris from 1621, he championed classical forms (he studied Graeco-Roman sculptures in royal collections), regal colours, stately compositions and triumphant heavenly cloudbursts influenced by his countryman Rubens. Champaigne painted for the king, the queen mother, powerful first minister Cardinal Richelieu (1585–1642) and the Church, and he was one of the founders of the *Académie Royale de Peinture et de Sculpture* in 1645 (see Chapters Two and Five). Yet as Champaigne matured as an artist, his work also became more introspective and ascetic, particularly after he underwent a spiritual transformation in the mid-1640s under the influence of the Jansenists, whom he credited with curing his daughter, a Jansenist nun, of paralysis. In 1662 he painted a famous ex-voto commemorating this event – it was a double portrait of his daughter and Mother Agnes of the Jansenist Convent of Port-Royal – an unusually austere painting in which the two sitters in their grey and black habits are posed like statues against a restrained grey background pierced by a beam of divine light from the right (44). His *Penitent Magdalene* (45) is more typical of this late style, in which he abandons his earlier cloudbursts, angels and ecstasies in favour of fervent introspection.

Mary Magdalene enjoyed a cult revival in the Baroque era because she had sinned, making her more approachable as a role model for ordinary Catholics (particularly women) than saints who lived lives of pious perfection, and the penitent Magdalene became one of the most popular subjects in Baroque

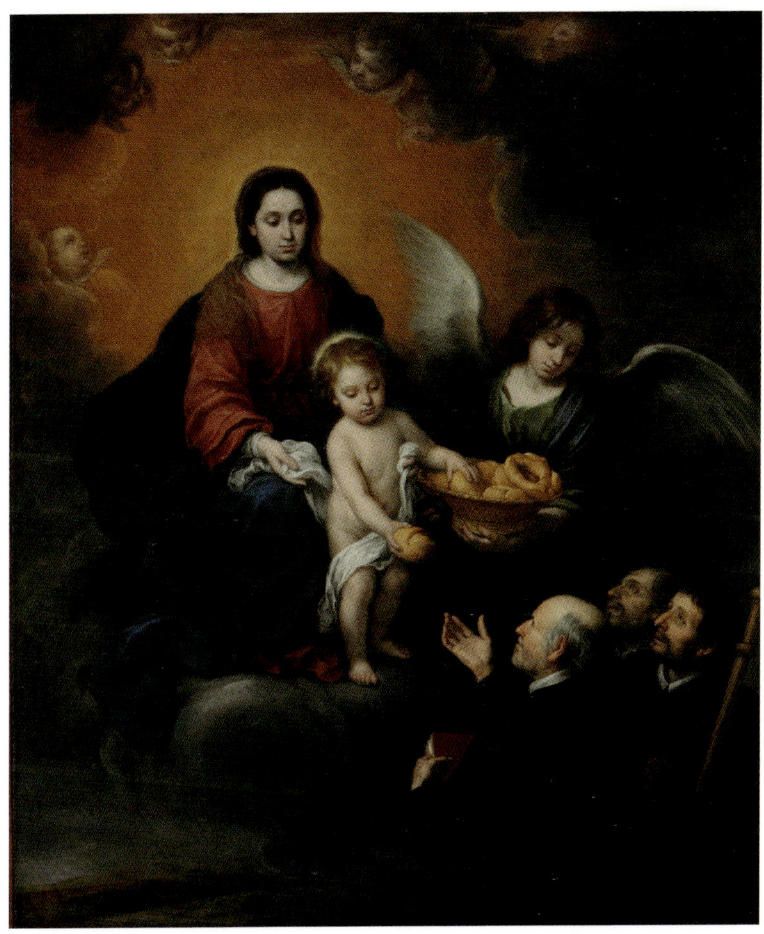

painting. In La Tour's version Mary is a simple country woman, sitting before a rustic table in a darkened room, the table adorned only with two old books, a lit candle, a penitential whip and a cross. Mary wears a rope around her waist as a symbol of her spiritual vocation, and she holds a skull on her lap as a *memento mori*. Although the skull commonly appears in Magdalene imagery, the skull and rope are both specifically Franciscan motifs, recalling the impact of that order on La Tour's spirituality. By contrast, Champaigne gives us a more traditional Magdalene, whose classical, idealized face and proportions, massive body and dramatic pose echo portraits of the Magdalene by such contemporary Bolognese painters as Guido Reni and Guercino. Franciscan symbolism is absent in Champaigne's Magdalene, which focuses instead on the more traditional emblems of the crucifix, ointment jar, skull and Scripture.

Whereas La Tour's Magdalene is passive and quietly contemplative – the
forms are so abstracted that they look more like a vision than reality –
Champaigne's is active and emotive, as she raises her tear-stained face
towards Heaven and crosses her hands before her breast. La Tour's trademark
candlelight serves as a focus for Mary's meditation and animates her face,
but it also enhances the picture's intimacy – more so even than Caravaggio,
whose principal light source always came from outside his paintings. La
Tour not only invites the viewer to join Mary in her solitude, but – by giving
his subject a contemporary setting and clothing – he allows her to place
herself in Mary's shoes, participating in the sacred tableau as if in real time,

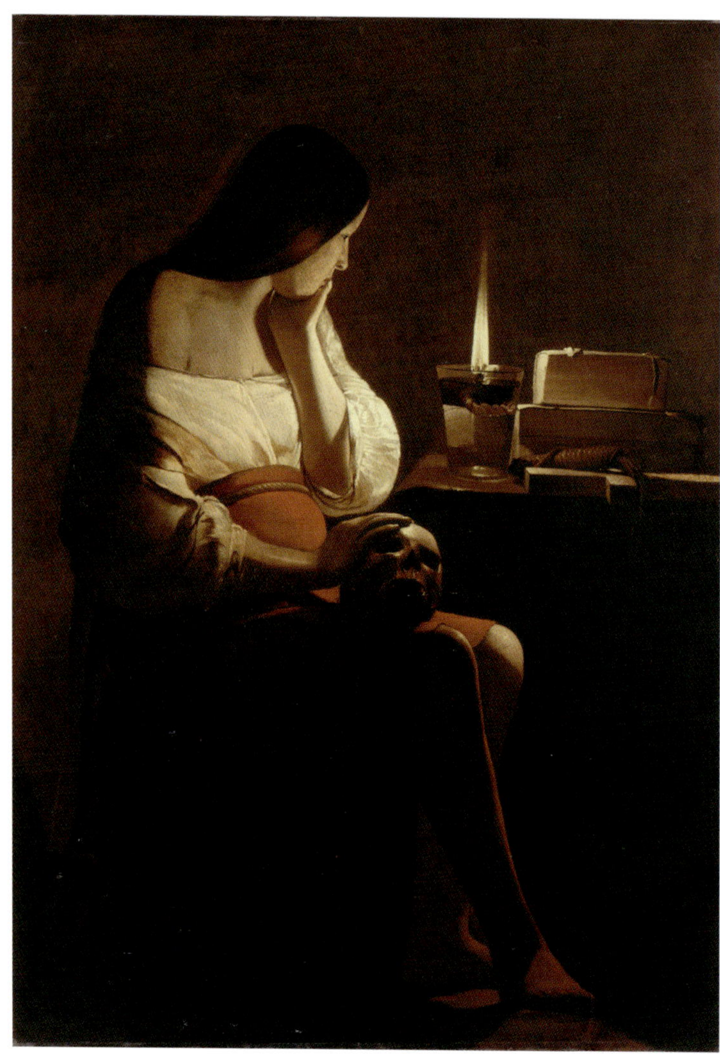

as with Caravaggio's *Martyrdom of Saint Matthew* (see 33). Champaigne's goals are quite different. Although his scene shares La Tour's sobriety, a more traditional divine light illuminates Mary from the upper left and her clothing and setting place her in a specific historical time and place, the cave in Provence, southeastern France, where she allegedly spent the last years of her life. La Tour radically simplifies his forms and palette, although his attention to surface textures allows the viewer to feel the contrast between the rough cloth of her gown and bodice and her smooth, young skin. By contrast, Champaigne revels in detail, as seen in the golden locks of Mary's hair, the delicate knuckles of her fingers and the facets of the rock, and his colours – although muted – still recall the royal blues and bronzes of his more triumphant early works.

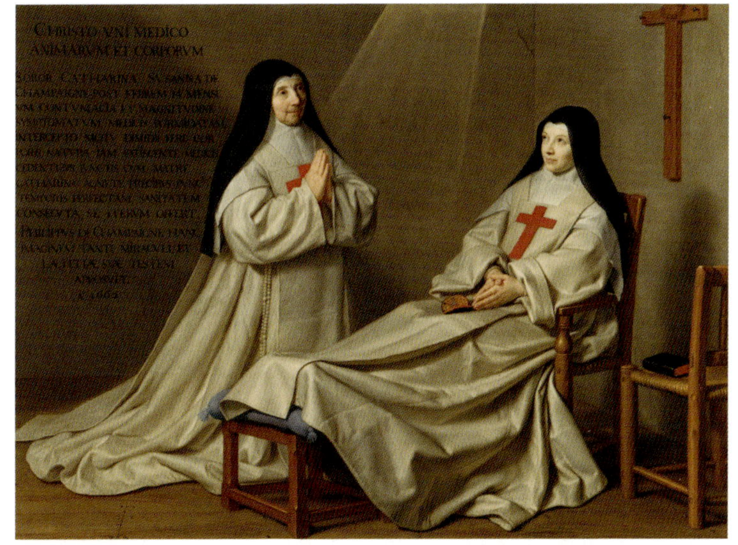

43.
Georges de la Tour, *Penitent Magdalene*, 1640–4. Oil on canvas; 128 × 94 cm (50½ × 37 in). Louvre, Paris

44.
Philippe de Champaigne, *Ex-Voto*, 1662. Oil on canvas; 1.65 × 2.29 m (5 ft 5 in × 7 ft 6 in). Louvre, Paris

Few parts of Europe were so directly and violently engaged in the struggle between Reformation and Counter-Reformation – and the war of images – as the Netherlands, divided between the Protestant north (Holland) and Catholic south (usually called Flanders, modern-day Belgium). The whole of the Netherlands had been a Spanish colony since 1551, but on the heels of the *Beeldenstorm* a civil war ensued between Protestants and Catholics that led to a declaration of independence by the Protestant northern provinces in 1581, although Spain was only forced to accept the secession at the conclusion of the Thirty Years War in 1648. Thus, unlike in France, the battle was still being fought well into the Baroque era, and the arts took a more militant approach to the conflict. More than any other country in this chapter, the art scene in Flanders was dominated by the towering personality of one man: Rubens. Painter, diplomat, spy and the seventeenth-century equivalent of a jet-setter, Rubens put his gregarious personality and prodigious talent to work, selectively synthesizing artistic traditions he encountered in Rome, Venice, Spain and France with those of his homeland and creating the first international Baroque style. Scholars have recently suggested that he was painting's answer to the sculptor Gianlorenzo Bernini, and his boisterous, dynamic and sensuous painting style, with its loose, fluid brushwork, came closer to what Bernini had achieved in sculpture (see Chapters Two and Three) than any Italian painter of his generation. Rubens the man was as complicated as Rubens the artist. Born a Calvinist, he converted with his family to Catholicism early in life and became its chief artistic spokesperson – and that of Flanders' Spanish viceroys. A socialite and sensualist at home in the royal courts of Europe, Rubens was also profoundly devout, bequeathing a substantial part of his energies and wealth to supporting Catholic confraternities and religious Orders, particularly those belonging to the Society of Jesus.

Rubens's largest commission in Antwerp was for the Jesuits, an Order he had worked for regularly during his 1600–8 sojourn in Italy. Antwerp was undergoing a Catholic revival in the first decades of the seventeenth century, as the Habsburg nobility commissioned new churches and artworks to replace the devastation of the *Beeldenstorm*. The most important was the grandiose new church of the Jesuits, dedicated to Saint Ignatius (now Saint Charles Borromeo), which Rubens may have helped design and for which he served as principal decorator. Although his series of thirty-nine ceiling paintings of saints and biblical subjects (done with the assistance of a young Anthony van Dyck) was destroyed in a fire in 1718, the two massive altarpieces, *The Miracles of Ignatius of Loyola* and *The Miracles of Francis Xavier*, survived the immolation and evoke the splendour of the church's interior (46). Adapting the monumentality of Venetian altarpieces – particularly those of Titian, his lifelong inspiration – Rubens heightens the grandeur

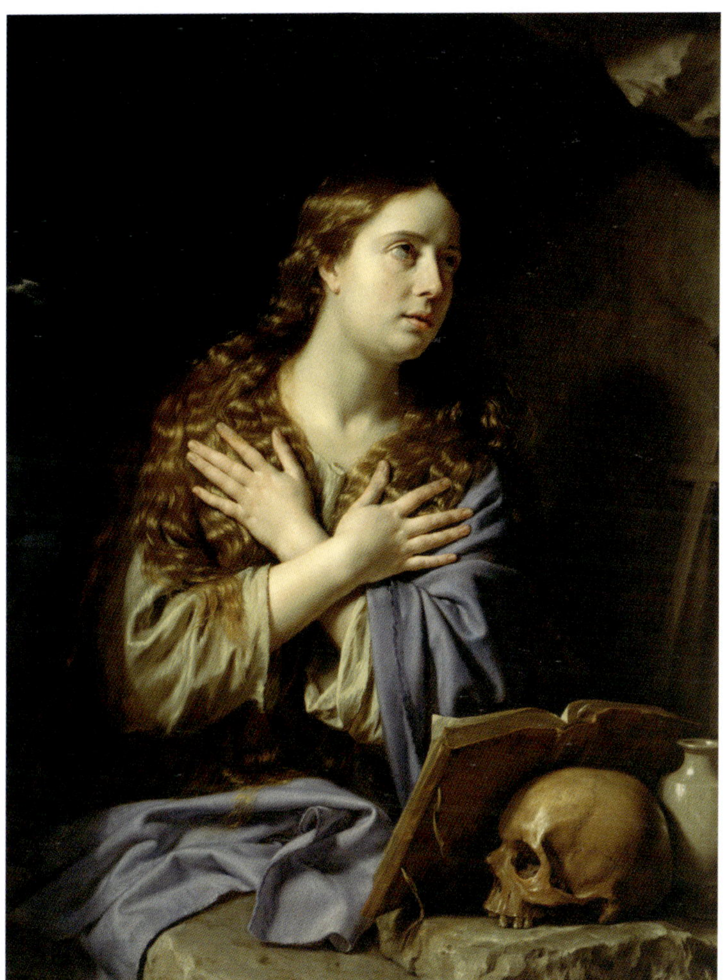

**45.
Philippe de
Champaigne**, *The Repentant Magdalene*, 1648. Oil on canvas; 115.5 × 87 cm (45½ × 34¼ in). Museum of Fine Arts, Houston TX

of the scene by allowing the columns and vault of the church to rise above the upper limit of the canvas. Also typical of Venetian painting is the way Ignatius stands halfway up the canvas in the middle ground on a staircase, allowing for a dramatic diagonal sweep from the crucifix on the upper right through Ignatius's head and down to the recumbent figure on the lower left. As Ignatius performs an exorcism on a man and a woman possessed by the Devil (a metaphorical reference to the Protestant heresy; see 22), the crowd at the lower left seethes with tension. The clamour of their bulky, muscular figures, fervent poses and facial expressions contrasts vividly with the gentle and orderly ranks of Jesuit priests standing behind Ignatius, representing the infallibility of orthodoxy. Rubens lavishes attention on the sparkling fabrics – particularly the splendid embroidered chasuble worn by Ignatius – and lavish interior (the golden bosses in the vaults recall the actual ceiling of the church of Saint Ignatius), as well as the cloudbursts, which serve as a vehicle for the victorious cherubs on the right and the escaping demons on the left.

If *The Miracles of Ignatius of Loyola* represents Rubens at his most triumphal and orthodox, his *Bathsheba at the Fountain* (47), a portrait of his young second wife Hélène Fourment, shows his sensual side. The Council of Trent condemned nudity in sacred painting, forbidding 'lasciviousness' and 'beauty exciting to lust', an attitude shared by many prominent clerics, including the earlier Dutch humanist scholar Desiderius Erasmus (1466–1536). Nevertheless, beginning as early as the first decade of the seventeenth century, Baroque painters from Artemisia Gentileschi (c.1593–1652; see Chapter Two) to Guercino routinely ignored that prohibition when painting certain episodes from the Old Testament that had been titillating audiences long before Trent: most notably *Susanna and the Elders, Joseph and Potiphar's Wife* and *Bathsheba at the Fountain* (see 12). These works fell outside the proscriptions of Trent because they were intended for private delectation and were never meant to be put on public view: this distinction between public and private often confuses present-day audiences, who are understandably surprised when faced with a 'religious' image that is frankly erotic. Rubens was perhaps the most flamboyantly sensual of them all, and made a speciality of biblical scenes featuring partially or fully nude women. In Bathsheba, Hélène – a far cry from Velázquez's demure tribute to his wife (see 41) – is an earthy seductress, the rosy tones of her skin and the ample proportions of her young body matched by the rich draperies surrounding her (black velvet, red satin and a glimpse of her white silk chemise still clinging to her right arm), as well as her palatial setting and attentive servants. Although she turns away from the viewer and modestly covers her lower torso, she fully exposes her bare legs and breasts, and plays seductively with her pearls, allowing them to slip down her left arm. Rubens's trademark loose brushwork here serves not only to energize the scene, but also to soften the edges, giving the whole a warm and inviting sensation.

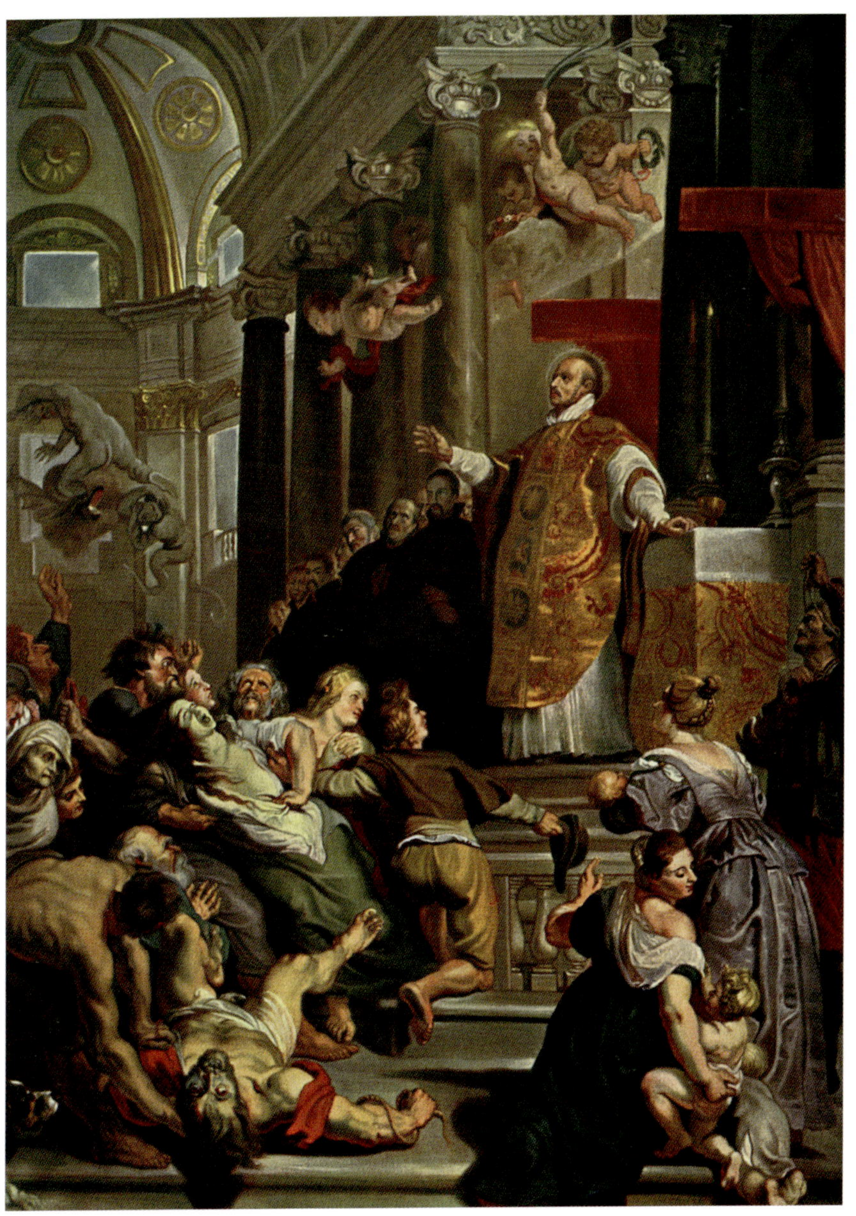

46.
**Peter Paul
Rubens**, *The
Miracles of
Ignatius of
Loyola*,
1617–18. Oil
on canvas;
5.31 × 3.91 m
(17 ft 5 in ×
5 ft). Kunst-
historisches
Museum,
Vienna

This chapter has been devoted to Catholic art, as the Catholic rejuvenation
of sacred imagery directly led to the creation of the Baroque. Yet, as we have
seen, Protestant leaders including Luther and Calvin were not opposed to
religious imagery outside churches, as long as it was didactic and did not
serve as an object of worship. In fact, Dutch painters produced thousands of
paintings and prints of biblical scenes to adorn peoples' homes, images that
shunned the triumphant bombast of such artists as Rubens in favour of quiet

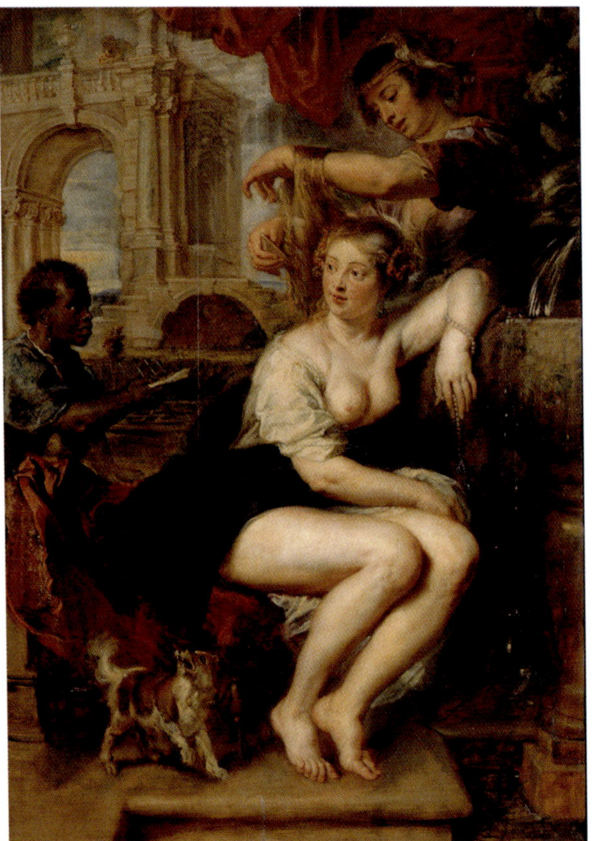

47.
**Peter Paul
Rubens,**
*Bathsheba at
the Fountain,*
c.1635. 1.26
× 1.75 m
(4 ft 1¼ in
× 5 ft 9 in).
Gemälde-
galerie,
Dresden
(Germany)

contemplation and humility more in sympathy with the meditative simplicity
of Caravaggio or de Ribera. I will close with a Dutch painter responsible
for some of the most moving sacred pictures in the history of Baroque art:
Rembrandt van Rijn (1606–1669). Although he painted biblical scenes as
early as the 1620s, Rembrandt's paintings, etchings and drawings increasingly
explored religious themes after the late 1650s, during the last decade of his

life. These works included episodes from the Bible and portraits of monks, hermits, saints, Christ and the Virgin Mary – he even painted a self-portrait as Saint Paul. Depictions of the Evangelists and Apostle Paul were especially appropriate for Protestants as they wrote the Gospels and Epistles and represented the primacy of text over image.

Rembrandt's dark and brooding *Apostle Paul* (48) – not the self-portrait – is a model for Protestant contemplation, its seated protagonist gazing introspectively but resolutely out of the gloom, resting his head in his left hand. Although the painting reflects Rembrandt's increasing fascination with the condition of the human soul, it also celebrates Scripture. Saint Paul is shown holding a pen with an open book on the desk before him, and Rembrandt uses light to link the Divine with the Word: the brightest passages are the Apostle's head, representing inspiration from God, and his writing hand and boldly foreshortened book, both overt references to his Epistles. The giant sword behind the desk would have further reminded viewers that Paul referred to the Word of God as the 'sword of the Spirit', a rare – but entirely appropriate – use of religious symbolism in his painting. Rembrandt may have executed these religious scenes for mundane mercantile reasons – such works were esteemed in private homes and the artist signed them in prominent places (in *Apostle Paul* the signature is on the foremost of the books) – but many scholars believe he painted them as personal explorations of spiritual contemplation. His interest in biblical scenes – several of them from the Old Testament – may also reflect his sympathy for Amsterdam's Jewish community, who lived in his neighbourhood, and some of whom scholars believe posed for his paintings of Christ and the Apostles.

The greatest – and one of the last – of Rembrandt's religious paintings is *The Return of the Prodigal Son* (49), painted during an acutely tragic time in his life when the artist was destitute and after he had lost his second (common-law) wife Hendrickje Stoffels (d. 1663) and his son Titus (d. 1669). Rembrandt has stripped the narrative down to one essential moment of love and redemption, as the rich man embraces – and completely engulfs – his tattered son, the envious brother and a pair of servants (much obscured) looking on from the right, while another figure can barely be discerned in the distance. Evoking

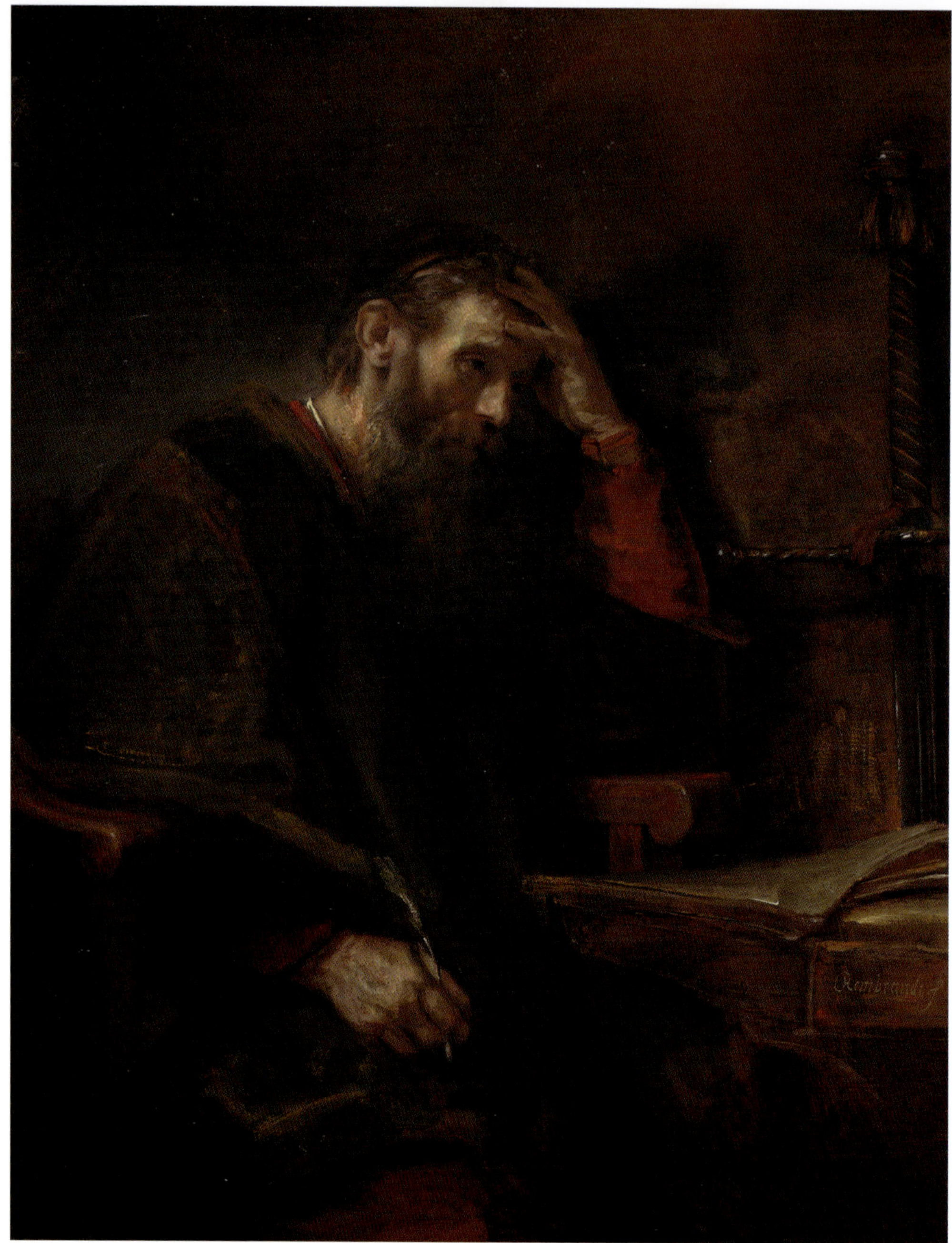

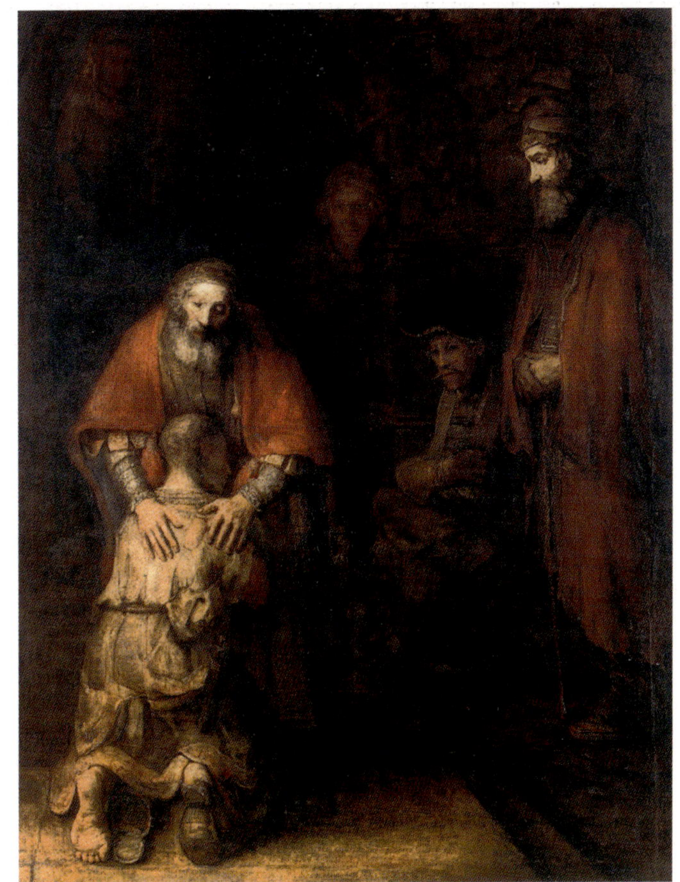

Caravaggio's tenebrism but transforming it completely through his sketchy

brushwork and heavy, almost sculptural impasto, Rembrandt has the two

protagonists emerge from a melancholy darkness into the viewer's space,

creating an intimacy, sense of quiet and an abstract quality comparable to

that of La Tour (see 43). The light, falling on the head of the father, the back

of the son and the face of one of the witnesses, punctuates the key moments

in the drama. The son – ruined, sick and worn, his bare feet and ragged

clothing echoing Caravaggio's pilgrims (see 34) – expresses contrition for a

life of vanity, one that Rembrandt may have intended as a reference to his

own youth. The father responds with a tenderness that commemorates mercy

as much as loss. This contemplative, introspective work of private devotion

serves as a fitting coda to a chapter that has considered some of the most

human responses to the sacred in the history of Western art: a heterogeneous

web of violence and love, torture and sensuality, and pessimism and triumph.

Profane Images   The Hierarchy of Genres and Proliferation of Worldly Subjects

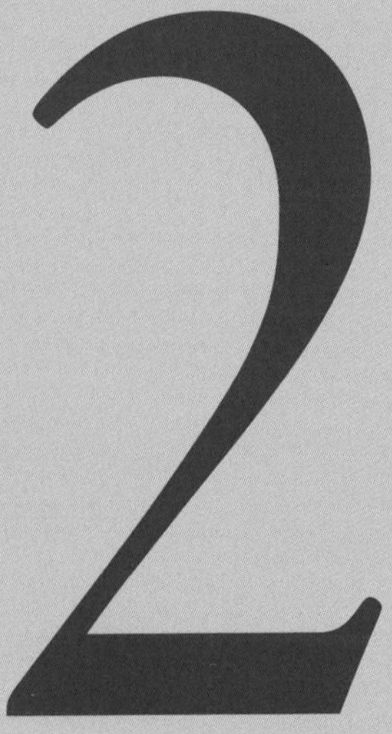

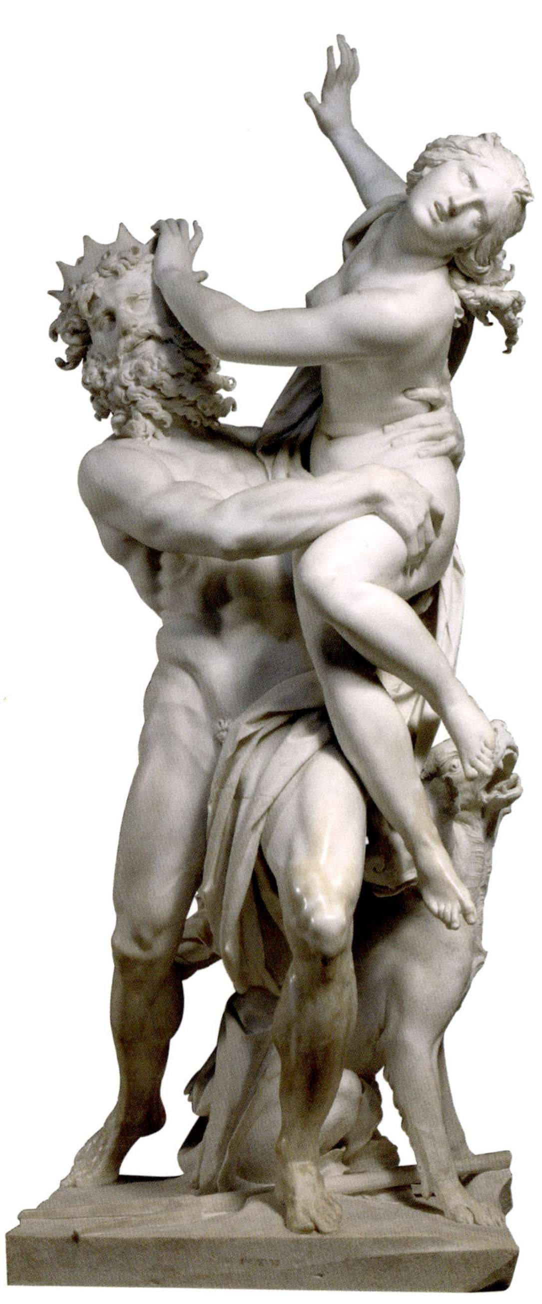

50.
Gianlorenzo Bernini, *Pluto and Proserpina*, 1621–2. Marble; 2.25 m (7 ft 5 in). Galleria Borghese, Rome

Profane Images   The Hierarchy of Genres and Proliferation of
Worldly Subjects

It might seem that the decrees of the Council of Trent and Protestant and
Catholic essayists would have put paid to profane imagery with its pagan
iconography, lascivious nudes and brazen manifestations of wealth. But
Protestant iconoclasm and Trent's condemnation of paintings depicting
'filthy lucre', 'lasciviousness' and 'beauty exciting to lust' were aimed solely
at sacred art: what we today call 'secular' imagery (the term was not coined
until the late eighteenth century) flourished on an unprecedented scale
in the seventeenth and eighteenth centuries, with artists and workshops
increasingly specializing in specific subjects, whether pagan allegory,
portraiture, landscape, scenes from everyday life, still life, exotica or erotica.
Two factors explain this explosion of imagery. In northern Europe practical
concerns for money and patronage in the wake of the Protestant banishment
of sacred art drove artists towards worldly genres with a more popular
appeal. Especially in Holland, views of familiar objects and surroundings
enchanted a mercantile class made newly prosperous with the rise of
international trade. The Catholic south also embraced northern genres
because of their accessibility and popular appeal so that landscapes and
still lifes – formerly only acceptable within religious or narrative paintings
– emerged as categories of painting in their own right. Especially in Italy
and France, the aristocracy's continuing enthusiasm for antiquity fuelled a
resurgence of Graeco-Roman mythological scenes (*favoleggiatura*). Even
clerics habitually indulged in such imagery, often passing it off as an allegory
of Christian virtues, as with Annibale Carracci's ode to love in his ceiling
for Odoardo Farnese in Rome (see 13). But most non-religious works of art
were kept from the eyes of the masses: destined for the domestic world of the
palace, country house and middle-class home, such images provided private
instruction, delectation and titillation.

With so many different kinds of subjects in circulation, art academies
such as the French Académie Royale de Peinture et de Sculpture (founded

1645) tried to arbitrate artistic taste through a hierarchy of genres divided into what they called the 'grand genre' (major genre) and 'petits genres' (minor genres) that still informs our notions of 'high' and 'low' art. French academician André Félibien (1619–1695) wrote in the preface to his *Conférences de l'Académie royale de peinture et de sculpture* (1667) that painting in which 'some Fable or Allegory, or History is represented' was the most noble of the genres, and he rated the lesser genres in descending order based on the worthiness of their subject, their amount of narrative content and their number of figures. Thus portraits are below history paintings because they depict a single person and lacked movement; landscapes are superior to paintings restricted to flowers, fruits or shells; and paintings of living animals are finer than still lifes showing the spoils of the hunt. The essential distinction is that the major genre is narrative – and therefore intellectual – while the minor genres are merely mimetic. The hierarchy of genres derives ultimately from Aristotle: in his *Poetics* the Greek philosopher placed dramatic literature (he called it 'tragedy') above epic, comedic and other lesser genres because of its ability to represent action, the seriousness of its subject, degree of introspection it demands from its listener, and sophistication of its audience. By conceiving a similar system of categorization for art, seventeenth-century academicians hoped to raise the status of painting to the level of literature – at the time considered a much more exalted medium.

The major genre (it became known simply as 'history painting') comprised allegorical, mythological, historical and religious themes – many of the paintings in Chapter One belong to this category – with allegory the noblest of all because it conceals within a narrative the virtues, mysteries and noble deeds of great men (and, more rarely, women). Definitions of history painting can be traced back to the treatise *On Painting* (1435) by Renaissance theorist Leon Battista Alberti. According to Alberti, *istorie* (histories), by which he means subjects of serious importance, should combine 'many figures together' arranged logically and with appropriate and dignified gestures (the idea of appropriateness, or decorum, comes from Aristotle). He is echoed in Félibien's insistence that in history paintings 'care must be taken that there be only one Subject in a Picture and though it may be filled with a great Number of Figures they must all have respect to the principle one'. The most significant champion of history painting was Charles Le Brun (1619–1690), one of the founders of the Académie Royale and a man of almost superhuman energy and organizational skill. Le Brun personally oversaw almost all of Louis XIV's commissions for paintings, sculpture and decorative arts over three decades, and was the country's premier arbiter of taste. Le Brun particularly promoted the artistic theories of painter Nicholas Poussin (see below), on whose ideas Félibien had based his *Conférences*, and he helped establish antiquity, Raphael and Poussin as the chief models for contemporary painters.

Although the discussions at the Academy focused on painting, the genres could be reflected in other media. The earliest mature works of Gianlorenzo Bernini (1598–1680) were literary mythological sculptures and therefore belonged to the major genre. The son of the sculptor Pietro Bernini (1562–1629), Gianlorenzo had the extraordinary advantage of growing up surrounded by the world's greatest collections of ancient art and bolstered by the encouragement of powerful patrons. As a boy he may have been subsidized by Maffeo Barberini (later Pope Urban VIII), but his most decisive early supporter was Cardinal Scipione Borghese (1576–1633), nephew of Pope Paul V, who invited him at the age of nineteen to live in his splendid villa just outside Rome in what is often referred to as *servitù particolare* ('private service'). With Scipione's premier Graeco-Roman sculpture collection at hand, the young Bernini perfected his craft, creating a series of classically inspired group sculptures between 1618 and 1625 that directly challenged the legacy of Michelangelo and the late Renaissance sculptor Gianbologna (1529–1608). It suited patron and artist alike to play this kind of intellectual game – distinguished by the term *novità* (novelty) – in which contemporary artists improved upon works by classical or Renaissance masters.

Bernini's *Pluto and Proserpina* (50) – a striking example of *novità* – tests Michelangelo's favoured medium of marble to its limit, endowing it with an unprecedented fleshiness and pliancy. The large-scale group with two human protagonists and the three-headed dog Cerberus, which guarded the entrance to Hades, represents the story of the rape of a young goddess by the King of Hades as recounted in Ovid's *Metamorphoses*, the source of much Baroque and Rococo imagery, including the Farnese Ceiling (see 13) and Bernini's own *Apollo and Daphne* (see 2). Bernini's group also challenges Giambologna's bronze *Rape of a Sabine* in the Loggia dei Lanzi in Florence (c.1585), countering Giambologna's slender bodies and dance-like gestures with bulkiness and strength. Bernini joins the protagonists together in a giant X, with Pluto's mighty grip as the fulcrum and the figures' heads and limbs – particularly Proserpina's flailing right arm – as the extensions. Hoisting his quarry on to his hip, Pluto grasps her so firmly that his fingers press into her waist and thigh, and in an opposing gesture Proserpina pushes so forcefully against her aggressor's face that it stretches his skin. Thus, in the kind of conceit beloved by Bernini, the flesh of both figures is violated, one by lust and the other repulsion. Like the slightly later *Apollo and Daphne*, also made for Borghese, *Pluto and Proserpina* depicts an action frozen in time, a favoured Baroque motif and one invited explicitly in Ovid's text, which reads: 'as if at one glance, Death [Pluto] had caught her up'. Both groups also juxtapose the bemusement of an assailant with the terror of a victim, manifested through her silent scream and visible tears – Proserpina's expression derives from Bernini's study of Caravaggio's paintings and shows that part of the *novità* of this group was its transgression of the *paragone*'s boundaries between painting and sculpture (see Introduction). Bernini kept close to the text: it refers specifically to her 'terror' and tears, and notes that Pluto had 'ripped the neckline of her dress' – the latter acknowledged superficially with the garment draped over Proserpina's right shoulder as the group is primarily a nude study. Although *Pluto and Proserpina* and *Apollo and Daphne* were meant to be seen primarily from the front (they were set against a wall), we can appreciate the way the action unfolds by walking around the sides, guided by the twisting movements of the torsos and legs and – in *Pluto and Proserpina* – Pluto's diagonal stride and the encirclement of his arms. At once violent and erotic, Pluto and Proserpina was the epitome of the private mythological scene, enlivened by a typically Baroque energy and sensuousness.

Large-scale mythological subjects like Annibale Carracci's ceiling at the Palazzo Farnese, still appearing exclusively in domestic settings, could be made more acceptable by clothing their Graeco-Roman themes and figures

in Christian garb, a convention of Renaissance origin that was temporarily
halted by the religious crises of the later sixteenth century. The first
resurrection of the Christianized mythological scene, in which pagan gods
serve as allegories for 'Religion', 'Charity' and 'Justice', was a ceiling fresco
by Giovanni and Cherubino Alberti for Pope Clement VIII at the Sala
Clementina in the Vatican Palace (1596–9). But the most influential ceiling
fresco of this type was Pietro da Cortona's *Glorification of the Reign of Urban
VIII* in the Palazzo Barberini in Rome (51). Pietro Berrettini (1596–1669),
known as 'da Cortona' after his Tuscan birthplace, also benefited from
high-level ecclesiastical patronage. During his first twenty years in Rome
he was supported by aristocratic patrons including Cassiano dal Pozzo
(1588–1657), the secretary to Cardinal Francesco Barberini, nephew of Pope
Urban VIII (r. 1623–44), arguably the most influential private collector of
his age. Cassiano was not only an influential patron of young artists but
also a dedicated encyclopedist, compiling what he called the *Museo Cartaceo*
('Paper Museum'), a vast collection of drawings, watercolours and prints of
classical art and architecture as well as geological, botanical and zoological
knowledge. Cortona's ceiling fresco in the Grand Salone at Barberini's palace
in Rome guaranteed his place within the triumvirate of High Baroque artists
(along with Bernini and Francesco Borromini). This paean to the Barberini
family was based on an erudite programme composed by a court poet, in this
case Francesco Bracciolini (1566–1645). Drawing upon classical mythology
and emblematic conceits, Bracciolini devised an allegory in which Divine
Providence, elevated above Time and Space, petitions Immortality to adorn
the Barberini family – represented by the heraldic device of a trio of bees –
with a crown of stars, while representations of the heroic deeds and virtuous
qualities of the pope adorn the sides.

Cortona builds upon the tradition of *quadratura* painting used at the Farnese
Palace and Michelangelo's Sistine Ceiling (1508–12), challenging them in the
tradition of *novità*. The main novelty here is the way the three levels of the
painting – the illusionistic architectural framework, the heavenly apparition
above, and the figures, landscapes and clouds below – interpenetrate to
increase the sensation of height, even though the frame itself is restricted to
the size of the vault (compare with 13). Cortona adorns the frame with false

stucco garlands, masks, herms, shells and false gold plaques in imitation of contemporary Roman palace architecture. He divides his ceiling into five sections, with the largest panel at the centre and four elongated landscape panels set flush against the four walls, allowing the perspective to be appreciated from different angles. A single sky, glimpsed through the clouds in all five sections, unifies the composition. The cloud-borne figures, rising from the earthly outer panels past the frame and into the heavenly central panel, gather into four principal pairs, their ascent accentuated by dramatic foreshortening inspired by Venetian painting. Providence – observed dramatically from below – rides on the apex of a triangular mass of clouds and figures. She raises her right arm towards Immortality, who rises on her right. A living version of the Barberini arms dominates the other half of the panel, the three golden bees enclosed in laurel wreaths supported by pagan god-like figures symbolizing Faith, Hope and Charity, and additional figures supporting the crowns of pope and poet. Further pagan deities (the figures emerging from the side panels) are also commandeered to portray Christian ideals, with Minerva representing Wisdom and Hercules symbolizing Strength, while the scene of Pallas destroying the giants mirrors the pope's struggle against Protestantism. Notably, Cortona's classical figures are mostly clothed: gone is the nudity that heightened the sensuality and eroticism of the Farnese ceiling or Bernini's sculptural groups, a reflection of a new cautiousness among some ecclesiastical patrons in their more visible private commissions.

**51.
Pietro da Cortona**, *Glorification of the Reign of Urban VIII*, 1633–9. Fresco, Palazzo Barberini, Rome

Cassiano dal Pozzo was also responsible for promoting Nicolas Poussin (1594–1665), the most significant French painter of the Baroque who paradoxically spent most of his life in Rome. Poussin was an ardent classicist and together with Claude Lorrain (about whom more below) he inspired an enthusiasm for that style in French painting that persisted – except in the work of the most radical Rococo painters – until the outbreak of Impressionism in the 1860s. As noted above, Poussin was also a passionate defender of the hierarchy of genres and his ideas were at the foundation of the Académie Royale. Some of his interests in antiquity derived from Cassiano – scholars are now suggesting that Poussin himself was less of an intellectual than previously assumed – and his later works increasingly

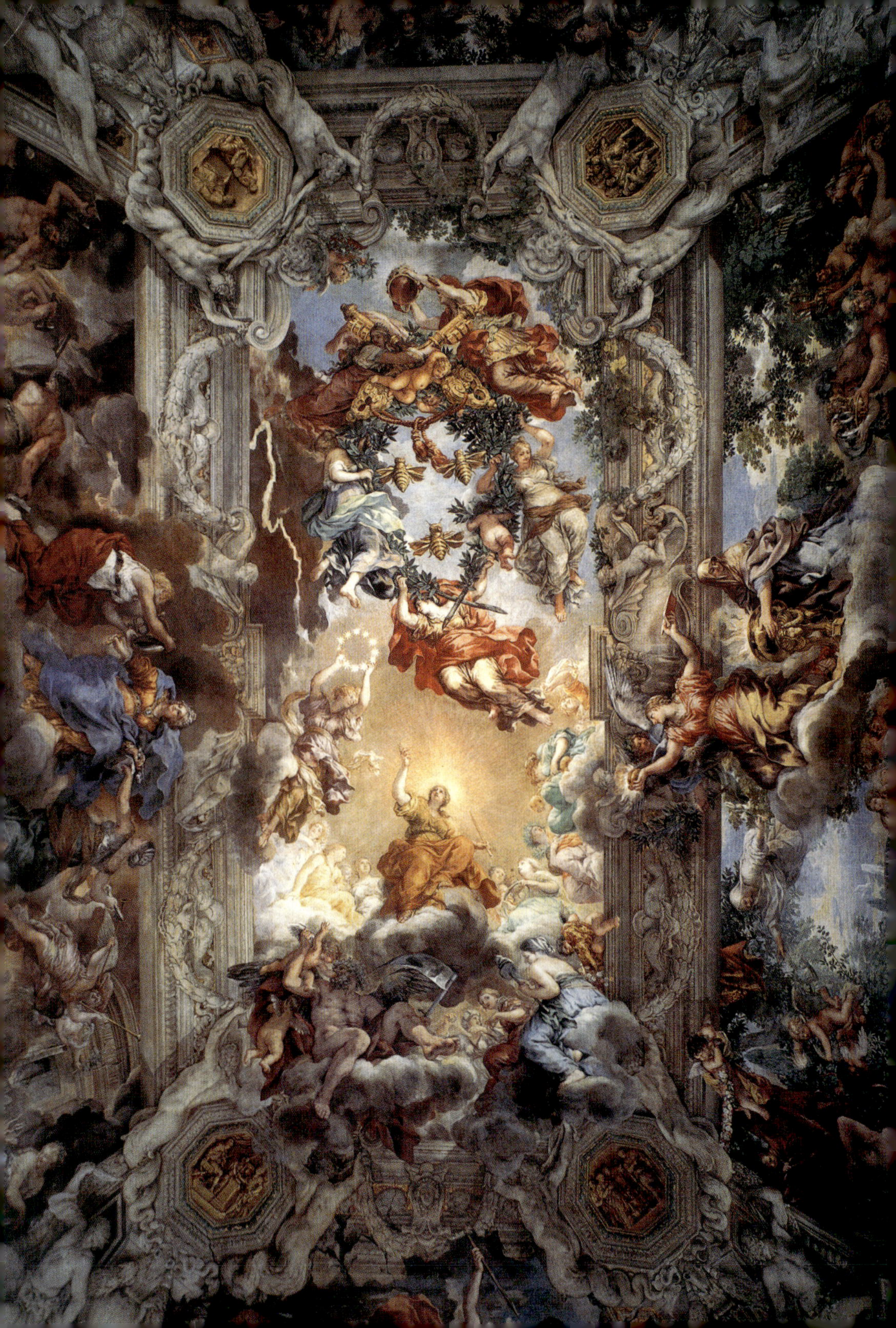

demonstrate a fascination with Graeco-Roman sculptural and architectural models. Stung by an early disaster with a heavily criticized altarpiece for St Peter's, Poussin abandoned ecclesiastical patronage and grander formats around 1629–30, devoting his time to easel paintings commissioned by a small group of intellectuals including Cassiano, as well as middle-class French patrons. Poussin's change of format also entailed some changes in subject matter as he introduced an increasing number of mythological scenes, based at first on the pastoral literature of Ovid and the Italian poet Torquato Tasso (1544–1595).

By the end of the 1630s and most notably in the following two decades, Poussin abandoned this bucolic world in favour of sombre, heroic subjects inspired by the Stoics, a group of Hellenistic and Roman writers who endorsed self-control and morality as a way to conquer the emotions. Poussin's settings and compositions became more balanced, his colour muted, and the poses and expressions of his figures more rigid. In his letters he declared – as would his biographer Félibien – that the noblest goal of painting is to depict serious and dignified human deeds: 'first of all … it is necessary that the subject be in itself noble, and that it give scope for revealing the painter's mind and industry'. Scenes were to be presented in a logical, idealized fashion, with restrained but appropriate emotions – a clear challenge to what he believed to be the excesses of High Baroque style. Going further, Poussin devised in 1647 a system of what he called 'modes', perhaps the least understood Baroque theory of art and one that has flummoxed generations of students. Essentially an adaptation of a 1589 thesis on the history of music by the Venetian Gioseffo Zarlino, Poussin's ideas borrowed the Greek music theory that certain modes – a proportional combination of notes like a scale – were used 'to arouse the soul of the spectator to various passions', namely, to evoke specific emotional reactions. As Poussin described them, the Dorian mode is 'stable, grave and serene', the Phrygian depicts 'pleasant and joyous things', the Hypolydian 'contains a certain suavity and sweetness which fills the soul of the spectators with joy; it lends itself to subjects of Divine glory and Paradise', and the Ionian is used 'to represent dances, bacchanals and feasts, because of its cheerful character'. The effect is created by a judicious mixture of all aspects of a painting, such as composition, proportions, gestures and expressions. The problem is that despite many scholarly attempts, it is virtually impossible to link these modes to any of Poussin's paintings: they cannot be related to specific combinations of elements, they likely do not conform to colour schemes as is commonly believed, and for us to recognize them we would need to experience the intended emotion – likely impossible at our temporal and cultural remove. Poussin's moral classicism is at the core of *The Arcadian Shepherds*, the latter of two versions (52). In this canvas he challenges the playful mood of his earlier paintings and of the pastoral scenes of his contemporaries (such as Pietro da Cortona's frescos for the Palazzo Pitti in Florence; see 153), by

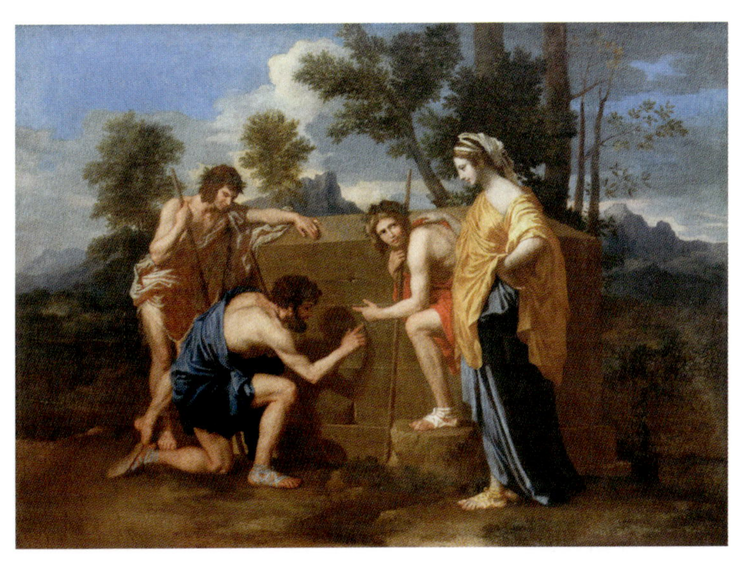

52.
Nicolas Poussin, *The Arcadian Shepherds*, 1638–40. Oil on canvas; 85 × 121 cm (33½ × 47¼ in). Louvre, Paris

introducing a jarring note of melancholy into Arcadia, a mythical land of rural pleasure and relaxation. In a forested glade three shepherds and a shepherdess, all dressed in classical drapery and arranged horizontally as if on a frieze, approach a sarcophagus bearing the Latin inscription *Et in Arcadia Ego* ('Even in Arcadia am I'). Both the female figure and the man to her right are based on Graeco-Roman statues, the latter a sculpture of Neptune. The inscription, not found in any classical source, serves as a reminder or *memento mori* (see Chapter One) that Death can occur even in a pastoral utopia, and some have interpreted the shepherdess, resting her hand gently on one of the men's shoulders, as another allegory of Death – her noble pose and

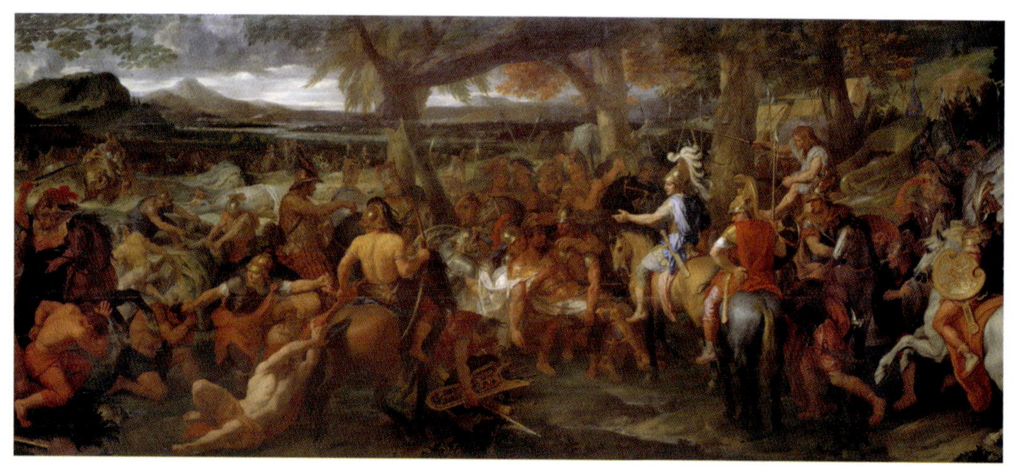

53.
Charles Le Brun, *Defeat of Porus by Alexander*, 1665–8. Oil on canvas; 4.70 × 12.64 m (15 ft 5 in × 41 ft 5½ in). Louvre, Paris

calm expression would seem to support this hypothesis. The sickle-shaped shadow cast by the kneeling figure has been interpreted as Death's scythe. In place of the dynamic, loosely painted forms of Cortona, Poussin gives us precise, sharply modelled figures locked in place like statues. Each has a subtly different emotional response to the inscription, from the intense curiosity and concern of the kneeling man and the shepherd on his left to the contemplative melancholy of the two outer figures.

Le Brun's *Defeat of Porus by Alexander* (53) – a gigantic canvas measuring 15 by 40 feet (4.7 by 12.6 m) and one of five celebrating the *Battles and Triumphs of Alexander* – was commissioned by Louis XIV and established Le Brun as his court's official painter and designer (see Chapters Four and Five). A tribute to the benevolence of the Greek conqueror, who allowed the defeated Indian king Porus to retain sovereignty over his realm, it epitomizes the French Academy's definition of history painting. As a scene from antiquity it is the noblest kind of subject, and it follows High Renaissance models such as Leonardo's unexecuted Battle of Anghiari (1503–5) and Raphael's *Meeting of Leo the Great and Attila* (1514). Other features are more Baroque, like the gentle Mediterranean landscape inspired by Annibale Carracci and Domenichino (see 66). Yet the canvas has a monotony common in institutional art, notable in the uniformity and blandness of the soldiers' gestures, the stiffness of the foreground figures, and the pedantically correct colour balance of their capes and tunics, a hackneyed reference to Raphael. The groups of soldiers add little depth to the picture, most of them lining up like bas-relief carving on a sarcophagus panel. Le Brun contrasts the crowd's turbulence with the regal calm of Alexander and his men to demonstrate the emperor's gentlemanly generosity in the face of adversity. Alexander is a stand-in for Louis XIV, who believed he shared many of the Greek conqueror's qualities, so it is no coincidence that Le Brun dresses his hero in light blue, the colour of the Bourbon family. Alexander is also the best-illuminated figure in the picture: the golden light symbolizes both divine approbation – a foundation of absolutist rule – and the Christian nature of clemency. Le Brun worked with a small army of assistants, but he oversaw every detail of the painting's design and intervened throughout the canvas in the kind of close scrutiny that would characterize his architectural and décor projects.

Although also commissioned by an absolute monarch – Philip IV of Spain (r. 1621–65) – Velázquez's *The Surrender of Breda* (54) is a world apart from Le Brun's stale institutionalism. One of the most vivid and minutely observed battle paintings in the Western tradition, it depicts a contemporary event, the defeat of the Protestant Dutch under Justin of Nassau by the Italo-Spanish general Ambrogio Spinola in 1625. Perhaps to compensate for its present-day subject matter, Velázquez gives his painting the kind of literary credentials usually restricted to classical subjects by basing it – albeit loosely – on the play *El sitio de Bredá* (*The Siege of Breda*) by the celebrated Spanish dramatist Pedro Calderón de la Barca (1600–1681). In fact, the central action, in which Nassau bows before Spinola and hands him the keys of the city, is taken directly from Calderón's play, in which the victor responds magnanimously, 'Justin, in receiving them I acknowledge that you are valiant, that the valour of the vanquished creates renown for the conqueror.' Yet the handing over of the keys never actually took place: the genius of the painting is the way its immediacy and naturalism can pull the wool over our eyes. As viewers we assume that something lifelike and emotionally genuine must be depicting the truth, even if we know or suspect otherwise.

If Le Brun's epic is an homage to classical idealism, Velázquez's picture is an essay in realism. Velázquez lays bare the brutality of war, concentrating on the psychological and physical repercussions of combat: the faces and gestures of the Spanish and Dutch soldiers reflect a wide range of emotions, from melancholy and nervousness to contemplativeness and confidence and the fires in the background bear witness to the ravages of war. Le Brun views his subject from above so that we remain aloof, but Velázquez places us on the ground with the soldiers, making us witnesses or even participants in the events. Similarly, Le Brun's conqueror towers over the supine Indian king, whereas Velázquez's victor dismounts to greet his adversary as an equal, placing his hand on his shoulder in a human gesture and looking sympathetically into his face. But there is no doubt about who has won this battle: Velázquez contrasts the vertical and orderly row of lances over the Spanish troops on the right with the disorganized jumble of halberds on the Dutch side on the left and the bowed head of the conquered leader is echoed by the lowered Dutch flag behind. His resonant colours bring the painting to life, particularly the cool greys of the landscape and the luminous blues of the sky, ironically inspired by Netherlandish Renaissance painting. Velázquez's mastery of texture comes through in the minute differences in costume: note the contrast between Nassau's rough herringbone wool and Espinola's shimmering purple sash, or the heavy beige coat of the second soldier on the left and the fluttering white sleeve and bloodied jerkin of the soldier to his right.

So far we have looked only at history paintings. Minor genres – paradoxically the very types of images that please audiences most today – occupied a lower position in the hierarchy because they were merely representational and did not aspire to the noble goals of the *grand genre*. Yet patrons appreciated them precisely for their technical skill, their ability to capture likenesses, and their sense of humour. Paintings that do little more than mimic nature seem antithetical to an era that took art so seriously, but illusionism was one of the most fundamental features of Baroque art in general, even in *grand genre* works such as Catholic religious paintings where it was at the foundation of the rhetorical *delectare*. Until recently most art historians paid attention to teasing out iconographic or moralistic meanings from landscapes, still lifes and domestic scenes, applying interpretive tools derived from study of

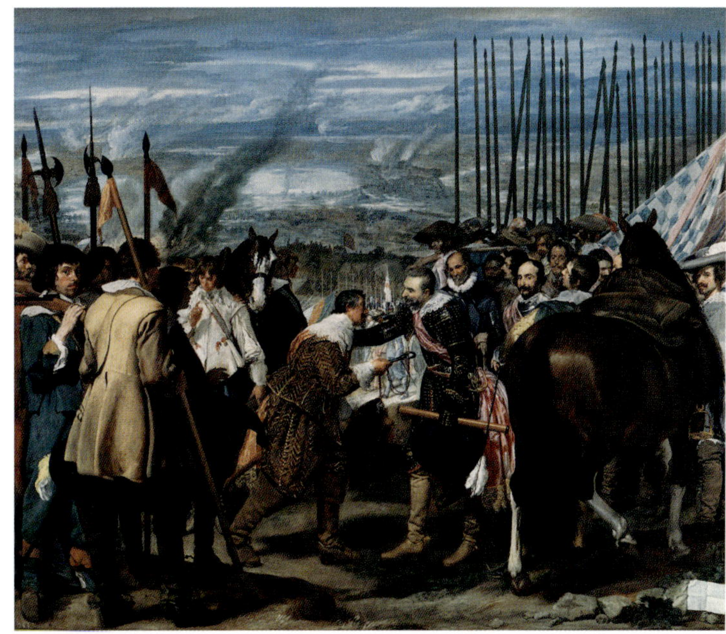

54.
Diego Velázquez, *The Surrender of Breda*, 1635. Oil on canvas; 3.07 × 3.7 m (10 ft × 12 ft 2 in). Museo del Prado, Madrid

the grand genre. In fact, the question of whether these paintings' mimesis precludes any symbolic interpretation remains controversial. But there can be no doubt that Protestant collectors in particular, for whatever reasons, preferred artless depictions of the material world to solemn homilies, and if some paintings combined realism with iconography – as I believe they did – the realism came first.

Patronage was one of the main differences between minor-genre paintings and those of the *grand genre*. Artists of history paintings would not usually begin a work unless they had a patron in hand, as such works tended to be large and expensive and might involve literary research beyond their abilities. Minor-genre artists did not have such restraints and frequently produced works in advance to sell in shops, street fairs, in their own homes or via art dealers – a new profession in the Baroque – but their struggle to make a living in the risky open market was acute. Rembrandt's volatile career is a case in point: although he put great faith in the market by creating specific, identifiable styles and subjects in response to the fiercely competitive Dutch art scene, he often bet on the wrong horse – he speculated actively on his own work – and even wound up in bankruptcy court. The minor genres enjoyed particular acclaim in northern Europe, particularly among the middle and even working classes who preferred views of the world around them to weightier *grand genre* subjects. Unlike the Catholic powers, the Dutch (and English) governments encouraged mercantilism: Holland was ruled by burghers called regents who promoted economic freedom and growth. Capitalism, or creating profit by selling goods at a higher price than their purchase value, had been on the rise since the Iberian empires flooded Europe's currency market with gold and silver, allowing merchants to accumulate capital on a larger scale. European powers also opened an increasing number of trade routes with Asia and Africa, allowing for new sources of products and an expansion of world markets. England and Holland were world leaders in international trade, facilitated by the activities of their two East India Companies (founded 1600 and 1602 respectively), begun by groups of merchant investors to dominate Asian trade. The rise in mercantile wealth was directly reflected in the proliferation of minor-genre painting and increasing specialization of artists in Holland and elsewhere in the Protestant world.

The minor genre that was most esteemed in Catholic and Protestant countries alike was portraiture, since its subjects included kings, popes and aristocrats, and it dated back to the Middle Ages when profile portraits of donors were frequently incorporated into altarpieces. In his 1590 treatise *The Ideal Temple of Painting*, Milanese painter Gian Paolo Lomazzo (1538–1600) enhanced portraiture's prestige by insisting, like the defenders of history painting, that it be restricted to noble and virtuous subjects such as emperors and princes, sages, heroes, 'or at least people who are important or remarkable in some way, such as beautiful women or men'. Portraits underwent many transformations between the Renaissance and Baroque. In the early Renaissance they were characterized by a rigidity and aloofness that corresponded to the high station of their sitter, but Leonardo and Raphael revolutionized the genre by having the subject engage the viewer directly (as in Leonardo's *Mona Lisa*, 1505) or reveal an emotional state (as in Raphael's *Pope Leo X with Cardinals Giulio de' Medici and Luigi de' Rossi*, 1518–19). Nevertheless, arrogance and idealism returned in the mid-sixteenth century, when Agnolo Bronzino (1503–1572) and Francesco Salviati (1510–1563) used portraiture as a tool for glorifying the despotic rule of the Grand Dukes of Florence and the reformist popes.

In the 1630s Bernini brought life back to portraiture with what we might call the action portrait, one in which the sitter is both animated and engaged with an invisible interlocutor in the viewer's space. Yet the apparent approachability of his marble busts belie the often authoritative and tyrannical nature of Bernini's subjects – men every bit as despotic as their late Renaissance predecessors. The portrait of his patron Scipione Borghese (55), one of the most powerful men in Rome, is one of the earliest and most lifelike, demonstrating Bernini's preoccupations with motion and speech. As with *Apollo and Daphne* or *Pluto and Proserpina* (see 2, 50), Bernini manipulates the marble so that it seems to breathe, and enlivens it further by introducing pupils into the eyes. Bernini meticulously replicates the different textures of Borghese's face: the knit brow, the sagging skin under the eyes, and the flaccid jowls and double chin. The urbane cardinal seems to have been caught in mid-sentence – his piercing glance cast over our left shoulder and his lips parted as though speaking – as if we are part of the group being addressed.

The bust is a clear manifestation of Bernini's celebrated remark that a portrait is most revealing when the sitter is depicted just before or after talking, a conceit known as a 'speaking likeness'. Bernini did not have Scipione sit still while making the preliminary sketches, as he wanted to capture the qualities that made him a man of action. Borghese's tunic is rumpled, with a button popping out of its buttonhole, and his biretta is slightly askew, in defiance of the formality traditionally associated with portraiture. But Borghese's casualness does not negate his authority: this kind of studied nonchalance, known at the time as *sprezzatura*, was affected by the nobility precisely so that they would appear elevated above the mundane world.

Executed during a brief sojourn in Paris at the behest of the king's first minister Jean-Baptiste Colbert in 1665, Bernini's magisterial portrait of Louis XIV of France (56) – a tyrant on an altogether different scale – shares something of Borghese's immediacy but none of its intimacy. The Sun King glances quickly to the left as if observing a courtier just entering the room, his movement emphasized by the billowing curls of his hair and a windswept sash (carved mostly by Bernini's assistant Giulio Cartari) that would become a cliché in later Baroque sculptural portraits. Louis shares nothing of Borghese's nonchalance or engagement with the viewer's space. His glance is aloof and regal – the idea of authority was the main conceit behind this sculpture – and his upper body is inaccessible behind his suit of armour. By widening the space between Louis's famously close-set eyes, enlarging his torso, and giving him a broad forehead like that in portraits of Alexander the Great, Bernini idealized his subject while appearing to create an authentic likeness through realistic textures and sense of movement – using naturalism to mislead the viewer as did Velázquez (see 54). Bernini has also exaggerated the king's thick and curly hair, deepening its texture through a clever manipulation of natural light, like chiaroscuro in painting. It should come as no surprise that Bernini was an avid caricaturist – in fact, he is considered by many to have invented the genre, although the Carracci made forays in that direction decades earlier. Bernini made light-hearted sketches of some of the very personalities he would later sculpt (such as Scipione Borghese), reducing their essential features to a few well-chosen lines. More remarkable are his uncannily contemporary-looking parodies of people he met on the street

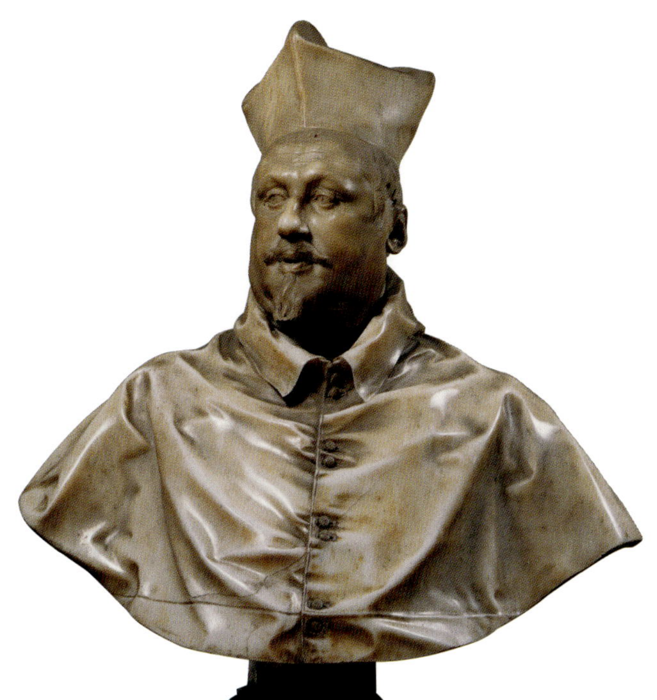

such as his *Caricature of a Captain in the Army of Urban VIII* (before 1644) with his turtle's neck and foppish curls (57). Bernini has reduced the face to five rapid strokes of the pen, hiding the eyes behind his hair and turning his nostrils, moustache and mouth into a second face. As his son and biographer Domenico Bernini put it, Bernini intended to 'deform, in jest, the images of others, in those parts where in some way nature had been wanting'.

Although he also sought absolutist rule, King Charles I of England favoured *sprezzatura* over more overt displays of authority, perhaps because he was wary of the domestic and foreign dangers that overshadowed his reign (he was beheaded in 1649). Anthony Van Dyck's Portrait of *Charles I at the Hunt* (58) introduced the kind of nonchalant full-length portrait that came to dominate English painting. Charles commissioned Van Dyck, court painter since 1632, to advertise his breeding but also his infallibility, as Charles promoted the doctrine of divinely guided kingship. But Van Dyck also stressed his gentlemanly demeanour in keeping with new ideas promoted by Henry Peacham's bestselling *The Compleat Gentleman* (London, 1622), a guide to courtly behaviour devoured by London's social-climbing public.

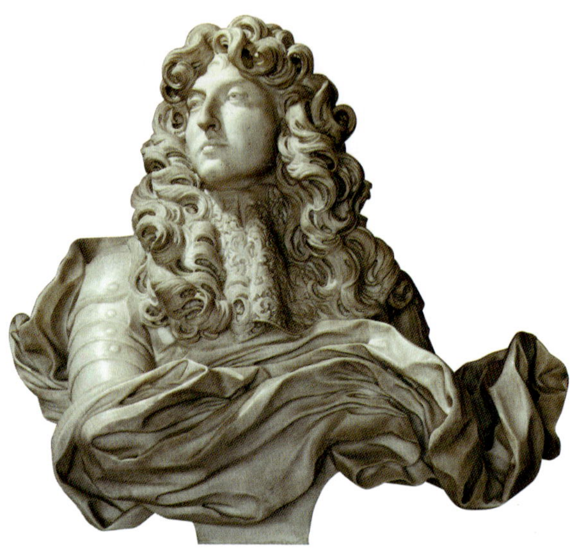

Charles stands ramrod straight, chest out and head held high, yet he casually bends his left knee and wears his hat at an informal angle. He also reveals none of the traditional symbols of royalty, whether crown or heraldic device. Charles's hooded eyes peer at us with lofty detachment, and in contrast to Bernini's Borghese (see 55) he makes no pretence of being a learned man. In fact, the king's grandeur appears superficial: the shimmering tunic and lush velvet trousers – too fancy for a hunt – compete with his face for attention, and his unnaturally slender body, anticipating a fashion in English portraiture, recalls the courtly exaggerations of Bronzino. The two grooms are youthful and move with grace, and Charles's mount is at once muscular and sensuous – the luxurious mane is one of the high points of the picture. Even the landscape is bucolic and classically balanced, with a massive tree on the right and open sky on the left, the tree reaching over the king like a canopy. Van Dyck gives us Arcadia, but without Poussin's *memento mori*; although historians are now demonstrating that Charles was well aware of the dangers that faced him, none of them are apparent here.

By the eighteenth century, well after the Rococo had taken root in England, *sprezzatura*, aristocratic disdain and impossibly elongated figures were standard fare even in portraits of the lesser nobility. The style's undisputed

**56.
Gianlorenzo
Bernini,**
*Portrait of
Louis XIV of
France*, 1665.
Marble; 80 cm
(31½ in).
Château de
Versailles
(France)

**57.
Gianlorenzo
Bernini,**
*Caricature of a
Captain in the
Army of Urban
VIII*, before
1644. Pen and
brown ink on
white paper,
sheet 18.8 ×
25.6 cm (7½ ×
10 in). Fondo
Corsini, Rome

protagonist was Thomas Gainsborough (1727–1788), Britain's high society
painter, who spent much of his career in the fashionable resort of Bath
transforming a prosaic clientele into beautiful, world-weary paragons. His
portrait of the gamine Honourable Mrs Graham (59), granddaughter of an
ambassador to Catherine the Great of Russia and wife of the future Lord
Lynedoch, shows us a figure as elastic as the stucco saints and cupids of the
German Rococo (see 103). In homage to Van Dyck, details of Mrs Graham's
costume – particularly her jagged lace collar – evoke seventeenth-century
dress. As comely as a Renaissance Madonna but as cold as a classical Minerva,
Mrs Graham glances loftily away from the viewer and her body seems
weightless – in fact, her tiny feet appear at first to float above the ground
like those of Caravaggio's *Madonna of Loreto* (see 34). Her rosy cheeks and
puckered mouth are at once a paradigm of beauty and an essay in triviality.
Gainsborough's brushwork is even looser than that of Van Dyck, softening
the figure, costume and landscape – the ostrich plumes are a tour de force –
and the staccato white highlights of the satin gown and rippled folds of the
velvet skirt are energized in a way that her expressionless face is not.

Self-portraiture, with its presumption of directness and honesty, seems
far removed from Gainsborough's deceptive idealism, yet it was no less
contrived. Self-portraits only revealed what artists wanted viewers to see,
and even when they seem to look into the very soul of the sitter they can be
subtly manipulative. The genre was relatively novel in the Baroque, as early
Renaissance artists tended only to include self-portraits in religious or history
paintings, often as a substitute for signatures. But by the mid-sixteenth

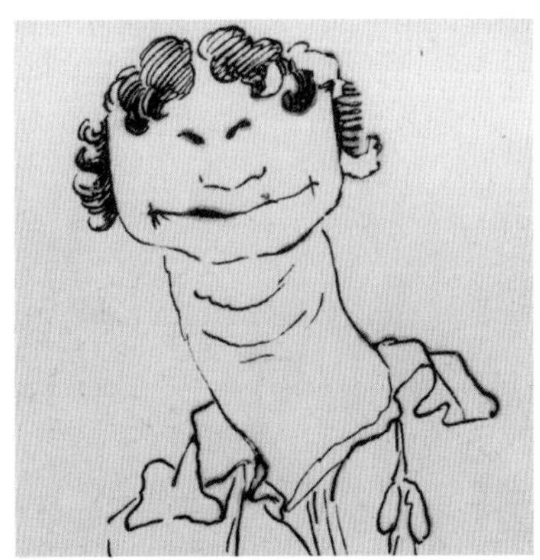

century self-portraiture had already acquired its own set of tropes and visual tricks. One of them was the notion of the artist's face as a mirror of reality: mirrors are very common in self-portraits since the artist's work supposedly 'reflected' truth. The self-portrait also flaunted the artist's ability to fool the eye and – in a nod to Pliny the Elder's biographies of ancient Greek artists – painters enjoyed obscuring the distinction between reality and illusion. Other self-portraits emphasized the artist's public persona, not only his or her intellectual and social achievements but also personality traits – such as melancholy or restlessness – that had been associated with genius since the publication of Giorgio Vasari's *Lives of the Artists* (1550; 1568). Many self-portraits celebrated the craft of painting, depicting the artist at work with paintbrush, palette and easel. This theme also relates to the *paragone* debates in which the proponents of the various media asserted the superiority of their tools and techniques and – as in the case of Michelangelo – emphasized the physical labour necessary for the creative process.

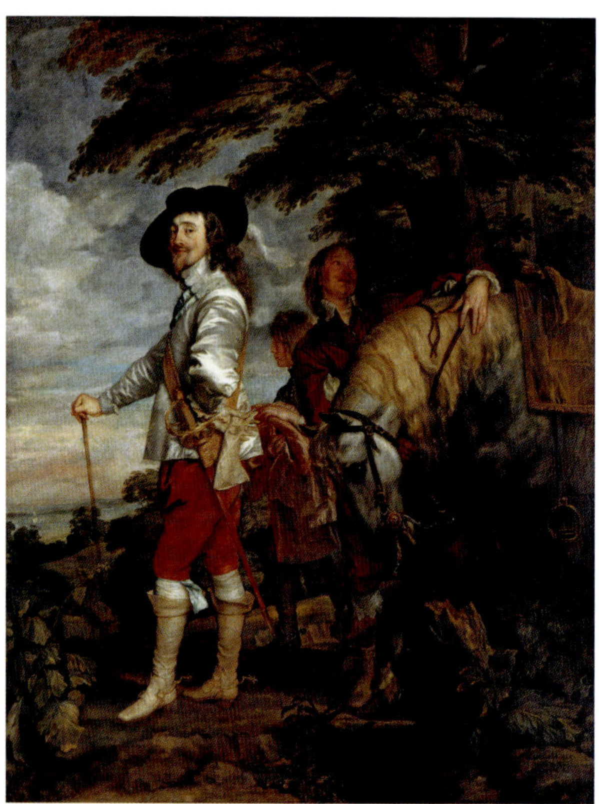

Four self-portraits, two by men and two by women, illustrate these various tropes. The first, by the Lombard painter Sofonisba Anguissola (c.1527–1625), was painted before the Baroque when self-portraiture had emerged as its own genre and also corresponds to a time when women were becoming more generally accepted as artists (60). Although women rarely painted history paintings or the other 'noble' genres of academic painting, they quickly achieved a niche market in the 'minor' genres, as painters of portraits, still-lifes, and women and children. Since one of the attractions women artists had for their often male patrons was their supposed ability to paint women and other 'feminine' themes better than men, their identity was crucial to their success. Some, like Anguissola and Elisabetta Sirani (1638– 1665), promoted themselves as the ideal of feminine chastity, while Artemisia Gentileschi – one of the few to specialize in history painting – capitalized upon her much-publicized rape trial in 1612 to paint both heroic, vengeful women and sensuous nudes (see 83). Other established woman painters of

58.
Anthony Van Dyck, *Portrait of Charles I at the Hunt*, c.1635. Oil on canvas; 2.72 × 2.12 m (8 ft 11 in × 6 ft 11½ in). Louvre, Paris

59.
Thomas Gainsborough, *Portrait of the Honorable Mrs Graham*, 1777. Oil on canvas; 2.37 × 1.54 m (7 ft 9 in × 5 ft). National Gallery of Scotland, Edinburgh

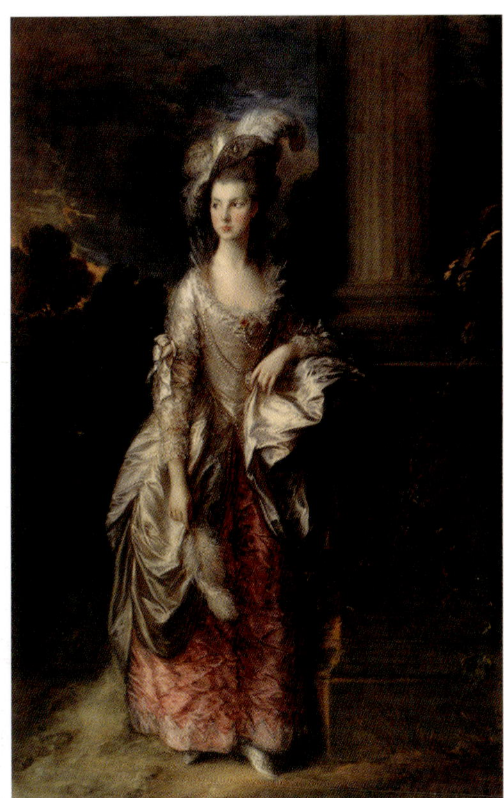

the era include Lavinia Fontana (1552–1614), Clara Peeters (1594–c.1657; see 79), Judith Leyster (1609–1660), Maria van Oosterwijck (1630–1693) and Rachel Ruysch (1664–1750; see 4), many of whom enjoyed international reputations – Anguissola herself was invited to Spain by Philip II to serve as a court painter in 1559.

In *Bernardino Campi Painting Sofonisba Anguissola* the artist introduces the novel conceit of representing her self-portrait as if it were being painted by her mentor, making it difficult to distinguish between the painter and the painted (60). It is both an homage to Campi – like Pygmalion he brings his pupil (or, more specifically, her artistry) to life – and an essay on the creative process. But there is no mistake about the principal subject of the picture: Anguissola is not only larger than her teacher but is also positioned at a higher level, signifying that she has surpassed him as an artist. Anguissola also demonstrates her social status through her rich velvet gown and lace collar – she was born into the minor nobility – and fondles her gloves like an aristocrat.

Painted 175 years later, Czech painter Jan Kupecký's *Self-Portrait with a Game Board* (61) was equally concerned with social status. One of the most celebrated Bohemian artists, Kupecký was forced to leave his native Prague as a child because of his Protestant faith and eventually worked for the imperial court in Vienna and then in Nuremberg. Having narrowly escaped becoming a weaver's apprentice in Slovakia as a youth, Kupecký was particularly eager to project a gentlemanly persona in keeping with the high level of his patronage. The artist stands proudly before the viewer, chest out and hand on hip like Van Dyck's Charles I (see 58), and his stern expression seems almost confrontational, as if challenging any doubts about his origins. Kupecký's costume is casual but elegant, his velvet hat set on an angle and his plush dressing gown tied at the waist with an intricately patterned Turkish sash. The inclusion of a game board shows him to be a man of leisure. Yet the picture is not all bravado. Kupecký was celebrated as a realist in an era of idealism, and his precise brushwork gave the features and outlines of his figures a sharpness that was absent in the looser handling of most of his contemporaries. Kupecký appears well past his youth, with prominent jowls,

**60.
Sofonisba Anguissola,** *Bernardino Campi Painting Sofonisba Anguissola,* c.1558–9. Oil on canvas; 111 × 109.5 cm (43½ × 43¼ in). Pinacoteca Nazionale, Siena (Italy)

a wrinkled brow and a receding hairline, and there is a hint of melancholy in his expression – precisely the kind of psychological element that inspired critics to compare him to Rembrandt.

Marie Louise Élisabeth Vigée-Lebrun (1755–1842) celebrated another trope often used by self-portraitists in her delightful *Self-Portrait in a Straw Hat* (62). Ever since Pliny praised the gracefulness of the Greek painter Apelles – the notion was revived in Vasari's biography of Raphael – the conceit of the

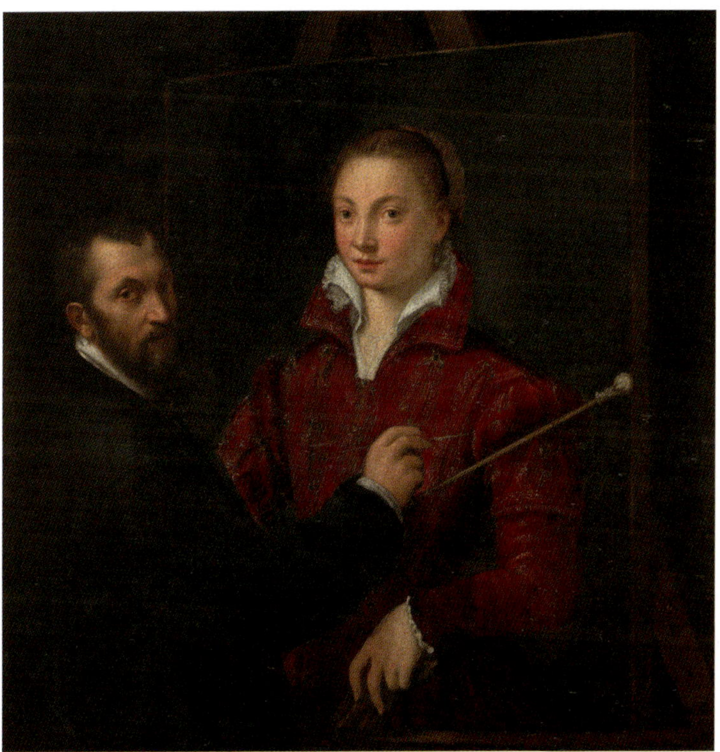

charming, gregarious artist gained general acceptance (Bernini was praised for precisely the same personality traits). Vigée-Lebrun was the ultimate society painter, exceeding all her female contemporaries in the extent of her royal patronage – particularly from powerful women. Not only was she the chief portraitist of Queen Marie-Antoinette of France (1755–1793), but she also served at the courts of Empress Maria Theresia of Austria (1717–1780), Czarina Catherine the Great of Russia (1729–1796), Queen Elizabeth of Prussia (1715–1797), and the Prince Regent (future George IV) of England

(1762–1830). Her honours would have done any of her male counterparts proud: she enjoyed memberships in the Académie Royale (1783) in Paris, the Roman Accademia di San Luca (1790), the Imperial Academy of Saint Petersburg (1800) and the Berlin Academy of Painting shortly afterwards. Vigée-Lebrun was also the first woman painter to write an autobiography, the droll and engaging *Souvenirs de ma vie*, in 1835–7. A description of her life after the French Revolution, it includes a set of instructions to portrait painters tempered by the cynical pragmatism of a seasoned courtier. This is her advice to the problem of fidgety female subjects: 'One must flatter them,

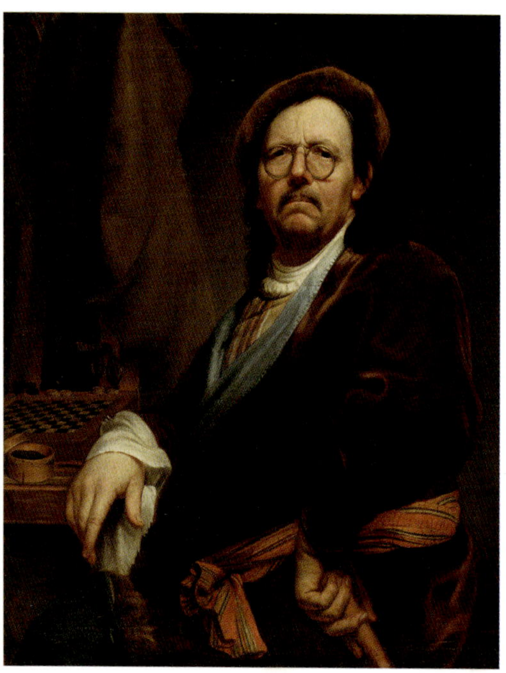

61.
Jan Kupecký,
Self-Portrait with a Game Board, after 1733. Oil on canvas; 94 × 74 cm (37 × 291/8 in). Staatsgalerie, Stuttgart (Germany)

tell them they're beautiful, that they have a fresh complexion … This puts them in a good mood and makes them more inclined to sit still.' Vigée-Lebrun's vivaciousness and commitment to her craft are both on display in *Self-Portrait in a Straw Hat*: standing close to the picture plane with her palette and brushes in her left hand, she looks engagingly at the viewer with open, smiling lips typical of a 'talking portrait' – but one that is far from the intensity of *Scipione Borghese* (see 55). This energetic, confident woman contrasts notably with Gainsborough's *Mrs Graham* (see 59), a passive, objectified beauty. Vigée-Lebrun projects a female *sprezzatura* – the attitude

was encouraged at Marie-Antoinette's court – her plunging décolletage tied
with a simple bow and whimsical straw hat adorned with flowers and an
ostrich plume, and her satin dress and lacy shawl advertise her courtly status.

Rembrandt's *Self-Portrait* of 1659 (63) is an entirely different kind of picture.
The most prolific painter of self-portraits of his time, Rembrandt painted,
etched and drew around a hundred of them from the age of twenty-three
until the year of his death in 1669. Many, particularly later ones like this,
have traditionally been seen as a kind of visual autobiography, in which the

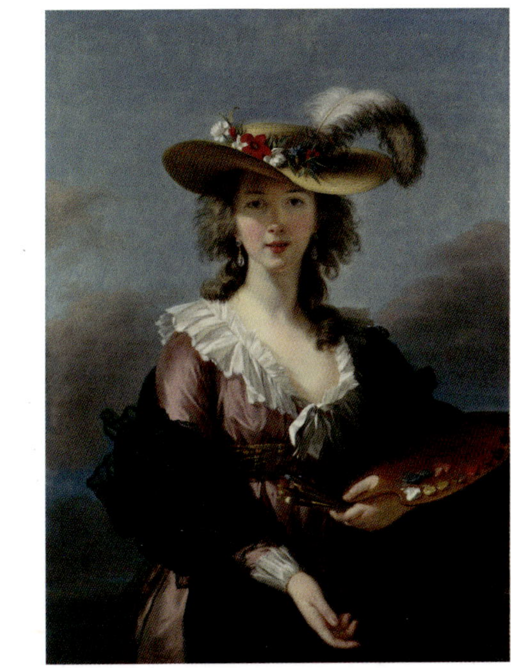

artist uses portraiture to carry on a dialogue with himself, his increasingly
melancholy facial expressions reflecting his progressively difficult and tragic
life. But this kind of self-analysis was more a product of the nineteenth and
twentieth centuries. More recent studies, focusing on Rembrandt's early
self-portraits, have revealed how they also served more mundane purposes.
On the one hand they satisfied a largely middle-class market for portraits of
famous people (Rembrandt enjoyed early renown and most of his portraits
sold right away), and on the other they gave the artist an opportunity to
test out a variety of emotions (sadness, fear, delight) as a way of perfecting

his painting technique. The scientific study of human emotions was a key aspect of training for many artists, as at the Carracci academy in Bologna (see Chapter One). Rembrandt's carefully crafted self-portraits not only celebrated his skill at depicting human sentiments but were also essays in self-promotion, making his image the most familiar of any artist of the time.

In this half-length *Self-Portrait* Rembrandt sets himself before a darkened oilcloth like that of Sebastiano del Piombo's *Christ Carrying the Cross* (see 23) and the painting evokes similar meditation from the viewer. A study in browns, the canvas uses gradating hues to trace the diagonal path of the light from the upper left to the front of the figure, which stops its progress and casts a deep shadow over the lower right corner. By contrast the bright flesh tones of his face and clasped hands focus our attention and bring us closer to the subject – this effect is aided by the contrast between the thick impasto in the face and the sparer application of paint in the background, in places scraped to the bare canvas. Yet this intimacy is illusionary, as the sitter's body is in fact turned to the side, flat against the picture plane, and the foreshortening of the shoulder – a common device for making a figure seem to enter the viewer's space – is diminished by the shadow. Even his glance is ambiguous: at first he seems to stare directly at us, but as we look longer at the picture his gaze becomes more introspective. Heavy brushstrokes trace the wrinkles on his deeply furrowed face, and Rembrandt heightens the sensation of vulnerability and softness – in his sagging jowls, woolly hair, wrinkled cap and the tactile fur lining of his garment – to make the portrait appear accessible and immediate. Its anguish and tragedy would seem to derive from the deepest reaches of the painter's soul.

But this portrait is more a work of self-promotion than psychological revelation. First, Rembrandt brands it as his own by placing his signature immediately to the left of his face in a prominent place in the canvas. More importantly, the pose, colour and costume – even the clasped hands – are an overt reference to Raphael's *Portrait of Baldassare Castiglione* (1514–15), not only implying that Rembrandt is equal to the Renaissance master but also proclaiming Rembrandt's status as a man of culture and breeding, as Castiglione was not merely one of the most influential writers of his age

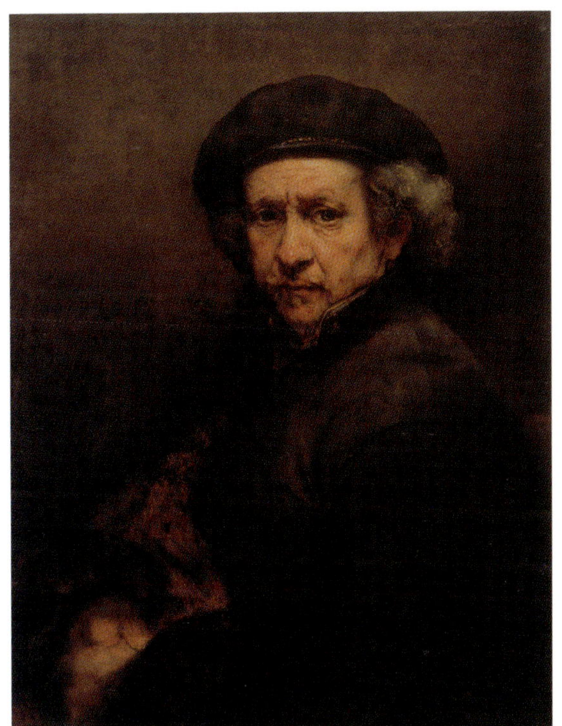

63.
Rembrandt van Rijn, *Self-Portrait*, 1659. Oil on canvas; 84.5 × 66 cm (33¼ × 26 in.). National Gallery, Washington, DC

but the author of the prototypical book on courtly manners, *The Book of The Courtier* (1528), from which we get the term *sprezzatura*. Even Rembrandt's disconsolate expression plays into the traditional iconography of melancholy, another artistic trope with a distinguished history. In Vasari's biography and Michelangelo's own writings the Florentine sculptor was portrayed as a melancholic, a carefully contrived personality trait based on Aristotle's statement that only melancholy men could achieve genius. By the dawn of the Baroque, with the publication of treatises like Timothy Bright's *On Melancholy* (1586), the conceit of the melancholic artist, particularly one who lived apart from society to devote his time to his work, became even more widespread.

One of the greatest innovations in Baroque portraiture was the Dutch *doelenstuk*, a corporate group portrait with late sixteenth-century origins that reached its apogee between the 1620s and 1640s. A fiendishly challenging genre, it involved incorporating individual portraits of usually large groups of people into a single painting so that they seem to interact naturally and – in the best ones – to participate in a single activity. The unchallenged leaders of the genre were Rembrandt and Frans Hals (c.1580–1666), and it was a direct product of the increasing prosperity and civic pride that came with the rise of capitalism. The *doelenstuk* became the genre par excellence for civic officials, trading companies, doctors, lawyers, guildsmen and other non-religious groups wishing to advertise their new wealth and prosperity. Civic guards, groups of upper-class men charged with protecting neighbourhoods, were the most common patrons of such works, placing them in their guard houses. Over 120 of them are known to have been painted. Hals's *Officers and Sergeants of the Saint Hadrian Civic Guard* (64), depicting a company of riflemen in the city of Haarlem, is a work of astonishing compositional dexterity. Anchored by a pair of sweeping diagonals that cross at the centre, the guardsmen separate into two groups on either side to form intersecting, right-angle triangles. Typical of Hals, the faces are both keenly observed and enlivened with a staccato brushstroke. They are also 'speaking portraits', as nearly everyone seems caught in mid-conversation. Hals enhances the boisterousness of the scene through gestures and props: several of the men accompany their discussion with hand movements, others hoist wine glasses in the air, and the man at the table is interrupted from his meal, knife in hand. The painting fairly bursts from the canvas, with its brightly coloured costumes, billowing flags and sparkling glasses and dishes – the latter a reminder of the Dutch supremacy in the art of still-life painting. Yet the apparent communality of this scene is misleading: a closer look at the faces shows that none of the men is looking at any of the others, making it a mere juxtaposition of portraits after all. In fact, each man paid for his individual likeness, and they were positioned in the painting according to rank. At the end of the day Hals and his patrons were more concerned with revealing the sitters' status than with creating a believable conversation piece.

Rembrandt's *Anatomy Lecture of Dr Nicolaes Tulp* (65) uses an even cleverer conceit to integrate his eight subjects, seven eager medical students and one of the most renowned physicians of Amsterdam. By treating his subject more as a history painting than a portrait and giving it an emotional centre, Rembrandt assimilates the figures' gestures and glances more successfully, allowing each man to react uniquely to the central action – another example of his lifelong fascination with the relation between emotion and facial response. Rembrandt also elevates his painting to a higher level of meaning than Hals. On the surface it depicts an anatomy professor demonstrating the function of the tendons of the arm and workings of the hand (note the way the doctor subtly mimics the dead hand's movement with his own). Five of his students hang onto his every word, staring at the teacher or the bloated corpse (of an executed murderer) with varying degrees of concentration and, in one case, revulsion, while two others look out into the viewer's space as if we were part of the class. A copy of Andreas Vesalius's manual *On the Workings of the Human Body* (1543) sits open in the right foreground, nearly within the sightline of the viewer, and the furthest student to the right checks his observations against his own handwritten notes. Yet all is not as it seems. The focus on the executed criminal and the way his corpse is being used to benefit society hints at the morality of crime and punishment. The student at the top who looks at the viewer and points to the body also turns this painting into a *memento mori*, reminding us of the corruptibility of the flesh. But most significantly, the painting possesses a sacred aura. Its brightly lit nude encircled by students recalls Entombment scenes (compare with 25, 32) in which the body of Christ is surrounded by grieving figures. A recent study has suggested that the picture's focus on the functional properties of the human hand is a more specific reference to divinity, since the Greek physician Galen (AD 129–216) wrote in Book I of his *De usu partium* (*On the Usefulness of the Parts*) that the human hand was the quintessential product of divine artistry. Tulp may well have proposed this interpretation, motivated by an understandable attempt to give his gruesome profession a more positive reputation.

Landscape painting first came into its own in the Baroque. During the late Gothic and Renaissance periods, landscapes served as backdrops to history paintings – particularly in the Northern Renaissance, where they attained an unparalleled richness and degree of naturalism. But in the seventeenth century artists began to explore the way natural settings could express moods or emotions, and they were taken more seriously. Baroque landscape painting took two forms, one promoted in Italy and France and the other in northern Europe, particularly Holland. The first was inspired by classical models and was characterized by warmer Mediterranean tones

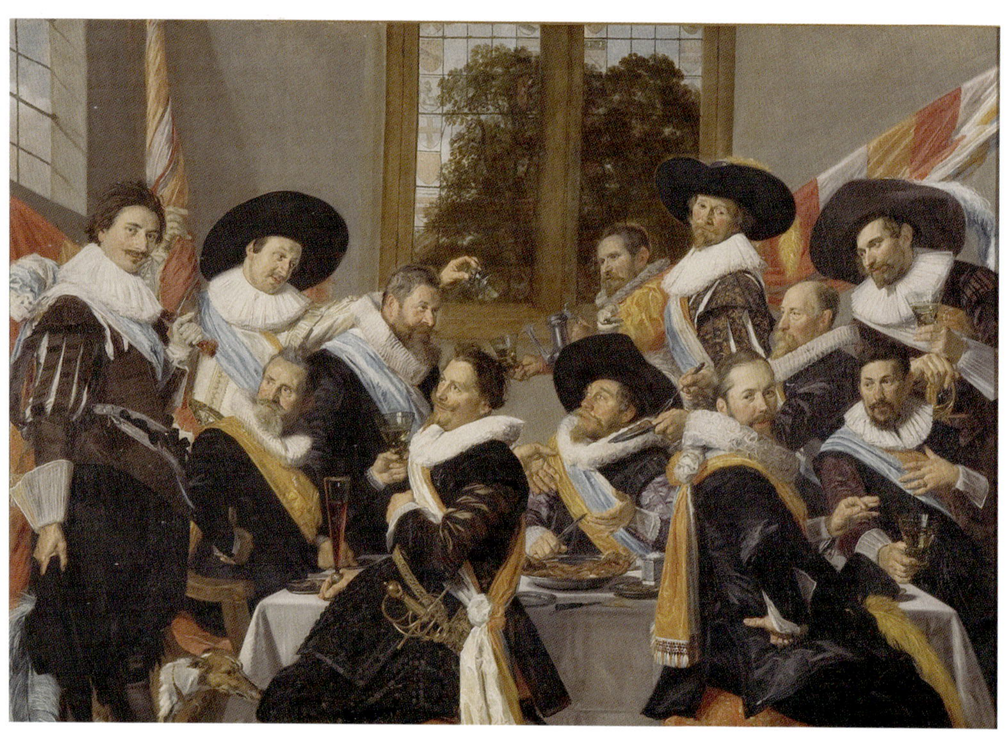

64.
Frans Hals,
*Officers and
Sergeants of
the St Hadrian
Civic Guard*,
c.1627. Oil on
canvas; 1.83 ×
2.66 m (6 ft ×
8 ft 9 in). Frans
Hals Museum,
Haarlem (The
Netherlands)

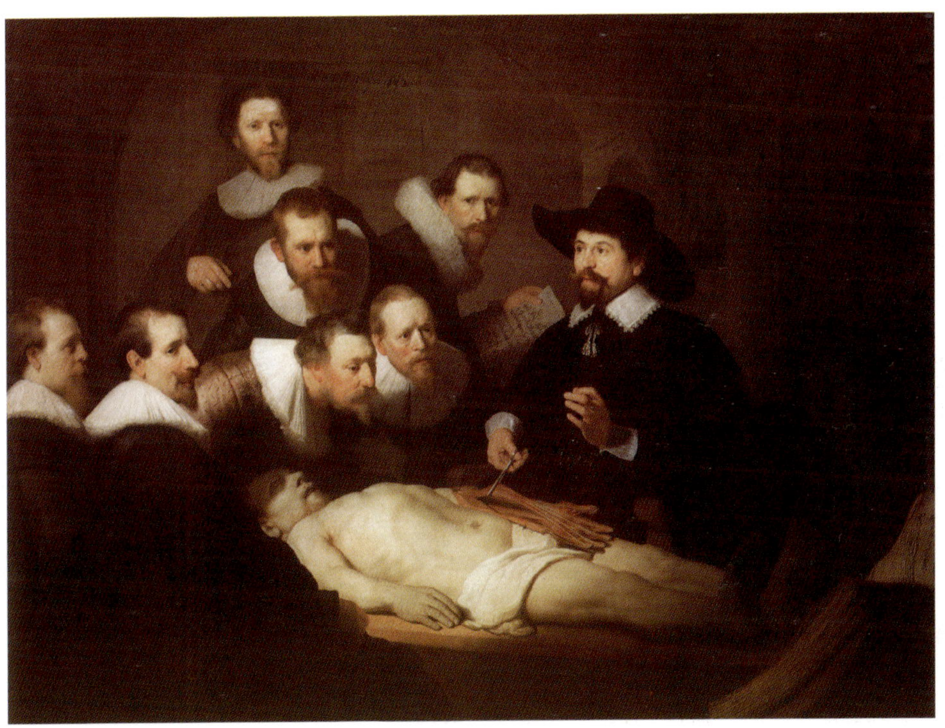

**65.
Rembrandt
van Rijn**,
*Anatomy
Lecture of Dr.
Nicolaes Tulp*,
1632. Oil on
canvas; 1.69
× 2.16 m (5 ft
6½ in × 7 ft
1 in). The
Royal Picture
Gallery,
Mauritshuis,
The Hague

and an idealized sense of harmony (a similar aesthetic prevailed in Poussin's *The Arcadian Shepherds*; see 52). Landscapists made sketches from life but always rearranged and 'corrected' them in the studio in keeping with classical precepts. Southern landscapes were only slowly extricated from religious painting, and even the most vivid early Baroque landscapes were dotted with tiny figures painted *alla prima* (directly onto the canvas without retouching) and given titles like *Rest on the Flight to Egypt* or *Tobias and the Angel*. Indeed, many churchmen believed that landscapes reflected the created world and therefore God's glory. The Dutch variety grew out of an entirely different socio-religious climate. In Holland, cleansed of public religious imagery by Calvinism, aristocrats and burghers alike gained an appreciation for the things of this world, commissioning views of their immediate surroundings. These artists reproduced more accurately the ink and oil sketches they made *en plein air*, and while they idealized the final product as well sometimes producing fantasy landscapes – and here etchings and engravings were as important as oil paintings – the aim was not a classical, perfected nature but a domesticated and human one, at times monumental and even ominous, but on the whole familiar and comforting.

Early Baroque painters such as Annibale Carracci and Domenichino, inspired both by northern masters and the rich landscape settings and moody skies of the paintings of the Venetian Renaissance, allowed landscape painting (*paesaggi*) as a genre to take root permanently on central Italian soil. Annibale experimented with landscapes early in his career, executing scenes of untamed wilderness with asymmetrical trees and hillocks and peopled with huntsmen and fishermen. But after arriving in Rome he incorporated these views into more 'acceptable' religious paintings. Choosing the Roman Campagna, or countryside, as his subject, Annibale painted tamed classical landscapes characterized by wider horizons, taller, more massive trees, subtler shading and golden light. *Rest on the Flight to Egypt* (66), a joint work by Annibale and Domenichino, is carefully balanced with a large open space at the centre framing a river below and a castle in the middle distance, the whole anchored on the left by a forested hillock and on the right by more distant trees. Yet the presence of humanity is always in the forefront: the castle is central and prominent and the Holy Family appears at the intersection of two diagonals,

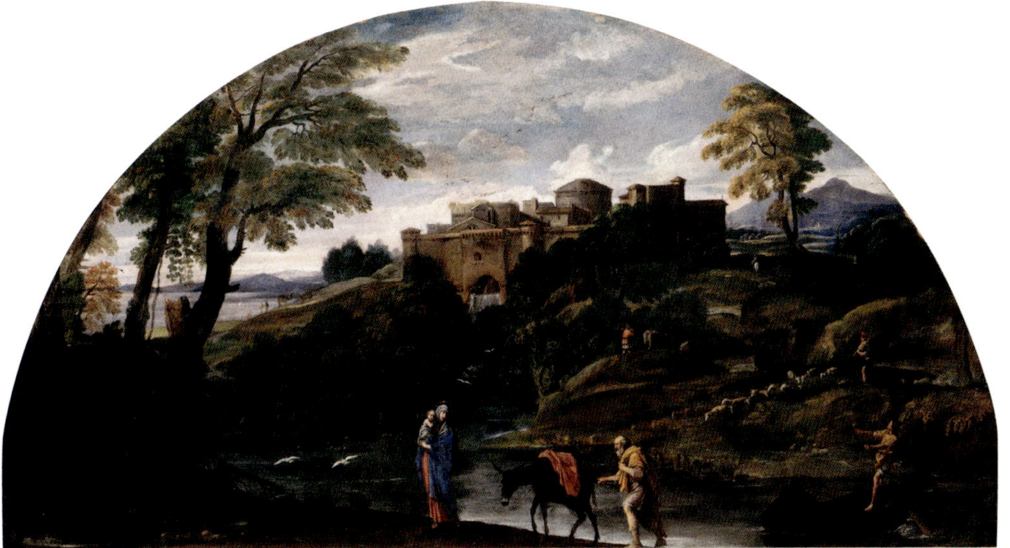

66.
**Annibale
Carracci and
Dominichino**,
*Rest on the
Flight to Egypt*,
c.1604–6. Oil
on canvas;
1.22 × 2.3 m
(4 ft × 7 ft
6½ in).
Galleria Doria
Pamphilj,
Rome

protected by the castle above and the trees on either side. This idealism is directly related to the theories of Giovanni Battista Agucchi, the advocate of 'nature perfected', who emphasized the connection between landscape and Graeco-Roman pastoral literature (Chapter One).

The search for a classical Arcadia also motivated the French exile and former pastry chef Claude Lorrain (Gellée, 1600–1682), better known simply as Claude. Like Poussin he spent almost his entire career in Rome (after 1627), and his work combines the classicism of Annibale with the keen realism and luminous light of such northern exiles as the Fleming Paul Bril (1554–1626) and the German Adam Elsheimer (1578–1610). Claude was soon favoured by the city's greatest patrons, Pope Urban VIII among them, and became the most sought-after landscapist in Europe – in fact, there were so many fake Claudes on the market that he compiled a book of drawings to help collectors verify genuine works (*Liber Veritatis*, or *Book of Truth*, first published in engraved form in 1777). *Seaport at Sunrise* (67) dates from the later part of his career, when he had tested out a wide spectrum of landscape types, many evoking ancient Roman pastoral literature, particularly the Roman poet Virgil's *Aeneid and Georgics*. Claude made long excursions into the countryside executing ink drawings enhanced by washes, and possibly also oil sketches. In his paintings he transformed them into scenes of classical harmony, working out compositional solutions directly on the canvas. *Seaport at Sunrise* is typical of Claude's later work, in which water, architecture, trees and people are gilded by the raking light of the rising or setting sun. It shows a southern Italian port in the last, decaying days of the Roman Empire, with its crumbling triumphal arch overgrown with plants and the partially ruined castles. The expansive, vaporous atmosphere of a sweltering dawn softens the rising sun (Claude was the first to paint the sun directly). The women and boatmen in the foreground – they move quietly from the casual conversations of dawn to the strenuous labours of the working day – are mere accents in a scene dominated by sky and seascape.

Dutch landscape painting (we get the term from the Dutch *landschap*) was a very different phenomenon. Instead of seeking an Augustan golden age, it celebrated the here-and-now: the familiar landscapes, cityscapes

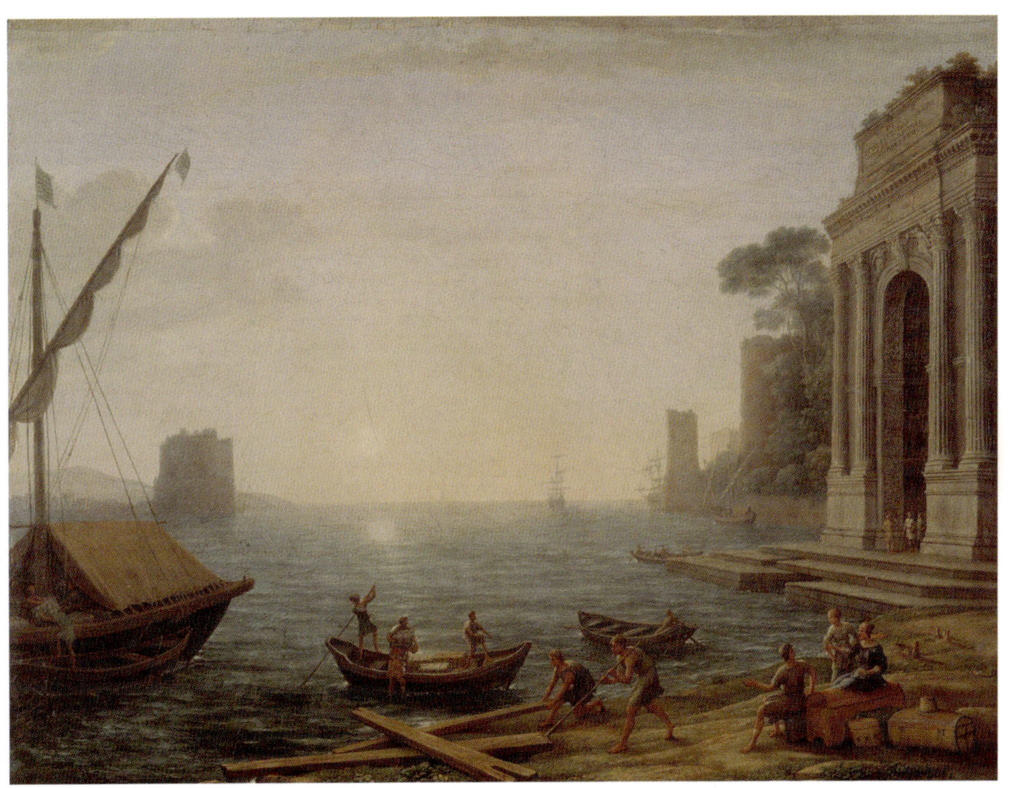

**67.
Claude
Lorrain,**
*Seaport at
Sunrise,*
1674. Oil on
canvas; 72 ×
96 cm (28¼ ×
37¾ in). Alte
Pinakothek,
Munich

and seascapes of a proud young republic and prosperous middle class.
Nevertheless, Dutch landscapes were often as contrived and idealized as their
southern counterparts, and were motivated by their own brand of 'nature
perfected'. Although scholars have recently attempted to read religious
symbolism about God's bounty into the wheat fields, waterfalls and sunbursts
by painters such as Salomon van Ruysdael (1600–1670) and Jan van Goyen
(1596–1656), there is little evidence either from the paintings' titles or from
contemporary commentaries that such a message was intended. Like Claude,
Dutch artists sketched *en plein air*, altering and correcting their compositions
in the studio, where they enlarged mountains, merged buildings or lowered
horizon lines. By constructing compositions along dramatic diagonals or
vertical axes, artists added drama and dynamism. Haarlem was the early
centre of landscape painting, where an interest in views of recognizable
locales developed in the 1610s, particularly in etchings. Claes Jansz
Visscher's (1587–1652) *Winter Landscape with Skaters* (68), from his series
of fourteen prints after designs by fellow Haarlem painter Cornelis Claesz
van Wieringen called *Amaeniores Aliquot Regiunculae*, shows a specifically
Dutch landscape, with dykes, frozen ponds and gabled and thatched houses
– Visscher referred to such scenes as *plaisante plaetsen* ('pleasant places') – but
also populated with ordinary people working or engaged in leisure activities
such as skating (the Dutch invented ice-skating) or building boats. Visscher's
etching also places great emphasis on the sky: with the horizon in the middle
it becomes as significant as the land, and the energy of Visscher's clouds
is equal to that of the figures below. As indicated by their name 'pleasant
places', such etchings aimed primarily at giving pleasure to the viewer. The
same goal continued to inform landscape art in its maturity, between 1650
and 1675, with the work of van Ruysdael and van Goyen.

This early painting by van Ruysdael, entitled *After the Rain* (69),
demonstrates a precocious ability to manipulate clouds, light and shadow
to create a sensation of expectation and foreboding – precisely the kind of
mood that has inspired scholars to read religious messages into his work.
The churning clouds, built up with deepening shades of brown and grey,
open up in the upper-left corner of the painting to reveal a burst of sunlight
that nevertheless illuminates only a small piece of the landscape below: some

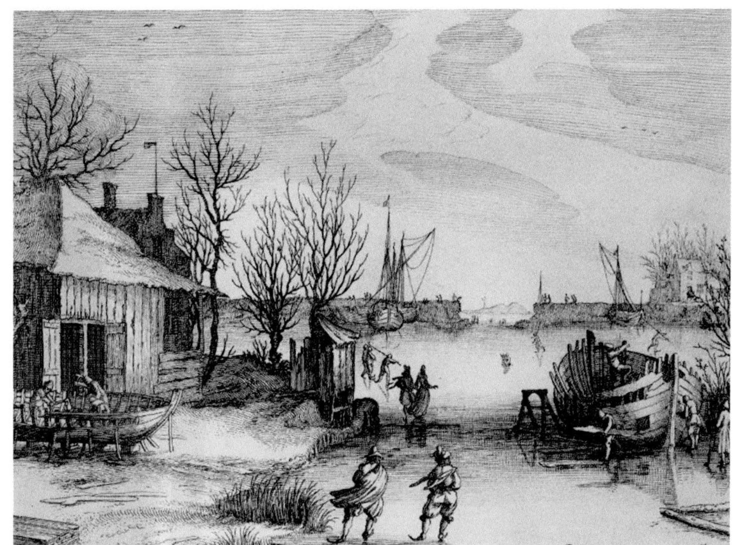

recently harvested straw and one of the horses. The cottage, wagon, straw cart and human figures are obscured by oppressively dark browns and greens: humanity and its accoutrements are mere details in a scene that showcases the vitality and frightening power of nature. Van Ruysdael carefully observes the effect of wind on trees and the dappled appearance of light filtered through clouds. He lowers the horizon further than Visscher so that the sky becomes the main organ of expression, and his rich and varied use of colour distinguishes his work from the nearly monochromatic world of van Goyen. The latter's *Haarlem Sea* (70) also features a low horizon line, agitated clouds and windswept rainy weather, but a significant proportion of the foreground is taken up by water, which van Goyen uses – through rippling waves and reflections – to mirror the movements of the clouds in a less dramatic, more human way than van Ruysdael. The waves threaten neither the boats nor the fishermen, who quietly go about their task, oblivious to the weather. But the human element still cannot match the power of nature, and van Goyen's sketchy windmill, cottage and distant spires are less substantial than those of van Ruysdael.

Even though the landscape was a genre based on drawing out-of-doors, drawings could be deceptively ingenuous. Salomon's nephew Jacob van Ruisdael (1628/9–1682) – they spelt the family name differently – is

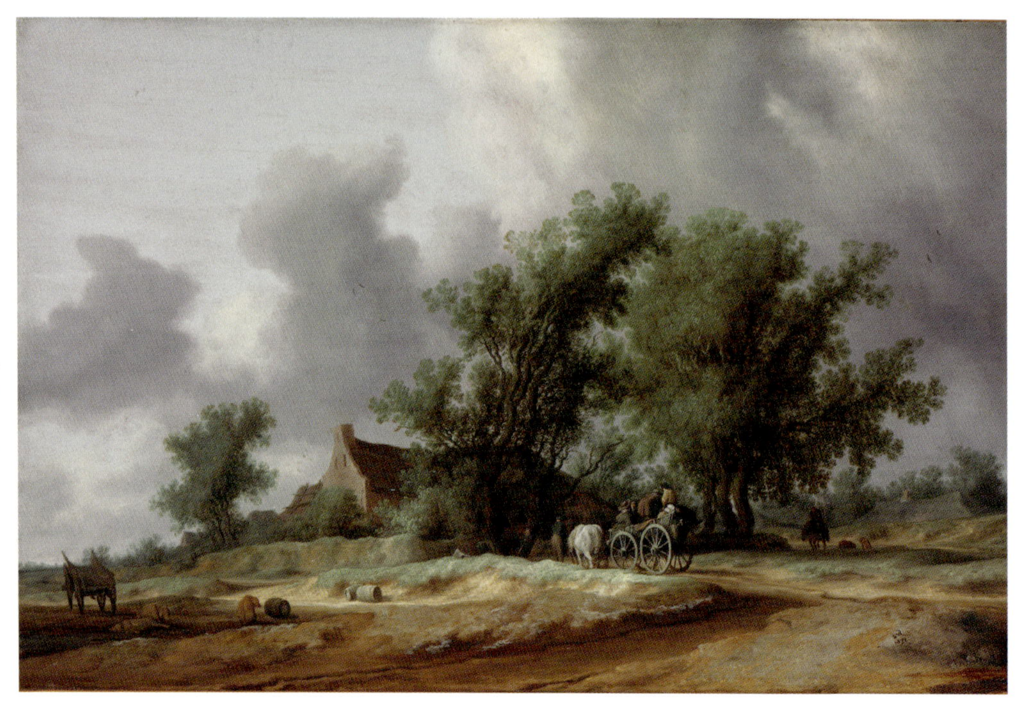

69.
Salomon van Ruysdael, *After the Rain*, 1631. Oil on wood; 56 × 86.5 cm (22 × 34 in). Szépmüvészeti Múzeum, Budapest (Hungary)

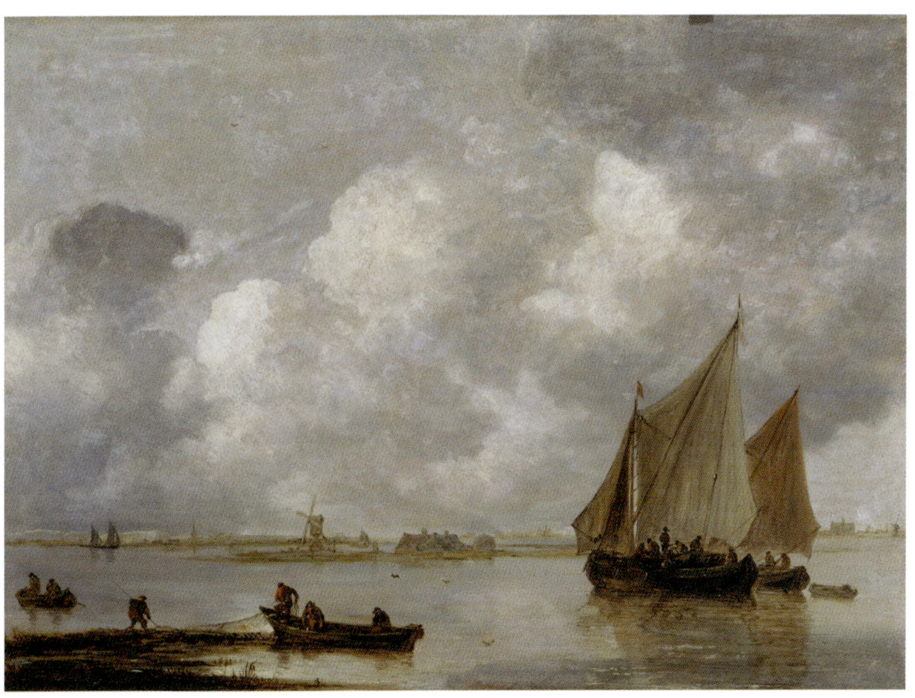

**70.
Jan van
Goyen**,
Haarlem Sea,
1656. Oil
on wood;
40 × 56 cm
(15¾ ×
22 in). Städel
Museum,
Frankfurt
(Germany)

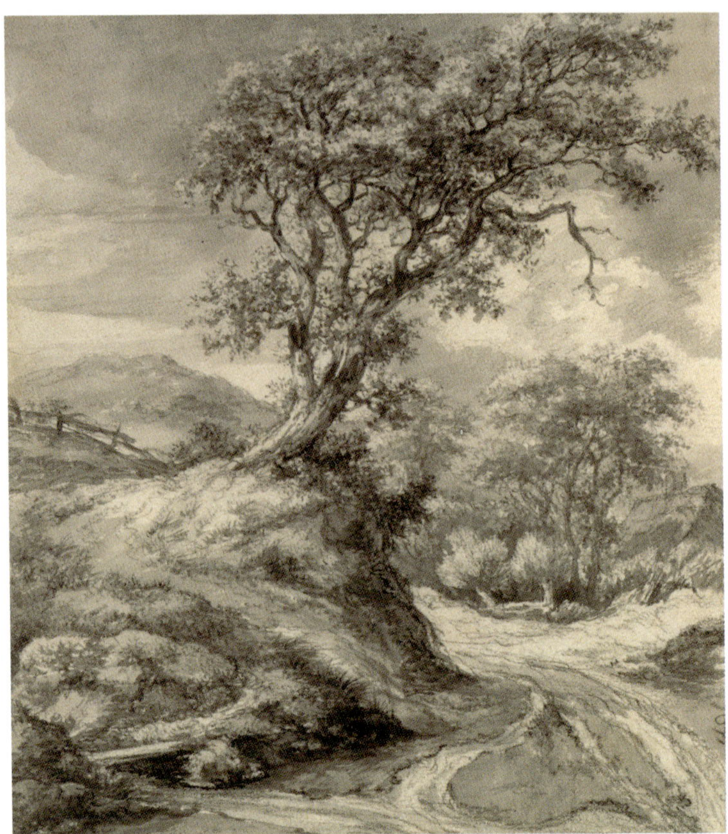

considered the greatest landscape painter of the Dutch Golden Age, and he
brought the kind of monumentality usually associated with history painting
to scenes of such quotidian objects as trees or windmills. His *Dune Landscape
with Oak Tree* would appear at first glance to be a *plein air* sketch executed
on an afternoon's stroll, but it is in fact a completed, monogrammed and
carefully constructed presentation drawing meant as a work of art in its own
right (71). He balances the forceful diagonal of the craggy tree and dune
with the subtler rivulet on the lower right and the footbridge on the upper
left, and he emphasizes the tree's height by allowing us to see it from below
and by crowding it against the frame at the top so that it blots out half the
sky. Through a careful interplay of chalk, washes and gouache van Ruisdael
gives this drawing the dramatic light effects he used more famously in his
oil paintings, and like his uncle Salomon he purposefully made the human
element – in this case the bridge and small thatched hut – seem trifling when
confronting the architectural majesty of nature.

A completely different kind of landscape painting developed in Rococo Venice and Rome. In contrast both to the emotive cloudscapes and seascapes of Dutch landscapes and the pastoral classicism of Domenichino and Claude, the scenes (*vedute*) of Giovanni Antonio Canal ('Canaletto', 1697–1768) and his teacher Giovanni Paolo Panini (1692–1765) aimed at crisp, detailed accuracy, faithfully rendering brightly lit views that approached what we would today call photographic realism (in fact, in his later work Canaletto used a *camera obscura*, or boxlike optical device, to project views directly onto the canvas before applying paint). Both artists prospered as a direct result of the Grand Tour, the eighteenth-century rite of passage in which young northern European aristocrats travelled over the course of months or even years through Italy studying the arts and culture of the Renaissance and antiquity and fostering important social connections. Joseph Smith, British consul in Venice and one of Canaletto's major patrons, helped sell the artist's paintings to this international clientele. Canaletto even worked for about ten years in London, beginning in 1746, before returning to Venice. *Grand Canal: Looking South-West* (72) is typical of Canaletto's views of Venice's canals and major monuments. Painted from nature directly onto the canvas, the cityscape is animated by a lively array of gondolas and boats. Like a photographer, Canaletto employs raking light to bring out the richer colours of dusk, highlighting the church of S. Simeone Piccolo on the left while S. Maria di Nazareth on the opposite side falls into shadow. As this painting was executed in the same year that S. Simeone was completed, it may have been intended as a commemoration of the event. The close observation of sunlight's effects on surfaces – particularly the flickering light on the waves – as well as the lack of a deeper, moralistic meaning anticipates French Impressionism. Panini's *Picture Gallery with Views of Modern Rome* (73) uses the illusionistic conceit of showing exterior views on the inside of a building: his glimpses of the Renaissance and Baroque architecture of Rome are paintings within a painting. Panini was not only a landscape painter but also painted portraits, frescos, stage sets and ephemera for festivals. As early as the 1710s, he executed *vedute* (views) and *capricci* (imaginary views) of Roman ruins in picturesque settings for clients on the Grand Tour, but he is most famous today for scenes of palace interiors hung to the rafters with framed paintings – by Panini – of views of Rome or Renaissance and antique sculptures. The structurally incoherent architecture with its dramatic perspective relates more to stage scenery than to architecture. At the foot of *Picture Gallery*, connoisseurs and art dealers observe the paintings and haggle over prices while kneeling and seated art students prepare their sketches.

Scenes of everyday life – confusingly, also called 'genre scenes' – ranked among the higher minor genres because even though they depicted lowly subjects they contained multiple figures and actions (they were equivalent to Aristotle's definition of 'comedy'). Like landscapes, their appeal lay in their familiar and contemporary subject matter, from placid domestic scenes to bawdy tavern capers. The genre began with the peasant scenes of Flemish

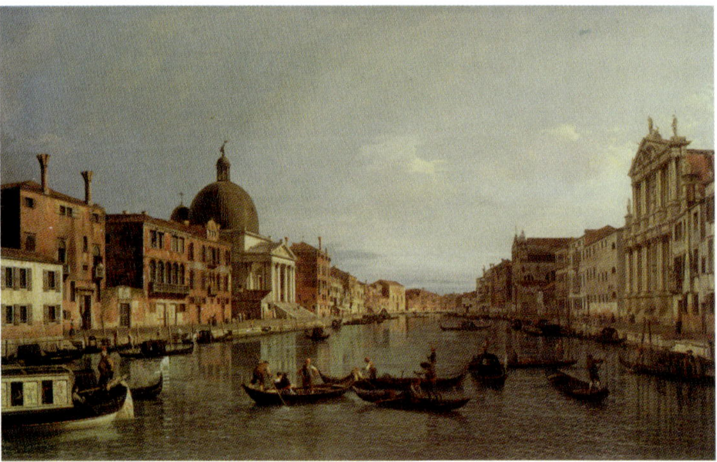

72.
Giovanni Antonio Canal ('Canaletto), *Grand Canal: Looking South-West*, c.1740. Oil on canvas; 1.24 × 2.05 m (4 ft × 6 ft 8½ in). National Gallery, London

painter Pieter Brueghel the Elder (c.1525–69), and although it was popular in early seventeenth-century Italy as a minor genre – Annibale Carracci and Caravaggio dabbled in genre scenes, and the *Bamboccianti* specialized in such paintings (see 18) – Holland quickly took the lead. Genre paintings were more prone to moralistic messages than were landscapes: the tavern scenes, which seem on the surface to be merely amusing or vulgar, often have admonitory functions, and the domestic interiors promoted family values like orderliness and celebrated the role of women in the home – homes that were, for the first time, freed of the labour and daily toils of less prosperous times. But this aspect is often exaggerated: these works were, above all, depictions of quotidian reality and appreciated for their mimetic qualities.

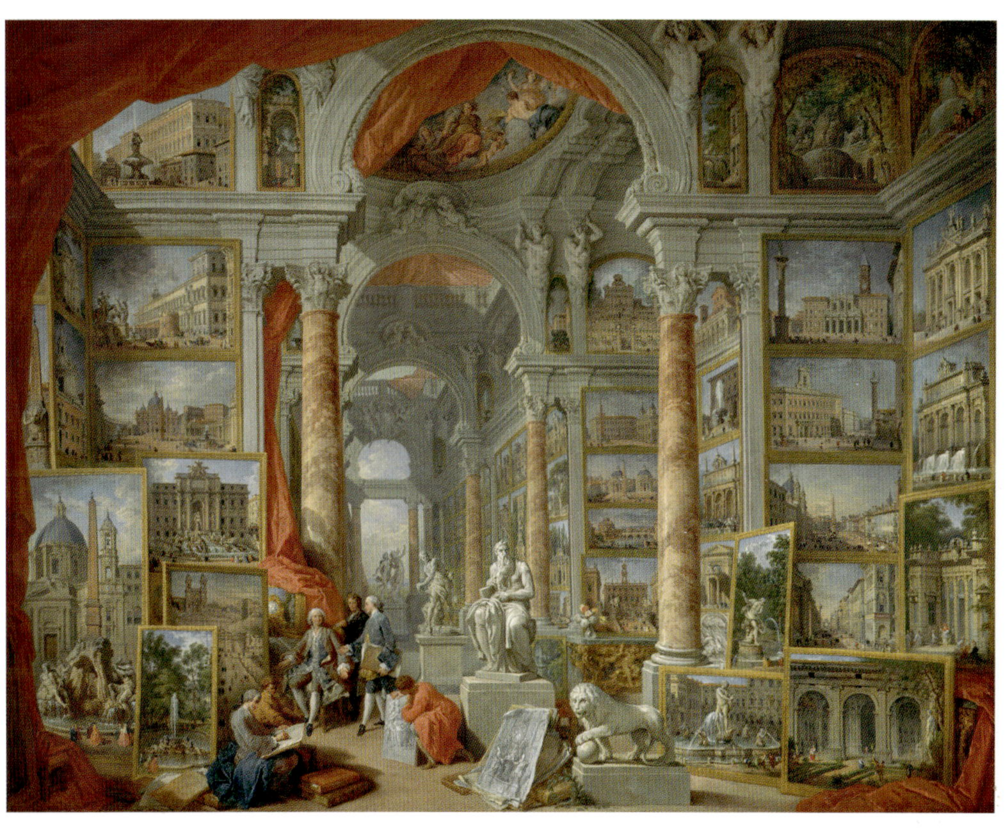

73.
Giovanni Paolo Panini, *Picture Gallery with Views of Modern Rome,* 1757. Oil on canvas; 1.7 × 2.44 m (5 ft 7 in × 8 ft). Museum of Fine Arts, Boston MA

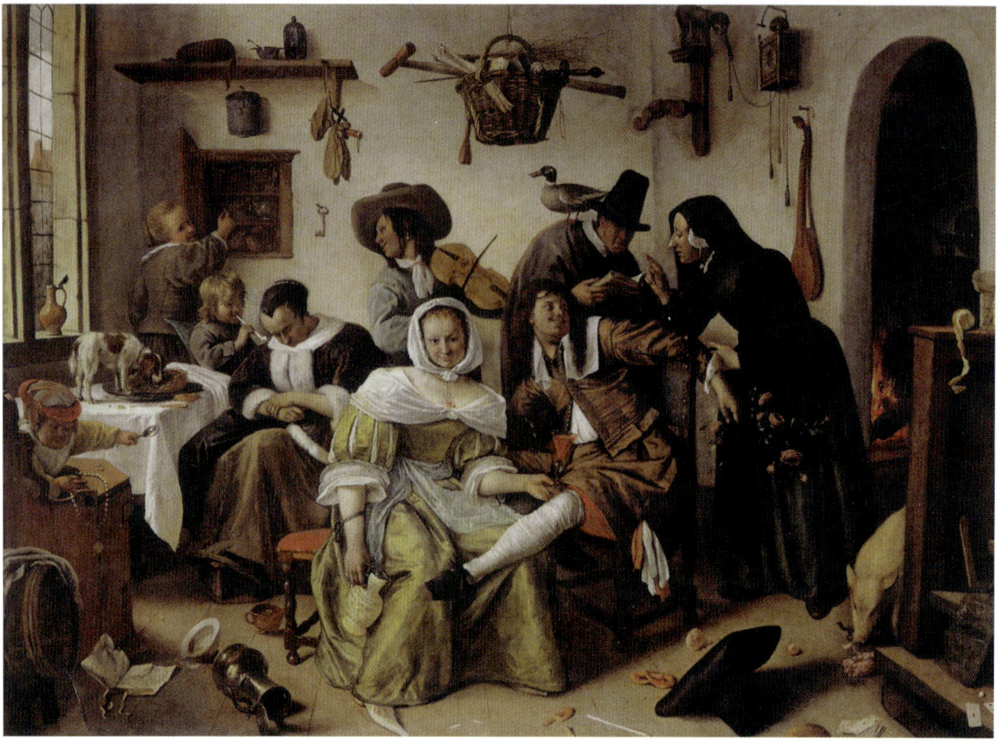

Jan Steen's *The World Upside Down* (74) and Jan Vermeer's *Girl Reading a
Letter at an Open Window* (75) represent opposite ends of the spectrum.
Steen's house is a shambles, the antithesis of the ordered household. Two
drunken and groping lovers in the foreground nearly fall off their seats while
a fiddler plays a song that – given the traditional association between music
and sexuality – is probably obscene. To the right a nun gossips with
a Quaker, while on the far left a girl steals money from the cupboard.
Her little brother – he is ignored by their sleeping, perhaps inebriated
mother – smokes a pipe and the unsupervised baby tosses household
valuables onto the floor. Elsewhere a small dog jumps onto the table and
gorges himself on a pie and (in the kitchen on the right) an abandoned roast
has fallen into the fire. A deck of cards strewn on the floor and a leaking
beer keg on the lower left (the pig has the spout in its mouth) add to the
debauched character of the scene. But none of these details are coincidental:
they are all symbols and allusions relating to proverbs, literature and plays.
The pig sniffing the rose recalls a Dutch proverb similar to the English one

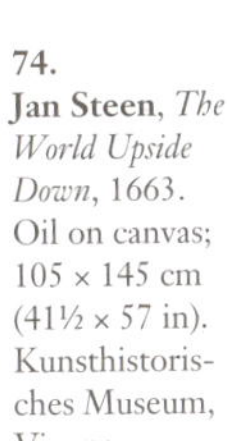

74.
Jan Steen, *The World Upside Down*, 1663. Oil on canvas; 105 × 145 cm (41½ × 57 in). Kunsthistorisches Museum, Vienna

75.
Jan Vermeer, *Girl Reading a Letter at an Open Window*, c.1657. Oil on canvas; 83.2 × 64.4 cm (32¾ × 25¼ in). Gemäldegalerie, Dresden (Germany)

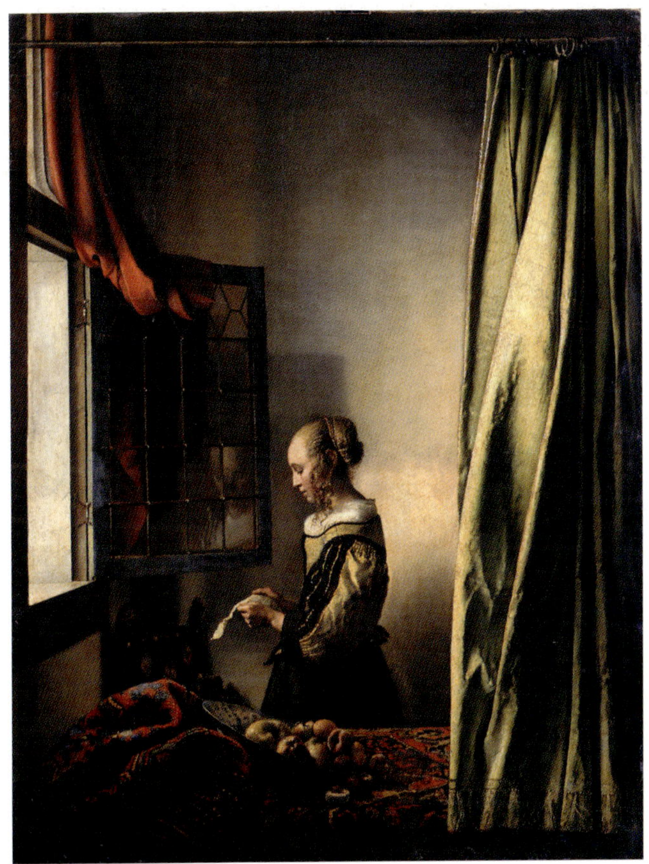

about pearls before swine, the duck on the old man's shoulder labels the Quaker as a 'quacker', and the monkey playing with the clock may refer to the saying 'life is no ape's game'. The title itself is the name of a game that questions the meaning of life and societal norms, and the artist has inscribed the words 'Beware of Luxury' on the chalkboard on the lower right. Steen was a Catholic in a Protestant country, and his faith may have led him to favour scenes with a moral message. Nevertheless, he is not entirely unsympathetic to his figures, and allows the lightheartedness and fun to delight the viewer.

Vermeer's is a very different world. *Girl Reading a Letter at an Open Window* is an essay on absorption: the girl standing in the centre of the composition is so engrossed in the letter that it is as if her spirit has left her body. In fact, she becomes another detail in a still life, along with the window, walls, curtains, carpet, furniture and bowl of gently spilling fruit. Her profile view prevents us from reading her thoughts, but by allowing a glimpse of her face's ghostly reflection in the window Vermeer invites us to pause and meditate as if before a sacred image. Typically, he applies his paint in thin layers and draws out textures and contours with subtle tonal variations rather than dramatic shading so that the image seems vaporous or out of focus. Nevertheless, the textures of the cloth and peaches, the effects of light on the window panes, and the decorative patterns of the carpet and bowl are painstakingly observed, giving inanimate objects a far greater prominence than in Steen's painting. Some are significant, like the Turkish carpet and Chinese porcelain, which hint at Holland's worldwide trading empire and at the prosperity of the household. Using prominent verticals (the curtain, the woman and the junction of window and window frame), Vermeer creates a rhythmic pattern of lines and spaces which he superimposes onto a diagonal that divides the picture into light and dark zones, and he suspends the bolder colours (red, green and gold) in perfect balance. The sunlight, which enters the room from the upper left, animates it, casting shadow, creating highlights, and reflecting against glass and porcelain as it goes. Some have tried to explain Vermeer's visual illusionism through his possible use of optical devices such as the camera obscura or pin-and-string system (whereby strings are pinned directly onto the canvas to assist with perspective), but such machines are beside the point: Vermeer's visual understanding overrode whatever methods he used, deviating from their mechanical perfection and creating a style entirely his own.

Absorption was also at the heart of the work of the Rococo painter Jean-Antoine Watteau (1684–1721). Although the French Rococo is often seen as a carefree and even frivolous era, as reflected in the prolifereation of scenes of relaxaton in the open countryside (called *fêtes galantes*), scholars are beginning to discover preoccupations with more serious themes such as conversation, raptness and spirituality. In Rococo pastorals asymmetrical groups of small figures dance, enjoy intimate picnics and engage each other in discussions. Common are figures from the theatre and musicians who often stand mute among the crowds of more animated figures. Even the loose handling of the paint evokes the glittering, constantly shifting nature of conversation. Yet there is a mysterious quality about these tableaux that defies narrative: they depict conversation but not specific stories, and even though the figures interact with great liveliness the viewer cannot know what they are talking about. In works such as *The Pleasures of the Ball* (76) Watteau highlights the interactions between the groups of people on the sides so that the dancers underneath the arch, whom the composition would imply are the main subject of the painting, seem rigid and characterless by comparison. Social interaction and conversation in particular were critical concerns in French society at the time: a proliferation of conduct books in the early eighteenth century focused on the importance of morality and decorum in human exchanges and conversation formed the centrepiece of the

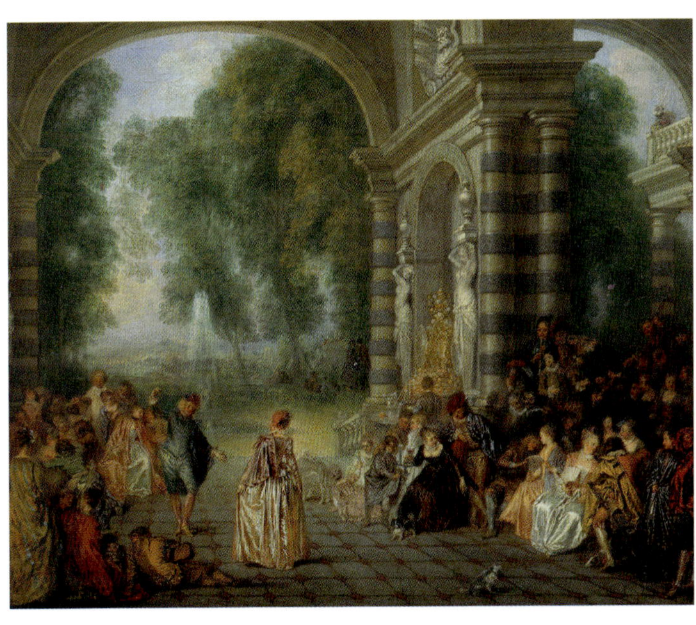

**76.
Jean-Antoine
Watteau**, *The
Pleasures of the
Ball*, 1715–17.
Oil on canvas;
52.6 × 65.4 cm
(20¾ × 25¾ in).
Dulwich
Picture
Gallery,
London

salon, a forum for polite debate and discussion hosted by aristocratic Parisian women that involved the most important intellectuals of the day, from Jean-Jacques Rousseau to Voltaire. Paintings such as these compel us to fill in the conversational gap ourselves, like a non-religious meditative image.

Genre scenes also commonly appeared in the more affordable medium of etching, a printing process in which a design is scratched onto a plate covered with acid-proof resin and then bathed in acid to bore it deeper into the metal. Rembrandt was one of the most prolific etchers of the Baroque – indeed etchings were the primary source of his fame – producing hundreds of religious scenes, allegorical studies, portraits and genre scenes. His *Beggars at the Door* (77) demonstrates not only Rembrandt's virtuoso technique but his empathy for the poor and oppressed, a theme we have already witnessed in his religious paintings. A beggar family stands before a doorway, receiving a coin from a wealthy man in the typical fur hat and fur-lined coat of the day. But the beggars are the centre of attention, not merely literally – they are in the centre of the picture and the rich man is mostly hidden behind the doorway – but by their poise. They wear their ragged clothes with dignity, the man's raked hat and boy's folded-back boots worn almost with an

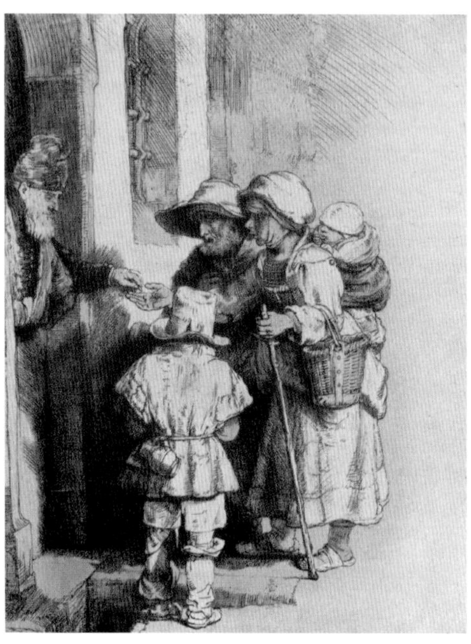

aristocratic *sprezzatura* (compare with 58), and the pair with their baby recall the Holy Family in Rembrandt's own depictions of the *Rest on the Flight to Egypt*. True to the ideals of genre imagery the beggars are represented with great accuracy, as with the hurdy-gurdy – the prototypical instrument of the wandering musician – held by the blind player. In its spontaneity of line the etching has the immediacy of a drawing, and its sensitivity to the effects of light and shadow stand up to any oil painting – the dark areas are enhanced by drypoint, a technique of scratching directly into the plate but leaving the scrapings, or 'burr', along the sides to hold more ink and create a velvety effect.

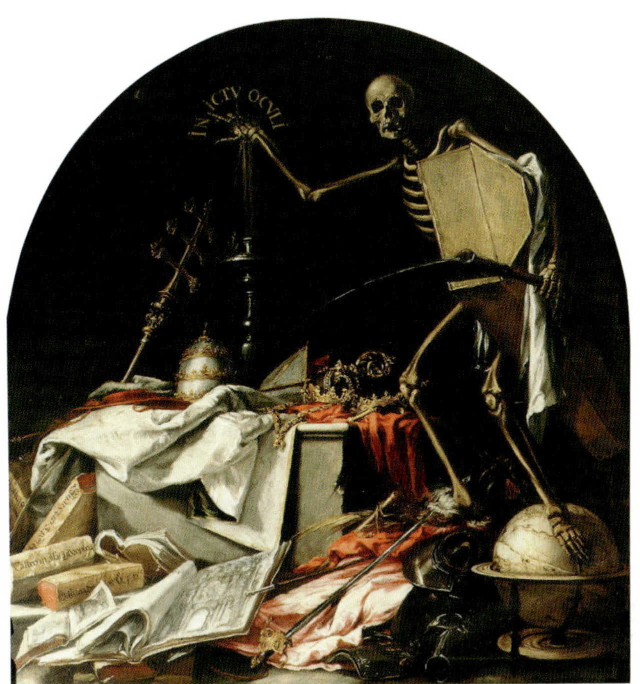

**78.
Juan de Valdés Leal**, *In Ictu Oculi*, 1670–2. Oil on canvas; 2.2 × 2.16 m (7 ft 2½ in × 7 ft). La Caridad, Seville

Still-life paintings, in which a selection of objects is laid before the viewer close to the picture plane, also began as details in religious works, and they emerged as their own genre first in the Netherlands and then, by the turn of the seventeenth century, in Italy and the rest of southern Europe. The term 'still life' – it comes directly from the Dutch *stilleven* – literally means 'dead life', and painters used this paradoxical conceit to communicate messages about vanity and the imminence of death (many served as *memento mori*). The more ghoulish extreme of the genre is epitomized in the work of Spanish painter Juan de Valdés Leal (1622–1690), Murillo's main rival in Seville. His *In Ictu Oculi* ('In the Blink of an Eye'; 78) – the inscription is in the upper part of the painting – depicts a tomb littered with a jumble of earthly vanities including satin gowns, a papal tiara and crown, swords, armour, books, a crozier and a globe, while a skeleton bearing a shroud, coffin and scythe looms above, mounting the globe and extinguishing the candle of life. The costume, objects and books – these can be identified precisely by their titles and the engraving in the open volume – refer to the papacy and Spain's Habsburg dynasty: Valdés's message is that even the great and powerful cannot escape Death, and that mortals should prepare to meet their Maker.

Dutch and Flemish still lifes feature a bewildering variety of subjects, some
with moralistic overtones and others not. Clara Peeters's *Still Life with
Flowers, a Goblet, Dried Fruit and Pretzels* (79) – part of a series of four Dutch
meals – suggests an interrupted supper as a metaphor for the uncertainty
of life and the dangers of luxury. One of the first to combine flowers with
food, Peeters divides her scene into three vertical sections. The central one
is dominated by a gilt bronze goblet in front of a porcelain bowl filled with
nuts, figs and dates, and it is balanced on the right by a plate of haphazardly
arranged pretzels and nuts, a pewter pitcher and a glass of wine. An
earthenware vase of flowers and some scattered petals on the table balance

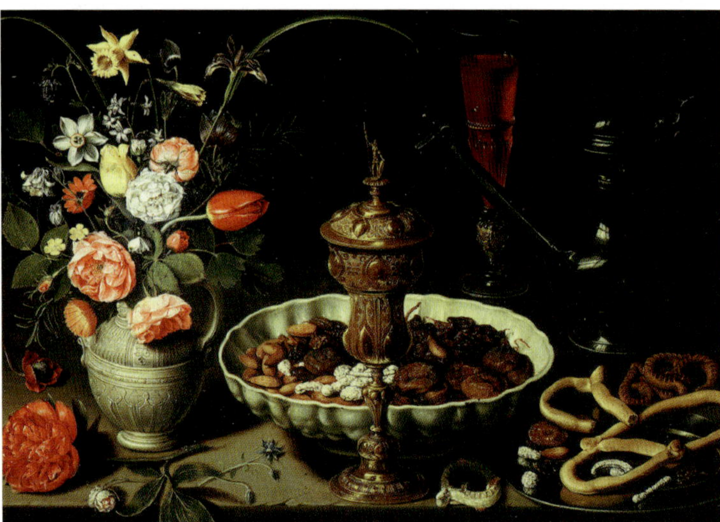

79.
Clara Peeters,
*Still-Life with
Flowers, a
Goblet, Dried
Fruit, and
Pretzels*, 1611.
Oil on panel;
52 × 73 cm
(20½ × 28¾ in).
Prado, Madrid

the composition on the left. The immediacy of the scene – most of the
objects are close to the picture plane and therefore the viewer – is enhanced
by the trick of having us look down upon the table as if seated there.
Although her bouquet is rendered in breathtaking detail, Peeters deceives us
by combining flowers – daffodils, tulips, poppies, irises, roses and peonies –
that bloom at different times of the year.

Flower paintings were the most popular kind of still life, fetching prices
higher than history paintings by artists as famous as Rembrandt. The Dutch
artist Rachel Ruysch, whose *Still Life with Roses* (see 4) was mentioned in the

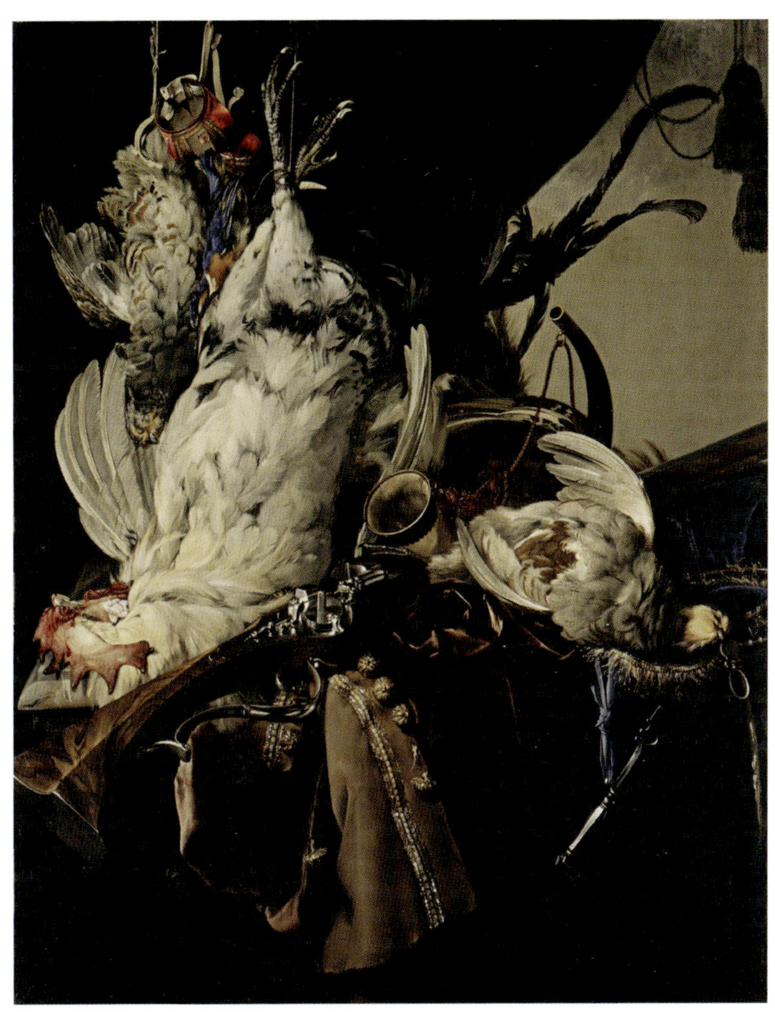

80.
**Willem van
Aelst**, *Still Life
of Dead Birds
and Hunting
Weapons*, 1660.
Oil on canvas;
86.5 × 68 cm
(34 × 26¾ in).
Gemäldegalerie,
Berlin

Introduction, was one of the most successful flower painters, satisfying her country's obsession with imported Middle-Eastern flowers, most notably the tulip, which was so valuable that people speculated on bulbs in the financial market. Ruysch was the daughter of a botany professor and was introduced to fine floral specimens from an early age, and her understanding of every nuance of texture, body and humidity of the flowers and fruit – note the way the light reveals different textures on the grapes alone – earned her an unparalleled reputation among the tulip-crazy merchant classes. Her teacher Willem van Aelst (c.1627–c.1683) specialized in quite a different kind of still life, one that again hinted at death and decay. At one time court painter to Grand Duke Ferdinando II de' Medici of Florence, van Aelst returned to Holland where he was in high demand for game pictures, painting over sixty of them between 1652 and 1681. His *Still Life of Dead Birds and Hunting Weapons* (80) combines an admonitory message with a celebration of the hunt, a prestigious activity and preserve of the rich. Three game birds are hung over a folded gentleman's coat, a hunting horn and a glistening, finely crafted matchlock. Van Aelst treats every feather with the same care and variety that Ruysch lavishes on her petals, and he expertly differentiates between the matte suede of the coat, the crisp, shiny metal of the gun and the plush down of the birds' breasts. He shocks us by contrasting the birds' downy feathers with their broken necks. Van Aelst leaves nothing to chance, arranging his composition around the pair of intersecting diagonals formed by the birds and the matchlock, and he balances the light areas with the darker earth tones to give the painting a sense of quiet harmony.

Although not differentiated as separate genres at the time, two subsections of genre painting – exotica and erotica – were typical of the age. The Baroque and Rococo were incessantly curious times, as the borders of the known world extended even further than they had during the sixteenth century's Age of Conquest (see Chapter Seven). Although some aristocratic families such as the Grand Dukes of Tuscany or the Habsburgs of Innsbruck demonstrated an early interest in exotica – more specifically, the natural wonders, peoples and products of Asia, Africa and the Americas – such imagery did not become diffuse in European art until the seventeenth and eighteenth centuries, when Asian princesses or Native American warriors adorned Roman ceiling

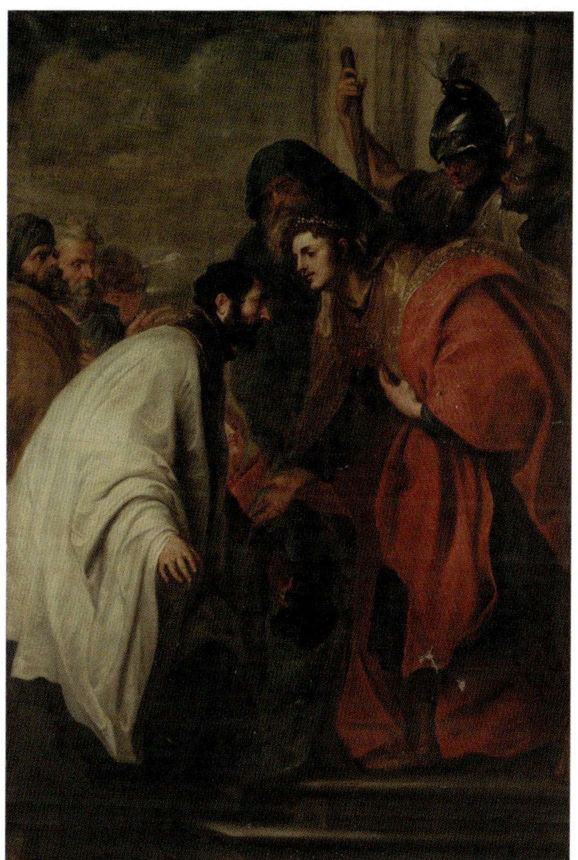

frescos or peeked out from Bavarian stuccowork. As we will see in Chapter

Five, Rococo interiors were especially favourable to exotica, particularly

with the introduction of the Chinese-inspired decorative movement known

as chinoiserie. Flemish and Dutch painters made portraits of dignitaries

from the furthest reaches of the European trading empires either (in the

Spanish Netherlands) to celebrate Christianity's spread across the globe or

(in Holland) in an attempt to make sense of the cultures upon which their

trade depended. At first glance, Van Dyck's *Saint Francis Xavier Meets Otomo

Sorin, Daimyo of Bungo* (81) would seem to show the Jesuit missionary paying

his respects to a European prince, not a Japanese warlord (the Daimyo of

Bungo was one of the most important early supporters of the Jesuits in

sixteenth-century Japan). The Japanese leader has the ruddy cheeks, red hair

and billowing robes of a Western potentate (he even wears the sandals of a

Roman emperor), and he is guarded by men in glistening European armour.

There is great drama in this painting, particularly in the passionate gazes and gestures of the protagonists, arranged along parallel diagonals, and in the compositional devices of a grand staircase and columns that extend past the frame – both used in Rubens's *Miracles of Ignatius of Loyola* (see 46). But Van Dyck's scene falls short as a work of anthropology. The artist may not have had access to accurate drawings of Japanese people or their costume, but accuracy was also not the point: Van Dyck's goal was to make this Japanese leader more sympathetic for a European audience that may have found it hard to empathize with people who did not look like them.

A different approach characterizes Dutch painter Jan Verelst's *Tee Yee Neen Ho Ga Row* (82), one of four portraits of Iroquois warriors commissioned by Queen Anne of England to commemorate the visit of three of them (one died on the sea voyage) to London. Tee Yee Neen Ho Ga Row (Tejonihokawara) was a Mohawk of the Wolf Clan from what is now upstate New York, and as his British hosts found his name something of a challenge, he took on the alias King Hendrick or Hendrick Peters. The embassy was orchestrated by the Dutchman Pieter Schuyler – mayor of what was the Dutch trading colony of Beverwyck, later Albany – to gain royal support for the Mohawks as allies against the French in Quebec (its immediate result was that Queen Anne commissioned a Mohawk chapel in what is now Fort Hunter, New York, in 1711). While lacking the artistry or dynamism of Van Dyck, Verelst is painstakingly accurate, and by presenting his subject as a full-length portrait he implied that he was of high rank. The Mohawk leader has the facial features and skin colour of a Native American, and he holds an exactingly rendered wampum belt made of purple and white shell beads, a high-status Amerindian artwork woven to record peace treaties and other agreements between peoples. His costume is part-English part-Mohawk, with Western shoes, leggings and shirt but a Native American tunic with a beaded pattern around the waist. Tejonihokawara demonstrates his willingness to negotiate not only through the wampum, but through the hatchet on the lower right, which he has laid on the ground in a gesture of peace. Verelst has even made attempts to reproduce a forested North American setting in the background, and while it is not rendered with particular skill the wolf on the lower left serves as a heraldic symbol.

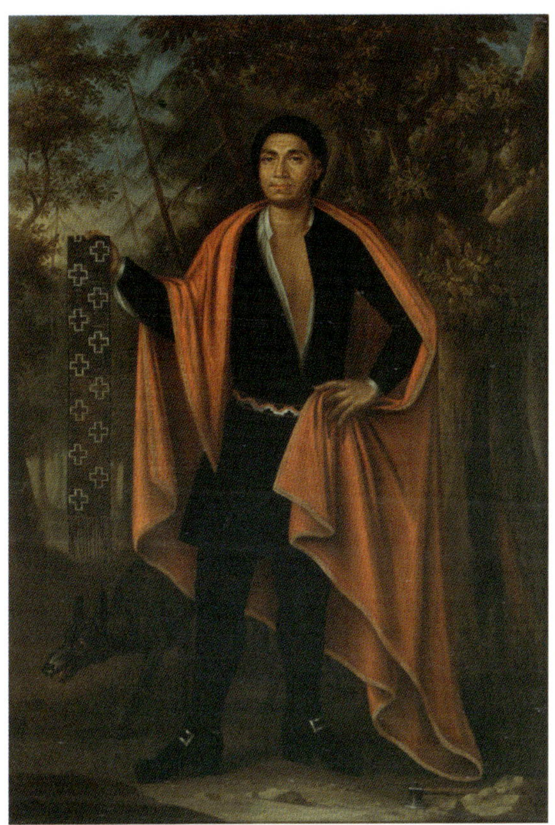

82.
Jan Verelst,
*Tee Yee Neen
Ho Ga Row*,
1710. Oil
on canvas,
91.5 × 64.3 cm
(36 × 25¼ in).
Portrait
Gallery of
Canada,
various
locations

Much exotic imagery, such as the fully or partially nude allegorical depictions
of 'the Indies' or their inhabitants found on many a palace ceiling, was of a
frankly sexual nature, and it fed into an already flourishing market for erotica.
Erotic paintings were common fare in the Renaissance, where scenes from
mythology or the Old Testament (Suzanna and the Elders or Salome were
among the most popular subjects) served as mere pretences for sexualized
imagery. German printmaker Hans Sebald Beham (1500–1550) specialized
in blatantly pornographic encounters, often between older men and younger
women. In the Baroque and Rococo, eroticism was still mostly enjoyed in
the guise of the Old Testament or pagan mythology (see 12), like Artemisia
Gentileschi's *Danaë* (c.1612), a depiction of the rape of the daughter of the
King of Argos by the god Jupiter in the form of a shower of gold coins (83).
It is painted on a copper panel, a small format very popular for works
intended for an intimate setting in which the oils appear more luminous than
on canvas (see also 27). Although executed by a woman who was undergoing

profound personal hardship during her own rape trial, the painting reflects none of her turmoil. Danaë does not resist her divine lover as she stretches fully nude on a sensuous, beautifully rendered, red velvet bedcover over a divan, her arm back and eyes passively closed. She crosses her legs to capture Jupiter's coins in her lap in one of Western art's least subtle representations of impregnation, and grabs other coins in her right hand (note how they are caught between her fingers), hinting that she receives money for sex and is therefore a fallen woman – in fact Gentileschi's painting is one of the very few depictions of Danaë in the midst of sexual climax. Meanwhile her maidservant holds out her cloak in hopes of catching any of the gold that misses its mark. Artemisia's nudes became especially popular among male patrons who found it titillating to have a sexualized nude woman painted by a woman who had herself 'fallen', and as a shrewd businesswoman Artemisia did not disappoint. Realistic details like the folds of skin where Danaë's right breast meets her arm and the folds under her belly were appreciated by the art world because female artists were reputed to paint their own sex more convincingly than men. They also had free access to a commodity that male artists had to pay for: a female life model.

But the Baroque also introduced paintings of a purely pornographic nature that – while intended for private courtly audiences – enjoyed wide exposure. Caravaggio's *Cupid, or Love Conquers All* (84), a lewd painting of a boy with false wings who gleefully exhibits his genitals (reportedly Caravaggio's lover, although this claim has been disputed), was commissioned by Cardinal Vincenzo Giustiniani (1564–1637), one of the great literary men and art collectors of Baroque Rome. Caravaggio's nude sits astride a pile of still-life objects symbolizing everything from lust to learning – musical instruments did both – blurring the distinction between eroticism and more intellectual pursuits. Never seriously intended as a scene from Graeco-Roman mythology despite its title from Virgil's *Eclogues*, the painting was created instead for its shock value, and the cardinal kept it behind a curtain and revealed it to select visitors with a theatrical flourish.

The dissolute and luxurious court of Louis XV of France was one of the most receptive to erotica, and some of the most favoured artists – notably Charles-

83.
Artemisia Gentileschi, *Danaë*, c.1612. Oil on copper; 40.5 × 52.5 cm (16 × 20½ in). St Louis Art Museum, MO

Joseph Natoire (1700–1777), François Boucher (1703–1770) and Jean-Honoré Fragonard (1732–1806) – painted sexual scenes that dispensed with references to antiquity. One of the finest is Boucher's *Brunette Odalisque* (85), which features an intimate back view of a naked young woman on her bed. The girl's flushed cheeks and buttocks and unkempt bedclothes imply that she has just been with her lover, who – since she looks into our space – might even be the viewer. With a coquettish yet introspective expression she toys with a string of pearls and stretches her right hand – it has the elongation of a Maniera painting – over a luxurious pillow. Everything about the painting is sensual. Her skin seems warm and pliant to the touch, the sheets and negligee caress her body, and the plush velvet and satin blankets beg to be stroked. The Chinese screen on the right even adds an exotic touch. Boucher's titillating canvas was intended for private delectation and was very far indeed from the naked but heroic mythological ode to love with which Annibale Carracci ushered in the Baroque almost 150 years earlier (see 13).

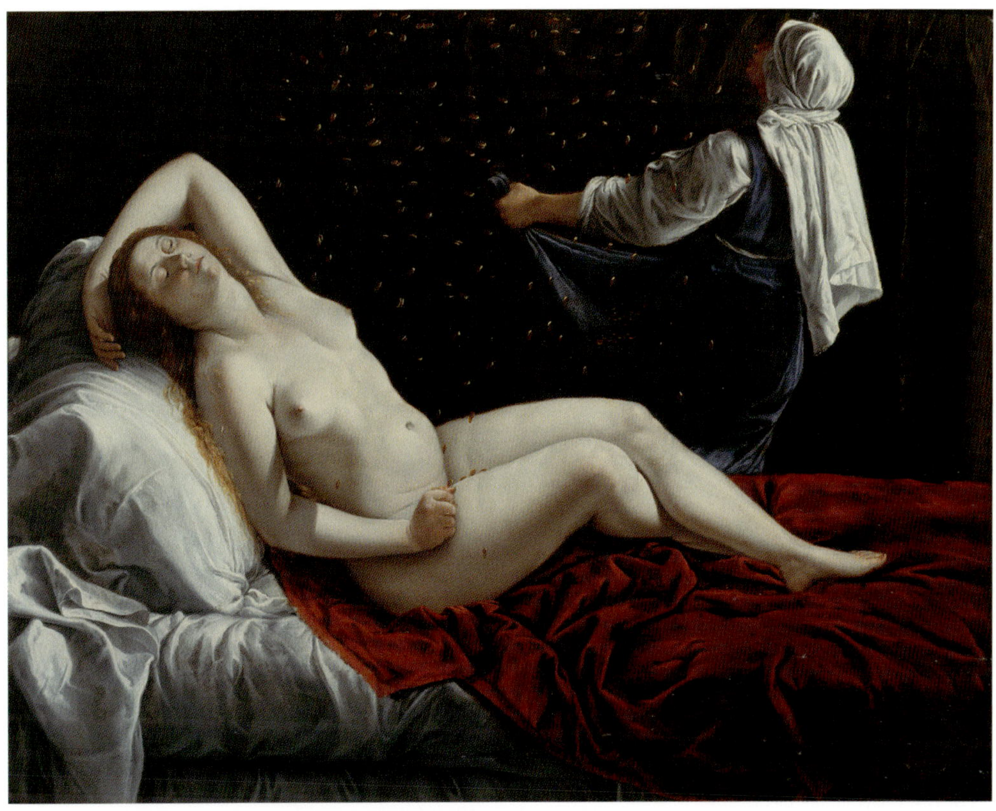

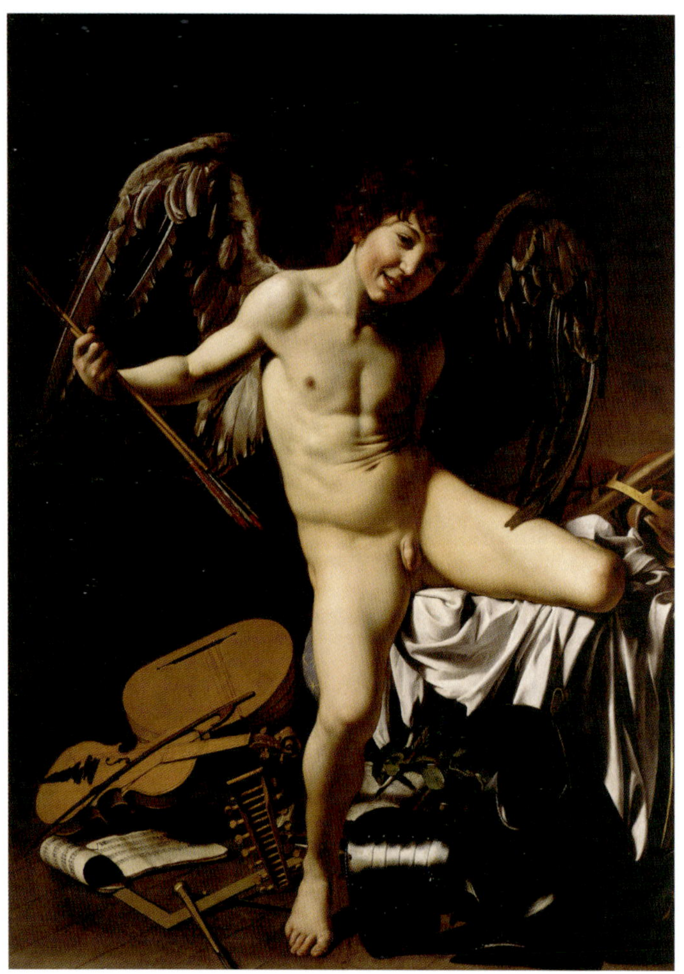

84.
Caravaggio,
*Cupid, or Love
Conquers All*,
1602. Oil
on canvas;
1.56 × 1.13 m
(5 ft 1½ in ×
3 ft 8½ in).
Gemälde-
galerie, Berlin

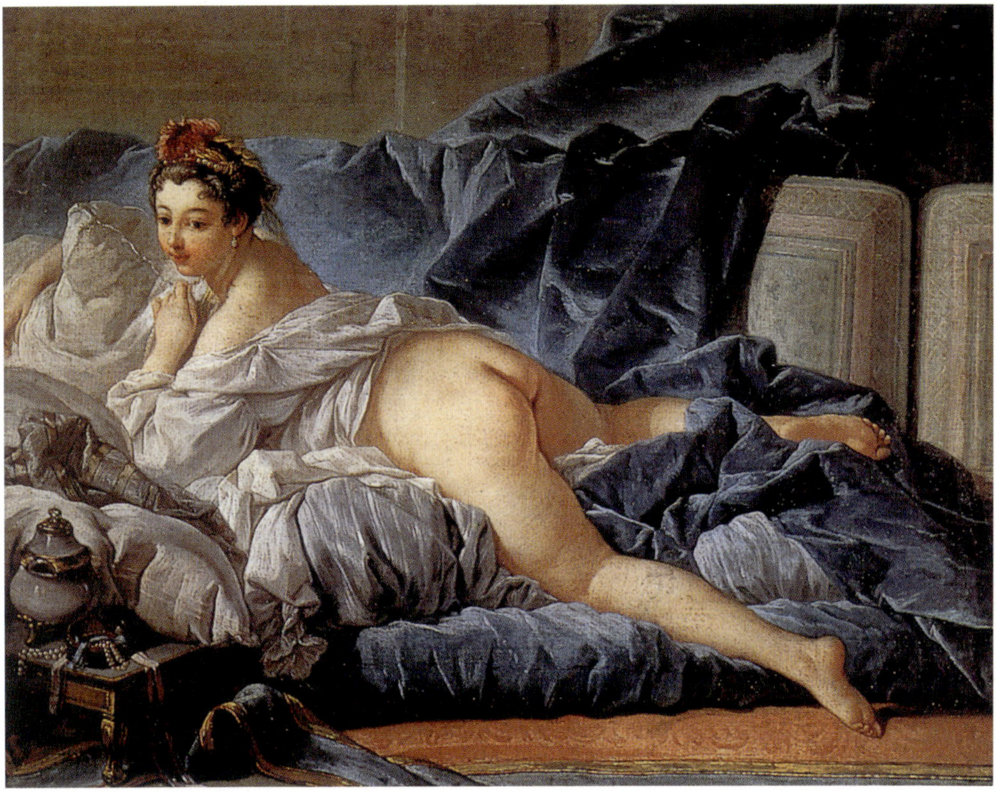

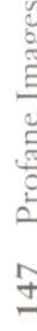

85.
François Boucher,
Brunette Odalisque,
c.1743. Oil on canvas; 53 × 64 cm (20¾ × 25¼ in). Louvre, Paris

The Bel Composto   Baroque and Rococo Church Interiors

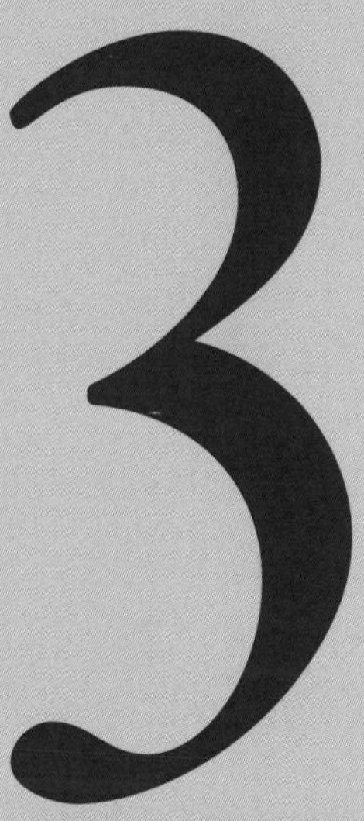

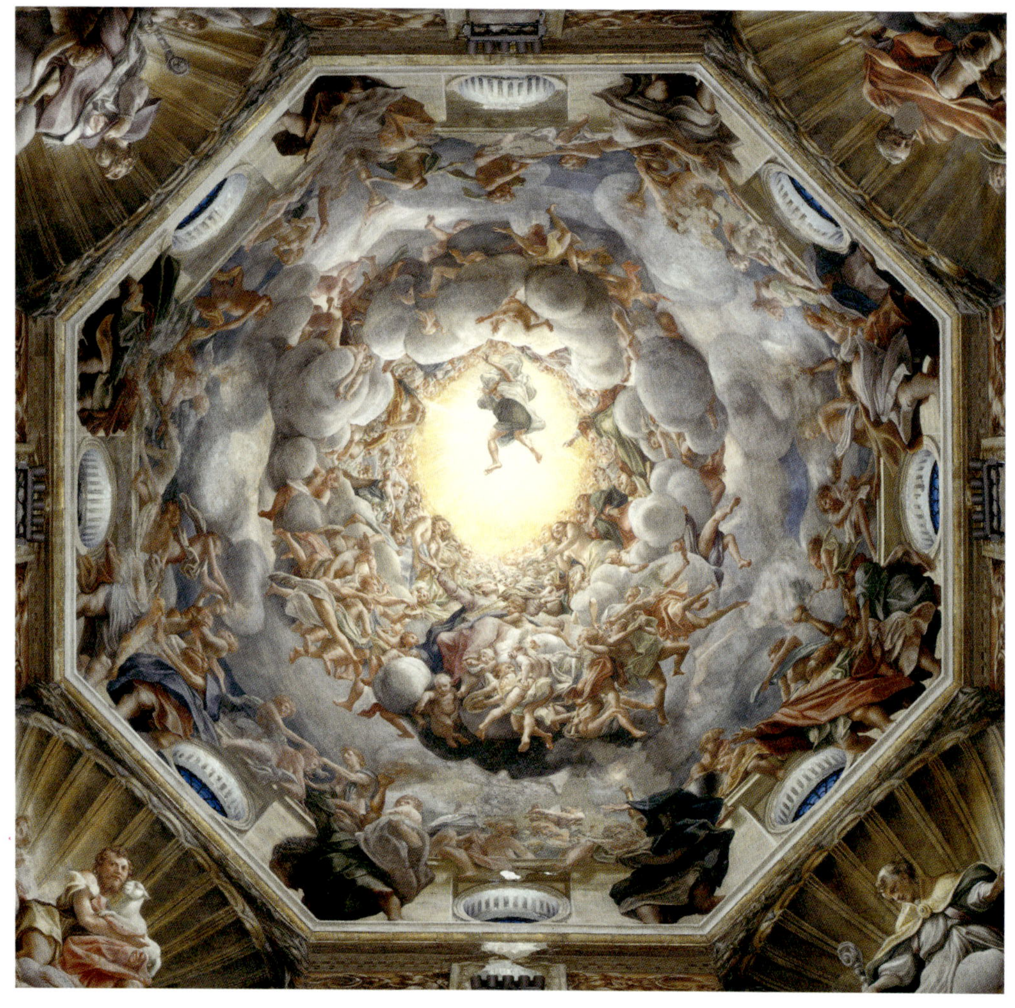

86.
Antonio da
Correggio,
Assumption
of the Virgin,
1526–30;
Fresco, Parma
Cathedral
(Italy)

The *Bel Composto*, or simply *composto* – a stylistically and thematically unified interior space that transgresses Renaissance boundaries between painting, sculpture and architecture – may be the quintessential form of the Baroque and Rococo. It is like a carefully choreographed dance, each medium playing its role in a fusion meant to elicit sensual, emotional and intellectual reactions from the viewer. In non-religious architecture, particularly the grand salons or staircases of palaces and town halls, such interiors communicated messages of royal splendour or municipal might, reducing visitors to bit parts in a larger drama of power and allegiance. But profane spaces cannot claim credit for one of the era's greatest inventions. The *composto*, born in church interiors and other sacred spaces, answered a need both for the directed public worship sought by Catholic theologians during the regeneration of the Church and for the more private, devotional practices craved by ordinary Catholics in this era of meditation, mysticism and ecstasies. Although Gianlorenzo Bernini conceived the paradigmatic *composto* in Rome in the 1640s, its roots extended much further, drawing upon interactions of space and iconography in use since the late Middle Ages. This chapter will explore sacred interiors, leaving the exteriors for Chapter Four. This division reflects an emerging duality in Baroque and Rococo architecture between the insides of churches, which focused on creating contemplative and visionary environments for worshippers, and the outsides, which promoted more civic messages of Christian community, the harmony between Church and State and the dominance of God over Nature. It will also concentrate on those parts of Europe where the *composto* had its strongest impact: Italy, Iberia, Flanders and central Europe.

The integrated church interiors of Baroque and Rococo Europe derive from two distinct traditions, one Italian and the other northern European, the two often merging in a single building – particularly north of the Alps and in Iberia. The better-known Italian variant grew out of the architectural and artistic ideals of the Renaissance while the northern variant emerged from a still-living late Gothic tradition. Although by the later seventeenth century both generally expressed themselves using the vocabulary of classical (Graeco-Roman) art and architecture, the underlying structures and aesthetics of the Gothic-inspired interiors and altarpieces could be quite distinct from their Italianate counterparts. Regionalism was a significant factor in determining the geographical limits of these two traditions, as Italians believed classicism to be part of their heritage and derided the 'German manner' at the same time that northerners claimed Gothic as their own – they also associated it with a pre-Reformation 'golden age' – and initially felt suspicious of imported styles. Spain and Portugal favoured the Gothic because of a long tradition of artistic influence from Flanders and a sense of pride in their late medieval age of exploration and conquest (their 'discoveries' of the Americas and the sea route to Asia occurred in the 1490s), and their Baroque and Rococo interiors – so different from those of Italy – clearly bear its stamp.

Stylistically, the Italian *composto* can been traced to Renaissance prototypes such as Michelangelo's interventions at S. Lorenzo in Florence – the New Sacristy (begun 1519), intended as a burial chamber for the Medici family, and the vestibule to the Laurentian Library (1530) – which broke the rules of classical architecture through their integration of the different visual media (87). Michelangelo ruptured the plane of the wall by pushing sections back and forwards as freely as if they were sculpture – in the vestibule they even advance past the columns that frame them – and in the New Sacristy the sculpture responds accordingly, pressing back into the wall or spilling out into the room, its massive scale giving it an architectural monumentality. Michelangelo originally intended to incorporate painting into his synthesis, but the frescos in the lunettes were never executed. The *composto* also owes something to illusionistic innovations in fresco painting. Michelangelo's Sistine Ceiling (1508–12) already uses perspective to create a false architectural framework with paint alone, and the dome frescos of Antonio da Correggio (c.1489–1534) surge with spiralling masses of figures depicted in dramatic perspective that seems to expand the height of the dome and break open to the heavens – a motif that became commonplace in the Baroque and Rococo (86).

The other feature of the *composto* – the idea of a thematically unified interior with a didactic and emotive function – emerged in the transitional period of the late sixteenth and early seventeenth centuries, and it was motivated in part by a groundswell of popular devotion, new meditative manuals, such as the *Spiritual Exercises* (1548), the *Litany of Loreto* (1558) and the *Litany of All Saints* (1601), and by the era's concern that art serve as a kind of visual rhetoric (see Chapter One). The imagery in these spaces served as a prompt for reflection and meditative prayer, and such interiors were also a suitable setting for sermons, catechisms and Lenten vigils. The Chiesa Nuova (decorated 1578–1620s) of the Oratorian Order, the Jesuit Church of the Gesù (decorated 1584–1608) and the long-demolished residence for Jesuit novices at S. Andrea al Quirinale (1597–1610) – all

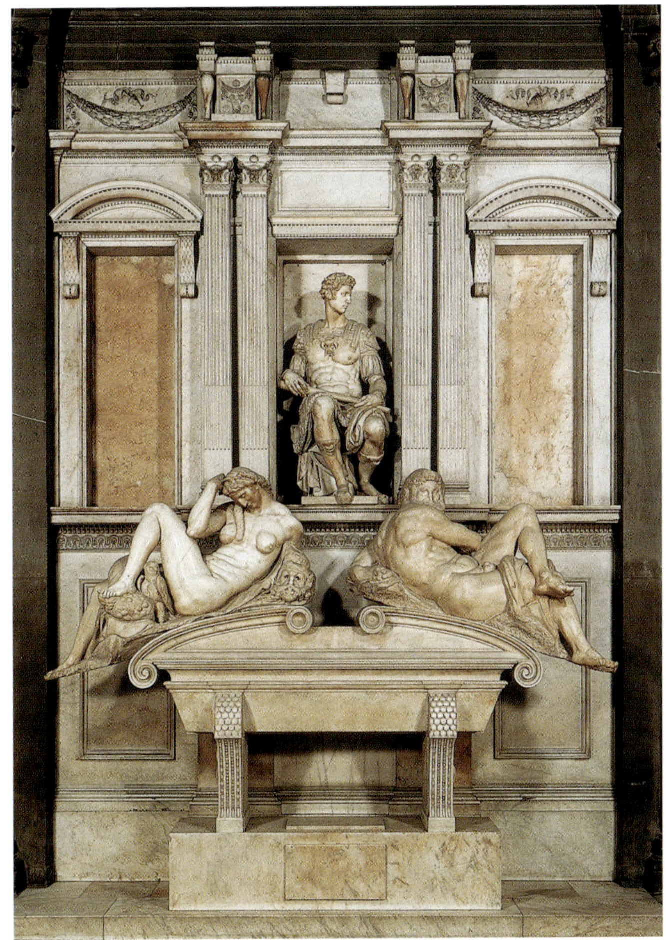

**87.
Michelangelo
Buonarroti,**
Tomb of
Giuliano
de' Medici,
1521–34.
New Sacristy,
San Lorenzo,
Florence

in Rome – provided opportunities for extended virtual pilgrimages and examinations of conscience. Within a framework of austere late Renaissance architecture these interiors communicated their messages through frescos, canvas paintings, stucco, marble revetments and sculpture in a variety of experimental new styles, combining narrative scenes, single figures, symbols, emblems and inscriptions. The reason scholars do not refer to such interiors as 'Baroque' is that they lacked the stylistic unity that would characterize Bernini's *composti* – even though the Chiesa Nuova housed works by early Baroque artists such as Caravaggio and Rubens.

The tightly woven iconography in places such as the Passion Chapel (88) in the Gesù, painted by Scipione Pulzone (c.1550–1598) and Gaspare Celio (1571–1640), contrasts violence with resignation, inspiring the viewer alternately to action and reflection. Most of the key moments in Christ's Passion are here, including the Lamentation (when Christ is removed from the Cross) on the altarpiece (it has since been removed), two vivid narrative episodes of his struggle to Calvary Hill on the sides, representations of the *Four Evangelists* as witnesses of the Passion, and four melancholy images of the tortured Christ in the tradition of Sebastiano del Piombo and Luis de Morales (see 23, 39), culminating with a triumphant *Apotheosis of the Cross and Instruments of the Passion* in the vault. The chapel can be used in many ways. It can serve as a backdrop for a Lenten sermon, a condensed Stations of the Cross (a devotion popularized by the Franciscans in which meditations and prayers are made at stages of the Passion), and as a reminder of the Passion meditations in works such as the *Spiritual Exercises* or Thomas à Kempis's *Imitation of Christ* (1418). Moreover, for the first time in an Italian interior the different painted sections of the Gesù chapels respond to one another beyond their frames: Christ gazes from the left wall at his fate in the altarpiece, the Evangelists look up to the Cross in the vault and the angels bearing that Cross thrust it forcefully down into our space. This kind of spatial interrelation would become a hallmark of the Baroque *composto*.

Thematically unified interiors were popular north of the Alps in the first three-quarters of the seventeenth century because their didactic and dogmatic content was ideal in the struggle against Protestantism. The

88.
Scipione Pulzone and Gaspare Celio, 1590–7. Frescoes, Passion Chapel, Gesù, Rome

Jesuit church in Antwerp, which Rubens adorned with a pair of altarpieces
(see 46) and thirty-nine ceiling paintings in 1620–1 (destroyed in a fire in
1718), told the story of Christ's victory over Heresy in such a way that it
could address visitors differently according to their level of education and
social standing. In Neuburg and der Donau, Germany, the former Lutheran
Court Church of Our Lady was adorned by its new Jesuit owners with
over a hundred stucco emblems (by Michale, Antonio and Pietro Castelli,
1616–19) illustrating the litanies of Loreto and All Saints to help visitors in

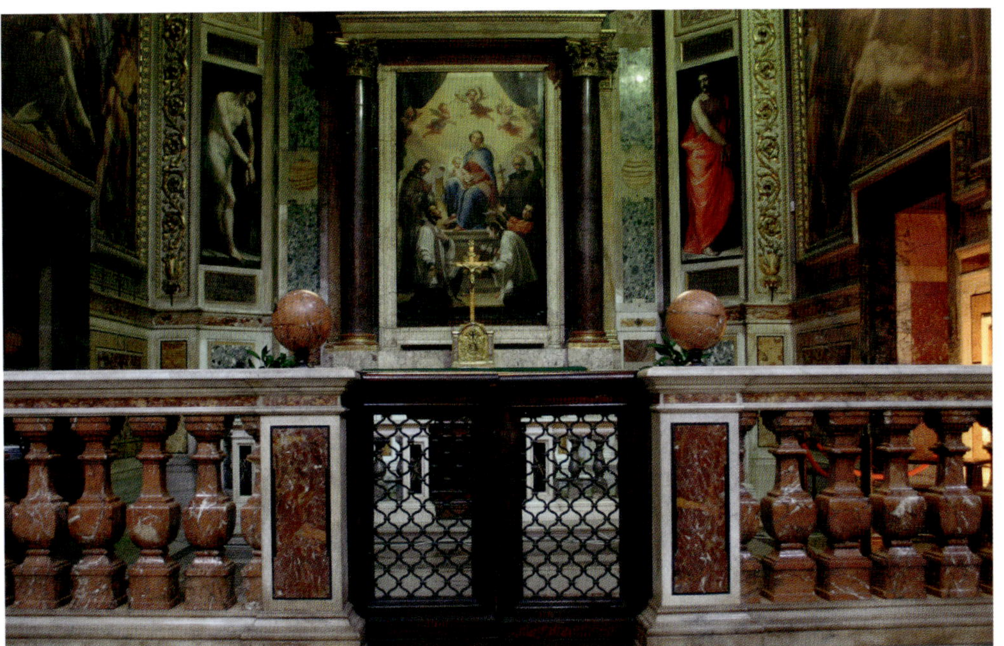

their devotions (89). One of the most thematically complex interiors is at
the pilgrimage church at Hergiswald (begun 1654), in Catholic Switzerland,
built at the same time Bernini was developing the Baroque *composto* in Rome
(90). Hergiswald underscores the crucial role played by viewer participation
in such spaces. The Capuchin monk Ludwig von Wyl hired a team led by
sculptor-carpenter Hans Ulrich Räber (c.1610–1664) to transform a modest
shrine of the Virgin with a lifesize replica of the Holy House of Loreto into a
multi-media extravaganza that interacted with the visitor like sacred theatre.
The spectacle unfolds from the moment pilgrims enter the building, when

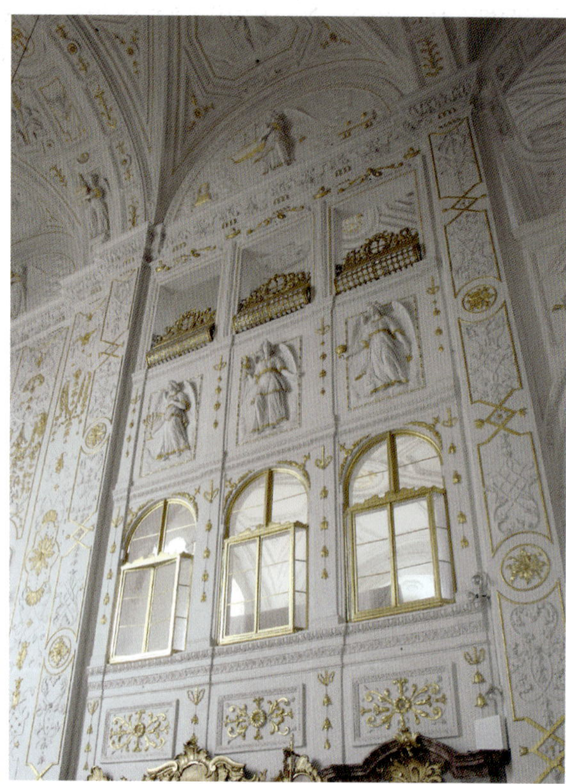

89.
Michale, Antonio, and Pietro Castelli, emblematic stuccoes in the Church of Our Lady, 1616–19. Neuburg and der Donau (Germany)

90.
Hans Ulrich Räber and others, Pilgrimage Church, begun 1654. Hergiswald (Switzerland)

they pass under a two-faced crucifix raised high on a beam with the bleeding Christ (of this world) on one side and the seraphic Christ (of the next) on the other, marking their passage from Earth into Heaven. Ahead they confront a sparkling gilded retable that combines sculpture, relief carving and painting to tell the story of the life of the Virgin in two and three dimensions, and the ceiling is given over to a heavenly apparition of Marian symbols – 321, to be exact, by Kaspar Meglinger – taken directly from the *Litany of Loreto* and other sources. Behind the retable a pair of angels create the illusion that they are floating on either side of the Holy House. Pilgrims then enter the Holy House, where they are greeted by sculptural groups of the Holy Family dramatically lit by hidden windows and candles as if in a vision, and opulent transept arches and side altars feature other theatrical apparitions of the Virgin and members of the Franciscan Order (Capuchins were Franciscans). Although these northern *composti* still lack the stylistic unity and integration pioneered in the Italian Baroque, they compensated through an unparalleled semantic richness.

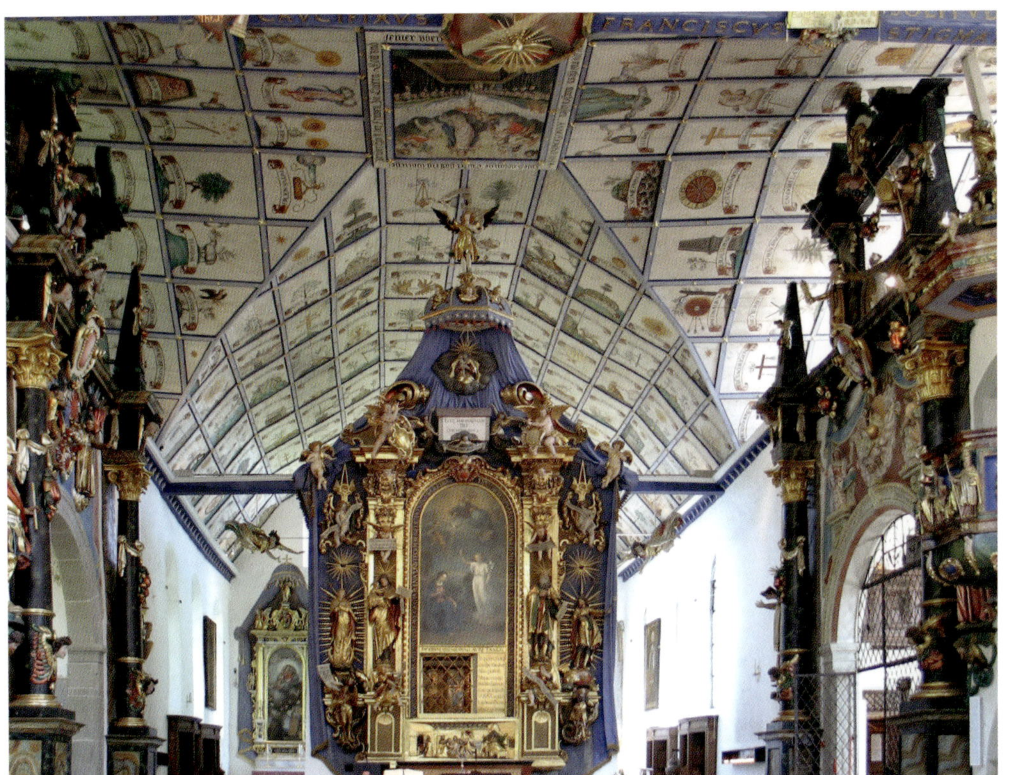

Northern European and Iberian interiors owed as much to the legacy of the
Gothic as they did to the classical tradition. Before the end of the Thirty Years
War (1648), central European architects continued to build essentially Gothic
structures, dressing them up with Baroque sculpture and altarpieces in a nod to the
renewed Church of Rome. The interior of the Jesuit church of the Assumption in
Cologne (91) combines soaring Gothic net vaults and piers with Baroque statues
of the Apostles by Jeremias Geisselbrunn (c.1594–c.1631) – their sweeping and
dramatic gestures run counter to the Gothic aesthetic – Italianate cherubs and
angels, and a Baroque pulpit and altarpieces that were among the grandest built in
Germany in fifty years. In later decades, as central European interiors increasingly
adopted Baroque and Rococo forms, the 'German manner' persevered in subtler
ways: medieval types of altarpieces continued to proliferate, as did building types
(such as the German Hall Church), intricate vaults and domes resting on tall piers,
geometrically complex ground plans based on triangles or stars, and an emphasis on
variety and proliferation in decoration, expressive realism in sculpture, and dramatic
use of natural light. The combination of Baroque and Gothic could be surprisingly

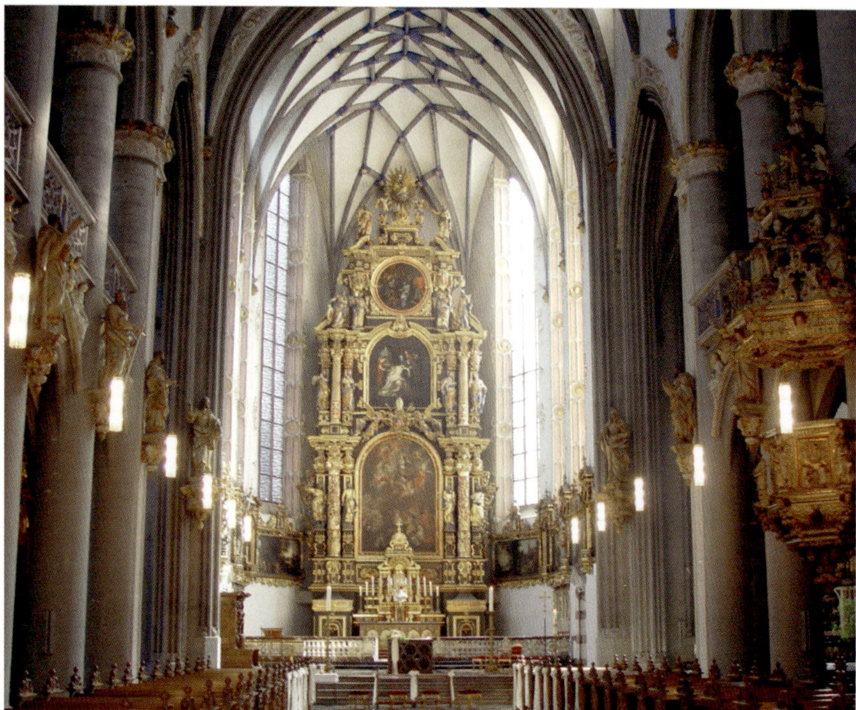

91.
Church of the Assumption, 1618–29. Cologne (Germany)

seamless because medieval interiors such as Ely Cathedral in England (see 109) sought strikingly similar effects to those of the Baroque *composto*. They combined a staggering variety of media – lacelike stone tracery and criss-crossing net vaults join forces with stained-glass windows, wall paintings, sculptures, reliefs and golden reliquaries – and they inspired devotion and conveyed a sense of mystery through illusion, surprise and sensual richness. Their manipulation of natural light, directed through coloured glass over liturgically important parts of the church, was a metaphorical reference to the Divine and the Heavenly Jerusalem.

Like their Baroque counterparts, Gothic sculptors elicited pathos in the beholder through striking realism and a vivid sense of emotion and pain. The Calvary scene in the central panel of the Passion Altar in the Herrgottskirche in Creglingen, Germany (92), a winged altar known as a *Flügelaltar*, features relief carvings painted in realistic colours to bring them alive for the viewer. Mary, the Magdalene and John the Baptist cry out or swoon in grief and the bloodied body of Christ and the two robbers shock us with their agonized poses. At the top of the altar the gnarled rotations and sharp spikes of the finial recall the Crown of Thorns. Like the Gesù chapels, the *Flügelaltar* operated on public and private levels, with seasonal liturgical ceremonies focusing on the different saints, relics and narrative scenes, and private worshippers using them as a stimulus for quiet meditation. When these altarpieces began to be executed in the Baroque style they adopted the classical architectural vocabulary, but their profile, use of gilded polychrome wood, and inclusion of Gothic-style relief panels betrayed their medieval origins. Such is the splendid trio of side altars at the Hofkirche in Lucerne, Switzerland (93), by Niklaus Geisler (1585–1663/5), in which the figures'

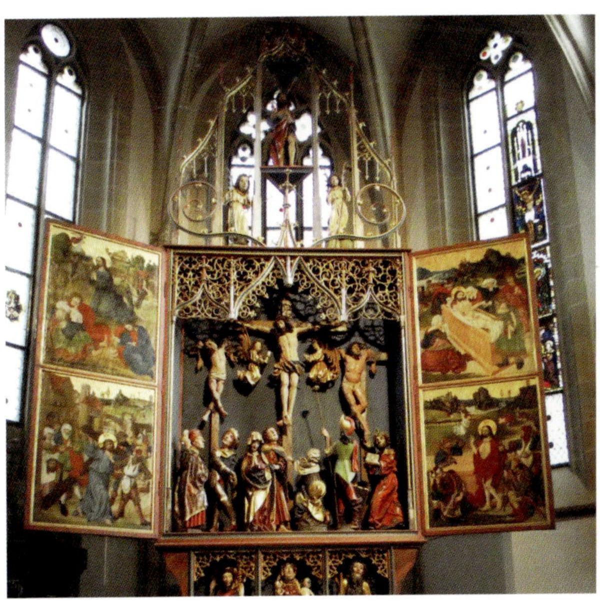

92.
Anonymous,
Passion
Altar, 1487.
Polychrome
wood; 9.3
× 3.73 m
(30 ft 6 in ×
12 ft 4 in).
Herrgottskirche,
Creglingen
(Germany)

drapery preserves the angular lines and flattened perspective of medieval sculpture but the framework features Corinthian columns, volutes, a broken pediment and globe-like finials. The Gothic decorative ingenuity perseveres as well, as in the way the curved cornices atop the 'wings' curve in opposite directions. Note also that like the Creglingen altar, the main panel is carved while the wings are painted.

Baroque sculptors in Spain and Portugal continued to favour Gothic-style hyper-realism throughout the Baroque era. Juan Martínez Montañés (1568–1649), Pedro de Mena (1628–1688) and Gregorio Fernández (1576–1636)

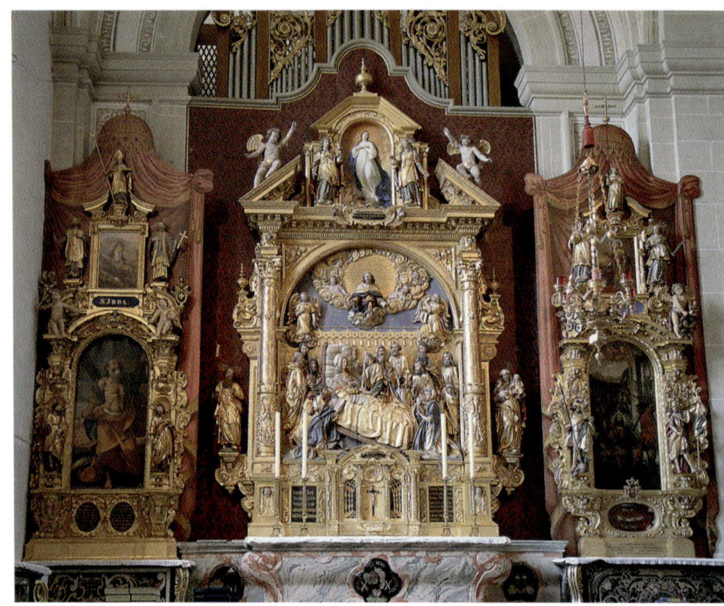

93.
Niklaus Geissler, Dormition Altar, 1640–4. Hofkirche, Lucerne (Switzerland)

specialized in such blunt imagery: the bloodied but muscular *Ecce Homo* by Fernandez from a *retablo* (altar) in the church of San Nicolás in Valladolid, Spain, shocks the viewer with a naturalism so intense and a crippling sense of pain so visceral that the statue appears to be sweating (94). Fernández's *Ecce Homo* also demonstrates the affinities and fundamental differences between the Spanish and Italian idiom. The statue's observant musculature and balanced classical pose recall Michelangelo's *Risen Christ* (1591–21) yet the slender, feminine body, balletic hands and deferential tilt of the head give it a vulnerability that confronts us with the mortality of the flesh. Although often displayed or published as a freestanding sculptures, these masterpieces of Spanish realism were made to be included in altarpieces that derived from the *Flügelaltar*, only taken out during feast days when they were processed through the city.

Gothic never completely disappeared in the period covered by this book. It flourished north of the Alps when Bernini was at the height of his powers; Italian stonemasons working on Milan's unfinished Gothic cathedral preserved it throughout the seventeenth and eighteenth centuries; and it re-emerged in Bohemia in the 1710s and 1720s with the hybrid Gothic-Baroque architecture of Giovanni Santini – about which more below. The key differences between

the classic and Gothic traditions – they would polarize buildings throughout
the Baroque and Rococo eras – were spatial and structural. The Gothic
aesthetic placed great emphasis on geometric order and numerical harmony
as a reflection of godly perfection – hence the emphasis on triangulation
and other geometrical forms – in contrast to the classical and Renaissance
tradition of basing the proportions of buildings on parts of the human
body and the design of a building on a single unit of measurement (called a
module) and its preference for circular and rectangular spaces.

The classic Italian *composto* began with Bernini's Cornaro Chapel (95),
one of the most virtuoso interiors of the Baroque, and its sculptural group
The Ecstasy of Saint Teresa (96), a work as subtle and tactile as his *Apollo
and Daphne* (see 2). Built as the tomb chapel for the Patriarch of Venice,
Federigo Cornaro, in the Carmelite church of S. Maria della Vittoria in
Rome, it is fitted into space so restricted and shallow that it surprises anyone

**94.
Gregorio
Fernández**,
Ecce Homo,
before 1621.
Polychromed
wood, glass
and cloth,
1.82 m × 55 cm
× 38 cm (6 ft
× 21¼ in ×
15 in). Museo
Diocesano y
Catedrálico,
Valladolid
(Spain)

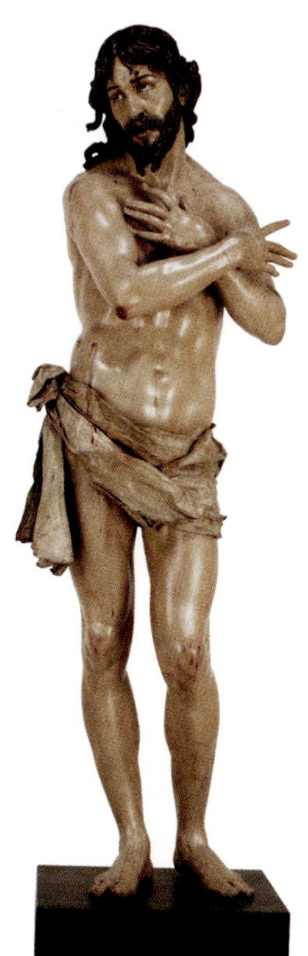

who knows it only from photographs. But Bernini did not let the chapel's diminutive size hamper his grandiose vision: at nearly fifty years of age, he chose this moment for his greatest challenge to the Renaissance *paragone* (see Introduction). Although using a basically Graeco-Roman language of architecture and inspired by the more classically inclined painters of his time, he stretched each medium beyond its limit, allowing painted stucco to overlap with architecture, and sculpture to use the techniques of painting.

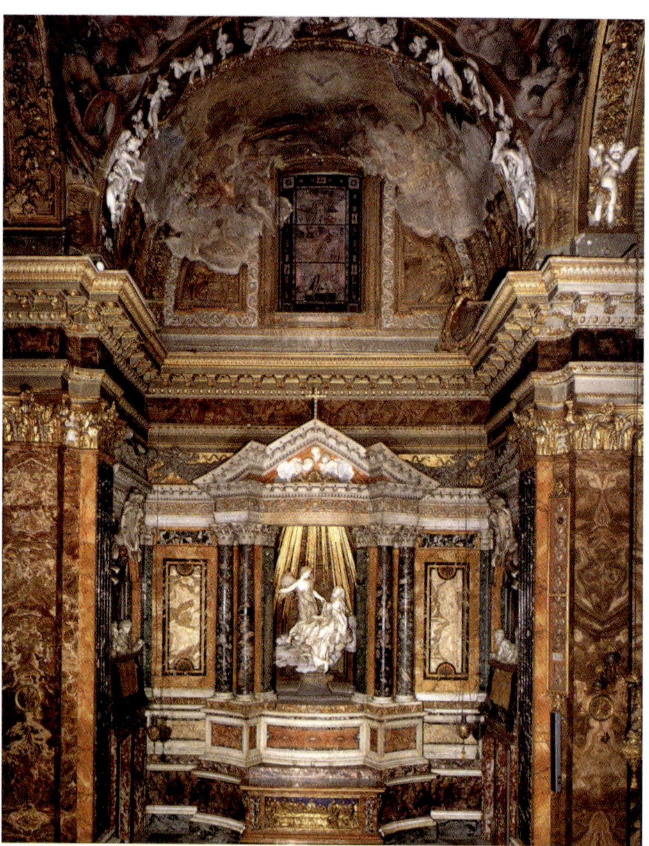

The most dramatic challenge was his reversal of the role of painting and sculpture in the altarpiece itself. Since the thirteenth century Italian altarpieces had traditionally been paintings on panel or – with the increasing use of oil painting in the sixteenth century – on canvas. Although he was inspired by the composition and rich shading of a painting of the *Ecstasy of Saint Margaret of Cortona* by Annibale Carracci's pupil Giovanni Lanfranco (97), Bernini outdid his predecessor's mere illusion of the third dimension

by transforming his altarpiece into an actual three-dimensional group –
yet one that could only be viewed from the front as in a painting. Bernini
emphasizes the third dimension by making the marble altar frame with its
paired columns and broken triangular pediment (such a portico-like frame is
known as an aedicule) expand into the viewer's space as if pushed forwards by
the sheer force of the ecstasy. This explosive sense of movement animates the
entire chapel.

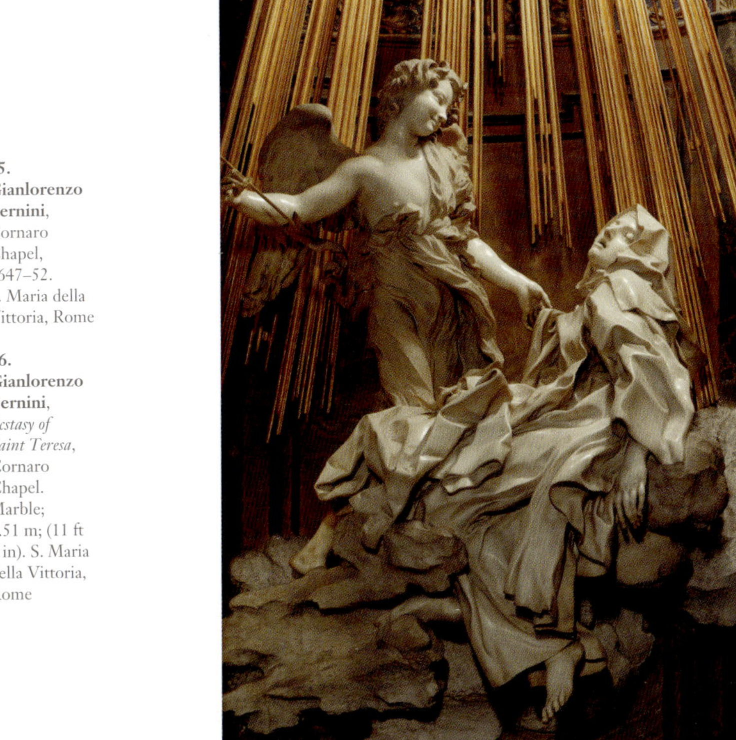

The Cornaro Chapel celebrates visionary ecstasy as a path to divine
communion. On a narrative level it represents a historical vision – that of the
sixteenth-century Spanish Carmelite mystic Saint Teresa of Ávila (1515–
1582) – but it is also meant to induce an ecstatic response from the viewer
(what we might call today an out-of-body experience). The chapel vibrates
with colour owing to its combination of cream, grey, greenish and rust-
coloured marble – most of it veined or dappled – as well as stucco, alabaster

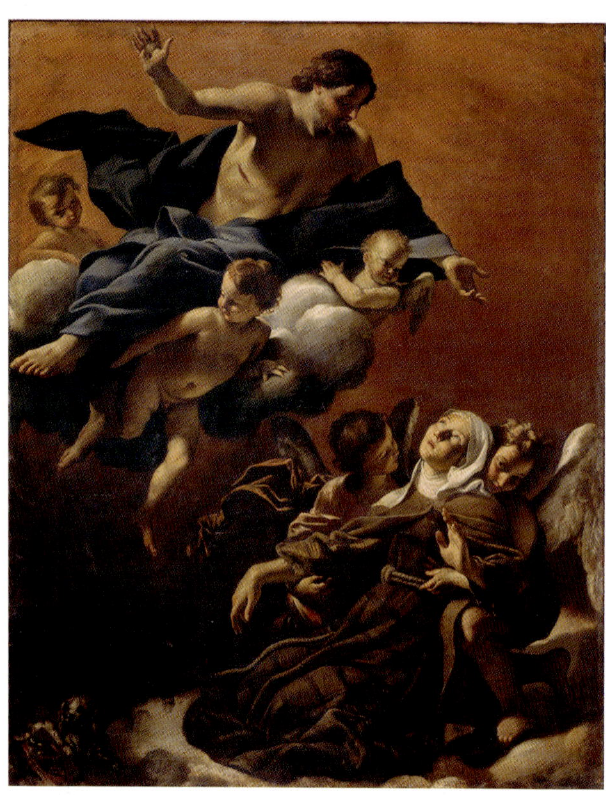

97.
Giovanni Lanfranco, *Ecstasy of Saint Margaret of Cortona*, 1622. Oil on canvas; 2.3 × 1.8 m (7 ft 6½ in × 5 ft 11 in). Palazzo Pitti, Florence

and gilt bronze. Its central sculptural group seems miraculously lit by a light from a hidden window inside the pediment of the aedicule – it can be seen on the outside of the church at the top of a projection of the wall made necessary to accommodate the sculpture – assisted by descending sunrays of gilded bronze. The lower part of the chapel encompasses the marble altar frame, panels of veined marble on the back wall, and a pair of false oratories (galleries in which the nobility attended services) on the left and right (98). These oratories appear to recede into the distance because Bernini used linear perspective – another technique borrowed from painting – when carving their low-relief vaults and colonnades. The group of spectators in the oratories – all but one of them dead at the time of the chapel's decoration – depict members of the Cornaro family, and in one of the first group portraits of the Italian Baroque they serve as an intermediary between the flesh-and-bones visitor and the heavenly apparition in the altarpiece. Although the churchmen react to Teresa's ecstasy through discussion, prayer or contemplation – a dedicatory text compares them to the Apostles at Christ's

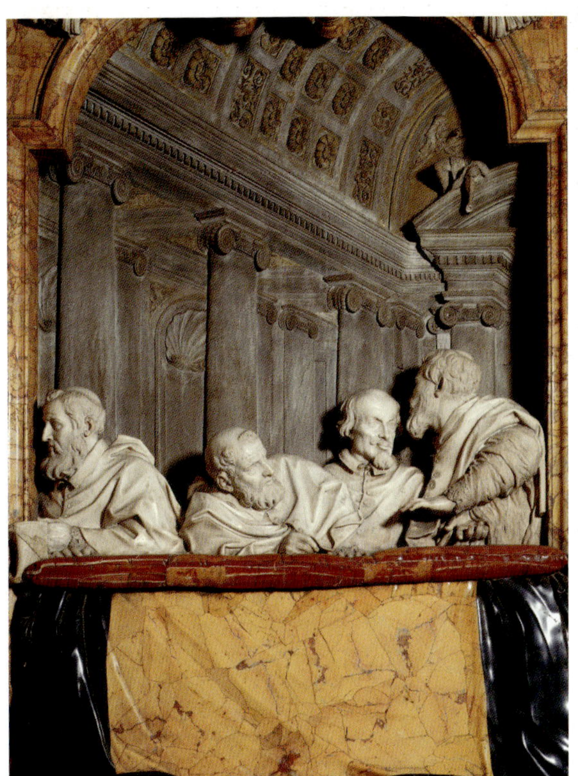

Transfiguration – they respond inwardly (none of them looks at the altar), motivating visitors to move beyond a dependence upon Bernini's vision to an interior ecstasy of their own.

A rectangular window, which once bathed the upper storey with white light (it is now filled with stained glass), is framed by architectural relief panels and a mass of painted stucco clouds that seem to descend from Heaven into the chapel, spreading out over the panels. The clouds are painted (by Guidobaldo Abbatini, c.1600–1656) with angels adoring the dove of the Holy Spirit, the lowest one dangling over the frame of the window, and three-dimensional stucco angels adorn the upper arch, the frieze dividing the storeys, and the central part of the broken pediment. Bernini first achieved the effect of focusing natural light through a hidden space onto a scene framed by artificial clouds and angels – it is usually referred to as a 'heavenly glory' or 'gloria' – in 1628 when he built a temporary plaster and wood *apparato* (backdrop) of false clouds lit by 'thousands' of hidden lamps for a Forty

Hours Devotion (a Lenten vigil: see Chapter Six) in the Pauline Chapel of the Vatican Palace. Ephemeral structures and theatrical perspective and light effects were critical models for Bernini's experiments in more durable media: as we will see he designed many temporary festival decorations and stage sets.

At the Cornaro Chapel, Bernini chooses a single moment in Saint Teresa's 1562 autobiography when she was visited by an angel who pierced her heart with a flame-tipped golden spear of divine love: 'This he plunged into my heart several times so that it penetrated into my entrails … the pain was so severe that it made me utter several moans. The sweetness caused by this intense pain is so extreme that one cannot possibly wish it to cease …' (see 96). Long conditioned by Freudian theory, viewers today have interpreted this moment as one of sexual release, a kind of mystic orgasm. They are partly right, as there is a sensual, even carnal element to this moment, but the 'sweetness' experienced by Teresa is a spiritual one. In a tradition going back to the thirteenth-century Rhineland, female mystics have used the erotic language of the biblical Song of Solomon, with its imagery of wounding love and the union of the bride (the soul) and bridegroom (God, or in the Christian tradition, Christ), as a means of contemplative communion with the Divine. As the thirteenth-century Saxon mystic Gertrude of Helfta (1256–c.1302) put it: 'no one ought to despise what is revealed by means of bodily things, but ought to study anything that would make the mind worthy of tasting the sweetness of spiritual delights by images of bodily things'. Teresa and Bernini participate in this same culture, using the sensual and even erotic as a way of releasing the soul from its mortal shell to achieve complete immersion in Christ.

Bernini faithfully follows Teresa's text – the equivalent of a bestseller at the time – in the composition of his group. The angel, a sexless youth with fiery drapery and a sublime smile, stands upright before Saint Teresa, a gilt bronze arrow delicately balanced in its right hand. Teresa herself falls into a passive swoon, although her upper body and face still thrust upwards as if yearning for God's light. Bernini reveals her soul's electrifying combination of pain and pleasure through her heavy, pulsating drapery, and he provides an erotic frisson by exposing the bare hands and left foot – surely one of the most sensual feet in the history of art. Teresa's ecstasy also shows in her face, her mouth opened in a moan and her eyes heavy-lidded and lacking irises. The principal drama in the group is the contrast between the calm of the angel (the spirit) and the rapture of the saint (the body). Bernini makes sure the viewer understands that this group – in defiance of the permanence of the marble – is an instantaneous and ephemeral vision. The figures cannot be approached or viewed from the back, and they float weightlessly on a bed of clouds.

If the Cornaro Chapel is a sensual overload, that was precisely the point. Typically for a *composto* interior, there are many ways of reading the space, depending upon the inclinations of the viewer. If we read it from the top down we see the heavenly apparition first, and watch as one of the painted stucco angels materializes into the marble angel in the sculptural group. If we begin with the sculptural group our eyes might move upwards with Saint Teresa's gaze to the light-bathed empyrean above and share her vision. Intermittently, we might turn to the Cornaro spectators, whose expressions and poses provide a paradigm of appropriate devotional reactions. The eye moves from one element to the next in a fluid yet serendipitous way – one scholar has compared it to cinematographic montage – and the mind wavers between the narrative and symbolic, the rational and emotional. Writers have long linked Bernini's use of the senses to the 'composition of place' in the *Spiritual Exercises* (see Chapter One), which were ideally to make use of all five senses. Bernini is known to have made the Exercises himself, was a close confidant of the Jesuit preacher (and later Father General) Gian Paolo Oliva (1600–1681), and regularly attended vesper services at the Gesù. I will not attempt here a lengthy comparison to the text – it has been done many times before – but will emphasize that Bernini's chapel shares with the *Exercises* an exhortation that the viewers use their free will and individual creativity in reassembling and interpreting the visual data that surrounds them.

Bernini explored the *composto* further in two larger spaces in Rome. One was a new Jesuit novitiate chapel at S. Andrea al Quirinale (99, 100) commissioned by Camillo Pamphilj, the nephew of Pope Innocent X, to replace a cramped and unstable sixteenth-century structure. As at the Cornaro Chapel, Bernini's challenge was to create opulence in a restricted space: he achieved it through

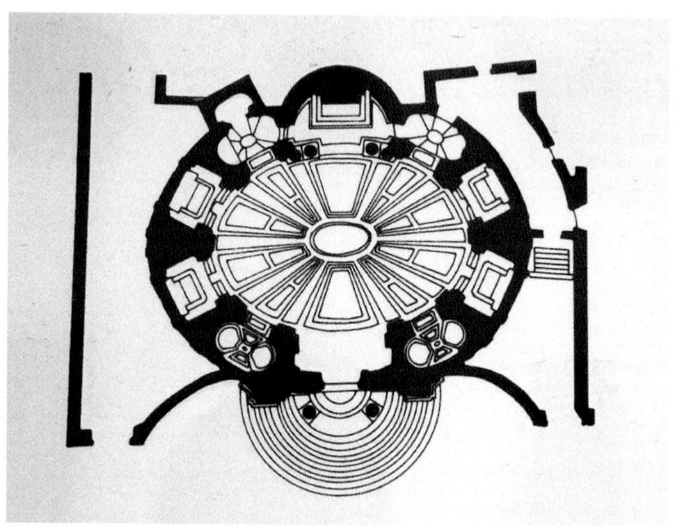

the combination of an ingenious floor plan and an overpowering *composto* that integrates the high altar, dome and lantern. For his plan Bernini chose an oval, a shape that was soon to become one of the most favoured of the Baroque and Rococo, and he placed it with the shortest axis between the entrance and high altar. Thus the chapel's magnitude reveals itself suddenly as we enter because the sides are unexpectedly deep and – because we do not realize immediately how close it is – the high altar seems larger than it actually is. Bernini gives the high altar even greater emphasis by placing solid piers instead of chapel openings at the ends of the oval's longitudinal axis, sending the eye instinctively back to the front. He uses light to divide the interior metaphorically between Heaven and Earth as the ground floor – except for the high-altar aedicule and lunettes at the back of the chapels – is darkened and the dome bathed with natural light.

The high altar is a variation on the Cornaro Chapel, but here it celebrates death and transfiguration. The high-altar aedicule has similar paired Corinthian columns and a broken pediment, and since it encloses a zone accessible only to priests it also impedes the lay spectator from entering. Yet the S. Andrea aedicule is plainer, lacking the Cornaro Chapel's stucco decoration, and is restricted to a single colour of striated marble in a muted pink. The greatest difference is that the altar frame recedes inwards, drawing the viewer unconsciously towards it. Instead of a sculpture posing as a

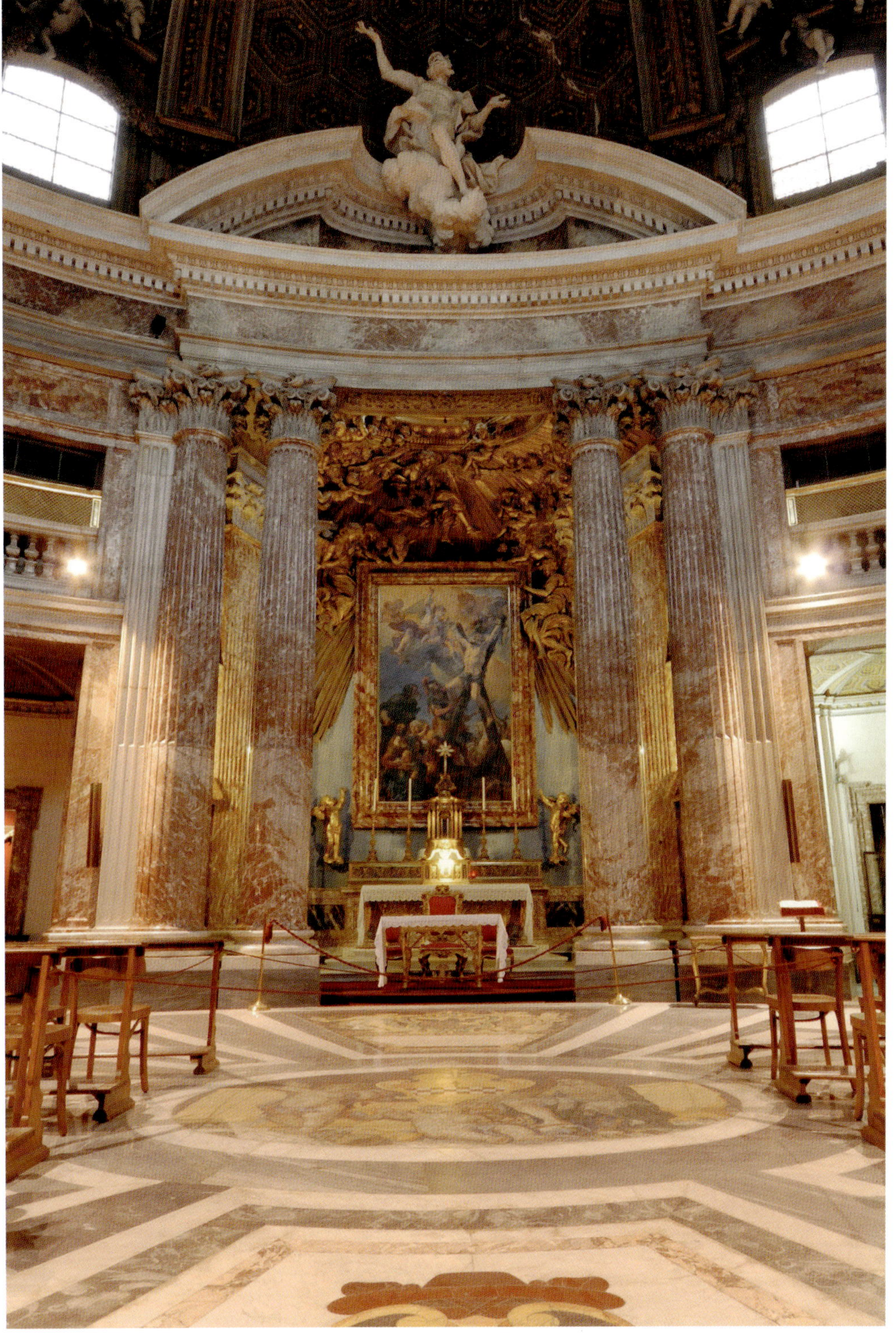

painting, Bernini chose for the altarpiece a painting (by Guglielmo Cortese, 1628–1679) of the *Crucifixion of Saint Andrew* whose bulky forms and intense shading lend it a pronounced sculptural quality. As at the Cornaro Chapel, the altarpiece is lit by a hidden light source, here a small oval cupola, and the natural light is reflected off a series of gilded sunrays, this time accompanied by cherubs and full-length angels, four of them supporting the painting while others seem to challenge the impermeability of stone by passing unhindered through the walls. The white veins in the marble of the painting's frame and the aedicule flicker as if penetrated by the light of the miracle behind it.

Saint Andrew's transfiguration takes place before our very eyes. The canvas shows the mortal man, a muscular near nude struggling against his torturers and looking to God for help. As we gaze up towards the source of the sunrays, we are startled to see Antonio Raggi's much larger sculpture of Saint Andrew – here it is his soul riding a cloud – bursting with volcanic force through the broken pediment of the aedicule. The miracle is underscored by Bernini's choice of media: the saint is in stucco – a lightweight, malleable medium – yet it is shown breaking through the heavy marble of the pediment. The upper part of Raggi's sculpture pierces the heavenly zone of the dome, with its gilt-edged hexagonal coffering and vertical ribs, themselves resembling sunbeams. Above the dome windows trios of stucco cherubs and pairs of stucco fishermen based on Michelangelo's nudes in the Sistine ceiling form a continuous garland and wait to receive the saint in Heaven. Finally, in the lantern, the now invisible Saint Andrew experiences union with the Holy Spirit (a stucco in the vault) as his soul passes through a second ring of winged cherub heads into the well-lit region above. One key difference between the Cornaro Chapel and S. Andrea is that in the Jesuit church Bernini provides an alternate vision for the priests officiating at the Mass within the aedicule. From this vantage point the priests can look directly up from the painting (at that time priests faced the altar at Mass and not the congregation) to the oval lantern hidden from the lay congregation. Surrounded completely by gilded sunrays and populated by a throng of gilded cherubs, the oval lantern culminates in a fresco of *God the Father*, who is also seen through a fiery circle of light – at least on sunny days. Thus the priest has the privilege of an unmitigated view of God that those outside cannot experience.

The grandest of all Bernini's treatments of interior space are in the new
Basilica of St Peter's, begun early in the previous century by Donato
Bramante (1444–1514) and enclosed by Carlo Maderno (1556–1629) only
in 1615. Bernini made two major contributions to the basilica's interior, the
Baldacchino (101) and the Cathedra Petri (102). Although only the second
is a true *composto*, both challenge the *paragone*: the first is a work of sculpture
on an architectural scale and the second a dazzling combination of sculpture,
marble, relief carving, painting and natural light. When designing the latter
of these structures, Bernini took great pains to ensure that the two could be
seen in a single gaze from a single viewpoint, the Baldacchino serving as a
frame for the Cathedra Petri.

Bernini's Baldacchino – it is named after an embroidered silk from Baghdad
(*Baldacco* in Italian) – is an adaptation of an early Christian structure called
a ciborium, a domed covering on four columns that sat over the altar.
Commissioned by Pope Urban VIII Barberini (r. 1623–44), Bernini's
Baldacchino is positioned directly over the tomb of Saint Peter and
underneath Michelangelo's monumental dome. In early Christian churches,
the ciborium was usually small, making up for its size with costly materials
(Pope Leo III's original ciborium at St Peter's was of silver). Although the
Baldacchino is nearly 95 feet (28.5 m) high, it also feels relatively small
compared to the stupendous scale of the basilica. In fact, the genius of
Bernini's structure was its ability to reconcile the alienating size of the church
with that of the visitor. The Baldacchino employs several early Christian
features, including the four twisting Solomonic columns (they imitate
four relics supposedly from the temple of Solomon and their use here was
probably not Bernini's invention) and the emphasis on costly materials.
Bernini merged two traditional forms by replacing the ciborium dome with
an imitation cloth canopy of the sort that was carried over dignitaries in
processions or that marked holy sites. But he broke with tradition by turning
the crown into a diaphanous pyramid formed of volutes joined at the top
and culminating in an orb and a cross – again creating permeability where
one would expect solidity. Bronze cherubs on high display the papal insignia,
and heraldic symbols of the Barberini family (bees, suns and laurel leaves)
punctuate the structure – notably the delicate laurel vine that wraps around

the upper two-thirds of the columns. Bernini's combination of twisting columns, gesticulating angels, dangling tapestries and scrolling volutes give the Baldacchino a sense of movement. Permanent yet apparently ephemeral, it explores a contrast that would become a leitmotif of the Baroque.

The Cathedra Petri, constructed decades later in the apse of the basilica, uses many of the same effects as the Cornaro Chapel and S. Andrea. Like the Baldacchino, it is a reliquary, this time housing a wooden chair believed to have been that of Saint Peter, which Bernini encased in a giant bronze

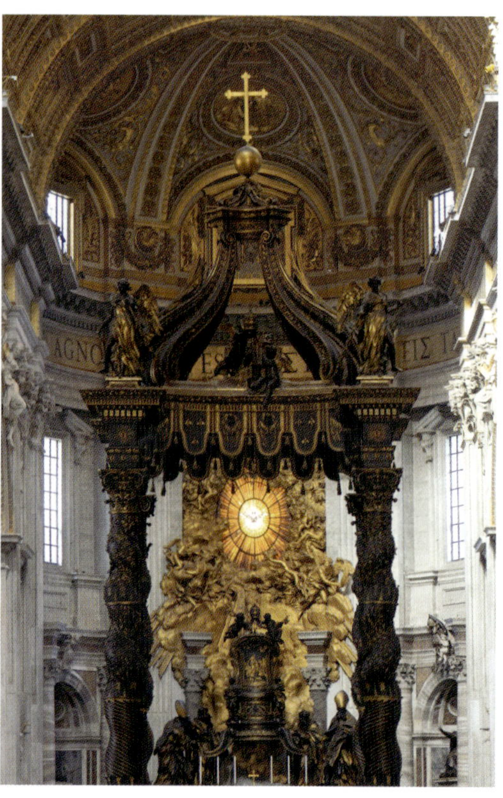

101.
Gianlorenzo Bernini, Baldacchino, 1624–33. Bronze and gilt; 28.5 m (93 ft 6 in). St Peter's Basilica, Rome

throne with a relief carving of *Christ's Charge to Peter* on the back and flanked by a pair of angels wearing fiery robes. As well as underscoring the legitimacy of the papacy (two putti crown it with a papal tiara), this empty chair also represents the return of Christ as the Messiah, an iconography with early Christian roots. Ever the subtle colourist, Bernini chooses for the main sculpture the same deep bronze with gilt highlights that he used in the

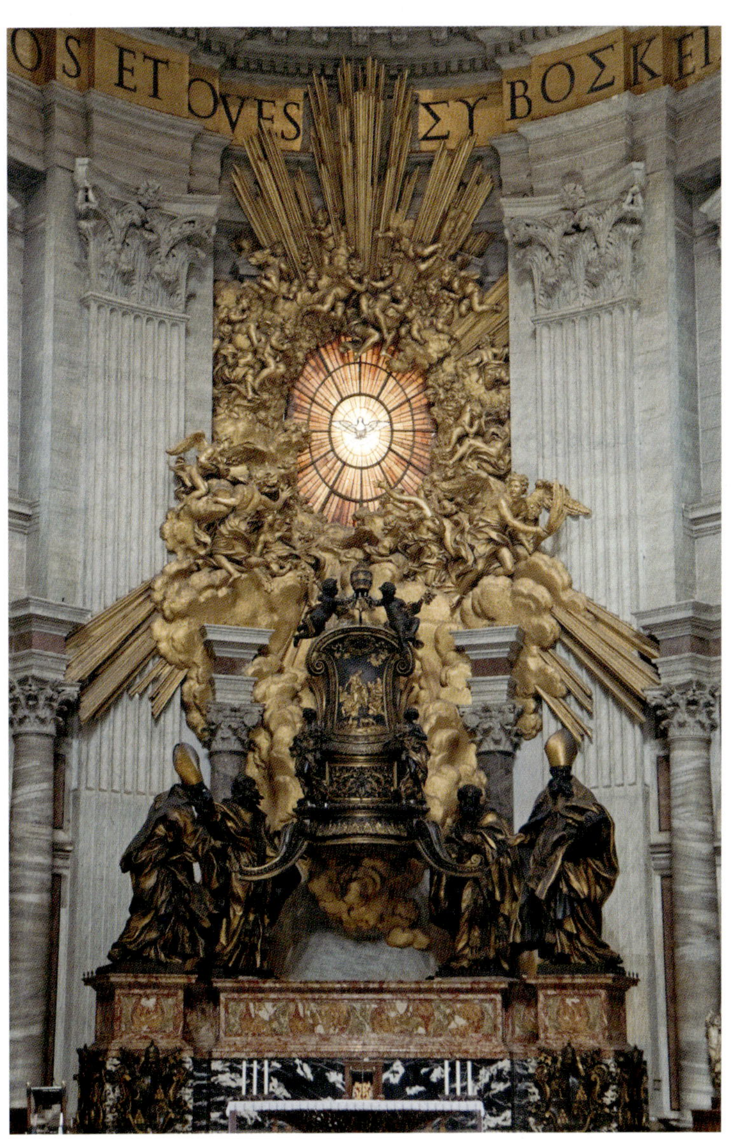

102.
Gianlorenzo Bernini,
Cathedra
Petri, 1657–66.
Parcel gilt
bronze, stucco,
painted glass;
St Peter's
Basilica, Rome

Baldacchino. Another reference to the Baldacchino is the pair of diagonal volutes under the throne. At first glance the chair seems to be supported by four animated figures of Doctors of the Church, however closer inspection reveals that the chair floats miraculously, like the Saint Teresa group and the painting of the *Martyrdom of Saint Andrew*. Bernini's grandest (and most frequently copied) visualization of Divine power appears just above, where an oval window bearing an image of the Holy Spirit effortlessly pierces the immensely thick apse, allowing natural light to bathe the ensemble – accompanied by an explosion of gilded sunrays and an avalanche of angels, cherubs and cloudbursts: the quintessential heavenly glory. In the Cornaro Chapel and S. Andrea, Bernini hid the source of light from the viewer, but here his blinding vision of Salvation is on view for all to see.

Bernini's 'heavenly glories' immediately inspired architects and sculptors beyond the Alps and Pyrenees. Perhaps the most astonishing is the sculptural group of the *Assumption of the Virgin* at Rohr (Germany) by the Bavarian sculptor Egid Quirin Asam (1692–1750), who with his brother the painter and architect Cosmas Damian Asam (1686–1739) were the chief decorating team of the central European Rococo (103). The Rohr *Assumption* is a variation on all three of Bernini's main *composti*. The massive white stucco sculptural group captures our attention as soon as we enter the church, even though – unlike S. Andrea or the Cornaro Chapel – we have to cross a long vaulted nave to reach it. This task is made easier by the church itself, which lacks frescos and is decorated in pastel tones and with subtle gilding. As in the Cornaro Chapel, the group at Rohr is raised above the viewer and kept at a distance, compelling us to look upwards. Egid Quirin replaces Bernini's bulging aedicule with a series of nesting, stage-like backdrops formed of paired columns and broken pediments that make the space look deeper than it is. A rich false tapestry in a dark eggshell blue and gold forms the backdrop for the ascending trio of figures (the Virgin and two angels), dramatically highlighting their whiteness and the gilding of their windswept drapery, an effect intensified by natural light from ample side windows. Down below the Apostles gesticulate wildly upon discovering the empty tomb and shroud, some of them looking into the sepulchre while others already behold the miracle above. Their expressions, ranging from incredulity to fervour, echo the viewer's reactions. The Virgin projects a powerful presence. Her stance is forceful and direct, her hands extend outwards as if encompassing the entire space (compare with 1), and her face turns towards Heaven like Saint Andrew at S. Andrea – yet she is bulkier, making it seem all the more miraculous that such a sculpture could float without any visible support. Egid Quirin takes a cue from the Cathedra Petri by allowing the sunburst and angelic glory to blast through the end wall and altar frame in full view. Flanking the window, Jesus and God the Father await the Virgin, reaching across the light to hold her crown in readiness. The Asam brothers took the theme of the permeability of architecture to a new height.

The most extravagant of all descendants of Bernini's *composti* is in Spain where, paradoxically, Italian influence was a rare intrusion into a Baroque infused with Gothic and even Islamic characteristics (much of Spain was under Muslim rule in the Medieval era). As in central Europe, Baroque and Rococo church interiors in Iberia and its empires continued to feature Medieval forms such as the retable (*retablo*), complex vaults and tracery, saturated decoration and hyper-realistic wooden sculpture. Narciso and Diego Tomé's (1690–1742) *Transparente* (104) in Toledo Cathedral was quite literally inserted into a Gothic context: it rests in the ambulatory of a thirteenth-century building, directly behind the late medieval high-altar *retablo*. Although the *Transparente* is a convex *retablo* of coloured marble, jasper and alabaster, with an altar of its own and two storeys of columns and broken entablatures, its main function is to serve as a frame for a glass window (hence the name) that illuminates the Holy Sacrament on the high altar behind it. It is thus a permanent version of the kind of Forty Hours apparatus that inspired Bernini's heavenly glories. The Tomé brothers gave the opening a Cathedra Petri-style sunburst with the rose of the Virgin at the centre, its gilded bronze sunrays accompanied by an unusually ebullient throng of archangels and putti. This burst of divine light – lit from above by a massive funnel-shaped lantern that replaced half the Gothic vault behind the viewer – seems less to break through the architecture of the altarpiece (as at Rohr) than to melt it. The entablatures droop down or curl up as if in a semi-liquid state and the white protective skin over the columns peels away to reveal the fluting underneath. Unfażed, the Virgin and Child sit regally on

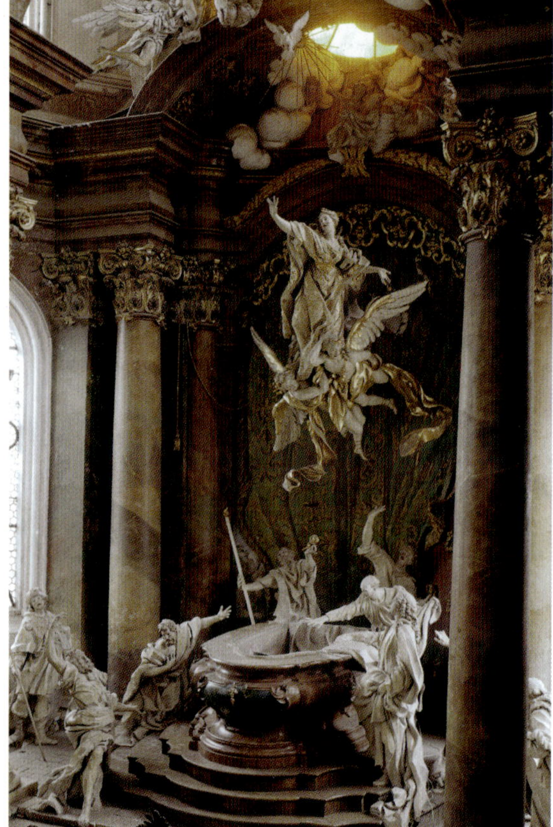

**103.
Egid Quirin
Asam,**
*Assumption
of the Virgin*,
1721–36 or
1717–25.
Marble and
stucco; Abbey
Church, Rohr
(Germany)

a throne below, and above the sunburst a lifesize alabaster tableau of the *Last
Supper* is placed so that Christ's blessing of the Eucharist is on the same axis
as the wafer below. Two narrative scenes showing predictions of the Eucharist
occupy gilt-bronze relief panels on either side of the Virgin, and above the
Last Supper another one depicts the Virgin presenting Saint Ildefonso with a
chasuble (a popular subject in Toledo). Statues of Hope, Faith and Charity
adorn the top like Gothic pinnacles. The commotion continues further
up, where a frescoed and stuccoed empyrean of angels, saints and prophets
spreads out over the vault and up into the lantern behind (at this point the
viewer must turn around to see it), where figures including the Lamb of
the Seven Seals and the twenty-four Elders of the Apocalypse shimmer in
natural sunlight. These images and the accompanying inscriptions from the
Book of Revelations provide the key to the *Transparente*'s meaning. One of

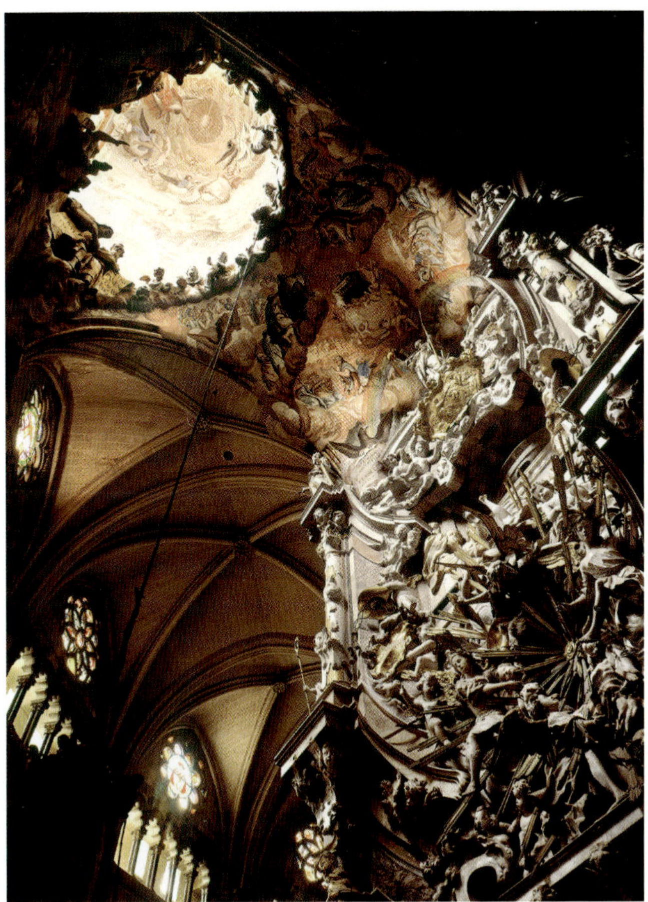

**104.
Narciso and
Diego Tomé**,
Transparente,
1721–32.
Marble and
bronze; Toledo
Cathedral
(Spain)

them reads 'after this I looked, and, behold, a door was opened in heaven'
(Revelations 4:1), and with Saint John the viewer mystically enters paradise
and encounters the throne of God. The reference to the throne in Revelation
is reflected in the use of jasper in the Transparente, since the throne was said
to be partly made of that material. Such imagery, whereby the altar or church
serves as a simulacrum for apocalyptic references to the heavenly Jerusalem,
was common in medieval architecture.

Bernini's influence is much subtler in the stupendous *Capela-Mor* (chancel)
in the Portuguese Dominican monastery in Aveiro, by António Gomes and
José Correia (105), which combines a riot of carved and gilded woodwork
with a Gothic net vault and a profuse kind of carved ornament that also
derives from late medieval interiors. The glittering, complex ornament and

the tunnel effect caused by the nesting arches on twisting columns behind the altar – inspired by Bernini's Baldacchino and his monumental staircase at St Peter's, the Scala Regia (1663–6) – draw the viewer inwards. The eye first focuses on a gilt tabernacle, which is flanked by a pair of Dominican saints in niches, and then is led up a pyramidal staircase of convex steps past another pair of Dominican saints to encounter a gruesomely realistic near life-sized statue of the Crucifixion, painted in flesh tones on wood and – like Bernini's Saint Teresa or the Virgin at Rohr – inaccessible to the viewer. The flickering effect of the natural light on the vaults would have been compounded by four layers of candles on the shelves below the Crucifixion, recalling an *apparato* from a Forty Hours Devotion (see 187). In buildings such as this the gilt woodwork spread out past the apse into the nave, where it formed ceiling

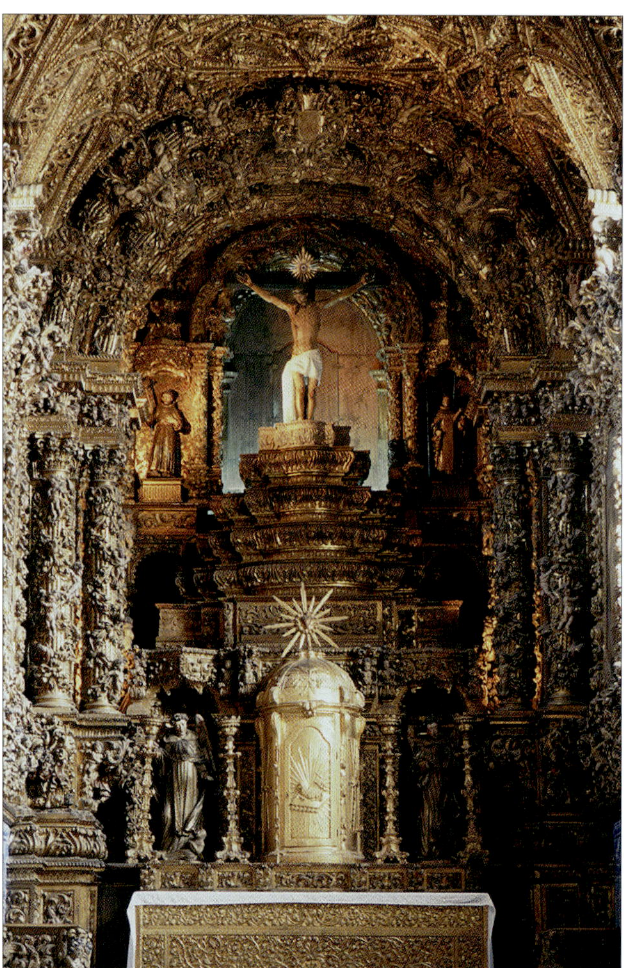

105. António Gomes and José Correia, Capela-Mor, before 1725. Dominican Monastery, Aveiro (Portugal)

panels and panel-like frames for paintings and pulpits, and it was often
combined with brilliantly coloured tiles – a Portuguese speciality.

Bernini's illusionistic stucco effects and medieval aesthetics also coexisted in
Spanish Sicily, where the taste for abundant ornament and hyper-realistic
sculpture distinguished some church interiors from Roman models (see 9).
Palermo sculptor Giacomo Serpotta (1652–1732) made a speciality of this
kind of *composto* in white stucco, many in confraternity chapels in which
narrative sculptures take over the role traditionally played by frescos. His
figures are smaller in scale and more naturalistic than those of Bernini,
and their arrangement along the walls is essentially flat and conservative.
His masterpiece is the Oratorio del Rosario di S. Cita in Palermo (106),
where the play of natural light on the high relief of his stuccos creates an
unparalleled textural richness. The iconography of the chapel is based on the
Mysteries of the Rosary (the life, death and resurrection of Christ and the Virgin)
and these form the subject of a row of *teatrini* – sharply receding, boxlike
dioramas with tiny figures in relief against landscapes and architecture
in perspective like panels in a *Flügelaltar*. Along the side walls pairs of
allegorical figures summarize the moral lessons of these episodes, and putti
mimic appropriate emotional responses. It is a striking example of Baroque
visual rhetoric (*delectare, docere, movere*) as discussed in Chapter One. The end
wall focuses on a spectacular miniature sea-battle representing the *Victory at
Lepanto* (attributed to the Virgin of the Rosary) surrounded by other *teatrini*
against a false curtain held aloft by an infinite number of twisting and leaping
putti – the sheer variety of their poses encourages the eye to linger. On the
sides we look upwards from the earthly row of *teatrini* to clusters of playful
cherubs between the windows and onwards to a series of allegorical female
divinities resting on top of the windows – the effect is very similar to Bernini's
dome at S. Andrea. Like the interior at Hergiswald (see 90), the visitor is
invited to participate in a guided yet serendipitous mystical experience.

Medieval forms inspired Italian architects further north to create an
alternative *composto* to that of Bernini, one in which architectural design
and symbolism took precedence over narrative. Although like Bernini
they used the vocabulary of classicism, they introduced an approach that

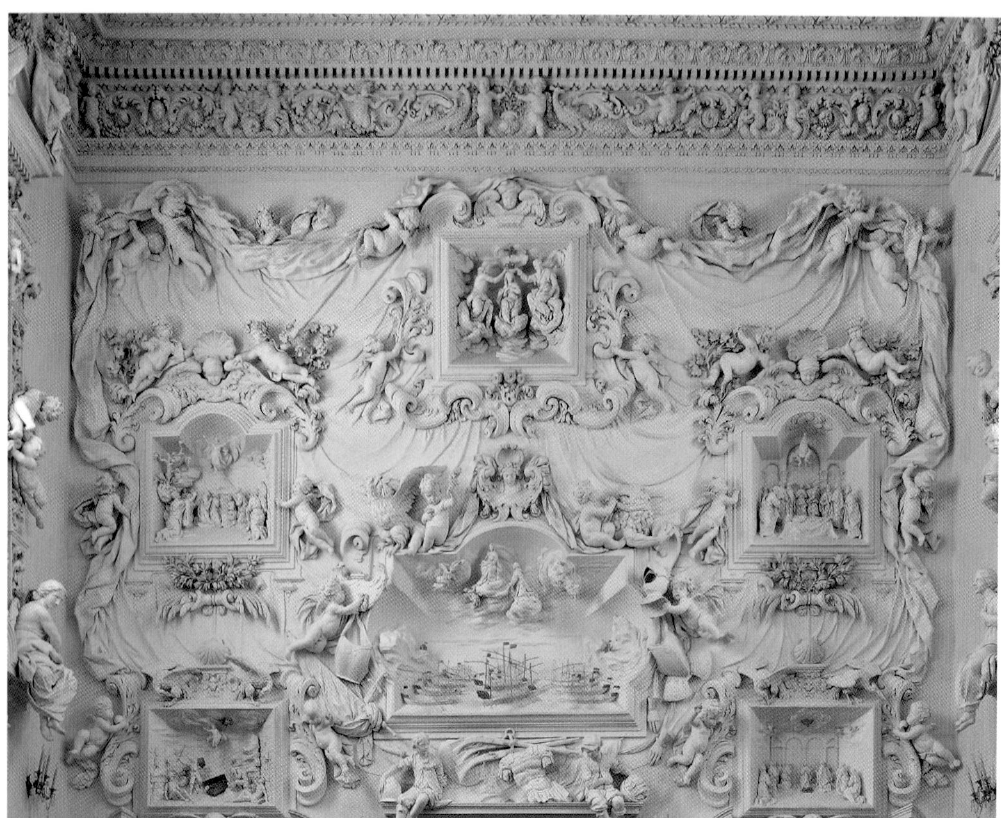

was fundamentally alien to the Graeco-Roman or Renaissance worlds.
Francesco Borromini (1599–1667) and Guarino Guarini (1624–1683) – both
northerners – brought to their churches in Rome and Turin, respectively an
emphasis on geometrical harmony, numerical proportions and translucence
that is essentially Gothic in spirit and helped ensure a hearty reception north
of the Alps. Both architects also explored other anti-classical forms, such as
the structurally innovative buildings of the Hellenistic age (c.300 BC) and
late Roman architecture in North Africa and the Near East, but Gothicism
was at the core of their most radical concepts of space. The two men made
strange bedfellows – Borromini was a tortured, anti-intellectual stonemason
who finally committed suicide by falling on his sword, whereas Guarini was
a refined and scholarly Theatine priest who wrote nine academic treatises
including *Disegni d'architettura civile ed ecclesiastica* (1686) and *Architettura
civile* (1737). Their *composti*, as exemplified at Borromini's S. Ivo alla Sapienza
in Rome and Guarini's S. Lorenzo in Turin, had little to do with the *paragone*,

sculpture in the round, or frescos. This is not to say that these architects scorned sculpture and painting, however with Borromini the stucco cherub heads, garlands and angels emerge from the structural elements and merely punctuate the architecture and in Guarini's interiors the sculptures, altarpieces and paintings play a secondary role and stay within their frames. The goal of these spaces was not always unity. At times Borromini and especially Guarini revelled in a kind of irrationality that encouraged disjointed and unpredictable viewpoints. However, in both buildings the most important direction to look was up: like Gothic cathedrals, the churches of Borromini and Guarini placed greater emphasis on their increasingly complex vaults. The mathematical abstruseness of these interiors has generated volumes of interpretation from the flabbergasted critics of the times to the more theoretically minded scholars of our day.

Like Bernini, Borromini faced restrictions when designing S. Ivo (the chapel of the Roman Archiginnasio, later University of Rome): here he had to work within a centralized plan at the end of an existing arcaded courtyard (107, 108). Instead of the round or oval solutions of his rival, Borromini based his plan on intersecting triangles forming a star hexagon with alternately convex and concave openings. Anchored vertically by eighteen giant Corinthian pilasters, the interior opens up laterally in all directions on the ground level, offering multiple viewpoints and encouraging the eye to circulate freely. Each bay divides into three recesses, with pairs of niches flanking larger niches, pairs of doors canted inwards to a point (a Gothic motif), an entrance arch and another arch framing the high altar – all milky white and unadulterated by statues, frescos, or paintings, except for the high altarpiece of *S. Ivo and Other Saints* (a late work of Pietro da Cortona finished by Giovanni Ventura Borghesi). The upper level of the wall abandons the flanking niches – in fact the opposition of open and closed space is the leitmotif of this level – but has a pair of convex oratories on either side of the altar and a corresponding window over the entrance doorway (together forming a triangle). The only sculptural elements are the cherub heads in the double doorway pediments, the heraldic martyr's palms below and under the entrance vault, delicate coffering in the niches, and the richly carved capitals. Borromini repeats the star-hexagon plan in a heavy entablature that wraps around the interior just below the springing of the vault. The vault prolongs the vertical emphasis of the pilasters, using pilaster-like ribs that recall those of the octagonal Gothic vaults at the cathedrals of Ely (see 109) or Milan (completed 1500) – the latter of which Borromini knew. At the top all is resolved in a circular lantern with a gilded dove of the Holy Spirit surrounded by sunrays. Although the surfaces are busier in the vault – stucco papal heraldic devices, stars, lilies, palm fronds and winged cherubs compete for our attention – they are all painted in the same milky colour and so do not hamper our eyes' rise towards the light of the lantern.

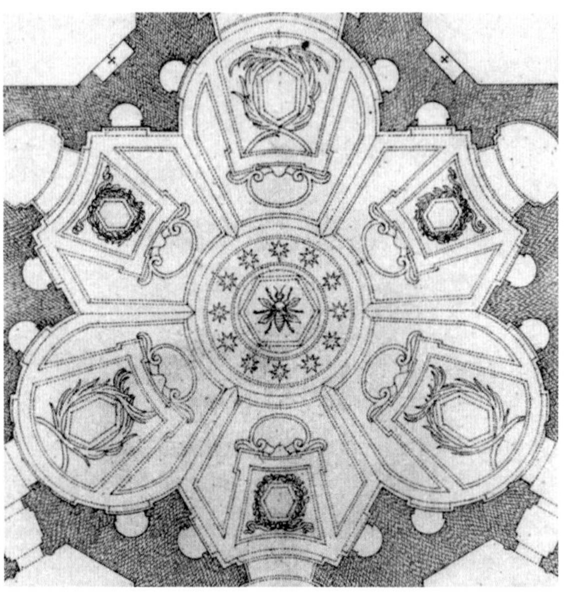

107.
Francesco Borromini, Project for S. Ivo alla Sapienza, Rome, c.1642. Etching by Sebastiano Giannini, 1720

108.
Francesco Borromini, S. Ivo alla Sapienza, 1642–52. Rome

The complexity of S. Ivo's design allows symbolic readings on two levels, one available to the average worshipper and the other to the more erudite students and lecturers of the Archiginnasio. Both are based on the doctrine that true wisdom is based on faith alone, as announced in the inscription above the high altar from Proverbs 9:10 – 'The Fear of the Lord is the Beginning of Wisdom' – and by the lantern, about which Borromini himself wrote: '[it] signif[ies] the coming of the Holy Spirit which brings the true Wisdom.' Unlettered visitors could understand the more generic symbolism of the martyr's palms and crowns and the lilies of purity, and the more educated could raise a knowing eyebrow at the references to the Star of

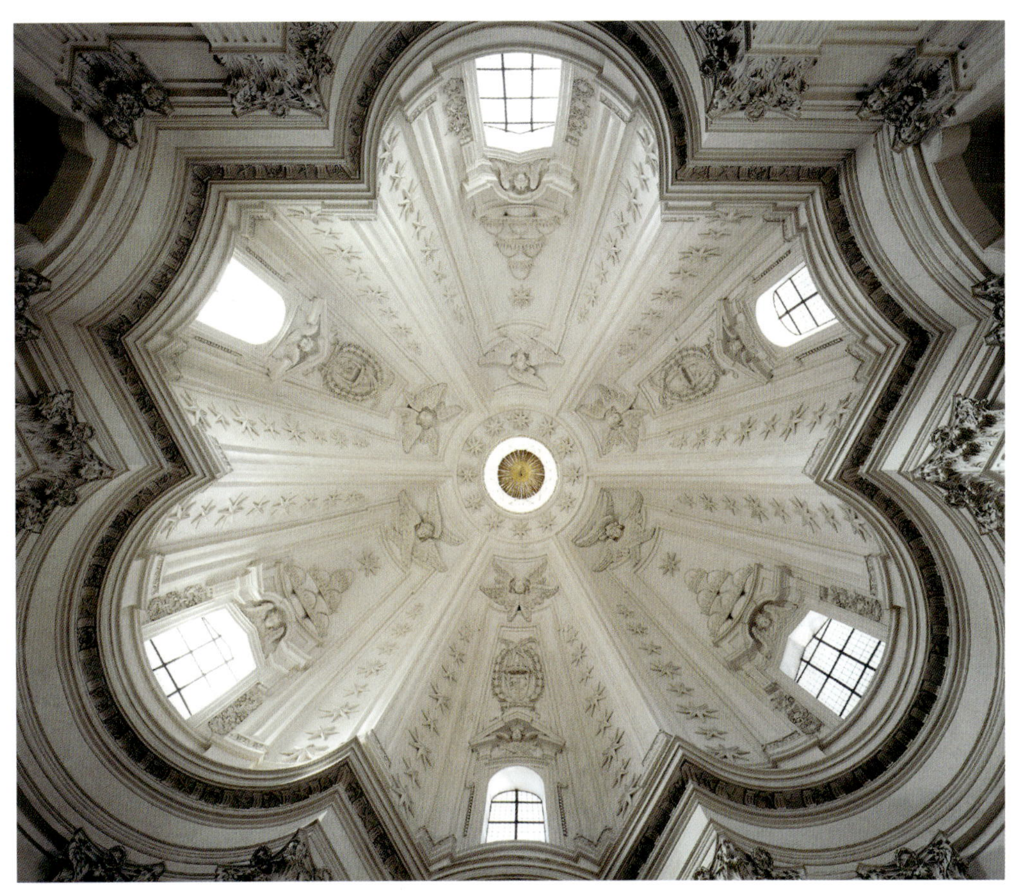

183   The Bel Composto

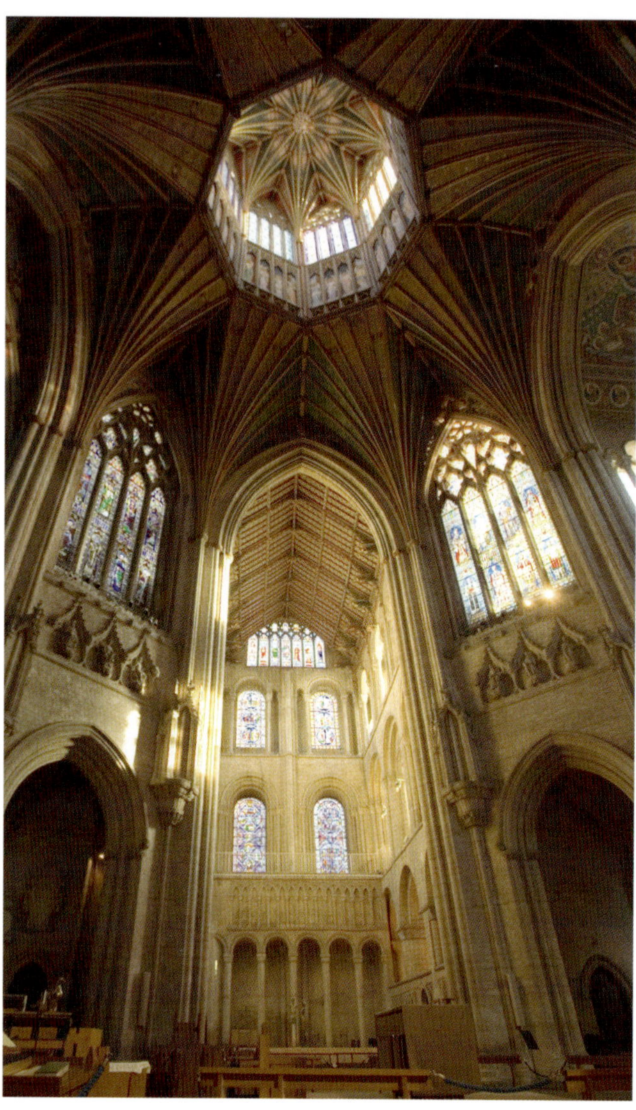

**109.
William
Hurley,** Octagonal
vault, 1326–34.
Ely Cathedral
(England)

Solomon, the Barberini bee and abstruse allusions to books of allegories
and the occult. Yet Borromini's genius was to unite all through the upwards
thrust of the pilasters and vault, provoking all visitors to gaze into the
cleansing light of God and silently complete that verse from Proverbs: 'and
the knowledge of the holy is understanding'.

Guarini's S. Lorenzo in Turin paid homage to S. Ivo but took its innovations
quite literally to new heights (110). Like S. Ivo, S. Lorenzo was built on a
centralized plan inscribed within a square. Guarini replaced Borromini's

six concave and convex openings with eight concave ones but he fronted them with an inner ring of convex arched units on pairs of slender columns to create almond-shaped chapels and shallow niches – yet allowed a nearly unbroken view of the interior in a single glance because the columns are not joined to the wall (the arched opening flanked by lower rectangular openings is popularly called a 'Palladian motif'). This inner ring seems both elastic – the wavelike repetition of the convex bulges is rhythmic – and diaphanous. The high-altar chapel and its vestibule are mostly contained in a separate annex. Unlike S. Ivo, S. Lorenzo is richly decorated with coloured marble, painted altarpieces, frescos and sculptures, and its walls are covered with putti, garlands and small-scale allegorical figures. Like Borromini, Guarini restates the main ground plan with a heavy, unbroken entablature at the top of the ground level. But then he jolts us by changing genres twice in quick succession. In the first storey, wide pendentives (curved trapezoidal supports) and shallow barrel vaults ending in convex/concave Palladian windows form a Greek cross (one in which both arms are equal) that – in apparent defiance of the laws of gravity – rests on the open arches below. Then, on top of a circular entablature pierced with oval windows we encounter a lacelike, diaphanous dome (111). An elegant criss-cross of double ribs, the dome forms a star shape like that of S. Ivo but with eight instead of six points and culminating in an octagonal instead of a circular lantern. Guarini departs from the classical ideal by allowing his web to be pierced by light at every juncture, in the drum, dome and the lantern, which is taller than the dome. The visitor is drawn up into this brilliant light and awestruck at the geometrical complexity that some scholars have interpreted as a symbol of infinity. Academics have sought Islamic and other precedents for this inspired piece of engineering – others have also insisted on looking at other Baroque models – but passages in Guarini's *Architettura civile* leave little doubt that Gothic architecture was a major inspiration. In an analysis of classical and Gothic architecture, Guarini praised Gothic churches for their seemingly miraculous defiance of the laws of gravity. He wrote of arches that seem to 'hang in the air', 'completely perforated' towers, 'vaults without the support of walls', and even mentioned that 'the corner of a high tower may rest on an arch' – precisely what he did with his second-storey pendentives. In his churches Guarini seeks a medieval atmosphere of divine mystery.

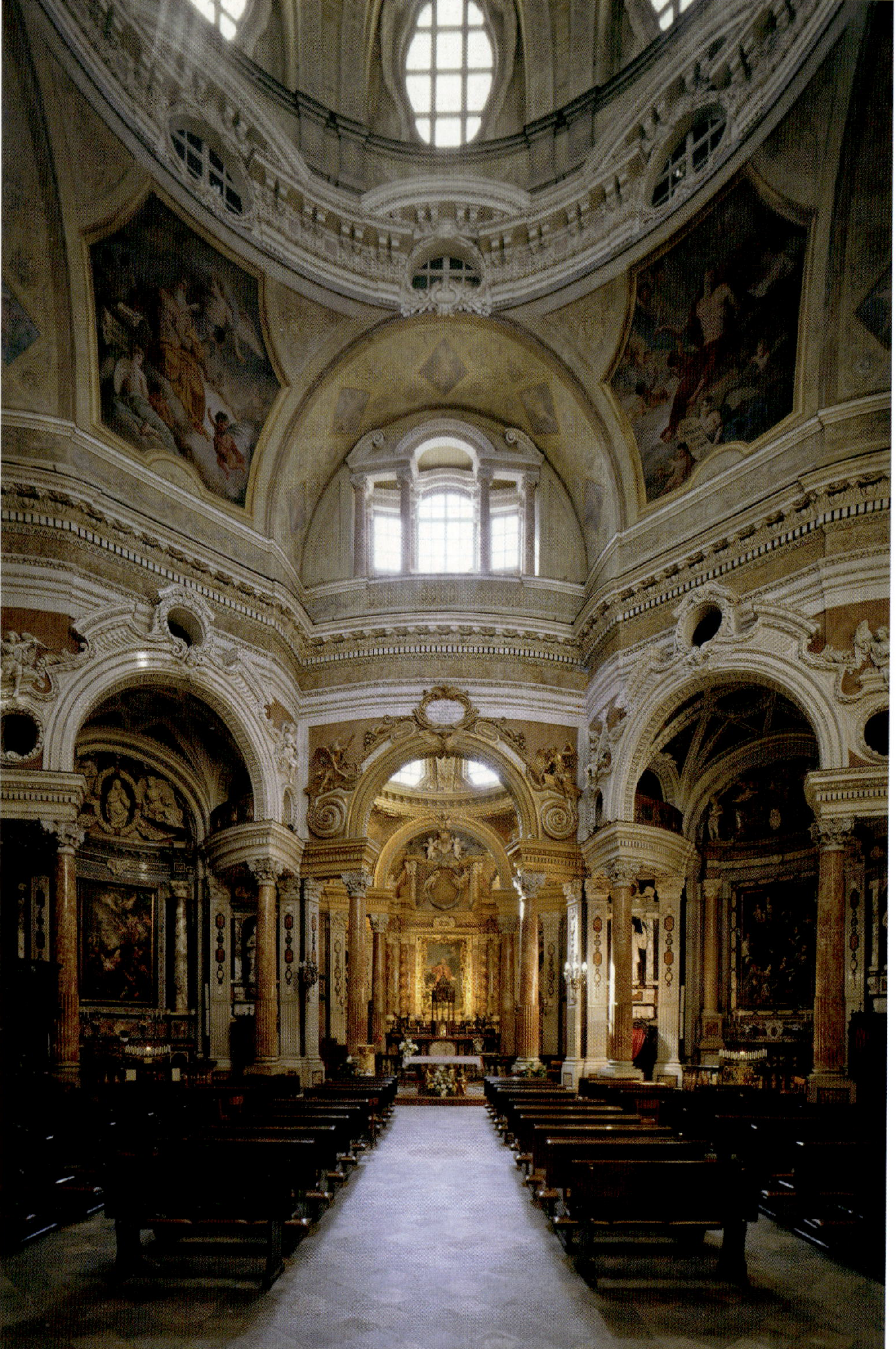

110.
Guarino Guarini, S. Lorenzo, 1668–87. Turin (Italy)

111.
Guarino Guarini, dome S. Lorenzo, Turin (Italy)

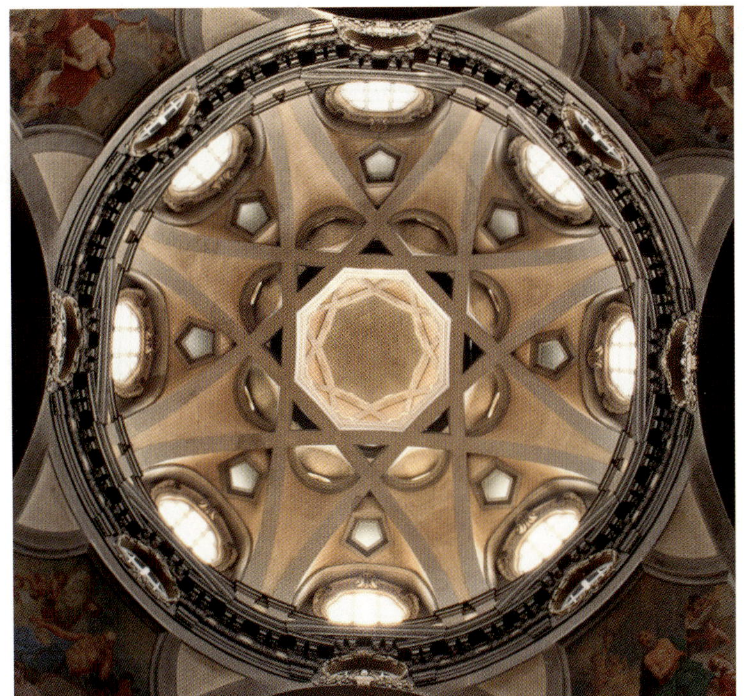

Guarini's church designs – thanks in no small measure to the popularity of his treatises – had many offspring in the north, especially because of his very practical solution to lightening the load through an inner circle of supports as at S. Lorenzo to achieve a more diaphanous interior. Perhaps even more inspirational than his centralized plans was a series of longitudinal schemes he designed and published in *Disegni d'architettura Civile* and *Architettura civile*, such as this metamorphosis of a rectangular Latin-cross church into one with an undulating profile based on oval vaults on diagonally placed pilaster piers in the nave, oval vaults forming concave side chapels in the aisles, and oval transepts (112). Such plans formed the principal inspiration behind Christoph Dientzenhofer's (1655–1722) masterpiece, the Jesuit church of Sv. Mikuláš (113) in Malá Strana (Little Quarter) in Prague, a city in which Guarini had worked. The Bavarian architect created a fluid, billowing structure with three interlocking ovals and angled pilaster piers in the nave – these prolong the rhythm of the curves – and side chapels and clerestory galleries with painted oval vaults. The crossing, with its circular dome resting on hemispherical transepts and apse, was added in 1737–53 by his son Kilian Ignaz, and is more conventional. The nave, with its striated pink-grey faux marble piers and galleries, its gilded capitals and crests, and its shimmering white statues with gilded highlights, provides the most striking *composto*. On the bases of the piers – just above eye level – we first confront the oversized statues of saints and angels, whose anxious gestures draw our gaze towards them. Next, our eyes follow the upwards thrust of the piers, made all the easier by the lack of a continuous horizontal entablature at the top (in contrast to Borromini's or Guarini's churches). Our eyes move past the well-illuminated galleries directly to the illusionistic fresco on the ceiling (1760), which is painted to look like a continuation of the piers with niches and a projecting cornice – it is very difficult to see where the real architecture ends and the fantasy begins.

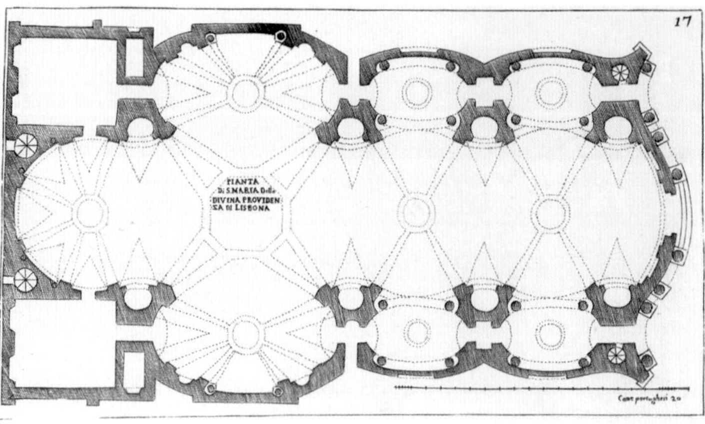

112.
Guarino Guarini, longitudinal church plan from *Architettura civile*, 1737. Engraving; 17.8 × 29.7 cm (7 × 11¾ in)

113.
Christoph Dientzenhofer, Sv. Mikuláš, 1703–11. Prague (Czech Republic)

In the ceiling (by Johann Lucas Kracker, 1760–1) we become lost in a vortex. Its confusing, wavelike contour seems to pulsate and the uneven surfaces confound attempts to gain our bearings. The borders, which are painted with powerfully foreshortened classical and medieval ruins, draw our eyes towards the centre and a heavenly apparition of the apotheosis of the church's patron, Saint Nicholas, riding high on a trail of blazing clouds.

The most overtly Gothic architect of the late Baroque, one as indebted to Borromini as he was to the medieval monuments of his Bohemian homeland and Moravia, was Johann Santin-Aichel (better known as Giovanni Santini; 1667–1723), born in Prague to an Italian family of masons. Discouraged

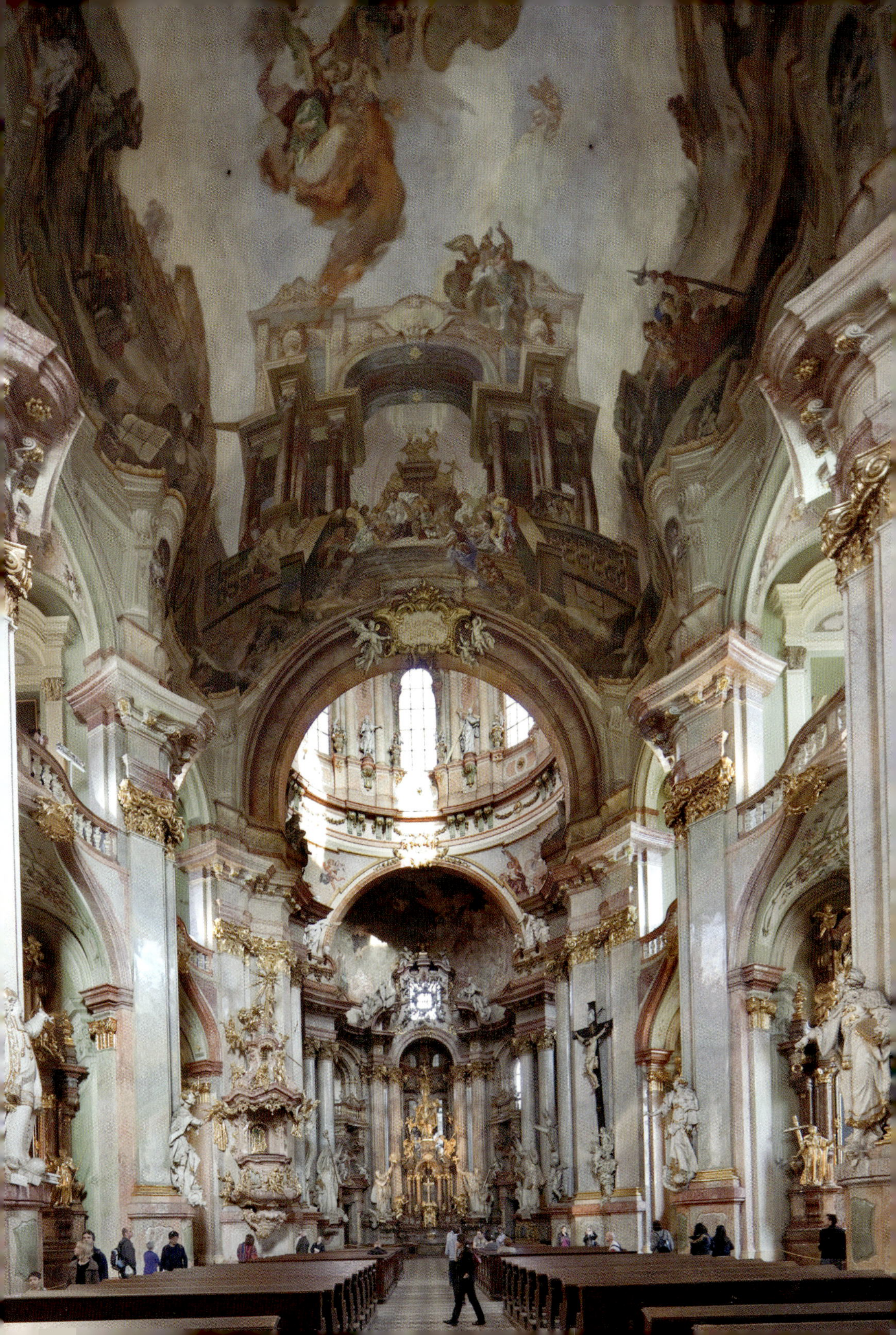

from a mason's career by partial paralysis, he trained initially as a painter and during a trip to Italy in 1696 studied Borromini's architecture. After his return to Bohemia in 1700, Santini began to develop a hybrid Gothic-Baroque style that was one of the most creative architectural innovations of the central European Baroque. His interest in Gothic was fuelled by the nationalistic medieval histories of the Czech Jesuit Bohuslav Balbín (1621–1688), who portrayed the medieval period as Bohemia's golden age and Prague's St Vitus Cathedral (begun 1344) as its crowning glory, and by a living local tradition of

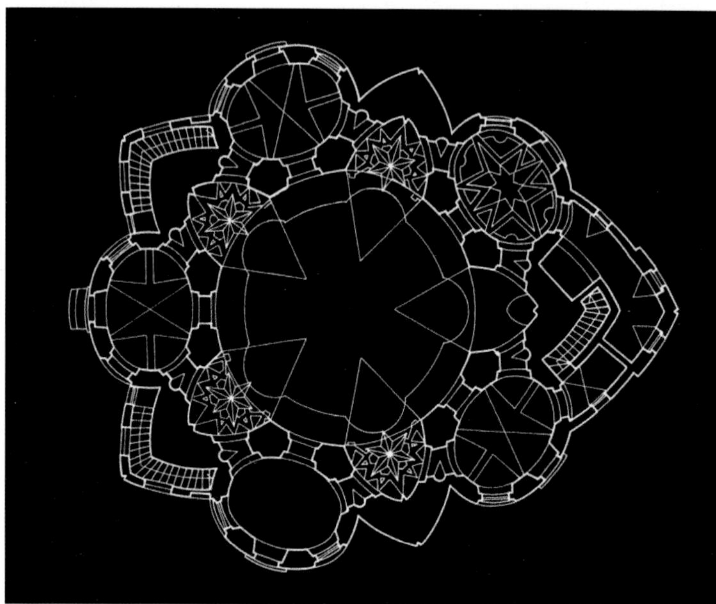

114.
Giovanni Santini, Pilgrimage chapel of St John Nepomuk, plan, 1719–22. Žd'ár nad Sazavou (Czech Republic)

115.
Giovanni Santini, St John Nepomuk, interior, Žd'ár nad Sazavou (Czech Republic)

Gothic masons. Although Santini designed several hybrid structures, mostly for rural monastic communities, his crowning achievement is his rocket ship of a pilgrimage chapel of St John Nepomuk at Žd'ár nad Sazavou in Moravia (114, 115, 116). The centrally planned chapel was commissioned by Václav Vejmluva, the abbot of the nearby Žd'ár monastery, as a commemorative pilgrimage site for the Bohemian martyr St John Nepomuk and was meant to draw pilgrims, and hence fame, to their foundation. He was inspired by the exhumation of the saint, in 1719, during which it was discovered that Nepomuk's tongue was still perfectly preserved. Consequently, the image of the living tongue was Santini's answer to the Barberini bee.

Santini replaced S. Ivo's intersecting triangle plan with an intersecting
pentagon one in which five radiating ovals interspersed with five pointed
tongue-shaped forms – the shape relates specifically to the chapel's relic
– create an ambulatory surrounding a centralized inner chamber, formed
of a lobed pentagon and five-pointed star. In fact, the five-pointed star
and tongue are the leitmotif of the church, and unite it from plan to vault
(even the outline takes on an elongated tongue form). The five vaulted
ovals were meant to be crowned with net vaults on a star theme – a highly

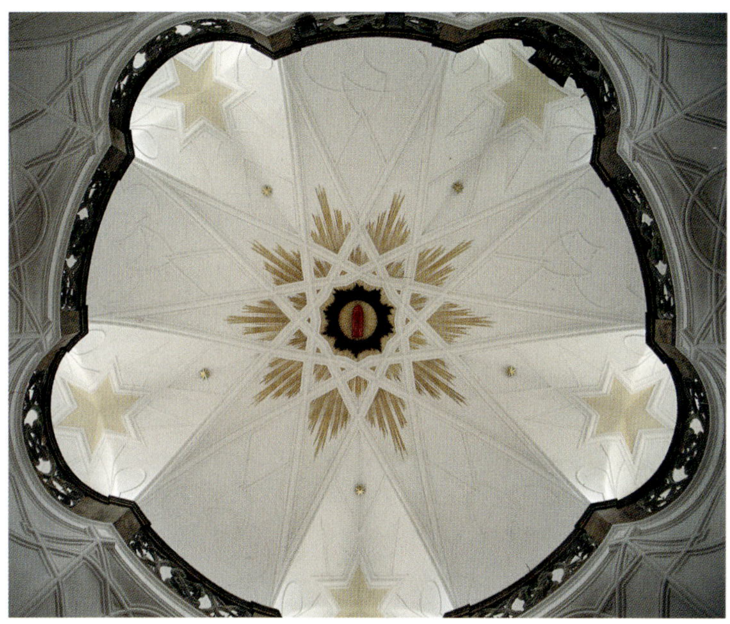

significant arrangement as pilgrims believed that a circle of five stars appeared
miraculously above the body of Nepomuk upon his exhumation – but only
four were completed. By contrast, hexagonal stars are the focus of the Gothic
rib vaulting in the niche chapels. Gothic is dominant in the upper part of
the church, with pointed windows, a playful tracery of ribs supporting the
base of the dome, and an intricate tangle of vaulting in the cupola. As in
a Gothic chapel worshippers are meant to look upwards, and at the very
top of the dome a giant red tongue, the object of the pilgrim's veneration,
appears inside a ten-pointed star and surrounded by gilded sunrays like
a heavenly apotheosis. Also medieval is the way the interior is unified by

light: it spills through the dome openings as well as from a ring of windows around the ground-floor and clerestory, and the openness of the plan and largely monochrome colour scheme allows it to permeate the whole church. However, Santini's expression of God's glory was much more sophisticated than a mere celebration of height and illumination. Taking a cue from Borromini, the ground plan of the central part of the church opposes openings of different shapes across diagonals: in this case half-teardrop-shaped niche chapels face sections of subtly rounded wall pierced by narrow passageways. In the dome this playful opposition is even more innovative as unbroken sections of vault cross over the dome only to open up into a wedge to accommodate pairs of pointed windows. However, unlike Bernini or Guarini, who often hid the complexities of their interiors behind misleading façades or box-like walls, Santini dispenses with anything that could properly be called a façade and allows the exterior directly to reflect its star-shaped interior, the knife-edged points of its buttresses contrasting with the rounded walls of its doorways and soaring up to its gilded spire (116).

The kind of illusionistic ceiling fresco that dominates the nave, side chapels and galleries at Sv. Mikuláš in Prague (see 113) has its origins in the last quarter of the previous century in Italy, where the generation after Bernini applied the *composto* to nave ceilings. The master fresco painters Baciccio (1639–1709) and Andrea Pozzo (1642–1709) – the former Bernini's pupil and the latter a Jesuit brother who specialized in frescos with false architecture in linear perspective – left Baroque Rome with its two grandest ceiling frescos. The tradition of painting a church dome to resemble the heavens went back to the frescos of Correggio (see 86), and Bernini had designed a heavenly ceiling in the vault over the Cornaro Chapel (see 95), as we have seen. After executing some spectacular palace ceilings, Pietro da Cortona transferred the heavenly ceiling to the nave of the church with his fresco at Rome's Chiesa Nuova (1647–51). Yet nothing anticipated the scale of Baciccio's project for the nave (1676–79), cupola (1672–1675), pendentives (1675–76), apse (1680–83) and left transept (1685) at the Gesù in Rome (117), or Pozzo's vault and dome paintings (1685–1702) at the other Roman Jesuit church of S. Ignazio (see 118, 119). Comprising his own frescos and stucco decoration by Antonio Raggi, Baciccio's vault in the Gesù boldly crosses media boundaries in a

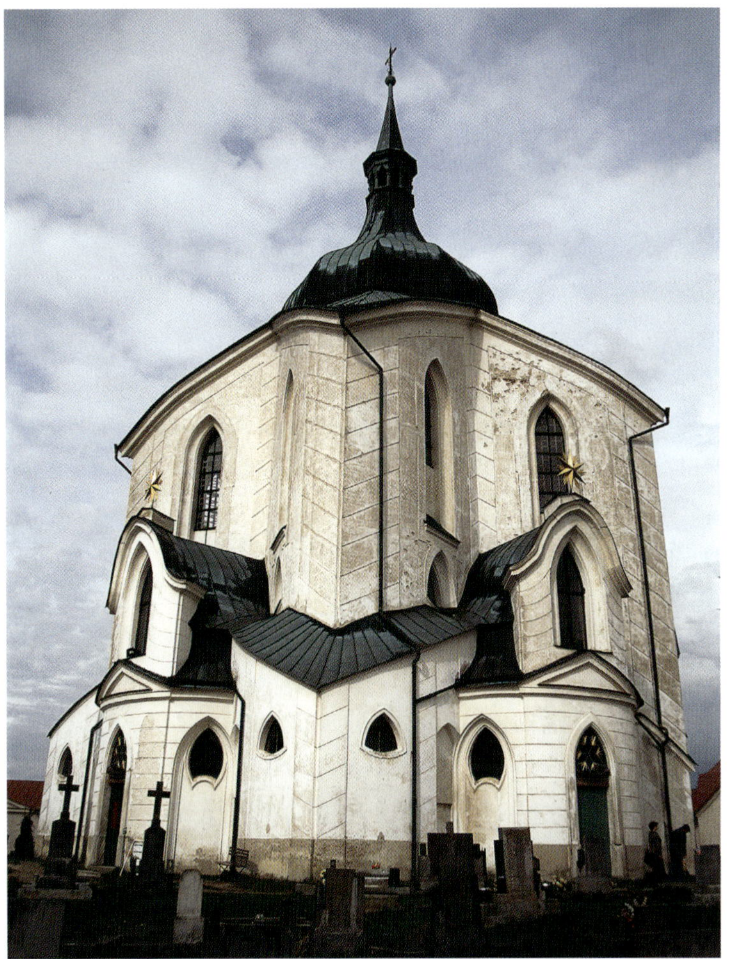

way Cortona hesitated to do. The frescoed sections of the nave vault bleed
into the gilt decoration of the ceiling and cast painted shadows onto it.
Although painted onto flat plaster, these sections of fresco seem to extend
into the viewer's space, enhancing the fresco's three-dimensional character.
The Triumph of the Name of Jesus focuses on a brilliant sunburst surrounding
the monogram of Jesus (I.H.S.) much as Bernini had framed the dove of
the Holy Spirit at the Cathedra Petri (see 102). A multitude of small figures
surrounds this illuminated area, arranged in loosely connected light and dark
zones that either ascend into Heaven on the rays of the sun (the elect) or
tumble down as if into the church (the vices). At the window level Raggi's
stucco figures, representing the geographic regions ministered to by the
Jesuits, reach upwards towards the light. The theme of Baciccio's fresco is

stated in a caption held by angels at the entrance of the church: 'at the name of Jesus every knee should bow, of things in heaven, and things in earth, and things under the earth' (Philippians 2:10–11), echoing the three different 'levels' suggested by the illusionism of Baciccio's ceiling.

Even more astonishing is Andrea Pozzo's *Allegory of the Missionary Work of the Society of Jesus* (118), a teeming apotheosis tamed by an intricate framework of feigned architecture so carefully calibrated for a single viewpoint (directly below) that it flattens out if viewed from the crossing. Pozzo's triumphal message is like Baciccio's but with a more specific focus on Jesuit missionary work. As at the Gesù, the light of the fresco emanates from a painted sunburst. This time it emerges from the head of St Ignatius, leading to Christ with the Cross and the God the father above, and simultaneously shining down upon St Francis Xavier (just below on the right), other Jesuit saints, non-European converts and four allegories of the continents underneath pairs of false columns on each side of the nave vault. These female figures wear costumes similar to those worn by actors during processions and other spectacles throughout the Catholic world (see Chapter Six). America is shown dressed in a feathered skirt and headdress and accompanied by a puma and toucan; Asia wears a turban and sits astride a camel while angels hand her a Chinese porcelain charger; dark-skinned Africa wears a feathered diadem and holds a tusk while riding a crocodile; while Europe, wearing a golden crown and holding a sceptre and an orb, sits atop a rearing stallion. All four continents expel figures representing Heresy and Paganism. Pozzo's other main contribution at S. Ignazio was the roof of the crossing, which he painted with an ingenious false dome (119), that looks startlingly real when viewed from the centre of the nave. Orazio Grassi, the main architect of the church, had initially planned a real cupola, but he died before the structure was begun and the Jesuits chose not to continue the work. Pozzo's solution, which he published in his architectural treatise *Perspectiva pictorum et architectorum* (Rome, 1693–1700), was such an ingeniously inexpensive answer to the problem that it was imitated throughout northern Italy and especially central Europe.

Like Guarini, Pozzo owes the success of his *composti* north of the Alps largely

117.
Baciccio,
The Triumph of the Name of Jesus, 1676–85.
Fresco; Gesù, Rome

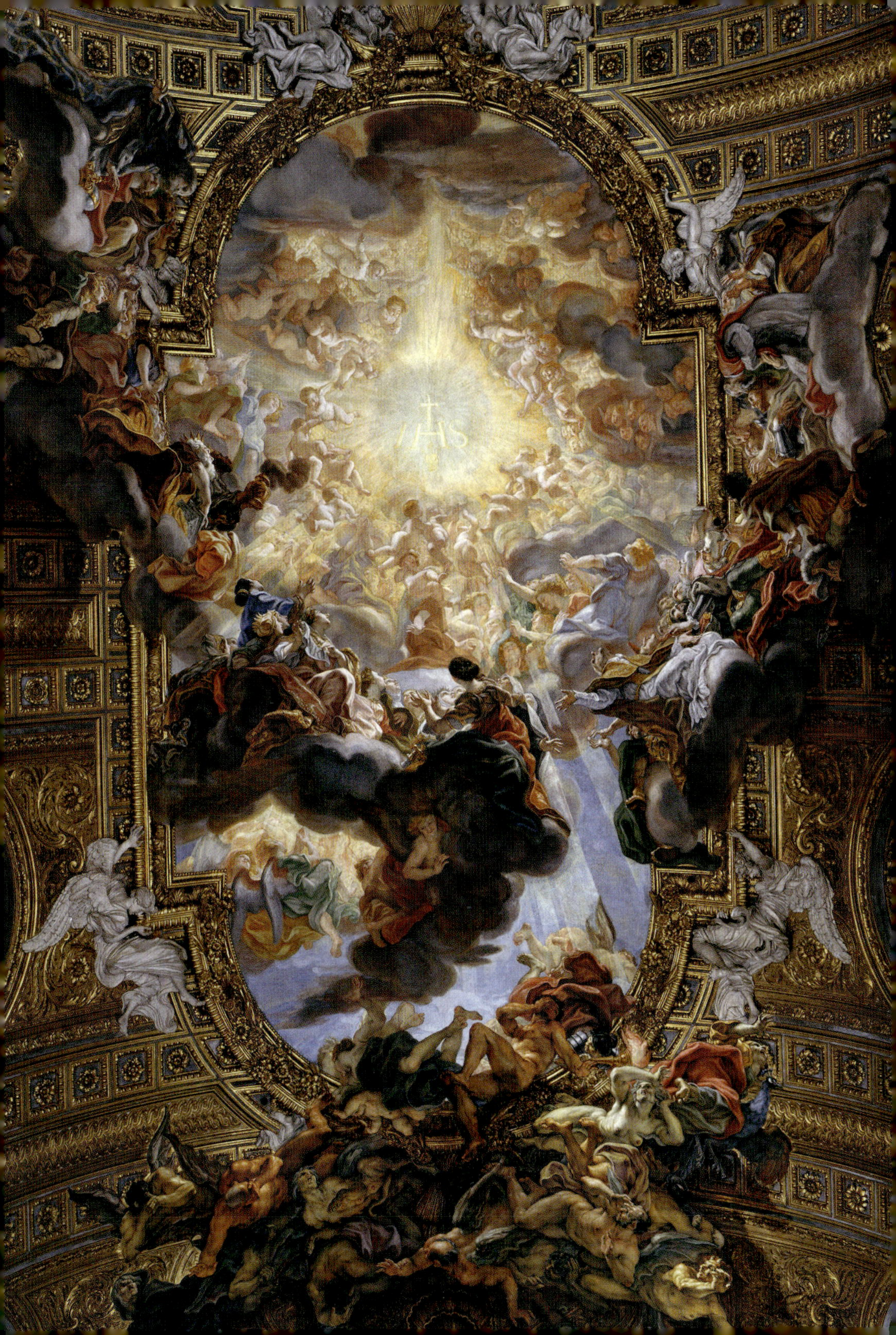

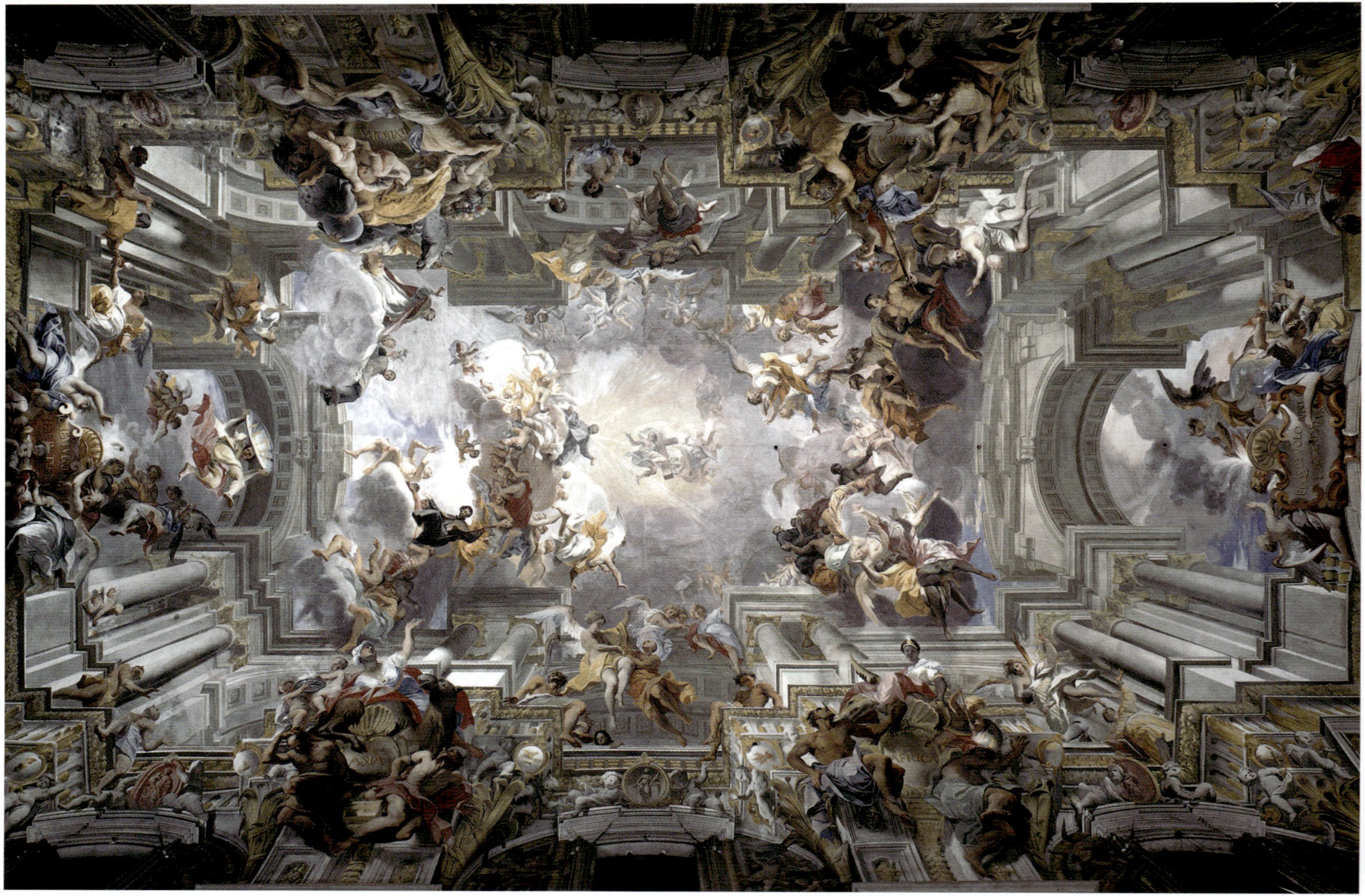

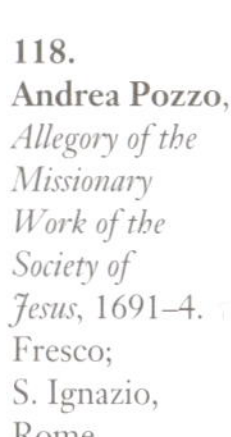

118.
Andrea Pozzo,
Allegory of the
Missionary
Work of the
Society of
Jesus, 1691–4.
Fresco;
S. Ignazio,
Rome

119.
Andrea Pozzo,
false dome,
1684–5.
Fresco;
S. Ignazio,
Rome

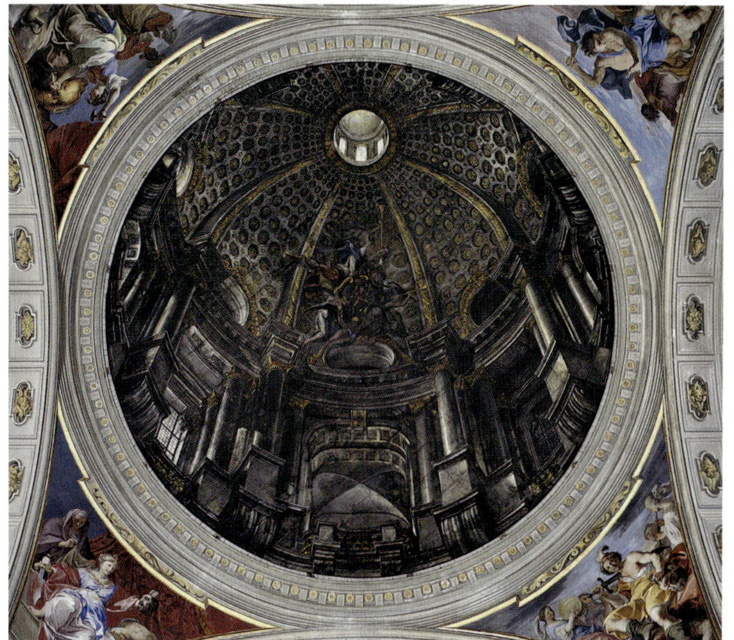

to the dramatic popularity of his manual (the royalties from the first volume alone paid for the S. Ignazio painting). His ideas spread far and wide, so that within a few decades the scenographic structures illustrated in his manual likely inspired the project for the new church of Saint John at the Jesuit university in Vilnius, Lithuania (begun 1737), one of the most important centres of learning in what was then the Polish-Lithuanian Commonwealth (120). Recent scholarship has suggested that Silesian architect Johann Christoph Glaubitz (Jonas Kristupas Gliaubicas, active 1737–1767) sought commonalities with eastern Orthodox tradition – the dominant form of Christianity in the eastern part of the Commonwealth – when he designed this church's extraordinary choir, which features a network of ten altars with bases and crowns of red and grey imitation marble, twenty-six columns of white stucco, eighteen free-standing sculptures (by Jonas Hedelis d. 1764), and white stucco relief panels on three levels. This splendid apparition – it contrasts sharply with the plain whitewashed nave and side aisles of this Hall Church – culminates with an angelic glory above the high altar featuring God the Father and the Holy Spirit showering sunrays onto a scene of the *Baptism of Christ*. An undulating entablature links together the three inner altars like the inner ring of arches at Guarini's S. Lorenzo, resulting in a diaphanous interior that allows multiple glimpses of the inner and outer altars from a single vantage point. This effect may be an attempt to emulate the effect of an *iconostasis*, the wall of multiple icons arranged in rows that separates the sanctuary from the nave in Orthodox churches (see 210). In another echo of Pozzo, the ceiling directly above the altar is painted with an illusionistic cupola featuring another *Baptism of Christ*. Pozzo's ideas travelled even further east when the Jesuits painted illusionistic ceilings and false domes on their mission churches in China.

However, it was in Germanic countries that Pozzo's illusionistic ceilings enjoyed their greatest success. One of the first to adopt this style – we have already seen it in the much later ceiling at Sv. Mikuláš (see 113) – was Cosmas Damian Asam in the abbey church of Weingarten in Swabia, Germany (1718–20), and Asam created infinite variations on Pozzo's ideas over the course of the next two decades. Asam's era was one of extraordinary renewal in Catholic central Europe. Over half a century had passed since the Thirty Years War, and the region was caught in a whirlwind of large-scale church building projects, particularly rural abbeys. By the third decade of the eighteenth century southern Germanic church architecture had firmly crossed the line between Baroque and Rococo, and these interiors reflect that style's lighter touch and pastel colours – pinks, light greens, sky blues and putty yellow – with whitewashed walls and false marble replacing marble and stucco acting as a whimsical organic accent. Inspired by Bacciccio and Pozzo, they allowed their illusionistic ceiling frescos to spill over their frames, but they do so more subtly. The painted figures are smaller, the colours are less intense with less shading, and the frames themselves are irregular, resembling shell or plant forms. Sculptures seem to float in the air. Although these churches evoke a vortex of activity, colour and light, it has less to do with urgency or striving than joy and triumph. The battle of the *paragone* has long been won and the media are now content with decorative play.

One of the finest Rococo descendants of the S. Ignazio ceiling can be found in Johann Michael Fischer's (1692–1766) Benedictine abbey church of Zwiefalten in Swabia (121), where fresco painter Franz Joseph Spiegler (1691–1757) and stucco worker Johann Michael Feichtmayr (1710–1772)

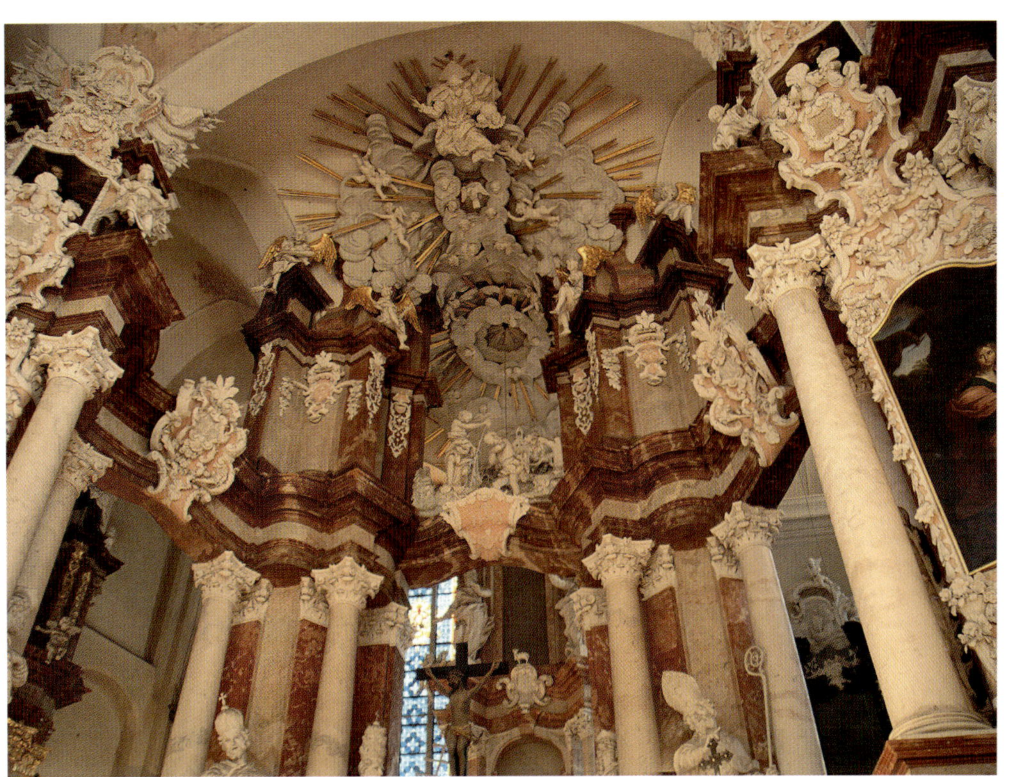

collaborated on the nave vault in the late 1740s and early 1750s. Entitled *Saint Benedict and his Followers Pay Homage to the Virgin Mary and the Holy Trinity* (1751), Spiegler's sprawling fresco dominates the entire nave of the church, drawing our eyes upwards into a dizzying spiral of clouds, bodies, angels and tongues of flame. Its muted tones – browns and greys predominate, along with chastened yellows and purples – harmonize with those of the false marble paired columns and the side altars and unify the main body of the church into a binary dialogue between colour and white, keeping the main focus on the ceiling. Spiegler's architectural setting, clouds and figural groups echo the asymmetrical distribution and licking, flame-like edges of Feichtmayr's masterful Rococo stucco work, which clings like seaweed to the borders of the fresco. Precipitous staircases with concave edges rise from both ends in an irregular zigzag, leading to a ring of pilgrims crowding around the sides of the fresco, including men and women, popes and kings, nuns and monks. These people represent the adherents of specific Benedictine pilgrimage sites to the Virgin, from Einsiedeln (see 6) to Altötting (Bavaria) and Zwiefalten itself, and the royalty and ecclesiastical figures represent historic events surrounding their foundation. Clouds overwhelm the ceiling, offering only the barest glimpses of blue sky. Divine approbation rains down on the multitudes from the Trinity, who in turn acknowledge the Virgin Mary on a cloud below. From Mary's breast a zigzag of divine light reflects off a painting depicting her and the Christ Child (it is a copy of an icon in the Roman church of S. Benedetto in Piscinula), smites the heart of Saint Benedict, and dissipates into tongues of flames that ignite the mystical fervour of a jumble of Benedictine saints in the clouds below. The four stucco cartouches at the corners of the ceiling contain allegorical frescos of vices that must be overcome in gaining the favour of the Virgin Mary. Through the harmonious fusion of architecture, stucco and fresco, the interior of the Zwiefalten church becomes an essay on the benefits of pilgrimage to Marian sites, and of the Benedictine Order in helping ordinary Christians gain the forgiveness of God. Overcome by wave upon wave of sensual stimuli, viewers are assimilated into the mystical drama played out above them, their own imaginations joining the *composto* as surely as the false marble, gilding, stucco and frescos.

Spengler's fresco at Zwiefalten was the beginning of the end of the Rococo's extraordinary flourishing in central and eastern Europe, painted at a time when urban centres were already starting to embrace the soberer lines and visual clarity of Neoclassicism (see Chapter Eight). Its creative and spiritual potential exhausted, Rococo led to intriguing regional variations but not to new styles. For another thirty years or so, Rococo architects, sculptors, stucco workers and painters continued to find ready employment in the countryside, first in the great Benedictine and Premonstratensian abbeys and then in smaller wayside chapels and rural parish churches. In fact, as late as 1815 the Würtemburg painter Josef Anton Mesmer (1747–1827) painted an illusionistic ceiling painting of the *Sermon on the Mount* in the Church of Mary Magdalene in the Swiss lakeside village of Meggen. But instead of being surrounded by Feichtmayr-style stucco cartouches, his fresco is ringed by simple Neoclassical garlands that would be more at home in a library by the English Neoclassical architect Robert Adam (1728–1792) than a church in the heart of Catholic central Europe (see 241).

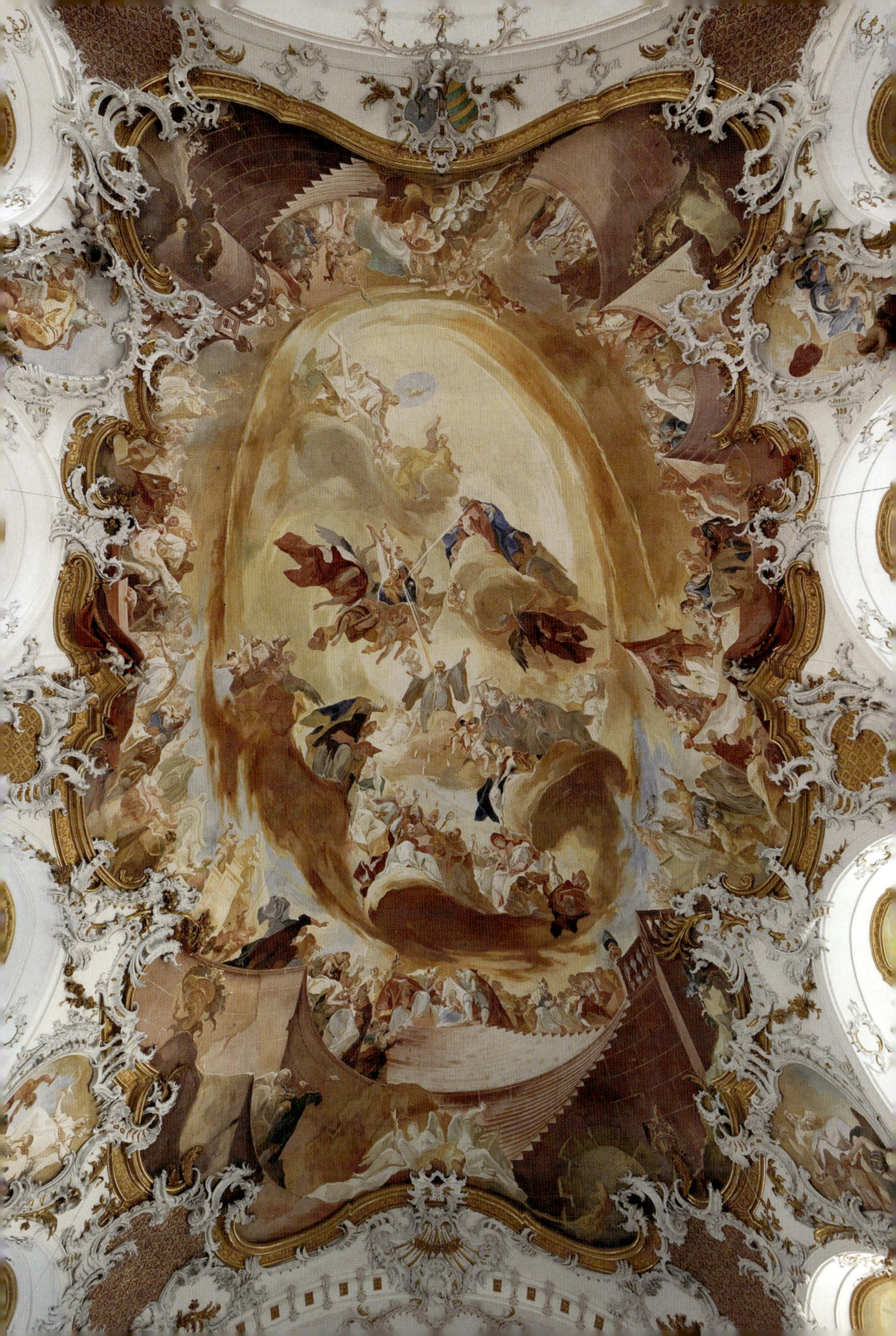

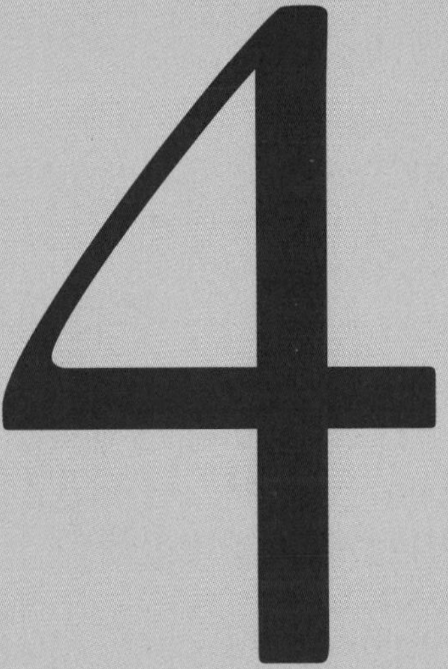

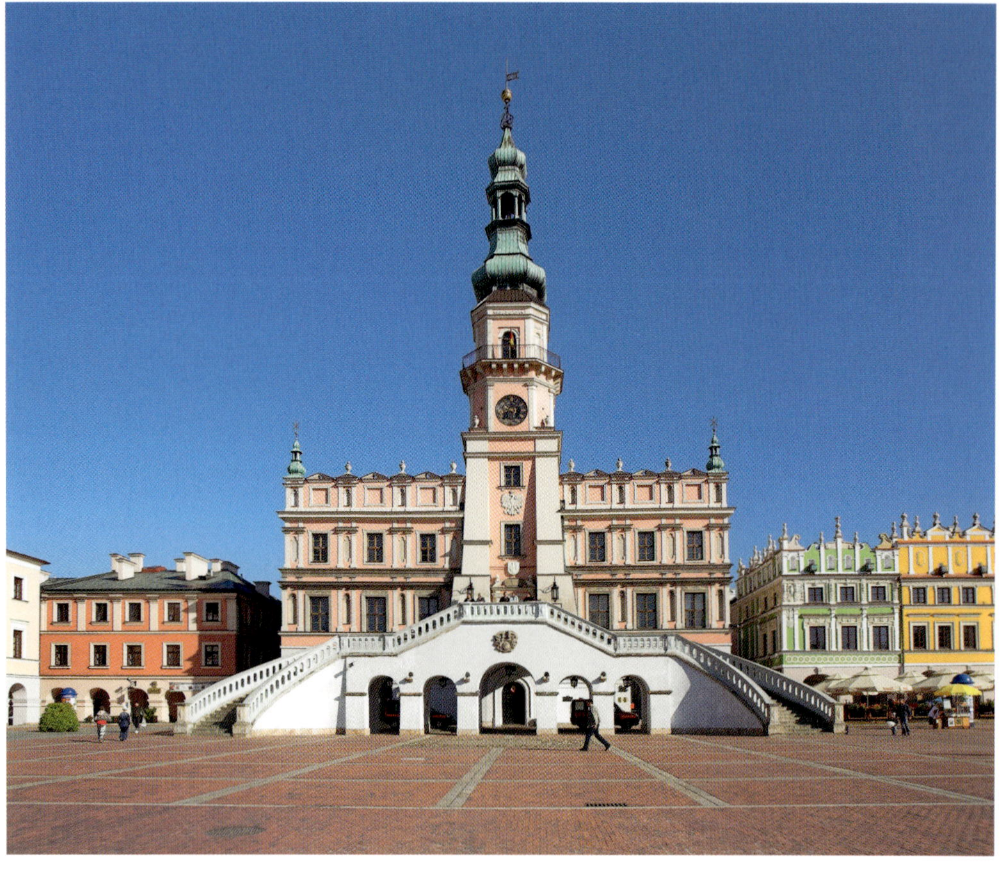

If church interiors provided a meditative space for the next world, their
exteriors were firmly rooted in this one: the city, town and countryside.
In fact, their setting and appearance related them so closely to profane
architecture that this chapter will consider the Baroque exterior as a
whole – encompassing urban spaces, palaces, civic buildings and churches
– concentrating on the complex interrelationship between architecture and
context. Baroque and Rococo buildings sought to seize viewers' attentions
and most tried to dominate their surroundings, whether on a modest scale
such as Francesco Borromini's S. Carlo alle Quattro Fontane in Rome with
its pulsating, outsized façade (see 3) or a mammoth one like the new façade of
the pilgrimage church of Santiago de Compostela, designed to tower over the
city (see 8). However as architects rarely had the advantage of unrestricted
plots with spectacular views, they were also occupied, especially in the cities,
with assimilation. Awkward, puny sites in medieval quarters with congested
streets provided acute challenges, but the best architects rose to the occasion,
turning disadvantages into opportunities, as with the restructured approach,
false wings and protruding porch of S. Maria della Pace, one of the most
original adjustments to demanding surroundings in the annals of architecture
(see 143). Both kinds of building, whether massive citadels on hilltops or tiny
churches in side alleys, used the tricks of the stage to intensify their sense of
awe and wonder – illusionistic perspectives and false backdrops, manipulated
viewpoints and angles of approach – drawing everyday people to participate
in the daily theatre of Church and State and to have faith in the security and
legitimacy of its institutions.

Many of the buildings chosen here are the superstars of Baroque and Rococo
architecture, often the largest, most bombastic, most heavily decorated – and
in many cases most famous – representatives of the style in Europe. Some
attracted attention through the intensity of their ornamentation, notably
in southern Italy and Iberia, where a medieval aesthetic persevered (see
Chapter Three). Such is the Cathedral of S. Agata in Gallipoli, Italy, with

its luxuriant embroidery of garlands and scrolls (see 144) or the jungle-like doorway of the palace of the Marquis de Dos Aguas in Valencia (see 10). But most buildings dominated by scale alone, their exteriors projecting an unexpected sobriety that contrasted markedly with their interiors and intensified the surprise experienced upon entering. Architects employed different strategies to enhance a building's prominence. Some evoked Gothic architecture by exaggerating height and breadth, at times introducing fortress-like appendages such as twin façade towers or bulwarks (see 138, 150). Most reinterpreted and manipulated the building blocks of classical architecture – pilasters, columns and window dressings – transforming them into expressive, sculptural forms. Some architects increased a building's scale or enhanced its surface texture by multiplying these elements and arranging wings and courtyards into enfilades to create the sensation of infinity (see 136). Galleries, colonnades, porches and staircases projected into public spaces, drawing visitors inwards and obscuring the distinction between indoors and outdoors. And by aligning balconies and loggias with sweeping avenues, staircases and garden paths cut out of the surrounding towns and countryside, architects gave their buildings a quintessentially Baroque command over their surroundings – a blunt metaphor for the all-powerful gaze of the functionaries of Church and State. The grandest abbeys and palaces such as Mafra (see 148) or Caserta (see 16) were so gigantic and their exterior decoration so repetitive and impersonal that they recall the Grand Hotels of the nineteenth century or the factories of the Industrial Revolution.

Controlled vistas, regulated traffic and imposed order began with the city itself. A manifestation of power and authority on the grandest scale, Baroque urban planning and renewal was promoted by Church and State alike. It was the first era since antiquity to experience mass migrations into cities, and urban planners took idealistic and sometimes draconian measures to regulate them. The most notable early example was Domenico Fontana's restructuring of Rome's street plan for Pope Sixtus V (see Introduction). But architects had experimented with idealized city schemes since the early Renaissance. Leon Battista Alberti (1404–1472) planned a centralized model city with streets leading to a central piazza and church like the orthogonal lines of linear perspective, and Filarete (Antonio di Pietro Averlino,

c.1400–c.1469) designed a round city named Sforzinda (1451–6) that he
based on the parts of the human body in the belief that a healthy city should
reflect the physiognomy of its inhabitants: like the promoter of a nineteenth-
century sanatorium, Filarete described Sforzinda as 'beautiful and good and
perfectly in accord with the natural order'. But neither of these idealistic
cities saw the light of day. In fact, few such projects came to fruition in
Europe as new cities were prohibitively costly and existing urban areas were
hampered by haphazard street plans and existing churches and palaces that
could not be demolished – only in the Americas, where architects often had a
clean slate to work with, were such cities possible, as in Lima, Peru or Buenos
Aires in present-day Argentina. Even Fontana's avenues in Rome were far
from symmetrical and look nothing like the spokes of a wheel as they are
often described. A rare exception is Palmanova, built in the Veneto in the late
sixteenth century to guard Venice against the Turks, with a centralized, star-
shaped plan and streets radiating at even intervals from the central piazza.

The earliest Baroque ideal city is Zamość (122), built north-east of Krakow
(Poland) by the Italian architect Bernardo Morando (c.1540–1600) for his
utopian patron Lord Chancellor Jan Zamoyski (1542–1605). A centralized
town focusing on a square with radiating streets, Zamość achieves even
greater unity through standardized arcades, yet allows for individuality in
the profiles and ornamentation of the upper storeys. Although the town
had multiple places of worship – extraordinarily, it included churches for
Catholics, Lutherans, Armenians and Ukranians, as well as a synagogue – it
converged on the splendid town hall in its main square (1639–51). Raised
on a giant basement level and fronted by a sweeping double staircase
(added in the eighteenth century), it projects civic authority, enhanced by a
soaring, thickly buttressed tower that contrasts pointedly with the horizontal
streetscape. As with so many central European towers after the mid-sixteenth
century, it is crowned with an intricate onion dome, an architectural feature
originating in Prague that – despite its similarity to Eastern Orthodox
church towers – is a combination of Italian Renaissance and Gothic forms.
Another ideal city was only made possible by an earthquake. The southern
Sicilian city of Noto, flattened in 1693, was rebuilt 10 kilometres (16 miles)
away according to a scheme by Jesuit architect Angelo Italia (1628–1701),

and construction lingered well into the eighteenth century under Rosario
Gagliardi, Vincenzo Sinatra and Paolo Labisi (123). Built on a grid plan
converging on the cathedral square, bisected by straight avenues, and
peppered with symmetrically disposed *piazze*, churches and government
buildings, Noto drew as much on Renaissance models as on Baroque
renovations in Palermo, Italia's home town. But Noto was far from utopian.
The Spanish viceroy had made the decision to move the city over the protests
of the townspeople, chaotic slums were kept hidden behind elegant façades,
and town planners refused to plant trees despite the sweltering heat because
aristocrats used carriages and the architects felt that trees would spoil their view.

Where entire cities could not be rebuilt, patrons and architects compensated
by carving out spacious and symmetrical squares, often with avenues
radiating out at perpendicular angles and focusing on a fountain, statue or
obelisk. One of the earliest, and the oldest public square in Paris, is the Place
des Vosges (formerly Place Royale), commissioned by Henry IV probably
after plans by Baptiste du Cerceau (1545–1590; 124). This gated residential
park in the fashionable Marais district was surrounded by terrace houses
and became a model for the rest of Europe, particularly London where such
spaces are known as 'garden squares'. All four sides are enclosed by uniform
red-brick houses on a continuous arcade – unlike Zamość (see 122) the
façades are relentlessly similar with their tall windows, grey stone quoins and
bands, their individuality marked only by dips in their pitched roofs. The
only departure from this pattern is the pair of higher pavilions that confront
each other across the north/south axis, dedicated to the king and queen.
Although originally meant to house artisans, the square and surrounding
Marais district quickly became the preserve of the nobility. Today trees make
it nearly impossible to appreciate the logic and unity of the Place des Vosges
– in the final analysis, the planners of Noto may have had a point.

The most famous Baroque space in the world is Gianlorenzo Bernini's
St Peter's Square. The largest in western Europe, it was built for Pope
Alexander VII in a miraculously short time between 1656 and 1667 (125,
126). Like a pair of arms embracing all Christendom – the conceit of the
church 'stretching out its arms maternally to receive Catholics' was Bernini's

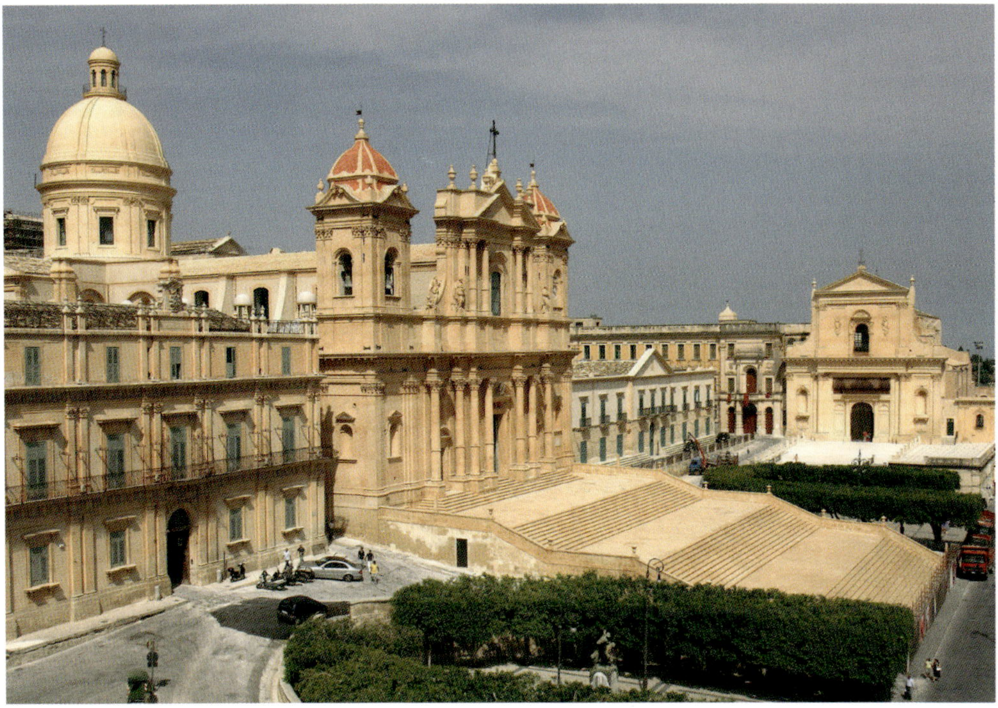

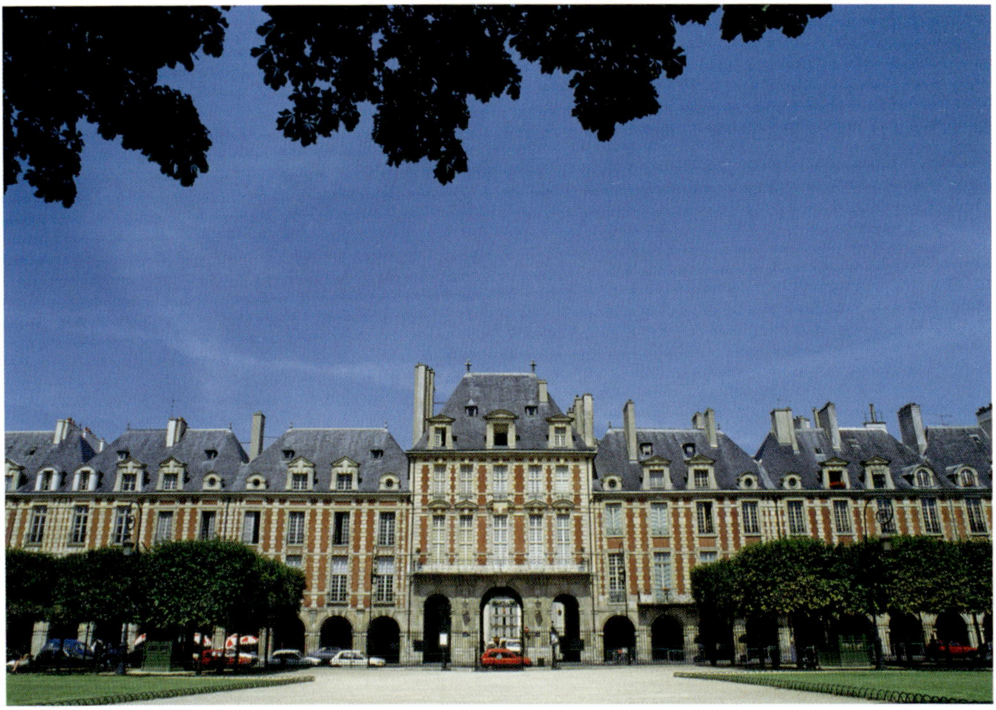

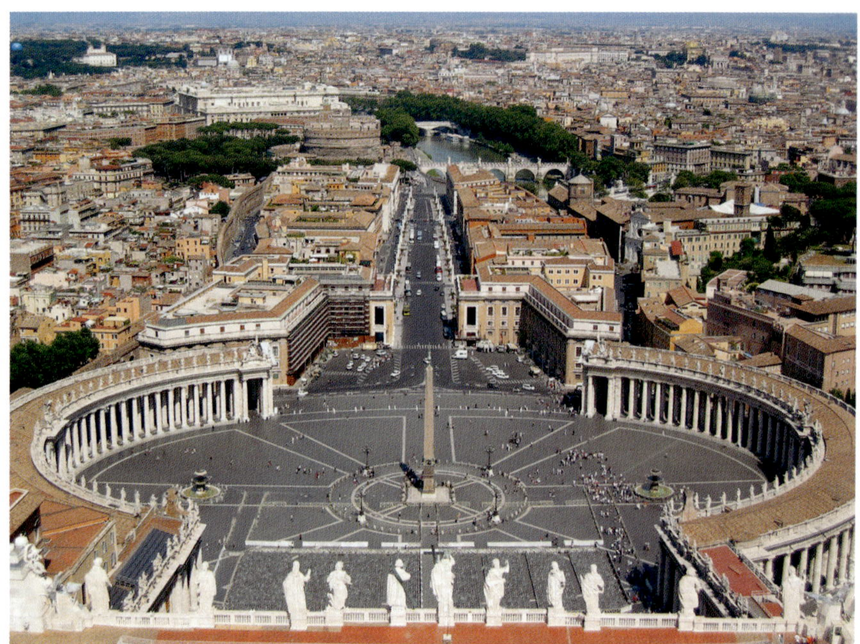

own – the sweeping wings encompass an oval outer piazza called the *piazza obliqua* and an inner trapezoidal square known as the *piazza retta*. The 284 free-standing Doric columns that make up the colonnade around the *piazza obliqua* are massive yet permeable. Lacking an outer wall they allow free access from all sides and form two covered walkways, an effective way of accommodating huge crowds of pilgrims – as crucial a need then as now. As visitors walk across the piazza the columns slip behind each other like the shutters of a camera lens, at times lining up to reveal a view of the streets behind them – once open gardens – and at times overlapping to block it. Another surprise awaits those who stand on either of a pair of porphyry stones in the pavement between the obelisk at the hub of the square and a pair of lateral fountains (1614, 1667) on the cross axis. Here, as if by magic, the four rows of columns in the nearest arm line up to create the illusion of a single colonnade. Ninety-six statues of saints on the colonnade's entablature greet the faithful and enhance the square's festive ambience, an appropriate sensation for a covered walkway intended in part to provide shelter for religious processions. Bernini wanted to heighten the sense of surprise by adding a third arm between the ends of the other two so that the immensity of the square would be concealed until visitors pass through

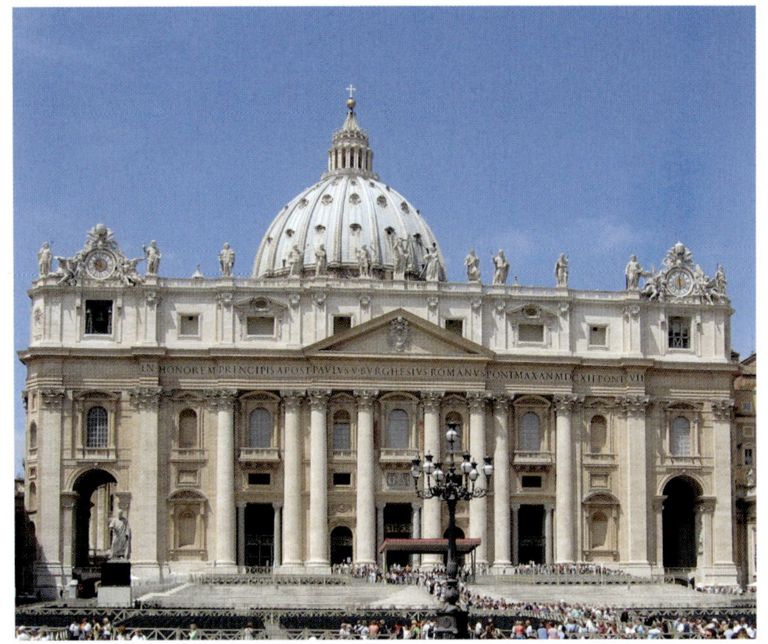

narrow passageways. This structure was never built and the hoped-for effect forever destroyed when Benito Mussolini carved the oversized Via della Conciliazione out of the surrounding neighbourhood to allow a direct view of the basilica from the River Tiber.

Bernini's creation gives the illusion of geometrical purity, a circle (in fact an oval) leading to a square (in fact a trapezoid) – *the piazze retta* was constricted by the position of the medieval Vatican Palace on the right, as you approach the church. Bernini 'improves' the proportions of the basilica (the façade was generally considered too wide) by keeping his colonnades low in relation to the church to enhance the basilica's verticality. As the *piazza obliqua* appears to be circular it makes visitors feel that they are advancing more quickly towards the basilica than they actually are – as if by magnetic attraction. Bernini played the same optical trick on a much smaller scale at S. Andrea al Quirinale (see 99, 100). The *piazza retta* has a similar effect when viewed from the basilica, looking longer than it actually is. Thanks to a natural incline in the ground, the façade and its prominent benediction loggia seem to tower over the viewer like an enormous theatrical backdrop, with the pope's addresses being the main performance.

At St Peter's Square fountains were used to align the cross axis with the obelisk. Monumental fountains are one of the most characteristic forms of the Baroque, not only as foci for public spaces but also as a metaphor for the Church's or State's capacity to control the waters and provide sustenance to the people. The aqueduct and twenty-seven fountains built by Sixtus V as part of his restructuring of the city are the most ambitious pre-Baroque examples of this idea. No longer mere basins surmounted by pedestals and statues, Baroque fountains took on architectural proportions capable of competing with churches and palaces for attention. One of the largest and most influential was the Fountain of the Four Rivers in Rome's Piazza Navona, Bernini's celebration of the reign of Pope Innocent X Pamphilj (r. 1644–55; 127). Although the Piazza Navona long pre-dated the Baroque – it was a Roman racetrack renovated by Pope Sixtus IV in the late fifteenth century as a market – Innocent transformed it into a statement of papal and dynastic authority that also incorporated a family palace (1644–50). Although not connected to a network of radiating streets that could provide dramatic angles of approach, the piazza astonished visitors by its sudden emergence from its congested surroundings. Bernini's fountain is at the centre of the square and aligned with the (at the time unfinished) church of S. Agnese in Agone (see 142) to form its cross axis. If Sixtus V's aqueduct and fountains symbolized his power over the waters of Rome, Bernini's represented the papacy's command over those of the entire world. The four rivers – the Danube (Europe), Nile (Africa), Ganges (Asia) and Río de la Plata (America) – represented the three continents where Catholic missionaries operated as well as Europe, where the Danube symbolizes the papacy's victory over Protestantism and the Ottoman Turks (the river ran through Lutheran and Turkish territory). The Roman river gods that serve as allegories for the rivers underscore the papacy's repossession of Rome's imperial past, and the dove crowning the obelisk, a Pamphilj heraldic symbol, more specifically links that reclamation to the papal family.

The Fountain of the Four Rivers is an impressive accumulation of Baroque conceits. Its base, carved of travertine marble by Bernini's pupils, looks like a natural rock form – drawing upon the Roman tradition of nymphaea, or artificial grottos in suburban palaces – yet it is carved by human hands

**127.
Gianlorenzo
Bernini,**
Fountain of the
Four Rivers,
1648–51.
Rome

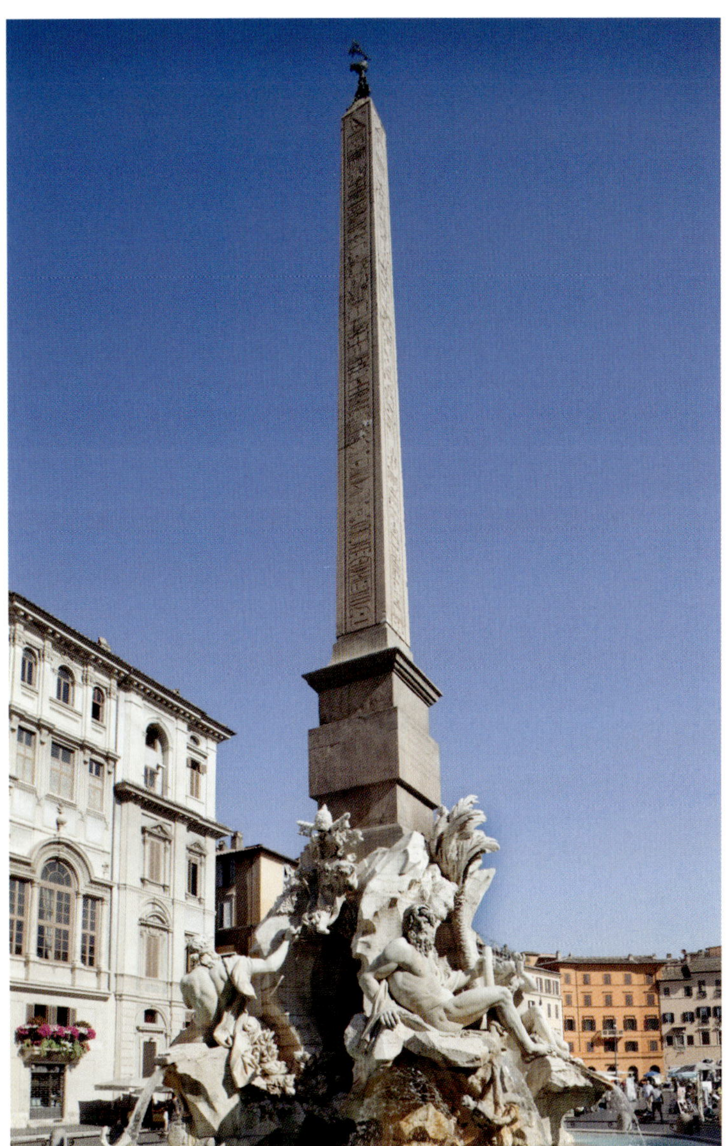

(compare with 5). Likewise, its churning waters were planned like a work

of sculpture. The fountain supports a 54-foot-tall (16.5 m) Egyptian obelisk

rescued from the Circus of Maxentius with a linear profile that contrasts

with the craggy rock face below and responds to the church across the

square. Yet the fountain is tunnelled out at its base, making it seem too weak

to support the obelisk – like Guarini's pendentives at S. Lorenzo in Turin

(compare with 110). Even the way the architect presented his design and

finished fountain to the pope was calculated to astonish and delight. In 1648
Bernini arranged to have the model secretly deposited in a room in the papal
palace where Pope Innocent stumbled upon it by accident, winning him the
commission over his rival Borromini. Bernini's biographer Filippo Baldinucci
(1624–1696) immortalized the pope's famous response: 'it will be necessary
to make use of Bernini … since those who do not want his works must not
look at them'. Likewise, when the pope visited the fountain at its unveiling in
1651, Bernini pretended that the waterworks were not complete, and as the
pope departed in disappointment Bernini turned them on as if by magic. Like
his *Pluto and Proserpina* (see 50), the Fountain of the Four Rivers is best seen
from all sides, revealing diverse prospects to viewers as they circumnavigate
it: each of the cave-like openings is different, as are the physiognomies and
gestures of the flanking river gods who become increasingly agitated as
we walk around it clockwise. The apparent lightness of the materials, the
theatricality of the roaring waters, and the accretion of allegorical figures
and symbols – in addition to the gods there are natural wonders from the
four corners of the globe including an armadillo and a cactus – all recall
ephemeral festival and processional structures with their plaster sculptures
and imitation marble walls. Bernini was an enthusiastic designer of such
structures, as we will see in Chapter Six.

Exactly a century later, French sculptor Barthélémy Guibal (1699–1757)
built two of the most sumptuous fountains of the Rococo, the Fountains of
Neptune and Amphitrite in the Place Royale (now Place Stanislas) in Nancy
(128), for the ex–King of the Polish-Lithuanian Commonwealth and Duke
of Lorraine, Stanisław Leszczyński. The marble and bronze fountains with
their bronze sculptures of the two Greek sea deities stand before delicate
gilded wrought-iron grilles by Jean Lamour (1698–1771). The fountain of
Amphitrite is flanked by gates leading from the *place* to a formal garden,
a transition from the rigid world of royal authority to the placid, carefree
domain of nature. The lilting contours and permeability of the grillwork
dramatize this shift through their contrast with the imposing and classically
severe architecture of the square. The Fountain of Neptune, flanked by two
smaller fountains instead of gates, allows generous views of the now ruined
garden through grilles sprinkled with gilded motifs that look, appropriately,

128.
Barthélémy Guibal, Fountain of Neptune, 1752–5. Nancy (France)

like shells and marine plants. Like Bernini's Fountain of the Four Rivers
(see 127), the fountains feature artificial rock formations, complete with
clinging stalactites, palm fronds and seaweed. Leaning over an oyster
shell-shaped cascade surrounded by river gods, animals and a conch-playing
putto, Neptune pulls his trident back as if about to hurl it into the square.
One of the two boys in the smaller fountains spears a dolphin and so
teasingly mimics Neptune's pose. But despite the sculptures' playfulness
and the graceful lines of the metalwork, the setting of the Fountain of

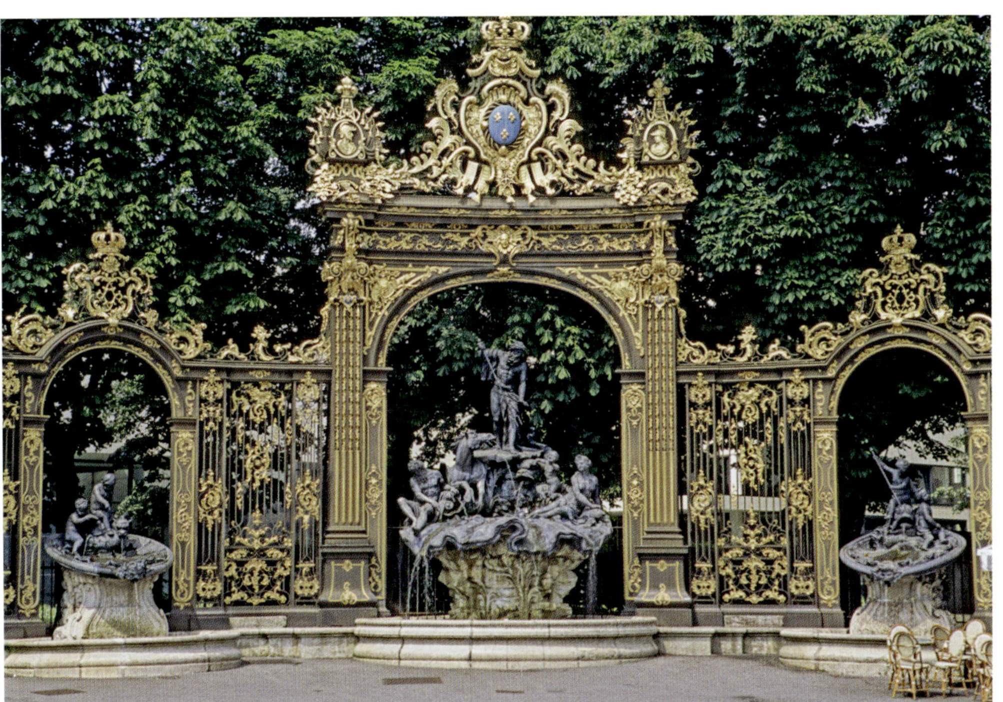

Neptune is no less a celebration of royal authority than the formal square
it faces: the grille has three arches like a Roman triumphal arch, its
ornament is symmetrical and ordered, and it is adorned with martial,
trophy-like finials, and lavish gilded crests dominated by the brilliant blue
of the Bourbon arms.

Fountains were only one way to draw attention to the centre of a public
space. Another common structure is the monumental votive column,

built in thanksgiving for protection from military attack (as with the Trinity
Column in Linz, Austria, 1723), earthquake (for example, the *guglia*, or
spire, of the Virgin Immaculate in Nardò, southern Italy, 1743), or plague
(the *guglia* of Saint Dominic in Naples, 1656–1737). As noted in earlier
chapters, the bubonic plague was the scourge of Europe, decimating cities
with grim regularity. The Trinity Column, or Pestsäule (Plague Column),
in Vienna was commissioned by Emperor Leopold I during the catastrophic
pestilence of 1679 (129). It was begun by Matthias Rauchmiller (1645–1686)
and completed after his death by Johann Bernhard Fischer von Erlach

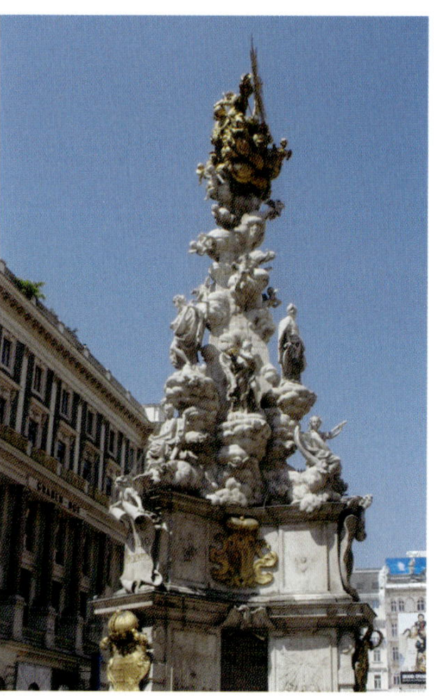

129.
Matthias Rauchmiller and Johann Bernhard Fischer von Erlach, Pestsäule (Plague Column), 1682 and 1694. Vienna

130.
Gianlorenzo Bernini, Angels with the Instruments of the Passion, 1668–9. Marble; over lifesize. Ponte Sant'Angelo, Rome

(1656–1723), arguably the most important Baroque architect in the German-
speaking world and designer of the city's cyclopean Karlskirche (begun 1716)
and the Great Hall of Vranov Castle (see 160). The Pestsäule occupies the
Graben, an oblong public space that is like a rectangular Piazza Navona, and
it recalls Bernini's Fountain of the Four Rivers (see 127) in its obelisk-like
profile and illusionistic sculptural work. However there is no sensation of
lightness here: Rauchmiller and Fischer von Erlach place the column on a
solid, three-winged plinth with bas-reliefs, inscriptions and gilded heraldic
devices. Here the illusion is not of rock face but of cloudbursts teeming
with allegorical figures and angels and incorporating an image of Leopold

I at prayer. At the top a gilded bronze Trinity – the focus of the king's supplications – seizes our attention through its sparkling contrast with the matte grey of the column. The clouds of the obelisk echo Bernini's Cathedra Petri (see 102), and like its model the Vienna column was inspired by ephemeral structures, in this case sets by the opera stage designer Lodovico Burnacini (1636–1707), who helped Fischer von Erlach complete the column. Burnacini's clouds give the sensation of a miraculous vision descended from Heaven, turning the Graben into a giant *composto* – and thereby transforming an exterior into an interior space.

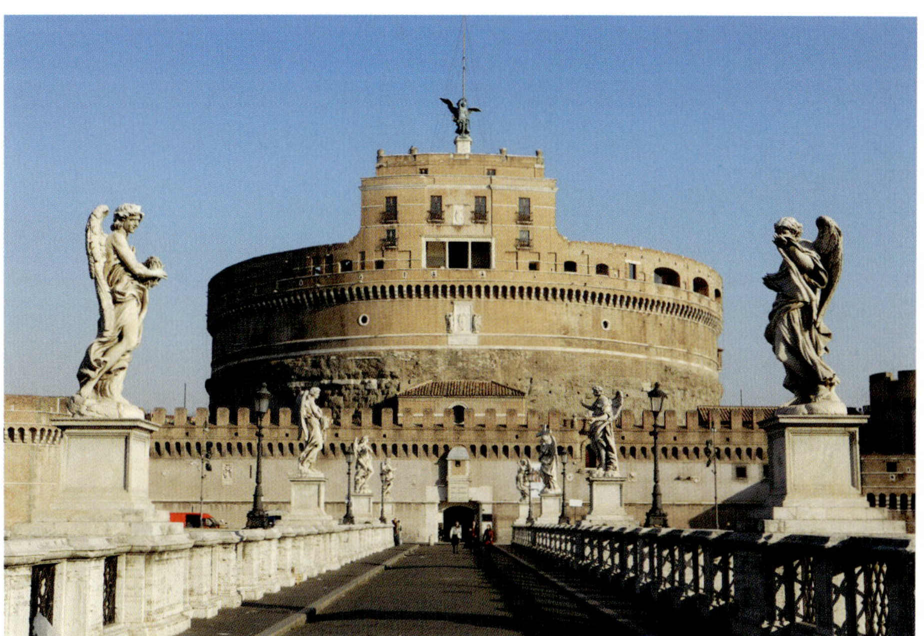

The *bel composto* also inspired another Baroque genre, the bridge of statues. The earliest was the Ponte Sant'Angelo in Rome (130), adorned by Bernini with a series of marble angels carrying the instruments of the Passion carved by his pupils, and now replaced with copies. A bridge provides an ideal setting for a *composto*, as viewers' movements are restricted and their experience of the sculptures is easier to manipulate. Sculptures on bridges also have the added benefit of evoking a sacred procession as people walk past them, an effect Bernini achieved here with his sequence of sorrowful angels clad in windswept drapery who seem to be swaying to and fro in lamentation. A much more ambitious project, if not as coordinated, was the

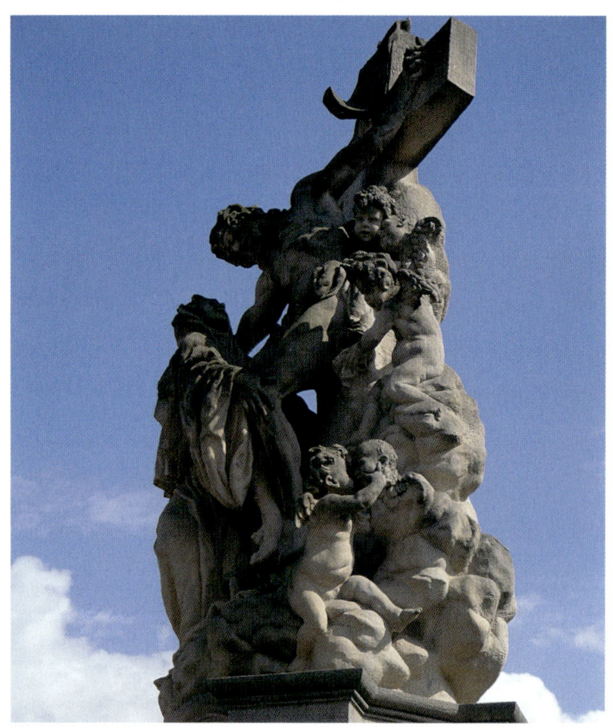

series of statues designed mostly by Johann Brokoff (1652–1718) and his son Ferdinand Maximilian (1688–1731) for the fourteenth-century Charles Bridge (Karlův Most) in Prague between 1682 and 1711. The earliest is Johann's bronze *St John Nepomuk*, a Czech martyr who fell to his death off this very bridge – it became the model for countless central European wayside statues – but later contributions tended to be group pieces like Matthias Bernhard Braun's *Saint Luitgard* (131), in which the saint embraces the Crucified Christ surrounded by grieving *putti* and emerging from a spiralling nest of clouds like those of the Vienna Pestsäule (see 129). Her expression is muted, her emotions revealed by the exaggerated gestures of the *putti* and the heavy, flame-like folds of her cloak that recall the cowl of Bernini's Saint Teresa (see 96). The sequence of biblical and saintly figures on the Charles Bridge evokes popular devotions such as the Litany of the Saints and recalls the organization of iconography in early Baroque churches (Chapter One).

So far this chapter has considered public spaces and the ways they focused peoples' attention, directing their gazes through angles of approach, emotive statues, massive columns and noisy fountains. However, of all the architectural types treated in this book none is as consistently domineering as the palace, the most palpable symbol of temporal power. The largest and most visually impressive were in rural or suburban settings where they could expand as far into the countryside as finances would allow. By contrast, urban palaces faced the challenge of assimilating into pre-existing townscapes, particularly in Rome where even the palaces of the most powerful were wedged into small and difficult plots. There was little opportunity to build structures comparable to the great Renaissance palaces like the Palazzo Farnese (1517–89), a massive rectangular block open on all sides that towers over an entire neighbourhood. Baroque architects were challenged to overcome their constricted surroundings and make their buildings compete with neighbouring palaces, churches and piazzas. Bernini's Roman Palazzo Montecitorio (formerly Ludovisi; 132) is an early essay in this kind of urban accommodation. Faced with a demanding plot of land – awkwardly wide, on the slope of a hill and restricted by houses on the south side of the square – Bernini created a building that projected a seemingly effortless image of authority and grandeur. The palace was begun for the Pamphilj family, and although work was interrupted on the death of Innocent X Pamphilj and the building only completed in 1694 by Carlo Fontana (1634/8–1714), much of Bernini's original conception is preserved, particularly in the façade.

Bernini turned the site's drawbacks into opportunities. In spite of its irregular shape the square afforded a dramatic view of the palace from a distance. The length of the site allowed him to design the longest palace façade in Rome – it is twenty-five windows wide, compared with thirteen at the Palazzo Farnese – and as he was unhindered by height he was able to make it tower over the adjacent Palazzo Aldobrandini-Chigi (begun 1588), thus downplaying the palace of a rival papal family. Even the buildings restricting the structure across the square – they made a flat façade impossible – became an advantage. Bernini took the unprecedented step of having both wings of the palace slope back from the central block, so that the wall sections meet at obtuse angles. Set in the middle of this convex façade, the main entrance seems to advance into the piazza, particularly when the building is approached from the sides. Bernini further stressed the building's width

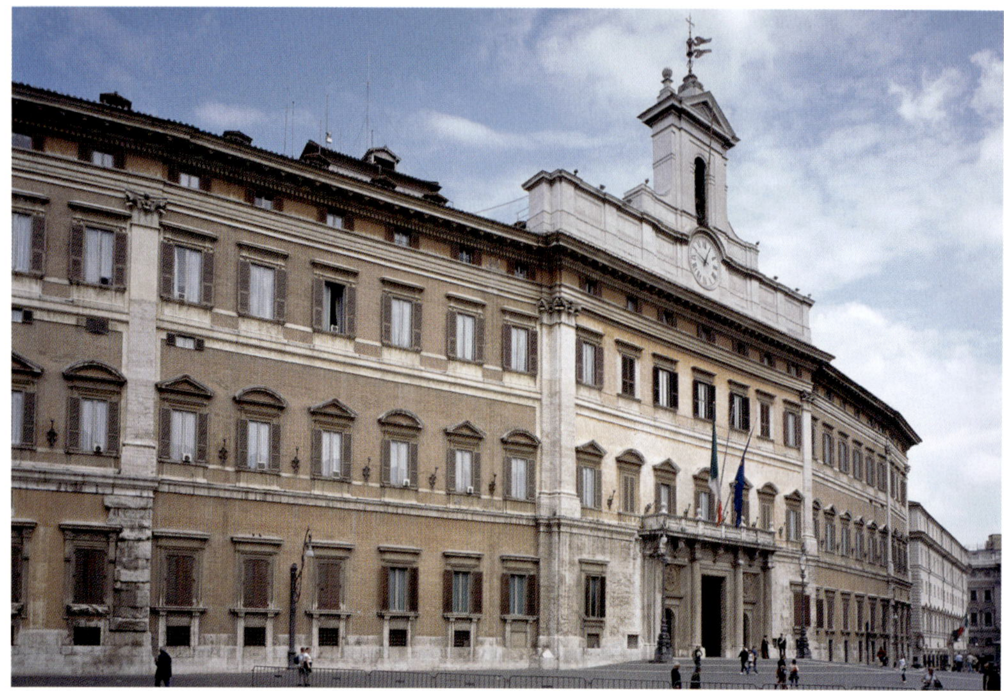

by removing vertical divisions between the windows, allowing the thick, belt-like entablatures separating the three storeys to draw the eyes in a horizontal sweep. The only vertical elements are the giant order pilasters on high plinths that frame the façade's two tower-like terminations and its central block. This use of giant order pilasters not only draws attention to the building's scale but also provides frames for the five sections of the façade. Bernini has the corner 'towers' incorporate components of fortification architecture such as rusticated pilasters – a decorative approach more suitable to an opera set than a building. The rustication is especially creative: carved to look like natural rock face (like the Four Rivers Fountain) it crawls into the window sills and pediments. The simplicity and vigour of the Montecitorio façade made it one of the most influential Baroque façades in Europe.

An even more challenging palace project – and ingenious solution – was Francesco Borromini's reconstruction of the Collegio di Propaganda Fide (133), the office of the papal congregation in charge of handling global missionary work. Borromini was challenged to enlarge an existing building on an irregular plot that was attached to adjacent structures on either side and open onto the Via di Propaganda – a street so narrow that it is nearly impossible to photograph the whole façade at once. The façade was his most significant intervention. Since he could not attract attention from the front, he advertised the building from the sides, pushing the language of classical architecture to its limit in his desire to dominate the street. Together with his giant order of pilasters (possibly an homage to St Peter's Basilica, see 126, and therefore a symbol of Papal power) he uses a dramatically projecting cornice and oversized window and door dressings to cast deep shadows over the wall: the façade is like a giant confined to a small cage. Borromini makes the central bay dip back from the street yet push outwards in the entablature, the cornice and angled pilasters of the door, and the cornice and convex central bay of the window frame to draw attention towards the middle of the building, a characteristic interplay of concave and convex surfaces like that of S. Carlo alle Quattro Fontane (see 3). He distinguishes the palace from the adjacent buildings by canting the outer pair of pilasters on a diagonal, suggesting that the façade projects forwards in a way it cannot. Borromini invents unorthodox capitals, removes the traditional architrave or frieze from his cornice, and transforms pediments into fancifully shaped, permeable window caps (the attic was added in the eighteenth century and draws attention away from the cornice). He further enlivens the façade by alternating the window dressings – those of the flanking six bays are also concave to counteract the convex central window – with the most complex variation in the centre. No one walking down the Via di Propaganda can fail to be impressed by this bold, looming creation, either coming from the Spanish steps, where it is best seen from a distance, or the Via di S. Andrea delle Fratte, where it appears suddenly around a corner.

Few obstacles faced architects of country palaces, and as a result they are vastly different in scale. The largest – and most influential – of all Baroque palaces is the Château of Versailles, Louis XIV's megalomaniacal statement of royal authority outside Paris (see 135). But Versailles was not the earliest palace in the grand Baroque manner that became known as the 'Louis XIV style'. In fact, Louis (r. 1643–1715) and his avaricious advisor Jean-Baptiste Colbert (1619–1683) quite literally stole that style from someone else, the former *Surintendent* of Finances, Nicolas Fouquet (1615–1680). An unwisely

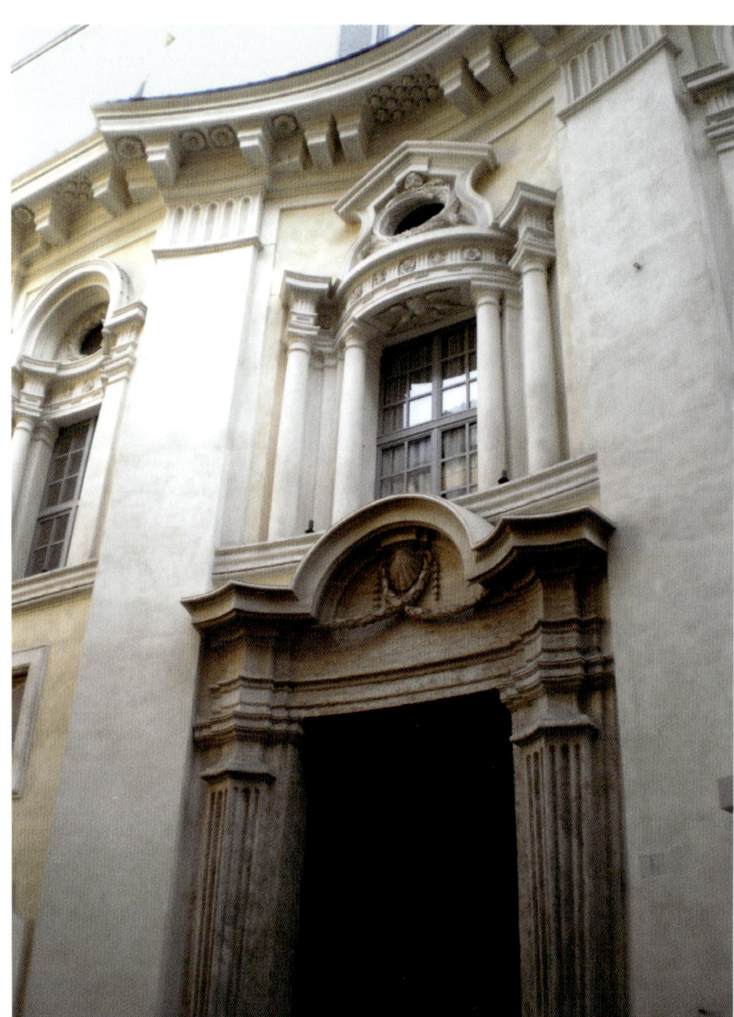

**133.
Francesco
Borromini**,
Collegio di
Propaganda
Fide, 1654–67.
Rome

ambitious man, Fouquet flaunted his wealth not only by commissioning
the splendid and innovative château and gardens at Vaux-le-Vicomte (134),
a few hours' ride from Paris, but also by inviting the king and his entire
court to a housewarming party, complete with a ballet and fireworks, on
17 August 1661. Not to be outdone by a mere finance minister, the young
king arrested Fouquet for embezzlement three weeks later, imprisoned him
for life, confiscated his château and lands, and arranged to have Colbert (now
the new finance minister) requisition Fouquet's entire team of architects,
garden designers, sculptors, painters, poets and musicians. He even took
some of Fouquet's garden statues and trees.

Vaux-le-Vicomte was the first collaboration between three of France's greatest artistic talents – all would work again at Versailles – architect Louis Le Vau (1612–1670), painter Charles Le Brun (1619–1690) and one of the most influential garden designers of all time, André Le Nôtre (1613–1700; see Chapter Six). Built with alacrity, Vaux was an amalgamation of architectural solutions adopted from contemporary country mansions, notably Le Vau's own Le Raincy (begun 1643), which introduced the idea of an oval *grand salon* in the centre. But whereas the oval at Le Raincy projected from both the front and garden façades, at Vaux it is only visible on the garden side, a surprise awaiting visitors as they walk around the rectilinear house and the focus of the entire formal garden. The *salon* is preceded by a square vestibule and flanked by two apartment wings, one for visiting royalty and the other for Fouquet and his family. Viewed from the garden side, the steep, traditionally French, roofs of the wings (compare 124) balance the dome of the oval, and the principal part of the château, separated from its service wings, rises like an island at the top of the gently sloping garden parterre. The house is best seen from the top of the grotto, across a canal on the same axis as the oval, or even more dramatically from the grassy heights of the hill behind the grotto, 1,500 metres (4,900 feet) away at the base of a giant statue of Hercules. Although the restored fountains, statues, reflecting pools and topiaries visible today give us a sense of the grandeur of the original garden, much of Le Nôtre's vision has been destroyed after centuries of neglect.

Louis XIV's remodelling of the Château of Versailles (135), formerly his father's comparably modest hunting lodge (1624), was the Baroque's prototypical symbol of divinely guided authority. Nearly bankrupting the nation and employing 22,000 workers a day to construct, it also revealed the dark side of such grandiose schemes. Like other absolutist monarchs, Louis demanded in 1682 that the landed gentry spend part of the year in his palace – allowing him to keep their independence in check – and he compelled them to take part in elaborate rituals focusing on the king as an embodiment of Apollo, the ancient Sun God. Such rituals, including the infamous *lever*, the rising of the king in the morning that involved nobles handing him his clothes and staff attending to his toilette, turned the palace into a giant theatre, with the king's bedchamber at the literal centre of the far-flung structure. The palace was enlarged in several stages, including an intervention by Jules Hardouin-Mansart (1646–1708) in 1678 that involved the addition of the Hall of Mirrors and the gigantic north and south wings. Like most despotic architecture, Versailles is oppressive and monotonous, lacking the charm of Vaux despite being built, decorated and laid out by the same team. As the courtier Duc de Saint-Simon aptly put it, 'it presents the distressing appearance of some vast hearse … one might be forever pointing out the monstrous defects of that huge and immensely costly palace'. On the entrance side, a vortex-like trio of courtyards, flanked by the palace's

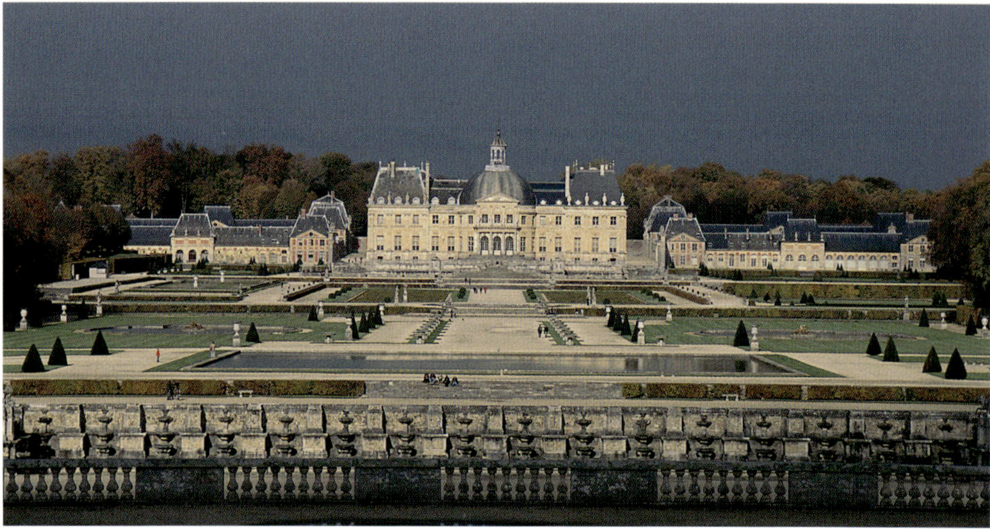

two elongated wings, draws the visitor forwards in an authoritarian twist on Bernini's arms at St Peter's (see 125). On the garden side, a 2-mile (3 km) vista of parterres, *alleés*, pools and canals symbolized the Sun King's command of the furthest reaches of his realm (see Chapter Six).

Although mitigated by the golden colour of the stone, the garden façade – it consists of a projection of the main palace block and Mansart's two side wings – is cold and repetitive, with a rusticated ground floor, Ionic pilasters flanking monumental windows on the first floor, and an attic with square windows and pilasters. Its sobriety was directly inspired by Louis' renovations of the Palais du Louvre in Paris, where Le Brun, Le Vau and Claude Perrault designed a Corinthian colonnade on the east front (1667–70) using a strict academic classicism that was to dominate French architecture for nearly a century and a half. Decoration on the Versailles garden façade is minimal, with a few statues marking the colonnaded projections from the façade and finials and trophy-like bundles of arms punctuating the roof. The seemingly endless horizontal extension of the palace – the walls have a total length of 580 metres (1,900 feet) – is created by the continuous rustication, a heavy, plain entablature on the first floor and a flat Italian-style roof and balustrade – possibly influenced by Bernini's rejected plans for the Louvre. Few pre-

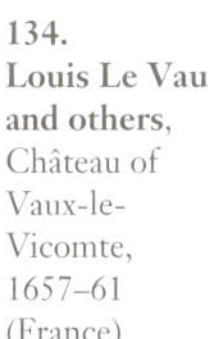

134.
Louis Le Vau and others,
Château of Vaux-le-Vicomte, 1657–61 (France)

135.
Louis Le Vau and others,
Château of Versailles, 1668–71 (France)

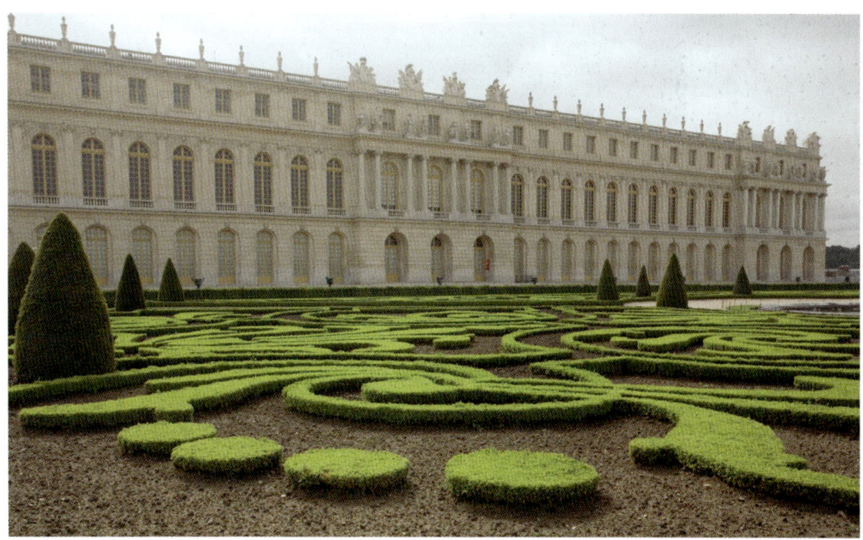

modern monuments were able so effectively to suggest the infinite. Only Le Brun's interiors (see Chapter Five) and Le Nôtre's splendid gardens (see Chapter Six) do something to mitigate the palace's monotony.

The Château at Versailles generated countless imitations, ranging from the dull and ponderous (as at Caserta, see 16) to the capricious (as at Queluz). One of the most original variations on the conceit of Versailles of infinite extension is the Rococo royal hunting lodge of the House of Savoy at Stupinigi, 6¼ miles (10 km) southwest of Turin (136). Built by the Sicilian architect and set designer Filippo Juvarra (1678–1736) for the Duke of

Savoy and King of Sicily Vittorio Amedeo II, Stupinigi is the most literal architectural embodiment of the Baroque motif of spokes extending from a hub. The hub is a grand oval ballroom, from which four wings of royal apartments extend at obtuse angles into the park, forming a giant X and integrating the complex with its surroundings. The front pair of wings connect to lower wings that proceed, crab-like, around the hexagonal forecourt, and two more reach out diagonally from the junction of the principal wings and the hexagon. A further arrangement of wings links the hexagon to a smaller forecourt, opens up to a giant half-moon shaped piazza, and then flanks a long *allée* leading towards the city, the latter accommodating service buildings including stables and barns. As visitors enter the palace precinct from the far end, the ensemble looks like a stage set, with wings and a distant backdrop arranged according to linear perspective. This theatrical sensation extends to the very fabric of the complex beyond the main palace, which consists of a veneer of stucco over brick in imitation of stone. The oval ballroom draws our attention in several ways. It presses towards us as if responding to our presence, it is the most decorated part of the complex with its Ionic pilasters and elaborately dressed French windows, and it is crowned with a high faceted dome and a figure of a stag. The oval domed chamber recalls Vaux-le-Vicomte (see 134), and Juvarra looked to several French palaces for inspiration – appropriately since Savoyard territory comprised a small corner of France.

The most extraordinary Rococo palace was the Dresden Zwinger (137), which like Stupinigi integrated the natural and built worlds and was intimately tied to the theatre, in both design and function. Its patron, Augustus II, Elector of Saxony (1694–1733) and King of Poland (r. 1697–1706) – better known by the aptly thespian title 'Augustus the Strong' – was one of the most spectacular personae and benefactors of his age. His cosmopolitan tastes ran to exotica, whether in concubines or costume, and his obsession with East Asian ceramics motivated him to found the first European porcelain factory at Meissen (181). During a youthful stay at the court of Louis XIV, Augustus fell in love with Versailles and the nearby Grand Trianon (by Hardouin Mansart, 1688–1715), a part-palace, part-garden pavilion comprising a series of narrow wings with large windows flanking a courtyard and extending into the park. During his reconstruction

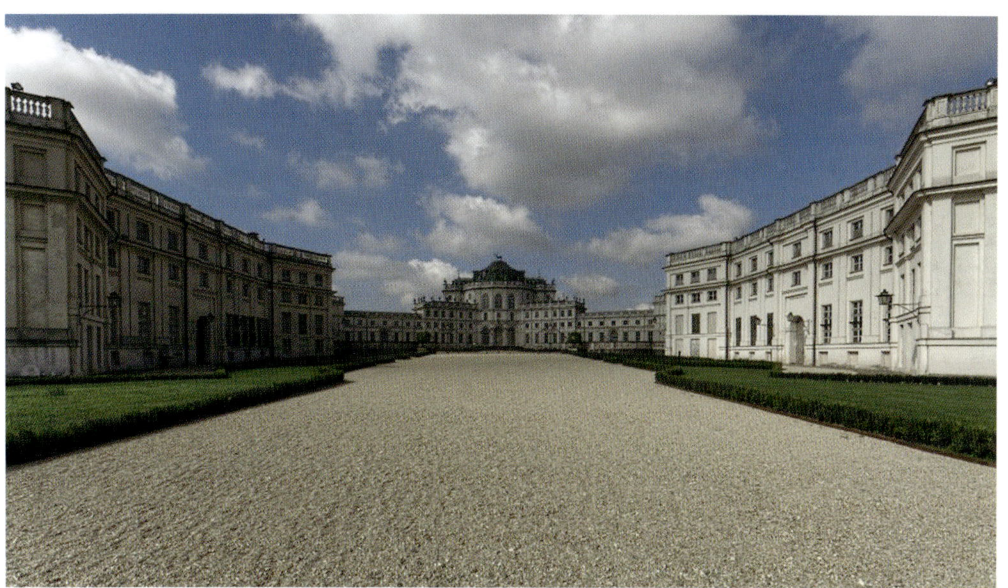

of Dresden into a royal capital he kept these structures in mind, scattering his
city with small palaces, pavilions and gardens that would serve as a setting for
splendid court ceremonies and distract attention from his spectacular losses
in the battlefield. The Zwinger, a Trianon-like network of garden pavilions
arranged around a courtyard, is his greatest legacy.

The Zwinger combines the ephemeral and permanent, and the artificial and
natural (it once opened directly onto the River Elbe). Structurally, it is an
outdoor *composto* in which the architect Matthäus Daniel Pöppelmann (1662–
1736) and sculptor Balthasar Permoser (1651–1732) achieved an intimate
interplay of architecture and sculpture. They transformed a tournament field
surrounded by wooden buildings into a three-sided cloister of one-storey
galleries and pavilions around a square courtyard (the cumbersome fourth
wing dates from the nineteenth century), with apse-like extensions on both
sides called exedrae. The designers give it an ephemeral sensation through
seemingly permeable architecture, an effect achieved by de-emphasizing the
wall and architectural forms such as Ionic pilasters in favour of an arcade-like
row of giant windows and sculptural decorative devices. Similarly, the tower-
like Crown Gate (1713) is open on both storeys and the oval pavilions at the
ends of each exedra (the Wall Pavilion, 1716, and Carillon Pavilion, 1780–4)

comprise an open arcade on the ground floor and a crown of windows so
tall they pierce the entablature – they recall the glass jewellery cabinets in
which their patron displayed his *objets d'art*. Pöppelmann also used giant
windows in the rectangular two-storey pavilions that flank the exedrae.
Permoser's sculptural decoration brings the pavilions, towers and wings to life:
mythological and allegorical figures and flowerpot finials sit atop the roof
balustrades; swags, fruit and shells punctuate the galleries and rectangular
pavilions; half-length male herms serve as pilasters on the lower level of
the pavilions; and angels and scrolls encircle the royal arms above in a giant
projecting cartouche. Decoration is subtler in the galleries, intensifies in
the rectangular pavilions, and reaches a crescendo in the Crown Gate and

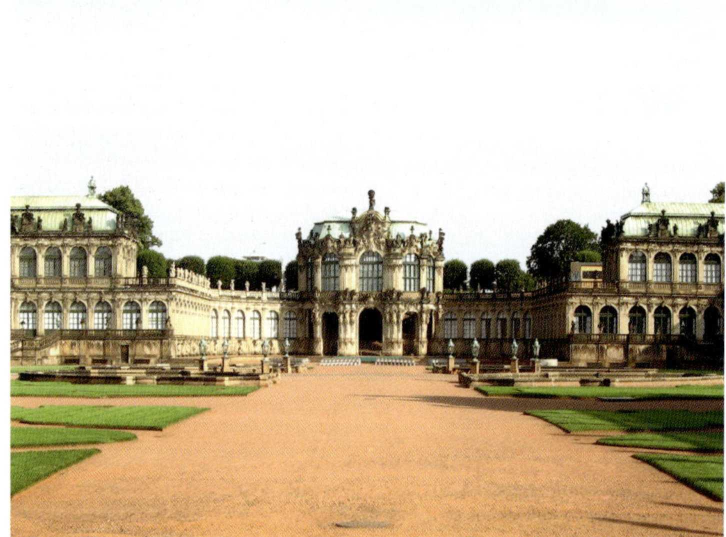

**137.
Matthäus
Daniel
Pöppelmann
and Bathasar
Permoser**,
Dresden
Zwinger,
1709–32
(Germany)

**138.
Caspar
Vogel and
Nicodemus
Tessin
the Elder**,
Skokloster
Palace,
1654–67
(Sweden)

Carillon and Wall Pavilions, especially the latter with its statue of Hercules,
Augustus the Strong's alter ego. Pöppelmann and Permoser added an aural
dimension to the visitor's experience of the Zwinger with fountains in the four
reflecting pools and the gushing waterfall in the Nymphaeum Fountain in the
north corner of the courtyard. It takes little imagination to imagine the pageants,
musical performances, tournaments and firework displays that once took place
within its confines, the most famous a massive equestrian event called the Carousel
of the Four Elements (1709) under the patronage of the god Jupiter, and event
so spectacular that 170 paintings were made to commemorate it.

In central Europe and Scandinavia, indigenous models for palace architecture
offered an alternative to those of France or Italy. Chastened and guarded
after the disastrous Thirty Years War (1618–48), which was fought in central
Europe and had Sweden as one of its main protagonists, these regions
often opted for plain, sometimes dour structures that evoked the military
architecture of the Middle Ages and Renaissance through their plans
and elevations. Such was the Skokloster Palace outside Stockholm (138),
built between 1654 and 1667 on plans by Caspar Vogel (1600–1663) later
renovated by Nicodemus Tessin the Elder (1615–1681) for Commander
Carl Gustaf Wrangel (1613–1676) a veteran of the Thirty Years War.
Wrangel was one of Scandinavia's great collectors, amassing a treasury of

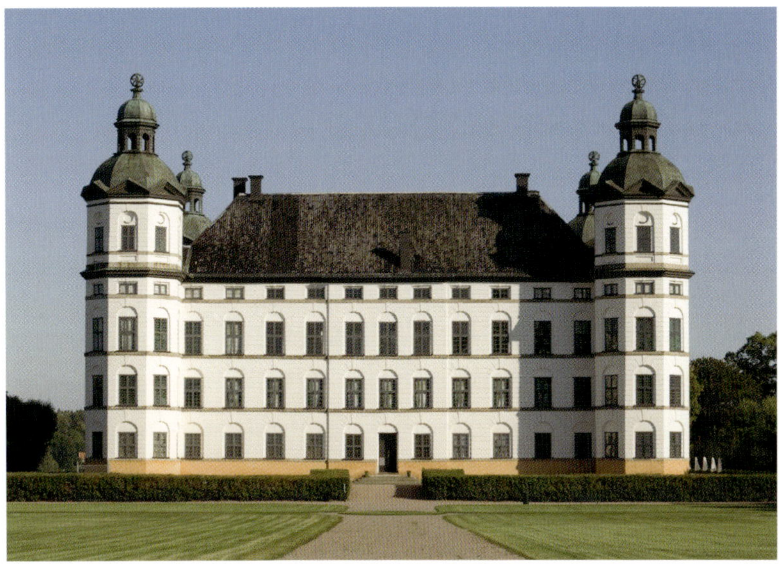

arms and armour, exotic goods from the Americas, and decorative accents
for his interiors. The plain palace does away with pilasters and columns
in favour of rustication – a block-like, pseudo-fortification construction
– on all three storeys, the attic and even the towers. Yet Vogel and Tessin
alleviate the palace's austerity by opening up the walls with large rectangular
windows so that light can permeate from the far end of the building, and
by choosing narrow towers with delicate crowns instead of hefty bulwarks.
The double cupolas are crowned with armillary spheres, an instrument used
by navigators and astrologers and a symbol for Wrangel's interest in the

non-European world. In the Rococo the fortress palace abandoned nearly all of its military associations. Such is the Rogalin Palace in Poland (139), the country seat of Kazimierz Raczyński, the future Royal Marshal, built by a Polish or Saxon architect between 1768 and 1774 and modernized inside by Domenico Merlini (1730–1797) and Jan Christian Kamsetzer (1753–1795). Like Skokloster, the Rogalin Palace has projecting corners (here they are rectangular), and it is also rusticated – although only on the ground floor and in the quoining of the central block. But the façade has a more welcoming appearance, not only because the main block projects gracefully towards the visitor but also because an elegant convex bay projects even further, taking all three storeys and the roof along with it, and allowing for a sweeping double staircase in front.

Civic buildings shared the same challenges as urban palaces. Like Rome, Paris suffered from an awkward medieval road plan (the wide boulevards of today are a product of the nineteenth century), presenting Louis XIV's architects with a particular challenge in imposing his absolutist vision onto the city. Louis Le Vau, the architect of Vaux-le-Vicomte and Versailles (see 134, 135), had to work on a modest scale in his Collège des Quatre-Nations (now the Institut de France, 140), on which he collaborated with his pupil François d'Orbay (1634–1697). The Collège was founded by Cardinal Mazarin (1602–1661) to house his tomb and as a satellite of Sorbonne University, serving students from the nations newly acquired by France after the Treaty of Westphalia (1648). Fronting the River Seine across the Quai de Conti and on a direct axis with the main court of the Louvre on the other side of the river, the Collège enjoyed more advantageous surroundings than the Propaganda Fide (see 133) and could be seen from a greater distance, although Le Vau had a bigger challenge at the rear of the building where the Rue de Seine took a giant bite out of the right wing and the Rue Mazarine compelled what was left of the rear façade to extend along a diagonal instead of a straight line. Le Vau gave the building its grandeur by carving out a shallow U-shaped courtyard in front (like Borromini's S. Agnese in Agone, see 142), which allows space to appreciate the projecting porch of the church and its dome, and by using the side wings of the Collège to provide the illusion of a symmetrical, unified block. Unlike Borromini's fantasies,

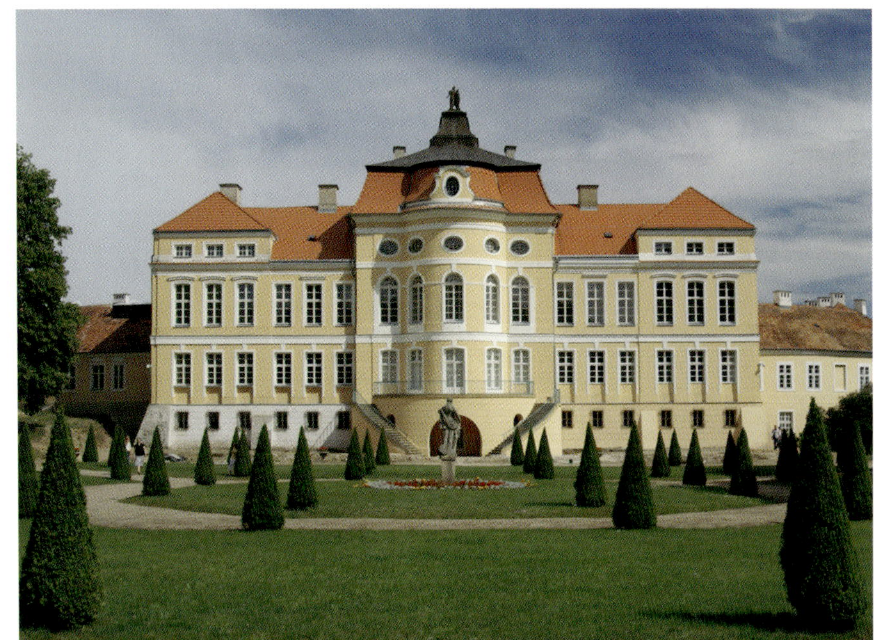

139.
Rogalin Palace, 1768–74 (Poland)

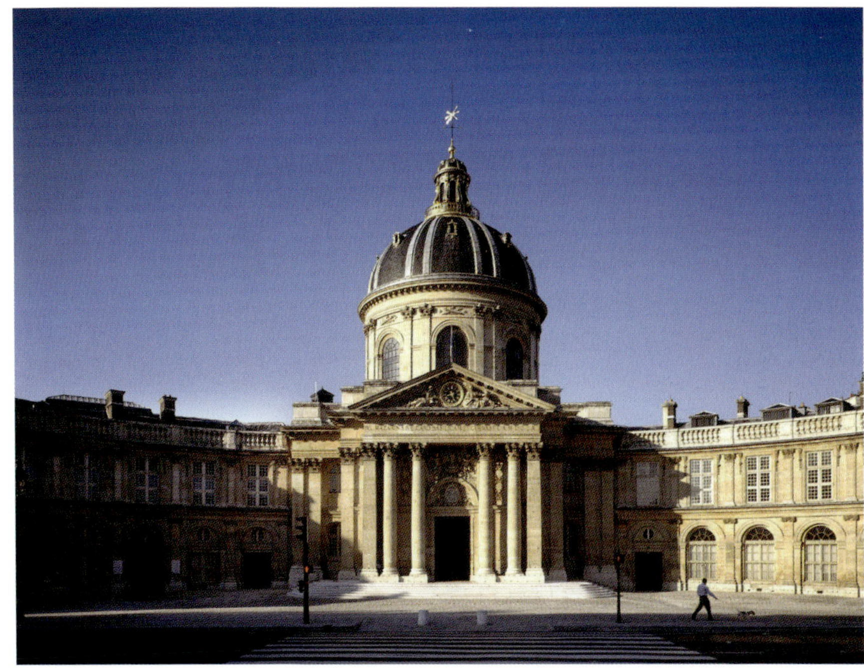

140.
Louis Le Vau and François d'Orbay, Collège des Quatre Nations, 1668–88. Paris

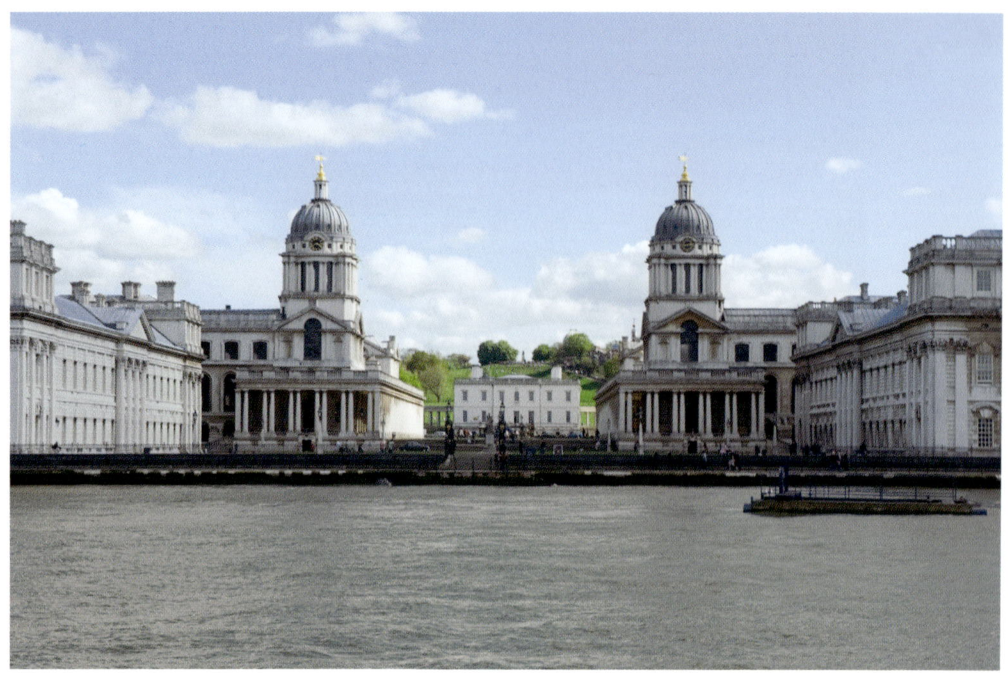

Le Vau's classicism is academic, his subtle Ionic and Corinthian pilasters on the wings contrasting with a Corinthian giant order of pilasters on the side pavilions and church, with two pairs of giant order columns flanking the church portal. His low, horizontal wings harmonize with the roofline of adjacent buildings while his dome – its paired Corinthian pilasters drawing the eye upwards by aligning with those below – emphasizes the building's verticality and competed with others in the neighbourhood.

Christopher Wren's (1632–1723) Greenwich Hospital in London (formerly the Royal Naval Hospital; 141) enjoyed a more forgiving suburban setting but was still hampered by existing buildings. It is composed of two pairs of palace-like blocks with courtyards, each pair flanking a green, the wider one on the banks of the River Thames and the narrower one further inland on a slight incline. Wren had to adapt his plan to incorporate John Webb's existing King Charles's Block (begun 1664), and it had to focus on Inigo Jones's Queen's House (1616–35), which stands at the other end of the hospital from the river on a direct longitudinal axis. The former posed little problem as it was on the grand Baroque scale Wren had in mind, but the latter's modesty spoiled his original scheme. Wren wanted the two courtyards, when viewed from the river, to culminate in a semicircular colonnade fronting a combination chapel/hall with a tall dome and classical portico – the design is very similar to the Collège des Quatre-Nations (see 140) – however King William III refused to have his view of the river from the Queen's House blocked. Since the Queen's House is not only small but plain, it was inappropriate as the focus of a grand Baroque vista. So Wren switched his design from back to front. He built a pair of rectangular halls (the chapel and Painted Hall) at the river end of the narrower green, placing domes at the junctions of the two greens. More ingeniously, he fronted the façades of the blocks flanking the narrow green with a low and austere colonnade of paired Doric columns that lead to the two-storey Queen's House without dwarfing it or overwhelming its subtle classicism. The colonnades recall both the Grand Trianon (the latter uses the Ionic order and also has arches) and the Doric arms of St Peter's square (see 125). Such references are not unreasonable as Wren had first-hand knowledge of French royal architecture during a visit to Paris in 1665 where he also met Bernini and had a very brief glimpse of his design for the Louvre: 'I would have given my skin for it, but the reserved old Italian gave me but a view … I had only time to copy it in my fancy and memory.' The two outer blocks and the larger green at Greenwich were much as Wren intended in the first scheme, and together with the new location of the great domed halls the hospital concentrates its grandeur on the riverfront.

As Baroque and Rococo churches and monastic buildings were a reflection of divine authority, only the grandest palaces could compete with them in size, height or – in Iberia and its colonies – elaborateness of decoration. No period since the Middle Ages witnessed the construction of so many churches, whether abbeys, pilgrimage centres or urban parishes, as the Church intensified its hold on Catholic Europe and Protestant faiths conceived new kinds of building to accommodate alternate forms of worship. Like palaces, the largest were in the countryside where they did not face urban space restrictions. In the city, churches like the Roman church of S. Agnese in Agone (142) confronted the same challenges as urban palaces. Commissioned by Innocent X Pamphilj as part of his transformation of the Piazza Navona into a Pamphilj arena (it was the family church), S. Agnese is adjacent to the

Pamphilj Palace on the left and on a direct axis with Bernini's Fountain of the Four Rivers (see 127). Although Borromini executed the most revolutionary features of its design, S. Agnese was really a group project: it was begun by Girolamo Rainaldi (1570–1655), involved both Bernini and Borromini, and was completed by Girolamo's son Carlo (1611–1691). S. Agnese is the largest High Baroque church in Rome and it refers explicitly to St Peter's Basilica – appropriately since it is a papal commission – even taking the opportunity to remedy some of the latter's faults. It is based on a Greek-cross plan like Donato Bramante's original design for the basilica crossing (begun 1506), thus rejecting Carlo Maderno's longitudinal nave (1607–15), which distorted St Peter's proportions. As one of the most common criticisms of Maderno's nave was that it obscured the dome except from a distance, the elder Rainaldi ensured that there would be no danger of missing the dome at S. Agnese: mounted on an unusually high drum, it remains one of the highest in the city. Borromini's flanking towers (completed by Giovanni Baratta and Antonio del Grande) also allude to St Peter's, as a pair had been planned for the basilica but were never successfully built – had he lived to see them finished Borromini would have taken some pleasure in this particular improvement as the failure of the St Peter's towers was blamed on his rival Bernini.

Borromini's façade (1653–5) – he demolished what had already been built by Rainaldi – makes ingenious use of its surroundings. The plot is narrow and hemmed in by palaces on both sides, and it is so close to the square that a forecourt was out of the question. Borromini solved these problems by having the central part of the façade step back to create a small concavity – although it is very shallow it has the feel of a patio – and by raising the portal higher than the level of the square and preceding it with a staircase he amplified the church's majestic approach. The gently curving walls of the concavity and the way they balance the circular drum of the dome were copied throughout Europe, as we have already seen at the Collège des Quatre-Nations in Paris (see 140). To make the church seem bigger than it actually is, and to make the façade proportionate with the height of the dome, Borromini added illusionistic side 'wings' – they are also the bases for the towers – that are mere veneers over the ends of the abutting palaces as the furthest lateral stretch of the church interior does not extend as far as

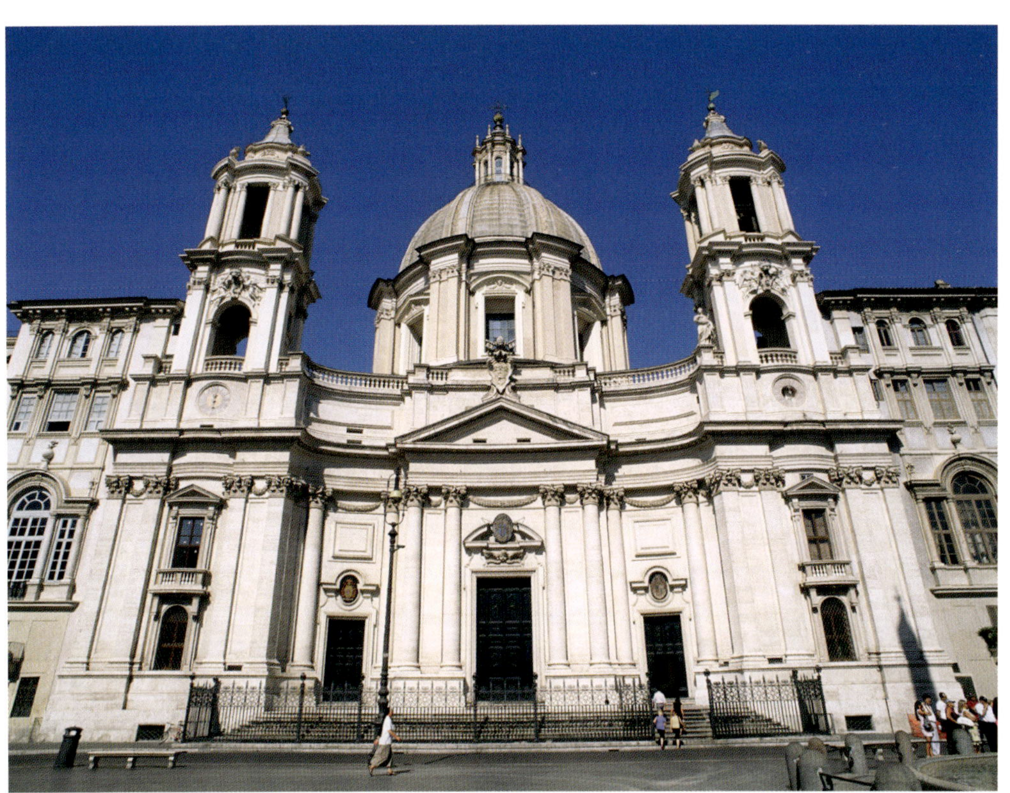

their windows. The central bays of the wings and towers are slightly convex, contrasting with the concave 'forecourt' and enlivening what could have been a monotonously long façade. The façade was not finished by the time Borromini was replaced by Carlo Rainaldi upon Innocent's death in 1655, and Rainaldi's team distorted Borromini's concept by adding a high attic and the triangular pediment.

A less influential but more inventive response to tight spaces is Pietro da Cortona's façade for the diminutive Roman church of S. Maria della Pace (143), two streets to the west of the Piazza Navona and facing onto an oblique junction of three narrow streets. Here a Renaissance church (built in 1482) stood in one of the most congested parts of the city and could only be appreciated from the Via della Pace, the street approaching it diagonally from the southwest. Pope Alexander VII ordered Cortona not only to replace the façade but also to help traffic circulation by demolishing some of the buildings on the south and opening up a small (14 by 30 metres; 10 by 46 feet)

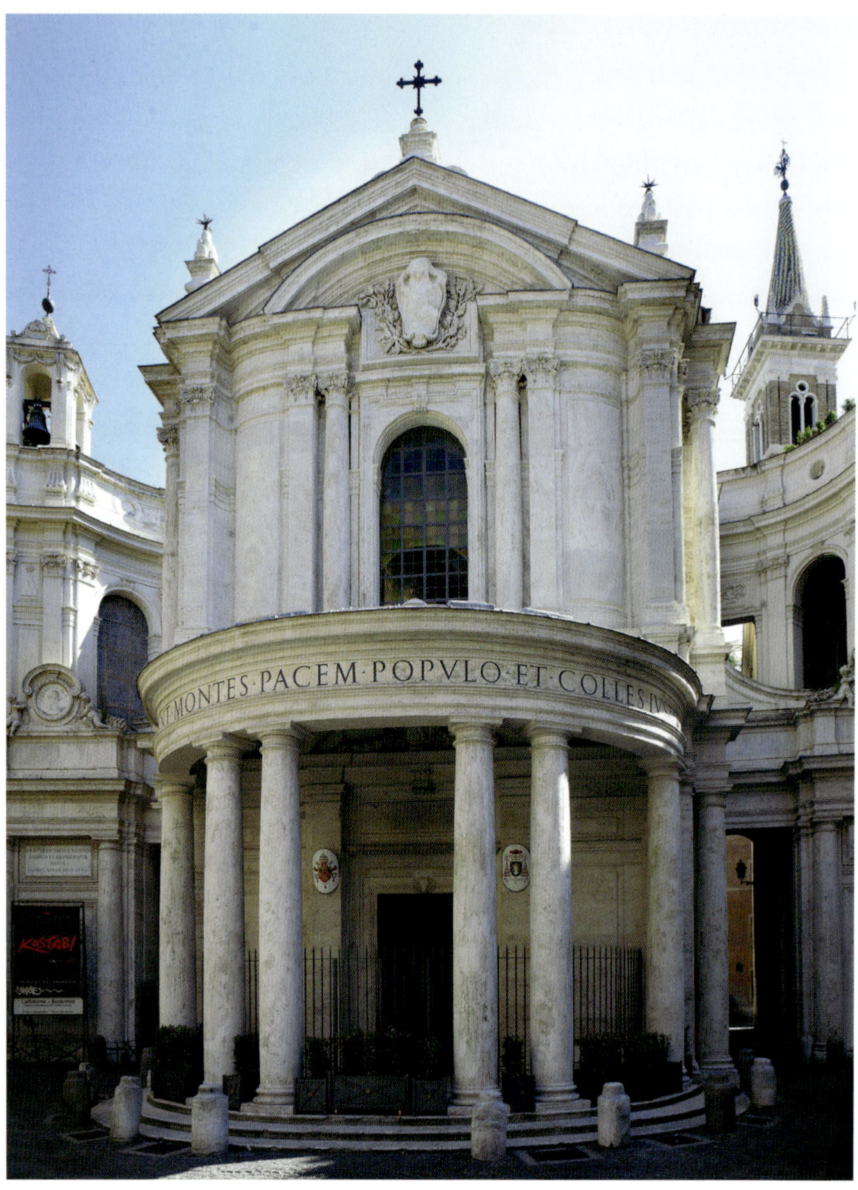

trapezoidal piazza in front of the church. The commission also had a spiritual motive, as it was an offering to the Madonna of Peace to protect Rome from the plague and invasion from the French. The pope seems to have been genuinely impatient to appease the Virgin, as Cortona finished the façade in two years, although construction of the piazza lingered into the next decade.

The architect modelled the interrelationship between façade and square on theatrical structures, so that the semicircular portico pushes into the piazza like a stage – it transforms foot traffic into an audience and draws people into the church – and the upper wings, curving outwards from well behind the façade, look like theatre boxes. The portico can be appreciated from all three approaches, and the paired columns are spaced at even intervals to allow an access for each of the three streets. Cortona also maintained unity between the church and the surrounding houses by linking their cornices, although the houses used pilasters instead of columns and were on a slightly lower level so as not to compete with the church. The wings on both levels are also illusions, as they do not reflect the actual width of the church (it is only as wide as the central section) but instead conceal other structures as at S. Agnese. The left one fronts a sacristy and oblique courtyard, the right one crosses over a narrow street accessed by the opening below, and the upper sections of both actually belong to the abutting buildings. By sweeping backwards the upper wings also help alleviate the square's claustrophobic sensation, both by suggesting an extension of space and by receiving more sunlight, as only the upper façade is illuminated in the late afternoon. Cortona compensated for the church's meagre dimensions by making the upper, central part of his façade the most visually alluring and architecturally complex. A convex wall presses forwards like a lung while the central window frame and rounded keystone-like pediment above it recede inwards in an interplay of shifting wall planes inspired by Michelangelo's New Sacristy (see 87) and Laurentian Library at San Lorenzo. Like bookends, a pair of projecting piers keeps the expanding wall in check. Architectural forms take on decorative functions, like the entablature halfway up that slips behind the columns and pilasters but is absent on the curving wall, or the upper façade with its spectacular nesting, or encased, pediments. A circular pediment (the 'keystone') is set into a larger triangular one, so that the lower part of the triangle passes underneath it, and the triangular one responds by projecting forwards in the middle in a section as wide as the circular pediment. Taken as a whole, the juxtaposition of the convex centre with concave wings gives the façade a curvilinear effect similar to that of Borromini's at S. Agnese (see 142).

Churches on constricted sites did not always rely on bold architectural innovations to draw attention to their façades. Particularly in Iberia, Southern Italy and Latin America, rich, saturated ornament compensated for more conservative, rectilinear plans and flat façades (e.g. see 216). The Salentine Peninsula, a Spanish colony in the heel of Italy with a unique, highly decorative architectural style, was richly endowed with such buildings, and the seventeenth-century cathedral façade of S. Agata in the fishing town of Gallipoli is one of the most lavish (144). Like Borromini's Coleggio di Propaganda Fide (see 133) S. Agata faces onto an extremely narrow street

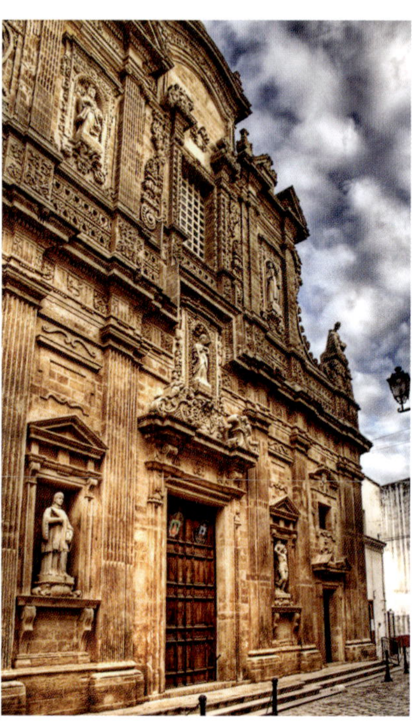

144.
Cathedral of S. Agata, façade, 1696. Gallipoli (Italy)

145.
Jules Hardouin-Mansart, Dôme des Invalides, 1677–1706. Paris

and its façade can only be appreciated from the sides. But instead of using bold cornices and undulating walls to draw visitors' attentions, S. Agata overwhelms us with a complex tapestry of decoration rarely equalled in Italy. Rosettes, scrolls, acanthus leaves, floral bouquets, vines, monsters, *putti* and myriad other forms join forces with figural sculptures in a luxurious ensemble enhanced by the use of both golden and cream-coloured stone. This approach to decoration is particularly suited to the church's location, since the carving is best seen sequentially and at close quarters, unlike churches with façades that can be seen at great distances.

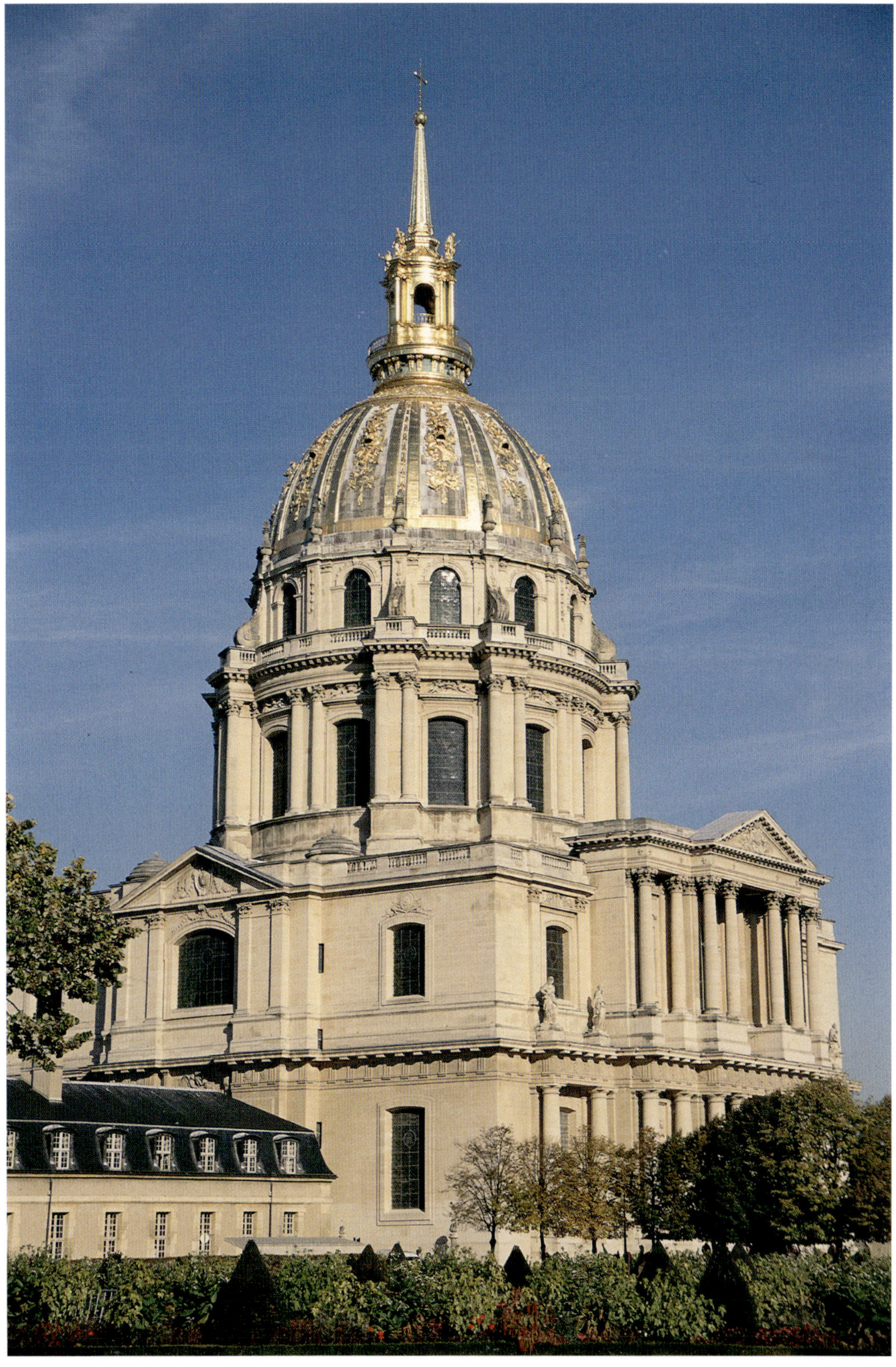

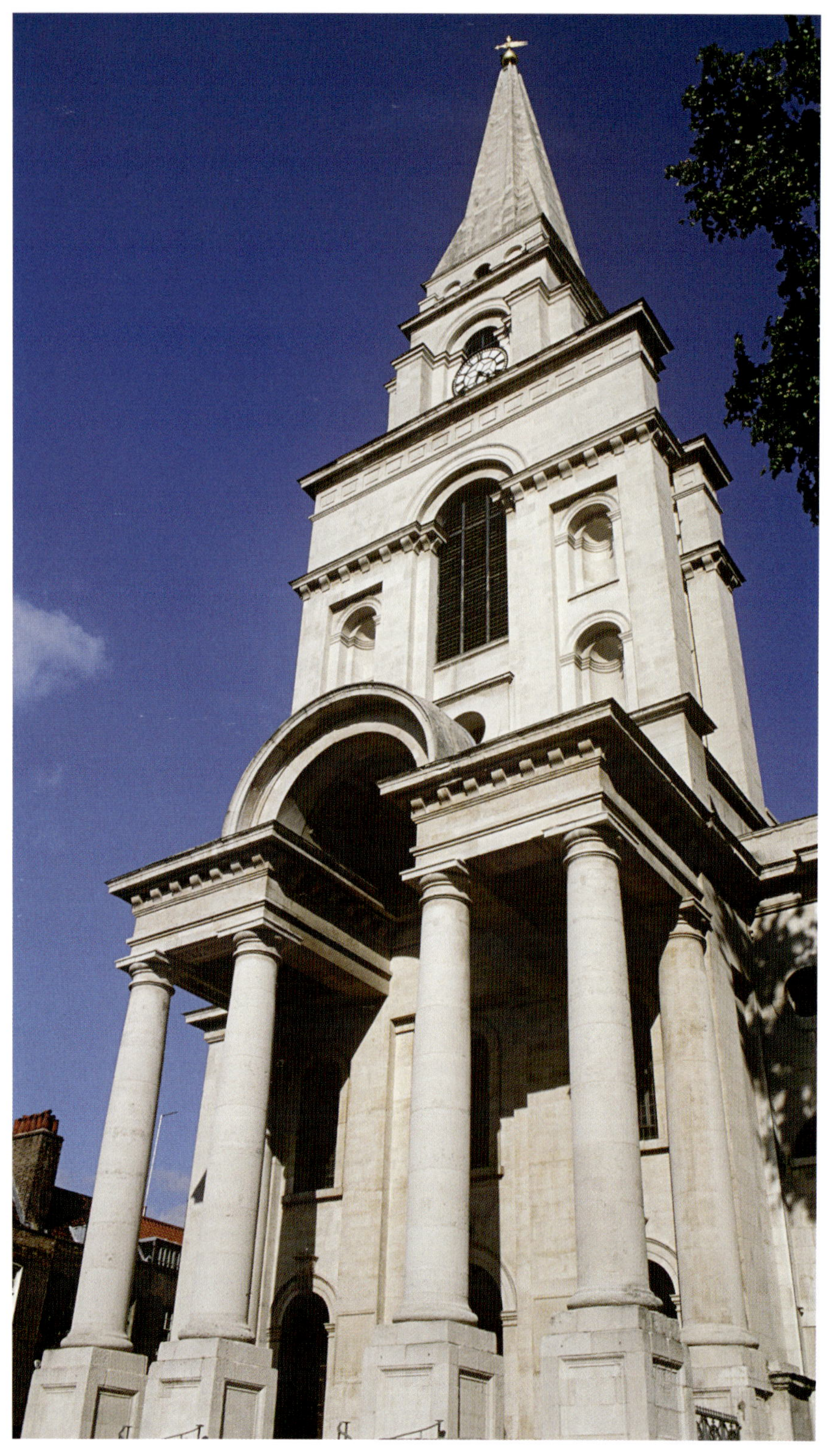

**146.
Nicholas
Hawksmoor,** Christ Church
Spitalfields,
1714–29.
London

An extreme case of the latter is the Dôme des Invalides in Paris (145), the centrepiece of one of the city's most grandiose architectural complexes: the Hôtel des Invalides (begun 1670). Located in the Faubourg Saint-Germain, formerly farmland belonging to the Abbey of Saint-Germain-des-Près, it was free from the congestion that usually plagued urban sites. The Hôtel was founded by Louis XIV as a hospice for wounded soldiers (a role it still plays), and at its height it was capable of accommodating between four and five thousand patients. The complex was begun by Libéral Bruant (d. 1697) and finished by Jules Hardouin-Mansart, who in 1677 began the Dôme itself – a centrally planned chapel royal attached by means of an oval sanctuary to the end of a church dedicated to Saint Louis. It was Paris's answer to St Peter's (see 126) and marked France's ascendancy over Italy as Europe's cultural capital. Although proportionately narrower to its height than the dome of the Roman basilica – perhaps owing to lingering Gothic aesthetics – the dome is only 30 metres (98½ ft) lower and is the focus of one of the world's great urban vistas: from the other side of the Seine down the 487-metre (1,598 ft) -long Esplanade des Invalides (laid out 1704–20). On the other side the Dôme's main façade gives onto an ample square now called the Place Vaubin. The vertical ribs in the dome and paired columns in the drum are further echoes of St Peter's, but Hardouin-Mansart added an attic level in between to increase the total height and scrolling buttresses above the pairs of columns as a transition between the two zones. Like S. Agnese in Agone (see 142) the Dôme can be seen as a 'correction' of the Roman basilica, since it preserves the Greek-cross plan and eliminates the nave, but the chapel façade is narrower and rectilinear, forming a plinth-like base for the dome. The elevation of the lower two storeys is stately and sparingly decorated in the kind of cool classicism typical of Louis XIV's public buildings in Paris (see 140), and the façade advances towards the centre in three stages, from the wings to the central block and culminating with the portico. The giant portal and windows of the façade, not to mention those of the drum and dome, give the building an openness that belies its daunting scale. But the Dôme is not a very forgiving building. Like the regime that built it, the chapel is meant to be admired from a respectful distance.

English architect Nicholas Hawksmoor (1661–1736) did not have to worry much about urban congestion either, as central London had burnt to the ground in 1666 and presented a clean slate to the group of architects hired, under Wren's supervision, to rebuild its churches. In 1711 an Act of Parliament released the coal tax to finance fifty new churches for London (only twelve were built), including one of Hawksmoor's most original creations, Christ Church Spitalfields (146). Although the two churches share a prominent position at the end of a long approach and both use the language of classical architecture, Christ Church could not be less like the Dôme des Invalides. A Protestant church in a country where absolutist bombast was disdained, Christ Church substitutes references to the papacy with reminiscences of English medieval architecture – most notably by replacing the dome with a massive steeple. Hawksmoor's classicism is eclectic instead of academic, inspired partly by Borromini but also by the English preference for Palladianism, a plain, proportionate style based on the inventions of the Italian Renaissance architect Andrea Palladio (1508–1580) and first championed in England by Inigo Jones (1573–1652). Hawksmoor's churches combine biblical, early Christian and classical features, the latter deriving more from Rome's exotic colonies such as Baalbek (Lebanon) than Rome itself. His interest in early Christian monuments responded to new movements in Anglican theology, which recognized the primitive Church as a purer alternative to contemporary Catholicism.

The prominence of the façade/steeple at Christ Church can partly be explained by two clauses in the 1711 commission. Although one demanded 'that one General Modell be made and Agreed upon for all the fifty New intended Churches', it added that 'the steeples or towers [are] excepted', allowing architects free rein above the roof line and encouraging a variety of silhouettes. The other specifically called for monumentality in the façades: 'that, there be handsome Porticoes at the West end of each Church where the Scite will admit of the same'. Completed in 1729, Hawksmoor's steeple mimics those of the destroyed Gothic churches of London, although after nineteenth-century renovations that removed its dormer windows and crockets (leafy Gothic finials) it looks more like an Egyptian obelisk – as it happens another of Hawksmoor's inspirations for the steeple. Both the tower and façade showcase the so-called Palladian Motif, an arch between two rectangular openings: it occurs in the portico below and – replacing the openings with paired blind niches – in the tower, and it is also repeated in the east window. This use of the motif on a massive scale, particularly as a projecting portico, is bold and original – Hawskmoor even creates a giant order when he makes the portico columns ascend past both window levels of the façade. Like Borromini – both architects shared a penchant for Near Eastern models and complex spires – he chose the curve as a leitmotif of his church, from circular portholes to round headed arches, the largest in the Palladian motifs of the façade and east window. But unlike Borromini, these curves are vertical and do not result in the kind of curvilinear plan so favoured by southern and central European churches. Christ Church is full of surprises for the visitor, such as the deep grooves that open up in the sides of the tower – only visible from the side of the church – and the tower's unexpected narrowness. It is this interest in the unanticipated, along with the daring and unexpected combinations of classical prototypes, that makes this Protestant church as Baroque as any in this book.

Of all the above urban churches only the Dôme des Invalides reached a scale comparable to the greatest churches, abbeys and pilgrimage shrines outside the cities. Two of the most stupendous are the abbeys of Melk (147), in Austria, and Mafra (see 148), in Portugal, so immense that they compete in size with Versailles (see 135) or Caserta (see 16). The Benedictine abbey of Melk is the holy grail of Baroque enthusiasts, a cyclopean combination of church and palace-monastery jutting out like a giant ship on a natural spur of land high over the Danube. The ship metaphor persists on the south side, where a 320-metres (1,050 ft) -long wall looming over the town and bearing three rows of plain windows bears an uncanny resemblance to the flank of an ocean liner. This marine association was likely intentional: the abbey was meant to be seen from barges on the Danube and the symbol of the 'Ship of the Church' was a common reference to the triumph of Catholicism. Melk's dramatic site was matched only by its political significance. Beginning life as a tenth-century castle to defend Bavaria from the Turks, it was associated with the royal family, and the abbey maintained palatial guest quarters for imperial visitors. Abbot Berthold Dietmayer (in office 1700–39) seemed an unlikely patron for the abbey's extravagant reconstruction, as he

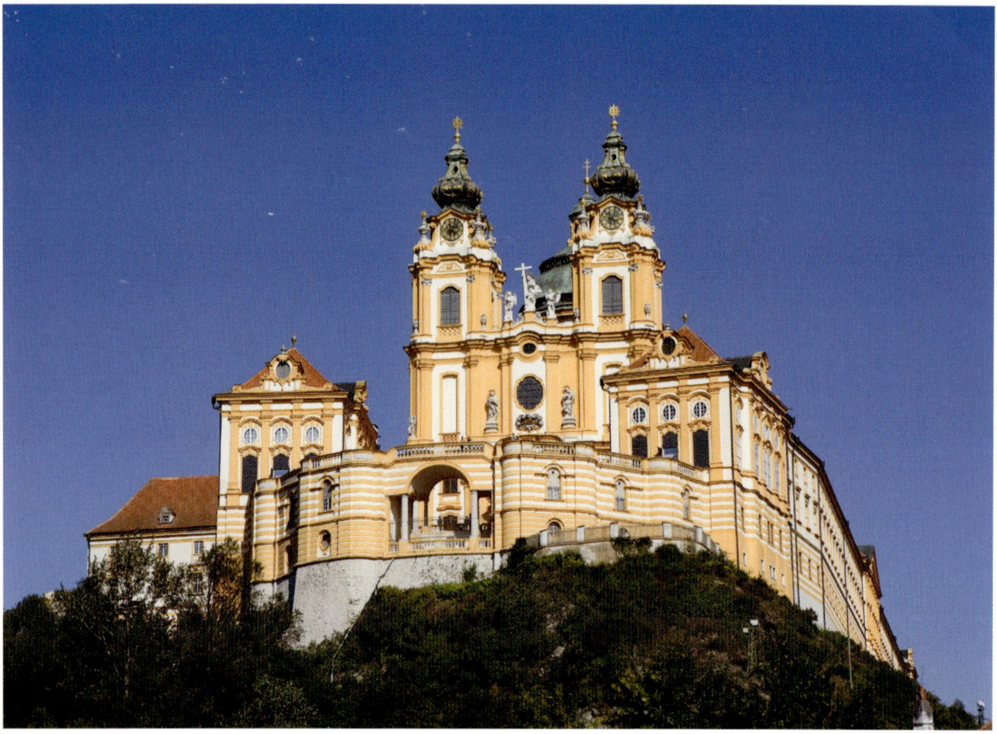

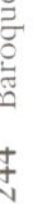

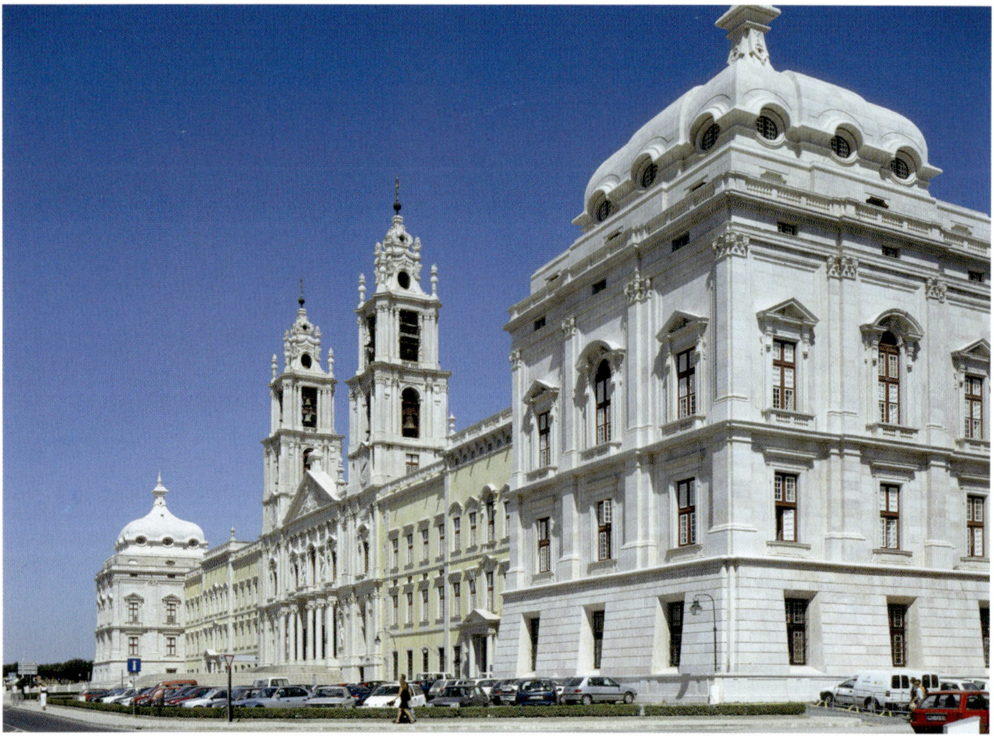

was known for his simplicity and strict monastic discipline, but like so many clerics before him he believed that opulence in a church was an appropriate exaltation of God.

Tyrolian architect Jakob Prandtauer (1660–1726) rebuilt the fortified medieval abbey, preserving its military appearance through the high, flat walls and the battlemented towers on the northeast flank of the complex. He also aligned the walls with the contours of the cliffs to enhance the sensation of height when viewed from below. The new building combined an abbey church and five courtyards surrounded by libraries, grand halls, the imperial residence, the abbot's residence, monastic dwellings, working quarters and a school. It was so sumptuous that the monks revolted and were only appeased when Dietmayer demonstrated that the expenses could be covered by the abbey's revenues. The church is the centrepiece of the complex, rising separately from within the enclosing wings and balconies. Its twin-tower façade (known as a 'west work', or *Westwerk*) is a symbol of the Church Triumphant and hearkens back to the fortified churches of Emperor Charlemagne (742–814). Such façades are ubiquitous in Baroque central Europe and Iberia (e.g. see 149, 150), although rare in Italy and France. Prandtauer let viewers appreciate the façade from below by lowering the horseshoe-shaped terrace in front – the 'prow' of the ship – and opening it up with a Palladian arch in the middle. The terrace plays a dual role because it also offers commanding views from above and serves as a metaphor for the all-knowing eye of the Church. The terrace also incorporates a library and a royal hall, which, taken together with the church symbolically unite Faith, Power and Knowledge. The façade's interplay of convex and concave walls is like a billowing sail and the tall bundled pilasters that rise to the top of the towers emphasize the church's height. Prandtauer has left us one of the most imposing complexes of the Baroque, yet its flowing lines, openness and large windows of the royal hall and library in the forward wings make the building seem more approachable than its walls or bastions would suggest. Despite its staggering scale, Melk is no Caserta.

The same cannot be said of the palace-abbey of Mafra in Portugal, which replaces sinuousness and openness with flatness and rigidity (148). One of the largest buildings in Europe, Mafra is more remarkable for its statistics than the quality of its architecture: each façade is about 220 metres (722 ft) long (slightly smaller than Caserta), the complex has 1,200 rooms and eight courtyards, and it took an army of as many as 45,000 builders and craftsmen to construct. Its patron was the profligate King Dom João V (r. 1706–50), perhaps the wealthiest monarch in Europe thanks to the royal fifth tax he claimed on the gold and diamonds that poured in from Brazil's Minas Gerais during the colony's greatest mining boom. He commissioned ambitious building projects throughout Portugal, imported sculpture and *objets d'art* from Italy by the ton – as well as some of Italy's and Germany's most talented architects and artists – and created a Roman and central-European-inspired Late Baroque style known as Joanine (*estilo joanino*). He invited Filippo Juvarra, designer of the Stupinigi Palace (see 136), to build the new royal palace in Lisbon in 1719, but the project never got beyond the planning stage and the king soon decided upon a country seat in the small town of Mafra, officially in gratitude for the birth of an heir but also in emulation of Louis XIV's Versailles and Philip II's Renaissance Escorial Palace (1563–84) in neighbouring Spain. The location is ideal for an imposing building, as it is relatively flat with grassy fields and low trees, and it offers unobstructed views for a great distance. Like the Escorial, Mafra combines a palace with a monastery (at the beginning it housed a mere thirteen capuchin friars) and is composed of a square block containing multiple courtyards and a church on the central axis (unlike the Escorial the Mafra church is at the front of the complex). But as Mafra was built quickly, corners were cut: only the towers, church façade and window surrounds are limestone, while the rest is plastered brick. The Escorial, by contrast, is solid granite.

Although the king's tastes ran to Italian style – Mafra has the first large Italian-style dome in Portugal and the vestibule showcases sculptures imported from Rome – the chief architect was the Bavarian Johann Friedrich Ludwig (1670–1752). Central European features dominate, including the square corner towers (compare with 139), the bulbous domes on the corner towers and steeples, and the placement of a twin-towered church façade between two transverse wings (as at Einsiedeln in Switzerland, 1704–7, which also has nearly identical corner towers). The church, a conservative

**149.
Carlos Luís
Ferreira
Amarante
and others,**
the Grand
Staircase,
c.1784.
Pilgrimage
Church of
Bom Jesus do
Monte, Braga
(Portugal)

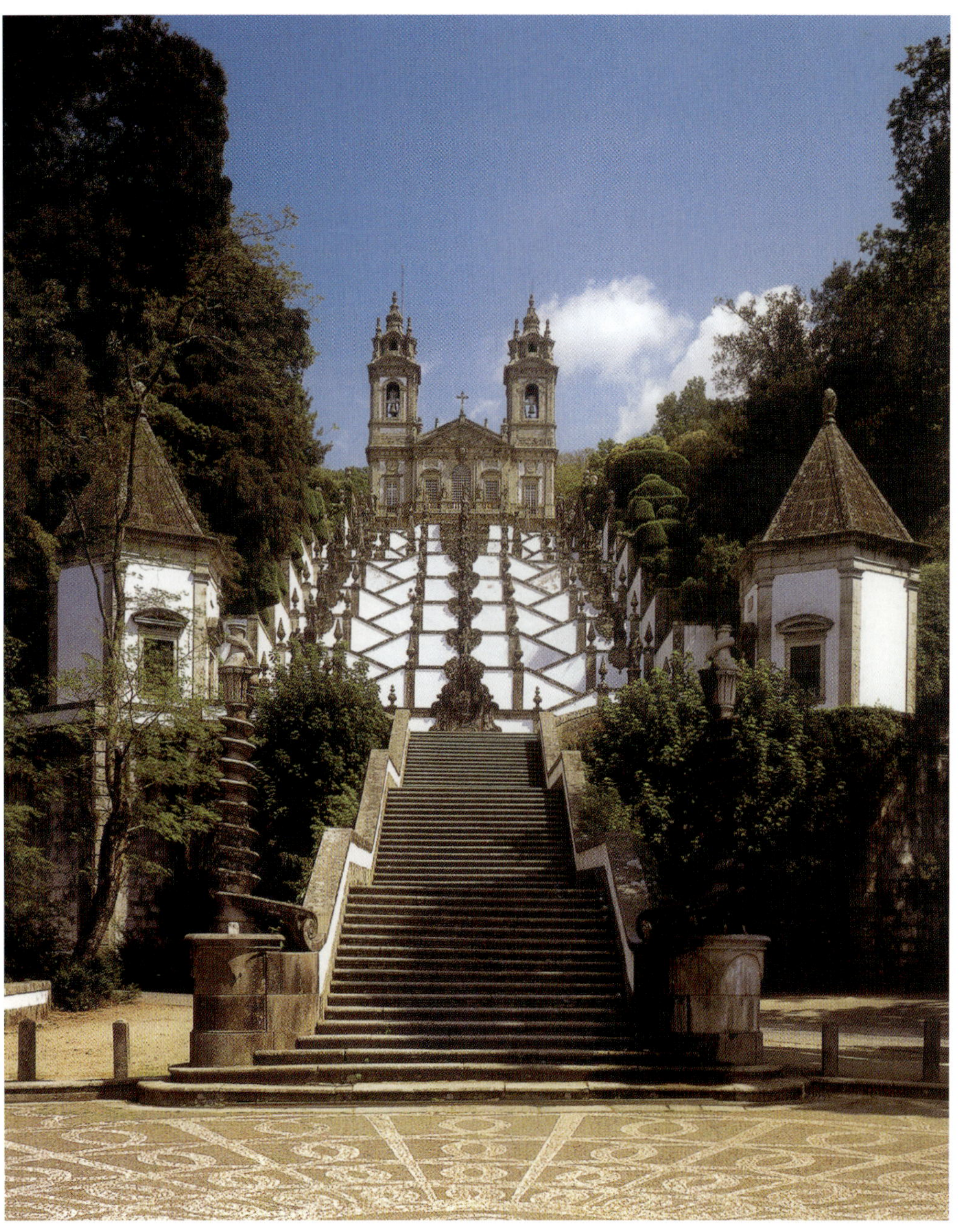

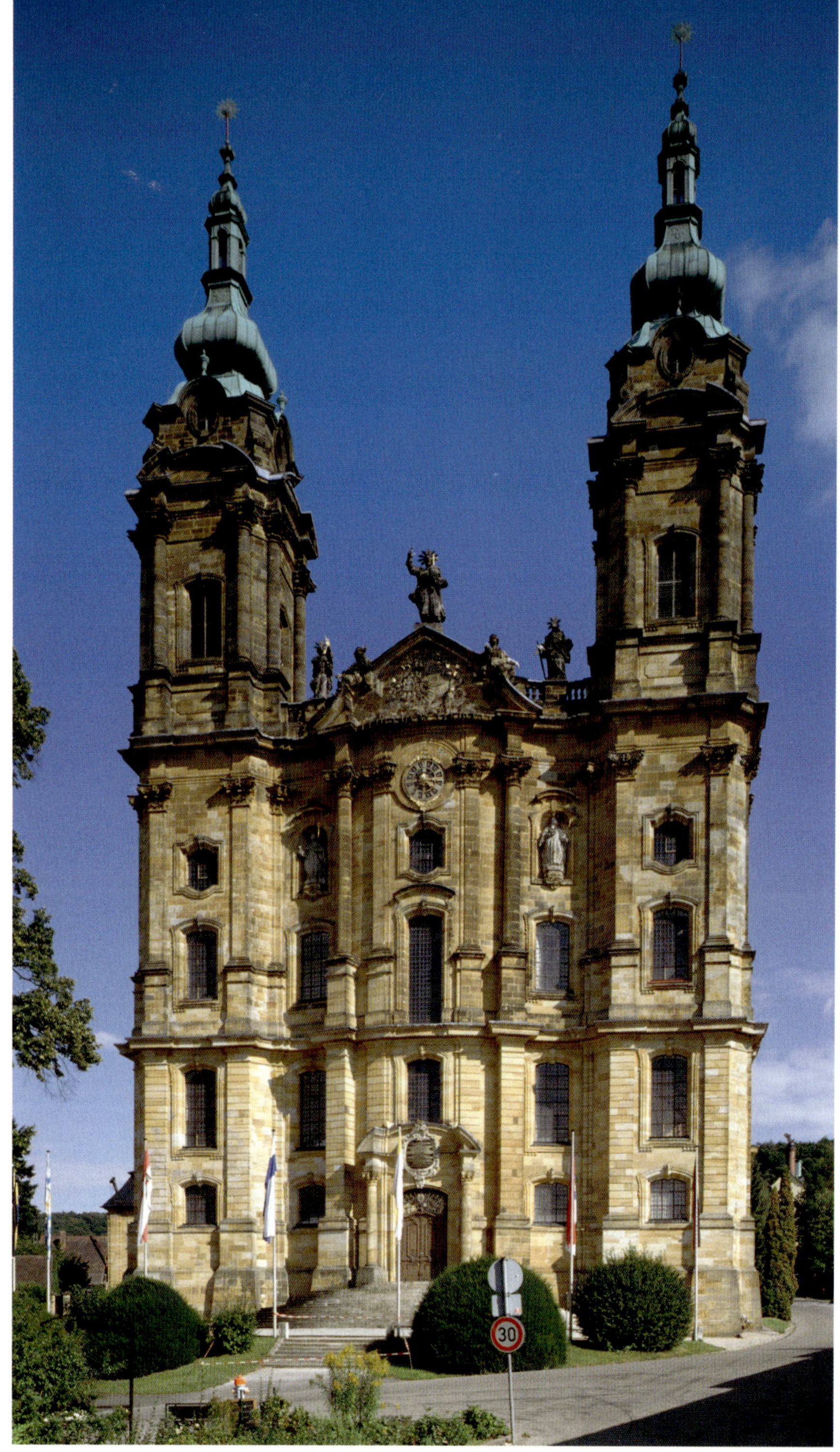

**150.
Johann
Balthasar
Neumann,**
Pilgrimage
Church of
Vierzehn-
heiligen,
1743–72
(Germany)

Latin-cross plan, has convex walls at the transepts and apse – they cannot be seen from the outside – and a flat, monotonous façade enlivened only by a portico of Ionic columns, engaged Corinthian columns above, a few garlands and a pair of sculptures in niches. Scholars have pointed out similarities with Borromini's S. Agnese in Agone (see 142) and Bernini's Palazzo Montecitorio (see 132). But if Mafra is a copy of these models it is a spiritless one, lacking their curving profiles, liveliness and originality of design.

Some of the most striking combinations of church and landscape occur in the abundant pilgrimage churches built or rebuilt in the Catholic world in the century after the end of the Thirty Years War (1618–48), when the Church entered a triumphant phase and hastened to commemorate even the least plausible miracle. The most spectacular is the shrine of Bom Jesus, a few miles outside the northern Portuguese town of Braga, although it is more noteworthy for its staircase – surely the most magnificent in Europe – than its church (149). In fact, the staircase was begun much earlier, and took nearly a century to complete. As visitors ascend, it provides the remarkable sensation of witnessing the passing of time: the sculptural decoration slips from Baroque into Rococo and the church façade hints at Neoclassicism. Archbishop Dom Rodrigo Moura Teles (r. 1704–28) began construction of the staircase in 1723 as the culmination of a Sacred Way, or a penitential and contemplative climb past scenes of Christ's Passion (in individual chapels in the forest below), and then, on the staircase, allegories and biblical figures are accompanied by scriptural quotations. The monument eventually featured sixteen zigzagging double staircases atop a long cascade of steps itself perched on the top of an exhausting climb (today all but the most devout ascend via a funicular train). The top section was designed by Carlos Luís Ferreira Amarante (1748–1815), one of the most distinguished architects of northern Portugal. Each of the eight upper landings, juxtaposing grey granite with dazzling whitewash, features a sculptural wall fountain, the lower ones with allegories of the five senses (delightfully, the spouts are hidden in their eyes, noses, ears or mouths) and the upper ones with allegories of Christian virtues. These fountains are flanked by Old Testament prophets, many of them wearing Asian garb – the latter a reference to Portugal's vast Asian trading network, ironically nearly moribund at the time the staircase was begun. By contrast,

the church is a tall but restrained building, with twin towers, an elegant grid
formed of stately columns/pilasters and prominent entablatures but otherwise
flat and sparsely ornamented. Only the pediment is adorned, with a heraldic
collection of the instruments of the Passion. Amarante designed the church
in 1784 for João de Almada e Melo (d. 1786), a well-connected Governor of
Oporto, but it was only completed in 1811 after the Rococo was no longer in
vogue. Only the cupolas on the towers, with their scrolling profiles and onion
domes, recall that by-then unfashionable style (compare with 147).

Baroque and Rococo pilgrimage churches include many of the most original
buildings and eye-catching settings. The prize in central Europe might
easily go to the shrine of Vierzehnheiligen (literally, 'fourteen saints') near
Bamberg in Bavaria, Germany, the soaring façade of which is lodged on a
challengingly lofty hill and perfectly orientated to receive the golden glow of
the summer sunset (150). Built between 1743 and 1772 to celebrate one of
the most contrived miracles in an era of contrived miracles, it commemorates
a shepherd's discovery of fourteen child saints who called themselves the
'emergency helpers', a cult that probably originated in the aftermath of late
medieval plagues. Its architect was one of the greatest of central Europe,
Johann Balthasar Neumann (1687–1753), who also built the Würzburg
Residenz (see 162). The plan is an ingenious incorporation of ovals and circles
– there are two ovals in the nave, one in the choir, and circles in each of the
transepts – into a relatively rectilinear Latin-cross scheme, a solution like that
of Christoph Dientzenhofer's Sv. Mikuláš in Prague (see 113). Neumann's
was the last of three plans presented to the patron, Stephan Mösinger, Abbot
of Langheim, including a centralized one with the miracle-working altar in
the centre, a Latin-cross plan enclosed in a rectangle as at the Roman Gesù,
and a scheme by Jakob Michael Küchel that introduced the idea of an oval
crossing. Neumann's brilliant proposal – it maintained a central oval within
a more elongated church – won the commission. The curvilinear façade is
far and away the most impressive feature of the exterior, and it is designed
to contrast with the sober flatness of the side walls. Neumann moderated
the façade's formidable scale through four rows of large windows, decorative
onion-domed spires, slender pilasters and columns on elevated plinths, and
narrow towers – an effect that also gives it a commanding verticality.

151.
John Rind,
Town Hall
(Tolbooth),
1737–47.
Kintore
(Scotland)

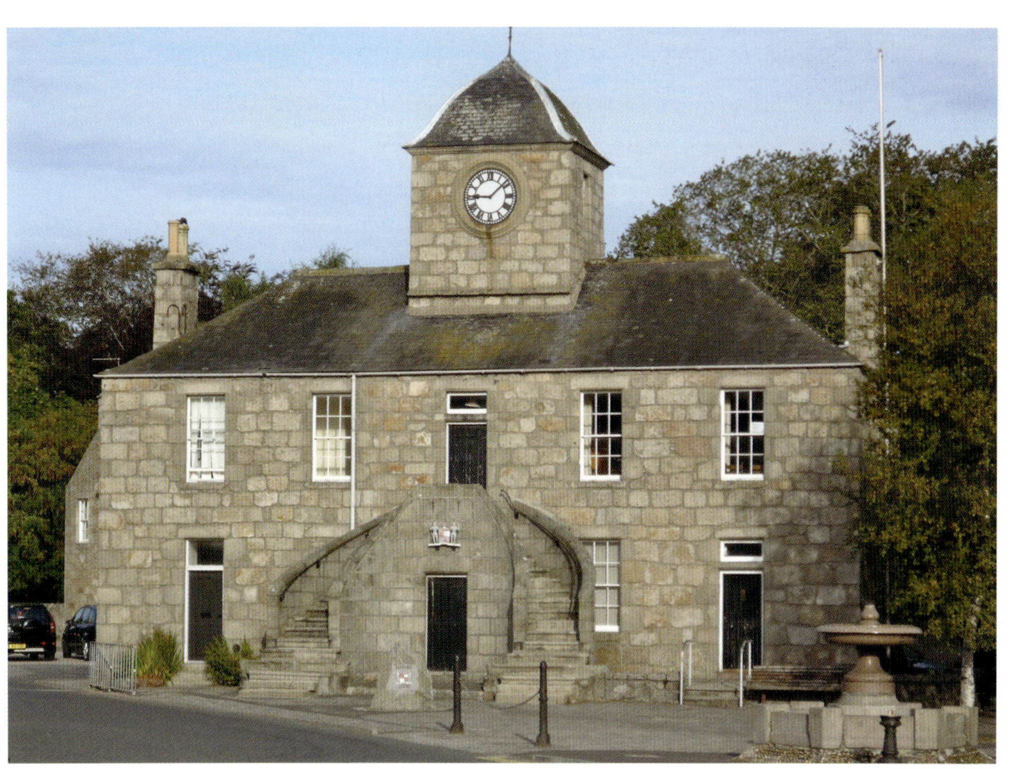

This chapter has mostly been concerned with giant buildings, which when viewed consecutively can be overwhelming. But given the right setting even the smallest structures were just as capable of grandeur and bravado, particularly in tiny villages, on hilltops or amid flat countryside where there are no larger structures to compete with them. In such propitious settings these buildings could look larger than they are, and architects manipulated this effect by exaggerating the relative size of towers and staircases and by making them unusually narrow so as to seem taller. I will conclude with two miniature monuments of the Baroque, one civic and Protestant and the other religious and Catholic. A reticent air of authority emanates from the Town Hall (Tolbooth) in the modest royal burgh of Kintore in northeast Scotland (151). Built by the mason John Rind for the Earl of Kintore, it contained a prison, school, council hall and a dwelling, and it still dominates a small market square that once hosted the important annual Marymass fair. Here the rough, unadorned simplicity of its pink granite – appropriate to its rugged northern setting and the strict Calvinism of its citizens – lends the building an illusion of massiveness. But its coarseness is mitigated by the delicate Dutch-style gambrel cupola on the tower and especially the sweeping

semicircular staircase, which has the elegance of the Town Hall at Zamość

(see 122) – perhaps no coincidence as merchants from this part of Scotland

traded directly with Poland. The staircase is made very narrow to exaggerate

its height and it reaches out dramatically into the square. Although now

surrounded by housing developments, it would have presented an impressive

sight from the gently rolling hills and riverbank nearby.

Even more extreme in its illusion of massiveness is the diminutive parish

church of St Aegidius in the village of Frauendorf, Germany (152), a handful

of houses on a millstream near Vierzehnheiligen. St Aegidius packs all of the

bombast of a great abbey into a building that can barely hold fifty people.

By inverting the expected ratio of tower to nave and giving it a precipitously

pitched roof, the architect makes St Aegidius appear immensely tall from

a distance, an effect enhanced by what may be the most elaborate onion

dome in central Europe, composed of eight separate concave and convex

sections (nearly twice as many as Vierzehnheiligen). St Aegidius also directly

quotes Vierzehnheiligen (see 150): the rusticated pilasters on the ground

floor and tall, plain pilasters above exaggerate the vertical to draw the eye

heavenwards. The greatest surprise, aside from how small the church really

is when approached, is that such a sophisticated work of architecture should

appear in a place of such little importance. Frauendorf owes its good fortune

to Johann Thomas Nissler (1713–1769), the architect who carried out

Balthasar Neumann's plans at Vierzehnheiligen, who was born in the village

and gave this delightful building to the community. When viewed from the

low fields and modest hills around it, this miniature Vierzehnheiligen has

the same illusion of grandeur that English garden designers instilled in their

'follies' (see Chapter Six), miniature false castles or temple ruins that appear

massive when glimpsed through carefully manipulated perspectival vistas.

The Kintore tolbooth and little Frauendorf church, with their ability to make

the small seem big, are particularly charming testaments to the potential

of Baroque stagecraft and a welcome counterbalance to the era's more

gargantuan monuments.

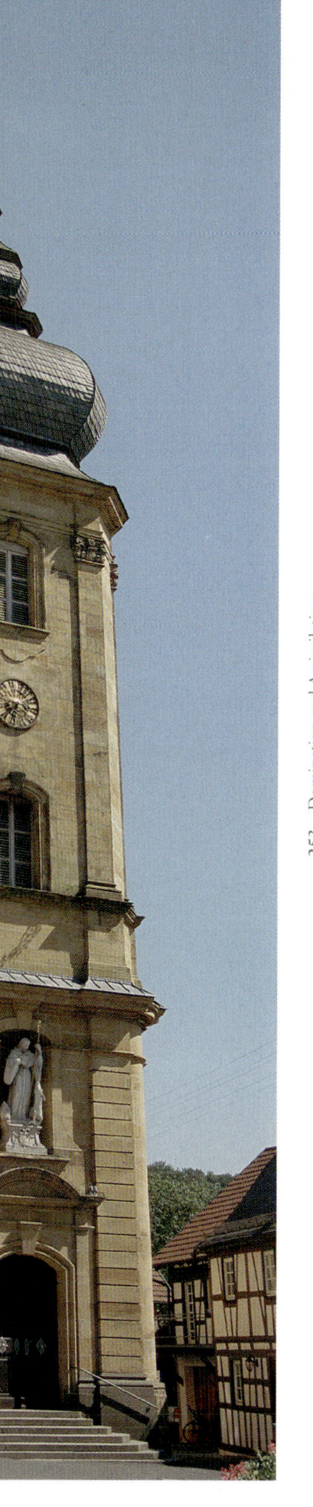

152.
Johann Thomas Nissler, St Aegidius, completed 1763, Frauendorf (Germany)

In Apollo's Realm   Baroque and Rococo Palace and Domestic Décor

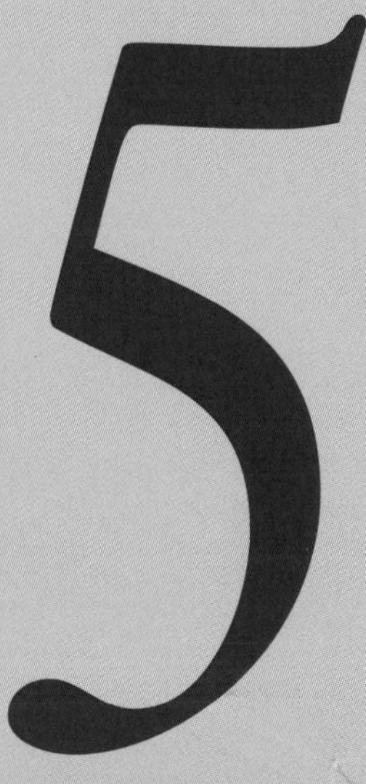

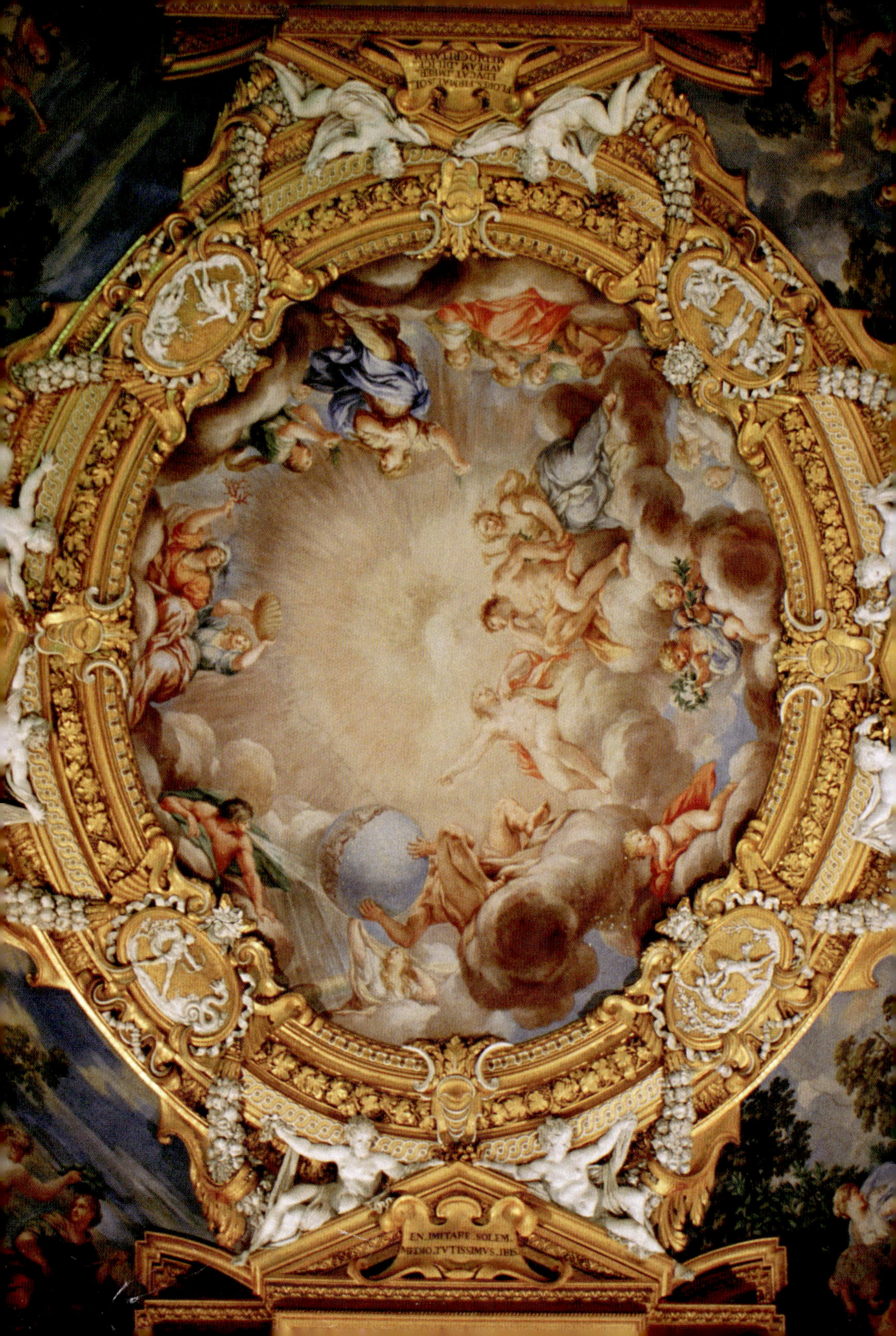
EN·IMITARE·SOLEM·
MEDIO·TVTISSIMVS·IBIS·

153.
Pietro da
Cortona,
Hall of Apollo,
Pitti Palace,
1647. Florence

Church interiors were calculated to overwhelm the faithful and exercise their emotions, fusing the media and using illusionism to encourage meditation and break down peoples' defences. Despite stylistic similarities between sacred and profane interiors, the latter served a very different purpose. The mundane world was concerned with external appearances, and in a culture defined by strict hierarchies and choreographed ceremonies the last thing designers wanted was to ignite the potentially destabilizing fervour of the human soul. If the Cornaro Chapel (see 95, 96) veiled distinctions between the media by synthesizing stuccos, frescos and sculpture, Baroque palaces and civic interiors maintained the inviolability of the frame, keeping the media – like the courtiers who dwelled there – in their place. Palace interiors upheld an essentially classical logic. But aesthetic rigour did not preclude richness of materials, exuberance of design, or love of illusionism, all in the service of worldly might and splendour. If sacred imagery with its visions and ecstasies dominated church interiors, palace and civic interiors made their impact through Graeco-Roman mythological scenes, allegories and martial and heraldic imagery. This conceit served its patrons well: monarchs such as Louis XIV and Augustus the Strong promoted themselves as a new Apollo and new Hercules respectively.

Styles changed radically in the 1720s with the advent of the Rococo, as the ponderous grandeur of marble columns and cornices, high-relief gilded stuccos, and richly embroidered tapestries gave way to pastel-coloured walls partitioned by spidery scrolls, garlands, shells and plants. Rococo interiors increasingly brought the outside indoors, evoking gardens and pastoral landscapes, grottos and languorous groves. But they were no less strictly structured. Although the Rococo increasingly toyed with asymmetry, the frames of the panels, windows, fireplaces and mirrors of Rococo salons were clearly defined, preserving the rooms' sense of order – even though they often concealed divisions between wall, spandrel and ceiling. Indeed, the frame is the defining feature of the Rococo, from the smaller cartouches used as accents to the sinewy panels partitioning walls and ceilings. Like their Baroque counterparts, Rococo domestic interiors rarely allowed the media to merge to the same bewildering – and potentially volatile – extent as church interiors such as Zwiefalten (see 121) or Einsiedeln (see 6).

The first moment in Baroque palace décor was Annibale Carracci's Farnese ceiling (see 13). Although a tour de force of *quadratura* illusionism, with false frames, medallions and sculpture, the ceiling merely mimics the architectural elements of the walls below – the cornice, niches and relief sculpture – and never invades their space. The same was true of the next comparable interior, Pietro da Cortona's *salone* in the Palazzo Barberini (see 51), where the frames are fictitious, the overlapping of media a painterly illusion, and the *quadratura* a reaffirmation of the profile of the vault. However Cortona changed tack in his designs for the apartments of Grand Duke Ferdinand II at the Pitti Palace in Florence (1640–7) – notably the Hall of Apollo (153) – where he turned his painted frames into stucco. An astrological celebration of the reign of the Grand Duke's ancestor Cosimo I, the rooms are named in turn after Venus, Jupiter, Mars, Apollo and Saturn, and they combine airy frescos with a heavy gilded framework overlaid with a jumble of garlands, shells, cameo scenes and figures, many left white to contrast with the gold. Although the frescos in the ceilings and upper walls are animated with cloudbursts, dramatically foreshortened figures and sweeping brushwork, the frames – a three-dimensional antidote to the frescos' illusionism – keep the celestial energy firmly in check. This marriage of exuberance and reason, of divine glory and earthly pomp, became the prototype for Baroque décor throughout Europe, notably in the rooms designed for Louis XIV at Versailles.

As noted in the last chapter, the Louis XIV style began at Vaux-le-Vicomte, and it was here – in the King's Bedroom to be precise – that the Pitti Palace apartments made their first impact on French soil (154). Although Vaux was not a royal residence, it was traditional in French palaces to set aside a room for the king, even if, as at Vaux, no king ever stayed there: the King's Bedroom is not so much a practical 'guest room' as a symbol of royal authority. The chamber was created by the château's team of Louis Le Vau (architect and supervisor), Charles Le Brun (painter and decorator) and

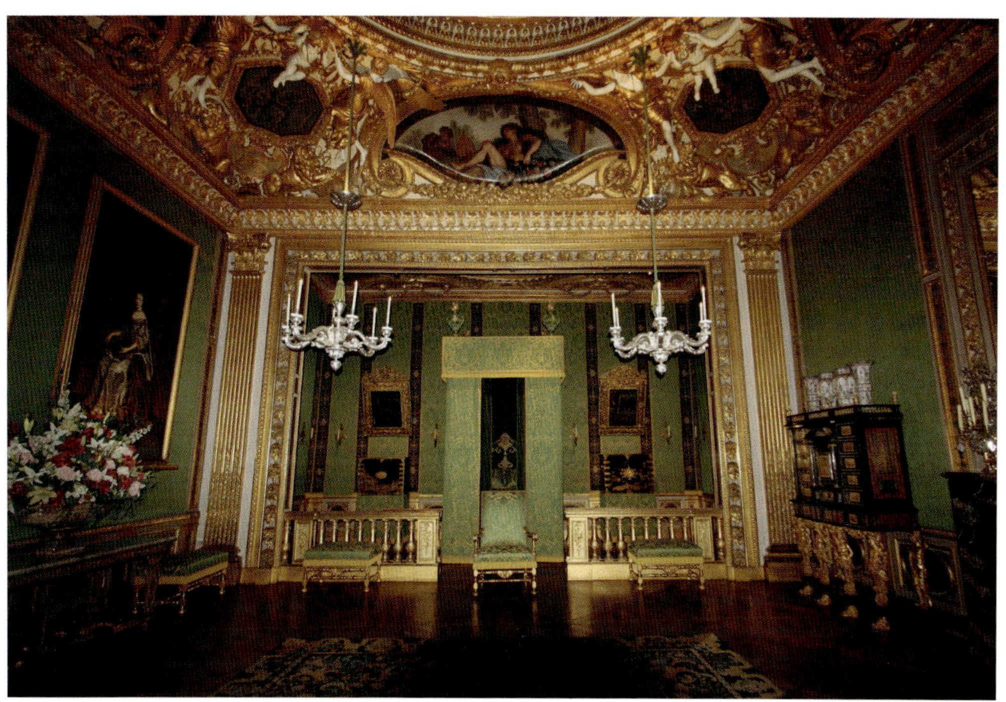

Gilles Guérain and Thibault Poissant (sculptors), and it includes a square
antechamber and a rectangular bed alcove enclosed in a gilded bronze
balustrade. The modest antechamber is overpowered by a ceiling so heavy
that it seems out of scale. Mythological-allegorical frescos are set into the
kind of gilded frame Cortona used at the Pitti, with high-relief stuccos of
garlands, shells, flowers, *putti* and larger-than-life winged figures, their white
skin contrasting with the gilding. Le Brun's fresco of the *Triumph of Truth
Supported by Time* in the centre roundel is surrounded in the four lunettes
by *Vertumnus* (abundance), *Mercury* (vigilance), *Jupiter* (power) and *Mars*
(valour), and, in the false medallions, *Leda*, *Diana*, *The Fates* and equestrian
battle scenes – all celebrations of the wisdom and prosperity of Louis's reign.
However, Le Brun's frescos more closely reflect the more staid style of
Nicolas Poussin than the dynamic apotheoses of the Italian High Baroque.

Le Brun executed this decorative scheme on a grander scale in the Salon
d'Apollon (Hall of Apollo) in Versailles, the Sun King's throne room (155).
The hall is the culmination of a series of seven *appartements* (1671–81)
dedicated – as at the Pitti Palace – to mythological figures with astronomical

associations, this time Apollo and the loves and deeds of kings of old. The rooms were organized along a single axis separated by open doorways to form an enfilade, an arrangement that would become typical of French palaces. The walls of several rooms are encased in coloured marble panels, pilasters and cornices in the Italian style, but Le Brun has arranged them into a more classical grid-pattern. The ceiling of the Hall of Apollo closely echoes that of the King's Bedroom at Vaux, its frescos (by Charles de la Fosse) enclosed in thick, gilded frames formed of scrolls and adorned with stucco angels, garlands and acanthus bands. Yet the effect is lighter: the frames are narrower, the figures are smaller and there is no white stucco to offset the gilding. The central ceiling roundel depicts Apollo – Louis's mythological alter ego – in his chariot accompanied by the Four Seasons, and it is positioned to be seen at best advantage by those standing directly before the monarch. Le Brun introduces a new kind of wall decoration in which patterned velvet serves as a backdrop for pictures from the king's collection – a style that a century later would be imitated by the first public art museums. The throne, replaced in 1689, was originally solid silver – it was made by the Gobelins workshop (see below) – as was all the furniture in the Salon de Mercure (Hall of Mercury), the state bedroom. All was rashly melted down to pay for Louis's disastrous war campaigns, so that we can only have a partial idea of the room's splendour today. As the chancellor of Pontchartrain, Louis Phélypeaux, lamented twenty years later: 'Very little … was gained from that transaction and, more precious than the metal itself, the loss of that magnificent craftsmanship … had proved irreparable.'

Less subtle were the Salon de la Guerre (Hall of War) and Galerie des Glaces (Hall of Mirrors), added to the palace by Jules Hardouin-Mansart and decorated by Le Brun between 1678 and 1686 (156, 157). The Salon de la Guerre contrasts walls of coloured marble and gilded and white stucco – the centrepiece is Antoine Coysevox's equestrian portrait of Louis XIV in a stucco wall panel – with painted ceilings divided by gilded frames and heraldic devices. The richness of materials – it is the only room that uses high-relief sculpture so extensively on the walls – surpasses Cortona's prototypes, yet it is also tempered by French classicism, with its regulated, grid-like components. The ceiling fresco, *France Armed*, eschews *quadratura*

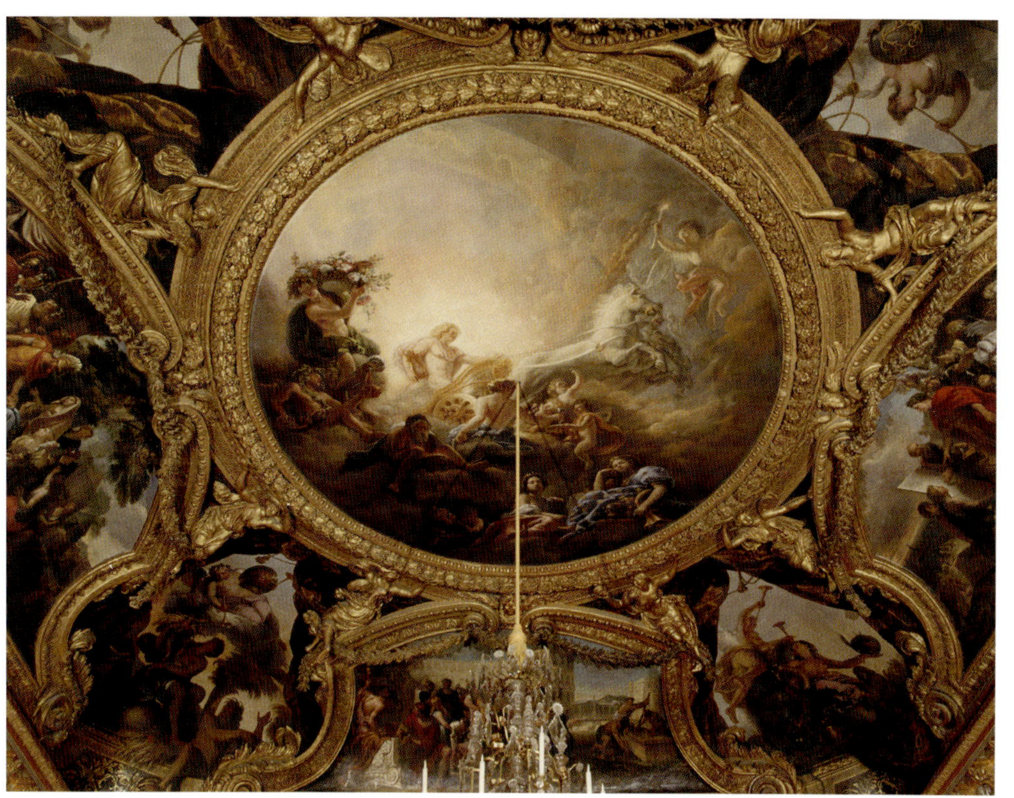

and the figures substitute Italian vitality with Le Brun's stasis (see 53). The
Hall of Mirrors, which replaced Le Vau's garden terrace and spoiled the
garden façade (see 135), may be the most imitated gallery in Europe (see
164, 167). A vestibule for courtiers to wait upon the king and his family as
they passed through on their way to Mass, the hall was also the scene of
the palace's most important receptions. Hardouin-Mansart and Le Brun
introduced few novelties here, stretching the type of salon developed in
the seven *appartements* and Salon de la Guerre into a tunnel-like gallery.
The Hall of Mirrors is faced with coloured marble walls framing rows of
seventeen windows on the garden side and seventeen mirrors on the inside,
each divided into threes and interspersed with sculpture panels. The lightness
of the windows and mirrors and the narrowness of the stucco ceiling frames
mitigate the oppressiveness of the hall's scale and materials. The ceiling frescos
revive some of Cortona's *quadratura*, with false cornices, medallions, frames
and curtains, as well as coffered ceilings that appear to extend past the vault,
but every section is clearly demarcated. The most opulent stuccos appear over

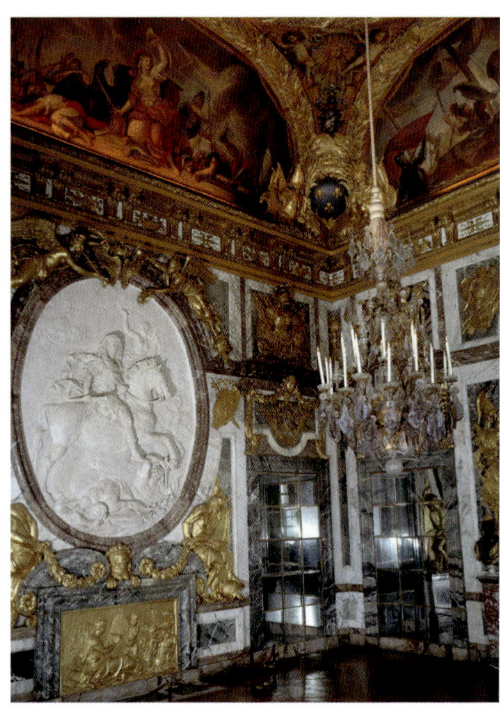

the cornice, including gilded high-relief heraldic motifs and cherubs. Although the frescos were originally to depict scenes from the legends of Hercules or Apollo, the king eventually decided on more palpable representations of his glory such as the *Conquest of Ghent and the King Governs Alone*.

If Cortona and Le Brun used *quadratura* sparingly, another Italian tradition, originating in Bologna, wrapped walls and ceiling alike in illusionistic architecture so elaborate that – like the theatrical backdrops that inspired them – the painted structures give the sensation of a nearly infinite expansion of space. The method was perfected by Girolamo Curti (1570–1631), and his pupils Angelo Michele Colonna (1600–1687) and Agostino Mitelli (1609–1660) became Europe's most sought-after *quadratura* team, working on projects from Rome to Madrid. One of their most impressive collaborations is the third room in the present-day Museo degli Argenti in the Palazzo Pitti (1641), painted in the same decade that Cortona executed his Pitti apartments (158). A fictive structural framework opens up the walls to reveal fantasy rooms and passageways, providing glimpses of sweeping staircases, open-air courtyards and great coffered domes. Larger-than-life

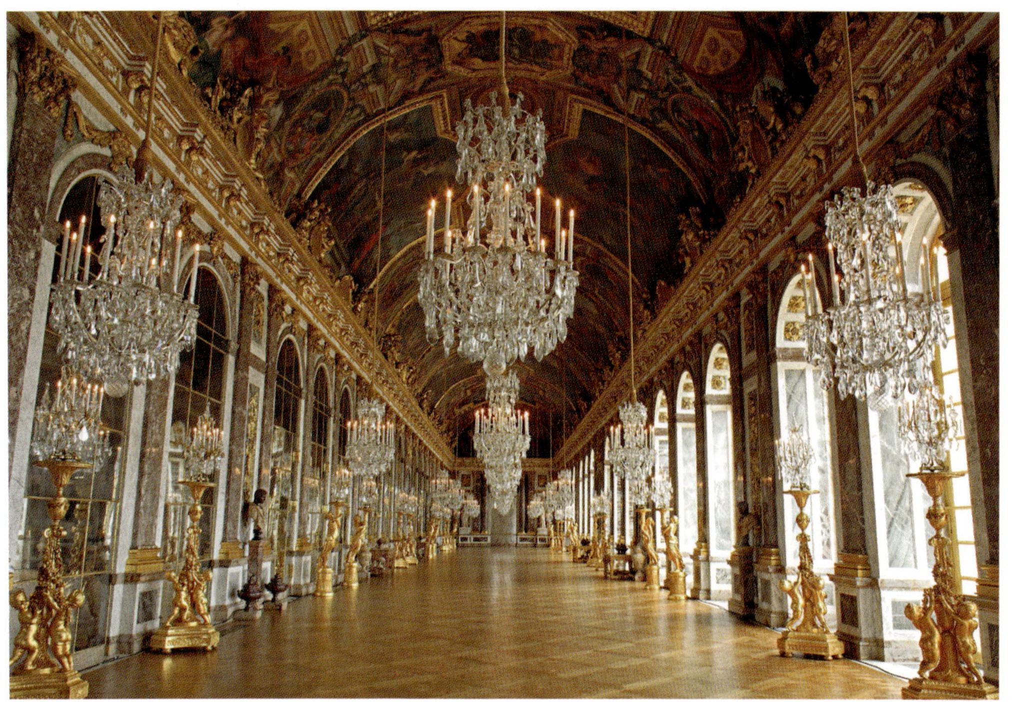

'marble' herms support 'bronze' flowerpots, low 'balustrades' give views of a non-existent mezzanine, and the ceiling vault reveals a feigned sky. Although *quadratura* had few enthusiasts in France, it flourished in England and central Europe, although rarely on the walls. Among the earliest are the ceilings of the Single and Double Cube rooms at Wilton House (designed by Inigo Jones and John Webb after a 1647 fire), one of the most opulent Baroque interiors in England (159). Although the Double Cube has ivory-coloured walls and French-style gilded stucco ornamentation, its illusionistic ceiling (by Dutch painter Thomas de Critz, 1607–1653) is the heir to Curti's creations. The centre features an oval flanked by rectangular panels with depictions of Perseus and Andromeda, while the cove (the vaulted link between wall and ceiling) is frescoed with a continuous band of heraldic devices, cherubs standing on plinths, brightly coloured fruit garlands, vases and decorative scrolls. Although the scenes in the rectangular panels are shown from the front like the framed 'paintings' of Annibale Carracci's Farnese Ceiling (see 13), the scene in the oval painting – *The Marriage of Perseus and Andromeda* – takes place under a spacious coffered false dome inspired by the Roman Pantheon and uncannily similar to that devised by

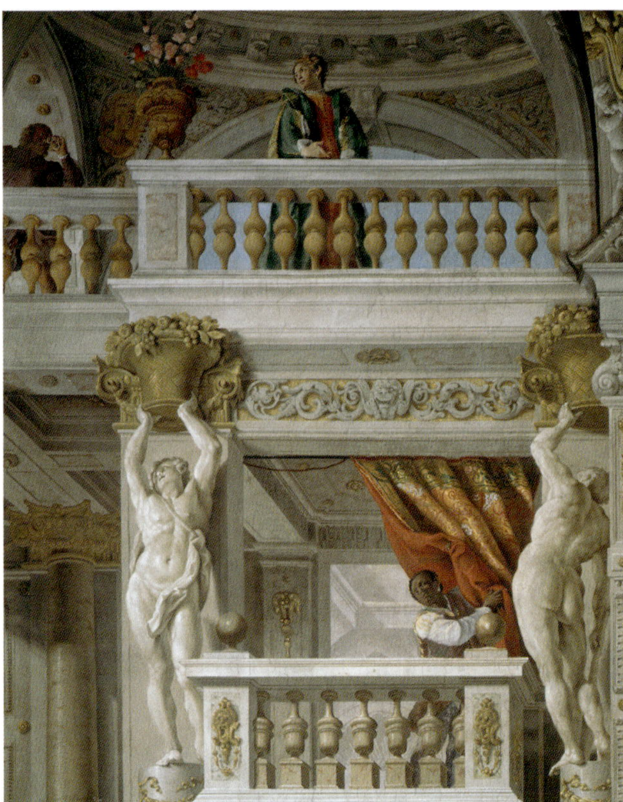

158.
Angelo Michele Colonna and Agostino Mitelli, apartment in the Museo degli Argenti, 1641. Palazzo Pitti, Florence

159.
Inigo Jones and John Webb, Double Cube room with ceiling painting by Thomas de Critz, after 1647. Wilton House (England)

Andrea Pozzo for the Roman church of S. Ignazio nearly fifty years later (see 119) – both ceilings even distort the dome in the same way so that it can only be appreciated from a single viewpoint.

Italian models inspired one of the most spectacular *quadratura* ceilings north of the Alps. Built in 1690–4 by Johann Bernhard Fischer von Erlach and frescoed by Johann Michael Rottmayr in 1695, the Great Hall of Vranov Castle, now in the Czech Republic, is conceived as a giant oval from plan to vault – the latter is even pierced by oval windows (160). Although Fischer von Erlach was inspired by Gianlorenzo Bernini's and Francesco Borromini's oval churches (see 3, 99) and would have known Guarino Guarini's 1686 treatise with its oval-based plans, the oval dome (known as a *Platzlgewölbe*) was already a familiar form in central Europe. Fischer von Erlach would have been exposed to Baciccio's Roman frescos (see 117) – they were underway during his stay in the city – and his enthusiasm for illusionistic ceiling

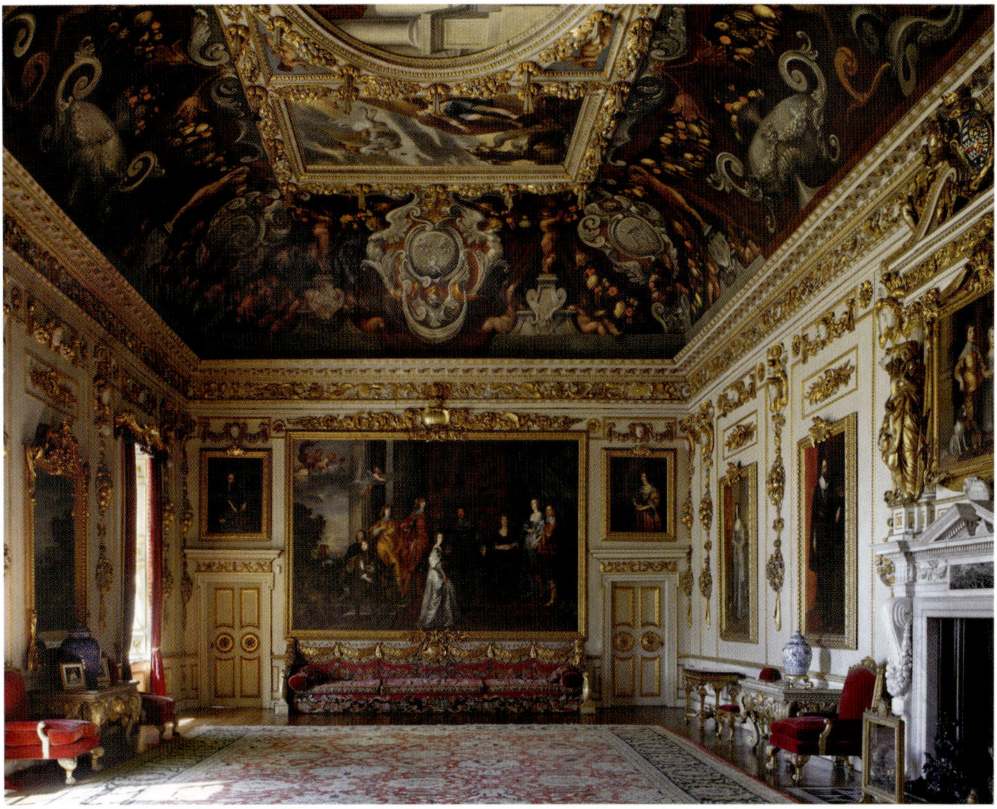

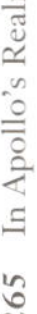

160. Overleaf Johann Bernhard Fischer von Erlach and Johann Michael Rottmayr, ceiling of the Great Hall, 1690–6. Vranov Castle (Czech Republic)

painting had a powerful infulence in central Europe. The light marble walls of the Vranov salon, with their low-relief stuccos, defer to the much more bombastic and vividly coloured ceiling. Prompted by his own experiences in Italy, Rottmayr creates an illusionistic extension of the wall's architecture, culminating in a *Glorification of the House of Althan* surrounded by a feigned marble cornice. The *quadratura* is dramatic and complex: the window frames contain false balustrades and illusionistic stucco work, scattered groups of figures ascend past artificial columns between the windows, and sham stucco heraldic devices and a fictitious acanthus band adorn the cornice. In an inspired attempt to unite the upper and lower sections of the vault more convincingly a luxurious fantasy carpet drapes over the edge of the cornice, hoisted in the middle by a cherub. But despite the similarities this fresco has with Baciccio's, it makes no attempt to fuse the media: the real entablature below the vault remains untouched by the illusionism above, and no stuccos emerge from the painted decoration.

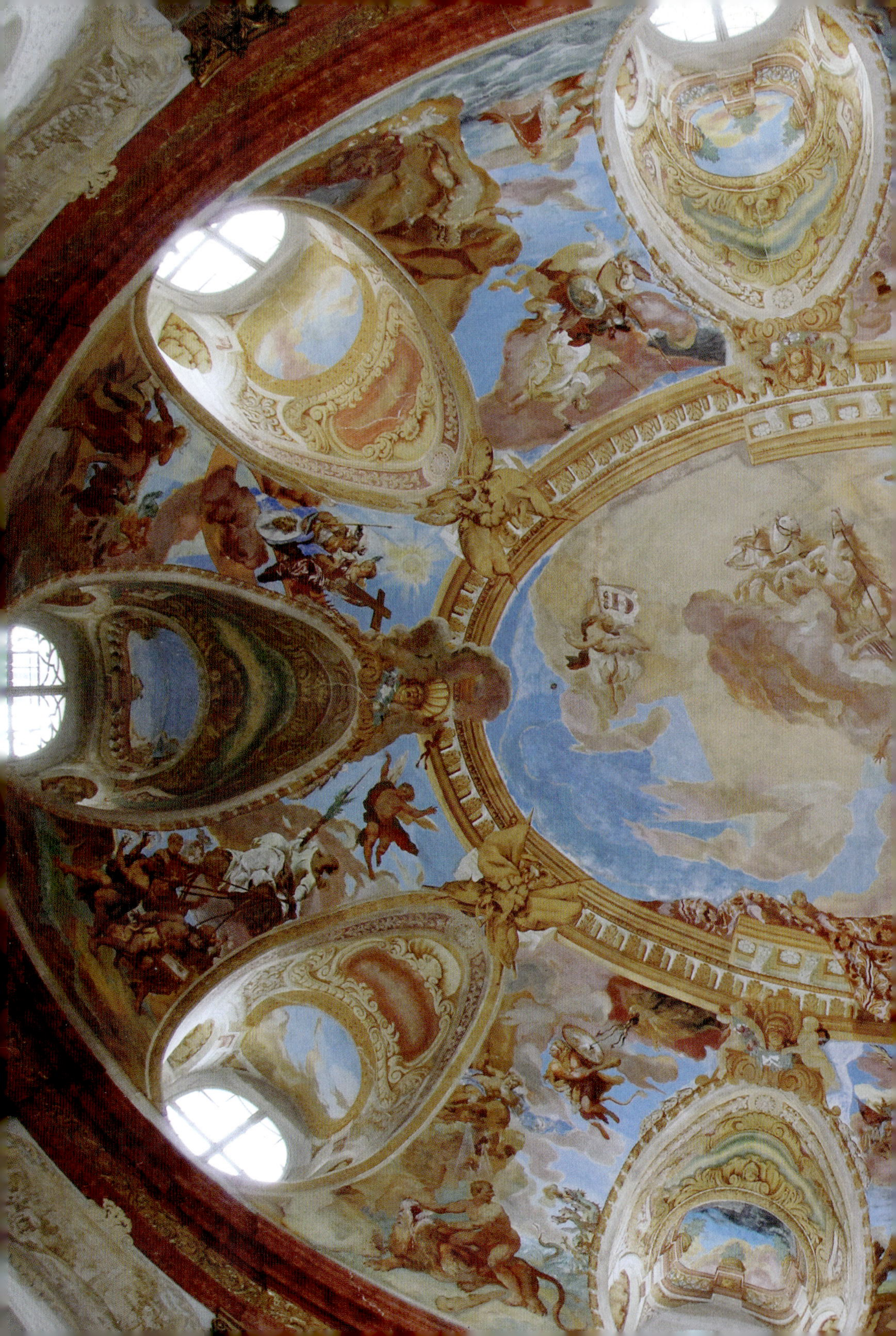

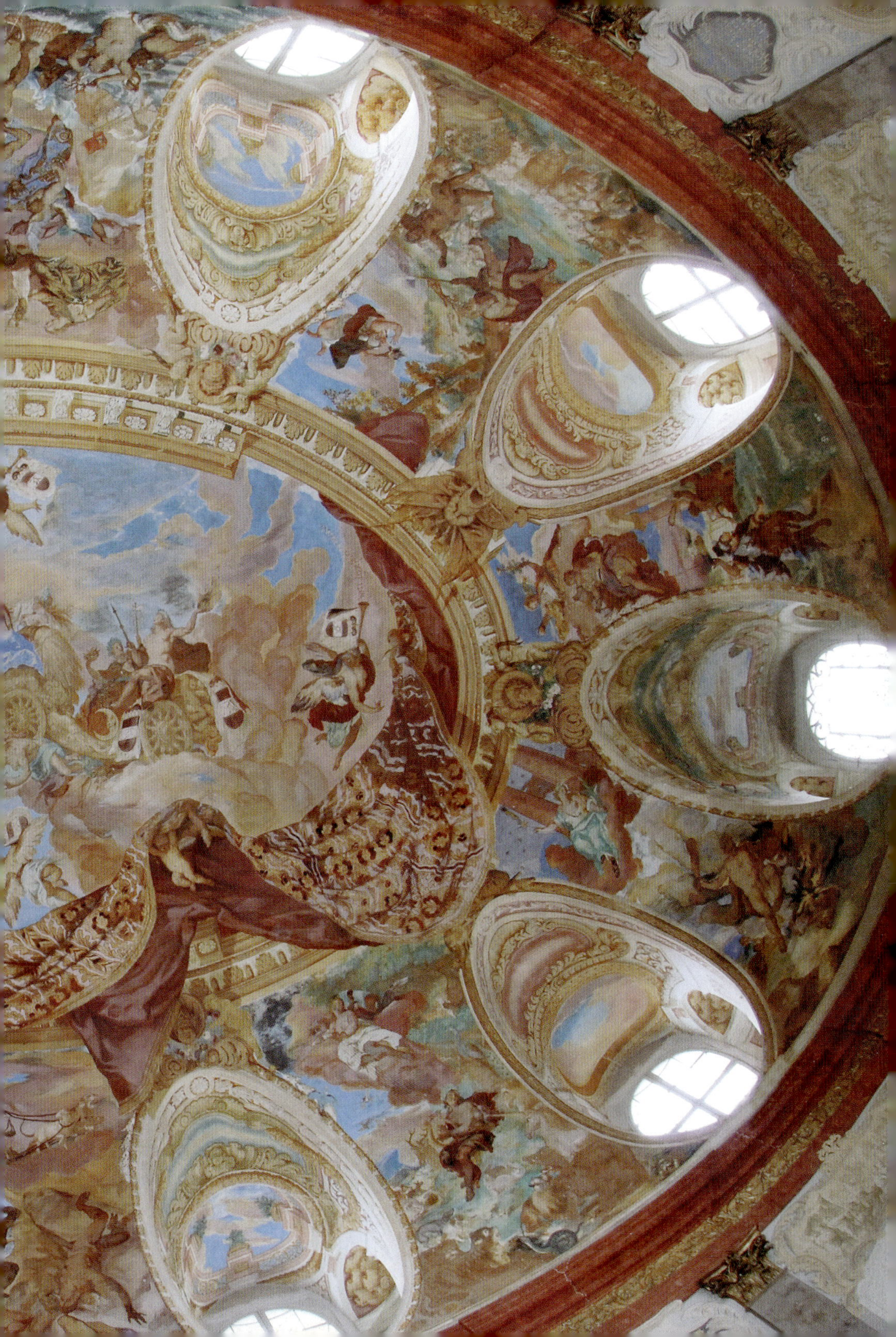

Another enthusiast for Italian styles was King João V of Portugal, the patron of Mafra Palace-Abbey (see 148), who on the eve of the Rococo commissioned one of the largest and most splendid Baroque libraries in Europe. The university library at Coimbra (161), the work of local architect Gaspar Ferreira, features imitation Italian-style coloured marble walls enlivened with heavy gilded scrolls, garlands and coats of arms comparable to Louis XIV's Hall of War (see 156). In each room a spacious *quadratura* ceiling in the Pozzo mode by António Simões Ribeiro and Vicente Nunes fictitiously extends this architectural framework past the vault into the heavens above – as if there were any need to augment the library's already staggering sensation of height. The library's three rooms are arranged like an enfilade of apartments, creating a telescope effect that ends in a portrait of the founder by the Italian Giorgio Domenico Duprà (1689–1770). Like stage wings, these successive archways draw the eye directly to the painting, which is framed like a shrine with gilded stucco curtains pulled aside by cherubs and mounted by trumpeting angels. The library has some of the impersonality of Mafra (see 148), but the wooden bookcases that line the walls (1719–24) – by Gaspar Ferreira and a team of carpenters – soften the effect with their leafy balustrades, wooden flowerpot finials and slender columns shaped like inverted pyramids (derived from French furniture). The side panels (1723) are painted by Manuel de Silva with Japanese-style patterns in imitation of the Asian lacquers that had become fashionable in Portugal as a direct result of its extensive eastern empire. One of the first European nations to acquire a taste for Asian ornament, Portugal anticipated the chinoiserie movement by a few decades (see below). The Coimbra Library's combination of Italianate architecture and frescos, French-inspired carpentry and gilding – the gilding is probably by the French émigré sculptor Claudio de Leprada (1682–1738) – and Japanese ornament was the perfect expression of King João's ambition to be recognized as a global ruler.

The staircase is one of the most characteristic Baroque spaces, partly because of the era's fascination with processions and the way people move through space (see 5, 149). Again Versailles was the pioneer, with the Escalier des Ambassadeurs (Ambassadors' Staircase) that formed part of Le Vau's and Le Brun's renovations in the mid-seventeenth century but has since been

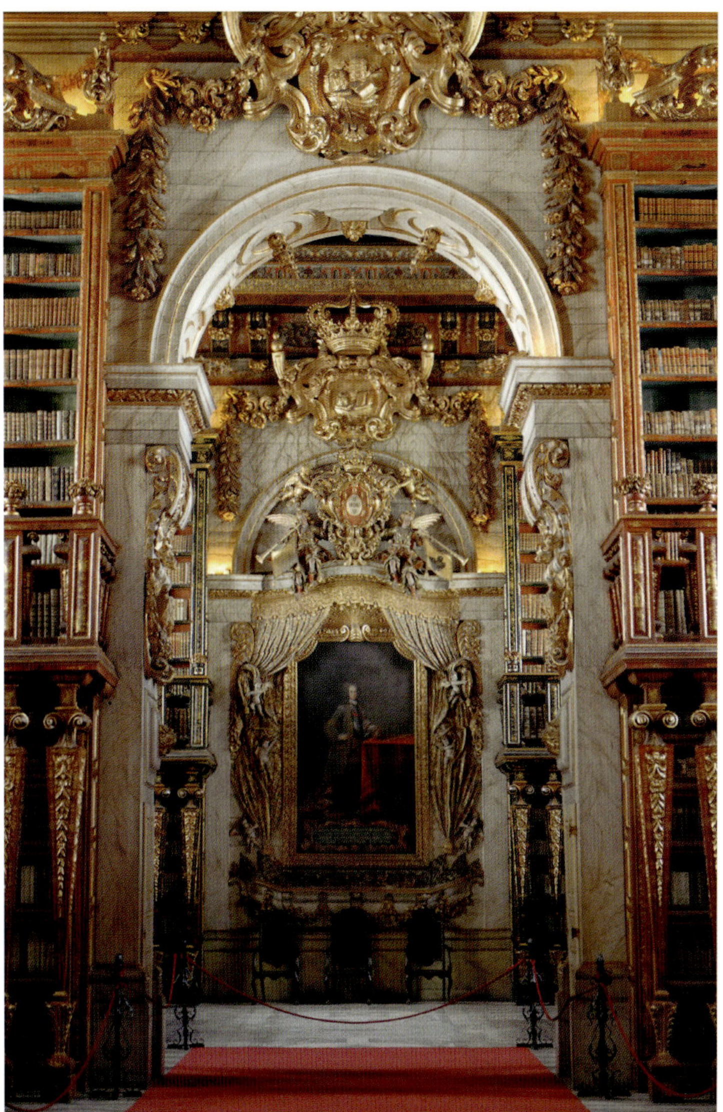

destroyed. The most impressive surviving staircase is the mid-eighteenth-
century Treppenhaus – the name means 'staircase' but it is really more of a
hall – in the Würzburg Residenz. In spite of its late date the Treppenhaus
is untouched by the Rococo décor flaunted elsewhere in the palace (162).
Home to the Prince-Bishops of Würzburg, the Residenz was built in a
single generation (1720–44) on designs by Balthasar Neumann, the architect
of Vierzehnheiligen (see 150). It combines architectural styles from Italy,
central Europe and Holland, reflecting the origins of his assistants and

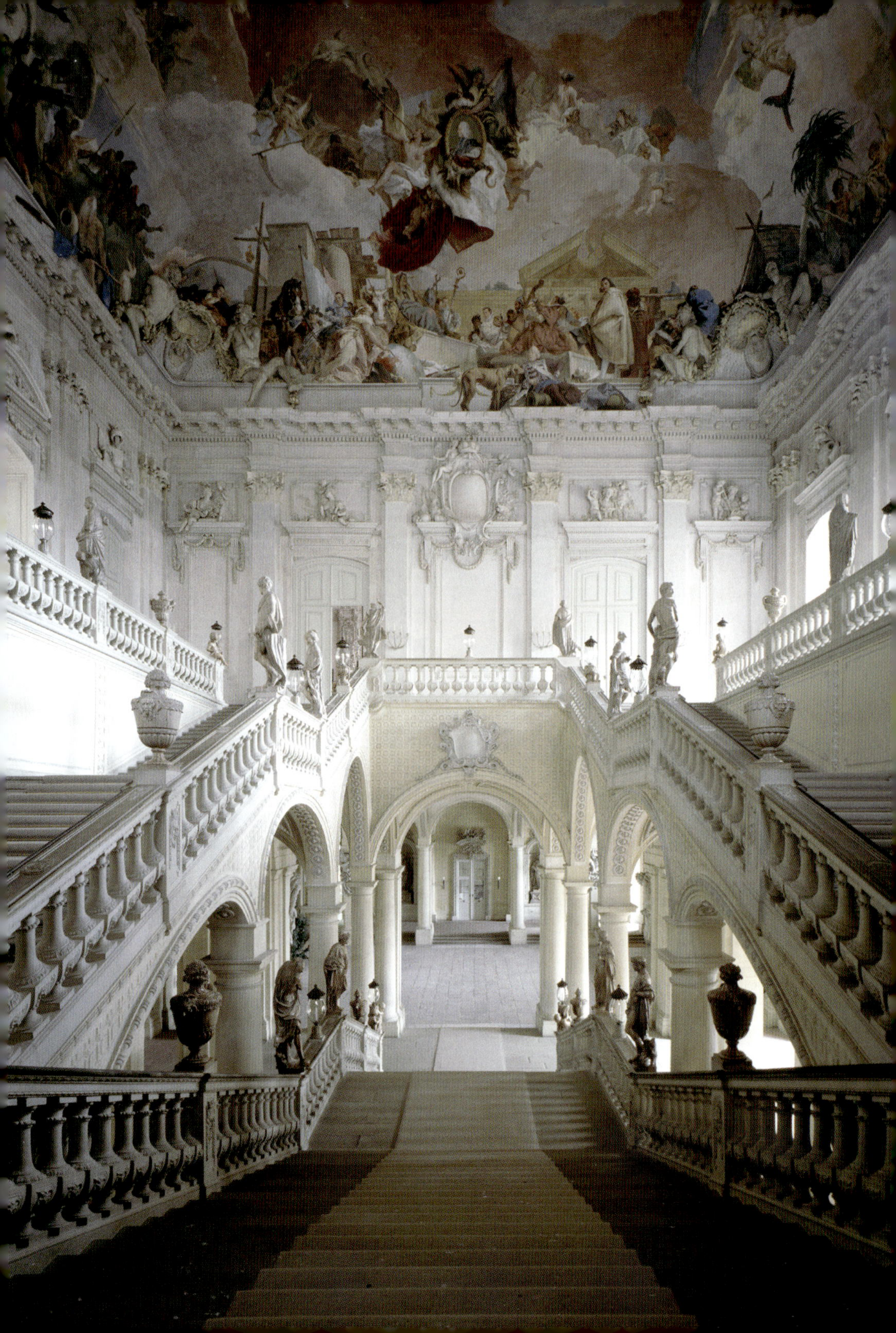

the painters and sculptors who adorned its interiors. The design of the staircase, a prototype for the manipulation of human reactions, was invented by Neumann in collaboration with the French royal architects Robert de Cotte and Germain Boffrand. The walls use the sober classicism of the French Baroque and Fischer von Erlach to set off the vividly frescoed vault by Giovanni Battista Tiepolo (1696–1770; see 162) to maximum effect. The design is also innovative. Instead of two flights of stairs on the side walls of the vestibule as originally planned, Neumann inserted a single staircase in the centre. This flight leads to a mezzanine landing from which visitors must make a 180-degree turn to continue, on either of two flanking staircases, to the first floor. This arrangement guides their approach quite precisely, allowing the space to open up sequentially towards a dramatic, typically Baroque, climax.

The scale of the hall is revealed in stages. At the ground-floor entrance we see the grand sweep of the main staircase and the mezzanine but only a glimpse of the upper space. If we turn around after reaching the mezzanine we suddenly observe the juxtaposed diagonals of all three staircases, one of the most awe-inspiring uses of perspective in the history of architecture. At that moment we also have our first – breathtaking – view of the complete ceiling. Only upon arrival at the top of the staircase, where we can circumnavigate the entire hall of a gallery, do we finally appreciate its full size and the miracle of a vault that measures 33 by 19 metres (107 by 62 ft) yet is unsupported by columns. During our perambulation we survey the whole perimeter of Tiepolo's ceiling, *Apollo and his Chariot, the Planets, and Allegory of the Four Continents*. Tiepolo takes full advantage of this approach by distributing the tumultuous crowds of his continental allegories – the same subject Pozzo used at S. Ignazio but here merging mythological and Christian figures – just above the entablature crowning each of the four walls. The bright, warm colours of the figures under a brilliant noontime sky seem like a vision above the cool, putty-coloured walls. It is also one of the few in this chapter to use the kind of overlapping media seen in church interiors: subtly tucked into each corner a pair of stucco male nudes sit on the same false upper cornice as the painted figures and elsewhere stucco carpets spill out of the wall, borne aloft by cherubs.

162.
Balthasar Neumann and others, staircase, completed 1753; and **Giovanni Battista Tiepolo**, *Apollo Presides over the Four Continents*, 1753. Fresco. Treppenhaus, Würzburg Residenz (Germany)

The most significant stylistic revolution in well over a century took place in France twenty years before Tiepolo's ceiling: the birth of the Rococo, one of the few styles in Western art to derive from interior décor (most Rococo exteriors are surprisingly plain). During the War of the Spanish Succession (1701–14), which pitted nearly all of Western Europe against France, Louis XIV exhausted the nation's coffers and large-scale royal work projects nearly came to a halt. Louis XV (r. 1715–74) was unable to preserve his great-grandfather's style of autocracy, the French aristocracy escaped the stranglehold of Versailles during a brief window when the court returned to Paris (1715–22), and domestic interiors discarded stifling pomp for relaxed livability – in fact, the idea of comfort, or 'commodity', was an explicit justification for the new style. Domestic Rococo abandoned Baroque's high moral tone, its weighty allegories and its obsession with legitimacy: in fact, its abstract forms and carefree, pastoral subjects related more to notions of refuge and joy that created a more forgiving atmosphere for polite conversation (see Chapter 2). Rococo rooms were typically smaller than their Baroque counterparts, reflecting a movement towards domestic intimacy. Even the grander salons used for entertaining were more modest in scale, as social events involved smaller numbers of guests. Rather than serving as repetitive chains in grand enfilades, Rococo rooms were frequently arranged in clusters and took on increasingly specific shapes and appearances according to function.

The first phase of Rococo is also called *style régence* (c.1715–30), after the regency of the Duc d'Orléans (until 1722) during the childhood of Louis XV, and it found expression in the royal apartments and aristocratic houses of Paris and the provinces. Unlike palatial Baroque, the Rococo was also claimed by a rising mercantile and intellectual class, giving it a bourgeois support base like Dutch landscape and genre painting (see Chapter Two). Primarily a style of surface ornament, the Rococo relegated sculpture and painting to secondary roles and used gilding to compartmentalize walls, mirrors and ornamental panels. Rococo spread quickly throughout Europe and as far as Ottoman Turkey and China (see 231, 234) thanks to ornament books featuring cartouches (curvilinear, often asymmetrical, panels), arabesques (sinuous, interlacing plant-like forms) and shell work, as well as designs for wall panels and fireplaces. The most popular were by Juste-Aurèle

**163.
Germain
Boffrand,**
Salon de la
Princesse,
1738–40.
Hôtel de
Soubise, Paris

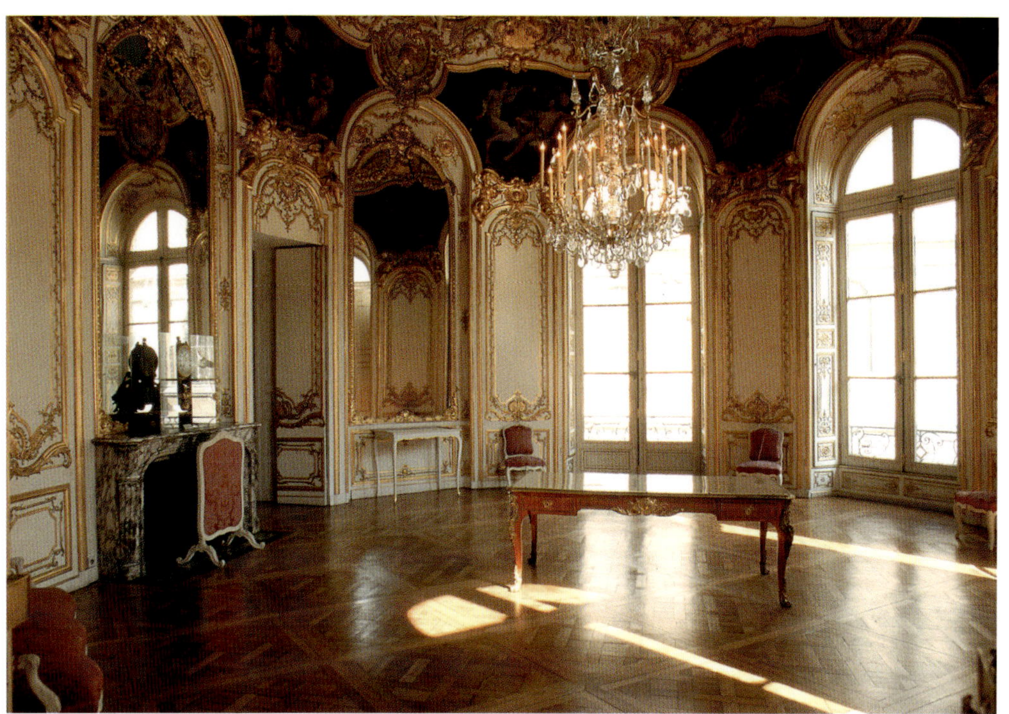

Meissonnier (1695–1750), Jacques-François Blondel (1705–1774), Pierre-Edmé Babel (1720–1775) and François de Cuvilliés (1695–1768). Over time Rococo décor became increasingly asymmetrical (the so-called *genre pittoresque*), and it gave way to a growing enthusiasm for exotica, especially the styles of India and East Asia. In the eighteenth century the nobility and bourgeoisie alike began collecting *objets d'art* on an unprecedented scale, and many Rococo rooms are designed with compartments in the walls to display porcelains, clocks and miniature sculptures.

The Hôtel de Soubise (a townhouse) in Paris, designed by Germain Boffrand (1667–1754), is the prototype of the French Rococo. Boffrand planned the interior on the basis of suites of *appartements* joined by oval salons – not abandoning the principle of the enfilade but giving it a more human dimension. The Salon du Prince and his apartments are on the ground floor and Salon de la Princesse and her apartments are on the first (163). The Salon de la Princesse, a late wedding present to Marie-Sophie de Courcillon, the nineteen-year-old wife of the Prince de Soubise, is the best in the house, with delicate gilded stucco panelling liberally doused with cherubs, cartouches and arabesques. Aside from the marble mantlepiece the only accents of colour are in the paintings of Cupid and Psyche by Charles-Joseph Natoire (1700–1777) above the wall panels and the deep blue ceiling. Note the dramatic change in relative size between figural paintings and wall when compared to the Salon d'Apollon (see 155) at Versailles. In the latter, as in most seventeenth-century palace interiors, the whole ceiling is frescoed and the lunette and spandrel paintings dominate the room. In the Salon de la Princesse, however, the ceiling is monochrome and the diminutive spandrel paintings (on canvas, not frescos) compete for viewers' attentions with the leafy cartouches above and between them. The plain, light-coloured panels, windows and mirrors make the room look larger than it is, and the fusion of spandrels, cove and ceiling disguise the transition between zones – an effect heightened by the white stucco cherubs and spindly gilded arabesques that extend beyond the upper moulding towards the centre of the ceiling. Although there is little new in the details – the 'bat's wing' motif that projects into the wall panels and the shape of the cornices and spandrels between the windows appear in earlier townhouses – their distribution around the room is uniquely harmonious, in part because of the appropriate scale of the room. And despite its capriciousness and the diminishing scale of its components, the Rococo framework in the Salon de la Princesse is as ordered and logical as that of the Salon d'Apollon.

The Soubise's modest scale was not always preserved in Rococo interiors, particularly in eastern and central Europe where the style blended uneasily with a Baroque concept of grandeur. The Francophile electors of Bavaria introduced Rococo to central Europe in the 1720s. Elector Max Emanuel recognized the architectural talents of the young François de Cuvilliés (1695–1768) – at the time his court dwarf – and sent him to study with Blondel in Paris in 1720–4. Back in Munich, Cuvilliés created a new Bavarian Rococo for Max Emanuel's son and successor Karl Albrecht in a series of apartments known as the Reiche Zimmer (literally, 'Rich Rooms') at the Munich Residenz. Faced with an imposing scale alien to Rococo principles – the rooms were meant to be worthy of Karl Albrecht's claims to the imperial throne – Cuvilliés made them more livable by splattering their walls with floral and foliate forms, diminutive figures, trelliswork, interlacing twigs

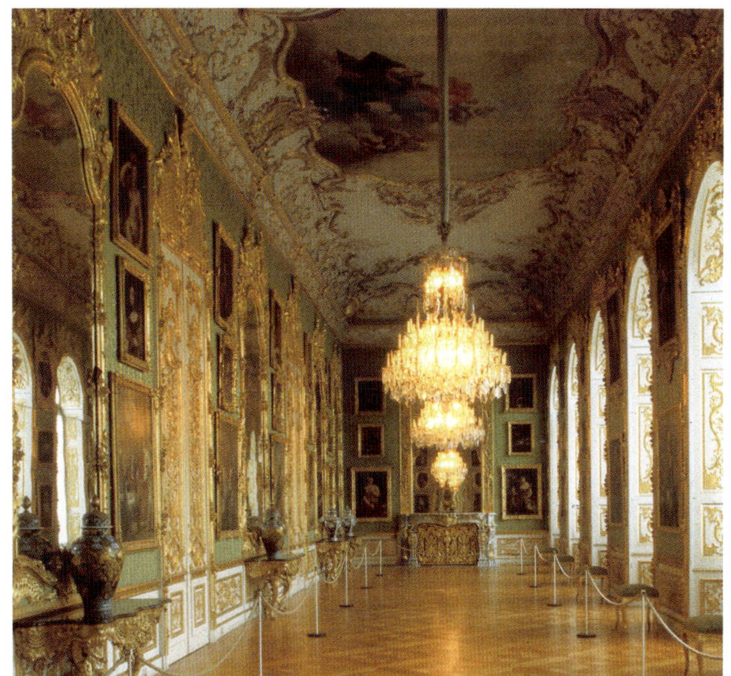

and sinewy palm leaves, sometimes arranged into climbing arabesques to compensate for the hall's length. Typical is the Grüne Galerie (Green Gallery; 164), a festive hall of green damask wallpaper and sparkling mirrors once lit by hundreds of candles. Arabesques in the door and window panels form into tall, narrow bands and the doorframes and mirrors culminate in entanglements of vines, trellises and shells. As at the Hôtel de Soubise, Cuvilliés uses delicate scrollwork to disguise the transition between wall, cove and ceiling, but it is finer and more arbitrary, incorporating naturalistic trees and vines that coil around the mouldings. In the centre of the ceiling they frame a painting of a familial apotheosis – it is more appropriate in a Baroque palace – with allegorical figures riding on clouds and ample views of the sky. Cuvilliés's style is more playful than that of the Salon de la Princesse (see 163), not only because of the naturalistic elements but also because his wall panels are less symmetrical. Cuvilliés was assisted by stucco master Johann Baptist Zimmermann (1680–1758) and sculptors Joachim Dietrich (1690–1753) and Wenzeslaus Mirofsky, and the hall once included bespoke furniture by the architect. Annihilated by Allied bombing in the Second World War, the rooms have been restored with painstaking accuracy.

Cuvilliés's most spectacular work is on a more modest scale. His Amalienburg (165, 166), the pavilion built as part of the Nymphenburg palace near Munich for the Electress Maria Amalia, was planned as two series of apartments flanking the Circular Salon. Using blue and yellow walls to differentiate the rooms, Cuvilliés substitutes silver plate for the more traditional gilding, giving the interior an icy sparkle very different from the Soubise (see 163). The decoration of the Salon echoes that of the Munich Residenz (see 164), with trelliswork framing the tops of the mirrors and tightly interwoven arabesques on the shutters. But the Amalienburg has more variety and naturalism, especially along the upper cornice and into the

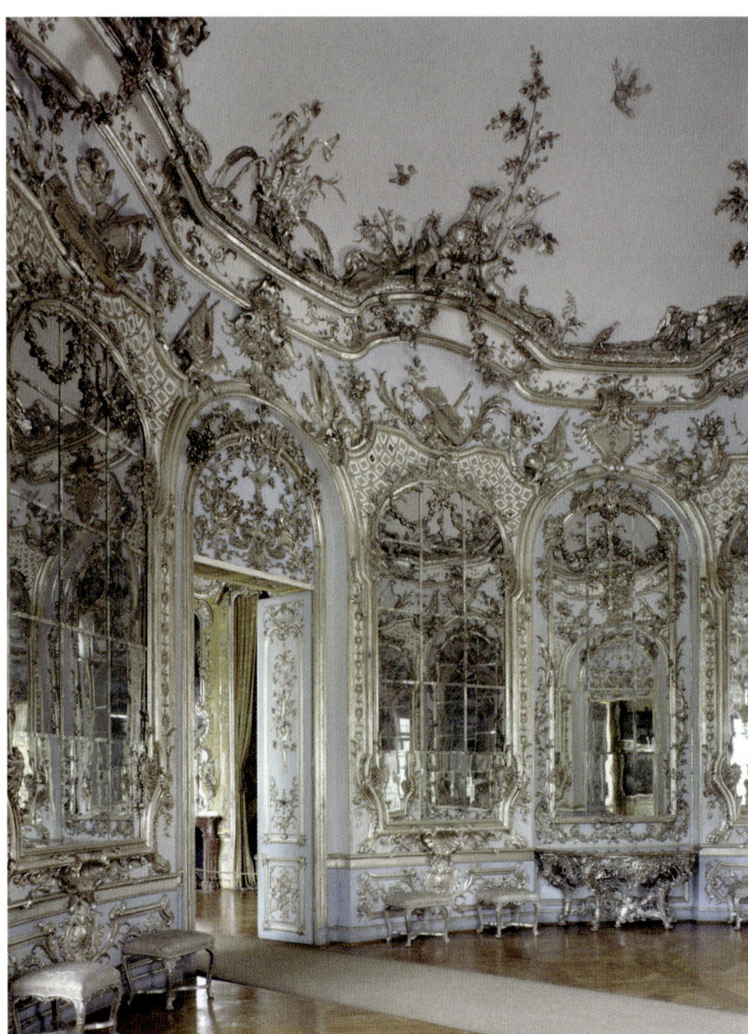

165.
François de Cuvilliés, Circular Salon (Hall of Mirrors), 1734–49. Amalienburg Pavilion (Germany)

ceiling where Cuvilliés presents us with an unbroken landscape of hunting and other country pleasures punctuated by cornucopias, musical instruments, trees, birds in flight, springs of water and high-relief pastoral figures. Here he explicitly gives stucco the role usually assigned to fresco painting, a typically Baroque/Rococo conceit of media substitution. Cuvilliés's stuccowork (executed by Johann Baptist Zimmermann) is also full of illusionistic surprises, as when the figures at the top lean an arm or leg out into our space or branches of leaves dip into the room. The yellow Bedroom (see 166), a modest chamber to the side of the Salon, is so saturated with ornament that it threatens to destroy any vestige of Rococo lightness and livability. Canvas

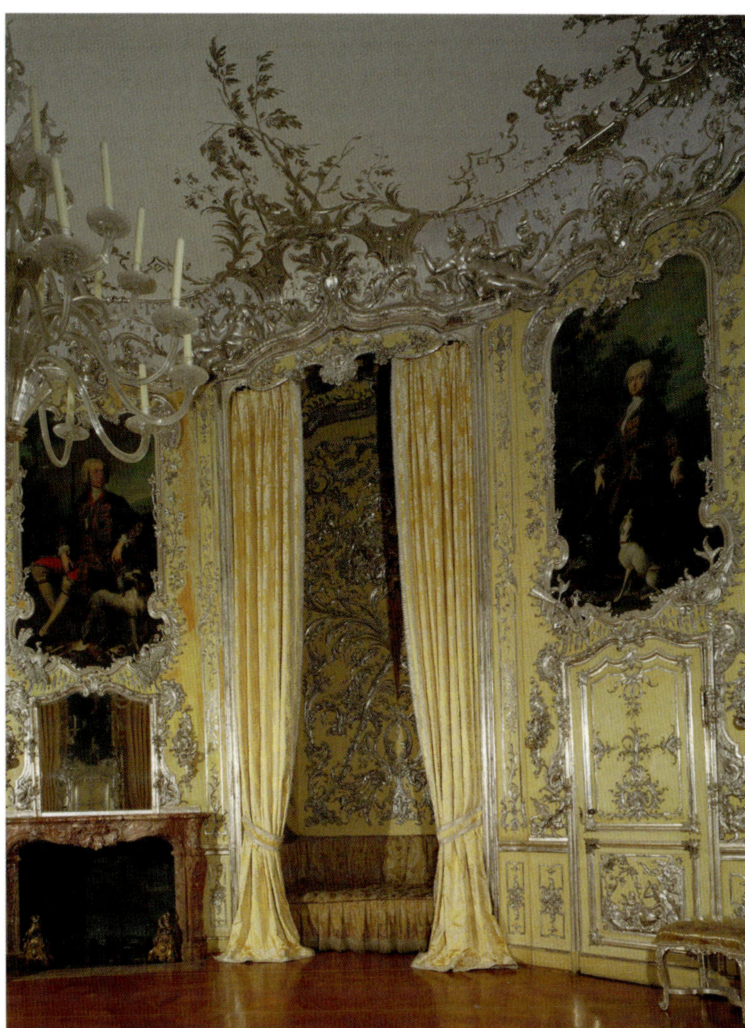

166.
François de Cuvilliés,
Bedroom,
1734–49.
Amalienburg
Pavilion
(Germany)

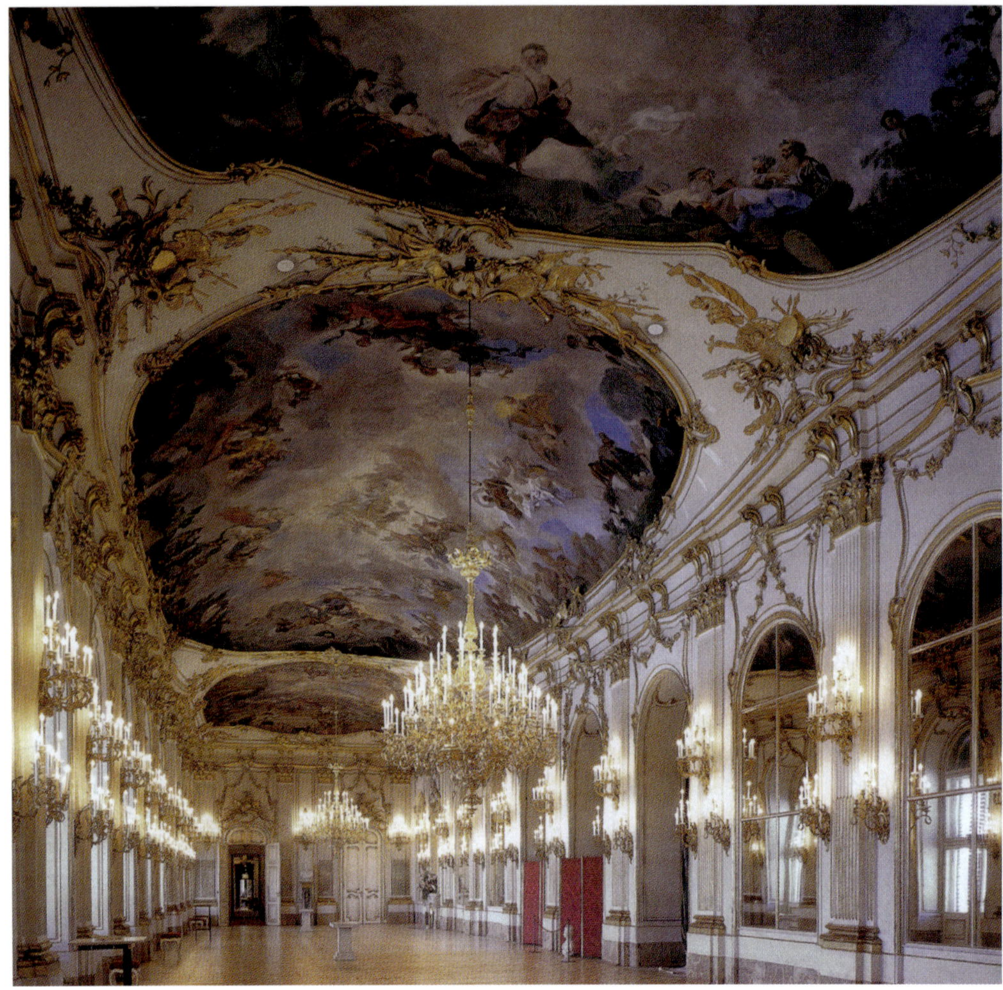

paintings of the patrons are invaded by silver branches, vines and figures, the doorways seem to recede into leafy grottos and the alcoves are plastered so heavily with silver ornamentation that it is hard to see the walls.

Another ostentatious example of central European Rococo, the Grand Gallery at the Schönbrunn Palace outside Vienna (167), contrasts notably with its Baroque model, the Hall of Mirrors at Versailles (see 157). The Schönbrunn was the summer residence of the Habsburg dynasty, and like Versailles it began life as a hunting lodge. Between 1696 and 1713 Emperor Leopold I commissioned Joseph Emanuel Fischer von Erlach to build a new palace on the site, which would have rivalled Versailles in scale had it been finished according to plan (for financial and political reasons it was not). In 1743 Empress Maria Theresia (r. 1740–80), one of the most enthusiastic patrons of the Rococo, hired the architect's son Joseph Emanuel (1693–1742) and the Italian Niccolò Pacassi (1716–1790) to update the style of the palace as she transformed it into the administrative and cultural capital of her empire. The focus of the renovations was a series of spacious reception halls evoking the palatial interiors of Baroque France, as well as more intimate apartments decorated in the 1760s (167). Although the Grand Gallery was Maria Theresia's answer to the Hall of Mirrors – a long, rectangular hall with a row of arched windows on one side and a corresponding row of mirrors on the other – it is a world apart from Hardouin-Mansart and Le Brun. At Versailles the walls are rectilinear and faced in coloured marble whereas at Schönbrunn they are painted white and – because of the curvilinear profile of the mouldings above – appear to dip back between the pilasters. The Versailles cornice is massive and loaded with high-relief sculpture, forming a definitive break between the wall and painted ceiling, whereas at Schönbrunn the stucco mouldings and decorations are much more delicate and the division between the two zones is confused by the trophy-like motifs that push into the ceiling. The painted ceilings are also very different, even though they both depict monarchical scenes. At Versailles the frescos are incorporated into a stucco framework that occupies the entire barrel vault, whereas at Schönbrunn, Gregorio Guglielmi's (1714–1773) paintings – they show Maria Theresia and her consort Franz Stephan surrounded by allegories of Virtues and the lands of the empire – are enclosed in delicate gilded frames and float freely over a plain ceiling the same colour as the walls.

As we will see later in this chapter, Rococo was intimately related to the decorative arts, and many of its motifs and forms were lifted from porcelains, gold and silverwork, furniture and textiles. Nowhere is this link more evident than in the late variation of Rococo called chinoiserie, which dominated European interior and garden design from the mid-eighteenth century well into the nineteenth, surviving the transition from Rococo to Neoclassicism. The Portuguese were the first Europeans to trade directly with the nations of East Asia, shortly after finding a direct route around Africa in 1498. Britain and Holland followed suit just over a century later with the foundation of

167.
Joseph Emanuel Fischer von Erlach and Niccolò Pacassi, Grand Gallery, begun 1743. Schönbrunn Palace, Vienna

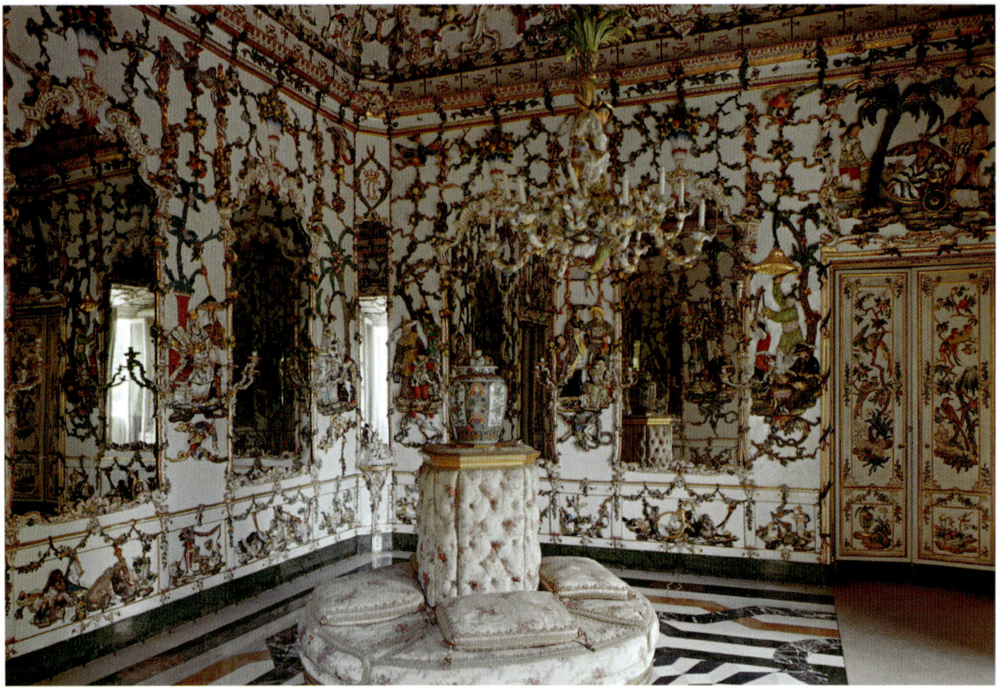

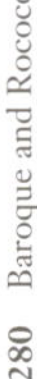

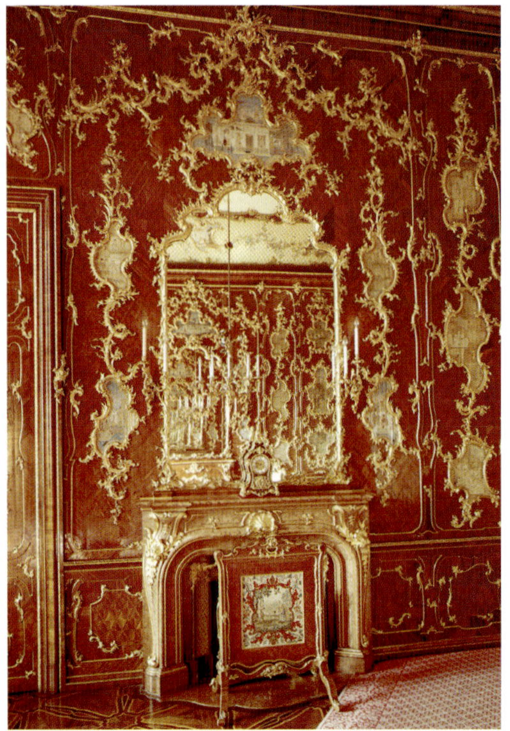

168.
Giovanni
Domenico
Tiepolo (?)
and others,
Porcelain
Room, 1759.
Royal Palace
of Aranjuez
(Spain)

169.
Million-
enzimmer
(Millions
Room),
c.1760.
Schönbrunn
Palace, Vienna

their East India companies – Protestant challenges to Portugal's power –
and Chinese porcelains, Indian textiles and Japanese lacquers flooded the
markets of Amsterdam and London. These items were sought after as objects
of prestige, symbolic not only of personal wealth but also of the influence
of the nations able to import them. European imaginations were fuelled by
perceptions of Asia as a place of wealth and luxury, and consequently patrons
from emperors to merchants vied with each other in adorning their living
quarters with Asian goods and decorating them in Asian styles. Where Asian
objects were hard to obtain, European craftsmen and painters stepped up to
fill the breach, creating a blend of Rococo forms and authentic Asian figures,
motifs and techniques. The vogue for Chinoiserie was ubiquitous: Asian-inspired
interiors swept over Europe from Sweden to Sicily and flourished in the
Americas from New England to New Spain (Mexico), Brazil to Argentina.

Chinoiserie interiors varied significantly, from the spring-like interior of the
Kina (Chinese Pavilion) at the Swedish royal villa at Drottningholm (1763),
with its classical reticence, cool green walls and delicate landscape and figural
décor, to the staggering pomp of the Porcelain Room at the Royal Palace
of Aranjuez in Spain (168). Commissioned by the newly crowned Spanish
king Charles III in imitation of a similar room he left behind at the Palazzo
Portici when only King of Naples, the Porcelain Room was crafted by the
same team of Capodimonte porcelain manufacturers he had used in Italy.
They interlocked thousands of specially cut pieces of china to form a puzzle
of high-relief sculptures against a gleaming white porcelain background.
The ceramic reliefs comprised large-scale representations of Chinese men
and women, generically exotic flora and fauna (the palm trees and monkeys
may derive from representations of Africa or the Americas), and Chinese
porcelains and *objets d'art*. Yet these 'foreign' motifs are bound together in a
quintessentially Rococo manner, the Asian motifs bundled into trophies, the
jagged bamboo branches woven into arabesques, and the narrative scenes
balancing asymmetrically – and precariously – on cartouches. The upper
frames of the mirrors and the scrollwork of the ceiling make no pretences
to Asian style except in medium. The highlight of the room is the massive
porcelain chandelier shaped like a palm tree and mounted by a Chinese
scholar and monkey: it and the large relief figures may be the work of

Giovanni Domenico Tiepolo (1727–1804), who was assisting his brothers and father Giovanni Battista fresco the ceilings of the Royal Palace in Madrid. The same team painted the Würzburg Staircase (see 162).

Many chinoiserie interiors functioned principally as cabinets for displaying Asian objects, their designers attempting to blend the surrounding décor with the porcelains, miniatures and lacquers on display inside them. One of the most unusual – in fact it is unique – is the Millionenzimmer (Millions Room) at Schönbrunn, commissioned by Maria Theresa around 1760 to house her collection of miniature paintings from Mughal and Deccani India (169). Approximately 266 watercolours of the emperors of Persia and India, royal hunts, congresses of sheikhs, scenes from Persian epics and holy men were cut into pieces by members of the imperial family and reassembled to fit into sixty-one specially made gilded rosewood cartouches set into walls of dark hardwood marquetry. The irregular cartouche frames differ dramatically from the miniatures' original setting in album books with rectangular borders, but court painters compensated by concealing the divisions between the paintings. They added landscapes and skies and highlighted facial features and costume elements so that they can be seen better from a distance – as a result the images are neither truly Indian nor European. The Millionenzimmer has a splendid chandelier, this time cast in bronze with Chinese-style enamel flowers (ironically, enamelling was introduced to the Chinese by Italian and French Jesuits).

The Millionenzimmer shows how intimately décor was linked with furnishings and art objects, and is a rare case where they survive in situ. As already noted, the absence of the original furnishings only allows us a partial idea of the original impact these interiors would have had on the visitor. The close affiliation between architectural interiors and furnishings should dispel any notion that the 'decorative arts' were dismissed – as they too often are today – as mere decoration. Gianlorenzo Bernini designed furniture and picture frames, Peter Paul Rubens provided designs for tableware, and we have seen that a member of Italy's most prominent fresco team did not turn down a commission to plan a gaudy porcelain interior for a place of private delectation. The alliance of the arts achieved official status under Le Brun, who invented the idea of

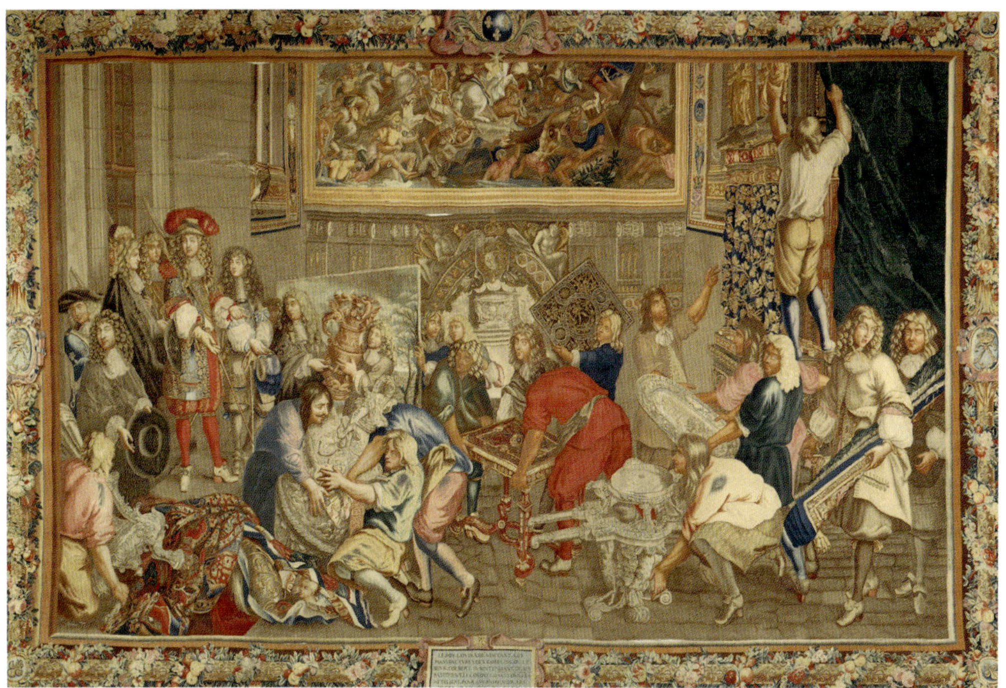

décor as we know it. Under the direction of Finance Minister Jean-Baptiste Colbert, he not only founded the Académie Royale (Chapter Two) but also industrial-scale royal manufactories such as the Gobelins Manufactory (1662) as part of a campaign to amalgamate the decorative and fine arts to produce official décor for the king's palaces and as gifts to foreign dignitaries – and to discourage imports. Monumental tapestries by Gobelins or the comparable San Michele Manufactory in Rome (founded 1710), too often seen out of context in museums today, rivalled canvas paintings and frescos in size and importance. In fact, one of the Gobelins' largest projects was a full-scale tapestry reproduction of Le Brun's Alexander series executed in the 1690s (see 53). Tapestries formed such an integral part of interior décor that wall ornament was kept at a minimum in places where they would be hung. In 1693 Swedish visitor Daniel Cronström remarked that in French palaces 'there are no bas-reliefs on the doors or fireplaces. Tapestries … prevail over everything.' Gobelins was much more than a textile workshop. Officially named the Royal Manufactory of Furniture to the Crown, it involved teams of specialized craftsmen who also produced paintings, bronzes, furniture, and gold and silverware, all for royal palaces or as state gifts.

The scale and variety of production at Gobelins is revealed by Le Brun's wool and silk *The King Visits the Gobelins Manufactories in 1667*, a tapestry by the LeFebvre workshop measuring 3.7 by 5.76 metres (12 ft 1 in x 18 ft 11 in) and part of his 1665–80 glorification of Louis XIV's reign entitled *The History of the King* (170). The king and his retinue are ushered into a palatial room to inspect the work of artisans who rush forwards to display carpets, furniture (some of it silver and other pieces featuring inlaid marble tops), paintings, ornamental silver and bronze vases, a silver brazier and platter, an embroidered curtain, and tapestries such as the battle scene displayed

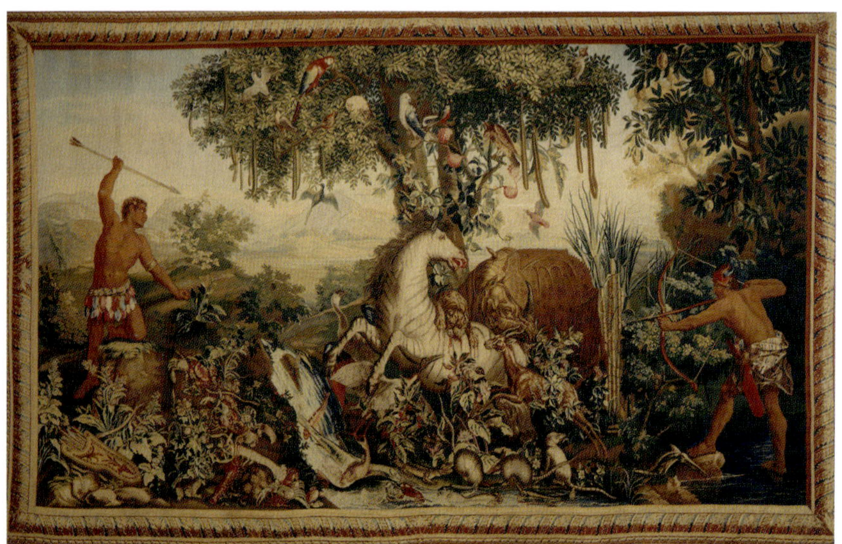

171.
Albert Eckhout and Franz Post, the *Striped Horse*, 1692–1730. Woven at Gobelins. Wool and silk; 3.3 × 5.74 m (10 ft 10 in × 18 ft 10 in) The Getty Museum, Malibu, CA

on the back wall. After 1699, Gobelins produced tapestries exclusively, and they were the best in Europe, employing artists such as Jean-Baptiste Oudry, Charles Coypel and François Boucher. The teams of weavers who transferred their designs into textiles were paid handsomely, the amount varying according to the complexity of the work (the highest paid were those responsible for the flesh tones of human figures). The workshop developed hundreds of dyes to match and compete with the colours of paintings. Another Gobelins tapestry reflects Europe's fascination for the exotic. One of several tapestries in the *Old India Series* (1690–1730), the *Striped Horse* was a Brazilian subject based on a cartoon by Albert Eckhout (c.1610–1665) and Franz Post (1612–1680), two Dutch artists who were among the first to

document the appearance of Native Americans and the American landscape
(171). Post actually spent time in Brazil during the Dutch occupation of the
northeast coast in the 1630s and 1640s, and his landscapes and botanical
studies are remarkably accurate, despite having been painted after his return
to Holland and to suit Dutch tastes. This scene, of a pair of hunters attacking
a zebra and rhinoceros, clearly takes liberties with Brazilian fauna, but the
trees above with their splendid parrots reflect the accuracy of their sources.
Louis XIV was enthusiastic about this kind of exotica not only as an armchair
traveller but also because its Dutch origin made it independent from the
more common American imagery provided by rival Iberian imperial powers.

Baroque and Rococo furniture could be as bombastic as the rooms they
were meant to adorn, and their motifs and techniques were carefully
calibrated to coordinate with the architect's overall decorative programme.
Designers from Le Brun to Boffrand all designed or selected furniture or
artworks specifically for royal salons, whether sconces to flank fireplaces;
chairs, settees and sideboards to be placed against the wall until needed; or
tureens and candlesticks to complement table settings. Throughout Europe,
furniture makers such as Antonio Chicari, Pierre Daneau and Thomas
Chippendale, and silversmiths like Paulus van Vianen, enjoyed the status of
sculptors or painters and were paid as handsomely for their work. Two of the
most characteristic types of Baroque furniture were the console table and
commode. Console tables, usually produced in pairs, were sideboards used
to display such works of art as clocks, porcelain vases or silver caskets. Often
they were directly attached to the wall and had only two legs, although others
were portable pieces with four. One splendid Dutch console, carved in linden
wood painted to resemble marble and surmounted by a marble table (172),
is imposing enough to stand up to the stuccowork at the King's Bedroom
at Vaux or the Salon d'Apollon at Versailles (see 154, 155), with which it
shares its sweeping scrolls and clinging *putti*. The four massive S-shaped legs,
formed of scrolls covered with foliage and ending in parrot heads – perhaps
a reference to the Dutch conquest of northeastern Brazil – are positioned
at oblique angles to extend dramatically into the room. The carving on the
table support denotes abundance, with pairs of cornucopias spilling fruit,
putti caressing grapes and garlands of fruit draped over each leg.

A strikingly opulent piece of furniture is this copy of a commode (173) made by André Charles Boulle (1642–1732) in 1708 for the bedroom of Louis XIV in the Grand Trianon (the copy is likely by the artist's own workshop, and dates from as early as 1710). One of the most prestigious furniture makers in Europe, Boulle was appointed Ébéniste du Roi (Royal Cabinet-maker) in 1672. Commodes – the term derives from the word 'commodious' – were chests of two drawers usually on stands, and they were the most prized piece of furniture in any room. Boulle's commode emanates sumptuousness through rich materials: carved of walnut with a veneer of ebony, it is inlaid with brass and tortoiseshell in a technique known as marquetry. In fact, Boulle was so celebrated for his marquetry technique – made by gluing sheets of tortoiseshell and brass together and cut to form the design – that it is now known as 'Boulle work'. The commode is further adorned with gilded bronze mounts such as the leafy lion's paws that serve as 'feet', and is mounted by a green marble tabletop evoking the coloured marble walls of Versailles's grandest apartments.

Although chinoiserie did not develop until the mid-eighteenth century, seventeenth-century patrons were just as interested in exotica, as we have already witnessed with the Brazilian imagery of the Gobelin tapestry (see

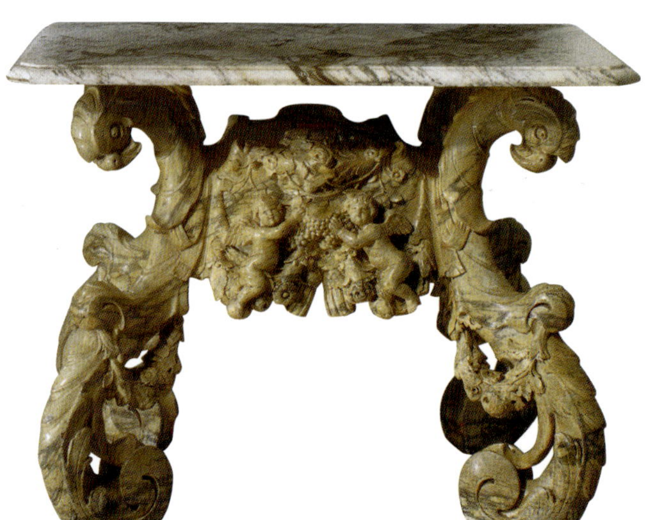

172.
Dutch console, c.1650–75. Wood and marble; 84 × 113.5 × 73.5 cm (33 × 44¼ × 29 in). Rijksmuseum, Amsterdam

171) and Dutch console. One Asian-inspired technique popular throughout Europe, known in English as 'japanning', imitates lacquered wood furniture from Japan and China. Asian lacquer boxes and other objects such as bookstands were available to the very rich in markets in Lisbon, Seville and Rome – the greatest of all was Lisbon's Rua Nova dos Mercadores (New Merchants' Street) – and European treatises on Asian lacquer technique were published as early as 1663. This English piece (174) combines a Japanese-inspired cabinet with a quintessentially Baroque stand reminiscent of the Dutch one just discussed, with caryatid legs, cherub heads, garlands and an eagle (see 172). Although bulky, the piece is carved mostly from lightweight pine, the stand plated in silver and the cabinet (partly of oak), painted in the Japanese style, with silver- and gold-painted designs of Japanese figures, floral bouquets and a pair of geese on a black background. European lacquer methods differed from those of Asia. First a size (sticky solution) and whitening were applied in layers onto wood, which was then painted black or red, varnished and polished. The decoration was often raised above the surface, a technique involving a paste of whitening mixed with gum Arabic and sawdust. The corner mounts and the lock plates for the doors were carved with Chinese designs. Japanning became more common and more sophisticated after John Stalker and George Parker published *A Treatise on*

173. André Charles Boulle, commode, French, c.1710–32. Walnut veneered with ebony and marquetry of engraved brass and tortoiseshell, gilt-bronze mounts, antique marble top; 87.6 × 128.3 × 62.9 cm (34½ × 50½ × 24¾ in). Metropolitan Museum of Art, New York

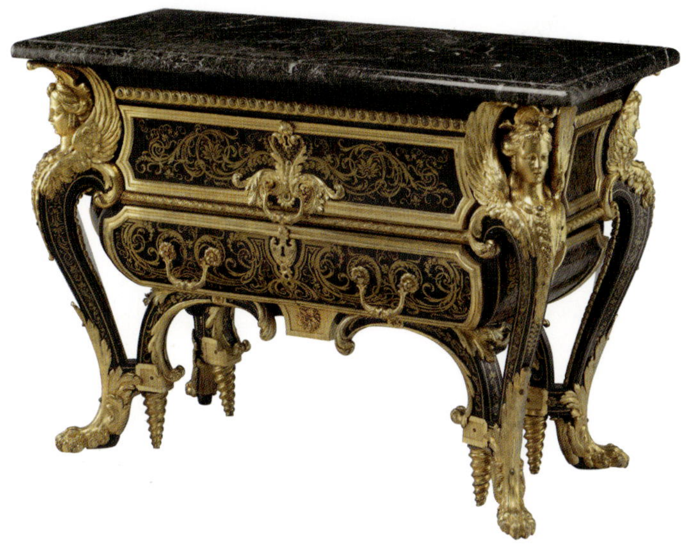

Japanning and Varnishing (Oxford, 1688), a popular guide to cabinet-makers, professional or amateur. Reflecting the enthusiasm for this new medium, Stalker and Parker remark: 'What can be more surprising, than to have our chambers overlaid with Varnish more glossy and reflecting than polisht marble?'

The Rococo introduced dramatic changes to elite furniture, as it favoured smaller pieces with narrow, sinewy frames and more delicate, often asymmetrical decoration, frequently including elements of chinoiserie. Such is this Queen's Armchair – the name refers to a category of furniture and does not necessarily denote a piece used by the queen – made by the Parisian master furniture maker Jean-Baptiste Cresson (1720–1781) for the court of Louis XV in 1755 (175). The piece reflects radical renovations undertaken by the king at Versailles to introduce suites of modestly sized private apartments for the royal family in the Rococo style. The chair, of painted *hêtre* wood, has an ample seat and averted arms to accommodate the wide tresses of ladies' court costume. In the subtle language of the court ceremonial an object like a chair could say a lot about the person sitting in it: a hierarchy of chair types, from stools to chairs without arms to armchairs related clear

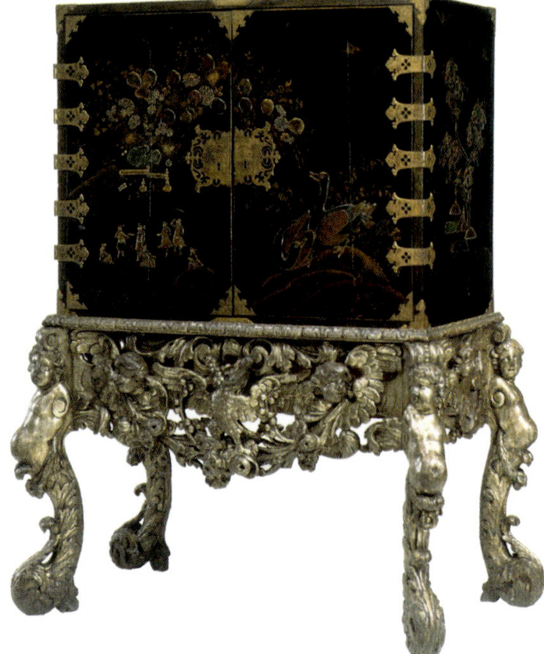

**174.
English
'japanned'
cabinet**,
English,
c.1688. Pine
and oak with
japanned
decoration;
stand of
silvered
pinewood, with
a yellow glaze
of gum resin;
159 × 109.4 ×
54.2 cm (62½
× 43 × 21½ in).
Victoria
and Albert
Museum,
London

messages about status and rank. Its frame imitates the scrolls and shells of the wall panels of Rococo interiors, the uppermost shell positioned so it pushes back over the frame. The tapestry upholstery on the back and seat, in petit point (fine embroidery), features asymmetrical frames formed of cornucopia, branches and flowers enclosing a loosely arranged bouquet of flowers and shell work. Although the pattern is purely European in inspiration, the blue and white colour scheme evokes Chinese porcelains, and is copied from a pattern by Jean-Baptiste Pillement (1728–1808), whose designs for textiles were among the most popular sources for chinoiserie in mid-eighteenth century France. A more obviously Asian-inspired piece is the two-drawer commode made in Paris around 1750 when the fad for chinoiserie was at its height (176). The wooden chest is painted with Chinese-inspired landscapes featuring mountains, pagodas, temples, bridges, willows and Chinese figures in red and white paint on a black background, all of which was varnished to resemble Asian lacquers. The asymmetrical arrangement of the landscape with overlapping mountains to suggest perspective is based on actual Chinese designs, most likely taken from porcelains or silks. The commode's curvilinear profile and thin, spindly legs are further reflections of Rococo style.

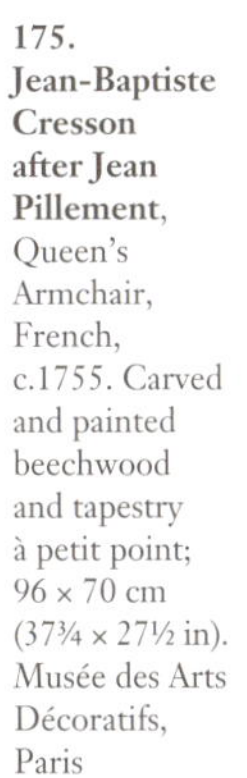

**175.
Jean-Baptiste
Cresson
after Jean
Pillement**,
Queen's
Armchair,
French,
c.1755. Carved
and painted
beechwood
and tapestry
à petit point;
96 × 70 cm
(37¾ × 27½ in).
Musée des Arts
Décoratifs,
Paris

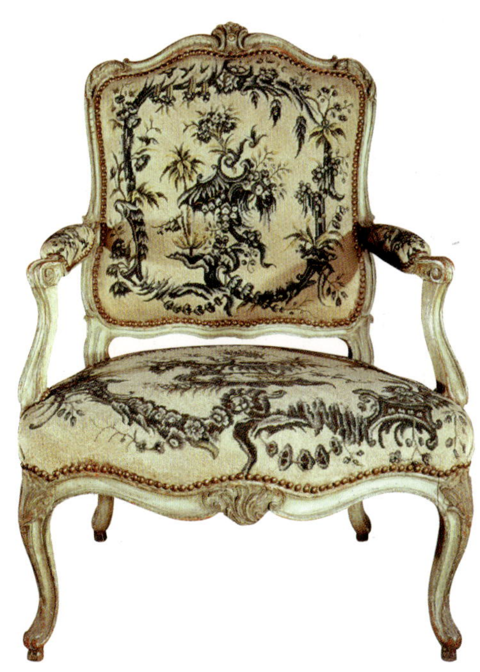

The highest paid decorative artists, in part because of the precious materials with which they worked, were metalworkers in gold, silver and bronze. Some specialized in miniature sculptures – after all, bronze was a sculptural medium with an ancient lineage and executed on a large scale by such Renaissance artists as Donatello and Gianbologna – including reductions of Graeco-Roman models. Miniature sculptures decorated sideboards, served as table centrepieces or *torchières* (figural candlesticks), or adorned treasuries and curiosity cabinets. Their makers, sculptors including François Girardon (1628–1715) or the eighteenth-century Roman artists Costantino Bulgari and Luigi Valadier, were commissioned and 'collected' by patrons as eminent as Augustus the

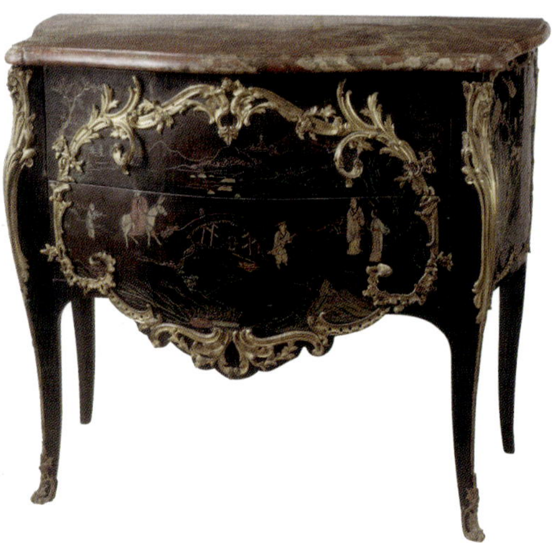

**176.
Jacques Dubois**, two-drawer commode, French, c.1750. Oak with red lacquer decorated in black; marble top and fittings in gilt bronze; 88 × 101 × 52 cm (34½ × 39¾ × 20½ in). Musée du Louvre, Paris

Strong or Pope Benedict XIV. Holland's premier Baroque silversmith was Paulus van Vianen (1570–1613) from Utrecht, who produced the splendid 'Diana Plate' in 1613 (177), so called because its central section, or tondo, is adorned on both sides with episodes in relief from the legend of Diana and her ill-fated admirer Actaeon – the sort of lightly erotic pastoral subject that was so popular in domestic painting cycles (see 163). The plate was made with a companion ewer featuring other scenes from the same legend. Van Vianen created the reliefs with a hammer and small iron rods, moulding the heated metal in a technique known as chasing – the fineness of the background vegetation and the sensuous skin textures demonstrate his mastery of the medium.

By contrast the rim of the plate features a kind of abstract ornament that
van Vianen made his trademark. Looking like melted wax that has dripped
and pooled into shapes reminiscent of Rococo shell work – but a hundred
years too early – this style became known as 'auricular ornament' because
some of the forms look like ear lobes. Auricular ornament was so closely
associated with van Vianen that when he died in 1613 at the court in
Prague, the Amsterdam Silversmith's guild commissioned his brother Adam
to make a silver-gilt tribute that is one of the most unusual metal objects
of the seventeenth century (178). A completely free-form jug with lid, it
includes a handle formed of a long-haired woman leaning over the side and

177.
**Paulus van
Vianen**,
'Diana Plate'
(scene from the
story of Diana
and Acteon).
Dutch, 1613.
Silver; 40.8
× 52 cm (16
× 20½ in).
Rijksmuseum,
Amsterdam

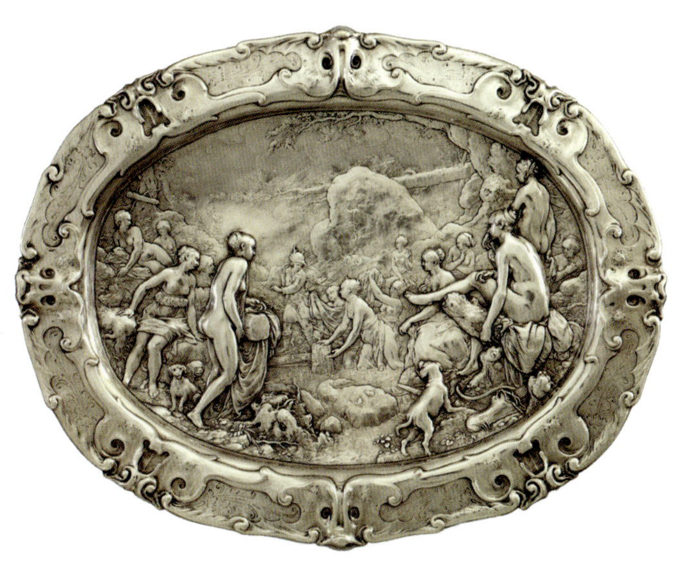

a crocodile snout; with a crouching monkey at the base; a pair or lizards
inside the cup and what looks like a giant dollop of melting chocolate, again
uncannily similar to Rococo, or even Art Nouveau. In fact, a very close match
is the Rococo French silver tureen and platter made by Pierre-François
Bonnestrenne after designs by Juste-Aurèle Meissonnier (179), a sumptuous
vessel for fish soups. Both the platter and tureen seem to be melting under
extreme heat, the platter formed of an asymmetrical accumulation of aquatic
forms and the tureen a bulging, shell-like bowl with a lid doused with
shellfish and seaweed. Not surprisingly gold and silversmiths had a profound
impact on the development of the Rococo.

The most important new Rococo medium was a direct consequence of European enthusiasm for Asian art. One of the most sought-after Chinese and Japanese products was porcelain, particularly blue-and-white vases and platters and green celadons, but also polychrome vessels ranging from the blue, red and gold porcelains of Japan to the sumptuously coloured *famille rose* (pink variety) or *famille verte* (green variety) porcelains. Even though these precious objects were extremely valuable and fiercely sought-after, European collectors could not resist enhancing them with

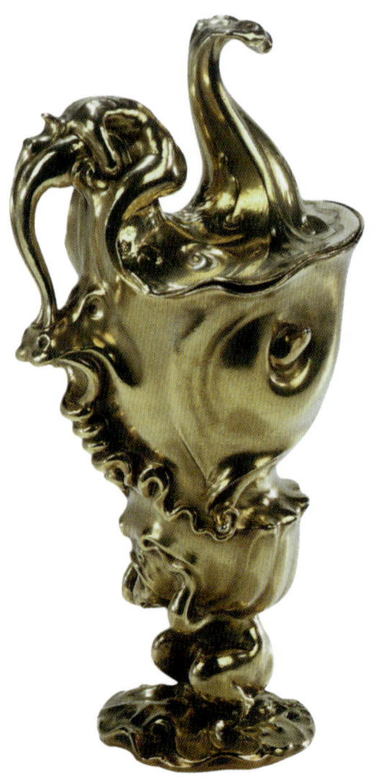

178.
Adam van Vianen, jug with lid, Dutch 1614. Silver gilt; 25.5 cm (10 in). Rijksmuseum, Amsterdam

Rococo appendages or stands, usually in gilt bronze (the medium was known as *ormolu*). Such is the case with this celadon bamboo vase from the Jingezhen kilns of China, which was clearly valued on its own merit but its French owners still felt it was incomplete without an *ormolu* stand rich in Rococo scrolls and shell work (180). Chinese connoisseurs (and modern-day collectors) would have considered this addition barbaric – we know this for a fact as the mid-eighteenth century Chinese scholar and critic Zhang Geng wrote that European style 'is not worthy of refined appreciation, and lovers

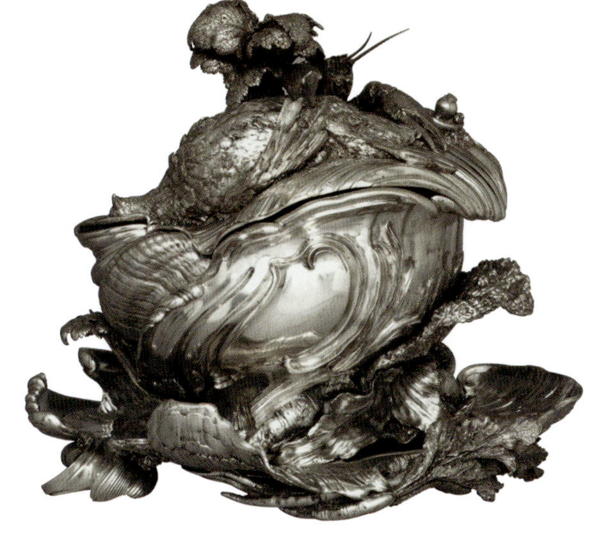

179.
Pierre-François Bonnestrenne after designs by Juste-Aurèle Meissonnier, tureen and platter, French, 1735–40. Silver; tureen: 36.8 cm (14½ in); platter: 8.9× 45.75 × 38.1 cm (3½ × 18 × 15 in). Cleveland Museum of Art, OH

180.
Celadon vase, Jingdezhen (China), 1700–20, with French mounts (1740–60). Porcelain and chased ormolu; 18 × 12.5 cm (7 × 5 in). Victoria and Albert Museum, London

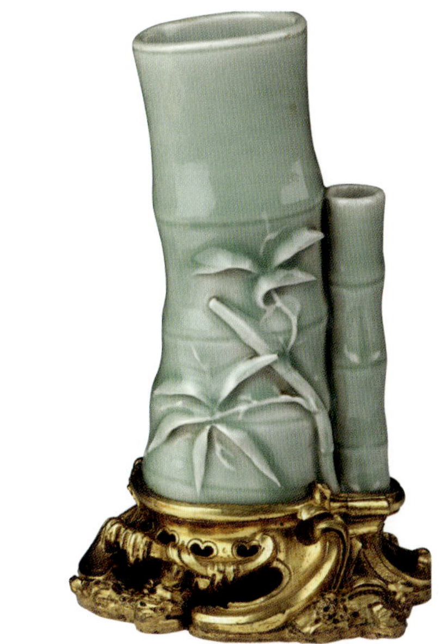

of antiquity will not adopt it.' True porcelain, a combination of white clay
and kaolin vitrified at extremely hot temperatures to produce a brilliant white
vessel, was developed in China in the ninth century, its recipe kept secret
from other nations and only successfully copied in the fifteenth century
by Japan and Vietnam (Annam). Europeans initially had to make do with
earthenware, course clay baked at lower temperatures, which was covered
with a white clay slip, painted and glazed before firing. Earthenware could be
made to look like Asian ceramics, but had nothing of the delicacy or sparkle
of the original. One variety of tin-glazed earthenware, called faience, was
adopted as the official dining services of Versailles in 1709, twenty years

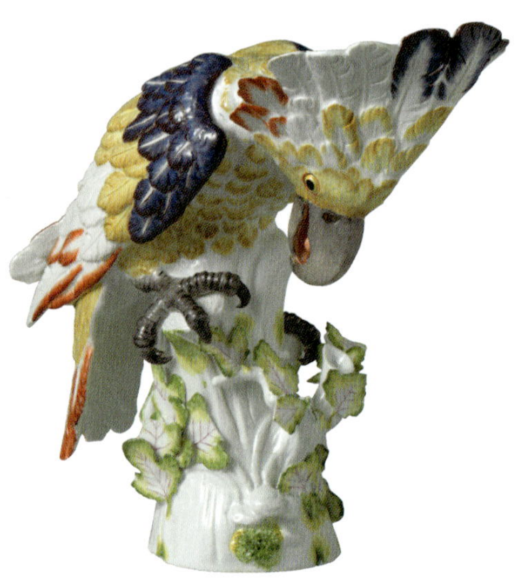

**181.
Johann
Joachim
Kändler,**
Cockatoo,
1734.
Porcelain;
34.7 cm
(13¼ in).
Rijksmuseum,
Amsterdam

after Louis XIV was convinced to begin melting down the silver furniture,
candlesticks and dishes of his early reign to keep France from lurching
further into bankruptcy. The Chancellor of Pontchartrain was disgusted,
stressing 'the shoddiness of the proceeding, for it would mean that the Court
and nobility ate off earthenware, while in the provinces private gentlemen
kept their silver plate'. During the eighteenth century, European kilns finally
figured out how to make true porcelain, beginning with the alchemist Johann
Friedrich Böttger and the physicist Ehrenfried Walther von Tschirnhausen,
who made the first European variety in 1709 for the most insatiable collector
of Chinese porcelains of his era, Augustus the Strong. Augustus was so

obsessed with amassing porcelains that he once traded an entire regiment of dragoons for forty-eight vases and emptied Saxony's coffers to acquire new pieces for his collection – Tschirnhausen called porcelain the 'bloodsucker of Saxony'. Later, other kilns stole the recipe or came up with their own porcelain technology – Augustus made the theft of the recipe punishable by death – including Rouen, Sèvres and Limoges in France, and Chelsea, Bow and Derby in England.

Augustus's Royal Saxon Porcelain Manufactory at Meissen (near Dresden), founded in 1710, became the premier source of European porcelains.

182.
Room fresheners, Rouen kilns, French, 1700–20. Tin glazed earthenware; 24.7 cm (9¾ in). Victoria and Albert Museum, London

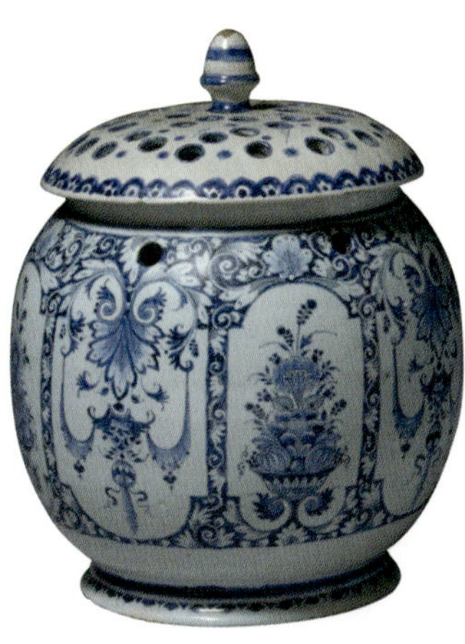
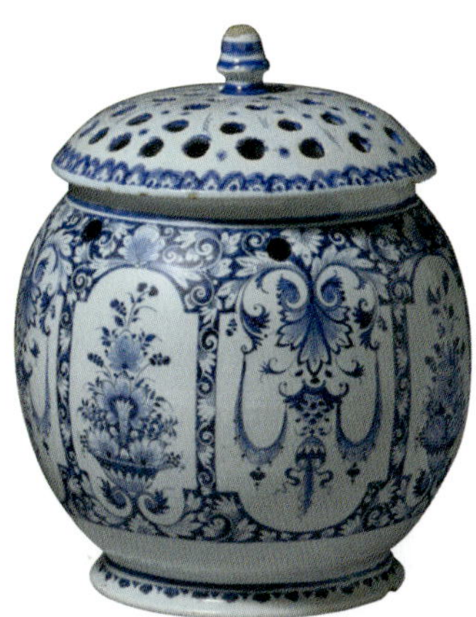

The kiln's first porcelains were Rococo in style, imitating silver pieces like Bonnestrenne's soup tureen (see 179), and decorated with over-glaze paintings of cartouches, masks and foliate scrolls. Johann Joachim Kändler (1706–1775) joined the Meissen workshops in 1731 as a modeller after having served Augustus as court sculptor – that a court sculptor would be sent to the porcelain workshops is further evidence of the prestige of the medium. As 'Master Modeller' (after 1733) he immediately became renowned for his large animal figurines, such as his whimsical *Cockatoo* of 1734 (181). In addition to its Asian obsession the Dresden court was fascinated with exotica in general, and kept a zoo at Moritzburg where Kändler sketched kingfishers,

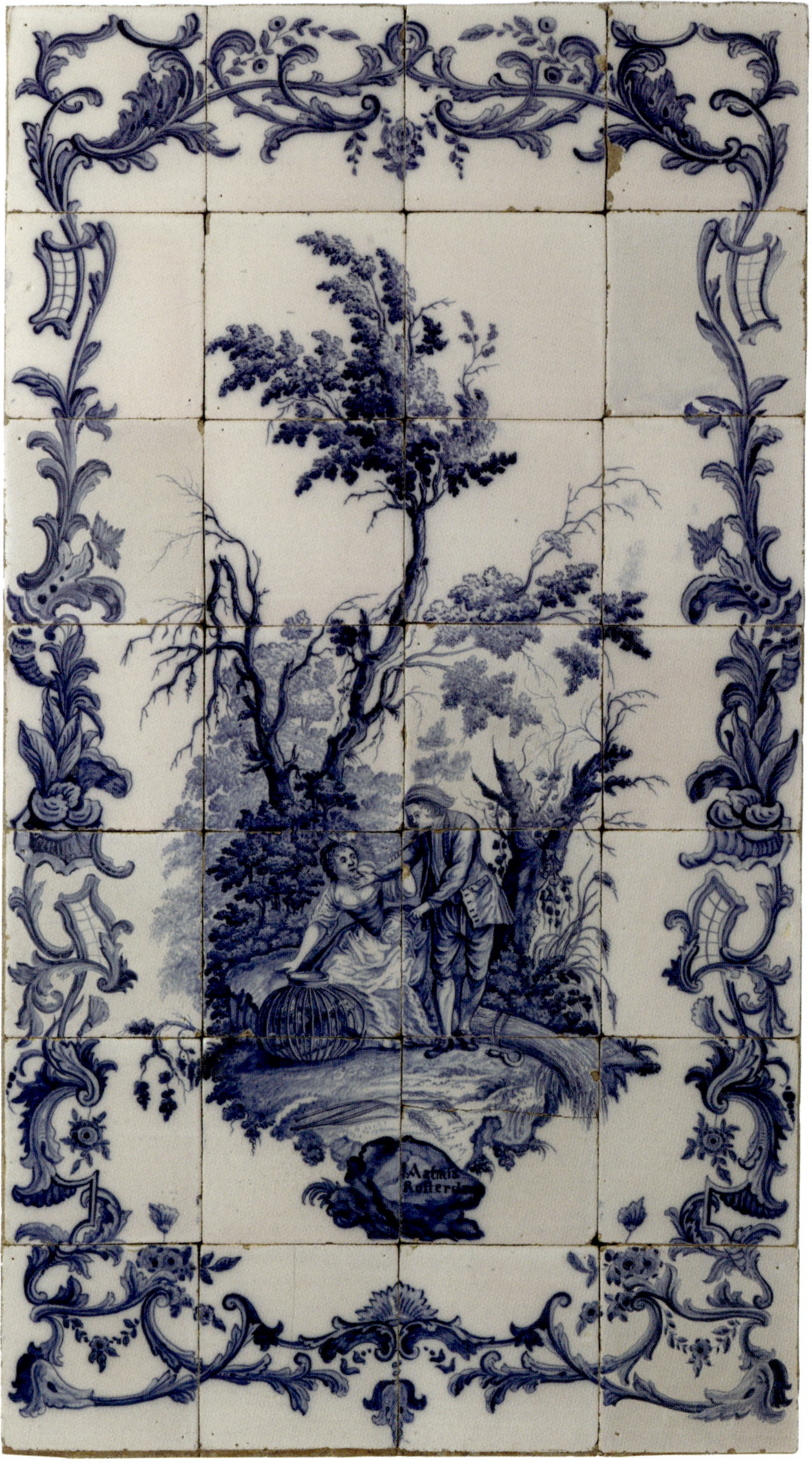

183.
Jan Aelmis,
Summer, panel
of twenty-eight
tiles, Dutch,
1760–80.
Ceramic; 91
× 52 cm (35¾
× 20½ in).
Rijksmuseum,
Amsterdam

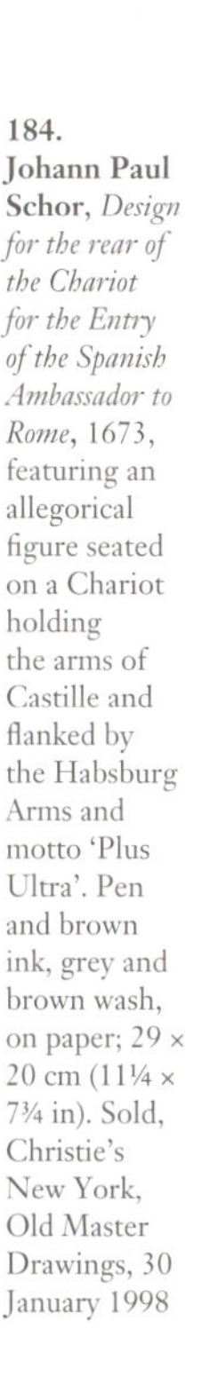

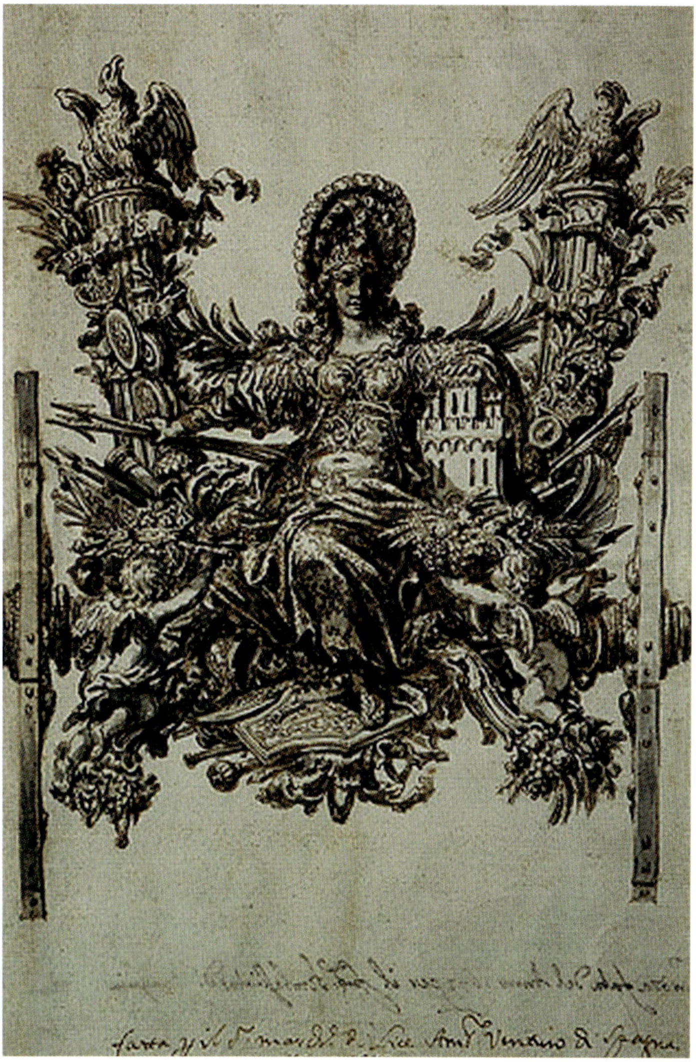

**184.
Johann Paul
Schor,** *Design
for the rear of
the Chariot
for the Entry
of the Spanish
Ambassador to
Rome,* 1673,
featuring an
allegorical
figure seated
on a Chariot
holding
the arms of
Castille and
flanked by
the Habsburg
Arms and
motto 'Plus
Ultra'. Pen
and brown
ink, grey and
brown wash,
on paper; 29 ×
20 cm (11¼ ×
7¾ in). Sold,
Christie's
New York,
Old Master
Drawings, 30
January 1998

parakeets and other tropical birds. In a diary entry dated June 1734 he
described spending two days there sketching a cockatoo, a bird he noted had
a particularly 'attractive appearance'. The resulting porcelain figure, which
he made in lifesize as well as reduced versions, testifies to the sculptor's keen
powers of observation: the lively pose, position of its body and intent gaze
on a grub reveal close study of its model – the piece is an animal equivalent
to one of Bernini's 'speaking portraits' (Chapter Two). Kändler specialized in
very busy surfaces, here seen in the texture of the bark, the ring of leaves and
especially the individual feathers. The painting was executed by another artist
underneath the glaze before the piece was fired.

French faience ware was made primarily in two kilns: Rouen operated on a more limited scale and its products are scarce today, whereas Saint-Cloud was a more industrial-scale manufactory. Nevertheless, Rouen faience was chosen by Colbert to replace silver services at the court of Versailles – a choice he made over actual Chinese porcelains, which would have been prohibitively expensive as they were not imported directly into France. This pair of Rouen room fresheners from c.1700–20 are not court objects but were made instead for the aristocracy or wealthy merchant class (182). In a world where people rarely bathed and bodily odours were masked with perfumes, room fresheners filled with *pot-pourri* (a blend of dried leaves, petals and spices) were a standard feature of Rococo interiors. This pair, made of clay that has been covered with a white slip, painted and glazed – the Rouen glaze has a characteristic blue tinge – is Chinese-inspired only in shape and colouration. The designs – floral bouquets, garlands and shell forms enclosed in panels and surrounded with scrolling vines – come straight from Rococo design books.

A similar combination of Chinese colours and European patterns also characterizes the tiles and other ceramic objects made in eighteenth-century Dutch kilns. Holland was exposed early to Chinese porcelains as its East India Company turned Amsterdam into one of Europe's leading markets for Asian goods, and soon Delft and other cities opened kilns to make earthenware copies of Chinese vessels for more impecunious patrons. They used cobalt from Saxony and fine French clay from Tournai. By the eighteenth century they became better known for Rococo forms and patterns, whether chinoiserie decorations taken from printed patterns or purely European motifs and subjects. Among their most popular and frequently exported products were blue-and-white tiles, either individually decorated or part of a field of tiles forming larger pictures. In spite of their Chinese colouring, tiles were not a Chinese import, deriving instead from an Islamic tradition that came to Portugal, Spain and parts of Italy via centuries of contact with the Islamic world. This panel of twenty-eight tiles by Jan Aelmis (1674–1755) is, typically, part of a series made for the open market to adorn domestic interiors (183). Entitled *Summer*, it is one of a series of the Four Seasons, and although painted in rich cobalt blue on a white background, the scene bears no trace of Chinese style, depicting instead a pastoral scene of lovers in the woods and a surrounding framework of shells, scrolls and trelliswork reminiscent of the interiors of Cuvilliés (see 164).

The final object in this chapter not only unifies the main styles and media discussed above but also serves as a bridge to Chapter Six. The *Oceans' Coach*, commissioned from a team of carpenters, sculptors, gilders and textile designers by King João V of Portugal in 1716, is one of the most opulent of a kind of contraption that epitomized the Baroque's lust for pageantry, combining the forms and styles of architecture, sculpture and the decorative arts (185). Ceremonial carriages, built to join convoys during public processions and other momentous occasions and sometimes used only once, partook more of the transient world of ephemera than the 'permanent' domain of palaces and their furnishings. Nevertheless, they were a kind of travelling palace and the artists who designed them also designed interiors, furnishings and even 'major arts' like sculpture, and their style derives closely from sources as varied as Cortona's stuccowork at the Pitti Palace (see 153), the statues at the base of Bernini's Fountain of the Four Rivers (see 127) or furniture like the Dutch console mentioned above (see 172). Rome was the foremost centre for carriage manufacture and its coaches rank among the greatest works of Baroque art, yet because they cannot neatly be categorized under any single medium they are unjustly overlooked. Generous archives of carriage designs survive by such designers as Johann Paul Schor (1615–1674) in the seventeenth century and Ignazio Stern (1680–1748) in the eighteenth (184). Schor, from Innsbruck and known in Italy as Giovanni Paolo Tedesco, was probably the most influential not only in carriage design but in the Baroque decorative arts in general. He worked with Cortona and Bernini, and the latter was so impressed that he shocked courtiers during his stay in Paris by quipping that Schor was better than Charles Le Brun.

Many of Schor's designs were inspired by Cortona's stuccowork with its combination of architecture, scrolls, foliage and figures. Schor developed a style known as 'vegetal-floral,' in which interlacing leaves and flowers – no longer mere decoration – assumed structural functions, as with the curling tendril-like spokes in the *Oceans' Coach*'s wheels. Although the carriage dates from the early eighteenth century, the influence of Schor and Bernini is

dominant in its design. Built by a Roman workshop, the coach may have
been designed by the Maltese architect Carlos Gimac and Portuguese
painter Vieira Lusitano, both based in Lisbon. One of only three surviving
Roman ceremonial coaches of the period, it was built for the Portuguese
ambassador at the papal court, Rodrigo Anes de Sá Almeida e Meneses, for
an audience on 8 July 1716. It formed part of a trio of allegorical carriages,
commemorating in turn Portugal's role in supporting the papacy, defending
orthodoxy, and spreading Catholicism to Asia, Africa and Brazil – ironically,
the purpose of this audience was to convince the pope not to suppress
Portuguese-sponsored missions in China that tolerated Confucian rites.
One was called the *Navigation and Conquest Coach*, the second the *Coronation
of Lisbon as the Capital of the Empire Coach*, and the third the *Oceans' Coach*,
representing Portugal's discovery of the connection between the Atlantic
and Indian Ocean in 1498. Its symbolism is every bit as complex – Almeida
was an intellectual and may have devised its programme – and its sculptural
groups just as monumental as Bernini's Fountain of Four Rivers to which it
was profoundly indebted.

The Oceans' Coach is built primarily of carved and gilt wood, with iron
fittings and silk furnishings. The sculptural group at the back (the most
important) represents the link between the oceans, and is formed of five
lifesize allegorical figures on two levels. At the top Apollo, emerging from
a globe of the world, plays his lyre and raises his right arm to signal the
friendship between the Indian and Atlantic Oceans. On either side a pair of
cherubs symbolize the north and south poles and female allegories represent
spring and summer – holding, respectively, a cornucopia and wheat sheaf –
themselves accompanied by *putti*. Below, two elders looking like Bernini's
river gods and representing the two oceans clasp each others' hands in a
gesture of friendship. On the front, flanking the coachman's seat, are two
lifesize female allegories of autumn and winter to complement those at
the back, the former crowned with fruit and the latter holding a brazier,
attended by another pair of *putti*. The cabin, where the ambassador and
his attendants sat, is open on all sides with a post at each corner to support
the roof – a lightweight canopy echoing the form of a *baldacchino* with all
its papal associations. The entire exterior of the cabin and finials is covered

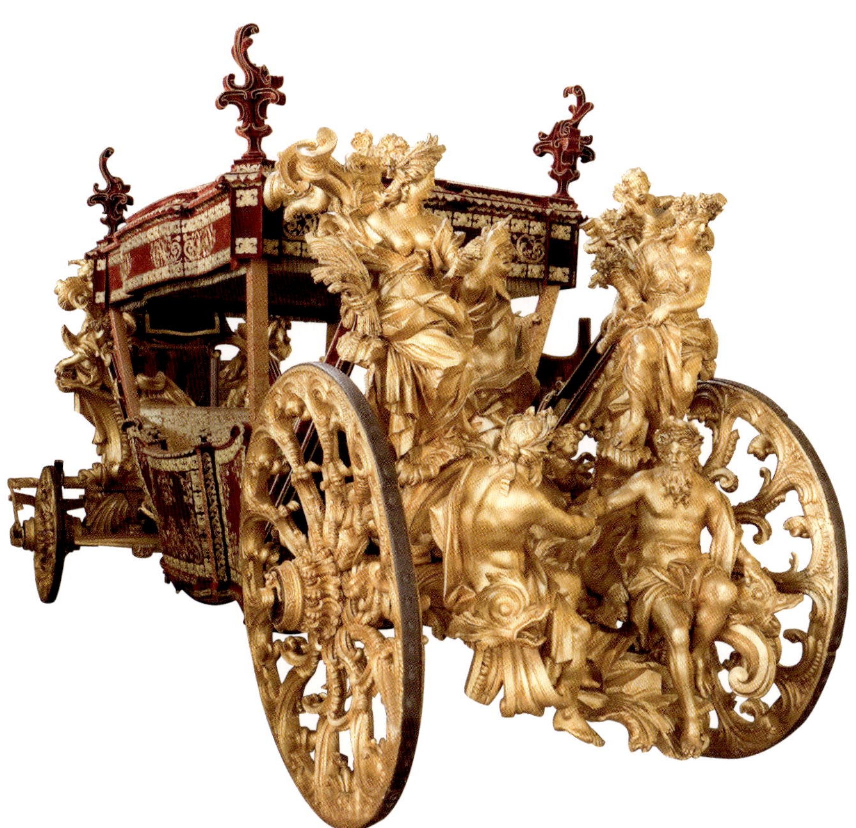

with dark crimson velvet embroidered with foliate and scroll designs in
gilt silver thread, partly in imitation of a kind of Indian casket esteemed in
Portugal that was made of tortoiseshell inlaid with mother-of-pearl – a fitting
reference to the riches of Asia that Portugal made available to Europe and
which would later inspire the chinoiserie design revolution.

The *Oceans' Coach* and the elaborate creations of Schor address the two main
spheres in which Baroque and Rococo culture operated: public and private.
Although their grandeur and costliness were meant to impress the crowds
who witnessed the processions in which they participated, recent scholarship
has revealed that the allegories and display of wealth on these coaches were
meant even more to impress the men and women of authority who received
them in their palaces – often in vast covered halls like indoor garages, as at
Caserta (see 16) – where they spoke of rank and privilege within the culture
of the court.

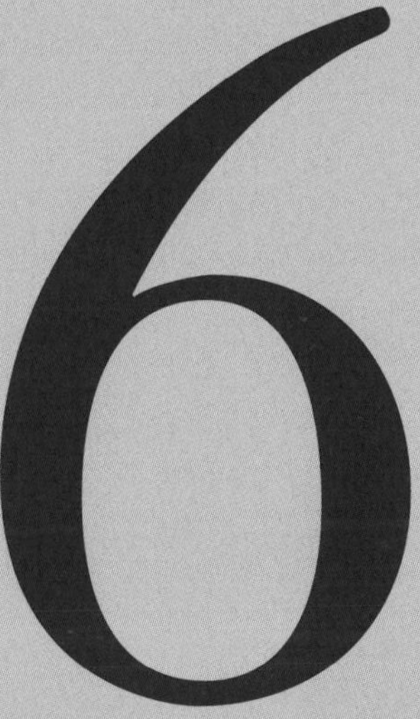

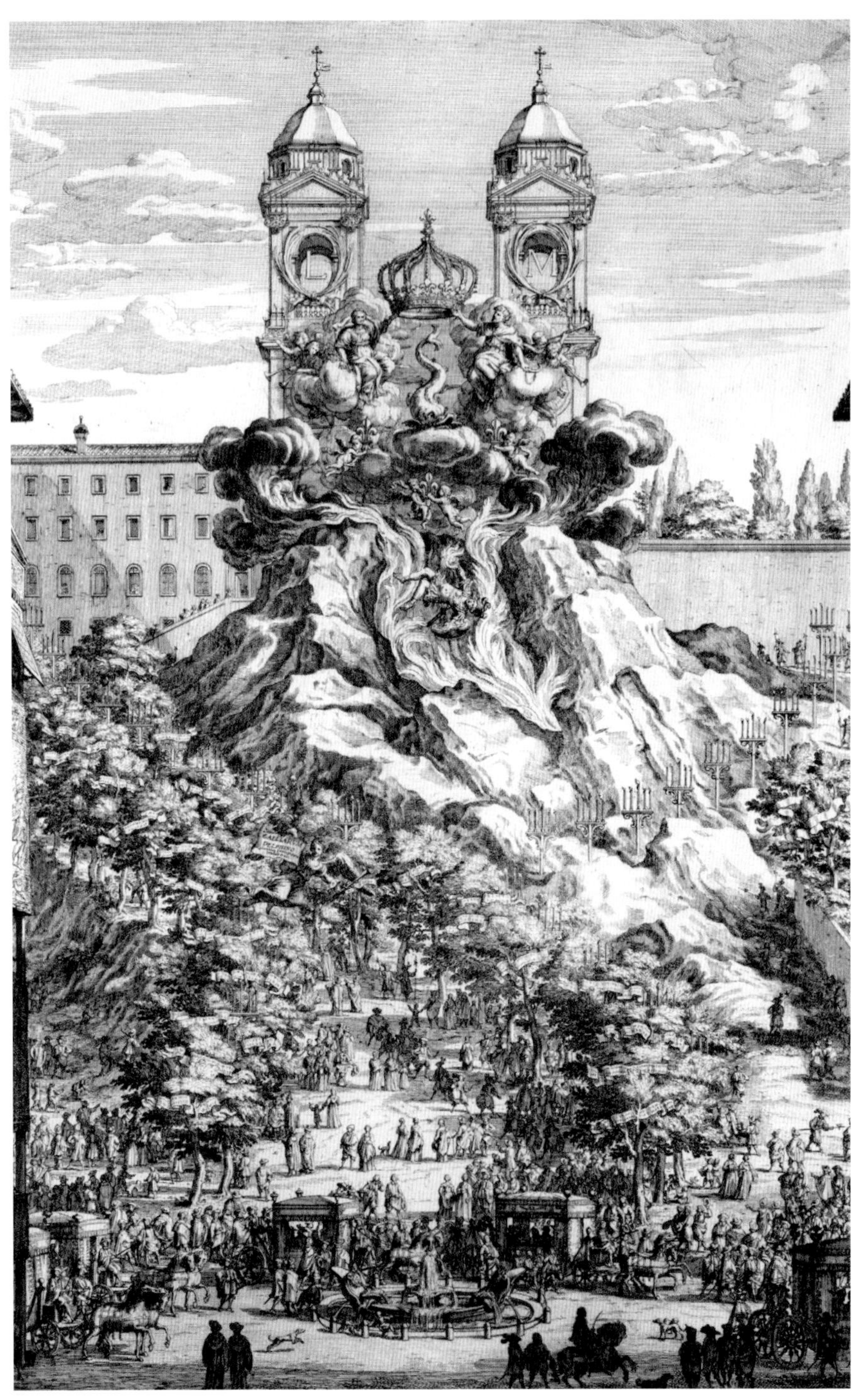

On the evening of 2 February 1662 all Rome turned out for one of the most awesome spectacles of the Baroque, an era so saturated with public festivals that patrons were hard-pressed to interest audiences (186). To honour the birth of the heir to the French Crown (the Dauphin), the Barberini hosted a multimedia paean to their French ally, Louis XIV – he had given the family sanctuary when they were wanted on embezzlement charges – in one of the city's most strategically located public spaces: the piazza facing the French church of SS. Trinità de' Monti, now the Piazza di Spagna, or Spanish Steps. The Barberini family – led by the robber baron Cardinal Antonio (1607–1671) – was Rome's most ambitious underwriter of public entertainments, from the operas and ballets mounted in their palace at the Quattro Fontane (see 51) to the processions, allegorical battles and fireworks displays that enlivened the streets and *piazze*. During the 1662 festivities the predecessor to the Spanish Steps was enveloped in a gargantuan illusionistic volcano – it was made, like any stage prop, of plaster and cloth on a wooden frame – which ascended from the lower square to the church towers. People could climb a sweeping staircase around the left flank lined with 'trees' dangling with allegorical texts while the right flank was lit by a ring of dazzling candelabra. At the top, obscuring the church façade, allegories of Peace and Fertility accompanied by trumpet-blowing angels balanced a crown over a silver dolphin (a pun on 'Dauphin'), while three others held a trio of illuminated fleurs-de-lis in a cloudburst in imitation of the Bourbon coat of arms – the effect was very similar to the Barberini bees in Pietro da Cortona's ceiling (see 51). The initials of the baby's parents ('L' for Louis and 'M' for Marie-Thérèse) sparkled in the church belfries while Discord, in the allegorical garb of a fallen angel, tumbled into the open maw of a flaming cave. On the evening of the event, Cardinal Antonio and other elite spectators sat above the crowds in a temporary three-storey viewing platform covered with red damask and decorated inside with tapestries. Responding to a signal by the impresario, the mouth of the volcano erupted into a torrent

186.
Dominique Barrière, after a drawing by Johann Paul Schor of a design by Gianlorenzo Bernini, *Fireworks Display at SS. Trinità de' Monti on 2 February 1662, for the Birth of the Dauphin.* Etching; 67.5 × 45 cm (26½ × 17¾ in). Gabinetto Comunale delle Stampe, Rome

of flame and explosions, rocking the entire city and visible for miles. Yet the spectacle's crowning moment was fleeting: three months of planning and untold expense brought the audience just over an hour's entertainment.

This short-lived monument to Barberini glory is an appropriate introduction to the subject of this chapter: the temporary architecture, sculpture, parade floats, stage sets and costumes designed for maximum astonishment but minimum lifespan, as well as gardens, an equally transitory medium at the mercy of the seasons, the delicacy of plants, the availability of labour, and the changing tastes and fortunes of patrons. Such creations are referred to as 'ephemera,' and are rarely studied in conjunction with the more permanent legacy of the Baroque and Rococo. Yet it would be a mistake to ignore them. The painters, sculptors, architects and designers of ephemera are the same people responsible for the buildings and works of art treated in the other chapters in this book – the festivities of 2 February 1662 were designed by Gianlorenzo Bernini and Johann Paul Schor, respectively the most celebrated architect/sculptor and designer of their day. Ephemeral artworks also competed with more permanent creations in importance and expense: this single event in honour of the Dauphin was celebrated in four published accounts (*relazioni*) and commemorated with a costly engraving. And most importantly, they influenced Baroque painting, sculpture and architecture through their manipulation of perspective and light, their ability to make the artificial seem real, their combination of the media, and through individual motifs like the heavenly glory, the hallmark of the Bel composto introduced in Bernini's Cathedra Petri (see 102). As noted in Chapter Three, the heavenly glory derived from temporary backdrops built every year for the Forty Hours devotion, or *Quarant'ore*, an event derived from medieval vigil ceremonies at Good Friday that was revived in Milan in 1527 and Rome in 1550. Beginning in 1595, the Jesuits held a sumptuous *Quarant'ore* every year at the Gesù in Rome – the intention was to compete with carnival and its more mundane pleasures – when the consecrated host was enclosed in painted wooden apparatuses, framed by damask hangings, surrounded by reliquaries, flowers in silver vases and candelabra, and brought to life through music and sermons. The Gesù *Quarant'ore* apparatus of 1650 (187), designed by Carlo Rainaldi – he completed S. Agnese in Agone (see 142) – is typical of

**187.
Carlo
Rainaldi,**
*Roman Gesù
Quarant'ore
apparatus
of 1650.*
Engraving.
Bibliothèque
royale de
Belgique,
Brussels

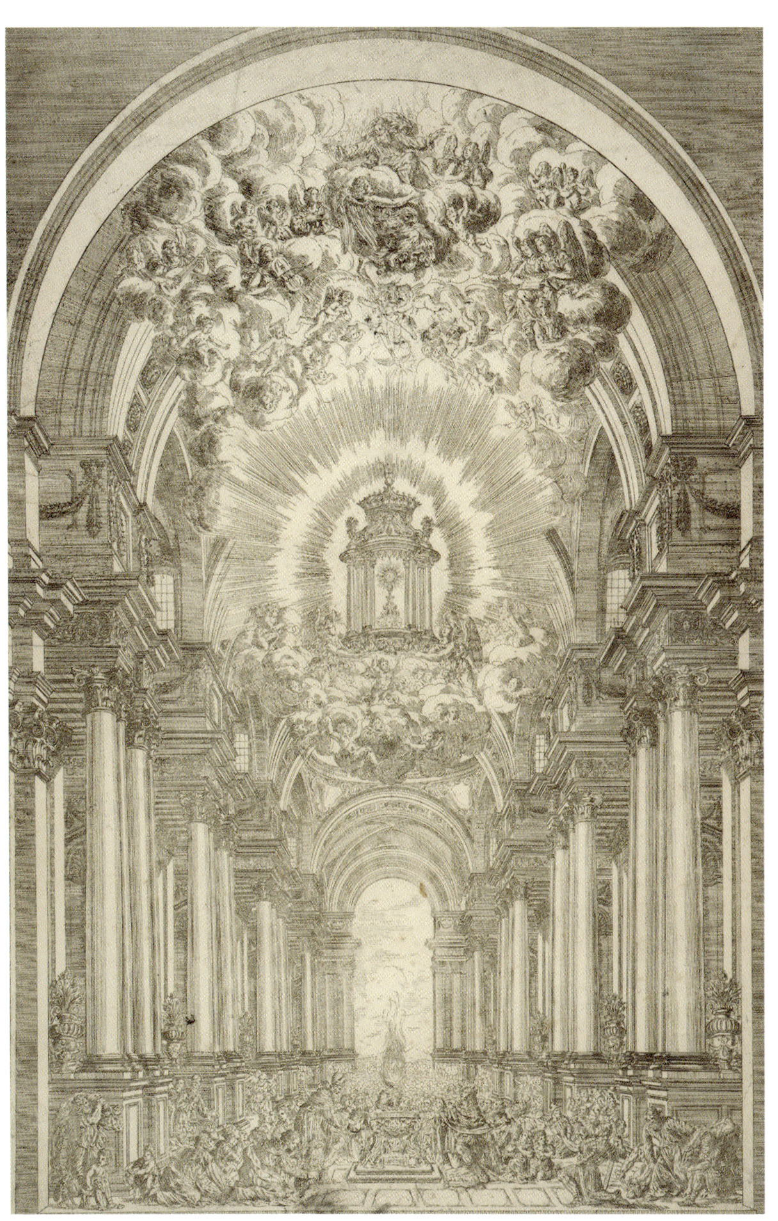

the genre, with its illusionistic perspective formed of stage-like wings and its overflowing heavenly glory at the top.

Ephemera and gardens employed armies of specialists – often members of the patrons' personal household – and brought together a wider variety of media than the more permanent arts. The most important experts were the project supervisor (in Italian, *corago*), usually a celebrity artist or architect, and the librarian, theologian or poet responsible for the abstruse allegorical programme and lengthy literary digressions in the commemorative volumes. The project supervisor selected the rest of the crew, including set designers and painters, carpenters and plasterers, engineers and pyro-technicians, waterworks experts and plumbers, coach makers and boat builders, scaffolders and bleacher builders, composers and musicians, choreographers and dancers, fencing-masters and firearms experts, drapers and costumiers, sommeliers and pastry chefs – not to mention the publishers and engravers responsible for the commemorative books. Patrons were also directly involved in the design and programme of these events and frequently performed in costume as allegories or heroes during plays, mock battles and other spectacles. Gardens involved collaborations on an even vaster scale: Versailles employed 36,000 people to build and maintain its grounds. Designers such as Louis XIV's chief gardener André Le Nôtre (1613–1700) hired architects, masons, sculptors, perspective consultants, earthwork and hydraulics specialists, canal builders, demolition experts, fountain designers, geologists, opticians, tree doctors, horticulturalists, gamekeepers, legal and financial advisors, and even astronomers.

Public spectacles and fireworks celebrations were nothing new in the Baroque era, but they occurred more regularly and on a substantially greater scale than in any period since antiquity. In cities plagued by overcrowding, poverty and violence, such as Rome, the elite resorted to the time-worn method of their pagan ancestors to ensure public submissiveness: bread and circuses. Festivals were also politically motivated, whether extolling the might of a ruler or nation, commemorating the death or marriage of a member of a royal or papal family, or celebrating an alliance between nations or families (which usually amounted to the same thing). The Dauphin's

birthday celebration proclaimed the primacy of the French faction in Rome
over that of the Habsburg Empire in a city that was still the principal arena
for European diplomacy. However, Rome was not the only venue for such
spectacles; they exalted their patrons and enlivened the drudgery of daily life
for the masses from Antwerp to Lima.

One of the most splendid early processions took place in December 1605 in
Krakow to celebrate the marriage of King Sigismund III Vasa of the Polish-
Lithuanian Commonwealth (and former King of Sweden) to Constance,
Archduchess of Austria, and it was commemorated on an extravagant scroll
possibly painted by Austrian court artist Balthasar Gebhard (188). One of the
most intriguing things about this procession is the way it blends European
and Islamic visual arts traditions. Not only did the Commonwealth share a
border with the Ottoman Empire but it also promoted an ideology known
as Sarmatianism, in which the nobility (*szlachta*) distinguished themselves
from commoners by claiming ancestry in Scythia, and they consequently
wore Ottoman-style long, fur-trimmed coats (*żupany*) and tall riding boots,
Islamic-style sabres (*szable*) and long Turkish moustaches. The wedding
procession combined messages of royal and aristocratic primacy, municipal
rivalry, military might and international diplomacy – above all the alliance
of two great powers. It was headed by diplomats and battalions from the
Commonwealth and its allies: the regiments of the Palatine of Poznán; the
king's own cavalry and hussar troops; the armies of the military commanders
of the state; Polish, Austrian and Muscovite dignitaries; the papal nuncio; and
Persian and Turkish envoys. The absent Austrian emperor was represented
by a proxy. The parade reached its climax with the most important
dignitaries: the king, the bride's elder brother Archduke Maximilian Ernst,
the child Prince Royal Ladislas – all on horseback – and a splendid open
coach drawn by eight horses bearing the principal women of the ceremony:
the bride, her mother Archduchess Marie, her sister Marie Christine
Batory and the king's sister Princess Anne Vasa of Sweden. It concluded
with coaches bearing ladies-in-waiting and the bride's dowry in trunks,
and a contingent of the militias of Krakow, Kazimierz and Stradom. Since
one of the main purposes of the procession was to proclaim the legitimacy
of the Commonwealth's rulers and their ability to look after its people,

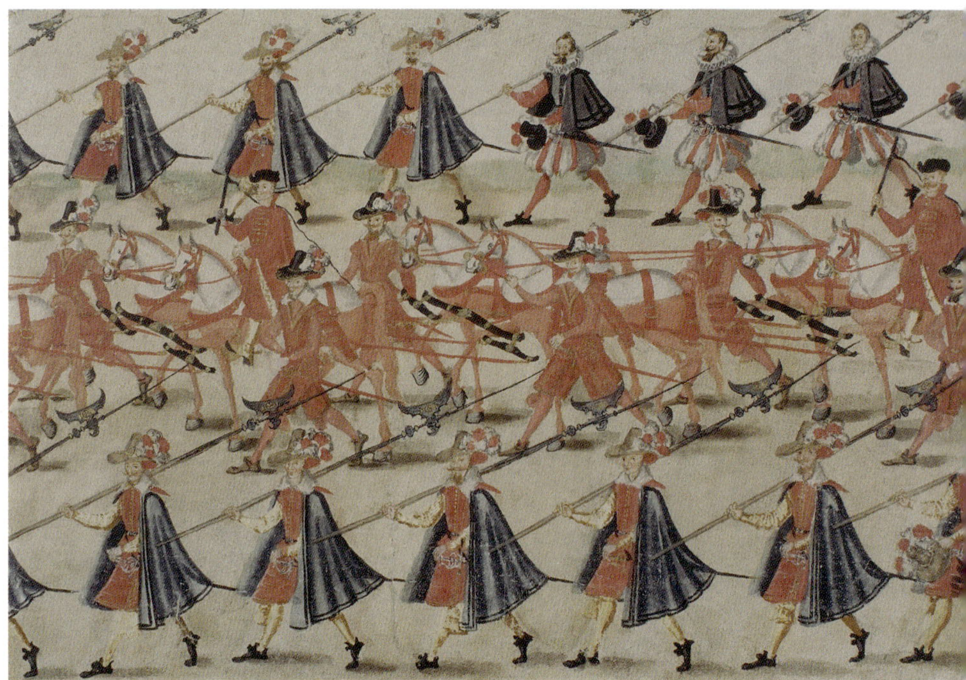

188.
Balthasar Gebhard (?), *Entry of the Wedding Procession of Constance of Austria and Sigismund III into Cracow* ('Stockholm Roll'), after 1605. Watercolour, gouache, gold paint, ribbed paper. Royal Castle, Warsaw

court officials scattered coins and medallions into the crowds of spectators (ironically probably inspiring a riot).

One of the most extravagant entertainments of the seventeenth century also had a Swedish connection. Ordered by Pope Alexander VII Chigi to celebrate the abdicated Swedish queen Christina Vasa's conversion to Catholicism, it was no mere devout exercise. Sweden was one of Europe's most powerful Protestant nations (the Catholic Sigismund III was long since deposed) and the nation had been a major player in the Thirty Years War (1618–1648). The Catholic Church considered Christina, daughter of Protestant warrior Gustav II Adolf, 'the Lion of the North', to be the era's highest-ranking rescue from Heresy. Mounted in February 1656, the celebrations were, like most, a combination of processions, theatrical pieces and outdoor spectacles. The Barberini were compelled to pay the bill – their suspect banking activities did not deter the pope from tapping into their fortunes – this time Cardinal Francesco and his plutocratic nephew Maffeo taking the helm. As conceived by Alexander and his secretary of state Giulio Rospigliosi (1600–1669), the events broadcasted the authority of the Catholic

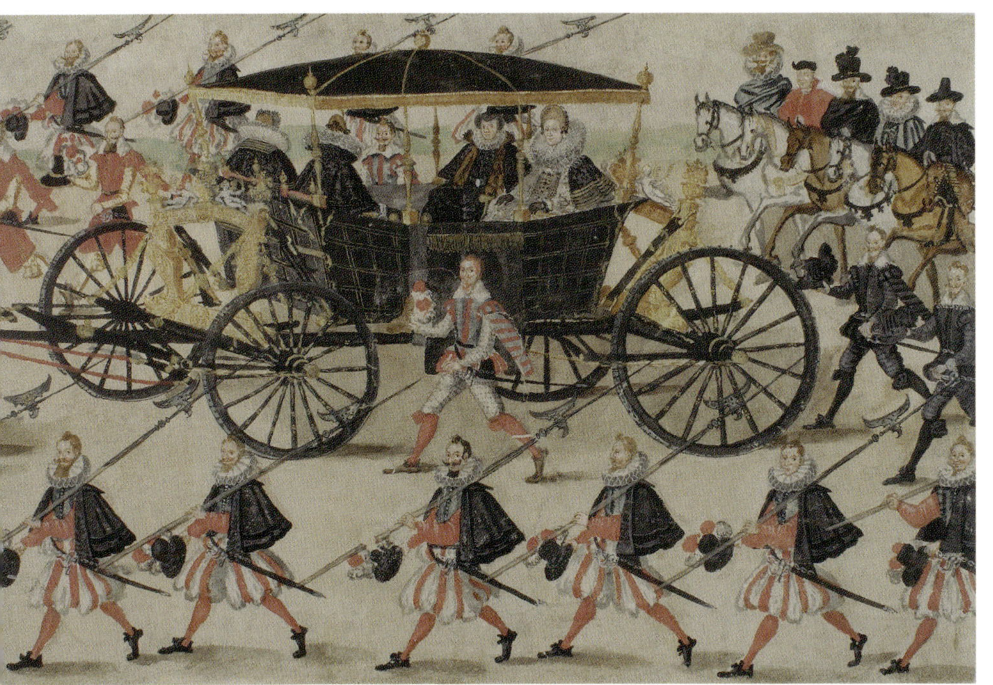

Church, promoted the contemplation of death (memento mori), the doctrine
of free will (in opposition to the Protestant doctrine of predestination), the
Holy Sacraments (also attacked by Protestants), and – ironically in the case
of a masculine queen who had inherited many of her father's leonine traits –
feminine modesty and submission.

The celebrations were timed at the beginning of Carnival season to take
full advantage of its ebullient atmosphere, and they included comedies and
sacred operas for the dignitaries and an outdoor mock battle for the public.
Both took place in or beside the Barberini Palace, demonstrating that despite
having to underwrite a spectacle for a Chigi pope the Barberini – the former
papal family – was able to use it to advance their own reputation. The mock
battle that ended the festivities, called the Giostra dei Caroselli (Joust of
the Chariots) – featuring Maffeo's celebrated stable of horses – combined a
procession with theatre, opera and ballet, and was witnessed by thousands
(189). The spectacle was set in a ready-built outdoor arena adjacent to the
palace's north wing, the façade transformed by Barbernini set designer
Giovanni Francesco Grimaldi (1606–1680) into a stage backdrop festooned

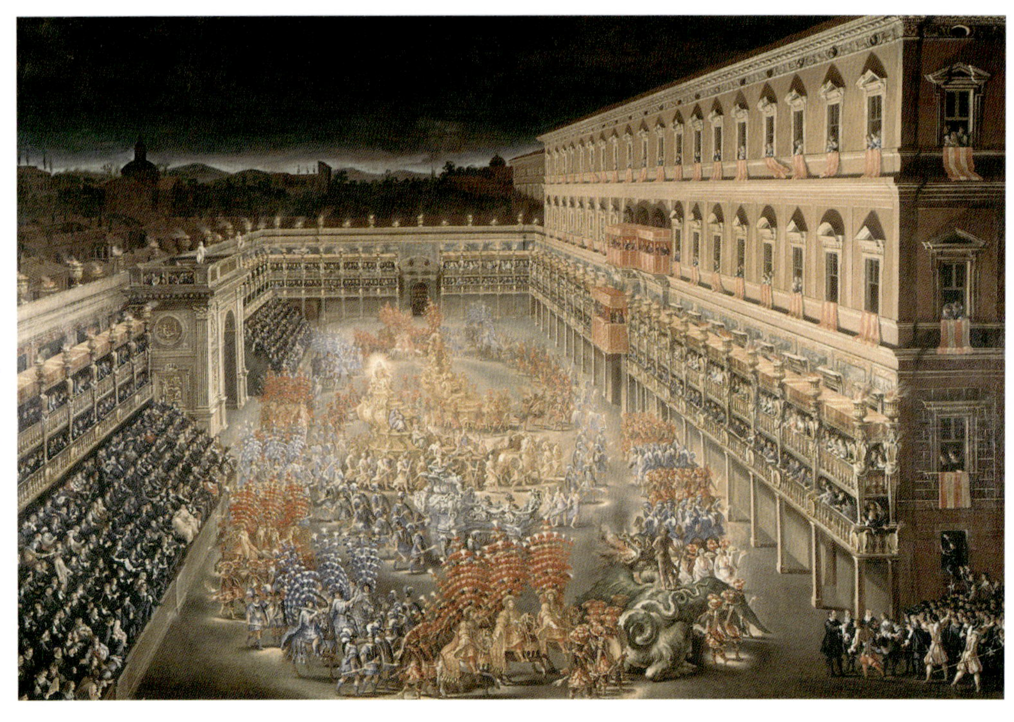

189.
**Filippo Lauri
and Filippo
Gagliardi**,
*Giostra dei
Caroselli*,
1656. Oil on
canvas; 340 ×
280 cm (133¾
× 110¼ in).
Museo di
Roma, Rome

with rented tapestries. Grimaldi constructed temporary boxes for the queen and dignitaries and surrounded the arena with a two-storey wooden gallery – men sat below, women above – as well as bleachers and a false triumphal arch opposite the palace. At nine o'clock in the evening over a hundred mounted trumpeters and grooms ushered in the squadrons of the 'Knights' and the 'Amazons'. The Knights, who wore Roman armour and feather headdresses in the Vasa colours of turquoise and silver, were followed by a chariot in the same colours drawn by three singers representing the Graces and driven by another singer dressed as an allegory of Rome and Love. The Amazons, led by Maffeo in an outrageous 600-feather headdress, were attired in 'Brazilian' skirts and feathers in the Roman colours of red and gold, and the four singers accompanying their chariot represented the Furies and Scorn. In an arabesque of processions, advances and retreats, the two groups presented themselves to the audience to the accompaniment of torches, singing, bagpipes and trumpets, and confronted each other in a battle using real firearms. Highlights included a singing Hercules and his dragon (a recycled opera prop given flame-throwing capacity by the Barberini plumber Signor Bolla), Apollo in his chariot singing of Rome's love for its new queen, and twenty-four local beauties representing the hours. Despite its complexity the message of this entertainment would have been clear to all: Christina's dual identity as woman and queen could only be synchronized under the guidance of Apollo – that figure beloved of tyrants everywhere – in this case Alexander VII.

Some processional entertainments took to the waters. One of the most elaborate was the mock sea battle that culminated the wedding of Cosimo II de' Medici and Maria Magdalena, another Archduchess of Austria, in Florence in November 1608 (190). It was merely one of a two-month-long series of nuptial events that included processions through temporary triumphal arches, the wedding mass, theatrical and musical presentations, a horse ballet, and a naval tournament performed by Pisan sailors in the River Arno. The sea battle represented the capture of the Golden Fleece by Jason and the Argonauts and its cast included Florence's and Austria's most prominent citizens. According to the commemorative volume, hundreds of spectators crowded on the two banks of the river between the Ponte S. Trinità and Ponte alla Carraia: 'the streets, for the whole length between the two bridges, were full of benches, which were placed on the riverbanks, and [others] rose behind them by degree, allowing for a marvellous view'. The north side included a three-storey viewing platform for the matrimonial couple and other dignitaries, and thousands more stood on the balconies and roofs of the houses and churches behind, as can be seen in the engraving. The Island of Colchis took the form of a floating platform anchored on both sides with a tent as the temple containing the Golden Fleece. The temple was guarded by a pair of fire-breathing bulls and a robotic dragon. When Cosimo gave the signal, a flotilla of little boats emerged from the sides, singly or in pairs, and encircled the island, displaying their finery to the audience on all sides.

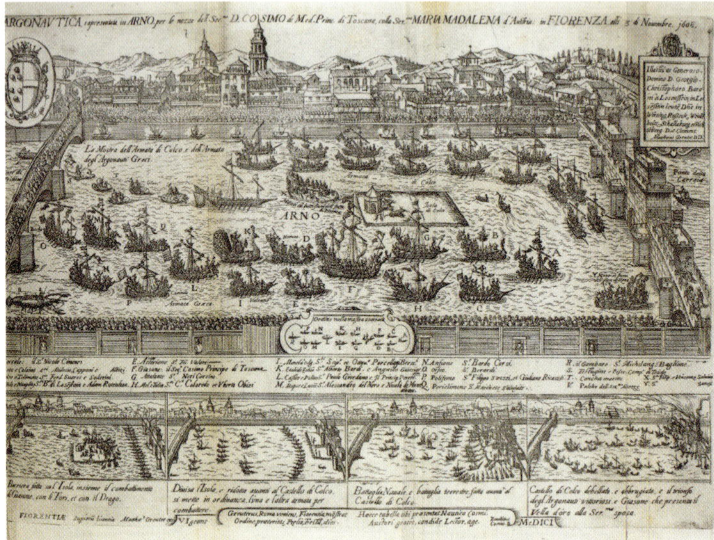

190. **Mattheus Greuter**, *The Argonautica Represented on the Arno for the wedding of … Cosimo de' Medici, Prince of Tuscany and … Maria Magdalena of Austria*. Engraving 12 from *Descrizione delle feste fatte nelle reali nozze*, Florence, 1608. British Library, London

Driven by the patrons who financed them – they included such prominent citizens as Ubertin degl'Albizzi and Filippo Strozzi – the boats were painted with allegories, gilded, and fitted with sculptures and figure heads. One ship was made to look like it was made of shells, sea sponge and dolphins; another looked like a giant lobster; and a third like a peacock. The patrons and sailors all wore masks and festival costumes, and they played musical instruments and fired off arquebuses in salute as they passed the nuptial couple. After the Argonauts defeated the Colchi armada, Jason took the island, subdued the beasts, and seized the Golden Fleece, provoking an ear-splitting combination of music, gunpowder and applause that echoed throughout Florence.

Like most processions in the Baroque world, Cosimo and Maria Magdalena's ceremonial entrance into the city was punctuated by wood, plaster and canvas triumphal arches – they were conceived around allegorical themes like the generosity and glory of Austria and Cosimo – before which the parade would stop and be acknowledged, sometimes with a Te Deum mass or a brief theatrical performance, before proceeding through the opening in the middle. In fact, temporary triumphal arches, produced for weddings, victories, funerals and coronations, were among the most common artistic commissions of the Baroque and provided work for legions of poets, scholars, carpenters, plasterers, painters and sculptors, including – as with the Dauphin's volcano (186) – the leading artists of the day. One of the most unusual is the Arch of the Mint designed by Peter Paul Rubens for the entry into Antwerp of Ferdinand, the Infante, or heir, to the Spanish throne, on 15 May 1635. A celebration of Spanish imperial might, it combined references to European, classical and Inca culture (191). The Arch of the Mint was only one of eleven arches constructed for the event, including a combination gate and arcade dedicated to the 'Austrian Caesar' (Philip IV) comprising statues of the king, his ancestor Emperor Maximilian of Austria and classical deities; another commemorating Portugal's submission to Spain (at the time they were under the same Crown) with figures of Hope and Safety; and a third celebrating the benign rule of the Spanish monarchy from Philip I to IV. Like all of the arches the Arch of the Mint was decorated differently on each side, but the front is the most remarkable in its mixture of Old and New World imagery and man-made and natural forms. As was traditional for such arches, it was financed by local interests, in this case Antwerp's Sodality (confraternity) of Mint Workers.

Although made of wood and plaster, the Arch of the Mint looked like a rusticated stone portal crowned with a mountain. The latter represented the Cerro Rico, or 'Rich Mountain', of Potosí (modern-day Bolivia), the most prodigious silver mine in history and one that turned Spain into one of the world's greatest economies. Two niches at ground level contained false marble statues of Roman-style river gods representing Peru (probably the Amazon) and the Río de la Plata (River of Silver) in present-day Argentina, one of the four rivers Bernini later chose for his Fountain of the Four

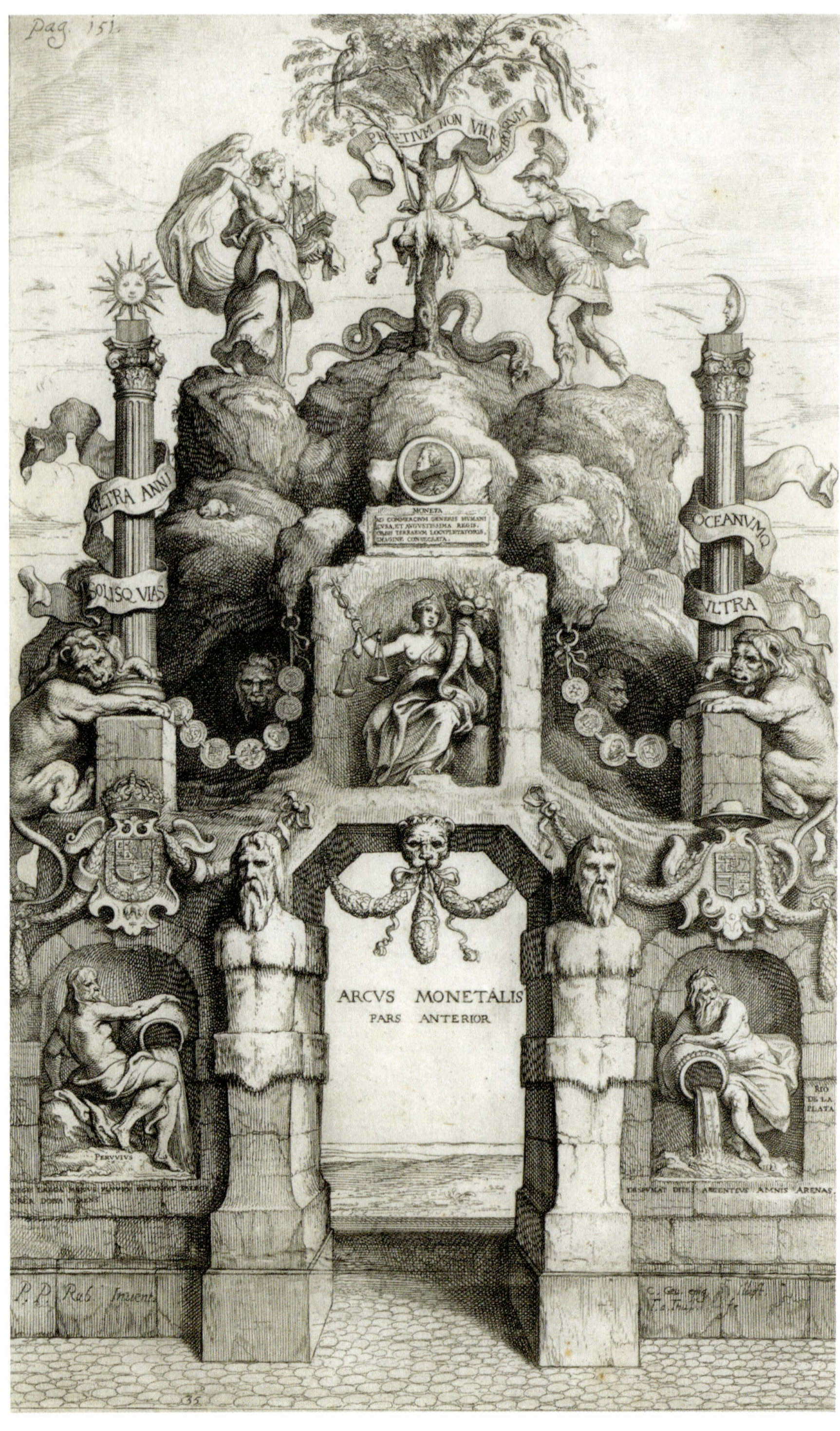

191.
Peter Paul Rubens, *Arch of the Mint*. Engraving; 52 × 36 cm (20½ × 14¼ in). From *Pompa Introitus Ferdinandi Austriaci* (Antwerp, 1635). Bibliothèque royale de Belgique, Brussels

Rivers (see 127). The mountain was framed by a pair of columns supported by lions representing the 'Pillars of Hercules', the entry into the Atlantic from the Mediterranean and a symbol of the Spanish Empire. The columns were crowned by a sun and moon to symbolize gold and silver, a metaphor that likely derived from Inca religion where the gold was the 'sweat of the sun' and silver the 'tears of the moon'. An allegory of the mint, with her cornucopia and pair of scales, sits in a niche at the centre of the mountain, flanked by garlands of coins bearing portraits of earlier Habsburg monarchs. At the very top Jason seizes the Golden Fleece from underneath a tree guarded by a snake (no dragon this time) while Felicity stands by holding a miniature ship. The arch features other South American imagery, including the pair of parrots in the tree and a vizcacha – a rabbit-like rodent exclusive to the highest reaches of the Andes. The Inca imagery and vizcacha go beyond the generic exotica of the age (see 171) and suggests that the author of the iconographic programme had access to first-hand knowledge of the region.

Some structures were meant to be destroyed before the audience's very eyes. During the Roman festivities celebrating the election of Ferdinand III as the Holy Roman Emperor in 1637, funded by the Spanish ambassador the Marqués de Castel Rodrigo to impress the pope with Iberian might, a false stone castle was erected on the final day in a public square – the text does not identify the location and the Spanish Embassy, Rome's first, was not built until 1647 (192). The 'castle' featured rounded bastions at each corner supporting female allegories of the Four Continents with their appropriate animals: a lion, alligator, camel and horse, three of which play the same role on Bernini's Fountain of the Four Rivers (see 127). A square tower rose from the middle, crowned with four corner plinths supporting fire-breathing dragons and a central plinth bearing the Habsburg arms. At nightfall the building was set ablaze to the accompaniment of trumpets and the castle blew apart with a terrifying explosion to reveal a round tower inside (193). The spectacle concluded when a shower of fireworks shot out of the top of the tower illuminating a lifelike image of Ferdinand in armour so that, in the words of the commemorative volume, 'the whole night was like day'. Another type of ephemeral structure was even more replete with dynastic and classical symbolism. The catafalque, or funeral bier, was a wood-

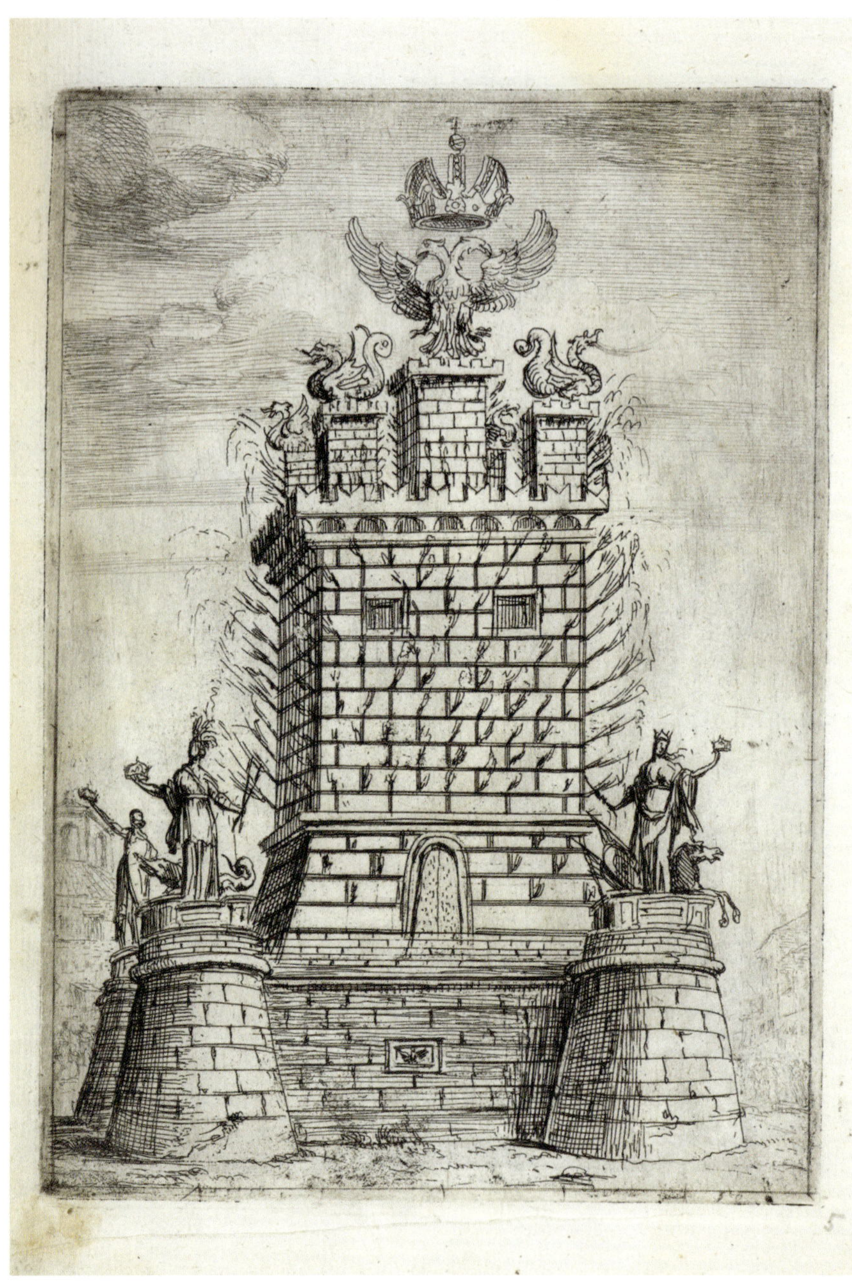

**192.
Miguel
Bermudez
de Castro,**
*Fireworks
castle (closed).*
Engraving.
From
*Descripción de
las fiestas que el
Sr. Marques de
Castel Rodrigo
... celebró en esta
corte a la nueva
del election de
Ferdinando III
de Austria Rey
de Romanos*
(Rome, 1637):
page 25.
British Library,
London

**193.
Miguel
Bermudez
de Castro,**
*Fireworks
castle (open)*.
Engraving.
From
*Descripción de
las fiestas que el
Sr. Marques de
Castel Rodrigo
... celebró en esta
corte a la nueva
del election de
Ferdinando III
de Austria Rey
de Romanos*
(Rome, 1637):
page 29.
British Library,
London

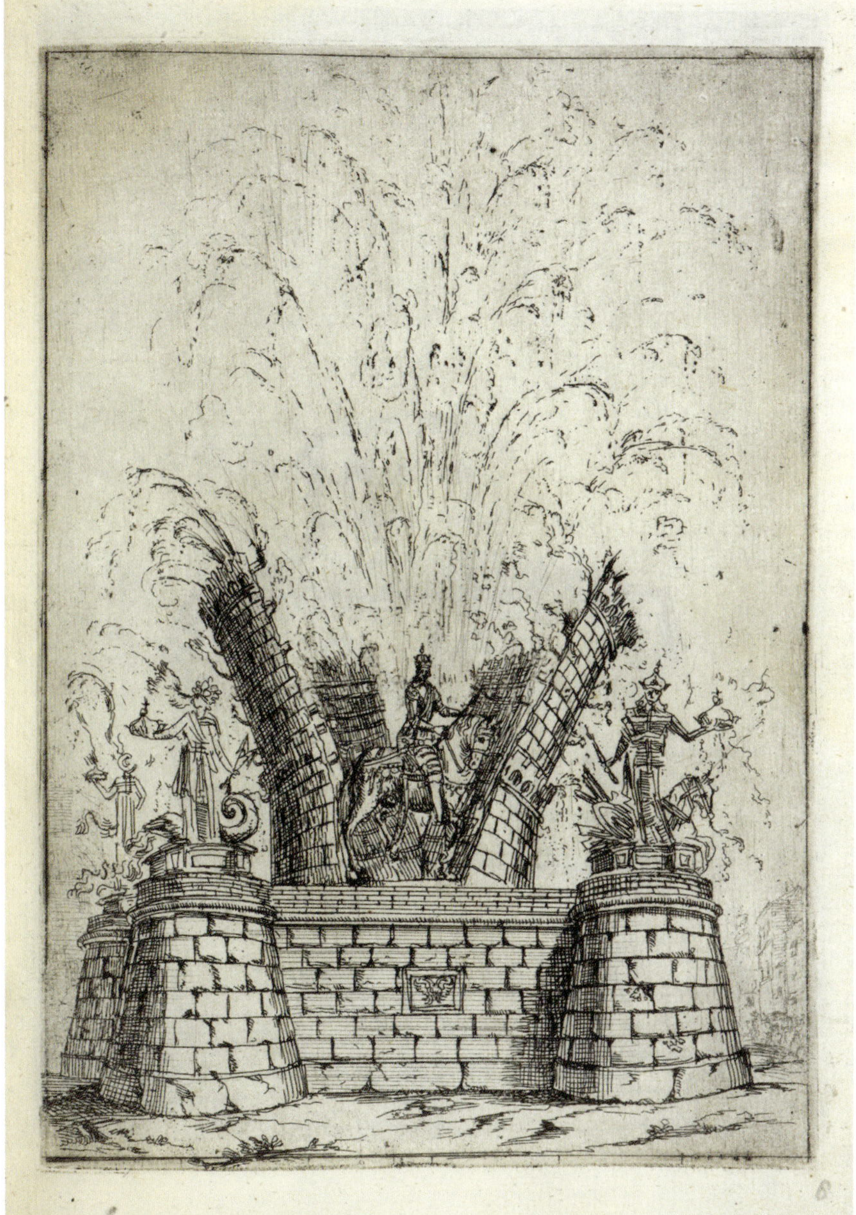

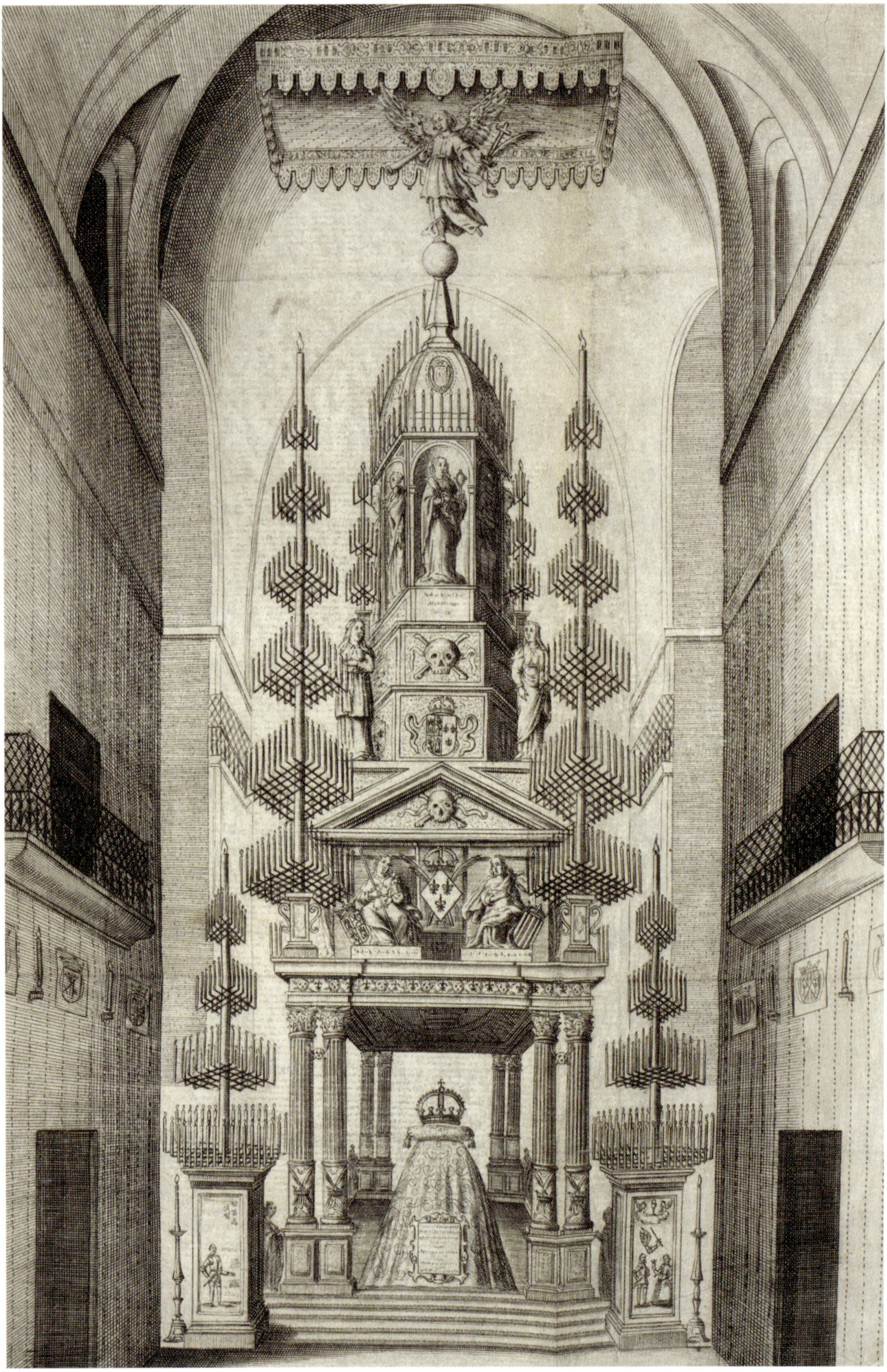

frame contraption built inside metropolitan churches to commemorate the deaths of important people, usually monarchs. They were the focus of elaborate funeral rites lasting several days and contrasted memento mori iconography with affirmations of the permanence of the royal line and the blessed status of the dead. The six-storey catafalque erected in the royal convent of San Gerónimo in Madrid in 1644 upon the death of Isabel de Borbón, Queen of Spain 'and the New World', is typical of the genre (194). Placed under the crossing of the church where it could be seen by the entire congregation, the roughly conical fake marble structure rested on a plinth of five steps and eight Corinthian columns. The enclosure formed by the columns contained the funeral bier draped in brocades and bearing

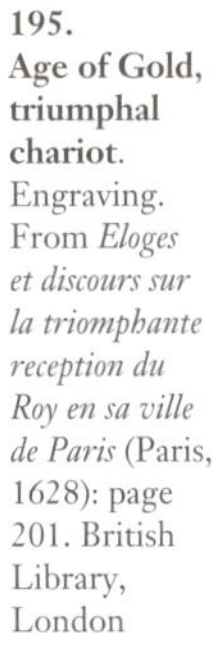

194.
Jan de Noort,
*Cat afalque
in the Royal
convent of San
Gerónimo in
Madrid to
commemorate
the death
of Isabel de
Borbón, Queen
of Spain, 1644.*
Engraving.
From *Pompa
funeral honras
y exequias de
la muy Alta y
Catolica Señora
Doña Isabel
de Borbon*
(Madrid,
1645): page 53.
British Library,
London

195.
**Age of Gold,
triumphal
chariot.**
Engraving.
From *Eloges
et discours sur
la triomphante
reception du
Roy en sa ville
de Paris* (Paris,
1628): page
201. British
Library,
London

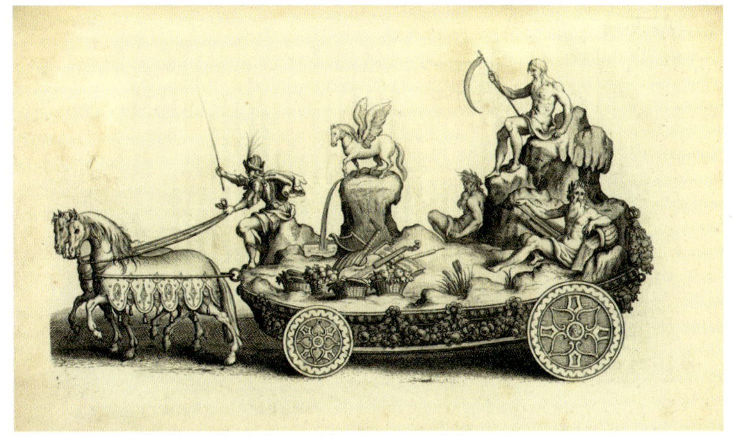

the royal crown on a pillow. As this catafalque was in the capital, the bier contained the body of the deceased: the catafalques erected in provincial churches and in colonial centres like Mexico City would have used proxy biers with no one inside them. Like Quarant'ore apparatuses, catafalques were lit with multiple candelabra, here on the four plinths surrounding the catafalque and above each pair of Corinthian columns. References to death punctuate the architecture, as in the main frieze, which is adorned with skulls and crossbones. Like the majority of ephemeral structures, the catafalque is covered with emblems, allegorical images or symbols that are often accompanied by inscriptions to help unlock their meanings. The Madrid catafalque had sixteen of these 'hieroglyphics' on the surrounding plinths alone, including depictions of the king in armour, death's heads bearing the date of the queen's passing, allegories of the queen's rule in heaven and earth, and memento mori such as the one showing a skull blowing on a tree and stripping it not only of leaves but also of crowns, mitres and papal tiaras – these all fall into open graves, demonstrating that status is no protection against death (compare with 78). Martyrs' palms, usually reserved for saints who died defending the faith, are employed here to represent the queen's selfless devotion to God and her subjects. The rest of the imagery was interchangeable with triumphal-arch symbolism: Bourbon coats of arms, gilded statues of the virtues and seasons, a trumpet-blowing angel, and gilded allegorical statues of the parts of the Empire weeping at her death (Spain, Italy, Flanders, Austria, Jerusalem, Tirol, Africa and the Indies).

Most festival processions involved chariots, allegorical parade floats laden with statues, imitation fortresses or caves, and real people performing in costume. The 1635 Antwerp procession was greeted with a chariot carrying elegantly attired young women who, as allegories of the city, descended from the vehicle to greet the Infante and hand him a laurel crown like a Roman victor. During the lengthy entry of Louis XIII into Paris following his victory over the Huguenots at La Rochelle in 1628 – it involved a veritable enfilade of triumphal arches – the king was greeted by three allegorical chariots, one depicting the Roman Circus (complete with a gladiatorial contest), and two representing the city of Paris and the Age of Gold, that Graeco-Roman utopia characterized by peace and prosperity (195). Saturn perches on an outcropping of rock at the back, not only as a synonym for the Age of Gold (the ancients alternately called this period the 'Age of Saturn') but also as a representation of the king's good government. At his feet are river gods – note the shiny cloth pouring out of their barrels instead of water – which serve as generic symbols of fertility, while in the front Pegasus indicates the Pierian Spring, the mythical source of knowledge and the arts. At the base of the rock baskets of fruit and vegetables and musical instruments symbolize fertility, harmony and civilization. The coachman in his classical garb was the only real person on the float.

We have already seen that many of these festivals included operas, opera-ballets, comedies and other theatrical performances, usually reserved for the nobility and other elites and held inside patrons' palaces. Not only did the opera evolve in the Baroque, but that era was also responsible for the idea of a purpose-built, permanent theatre. The earlier practice was to transform existing halls temporarily into theatres and disassemble them afterwards so that the room could be used for other purposes. Thus when the Barberini mounted theatrical performances such as the 1634 sacred opera *Il Sant'Alessio* in their palace at the Quattro Fontane, they converted a large *salone* into a theatre by building a proscenium stage, a pit for musicians, complex lighting

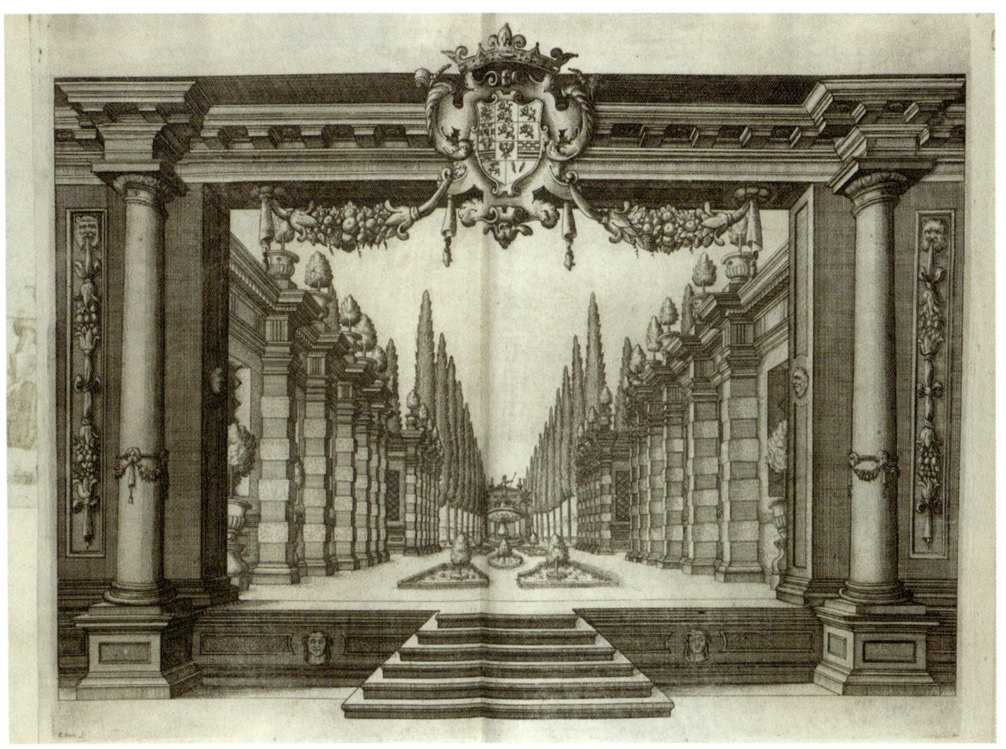

arrangements and accommodations for various special effects – including machinery to allow performers to descend from the ceiling, a mechanical flying angel, a trap in the floor for the Devil, and machines to produce clouds, thunder and lightning. The same held true for the opera-ballet *Triumphant Love Surrounded by the Victorious Virtues* mounted in the Ducal Palace at Celle in 1653 to celebrate the wedding of Christian Ludwig, Duke of Braunschweig-Lüneburg, and Dorothea, Duchess of Schleswig-Holstein-Sonderburg (196). The Celle Palace had been a flourishing centre for musical and theatrical events since the sixteenth century, and in the first half of the seventeenth it hosted regular performances by German theatre troupes, always in the Rittersaal (Knight's Hall), a large hall transformed as needed into a stage. This engraving of one of the three stage sets for the 1653 ballet is a rare record of such an event. Typically for opera-ballets at the time, the presentation involved a succession of small set performance pieces featuring allegorical figures: in this case Avarice, Lust and other sins were conquered by Justice, Moderation and other virtues. The performance also involved a more prosaic interlude with performers dressed as dancing bears carrying torches. The stage consisted of a rectangular proscenium frame formed of a heavy cornice raised on a pair of Doric columns on plinths and raised six steps above the floor to accommodate a trap for players to disappear under the floor. The stage was set on a raking angle, both so that the performers at the back were visible and because the perspective effects made the stage look longer than it was. The sets, comprising painted flats and a backdrop, were generic enough that they could be reused (one was a forest scene, another a palace arcade, and this one a formal garden).

As such performances became a more important aspect of aristocratic life, it was not long before the permanent palace theatre became an essential feature of the larger palaces. One of the earliest was the new theatre in the Barberini palace, which was completed in 1639 and included stage sets by Bernini. A permanent theatre was installed at Celle in 1670 by Duke Georg Wilhelm and is today the oldest working theatre in Germany. However, one of the most intact Baroque, or in this case Rococo, stages is the palace theatre at Český Krumlov (known by its then German-speaking inhabitants as Böhmisch Krummau, 197). It is one of only two – the other is at the Swedish royal summer residence at Drottningholm (1766) – that contains its original sets, flats and stage machinery. The first purpose-built theatre on the site was constructed by Prince Johann Christian I von Eggenberg in 1680–2 and the present one is a 1762–6 modernization undertaken by Josef Adam zu Schwarzenberg, when the theatre was fitted with the latest equipment and sets by the Viennese team of Lorenz Makh (carpenter) and set painters Hans Wetschel and Leo Märkl. The machinery includes devices under the stage for changing the wings, a mechanism to raise the footlights, elevators allowing

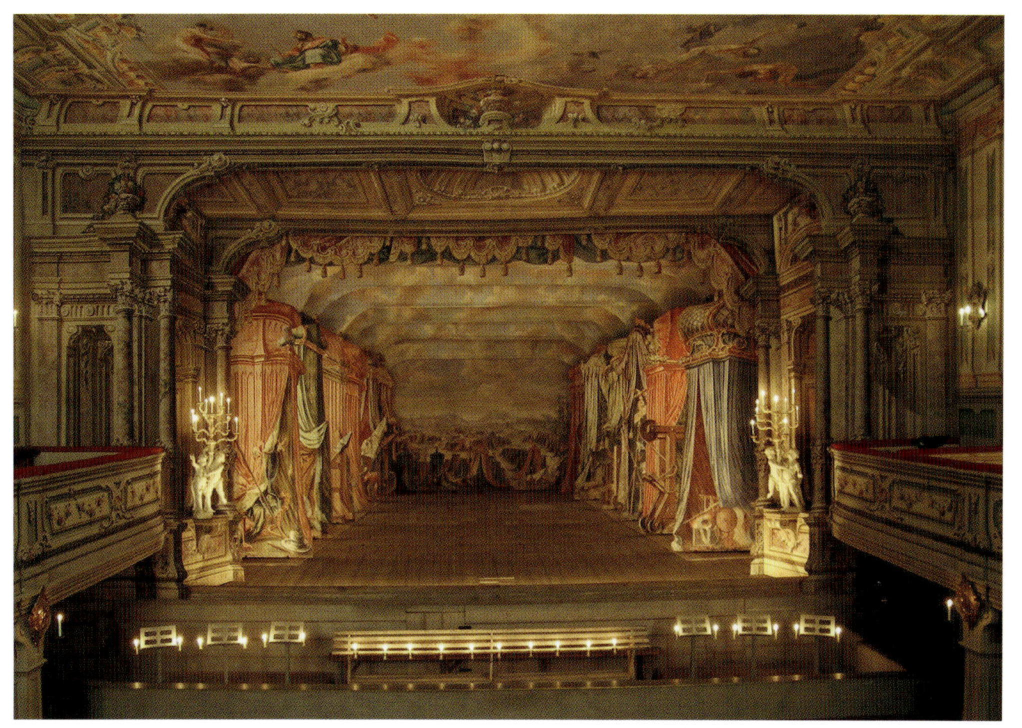

197.
**Josef Adam zu
Schwarzenberg,**
Palace Theatre,
1762–6. Český
Krumlov
(Czech Republic)

players to rise through trap doors in the stage, rotating proscenium doors, traps, as well as pulleys to operate the curtain and tracks in the upper part to accommodate a flying machine. As it appears today the theatre's proscenium arch, raking stage and full set of receding wings are strikingly similar to those used in the Celle opera-ballet a century earlier (see 196) – and in theatres the world over today.

Public spectacles were not confined to urban areas, the palace or the church. Some of the most spectacular took place in royal and aristocratic gardens, themselves one of the costliest and most labour-intensive temporary creations of the Baroque and Rococo. Although gardens are less ephemeral than festival structures – the land will always remain and their fountain structures, grottos and walls are relatively permanent – their most essential ingredients were much more delicate and very short-lived without constant attention. Flowers had to be replanted each year or, if perennials, protected against frost; fruit trees and tropical plants had to be taken indoors during the winter (gardens frequently have a separate building called a *limonaia* in Italian or *orangerie* in French to protect citrus trees in the cold season); trees and box hedges required constant pruning; and lawns had to be mown and weeded. Even trees were regularly cut down and replanted, usually every hundred years but often sooner since they were frequently introduced in haste or were not ideally suited to the region. In general, as plantings were meant to be appreciated immediately and changed at the whim of the landowner – during royal festivities at Versailles even several times a day – plants were forced and abused, incapable of surviving very long. The Duc de Saint-Simon commented about Versailles under Louis XIV: 'Who could help being repelled and disgusted at these violences done to nature?' With today's high cost of labour such gardens cannot be replicated. Few visitors to Baroque gardens today realize that they are visiting mere shadows of what they once were, like a palace interior stripped of its furniture, paintings and tapestries.

During the Renaissance, gardens served two main symbolic purposes: they were metaphors for the virtues or erudition of their owners and a setting for *otium*, a Petrarchan notion of rest and regeneration in the countryside inspired by ancient Roman villas. Nevertheless, early Renaissance gardens

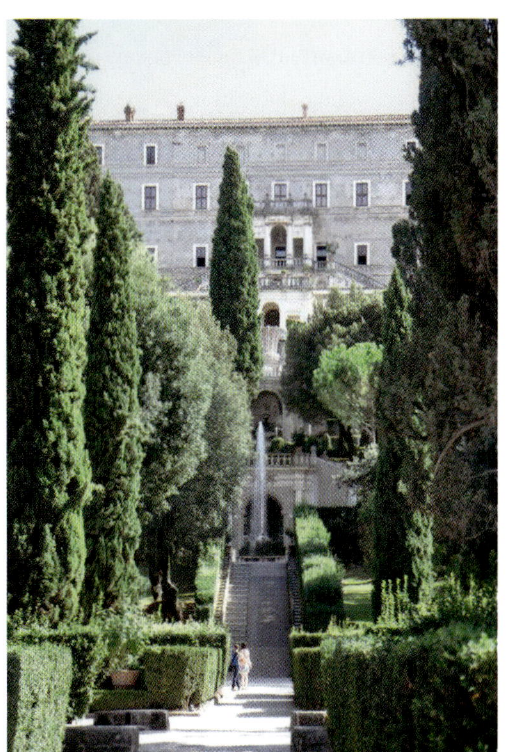

198.
Pirro Ligorio,
Gardens at the
Villa d'Este,
1560. Tivoli
(Italy)

remained functional, with herb and fruit gardens integrated into the main design, and they were arranged symmetrically to suggest balance and harmony. But by the sixteenth century, designers explored the idea of the capricious garden, with meandering walks into secluded groves (*selvatici* in Italian and *bosquets* in French) and hidden sculptures and machines (especially waterworks) to surprise and delight the visitor. The most celebrated late Renaissance garden is at the Villa d'Este in Tivoli, designed in 1560 by Pirro Ligorio for Cardinal Ippolito II d'Este (198). It combines symmetrical plantings arranged into parterres with artificial forest walks and caprices ranging from false waterfalls to a hydraulically operated pipe organ – all organized along a longitudinal and latitudinal axis. The progression from the rigid parterres near the palace to the 'untamed' forests beyond symbolizes the transition between the civilized world and the domain of nature, a juxtaposition that would be a favourite motif in the Baroque. Baroque designers gave increasing importance to the idea of infinite extension, providing seemingly endless vistas along axes or radiating outwards like spokes in a wheel, made possible by arrangements of ponds, canals, lawns and openings in the woods called *allées*. This ability to look over vast distances was a blatant manifestation of the authority of the monarchs, nobles or churchmen who owned the gardens.

As with the palace, the French led the way in Baroque garden design. This ascendancy is partly due to the publication of influential garden manuals in the sixteenth and seventeenth centuries, particularly Claude Mollet's *Théâtre des Plans et Jardinages* (published posthumously in 1652) and André Mollet's *Le Jardin de Plaisir* (1651), which were translated immediately into the major European languages. Manifestos of garden design, they emphasized the link between palace and garden, the supremacy of ornamental plantings over utilitarian ones, and the progression along an axis from parterre to bosquet, the latter pierced by allées. However, no one had as great an impact on the Baroque garden as André Le Nôtre, the Bernini of landscape design, and once again it was at Vaux-le-Vicomte that the new style was pioneered (199). The Duc de Saint-Simon proudly noted that Le Nôtre's designs for French gardens 'have so lowered the reputation of Italian gardens (which are really nothing by comparison) that most famous landscape architects of Italy now come to France to study and admire'. Le Nôtre came from a family of royal gardeners, working primarily at the Tuileries in Paris until qualifying as master gardener in 1637. No mere planter, he probably studied painting and perspective under Le Brun, and was conversant in everything from arboriculture to hydraulics. Although he became one of Louis XIV's favourite courtiers and was honoured as General Controller of the King's Buildings, the self-consciously practical Le Nôtre preferred manual labour in the gardens to court life at Versailles – he liked to be seen carrying a spade and when the king granted him noble status in 1681 he chose three snails and a cabbage for his coat of arms. Le Nôtre designed the most important gardens in France, worked for the pope and nobility in Rome, and landscaped several properties in England, including the park at Greenwich, behind Christopher Wren's as yet unbuilt hospital and the Queen's House (see 141). Yet when assessing Le Nôtre's legacy it is important to bear in mind the influence of his patrons, many of whom – Louis XIV in particular – initiated plans and paid very close attention to his gardener's designs, often rejecting or altering them (even after they were laid out) to suit his and his mistresses' whims.

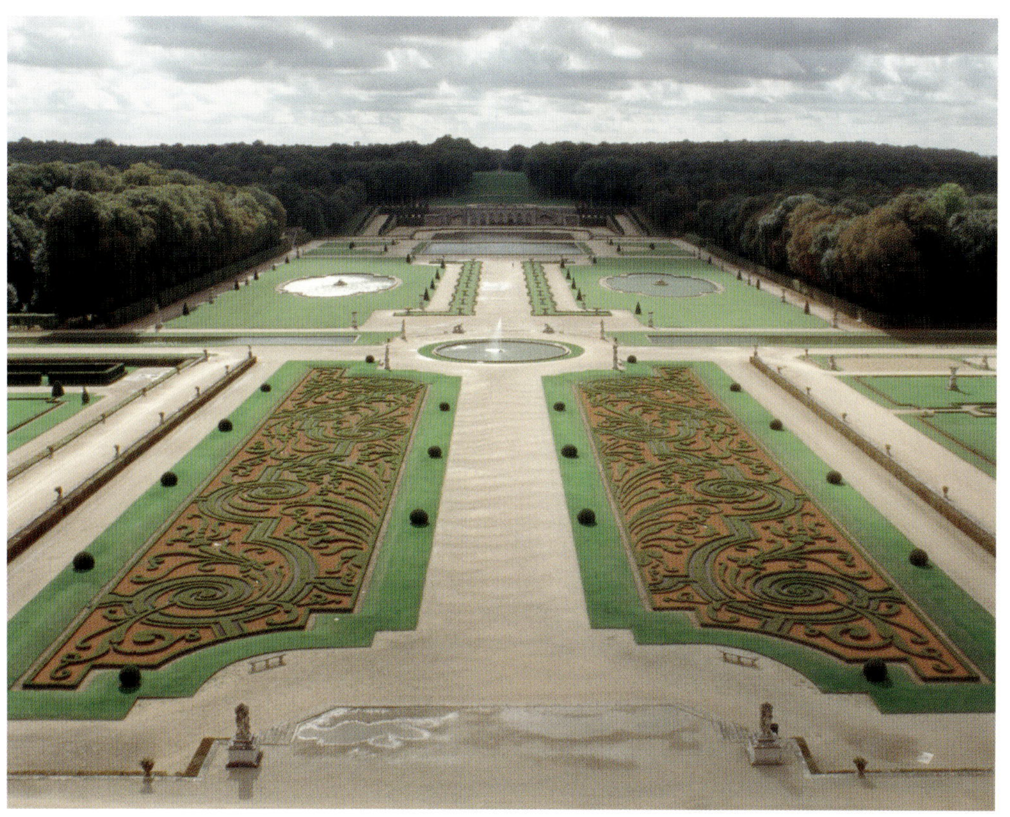

199.
André
Le Nôtre
Gardens
at Vaux-le-
Vicomte,
1657–61
(France)

Part of the genius of Vaux-le-Vicomte (1656–61) is the way Le Nôtre was able to impose his vision on an imperfect site (see 199). The palace grounds were uneven and constricted on both sides by villages, and the meandering River Anqueil passed directly through the middle. Although the problem of the villages was easily solved through demolition, Le Nôtre had to make the river work for him, straightening it 45 degrees into a kilometre-long (0.6 mile) canal that became the transverse axis of the rear garden. This canal also became the source of its many waterworks in the adjacent grotto and fountains. From the rear of the palace the garden sloped imperceptibly down to the river, and it was flanked by bosquets on the sides, a novelty since traditionally bosquets were placed behind the formal garden. From the chateau our glance first passes between rectangular parterre terraces – their Turkish-inspired designs of flowerbeds enclosed in box were referred to as broderies (embroideries) – across a water channel and pool that formed the first transverse axis, between a pair of rectangular lawns with fountains, across two large reflecting pools in front of and behind the canal (the canal is invisible at this stage), and ends at an oversized grotto and staircase. The grotto is built out of scale to appear correctly proportioned from the chateau, and its embracing wings invite the eye to pause before looking upwards through a wide avenue cut in the forest behind the grotto, first to a giant statue of Hercules on a hill 1.5 kilometres (1 mile) from the chateau, and then onwards for another 3 kilometres (1¾ miles).

Order is an essential theme in the garden at Vaux, the subduing of nature an expression of humankind's control over the elements. Le Nôtre also brings a Baroque sense of illusion and caprice to his garden, relating it to its Late Renaissance forebears. By means of a subtle manipulation of perspective we are fooled into thinking we can view the entire garden from the palace steps, yet we discover the deception as we walk towards the grotto. The grotto is much further away than it looks and seems to retreat as it is approached: the lawns turn out to be twice as long as the parterres, square pools are revealed to be rectangular, and – most dramatically – the hidden canal and cascades on its south bank suddenly emerge to block access to the grotto and further reaches of the garden. In fact, if visitors insist on going to the grotto it takes almost half an hour to walk around the end of the canal, and even longer to hike up to the Hercules statue. At the front of the chateau Le Nôtre provided a trio of paths radiating out from the door and forming a trident: known as a *patte-d'oie*, or goose foot, it became his most celebrated motif and is repeated in truncated form behind the canal in the rear garden. The same trident occurred in Italian villas but facing the other way: by turning it around, Le Nôtre invented another way of representing his patron's wide-ranging authority over his lands.

If the gardens at Vaux-le-Vicomte were an expression of order and permanence, Le Nôtre's landscape at Versailles (begun 1661) was more varied and adaptable, a response to Louis XIV's fickleness, the inevitability of changing tastes, and the variety of ceremonies, festivals and activities necessary in a garden that surrounded what became the administrative capital of the nation (200). Le Nôtre faced natural challenges as well. Not only were the grounds several times larger than Vaux – they occupied 60 square kilometres (23 sq miles) – but they contained a massive swamp and were too flat for gravity to run the waterworks. Versailles also placed more emphasis on fountains and statues to spell out its iconographical programme, to the extent that the formidable number of sculptors who worked on the site (among them Benoist Coysevox, Pierre Le Gros the Elder, Jean-Baptiste Tubi, Etienne Le Hongre and Thomas Regnaudin) had as much to do with the garden's appearance and iconographical programme as the gardeners and arborists. The garden's scheme was determined ultimately by Louis himself – he even wrote six personalized walking tours between 1689 and 1705 – and it revolved around certain key themes, including the idea of the 'Sun King', embodied mostly in references to Apollo; the monarch's rule over sea and land, with particular emphasis on France; the seasons and natural world; his ability to maintain peace; and his identification with the Roman emperors, manifested through copies of famous Graeco-Roman statues by students of the French Academy. Hunting imagery, embodied in statues of Diana and fights between animals, signalled the importance of such aristocratic pursuits at court. Louis was especially proud of the waterworks, which required four reservoirs filled by pumps and windmills, aqueducts and industrial-scale machines such as the Machine de Marly, a conglomeration of fourteen waterwheels and 221 pumps used to draw water 8 kilometres

(5 miles) from the River Seine. However, even these extremes of hydraulic creativity could not permit all of the fountains to run at once – a legion of young boys with whistles were employed to signal operators to turn on fountains so that all the waterworks in sight of the royal party would be working when they passed.

The immense plan is anchored in place by two axes facing the four cardinal directions. The north-south axis runs parallel to the palace façade while the east-west axis extends from the king's bedroom (before the construction of the Hall of Mirrors) nearly 3 kilometres (1.86 miles) to the west and setting sun (very important to a 'Sun King'). From the palace we look down a terrace, around the horseshoe-shaped Fountain of Latona (named after the mother of Apollo), along an extended, narrow lawn called the 'Green Carpet' or 'Royal Avenue,' across the Fountain of Apollo, through the entire length of the Grand Canal, and past another over 500 metres (1,640 ft) of gravel path. The Grand Canal (1667–80) – itself over 1.5 kilometres long (1 mile) – contained a permanent fleet of miniature French naval vessels and imported Venetian gondolas. The much shorter north-south axis comprised five rectangular segments including parterres, fountains and the Orangerie, linked by a central pathway and flanked on either end by the Fountain of Neptune (by Jules Hardouin-Mansart, 1679–84) and the gigantic Lake of the Swiss Guards – named after the army of mercenaries hired by the king to excavate it – a body of water large enough to accommodate the entire palace. However, from the king's walking tours we know that the east-west axis was more important, and that the visitor was to view it first, descending past the Latona Fountain to gaze across its entire length before turning around to contemplate the palace and parterres. The east-west axis also has the highest concentration of statues and therefore iconography, culminating in the Apollo Fountain – a symbol not only of the king but of dawn – with its gilded bronze statue group of Apollo in his Chariot by Jean-Baptiste Tubi (1635–1700). Le Nôtre played with the same division between 'tame' and 'wild' seen at Vaux, here by placing a mosaic of sixteen formal parterres, gardens, fountains and groves closest to the palace, and surrounding it on three sides by forested areas, the one opposite the palace – it is split in half by the Grand Canal – three times as long and four times as wide as the formal areas. The

200. André Le Nôtre, Gardens at Versailles, begun 1661 (France)

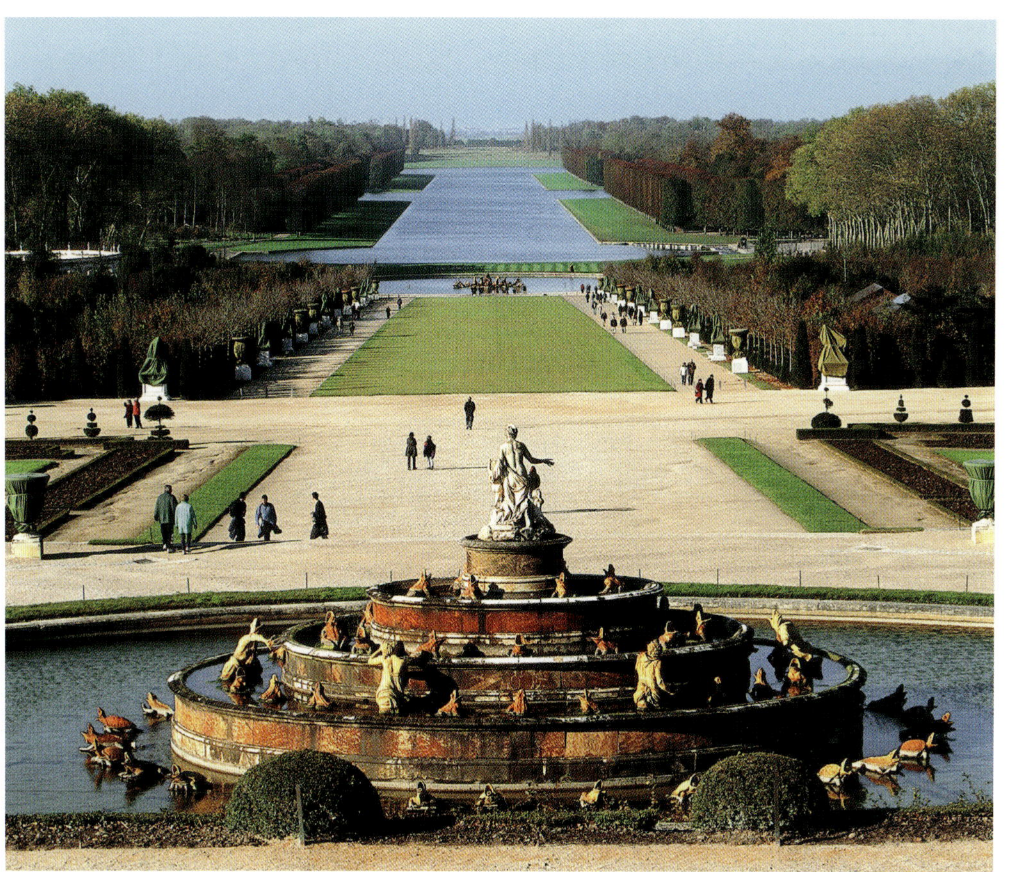

whole is criss-crossed by diagonal paths extending like spokes from hubs (including a very prominent *patte-d'oie* at the beginning of the Great Canal), more symmetrically and tightly arranged in the mosaic and more arbitrary in the bosquets. Because they were not as symmetrically planned as the formal areas, the forested zones could incorporate a variety of settings called *salles* (literally, 'halls') such as the 'Salle of Dance', the 'Green Salle', the 'Council Salle' and the 'Festival Salle', their names reflecting their roles in court ceremonial. Nevertheless, the forests are tamer than at Vaux, with adequate paths and openings to accommodate the frequent royal hunts (after breaking an arm the king hunted in a carriage). The bosquet to the south of the Apollo Fountain also once contained a menagerie, a symbol not only of the king's rule over the beasts (remember Augustus the Strong's zoo in Chapter Five) but also of his colonial empire, as many of its exotic denizens had been sent by colonial agents from Asia and the Americas.

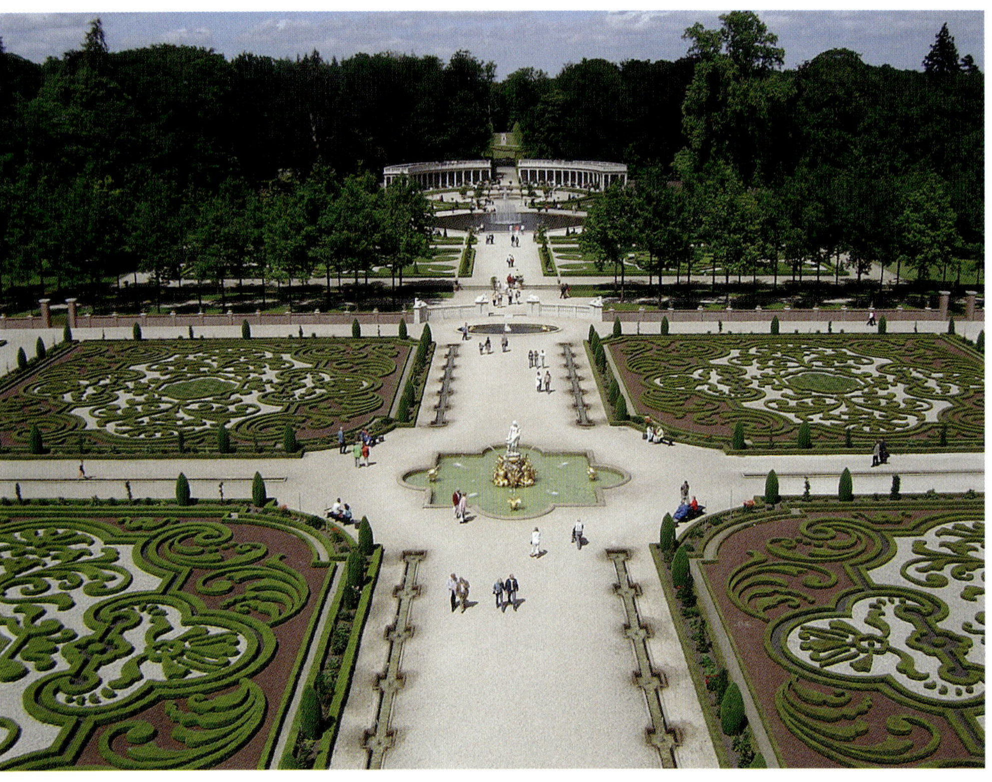

201.
Gardens at
Het Loo,
1689 (The
Netherlands)

Protestant gardens also fell under Le Nôtre's spell, as at Greenwich, but designers modified his absolutist vision to suit more modest budgets and anti-Catholic agendas. In Holland the French model was reproduced on a smaller scale, partly for economic and practical reasons – patrons were not as rich and gardens were often arranged along riverbanks so they could not extend as far – and partly to reflect the bourgeois identity of the new nation. A typical stretch of such gardens can still be visited along the River Vecht, just south of Amsterdam, where wealthy merchants built their summer retreats. These landscapes compensated for their size with a full complement of classical statues, fountains, grottos, spectacularly expensive tulips (see Chapter Two) and elegant clipped hedges. Dutch trade was commemorated by hothouse plants from the Indies, most of which had to be stored in orangeries during the northern winter. They also used some of Le Nôtre's perspectival effects, particularly his 'infinite vistas', even though the allées extended beyond the properties. The greatest of all Dutch gardens was Het Loo, built as a summer retreat for Louis XIV's enemy William of Orange (201). Since William was appointed *stathouder* (essentially the ruler of the Dutch provinces) and head of the federal army to protect Holland against the Catholic armies, his was a rare aristocratic garden – it even gained royal status when he assumed the throne of England in 1688 – in what was, after all, a republic. Although laid out by French garden designers Claude Desgotz (Le Nôtre's nephew) and Daniel Marot (1661–1752), it preserved such traditional Dutch features as a walled rectangular enclosure for the formal garden, which made it narrower than its French prototypes and relegated the bosquets to the zone outside the walls. At Het Loo there is more emphasis on the central axis, which leads the eye through the parterres and into the forests beyond, and the main garden was more rectilinear than Vaux or Versailles. Exotic plantings abounded, emphasizing surprising juxtapositions of colour, and the Het Loo fountains, focused on the central axis, were powered by a windmill. Although the garden is punctuated with militaristic and dynastic imagery – William modelled himself after Hercules and kept orange trees in honour of his family name – Het Loo emphasizes private pleasure over domination.

Garden designers in Sweden, another bastion of Protestantism, also modified Le Nôtre's model to suit local sentiments. Sweden's most prominent architect – indeed one of the most celebrated in Europe – was Nicodemus Tessin the Younger (1654–1728), architect to the royal family, who made radical changes to the Royal Palace in Stockholm (1680s–1700s) and to King Charles XII's country retreat and gardens at Drottningholm (1662–81). Drottningholm is his most overt homage to the Le Nôtre model, with a long vista along a longitudinal axis, a combination of parterres and bosquets, and canals, fountains and *allées*. But one of his most innovative designs is for the small garden and garden façade in his private home next to the Royal Palace, a work that blends Le Nôtre's landscaping with the architectural illusionism of Bernini and Carlo Fontana – he met all three architects during his apprenticeship in France and Italy (202). Departing from the classical sobriety that characterized his palace commissions, Tessin experimented with convex and concave curves, open and closed spaces, and perspectival tricks – the language of the Roman Baroque. The house and grounds are small and asymmetrical, and Tessin's challenge, using perspectival slight of hand, was to make the garden seem larger than it actually is. He divided the space into two trapezoidal gardens, one behind the other, with the formal garden of box hedge broderies and a fountain just behind the palace and a plainer lawn behind. The trapezoidal enclosures are wider at the far ends so that the enclosing walls receding at oblique angles made the spaces appear larger than they are. And since this shape was repeated, visitors experienced the illusion twice when passing between the two enclosures. The second trapezoid is a surprise since it can only be appreciated fully after walking through a narrow entrance flanked by two free-standing concave blind arches. At the far end of the second garden Tessin fools our eyes again. In the first storey of the wall he inserted an oversized Roman-style loggia with a tall arch in the middle flanked by smaller arches containing windows. The loggia gives the impression that there is another monumental palace wing behind the garden (there is not), and Tessin heightens the effect by telescoping the perspective inside the central arch to make it look like a long colonnade. It is a perfect piece of theatrical illusion. Few Baroque gardens of similar scale were able to aspire to such majestic effects.

However, majestic effects were not long to remain the ideal for garden designs with the arrival of the Rococo in the first quarter of the eighteenth

202. Nicodemus Tessin the Younger, Gardens and Garden Façade, 1692–1700. Tessin Palace, Stockholm

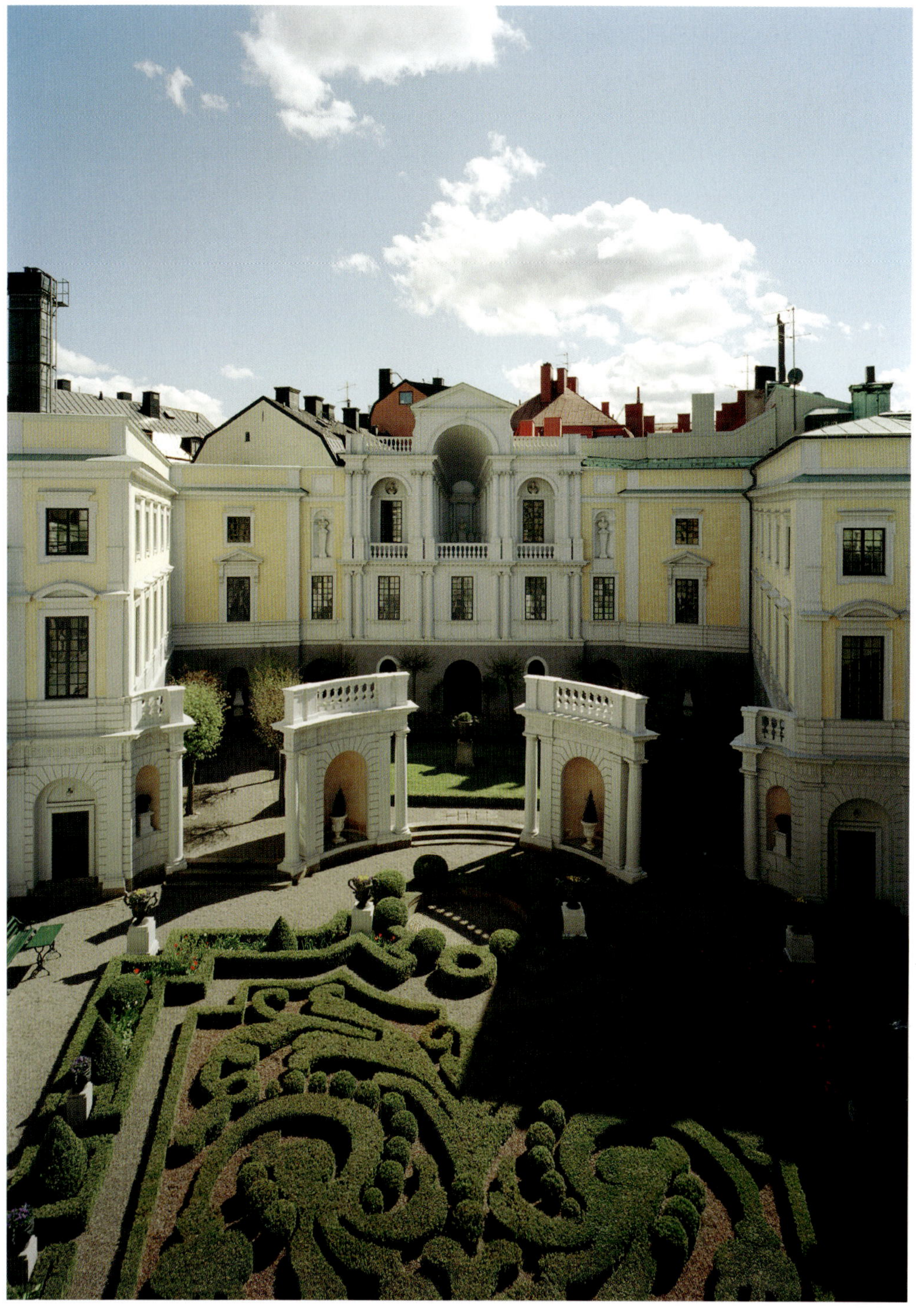

century. At first, designers merely reduced the scale of the garden's components, creating more intimate spaces and fewer grand vistas, although sculpture and fountains – now reflecting the asymmetrical and organic nature of Rococo design – were still an essential ingredient. Rococo gardens were inspired by the pastoral scenes made popular by Antoine Watteau and François Boucher in which languid young men and women listened to music or embraced in grassy slopes and forested glades (see 76). A first-rate Rococo garden surrounds three sides of the Queluz Palace (1747–80), the summer retreat of Dom Pedro de Braganza, King of Portugal, which employs Le Nôtre's canals, box-hedge parterres, grottos and fountains, but is divided into small enclosures and groves to allow for more private encounters and contemplation (see 14). However, Queluz was the end of a tradition, not a beginning. The design revolution that would forever change the way people thought about landscape was already under way in Great Britain – the only time during the Baroque and Rococo when that nation dominated European taste. Breaking from the stranglehold of the formal garden with its regular parterres, symmetrical canals and straight vistas, designers moved towards what they felt to be a more 'natural' garden, with uneven landscapes, asymmetrical stands of trees, meandering ponds, wandering paths and gracious lawns. Yet the so-called 'natural garden', or 'English garden', was as full of illusion and visual trickery as the most contrived of its Baroque predecessors.

Although the product of collaborations between numerous gardeners, patrons and intellectuals over the course of decades, the 'natural garden' is associated primarily with two master designers, William Kent (1685–1748) and his pupil Lancelot 'Capability' Brown (1715–1783), so named because of his optimistic assessment of the 'capabilities' of his clients' properties. It is also commonly tied to the rise of Neoclassicism and the so-called 'Age of Reason', particularly since classically minded writers such as Horace Walpole (1717–1797) and Alexander Pope (1688–1744) were personally involved in its development. Yet if we trace its origins, the 'natural garden' – at least in its earliest phases – fits neatly into the Baroque mould. It derived from the same Italian late Renaissance models (notably the gardens at Tivoli, see 198), contained elaborate waterworks and elements of 'surprise' for the visitor, was inspired by Baroque landscape painting (particularly Claude

Lorrain, see 67), and was deeply indebted to perspective studies and the theatre. In fact Kent, who was sent on the Grand Tour by wealthy patrons, had quintessentially Baroque credentials. He studied history painting with the late Baroque master Carlo Maratta (1625–1713), won second prize at the Roman Accademia di S. Luca in 1713, painted a turbulent cloud-filled ceiling fresco of the Apotheosis of Saint Julian for the Roman church of S. Giuliano dei Fiamminghi (1717–18), and was an enthusiastic set designer and promoter of Italian opera. Although ultimately a failure as a painter, when Kent returned to England he and his collaborators imposed these thespian forms onto their native landscape, creating a style that was as nationalistic as it was naturalistic. In fact, in the final analysis, the 'natural garden' was not so much anti-Baroque as anti-French.

The first manifestation of Kent's art – his Vaux – was the garden at Chiswick of 1729, the country villa of Richard Boyle, Lord Burlington (1694–1753), his lifelong patron, friend and one of his many companions on the Grand Tour (203). No mere dabbler, Boyle was a serious architect and was as involved as Kent in the garden's final appearance. The villa is a diminutive pavilion inspired by Andrea Palladio's Villa Rotonda in Vicenza (begun 1566) – less Neoclassical than neo-Renaissance – surrounded by relatively modest grounds to the north and northwest. Kent and Boyle's design deliberately avoided the symmetry, formal parterres and artificially trimmed hedges of Le Nôtre (Pope and fellow poet Joseph Addison both abhorred topiaries and broderies), but by sculpting out hillocks, rolling lawns, uneven ponds and canals, and strategically placed copses they created a 'naturalism' that was entirely illusionistic. There is even a giant *patte-d'oie* at the end of the garden, directly linked to the back of the villa by a straight *allée*, a caveat to those who maintain that the garden was a perfect manifestation of Walpole's ideal of a landscape without straight lines. Kent's concept of nature can be traced to the landscapes of Domenichino or Claude (see 66, 67) in which deceptively uneven hillocks and stands of trees created frames for views across water towards ruined temples and statuary. At Chiswick, Kent positioned statues, false classical ruins, a grotto, a sphinx, an obelisk and even a diminutive Pantheon so that they would appear as if by magic at the end of vistas that opened up as the visitor walked around the property. This apparently artless

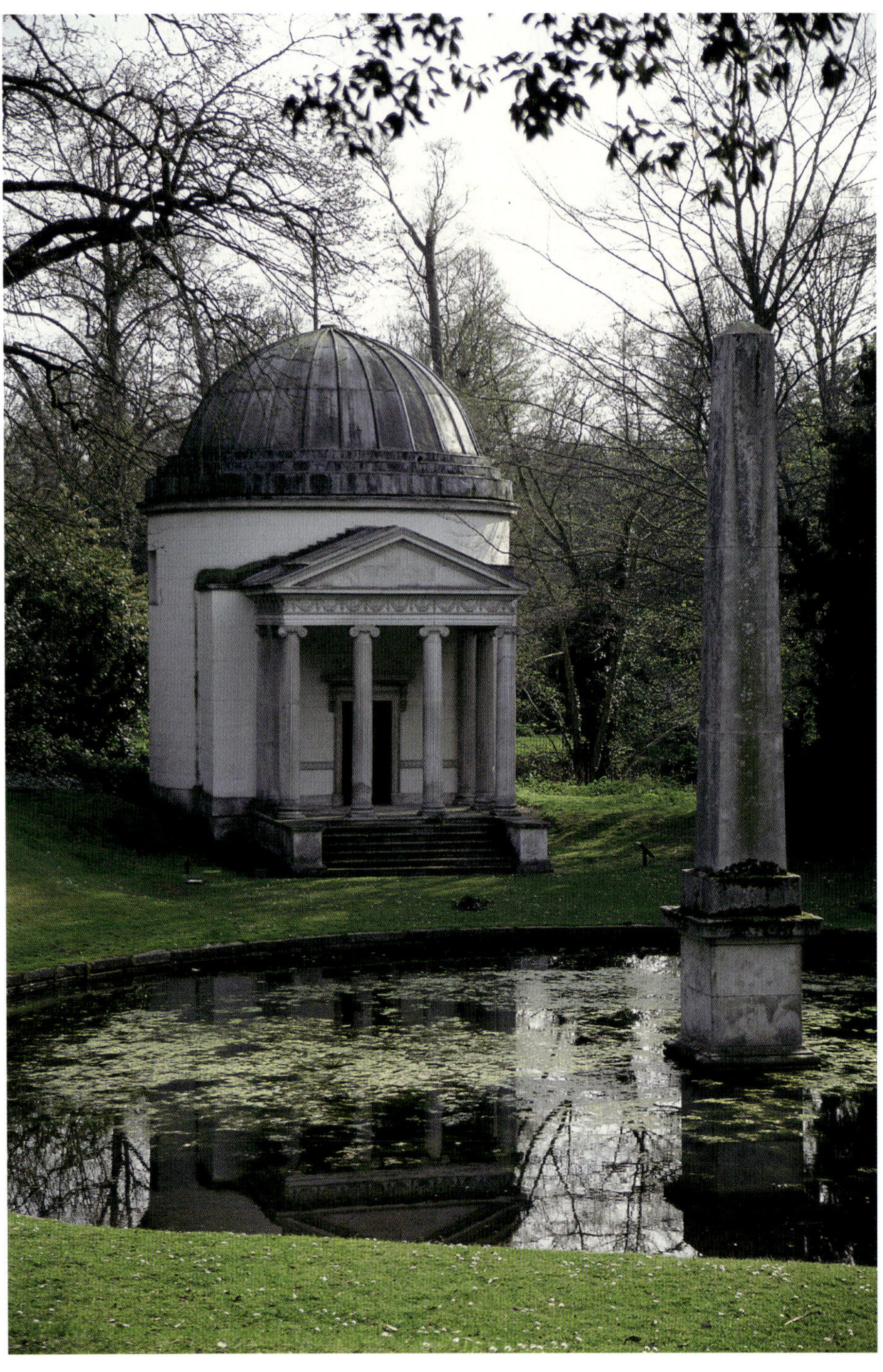

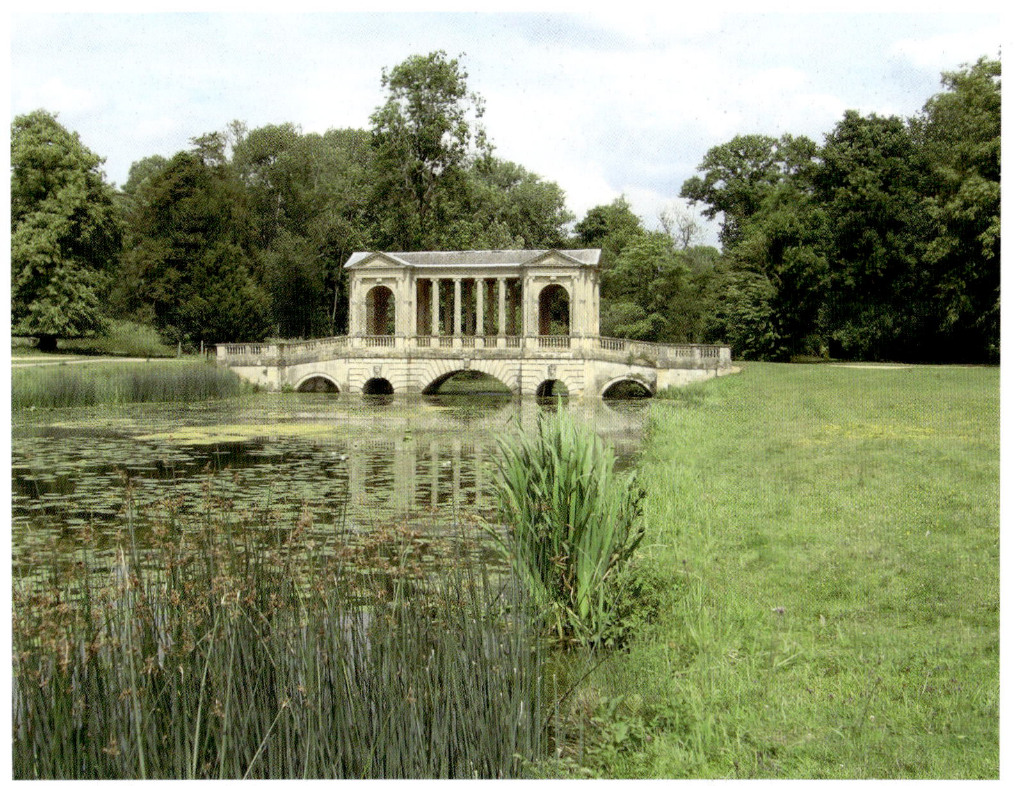

203. William Kent and Richard Boyle, Gardens at Chiswick House, 1729 (England)

204. William Kent, Lancelot Brown and others, Stowe Gardens, 1730s–40s (England)

distribution of structures (called 'follies') in a landscape was termed 'picturesque', and the buildings invited contemplation and melancholic reflection in a way that would have not been out of place in a Baroque composto. What Kent failed to achieve on canvas he ingeniously created in nature, treating the natural setting like a painter, his palette the water, trees, earth and sky.

Brown was a different matter, and it was he who gradually distanced the 'natural garden' from its Baroque prototypes, moving towards a more Rococo aesthetic. This process can be seen in a project to which both designers contributed, the magnificent gardens at Stowe in Buckinghamshire (204). Stowe was a long work in progress, having been redesigned several times since the 1680s, and when Kent arrived there in the 1730s to replace James Gibbs and Charles Bridgeman he was obliged to adapt to more than fifty years of ideas and compromises. Kent's main contribution, in the southwest and eastern part of the grounds – notably the 'Elysian Fields' – was the addition of several follies, including the Temple of Ancient Virtue (based on a temple in Hadrian's villa at Tivoli), the Temple of Venus, a rusticated Hermitage, and the massive, exedra-like Temple of British Worthies, bearing busts of its dedicatees and (in one case) a dog. When Brown was called in as head gardener for a decade beginning in 1741, he introduced his own manner. Together with his patron Lord Cobham he created the 'Grecian Valley', which, while containing a temple (1746–54) by Cobham after a design by Kent, was notable for the absence of follies. Instead, Brown gives us gently undulating greens and footpaths, and views of pools framed by stands of trees. In place of false exedrae he built an amphitheatre of earthworks and grass. Stowe gives us a hint of what was to come: during his renovations of Bridgeman and Kent's gardens at the royal gardens at Richmond in the 1760s, Brown transformed his predecessors' straight paths into meandering ones, and had all but one of his teacher's follies removed. In Brown's greatest gardens such as Longleat or Blenheim, he integrated the house with the property by bringing the parks as far as the house, eliminating hedgerows and fences, and inserting sunken trenches called 'ha-has' at the edge of the property to hide the boundaries between lawn and park. Ironically, given their Francophobe ideology, the innovations of Kent and Brown found fertile soil in France, where Rococo aesthetics had

**205.
Chinese
Summer
House**, Stowe
Gardens, 1738
(England)

already begun to favour asymmetry, pastoral settings and untamed nature. Political motives also came into play, as French intellectuals tired of royal extravagance looked towards England as a model for a more democratic government. Rococo designer Jacques-François Blondel published a manual for gardens in 1737 in which he celebrated the 'natural garden's' variety, unexpected juxtapositions and whimsy. Sixty-five years later Marie-Louise-

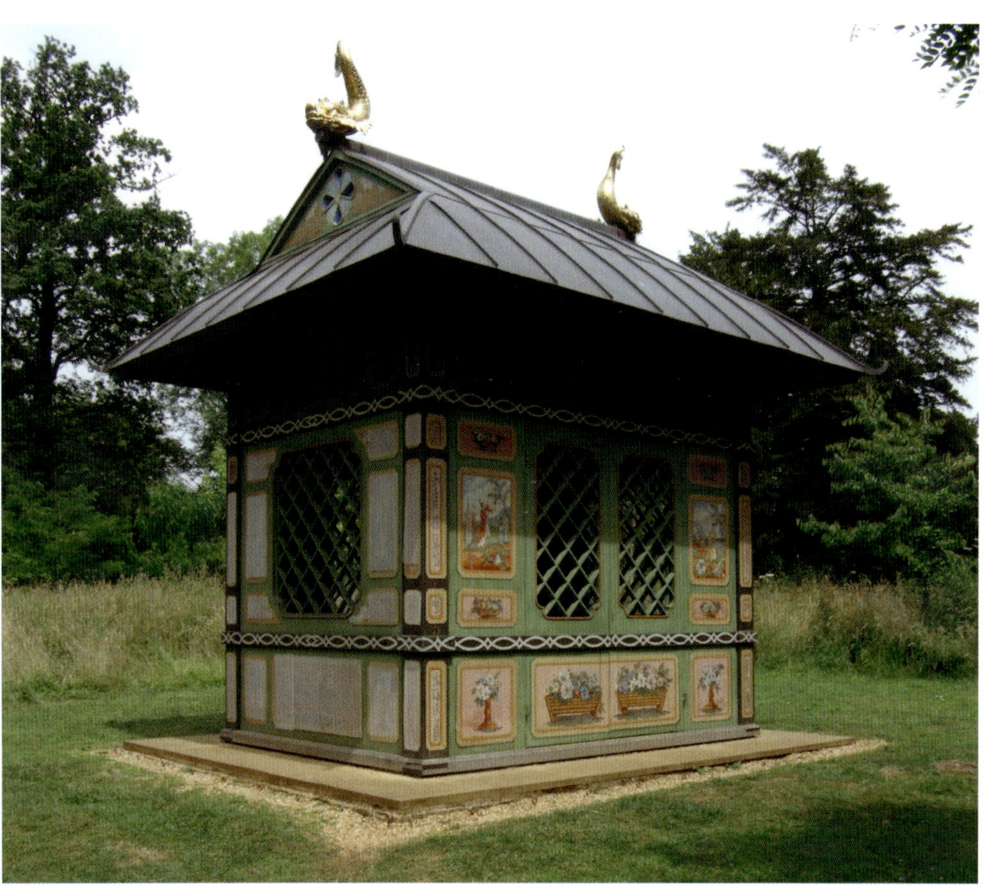

Élisabeth Vigée-Lebrun (see 62) was enchanted with Stowe, exclaiming that: '[t]he Park ... adorned with a temple, monuments, and every kind of structure, is of the greatest beauty'. Another Rococo feature soon associated with the 'natural garden' also came from England: the Chinese pavilion. The motif derived directly from British trade interests, as the East India Company had just established a trading office in Canton (Guangzhou) in 1711, and

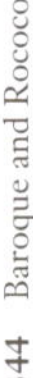

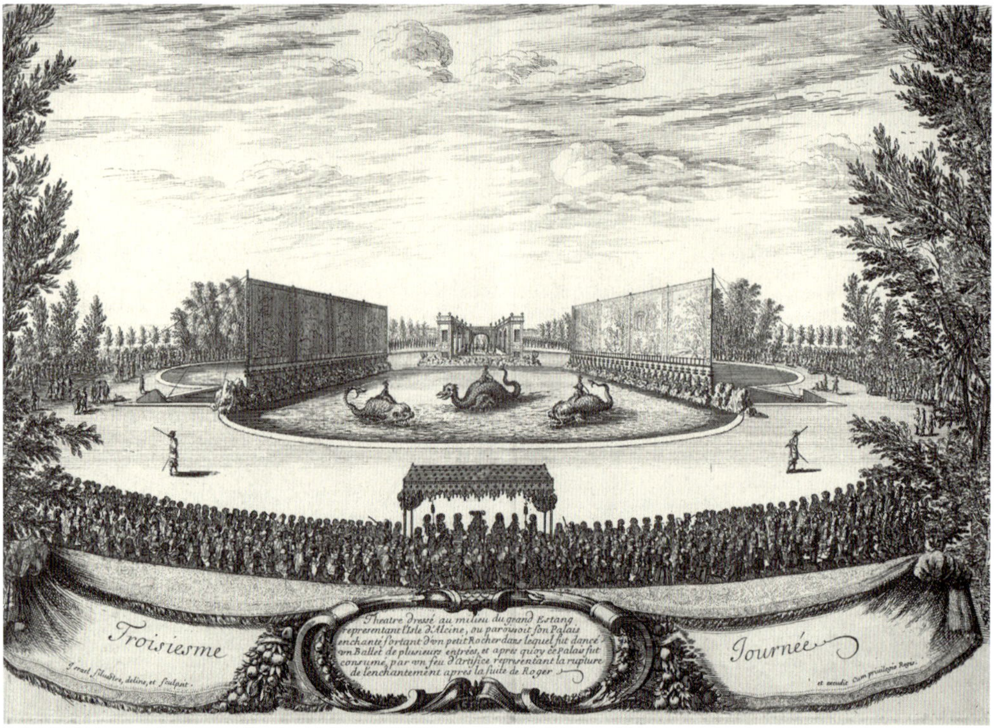

206.
Israël
Sylvestre
and François
Chauveau,
*The Palace of
Alcina* before
the firework
display
of 1664,
Versailles.
From *Les
plaisirs de
l'isle enchantée*
(Paris, 1674):
page 115.
British Library,
London

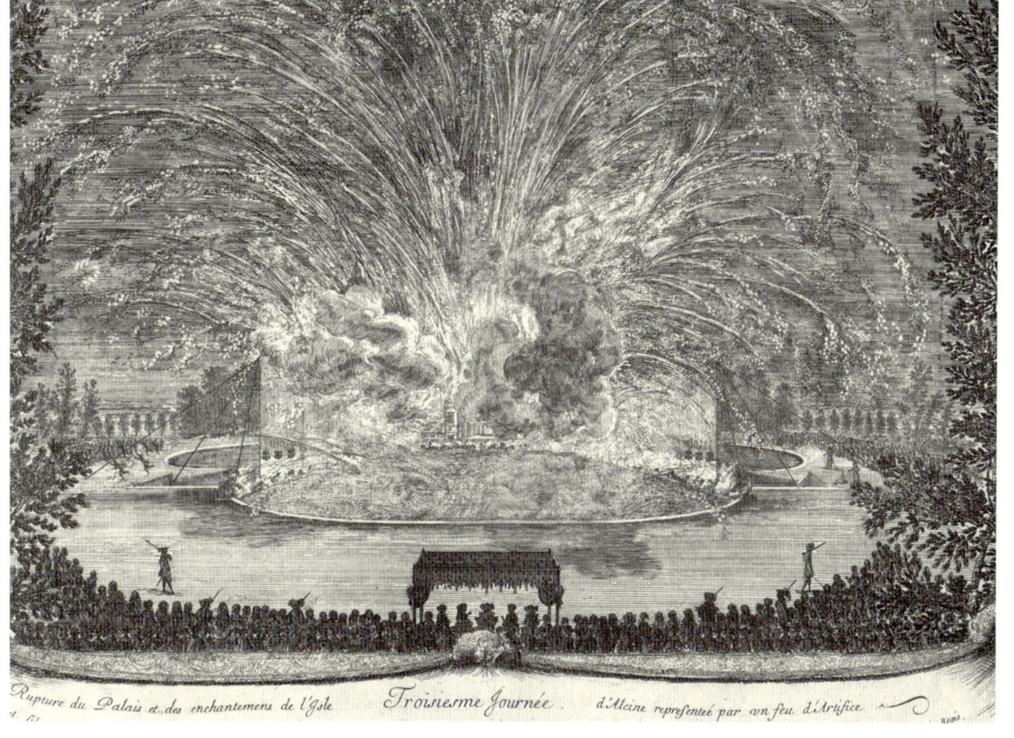

**207.
Israël
Sylvestre
and François
Chauveau,**
*The Palace of
Alcina* after
the firework
display
of 1664,
Versailles.
From *Les
plaisirs de l'isle
enchantée,*
(Paris, 1674):
page 123.
British Library,
London

tea and Chinese porcelains became readily available in London markets. Beginning with the Chinese Summer House at Stowe (205), fanciful wooden pavilions with hipped roofs, wide rafters, screened windows and brightly painted exteriors adorned the great gardens of Europe, from Palermo to Drottningholm. The Stowe pavilion, once in the middle of a lake and reached by bridges, is constructed of wood and canvas with paintings of Chinese landscapes by Venetian Francesco Sleter (1685–1775). Chinoiserie pavilions became so associated with the English garden that Blondel went so far as to assign the entire concept of the 'natural garden' to Chinese influence.

Kent understood the importance of people in garden design: a garden never really came alive until it was populated and its visitors participated in its views, sounds and entertainments. No one understood this better than Louis XIV, who hosted everything from banquets and ballets to operas and fireworks displays at Versailles, often set in front of one of the garden's larger pools or canals or in one of the many forested *salles*. In closing this chapter, I would like to return to ephemeral entertainments by looking at the most extravagant garden festival of the Baroque. On 7 May 1664, a multi-media celebration entitled *The Pleasures of the Enchanted Isle* was mounted to honour the two queens of France (the Queen Mother Anne of Austria and Queen Marie-Thérèse) and also to celebrate the commencement of the first building campaign at the chateau (1664–8), which included Le Nôtre's first suite of garden statuary, known as the Petite Commande. The event involved the greatest artists, writers and musicians of the day, including not only Le Brun and Le Nôtre, but playwright Molière (1622–1673) and composer Jean-Baptiste Lully (1632–1687), who collaborated on the allegorical themes and musical entertainments, and its sets were designed by the King's Engineer Carlo Vigarani (1637–1690). Over the course of three days the gardens played host to 600 guests – in his diary Louis 'thank[ed] God' that he did not have to lodge them in his palace – who watched solemn processions; diurnal and nocturnal outdoor feasts served by people dressed as shepherds and with dancers playing gods, the Four Seasons and the Four Continents (complete with mechanical animals); a cavalry tournament with a chariot of Apollo; a *course de bague* (a kind of jousting tournament); a sea-ballet about Charlemagne's battles with the moors entitled *The Palace of Alcina*; and the first performance of Molière's mythological comedy and ballet *The Princess of Elis*, with the king playing the title role (he was an accomplished dancer). Plants, landscapes and fountains took the place of walls, dining halls and backdrops. The banquets and jousts were held on a lawn in front of an exedra and three triumphal arches carved from box hedges, the comedy was mounted in a topiary proscenium stage set before a tree-lined *allée* – the first temporary stage ever constructed by the king – and the sea-ballet in a quatrefoil water basin on the site of the later Basin of Apollo. Another temporary theatre inside the palace hosted three additional plays by Molière.

Two of Israel Sylvestre and François Chauveau's illustrations to Félibien's commemorative volume depict *The Palace of Alcina*, performed on the Grand Canal, before and after the firework display (206, 207), both scenes reminiscent of the mock naval battles and fireworks displays performed throughout Europe in more public arenas (see 190, 192, 193). The palace, a wood and plaster structure with wings on oblique angles to enhance its perspective (compare with 196) – was built on a rock at the far end of the quatrefoil pond. Two screens of tapestries created a narrow perspective space to prevent the audience from seeing the sides of the pond and focus attention on the central axis. In the 'palace' forecourt a trapezoidal stage served the dancers, and the musicians huddled along the insides of the tapestry screens, violinists on the right and trumpeters and kettledrummers on the left. Three sea-monster machines moved about in the water in front of the castle, each ridden by a performer dressed in allegorical costume. Although the engraving shows the king and his family under the canopy in the centre of the multitudinous audience, he in fact played the title role of Ruggiero in the ballet, and his courtiers assisted, dressed in Grecian costume. Once the king had safely departed from the island, it went up in flames, ending the three-day festivity and astonishing all who watched it. Félibien wrote that 'it was as if the heavens, earth and water were all on fire ... the height and number of flying fuses, those which circled over the shores and those which emerged from the water ... created a spectacle so great and so magnificent that one could not have ended the enchantments better than with such beautiful fireworks'. The show concluded with a giant blast twice as loud as the preceding firestorm, ending in a resounding crescendo of explosions. The Sun King was pleased.

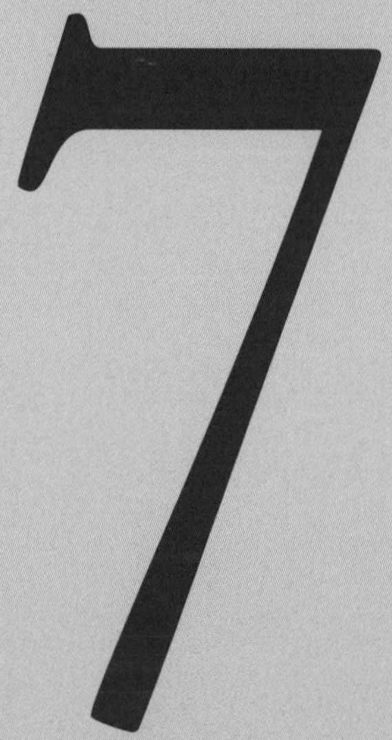

Global Baroque   Baroque and Rococo in Russia, Latin America, Africa
and Asia

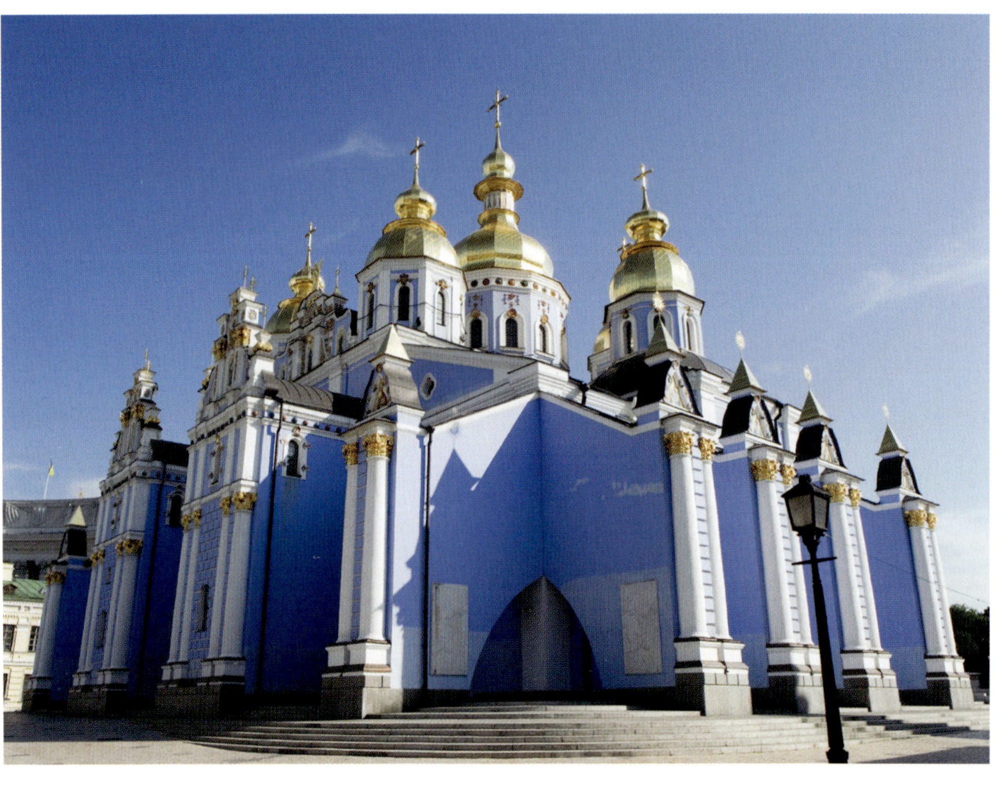

208.
Monstery of
St Michael, 1716–46. Kiev
(Ukraine)

The Baroque and Rococo quite literally encircled the globe in a way no earlier cultures had done. The ancient Romans spread Classical art from Scotland to North Africa, Iberia to India. Romanesque and Gothic followed the trail of medieval Christianity to Scandinavia and Cyprus, Lisbon and Lithuania. Following Iberia's forays into the Americas and Asia in the fifteenth and sixteenth centuries, Renaissance styles were broadcast further, into parts of Central America and the Andes, and as far east as Malaya. The great Asian empires, the Umayyad Caliphate (660–750) and Mongol Khanate (1206–1368), each dispersed their visual arts traditions across two-thirds of the territory between Morocco and Korea. However, with the expansion of Iberian territory and those of their French and Dutch competitors – combined with the even deeper penetration into the non-European world by Catholic missionaries – Baroque and Rococo was imposed on the Americas from California to Patagonia, the two coasts of Africa and India, and East Asian colonies such as Macao and the Philippines. The styles were also claimed by powerful nations outside the empire, in some cases avowed enemies of western Christendom: Ottoman Turkey, Ethiopia, Safavid Persia, Mughal India, China and Japan. Within Europe, Baroque and Rococo advanced beyond the Catholic and Protestant worlds into the heart of the expanding, increasingly cosmopolitan Russian Empire. This dissemination of western European styles was no mere stylistic conquest. Even in regions where it followed in the wake of brutal suppression of local cultures it was transformed by their civilizations and beliefs, either adapting to non-European aesthetic, formal and iconographic traditions or inspiring innovative regional variants as unique as those of Bavaria or Sicily.

This chapter will look at the often neglected Baroque and Rococo cultures outside Catholic and Protestant Europe, considering many of the forms and media that have been highlighted in the past six chapters. It runs the risk of oversimplification, since it might imply a global monoculture. However,

I hope it will show that nothing could be further from the truth. Baroque and Rococo outside western Europe emerged from within a dizzying array of cultures and geographic regions that reacted to the imported styles in different ways, with varying degrees of enthusiasm, and driven by diverse political aims and religious beliefs: Russian Orthodoxy, Islam, Hinduism, Buddhism, and a plethora of African and Native American faiths. Although some of the artists and architects responsible for these buildings, sculptures and paintings were western Europeans, the vast majority were not. The Baroque churches of the northern Andes were built by the Quechua descendants of the Inca Empire; the sculpture and architecture of Portuguese Goa were executed by Hindu and Muslim artists; and the Christian sculptures of Macao, China and the Philippines were carved by Buddhists or new 'converts' to Christianity who outwardly changed their faith to gain a market edge.

Russia was no exception in its transformation of Baroque and Rococo forms: the structures and decorative language of the Orthodox churches of medieval Muscovy dominated church architecture to such a degree that the imported styles at times seem like a veneer over indigenous forms. Russia first showed interest in western European styles during the Renaissance, when Grand Duke Ivan III the Great (r. 1462–1505), in his drive to introduce western European technologies and styles into Muscovy, invited Italian architects such as Aristotele Fioravanti (c.1415–c.1486) and Marco Ruffo (active 1485–91) to rebuild the Kremlin. Aside from the fortifications they were responsible for two of the cathedrals in the Kremlin's Cathedral Square, the Uspenski (1474–5) and Cathedral of the Archangel Michael (1505–8) – the latter introducing Renaissance forms on the exterior. But Ivan did not want these architects to import western-style churches wholesale. He insisted that the Italians immerse themselves in Russian architectural traditions to achieve a harmonious blend of Orthodox forms with Italianate classical decoration. Baroque forms first reached Russia and Ukraine not as the result of a royal decree but on the popular level, as the styles gained a foothold in the neighbouring Polish-Lithuanian Commonwealth and as printed books and engravings trickled into Moscow and Kiev. By the late seventeenth and early eighteenth centuries churches in those cities were dressed up with Baroque-style broken pediments, scrolls, baluster finials, pilasters and columns. The traditional plans of Orthodox churches, which featured a high central domed area surrounded by four or more lower domed chambers – a Greek cross within a square – made them receptive to the Baroque enthusiasm for centralized plans.

Such is the medieval Monastery of St Michael in Kiev, renovated on the exterior between 1716 and 1754, dynamited by the Soviets in 1936, and painstakingly rebuilt in 1997–9 (208). The church maintains its traditional centralized plan, with a high central dome surrounded by six lower domes, subsidiary apses, as well as buttresses on the sides and two rectilinear chambers flanking the main entrance. The gilded onion domes – all but the central one dated from the eighteenth century – have a traditional Russian Orthodox profile. Between 1746 and 1754 Ukrainian architect Ivan Hryhorovych-Barsky (1713–1785) covered the exterior walls with stucco and a facing of Baroque and Rococo features, including engaged columns topped by pilasters in the façade; volutes, floral scrolls and plant garlands surrounding the icons on the broken pediments; and shell-like cartouches over the windows that nevertheless retained their medieval rounded profile. Meanwhile a top-down importation of Baroque styles had been initiated by Tsar Peter the Great (r. 1672–1725), as part of a ruthless overhaul of Russian architecture associated with the construction of the new capital of St Petersburg in the first decades of the eighteenth century. Peter was determined to bring Russia up to date with western Europe, both by opening commercial and diplomatic links with countries such as Holland or the Austrian Empire, and by introducing western architectural techniques and styles. He invited legions of French, German and Swiss architects to design the capital and its fortifications, including Domenico Trezzini (1670–1734) and Jean-Baptiste-Alexandre Le Blond (1679–1719), the latter of whom – Peter called him 'a real marvel' – built the palace and gardens of the Peterhof, which was decorated in the rococo style by his countryman Nicolas Pineau (1684–1754), one of the leading figures of the Rococo in Paris. Peter's grand plans for the city were left unfinished at his death and most of the buildings of his western European architects have since been substantially altered.

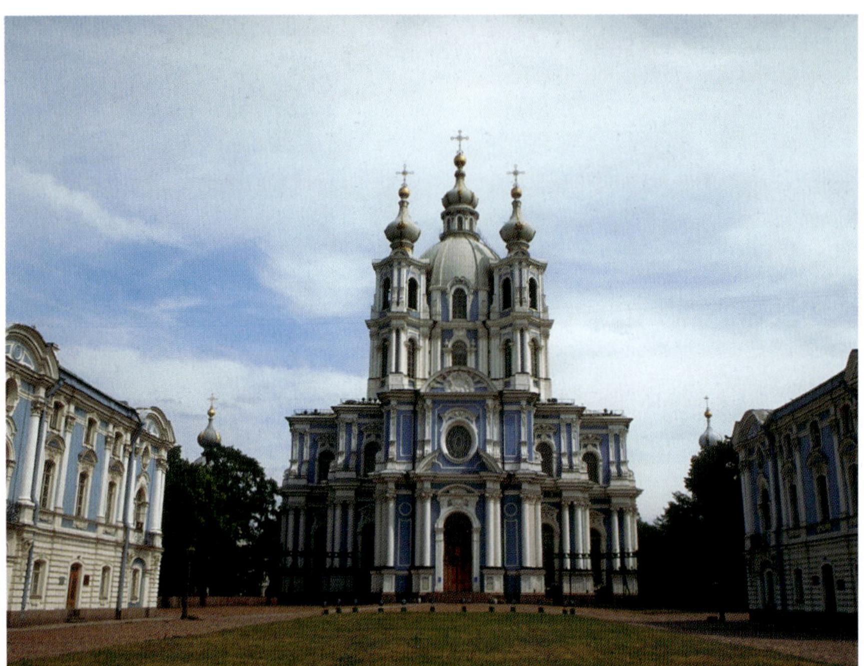

209.
Bartolomeo Rastrelli, Smolny Convent, 1748. St Petersburg (Russia)

210.
Bartolomeo Rastrelli, St Andrew's Cathedral, 1747–62. Kiev (Ukraine)

Peter's taste ran to simplicity and practicality, but his second oldest daughter, Elizabeth (r. 1741–62) was one of Europe's most enthusiastic Rococo patrons – in the same league as her Viennese contemporary Empress Maria Theresia (see Chapter Five) – commissioning a slew of wedding-cake palaces and jewel-box churches in St Petersburg, Pushkin and Kiev. Together with her favourite architect, the Russo-Italian Bartolomeo Rastrelli (c.1700–1771), Elizabeth developed a hybrid style far more sophisticated than the western veneers of Barksy and other vernacular architects, by substituting traditional domes, towers and other structures with equivalent forms from Baroque and Rococo Italy and central Europe. This wholly original style is best represented in Elizabeth's churches, notably the Smolny Convent in St Petersburg (209) and St Andrew's Cathedral in Kiev (210), both by Rastrelli. The Smolny Convent, which incorporates the Cathedral of the Resurrection, was built as an Orthodox nunnery for upper-class women and as a home for Elizabeth at a time when she was blocked from the throne and vowed to become a nun. The cathedral is painted sky blue with white trim, a typically Russian colour scheme (along with turquoise and white) that set Elizabeth's commissions apart from contemporary architecture in western Europe.

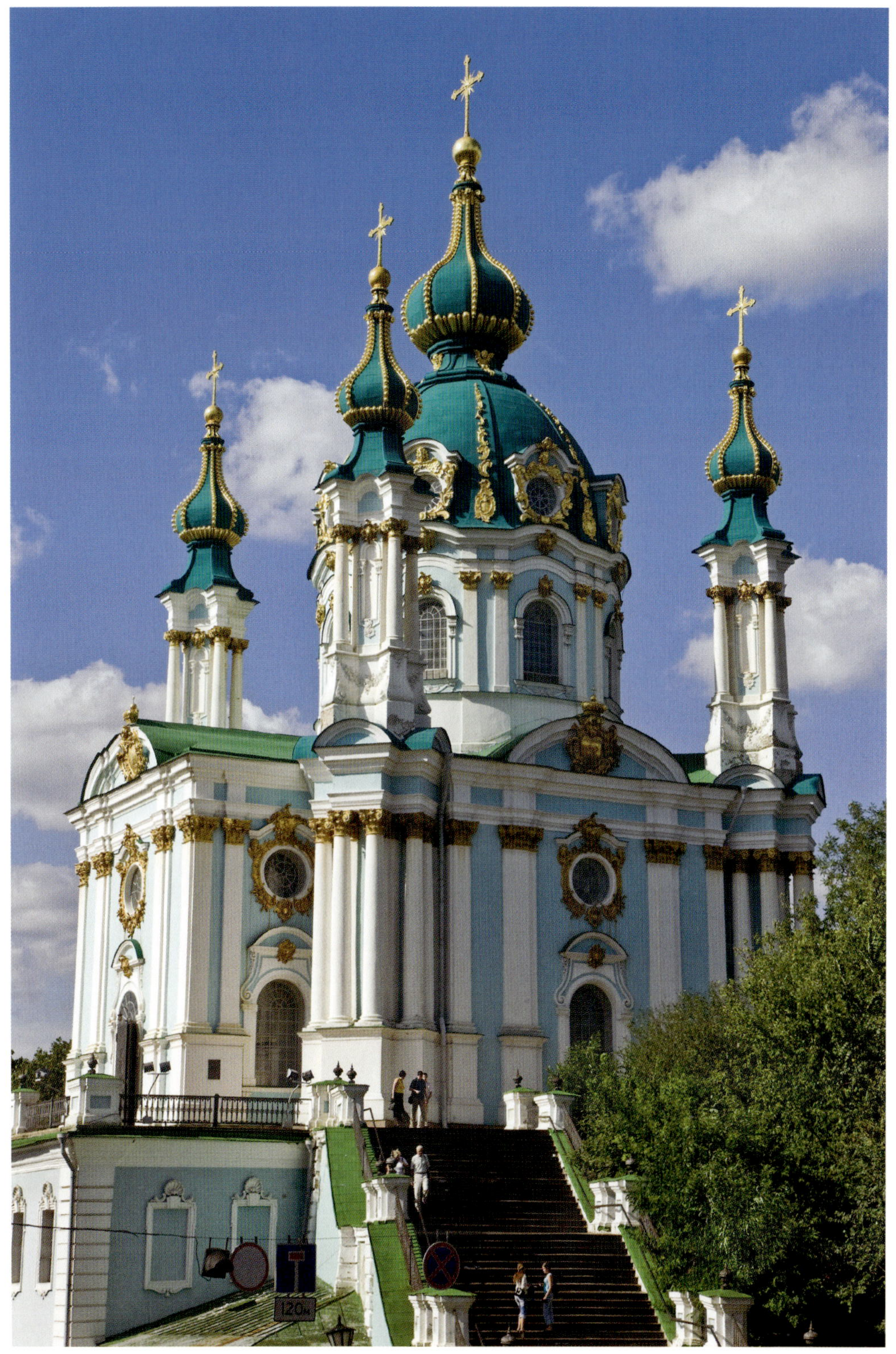

The way the Cathedral of the Resurrection combines western European structures within a Russian matrix is highly original. Although the dome has a Baroque rather than Orthodox silhouette and the church reinterprets other features from Italian models such as S. Agnese in Agone (see 142) or Filippo Juvarra's Basilica at Superga near Turin (1717–31), Rastrelli preserves the church's Russian profile by transforming the more traditional subsidiary domes into towers. The four towers are a more successful solution for a centralized church than the single pair at S. Agnese, since they surround the dome and the architect rotates each by 45 degrees so that they can better be integrated with its curvature. Other borrowings from western Baroque and Rococo include the window frames, inspired by Borromini (see 133), the profile of the onion domes, similar to Melk (see 147), and the oval window over the façade, typical of Baroque churches in Turin, such as Juvarra's S. Cristina (1715–18). Yet Rastrelli plays with Russian tradition in creative ways, as when he uses the Greek-cross-in-square plan of the church to make the planes in the façade step forwards in the Baroque manner to emphasize the central portal (see 145). When commissioned to build a typically Russian free-standing bell tower, he based his design on the tower gate of the Dresden Zwinger (see 137), making it two and a half times higher and crowning it with an obelisk and onion dome (work on this tower, which was to be the tallest in the city, stopped with Elizabeth's death in 1762). Rastrelli is similarly inventive in his church interiors. In the crossing of St Andrew's in Kiev he creates an Italian-style *composto* that incorporates the Russian Orthodox iconostasis, a screen of icons that separates the altar from the congregation (211). By distributing icons in gilded Rococo cartouches in the segments of the dome, the pendentives and the iconostasis, Rastrelli preserves the hierarchy of Orthodox imagery – it positions heavenly figures (the Sabaoth, Cherubim and Archangels) in the dome, Evangelists in the pendentives, and the traditional arrangement of Old and New Testament figures and narratives, archangels and sacraments in the iconostasis – yet turns the entire crossing into a stylistically unified meditative and liturgical space. He also draws our eyes upwards through a crescendo of gilded stucco ornament: spare against the plain white lower walls, becoming more profuse above the windows and culminating with the intensity of the gilded garlands and scrolls in the dome. Worshippers seated before the iconostasis interact

211.
Bartolomeo Rastrelli, iconostasis inside St Andrew's Cathedral, 1747–62. Kiev (Ukraine)

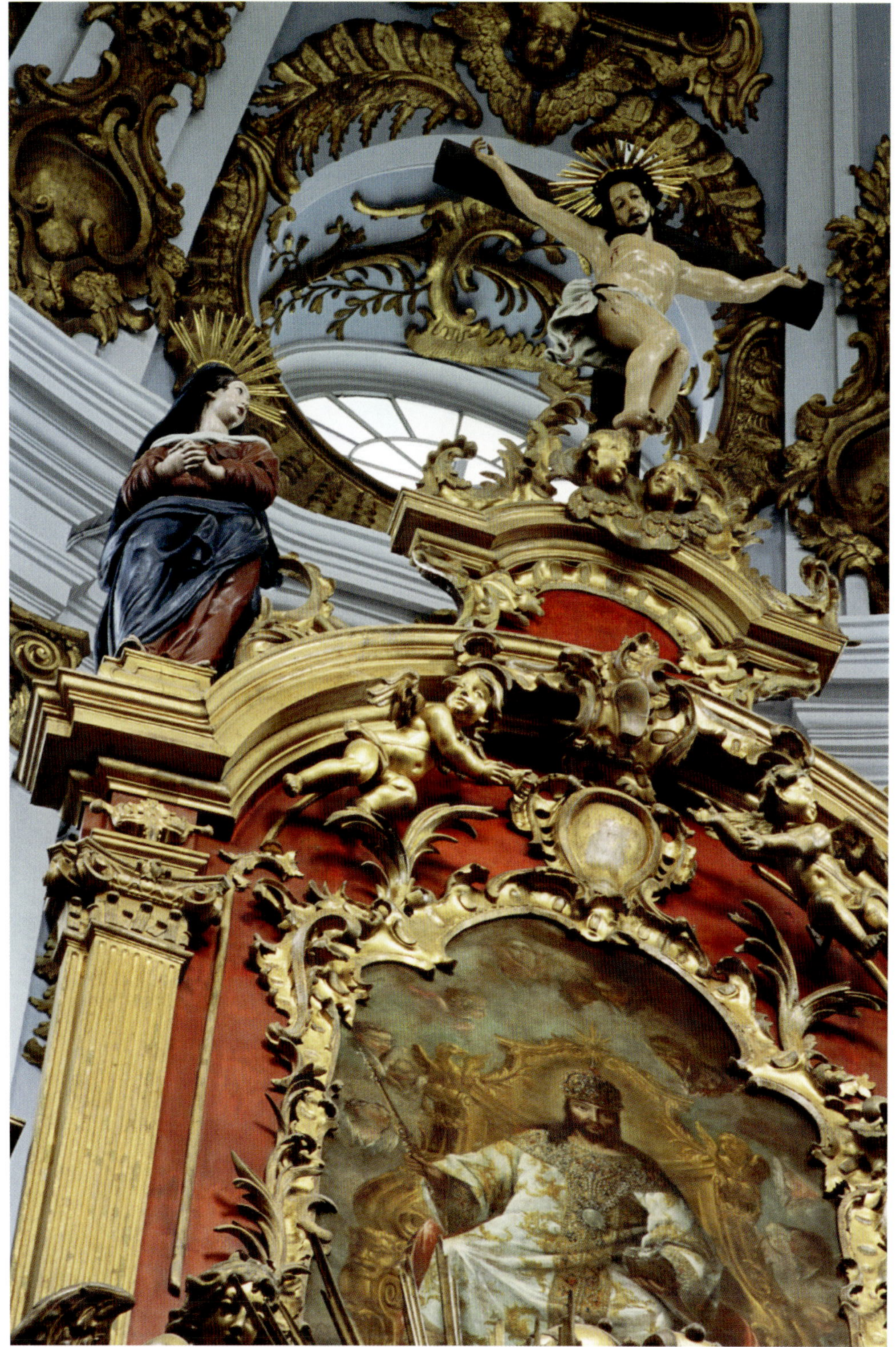

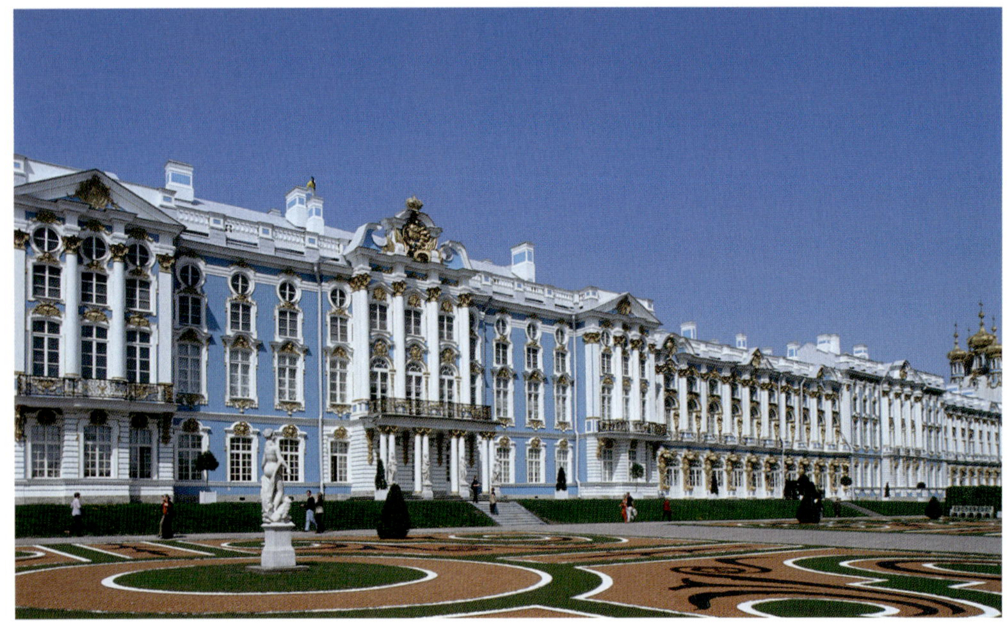

212.
Bartolomeo
Rastrelli,
Tsarskoe Selo,
1749–56.
Puskin (Russia)

with the paintings according to the customary Orthodox belief that they are a direct window onto the divine, but here the icons use a Baroque means to bring the faithful closer. Instead of the schematic traditional icon, which avoids realism to increase a sense of holiness, the paintings in the Kiev iconostasis and dome (by a team including Ivan Vishnakov, 1699–1761, and Oleksiy Antropov, 1716–1795) are naturalistic and emotionally engaging – even including landscape and genre elements – although they subtly retain the rigid stance and frontal pose of Orthodox practice.

Elizabeth and Rastrelli are best remembered for their staggering palaces: the Tsarskoe Selo Summer Palace in Pushkin (212), the Hermitage, or Winter Palace, in St Petersburg (213), and the radically reconstructed Peterhof outside St Petersburg (214). Although Tsarskoe Selo's turquoise and white façade is extraordinarily long, it avoids the monotony of the Versailles garden façade (see 135) by juxtaposing dramatically different styles. Two types of façade section – one taller and plainer and the other fantastically ornate – are strung together along a horizontal axis like railway cars. The differences in their roof lines give the whole a pleasing and rhythmic profile. The plainer sections juxtapose flat flanking walls with a bolder central ressaut (projecting section) using giant Corinthian columns on a rusticated base. In the middle section of the façade Rastrelli has placed the ressauts on either end and positioned an even grander ressaut in the centre – since it is the entrance it also has a portico and a high, ornate broken pediment. But despite their lower profile the more fanciful sections steal the show: they are lavished with gilded sculptural and decorative features, particularly a row of giant caryatids on the ground floor and herms in the first floor that form part of the window frames. The importance given to sculpture and the way the windows expand to meet the columns both recall the Dresden Zwinger (see 137). Protruding blocks anchor both ends of the façade, one end capped with the turquoise towers and sparkling gold domes of the palace chapel – curiously, the design of this ecclesiastical structure is more traditional than Rastrelli's other churches, its only debt to the West being its heavy Rococo window frames. The interiors of Elizabeth's palaces feature abundant gilded Rococo decoration and expansive illusionistic ceiling paintings, and they revel in colour variation through such media as inlaid amber (a Russian commodity) and room heaters covered with blue-and-white tiles. Halls with monochrome stucco contrast with rooms saturated in brightly coloured ornament.

The grand staircase in the Hermitage (213), while lacking the structural inventiveness of the Würzburg Residenz (see 162), has a delicate Rococo flavour with white walls, narrow gilded frames and mirrors. Although the ceiling features a dark apotheosis, the surrounding quadratura elements are brighter, the false sculptures and niches painted to resemble light-coloured stucco in white, lavender and grey.

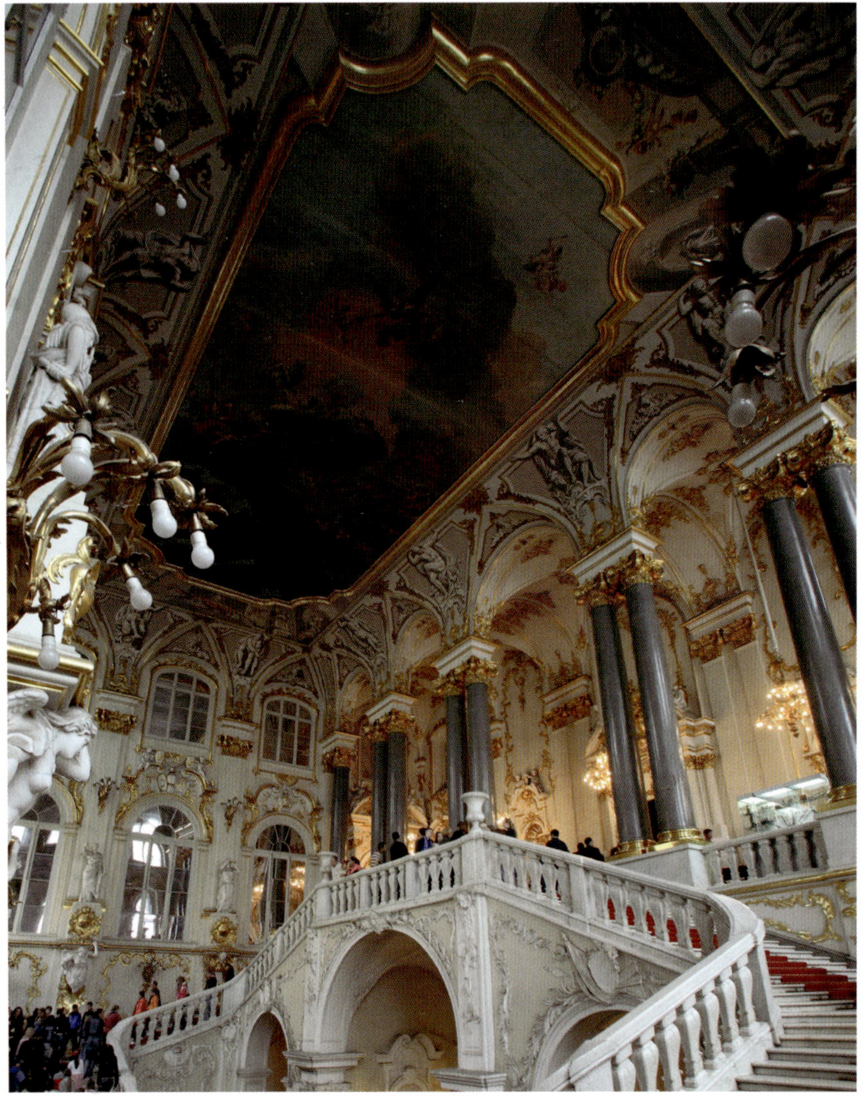

**213.
Bartolomeo
Rastrelli**,
Grand
Staircase,
Hermitage,
1754–68.
St Petersburg
(Russia)

**214.
Peterhof
Gardens**,
1746–58.
St Petersburg
(Russia)

Tsarskoe Selo and the Peterhof (214) boasted impressive gardens, based on Le Nôtre's model – at times refracted through Vienna – but also manifesting the Rococo taste for Chinoiserie and the more 'natural' style of William Kent. Built on a high bluff overlooking the shore of the River Neva, the Peterhof enjoyed a spectacular setting that could be manipulated to create dramatic waterworks and a breathtaking vista through the garden and out over the wide river. Unlike Vaux le Vicomte or Versailles, the waterworks were powered entirely by gravity, the water stored in cisterns behind the

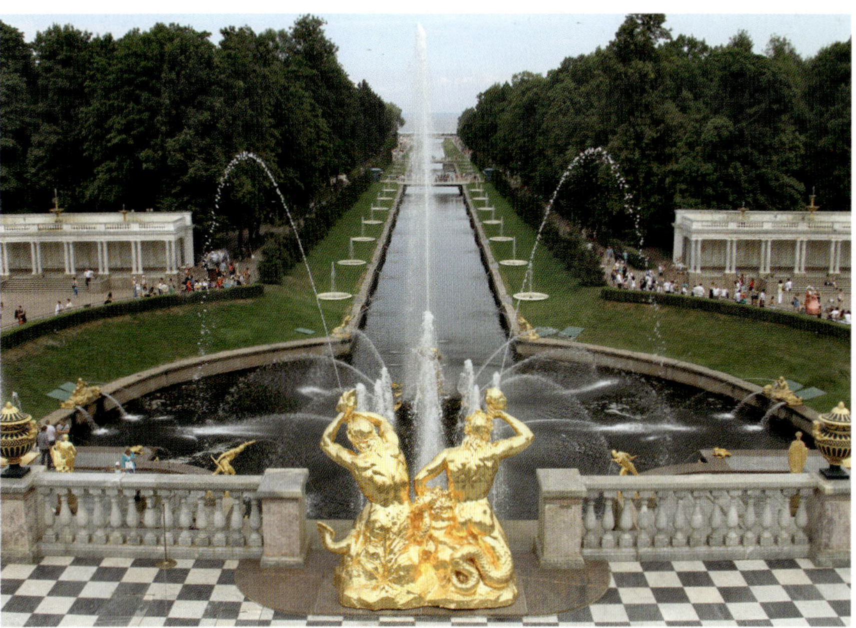

palace. The highlight is the double Grand Cascade that leads down the bluff from the castle, with staircases flanked by golden statues spouting water, a grotto, and two vertical chutes of water in the two ponds below, the latter emerging from a gilded statue of *Samson and the Lion* – a symbol of Russia's supremacy over Sweden. This kind of cascade may have been inspired by Le Nôtre's designs for the royal palace at Marly-le-Roi and also recall Italian examples like the Villa at Collodi (see 5) and the Villa d'Este (see 198). Another tribute to the Italian garden is the use of surprises, here taking the form of benches and 'trees' equipped with water pipes to spray visitors as they approach. The lower garden below the bluff contains the Sea Canal that draws the eye to the Neva and a number of smaller palace pavilions in imitation of Versailles. Elizabeth's and Rastrelli's age of Rococo ended abruptly with her death as Catherine the Great (r. 1762–96) introduced a more severe Neoclassical style into Russia.

Russians explored Baroque and Rococo styles and forms because they and their monarchs found them attractive or believed that they would help bring their isolated nation onto the world stage. A very different reality characterized the reception of Baroque and Rococo in the Iberian colonies in the Americas, Asia and Africa. Here the styles arose after a hundred-year policy of ruthless destruction of Native American, Asian and African religions, cultures and visual arts traditions. Yet, remarkably, those traditions did not die: even in some of the regions most heavily affected by colonial policy the indigenous majority preserved aspects of their faiths, languages, socio-political structures, iconography, and artistic and architectural practices. Many of the Baroque and Rococo buildings and artworks in the Americas reflect this indigenous heritage. Others, despite being executed for the most part by Native American and Mestizo (mixed blood) artists cannot be related to indigenous traditions but are no less original for it – the best are equal to the most extraordinary European variants of the style.

Spain first reached the Americas with Christopher Columbus' voyages to the Caribbean and Central America between 1492 and 1504, but large-scale conquest began with the destruction of the Aztec Empire in 1519–20 and the much more protracted annihilation of the Inca state between 1531 and 1581. Moving westwards across the Pacific, the Spanish also took the Philippine islands from their mostly Tagalog inhabitants (1571). Following Vasco da Gama's trip around the coast of Africa in 1498, the Portuguese carved out small colonies along the coasts of Africa and Asia: beginning in 1505, they founded settlements in places such as Mozambique, Diu, Goa, Macao and Malacca (in present-day Malaysia), and they explored the coast of Brazil (the colony would not gain much importance until the eighteenth century). In the first century and a half of rule in the Americas most Native American arts and architectural forms were systematically destroyed, however others were considered useful and were preserved in altered form: for example some buildings in Aztec temple compounds inspired structures in missionary church courtyards and the luxurious art of Aztec feather painting was recalibrated to make Christian pictures. Meanwhile, Native American artists and architects subtly perpetuated their own traditions by incorporating glyphs (the building blocks of Aztec picture-writing) or indigenous religious iconography into the margins of otherwise Christian façades or mural paintings executed for the missionaries. This phenomenon was more evident in Mexico than in South America: the Aztecs had a stronger figural arts tradition than the Incas and their stonecutters and painters passed down traditional styles and symbols from father to son. However, the phenomenon also died more quickly in Mexico, as Native American craftsmen perished in giant plagues and lost touch with their pre-Hispanic past. Few hybrid arts of this type in Mexico outlasted the Renaissance. By contrast, in South America, perhaps because the struggle for conquest lasted longer and also because the attack on indigenous religion – never won – was unusually vicious, there was little Native American content in the arts before the last decades of the seventeenth century. At this point the Baroque was in full swing.

The Baroque came early to South America. In the same decades that Bernini and Borromini were developing High Baroque architecture in Rome, the city of Cuzco, former capital of the Inca Empire, produced – in the wake of a devastating earthquake in 1650 – one of the most original Baroque monuments in the world. The Jesuit Church of the Transfiguration (better known as the Compañía), built by European architects and Native American stone masons, became the template for a vigorous new style characterized by a complex intersecting and layering of columns and entablatures that would be copied throughout the vast Bishopric of Cuzco through the end of the century (215). Strictly speaking, the Compañía was not the first building in this new style – the cathedral façade (1649–c.54) was earlier – but because the new Jesuit church (1651–68) possessed much greater unity, this more visually satisfying structure was destined to become the prototype for the *cuzqueño* Baroque. The Compañía may have been designed by the Flemish Jesuit Jean-Baptiste Gilles (Juan Bautista Egidiano) – so say the Jesuit chroniclers – or the retablo-maker Martínez de Oviedo, who was also responsible for the façade, and it included a main church, the Indian (Loreto) Chapel and Penitentiary Chapel, and a spacious college arranged around a courtyard.

The façade of the Cuzco Compañía – and here I mean the central section, called a 'retablo-façade' – was designed to seize the viewer's attention, both through its liberal use of ornamentation and its harmony of form. By having the wall and columns step forwards from the sides towards the centre it directs our gaze inwards much like a stage backdrop – the effect is not coincidental as musical performances, processions and other events took place in front of this very façade. There is also a typically Baroque emphasis on verticality, with tall towers, a relatively narrow façade, and a central section (that of the door) that rises well above those on the sides. Equally Baroque is the multiplication of elements, such as the paired niche/ windows on the sides of the first storey and the dollhouse-like finial towers that echo the real ones. The Compañía façade is richly layered and textured, with freestanding Corinthian columns, bold entablatures, elaborately carved friezes and panels, blind niches and multi-coloured stone, and it contrasts sharply with the plain walls of the tower bases framing it on either side. As at Borromini's S. Carlo alle Quattro Fontane (see 3), entablatures serve as the primary unifying element, but the Peruvian architects may have arrived at the solution independently given that the two monuments are nearly contemporary. Parallel entablatures on the ground and top storeys of the façade bind the towers to the façade, the upper entablature forming a soaring trilobe curve as it follows the contour of the niche below. Even the thinner entablatures of the tower window frames connect with the choir windows on the first storey of the façade, and – delightfully – the window frames mimic the form of the façade as a whole.

Hybrid Native American/European architecture first occurred in South America (as opposed to Mexico) in the late seventeenth century, after the indigenous symbols and styles that characterize this fascinating variant of the Baroque had been kept alive over the preceding century in other media, notably textiles. The prototypical example of this so-called 'Andean Hybrid Baroque' is also a Jesuit church, the façade of the Compañía in the southern Peruvian town of Arequipa (216). It is characterized by visual richness, deep relief carving, a mosaic-like distribution of decorative elements derived from Andean woven garments, and a plethora of indigenous motifs including references to Inca and pre-Inca cosmology, the Inca crown, or *mascaypacha*,

215.
Jean-Baptiste Gilles and Diego Martínez de Oviedo, Church of the Transfiguration, 1651–68. Cuzco (Peru)

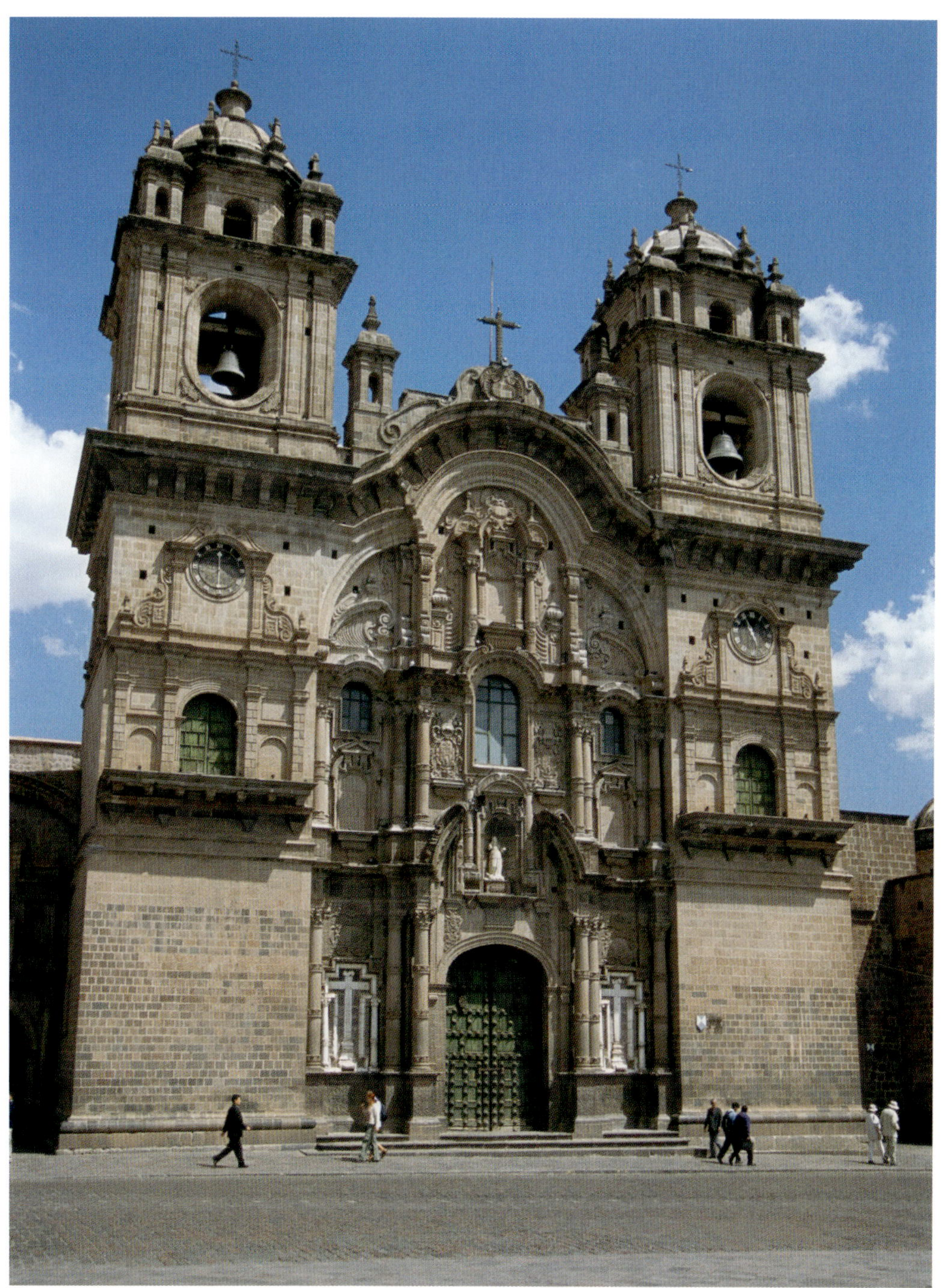

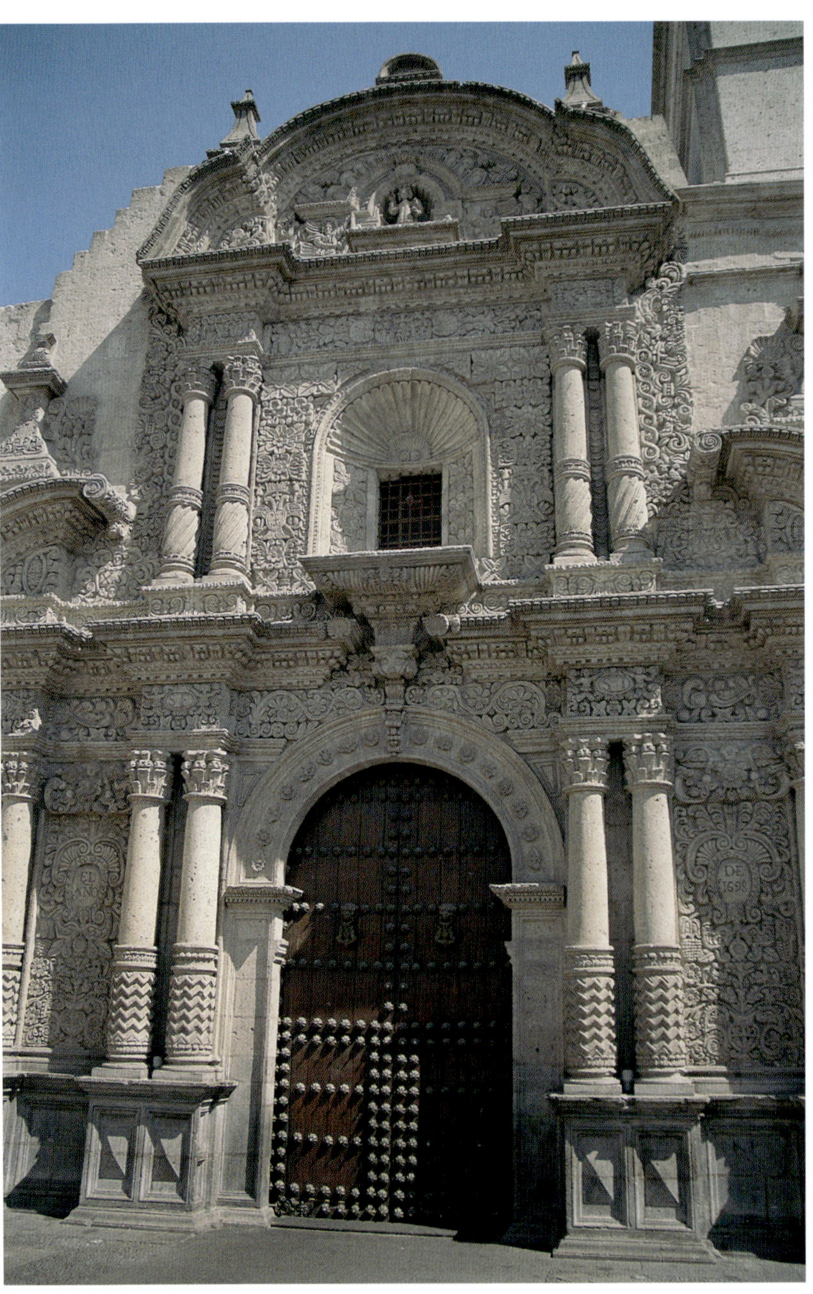

**216.
Diego de
Adrián and
others,**
façade of the
Compañía,
1698–9.
Arequipa
(Peru)

representations of Native Americans, and a panoply of local flora and fauna, from the tube-shaped cantuta and Inca lily to cactus flowers, pumas, hummingbirds and monkeys. Interestingly enough, the flora and fauna, while native to Peru, frequently come from the distant jungle lowlands, suggesting that they represent an idealized view of nature as a paradise garden. Typically of Spanish-American Baroque façades, it expresses a dynamic sense of movement through boldly projecting cornices and pediments and heavy columns rather than curvilinear planes.

The façade elevation was supervised by Spanish architect Diego de Adrián but – like nearly all Andean Hybrid Baroque monuments – the ornamentation was carved by Native American sculptors and masons who operated with surprising freedom in their choice of imagery. The portal is divided horizontally into two storeys and a large tympanum-like pediment that is almost a storey in its own right, and vertically into three bays with the widest one at the centre. This basic grid stands out against a tapestry of carved ornamentation, divided primarily into square or rectangular blocks. The lower storey is flanked by giant carved borders composed of serpentine monsters with giant mouths that disgorge pomegranates, tobacco-like leaves, cactus flowers, cantuta blossoms, scrolls and monster masks. Equally sumptuous panels appear between the columns, the areas surrounding the date inscriptions, the frieze over the lower storey, and the borders and mosaic-like panel around the window in the first storey, including winged cherubs wearing cantuta earrings (as women in Bolivia and Peru still do today), other human figures and masks (including one wearing the *mascaypacha*), tropical leaves and flowers, parrots and songbirds. The upper part of the façade – its frieze, tympanum-like pediment and finials – is also brimming with figures, plants and other motifs. This façade inspired variants from Cuzco far down into present-day southern Bolivia, and echoes of the Jesuit church appeared in remote villages as late as the early nineteenth century.

Many Latin American churches featured an especially lively treatment of the composto, derived from the richly decorated interiors of Iberian churches but producing unique results (see 105). Some of them combine European and Native American elements, as in the bewilderingly opulent interior of the eighteenth-century church of Santa María in Tonantzintla in Mexico (217). The crossing of this otherwise modest parish church is so overwhelmed with ornament that it has few equals anywhere. An intertwining stucco vine in high relief and outlined in gold leaf and polychrome paint covers the walls of the transepts and dome, incorporating angels, saints, caryatids, flowers, curlicues, birds, grapes and human heads. The stucco technique – it employs a type of plaster made of flour, egg-white and water – was devised by Native American craftsmen in the region and only appears within a short geographical radius. Many of the details found in the lace-like designs were probably adapted from printed books from Spain, Italy and Flanders, but the result is unique. The web of ornament spills over the architectural elements and engulfs the diminutive sculptures, achieving a unity of the arts as thorough as that of a Germanic Rococo church but employing an entirely different way of combining the media. There is no doubt that such spaces were meant to inspire wonder in their congregations: a commemorative volume of 1690 called a chapel in Puebla in the same style the 'Eighth Wonder of the World'.

Another *composto* is much closer to the Germanic tradition. In Brazil churches use much more daring Baroque structural forms than in Spanish America and their style relates to central European architecture – particularly in the states of Bahia, Pernambuco and Minas Gerais. This perhaps surprising connection can be traced to the influence of the Swabian architect Johan Friedrich Ludwig (1670–1752) at the court of King Dom João V in Lisbon (see Chapter 5) and also from German Rococo printed books and Germanic architects who immigrated to Brazil. After the 1720s Brazilian churches began to showcase oval plans, onion domes and convex façades as at Vierzehnheiligen (see 150). They also frequently boasted illusionistic ceiling paintings in the style of Andrea Pozzo and central European churches (see 6, 121). The chancel interior of the Benedictine Monastery of São Bento in Olinda (218), unites rich gilded Rococo woodwork with an illusionistic ceiling painting of the *Confirmation of the Benedictine Order* by José Elói (1785). Unlike German interiors, São Bento does not use stucco (unwise in a humid tropical climate; even the ceiling is painted on wood) but the gilded cedar carvings, by Master Gregório, achieve some of the

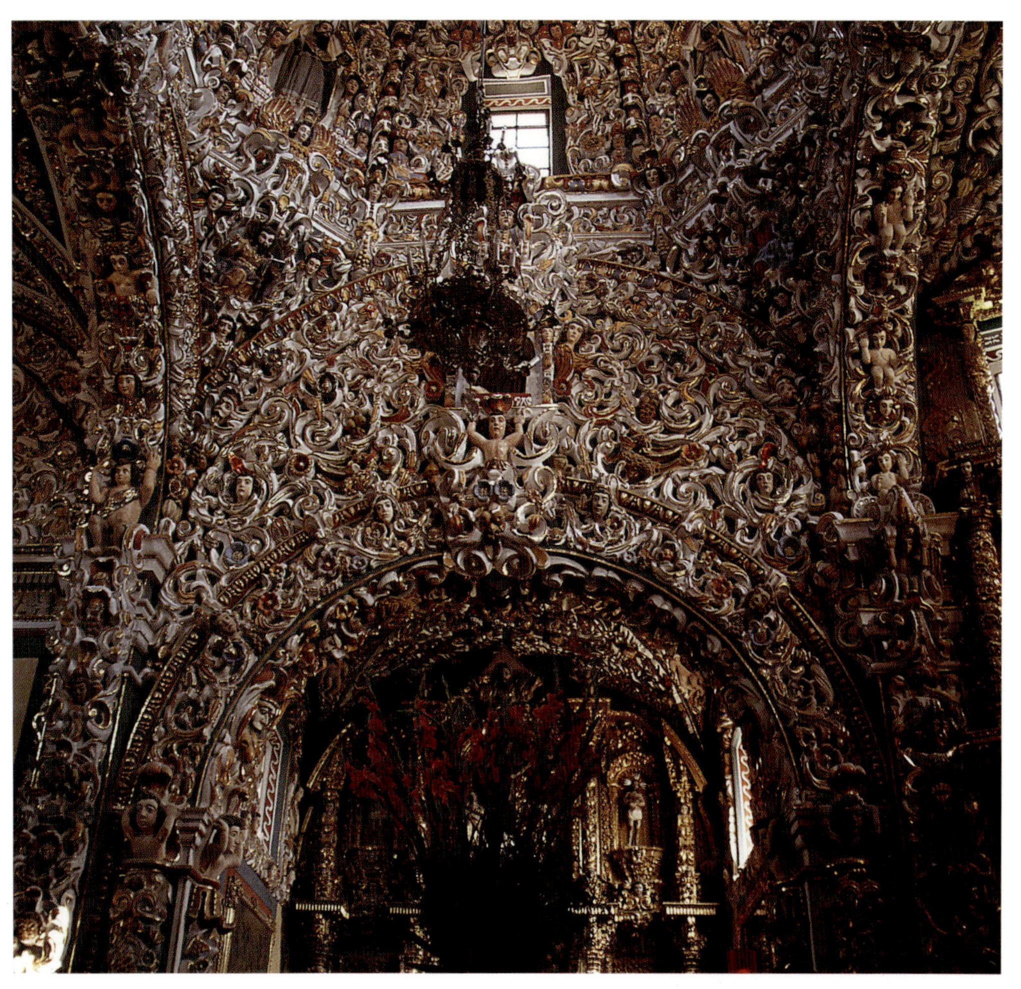

217.
Interior of
the church of
Santa María,
18th century.
Tonantzintla
(Mexico)

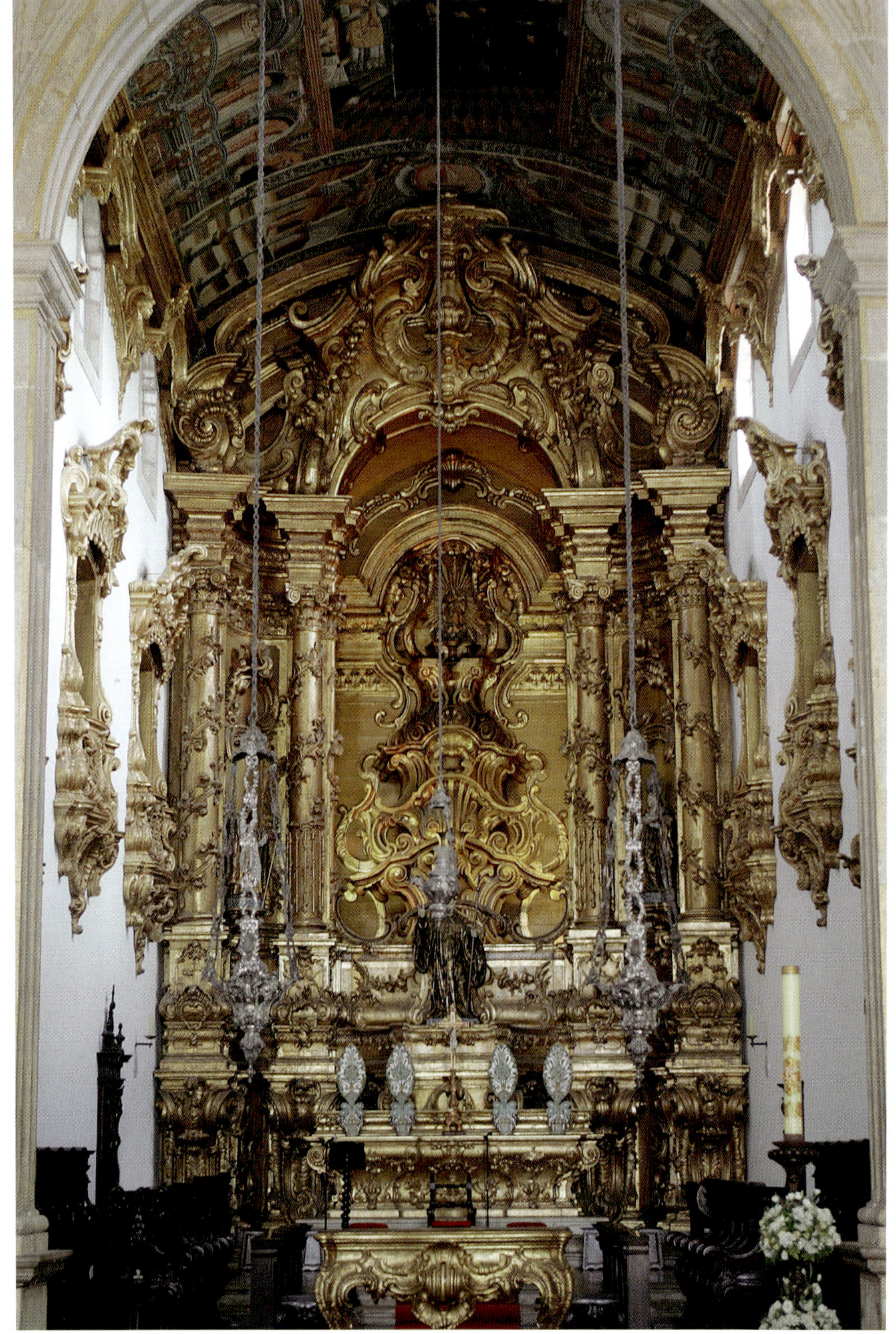

same effects: wooden 'drapes' dip from the ceiling over the wall and the ostentatious retablo pediment penetrates the frame of the ceiling, ending in an illusionistic bishop's mitre. The sculptures of saints Gregory, Benedict and Scholastica, by the Benedictine Frei José de Santo Antônio Vilaça, are small enough that they are consumed in the scrolls and vines of the retablo, as at the Transparente in Toledo (see 104). In the central niche of the retablo a triple plinth of Rococo scrolls serves as the base for a statue of the Virgin, the latter surrounded by a small Bernini-style sunburst (see 102). Although the style of the retablo and other wooden details was inspired by the interior of the Benedictine mother church in Tibães (Portugal), the carvings in the Brazilian church are much bolder and better integrated than its model.

Aside from architecture, sculpture was the most prolific and accomplished medium in Latin America, particularly in present-day Guatemala and Ecuador. The so-called School of Quito, a group of workshops in that northern Andean city active between 1660 and 1800, achieved one of the most delicate and moving sculptural traditions of the Baroque. Characterized by a humanity and gracefulness that rivals their Spanish prototypes (see 94), small-scale wood polychrome sculptures like this anonymous *Man of Sorrows* (second half of the eighteenth century) would have been placed in the private oratories of the wealthy to remind their owners of the fleetingness of life and the need to follow Christ's example (219). Its emphasis on the physical torture of Christ reflects themes found in popular Franciscan devotional manuals, and as with many Latin American Passion sculptures gruesomeness is exaggerated to provoke the viewer: here blood pours down Christ's body, the bones of his knees protrude from the skin, and even the hair and drapery are swept up in a fiery frenzy. Some scholars have suggested that Latin America's enthusiasm for gory images of the Passion reflect the Amerindians' projection of their own sense of oppression onto that of Christ. Quiteño sculptors used a highly developed system of labour distribution, each piece employing teams of artists specializing in heads, hands, bodies, painting, gilding, and the insertion of glass eyes and human hair that add immediacy to many of the pieces. The two best-known Quiteño sculptors were the *mestizo* Bernardo de Legarda (d. 1773) and the Native American Manuel Chili 'Caspicara' (active last half of the eighteenth century).

218.
Capela-Mor,
Benedictine
Monastery of
São Bento,
1783–6, with
José Elói
*Confirmation of
the Benedictine
Order*, 1785.
Oil on wood.
Olinda (Brazil)

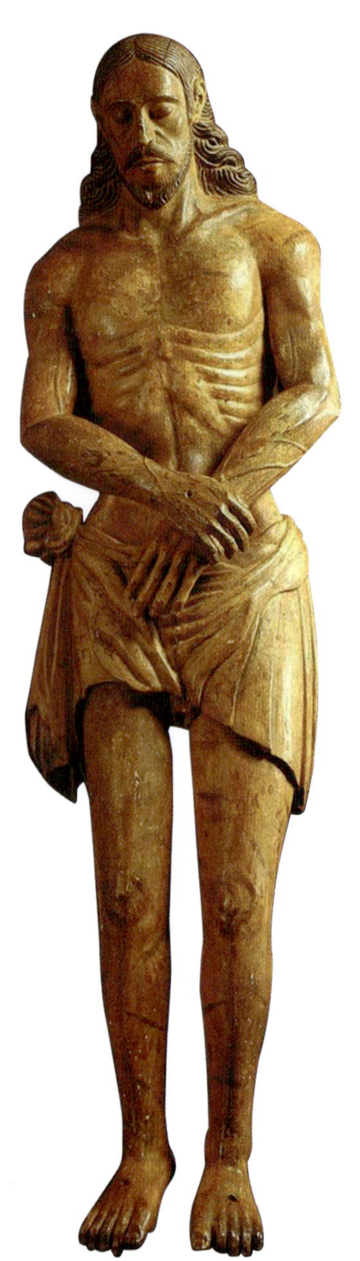

**220.
Guaraní
workshop**,
Dead Christ,
second half
17th century.
Polychrome
wood. San
Ignacio,
Museum,
Paraguay

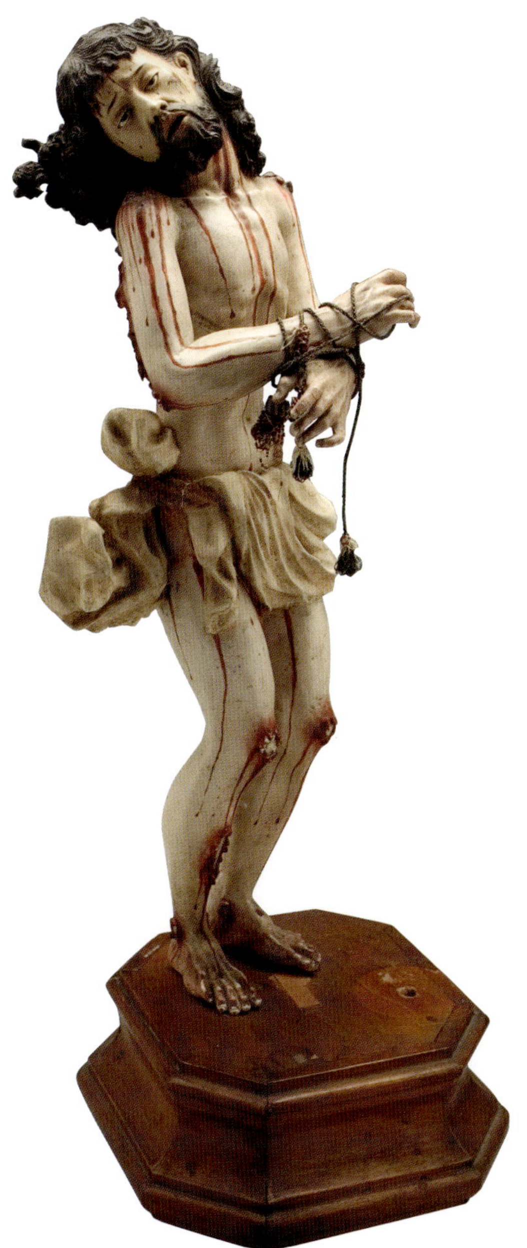

**219.
Quito workshop,** *Man of Sorrows*, Ecuador, second half 18th century. Painted and polychromed wood; 52 × 18 × 22 cm (20½ × 7 × 8½ in) Collection of Osvaldo Viteri, Quito (Ecuador)

Another Latin American sculptural tradition avoids references to physical pain, creating works of an otherworldly serenity that emphasize – like Orthodox icons – the holiness of the subject. The sculpture of the Guaraní Amerindians at the Jesuit missions in Paraguay (seventeenth–eighteenth centuries) was carved from hefty pieces of hardwood by elite carvers to whom the Guaraní attributed shamanic abilities derived from their indigenous faith. In fact, the sculptor was called a *santo apohava* – literally 'saint maker' – implying that the work of art directly shared the sanctity of the figure it represented. The late seventeenth-century *Dead Christ* (220) from the mission of San Ignacio Guazú betrays nothing of the torment of his Passion. Christ is rigid but calm, his musculature, bones, hair and beard reduced to geometrical patterns of strict symmetry when compared to the Quiteño Christ. The Guaraní Christ's detachment from the world of human suffering corresponds with the indigenous conception of Christ as a Great Shaman (Pai Guazú), a religious leader who leads people to the Guaraní paradise – a place that is reached without dying.

Other images that merge Christian and non-Christian readings do so more openly. The celebrated eighteenth-century painting of the *Virgin of the Rich Hill of Potosí*, painted by an Amerindian artist in what is now Bolivia (221), combines an Andean mountain deity known as Pachamama ('Mother Earth') with Christianity's chief mother deity, the Virgin Mary – her face and hands miraculously emerge from the mountainside. The mountain in this case is quite specific: the Rich Hill, or *Cerro Rico*, was the most important silver mine in the Americas and a place where Native Americans from all over the Andes were forced to work on a rotation basis in appalling conditions. Because of the horrors involved in their toils the Andeans sought the assistance of Pachamama as embodied in the Rich Hill, and missionaries reported clandestine sacrifices made to the mountain as early as 1559. The painting neatly divides into Andean and European spheres. The mountain contains figures of Andeans and their flocks of alpaca, as well as a depiction of an Andean shepherd named Gualpa telling the Inca Huayna Capac about his discovery of silver on the mountain. The artist took a risk depicting the Inca in his full imperial regalia, as the Spanish considered such images to be seditious. The mountain is also flanked by the sun and moon, the chief

deities of the Inca state (see 191). The European zone is at the base of the
mountain, where Emperor Charles V, Pope Paul III, a cardinal, a bishop and
a member of the Royal Order of Alcantará kneel on either side of a globe,
paying homage to the Virgin. Or are they paying homage to Pachamama?
Such an interpretation – it would have been lost on the Spaniards – would
have been very seditious indeed.

Chapter Six was devoted in part to the ephemeral arts of the Baroque and
Rococo, particularly to processions and the temporary structures that were
built to serve them. Such activities were at the very centre of colonial life in
Spanish and Portuguese America, from the *entradas* (ceremonial entries of
new Spanish viceroys) to the costumed processions of the so-called 'Kings
of Congo' by the black confraternities of Minas Gerais in Brazil. There
is less evidence than in Europe about what these events looked like – we
mostly have to rely on descriptions – however a handful of paintings like the
Entrada of Viceroy Morcillo into Potosí by the *mestizo* painter Melchor Pérez
Holguín (c.1660–after 1724) show that they were very similar (222). *Entradas*,
performed upon the inauguration of each viceroy, were complex ceremonies
that brought together European, Native American and even African
symbolism to emphasize the unity of the people, and they involved days of
processions, musical and theatrical performances, religious services, bullfights
and sermons. Holguín's canvas shows the entry into Potosí of Fray Diego
Morcillo Rubio de Auñón, a Trinitarian friar, who at the age of seventy-four
(in 1716) became not only Archbishop of Charcas (modern-day Sucre) but
the interim Viceroy of Peru, which meant a gruelling march over 1,000
kilometres (620 miles) from his mountain home in Potosí to coastal Lima.
The painting was commissioned by the municipality of Potosí to record his
triumphal march through the city, a celebration that cost them the massive
sum of 150,000 *pesos*. The parade route was decorated with a combination of
indigenous, classical and Euro-Christian symbolism that is typical of Spanish
American *entradas*. The walls and windows of the buildings lining the route
were hung with Andean textiles and paintings of Greek mythological subjects
like the *Colossus of Rhodes and the Fall of Icarus*. A wood and canvas triumphal
arch at the far right was decorated with false marble solomonic columns,
finials, plaster statues, gold-framed paintings and inscription panels – the

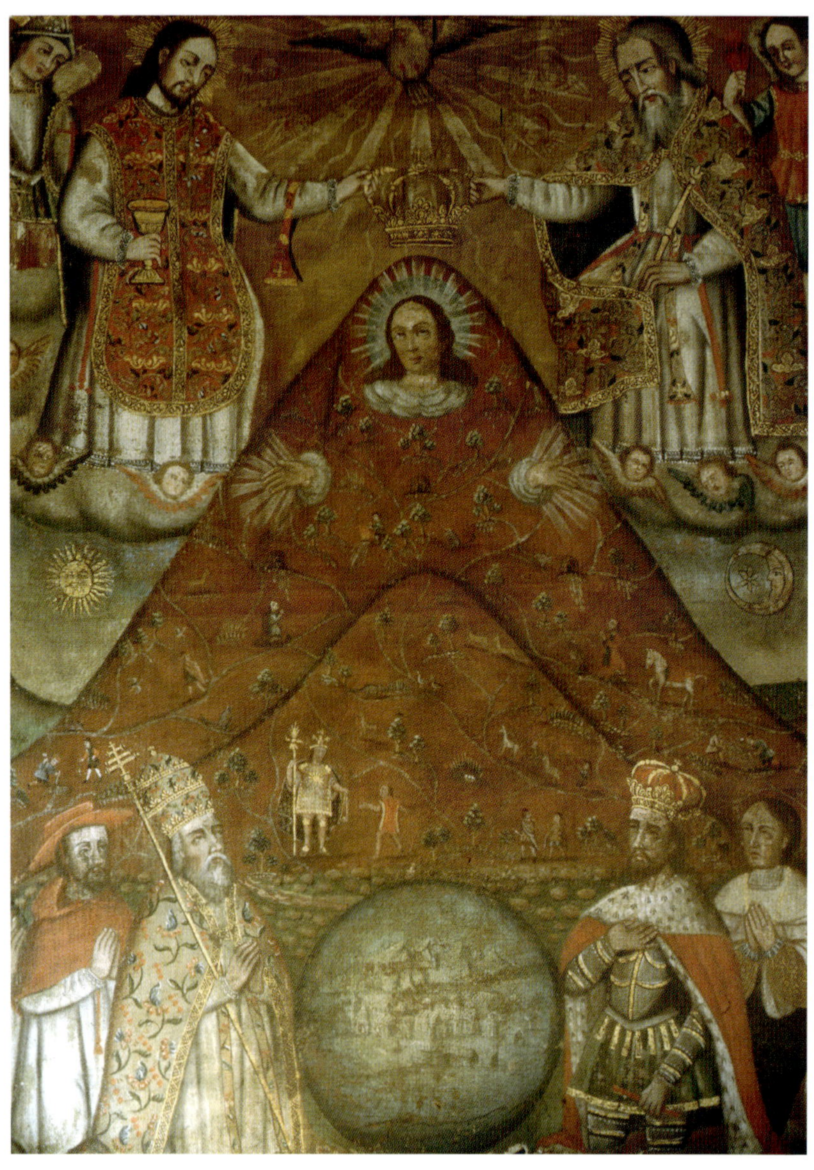

221.
*Virgin of the
Rich Hill of
Potosí*, Bolivia,
18th century.
Oil on canvas;
134.6 × 104 cm
(53 × 41 in).
Casa Nacional
de Moneda,
Potosí

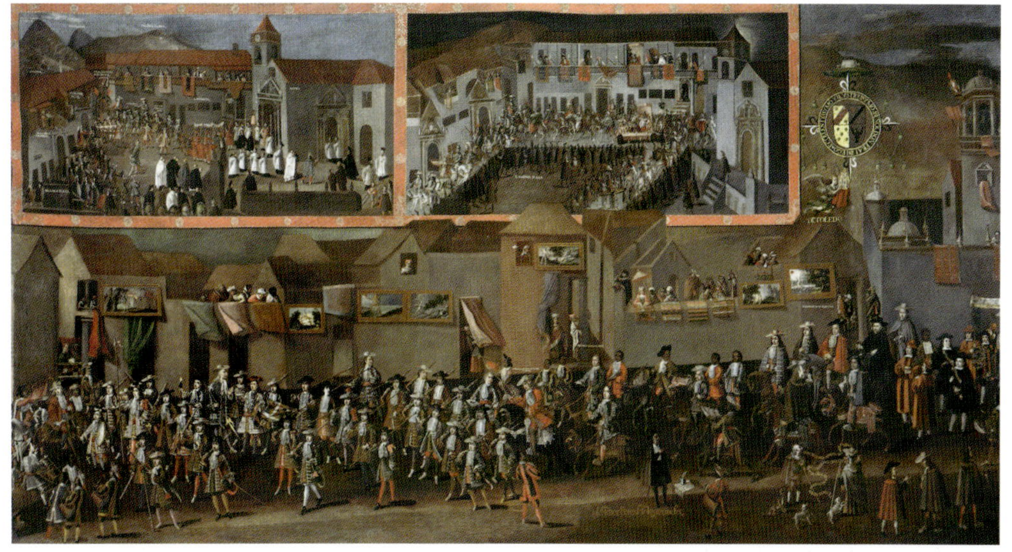

222.
**Melchor
Pérez
Holguín,**
*Entrada of
Viceroy Morcillo
into Potosí,
Bolivia*, 1716.
Oil on canvas;
2.3 × 6 m
(7 ft 6 in × 19 ft
8¼ in). Museo
de América,
Madrid

programme for the arch's iconography as well as the inscriptions would likely have been prepared by a local cleric. The Viceroy rides under a silk palanquin accompanied by battalions, local nobles (including Amerindian elites) and members of the church hierarchy. In the upper left-hand corner a pair of miniature scenes shows the Viceroy's arrival at the cathedral and a nocturnal play performed in his honour in the Plaza Mayor. Thus, although smaller and performed in a remote oxygen-deprived city at an altitude of 4,090 metres (13,419 feet) – by comparison Mont Blanc is 4,810 metres (15,781 feet) high – Viceroy Morcillo's procession echoes the Medici, Habsburg and Bourbon processions of Baroque Europe.

The earliest Baroque art and architecture in Asia appeared in the Portuguese colonies and at the Catholic missions outside Portuguese territory. The Dominicans were the first to arrive in India (Goa, 1510), followed closely by the Franciscans in 1517. But no one equalled the Jesuits (1542) in the volume of their missionary activities and arts patronage in India. The Jesuits built churches and colleges – frequently on a massive scale – throughout Goa and surrounding districts, as well as in the colonies of Bassein, Daman and Diu, home of the spectacular church of São Paulo (223). Although we no longer know their names, legions of Indian sculptors and painters contributed to these churches, many of them unconverted Hindus and Muslims from the villages outside the colonies. These people brought their centuries-old iconographic traditions to bear on the art they produced for the new religion, producing artistic hybridizations similar to those of the southern Andes (see 216). The architectural ornamentation, wooden sculpture, pulpits and choir stalls that survive reveal a blending of European iconography with indigenous motifs and figural styles, and they are overwhelmed with ornamentation based on native flora and fauna. The richly decorated façade of São Paulo combines Renaissance columns and pilasters, elaborate window frames formed of scrolls and caryatids, and an aedicule framed by fan-shaped scrolls. But the façade also displays Hindu rosettes and garlands, as well as Islamic geometrical arabesques in the frieze and the frames of the heraldic panels.

Another example of Indian hybridization is the eighteenth-century pulpit in the Church of Bom Jesus, the Jesuits' headquarters in Asia (224). Lavishly

223.
São Paulo,
1601. Diu
(India)

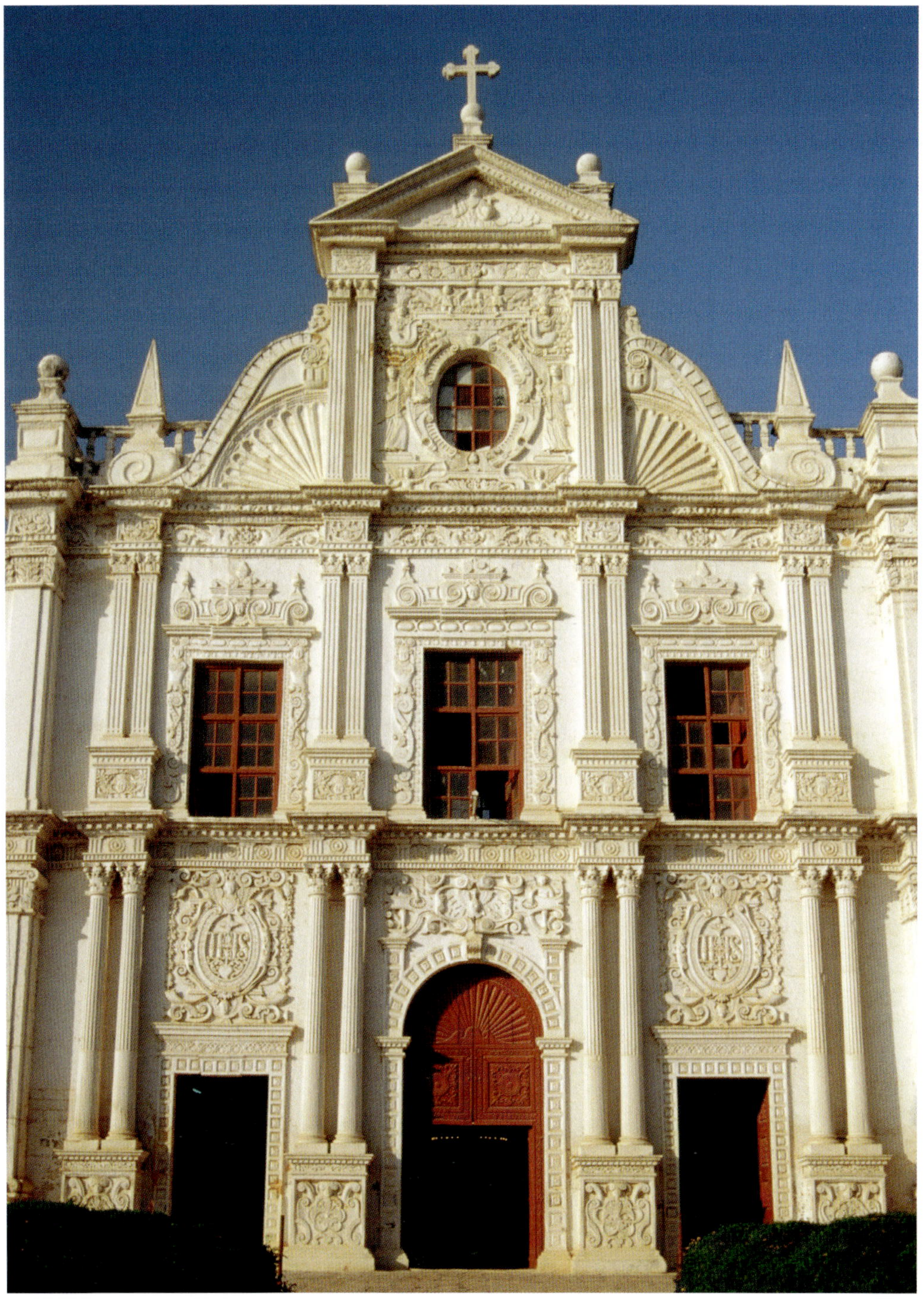

carved with Indian flora and fauna and a ring of voluptuous semi-nude caryatids, the carving obeys Hindu conventions as much as European ones: figures are stocky, rigid and generally depicted frontally; their expressions are impassive; and they wear elements of Hindu costume such as bead necklaces. As early as 1545, reports were praising the abilities of Hindu carvers in decorating the churches of the Indian colonies, and such carvers became so common that colonial authorities repeatedly tried to ban non-

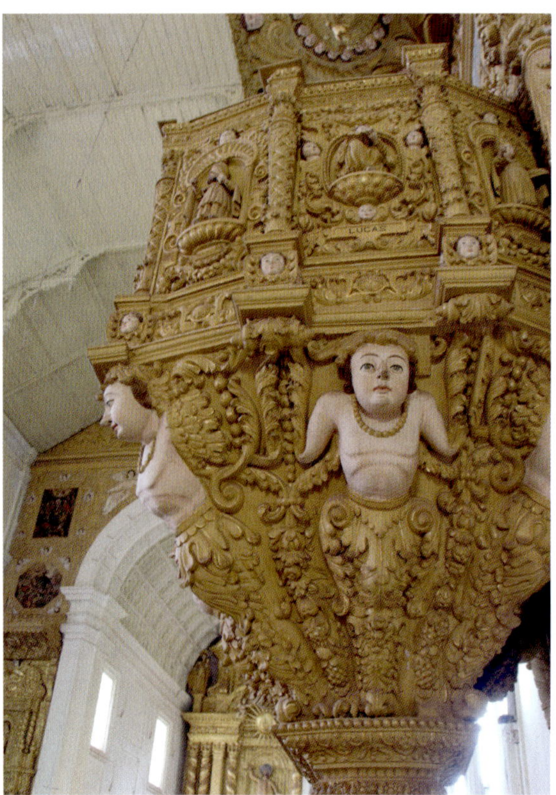

224.
Pulpit, 18th century. Church of Bom Jesus, Goa (India)

Christian sculptors for fear that they were corrupting Christian iconography, as in this 1588 decree: 'Seeing the great skill with which the gentile painters and other infidel artisans make images and figures of our Holy Christian Religion despite the hatred they have for it, [we] order that no Christian shall commission an infidel painter to paint images or any other thing pertaining to the Divine Cult.' Sometimes artists were asked to convert as part of their contract – as with the Hindu sculptor who carved the first pulpit in the Jesuit

collegiate church in Cochin in 1591 – however there is little evidence that any of them followed through. Influences also ran in the other direction over the decidedly porous colonial frontier: the sculptors who made works like the Bom Jesus pulpit incorporated Baroque architectural features into the Hindu temples in their own villages.

The Portuguese colonies in East Africa, administered from Goa, also mostly relied on Indian carvers to adorn their churches – the churches themselves

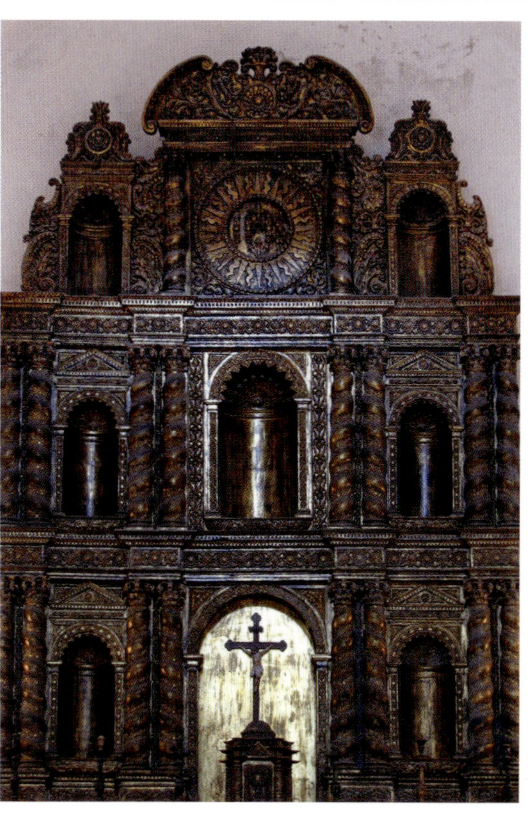

225.
Retablo,
late 17th or
early 18th
century. São
Paulo, Ilha de
Mozambique
(Mozambique)

were almost brutally plain as they were frequently constructed by military architects. But there is also evidence that local Swahili sculptors contributed to these projects, notably in the case of the retablo at the Jesuit church of São Paulo on the Island of Mozambique (225). The church was built between 1603 and 1634, and its three-storey wooden high altar has to have been in place at least by the early eighteenth century. The retablo's architectural language is Baroque, with Solomonic columns, an aedicule at the top, and acanthus leaves in the upper parts of seven of its niches. But the scrolling blossom motif that adorns the plinth, the main and upper frieze and the pediment relates to Swahili door carving, an industry that thrived in coastal towns such as Lamu, Jumba la Mtwana, and Mombasa (Kenya), Zanzibar and Kilwa (Tanzania), and other settlements in present-day Mozambique. Swahili culture combines African and Arab elements, and the defining features of Swahili doors – the arabesque-like floral scrolls and bosses – derive from Islamic prototypes introduced to the region by Omani traders. These works of art were greatly prized – during the Portuguese sack of Faza in 1587 villagers took the doors with them for safekeeping – and they also advertised the status of the owner. By placing such ornamentation on a retablo, Swahili carvers were investing it with the same prestige and value as their most treasured domestic possessions.

The most famous Hybrid Baroque building in Asia is the spectacular façade of the Madre de Deus Church, better known as the Church of São Paulo, in the Portuguese colony of Macao off the coast of China (226). The façade of the Jesuit church – the rest was destroyed in a typhoon in the nineteenth century – was designed by the Italian Jesuits Carlo Spinola and Giovanni Niccolò, and at first it seems to be a standard early Roman Baroque church with free-standing columns arranged to emphasize the central section, statues in niches, finials and a pediment. But the sculptural decoration of the façade, carved by Chinese and probably also Japanese sculptors, tells a different story. Chinese temple lions support the obelisks at the very top of the façade, peering down as if from a Buddhist temple. The drapery even of the figures of Christ and the Virgin Mary have the bevelled line and windswept quality of Buddhist sculpture, and motifs such as Chinese cloud scrolls and carp are adopted from traditional Chinese painting, porcelains and other arts. The angels closely resemble a flying Buddhist deity known as an *apsaras*. The façade's Chinese identity is further emphasized by explanatory texts in Chinese characters – the first in a Christian building.

Missionaries in China faced greater cultural challenges than in Japan or South Asia, particularly in the arts. The Chinese emperor and literati (intellectual elites) only tolerated missionary activity if it adapted to Chinese

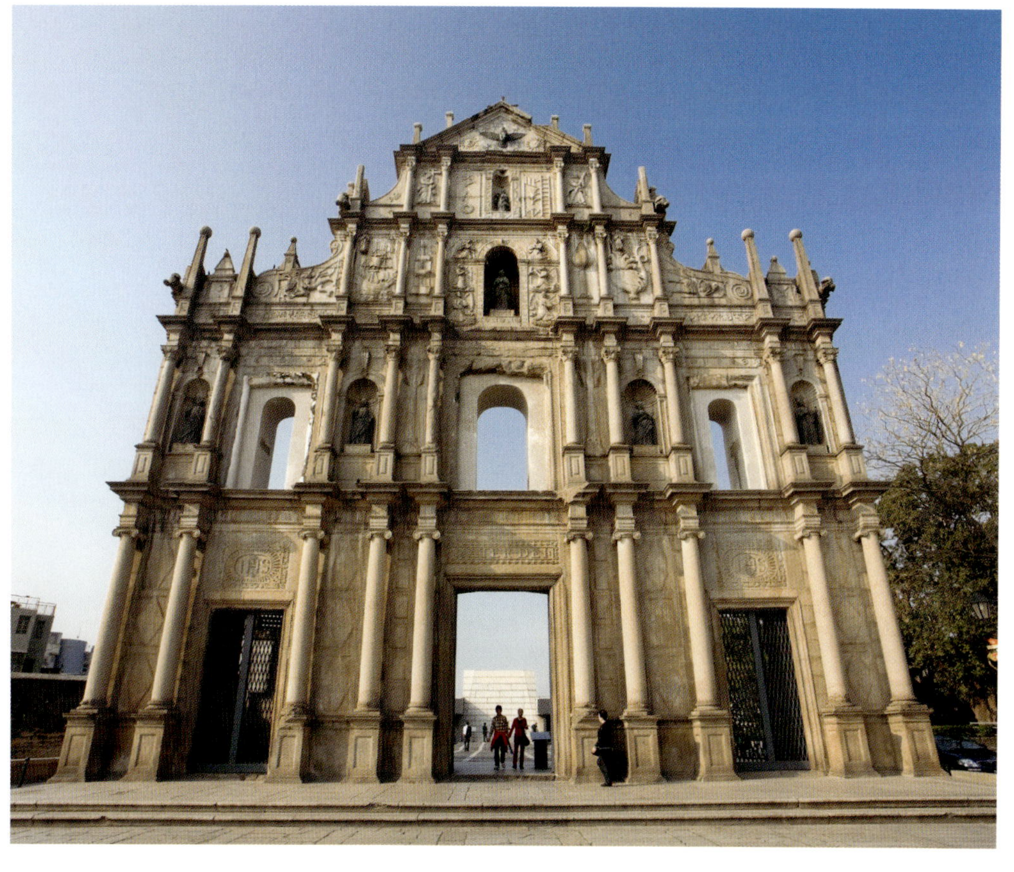

226.
São Paulo,
begun 1601.
Macao (China)

tradition, an imperative that held true for the arts of the mission, which had to conform to Chinese taste – at least officially. But meanwhile, in hopes of gaining a market advantage, non-Christian Chinese artists showed no hesitation in copying Christian imagery in a Western manner, like the Hindu sculptors of Goa. In December 1561, before the first Catholic mission was founded in China and only four years after the foundation of Macao, a Portuguese nobleman described a Chinese workshop that mass-produced Flemish-style Christian devotional paintings, including a processional banner as well as ivory carvings – it is one of the first accounts of the Chinese skill at imitating Western products in the name of trade. He wrote with self-righteous disdain that Chinese craftsmen 'never lose an opportunity for profit, which is virtually their only aim', yet this attitude did not prevent Iberians from purchasing thousands of Chinese-made Christian art objects over the next two centuries. Chinese craftsmen in Fujian, Macao and Manila knew their market, demonstrating a highly sophisticated knowledge of the specific iconographic needs of these strange foreigners. This moving statue of *Christ at the Column*, now in the Sacred Art Museum at the Church of São Domingos in Macao (227), demonstrates a profound understanding of Iberian and Latin American wooden sculpture and shares their sense of humanity, realism and representation of Christ's pain (see 94, 218). In fact, only its hint of Asian physiognomy indicates that it was made by Chinese craftsmen.

One of the most striking Baroque churches anywhere is the massive, earthquake-proof Augustinian church at Paoay in north Luzon, Philippines (228), commissioned by Friar Antonio Estavillo and completed sometime in the first decade of the eighteenth century. Its massiveness and wide, squat profile dominate the south valley of the River Wawa. The façade is very plain: it is divided into seven sections by flat pilasters and features only a handful of empty niches and a pair of scrolls in the corners of the pediment. What makes this church so extraordinary is the treatment of the roof line and the muscular, limb-like buttresses that line the sides like legs on a centipede. The façade roof is crowned with giant baluster finials and low wave-like crenellations while the buttresses are variations on the Baroque volute. They extend so far from the wall that the façade looks twice as wide as it really is. The seemingly endless repetition of this combination of sinuous contour and

227.
Macao workshop, *Christ at the Column,* 17th or 18th century. Museum of Sacred Art, Macau

baluster finial gives the church an uncanny similarity to the ninth-century Buddhist temple in Borobudur, central Java, and has prompted some scholars to suggest that workers from present-day Indonesia helped construct the church. While such an explanation seems unlikely, there is no doubt that this monument makes highly original use of the Baroque vocabulary, and its probably Chinese carvers added Chinese-style flowers and clouds around the side doorways. The buttresses' size

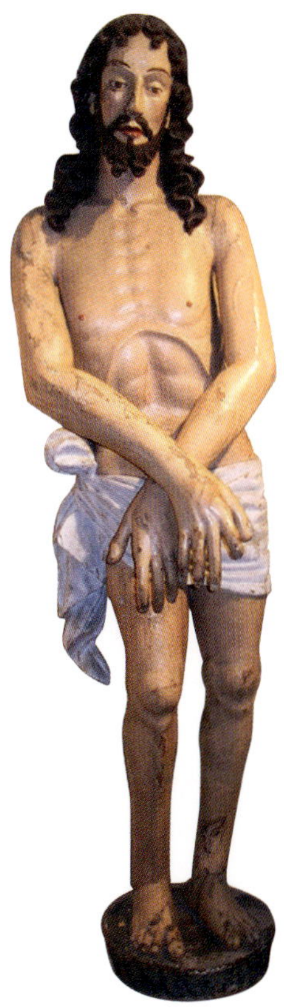

and height had more to do with protection against earthquakes and typhoons than with aesthetics, and they also helped people extinguish fires on the church's traditional thatched roof.

With the exception of Russia, the architecture and works of art discussed so far in this chapter were executed in a colonial setting – in parts of Asia, Africa and the Americas that were controlled by western European powers – and Baroque and

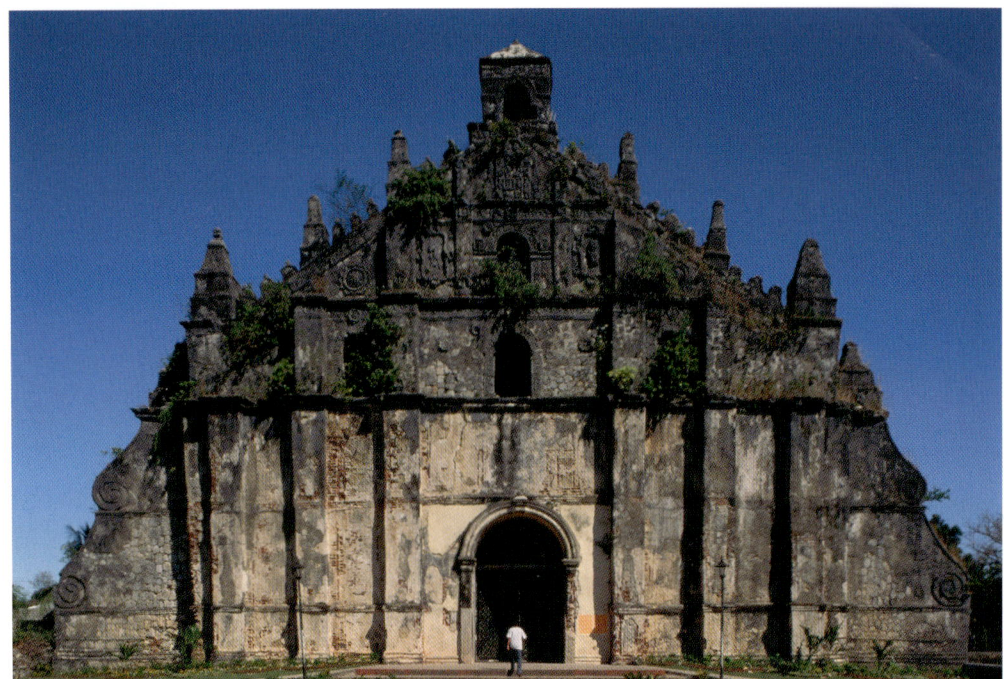

Rococo forms were, to varying degrees, imposed upon the people there. But other non-European civilizations adopted Baroque and Rococo forms by choice. Some, similarly to Russia, did so out of a desire to learn the latest technologies and styles from the West, while others sought out these imported forms for their aesthetic properties: their decorative quality and, in painting, their ability to suggest emotion and the third dimension. The most fascinating of these artistic encounters took place at the imperial courts of Ethiopia, Persia and Mughal India, in the castle compounds of the warlords of Japan, and – most substantially – Ottoman Turkey and Qing China. In the latter two, patrons and artists carefully selected Baroque and Rococo elements that suited their needs, grafting them onto essentially non-European forms. The decision to adopt European motifs should not be interpreted – as it too often has been – as a capitulation to Western culture. Turkey and China had nothing to fear from the West and their interest in foreign styles was no less a capitulation than Rococo Europe's fascination for the styles of China and Japan (see 168, 174) or Mughal India (see 169). The most flourishing hybridization took place where local traditions were still strong enough to keep the Western elements in check and when a confident and creative spirit of experimentation could prevail.

Although Ottoman Turkey was the bane of Mediterranean and eastern Europe's existence throughout most of the period of this book – in fact, images of Turkish captives and depictions of European victories like the Battle of Lepanto were perennially popular subjects for Baroque and Rococo artists – relations between the two regions improved by the early eighteenth century and the Ottomans began to exchange embassies with the French and other western European powers. Hoping to study European technological and military advances, Sultan Ahmed III (r. 1703–30) sent an embassy to Paris and Versailles in 1721. An Ottoman experimentation with Baroque and Rococo styles followed – it is called 'Turkish Baroque' or 'Turkish Rococo' – which was one of the most original and imaginative cultural fusions of the era. Ambassador Mehmed Çelebi's descriptions of the palaces, pleasure-gardens and furnishings of Louis XV's court set off a fad for Occidentalism that mirrored France's own vogue for Asian exotica. Among its leading proponents were Vizier (Prime Minister) Damat İbrahim Paşa (d. 1730), whose taste for European clocks, furniture and painting was widely imitated, and the Chief Black Eunuch Ağa Bektaş. The new trend was especially pronounced in architecture and architectural ornament, since this period was characterized by extensive building projects. Fountains, country villas, gardens, baths, kiosks and even mosques began to exhibit broken cornices, bundled pilasters, Corinthian capitals, extravagant volutes, shell-motifs, Rococo cartouches, and even some of the spatial arrangements of Baroque architecture.

This combination of styles was accelerated by a collection of western European printed books and engravings that may have been brought there by Mehmed Çelebi upon his return from Paris in 1721. They include treatises on waterworks by Carlo Fontana, works on architecture by Andrea Palladio and the Rococo master designer François Blondel, instructions on painting pastoral scenes by Jean-Antoine Watteau, a guide to designing gardens by Johann David Flücken, as well as several illustrated books about Versailles and other French palaces, including the engravings of fireworks displays discussed in the last chapter (see 206, 207). European artists such as Jean-Claude Flachat (in Istanbul from 1740) were also invited to court to advise on decorative schemes. Part of the reason why Turkish Baroque architecture avoids becoming a slavish homage to European style is that although Ottoman architects used Western books and engravings as a source of individual motifs for their buildings, they never reproduced a complete façade, plan or elevation from them, treating them instead as copybooks. The very idea of a full architectural elevation was foreign to Islamic tradition, although ground plans, often drawn on a grid-pattern, were widely used.

Turkish Baroque architecture can be divided into two phases. The first – a subtle blend of classical Ottoman and Rococo ornament – lasted from 1721 to the 1730 assassination of İbrahim Paşa and abdication of Ahmed III, and is characterized by a new interest in fountain and garden architecture. In the second stage, beginning around 1740, classical Ottoman elements give way to bolder experiments with Western forms in three dimensions. Not only do the new decorative motifs become heavier and more plastic – they now include Baroque-style pediments and entablatures – but the plans begin to bend and curve like their Baroque prototypes. Ahmed III revitalized Istanbul's aqueducts and drinking water and opened up public squares, possibly inspired by the *places* of Paris. He built two grand water pavilions, the most influential of which was at the gate of the Topkapi Palace (229). For the first time, an Ottoman *çesme-şebil* (a traditional drinking fountain) occupied the middle of a public square like a Baroque fountain – except here, following Ottoman practice, the water was inside the pavilion – and Rococo panels and relief ornament cover the undersides of the eaves. Otherwise the ground plan and elevation are entirely conventional, adorned with intricate arabesques and coloured tiles. Later fountains became lighter and suppler, constructed on an almost transparent Rococo structural skeleton. The Abdülhamid I fountain was built by Ahmed III's son in 1777 (230), next to the gate of the Zeynep Sultan Mosque (1763). Unlike the Ahmed III fountain it is entirely formed of European architectural members and ornament. The division of the walls into panels, and the framework and decoration of those panels, is inspired by Blondel's Rococo interiors – in fact, the fountain looks something like a French salon turned inside-out. The walls of the *sebil* press outwards like the architecture of Guarini (see 112), and curvilinear forms dominate the contours of the windows, cartouche panels, and the blind arches above the spigot. Yet the basic shape of the building is still classically Ottoman.

 Baroque and Rococo

229.
Ahmed III Fountain at the Topkapi Gate, 1728. Istanbul (Turkey)

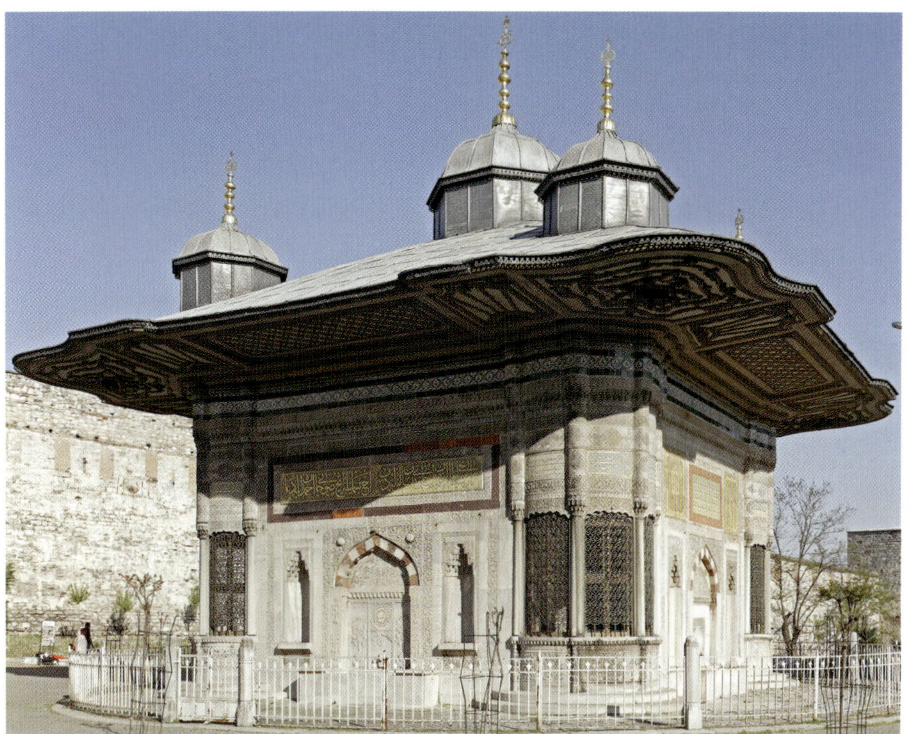

Baroque mosques would seem to be a contradiction in terms, since we would expect an Islamic religious structure to be immune to Western influence. Yet the Nuruosmaniye Mosque ('Osman's Light'), the imperial mosque begun by Sultan Mahmud I near the Grand Bazaar in Istanbul, incorporates not only the stylistic but also spatial ideas of the European Baroque and Rococo (231). Its courtyard replaces the traditional rectilinear plan with a curving one, and the semicircular apse and transepts evoke those of a Baroque church. The exterior of the mosque creatively adapts European features such as heavy, undulating cornices, curvilinear buttresses around the drum of the dome, and pilasters on the walls. The way the giant cornice dips to join the tympanum to the buttresses recalls the work of Borromini (see 3) – it is also coincidentally similar to the solution reached at the Compañía in Cuzco (see 215) – and the dome is supported by scrolling buttresses that may have been modelled after those of Hardouis-Mansart's dome of the Invalides in Paris (see 145), of which the court library included two monographs. The prominent cornice at the top of the drum with its pilasters and spreading capitals is also especially inspired.

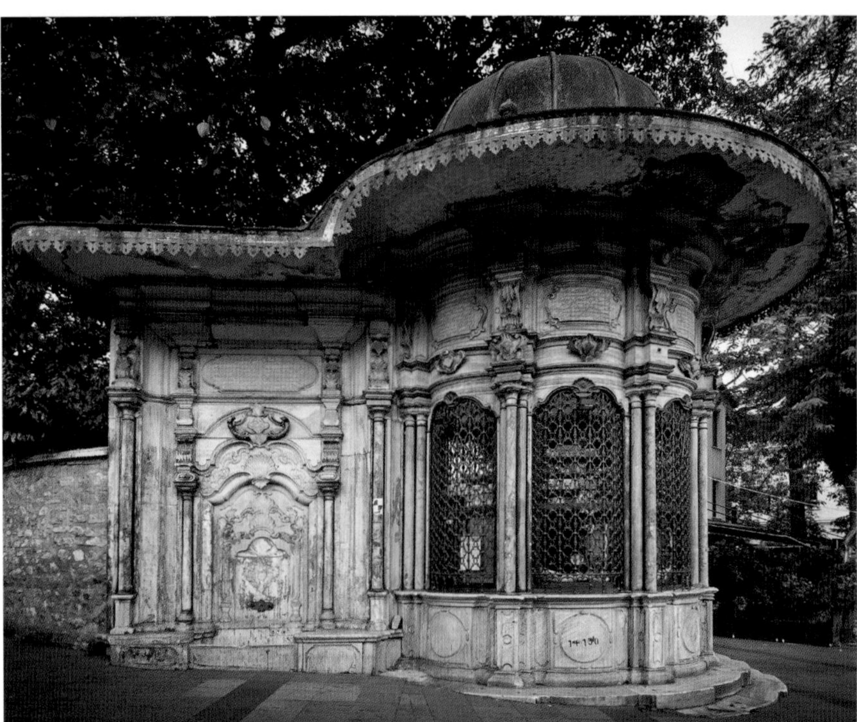

**230.
Abdülhamid
I Fountain**,
1777. Istanbul

**231.
Nuruos-
maniye
Mosque**,
1748–56.
Istanbul

Imperial China also toyed with Baroque and Rococo styles, partly out of a
desire to learn about techniques such as perspective but also because of a taste
for exotica at the Qing court that might be described as a reverse chinoiserie.
The Chinese court began to show a mild interest in Italian Renaissance art at
the end of the Ming Dynasty (1368–1644) thanks to the Western engravings
and paintings the Jesuit missionaries provided in bulk since 1580. However, it
was only in the succeeding Qing Dynasty, particularly under the patronage of
Emperor Qianlong (r. 1736–95), that the Chinese court embraced European
art – by now the Baroque and Rococo – as the taste for Western exotica
reached its apex. Jesuits were also involved at this stage, but largely against
their will as the emperor enlisted any Catholic missionaries with talents in
the arts to work at court in a kind of Chinese *servitù particolare*, executing
anything from portraits, enamelled metalwork, ceramic ornament, clocks
and architecture. The most famous were Giuseppi Castiglione (1688–1768),
Denis Attiret (1702–1768) and Michel Benoist (1715–1774). Since most of
their work was panegyric imagery extolling the power of the throne, it had
to be executed within traditional Chinese parameters – on silk scrolls and

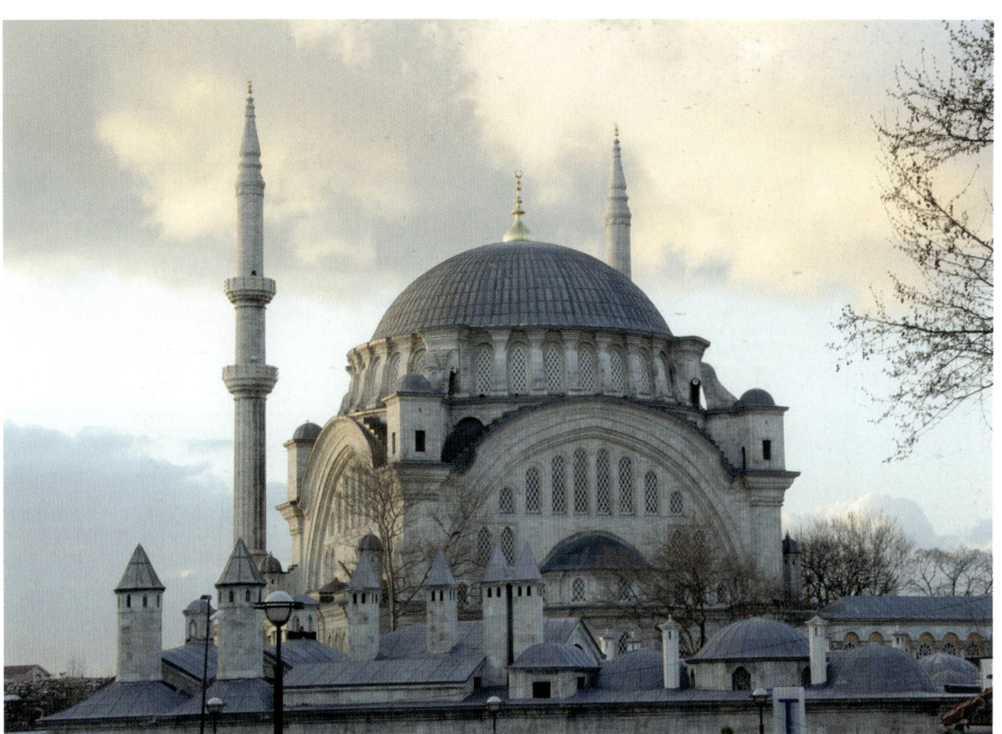

using a linear style with an emphasis on brushwork – and it was restricted to Chinese subjects. One French priest remarked bluntly about a colleague in 1769: 'it is necessary that he abandon his taste and his ideas in many aspects, so that he can accommodate to those of the country'. But privately, inspired by Louis XV, the emperor was enthusiastic about more openly Baroque and Rococo work in his palace and pleasure gardens.

Typical is *Xiang Fei in Military Costume*, a portrait of Qianlong's favourite concubine, part of a series of paintings of the famed courtier in Rococo costume and settings inspired by Watteau and Boucher (232). They have traditionally been attributed to Castiglione but are just as likely the work of one of his many Chinese pupils. Although painted on paper in the Chinese manner they are executed in oil – the medium was alien to China, where ink and watercolours were used – and feature brighter tones and deeper shading than the emperor's public commissions. Xiang Fei is dressed as the Roman war goddess Bellona, with her sparkling breastplate and plumed helmet, and the painting glows with colour: the bright blue sky and brilliant red sleeves, feathers and lips. The artist demonstrates a keen understanding of Western shading and other illusionistic techniques through the light effects on the armour and the subtle modelling on the face and hands, and the fire and churning clouds in the background enhance the work's Baroque sense of movement. In some paintings in this series Xiang Fei is dressed as a shepherdess, echoing a favourite pastime of the French queen Marie-Antoinette, who liked to wear the clothes of peasants in her imitation village called the Petit Hameau (1780) at Versailles.

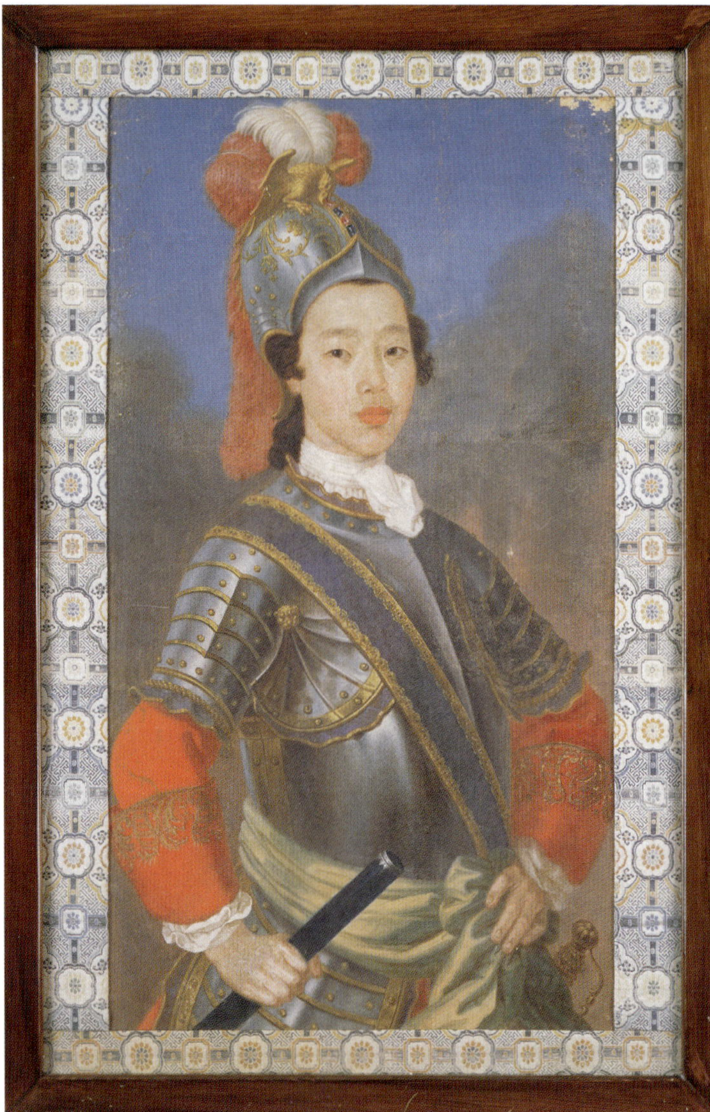

232.
Giuseppe Castiglione or follower, *Xiang Fei in Military Costume*, second half 18th century. Oil. National Palace Museum, Taipei

Qianlong's most ambitious Rococo project was the Garden of Perfect Clarity
at the imperial summer residence of Yuanmingyuan outside Beijing, a series
of garden pavilions, music halls, mazes, fountains, reflecting pools and
places for viewing perspective paintings that were conceived by the emperor,
designed by Castiglione and Benoist, and built by legions of Chinese
masons, bricklayers, gardeners and plumbers (233, 234). Like their Ottoman
contemporaries, Castiglione and Benoist had a library of European treatises
at hand, including three versions of Vitruvius' *De architectura*, Renaissance
architectural manuals by Giacomo da Vignola, Vincenzo Scamozzi, Andrea
Palladio, Giovanni Rusconi and Jacques Androuet du Cerceau (1520–1585),
and Baroque and Rococo design books by Andrea Pozzo – his *Perspectiva
Pictorum et Architectorum* was translated in 1729 into Chinese – and André
Félibien, as well as works on fountain architecture by Carlo Fontana and
Giovanni Battista Barattieri. At the Garden of Perfect Clarity the emperor
displayed his European paintings and Rococo clocks and *objets d'art* and
relaxed with his family, concubines and closest confidants in a Petrarchan
otium. Although destroyed by British and French troops in 1860, parts of
the white-marble masonry survive, with their floral garlands, shell forms,
scrolls and other *rocaille* details. Most of what we know about the gardens
comes from a series of commemorative engravings Qianlong commissioned
from Yi Lantai between 1783 and 1786, including this view of the *West
Façade of the Hall of Calm Seas*. Although the scrolling fountains, sweeping
staircases, projecting wings and Rococo window frames recall the Zwinger in
Dresden (see 137), the pavilion is an understated mixture of East and West,
with a traditional Chinese hipped roof, tiles, timber gates, some Chinese
decorative ornament and bronze zodiacal statues in place of Graeco-Roman
gods. The emperor also prohibited nude statues in his gardens as the nude
was not yet an accepted subject in Chinese art. Like Baroque and Rococo
gardens throughout Europe, the Garden of Perfect Clarity uses impressive
waterworks and calm reflecting ponds – one was a giant lake called the
'Sea of Auspiciousness' – to symbolize the emperor's supremacy over the
landscape, yet their treatment of Rococo style as a plaything unsuitable for
public settings underscores their belief in the superiority of the Chinese
styles that eventually put an end to this brief flourishing of Baroque and
Rococo art at the imperial court.

It is often remarked that Baroque and Rococo are 'forgiving' styles, and that their disdain for rules and boundaries made them unusually receptive to adaptation, artistic fancy and regional variety worldwide. To a certain degree this statement is true: their taste for novelty and creativity encouraged inclusiveness and openness, and their engagement with the human condition in its complexity and contradiction made Baroque and Rococo approachable in a way that many styles are not. This comprehensiveness extends to their geographic reach as emphasized in this chapter. Not merely the product of a handful of metropolitan centres, Baroque and Rococo originated as much in the valleys of Goa and Peru or the farmlands of Swabia and Moravia as in the streets and salons of Rome and Paris. Rather than provincial echoes of a mother style, Baroque and Rococo art and architecture outside the European cultural capitals were distinctive dialects of a global language, at once local and international, and they developed and flourished as much on the popular level as on that of official institutions. Baroque and Rococo were as much an art of the masses as of the elite, and could manifest both European and non-European values. Yet we must not paper over the oppressiveness of European authorities in imposing their unyielding vision of power and authority on the very people who made and consumed Baroque and Rococo art and architecture, most violently in places like Latin America, but also in Europe under the tyrannical regimes of Louis XIV and the more dogmatic of the Baroque popes.

233.
Giuseppe Castiglione and Michel Benoist, West Façade of the Hall of Calm Seas in the Garden of Perfect Clarity at the Imperial summer residence of Yuanmingyuan (China), completed 1783. Engraving, c.1785. Bibliothèque Nationale, Paris

234.
Ruins of European pavilions in the Garden of Perfect Clarity at the Imperial summer residence of Yuanmingyuan, completed 1783 (China)

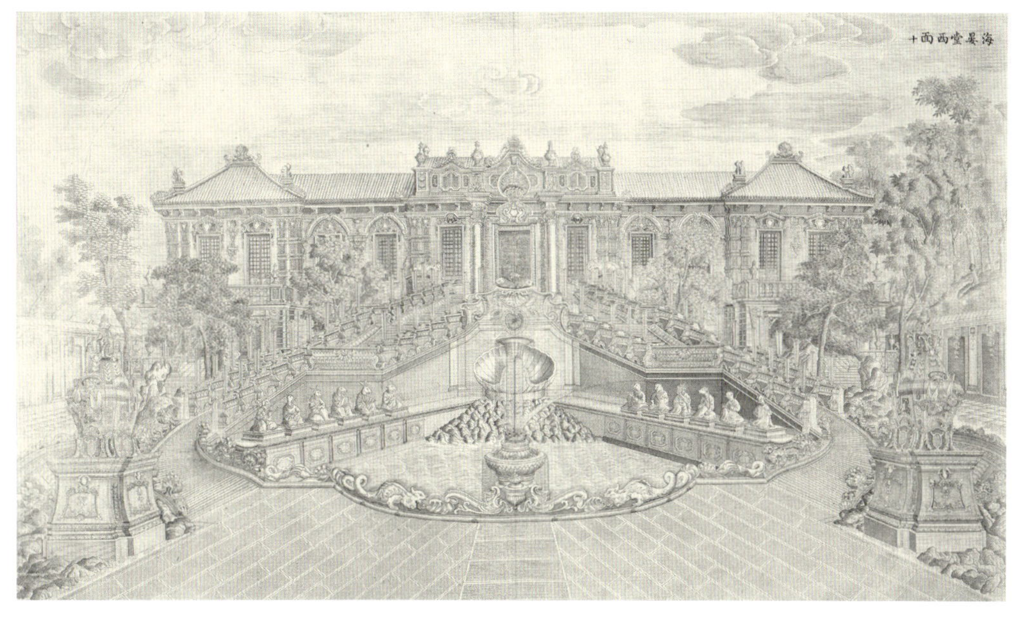

海晏堂西面十

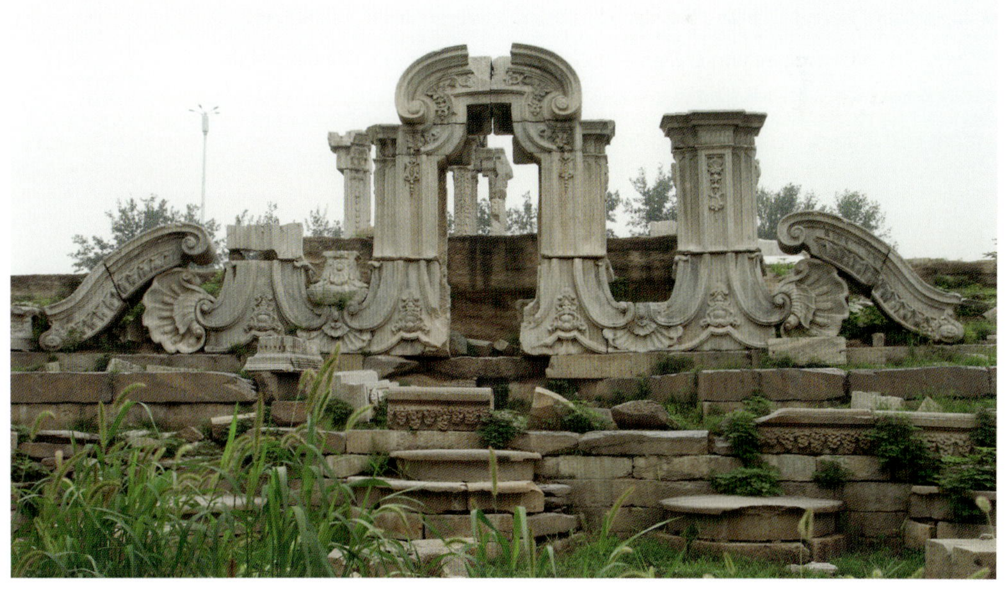

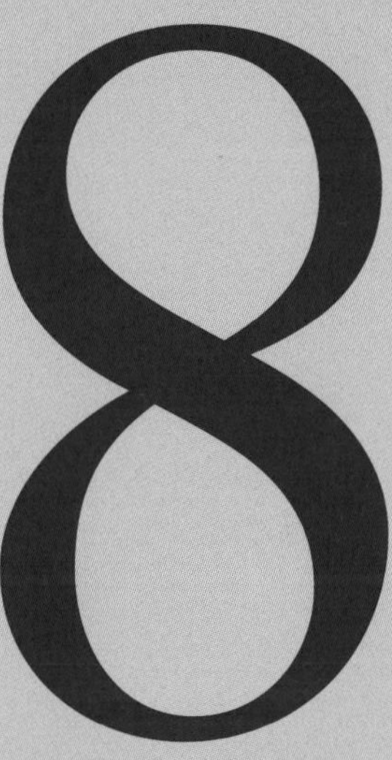

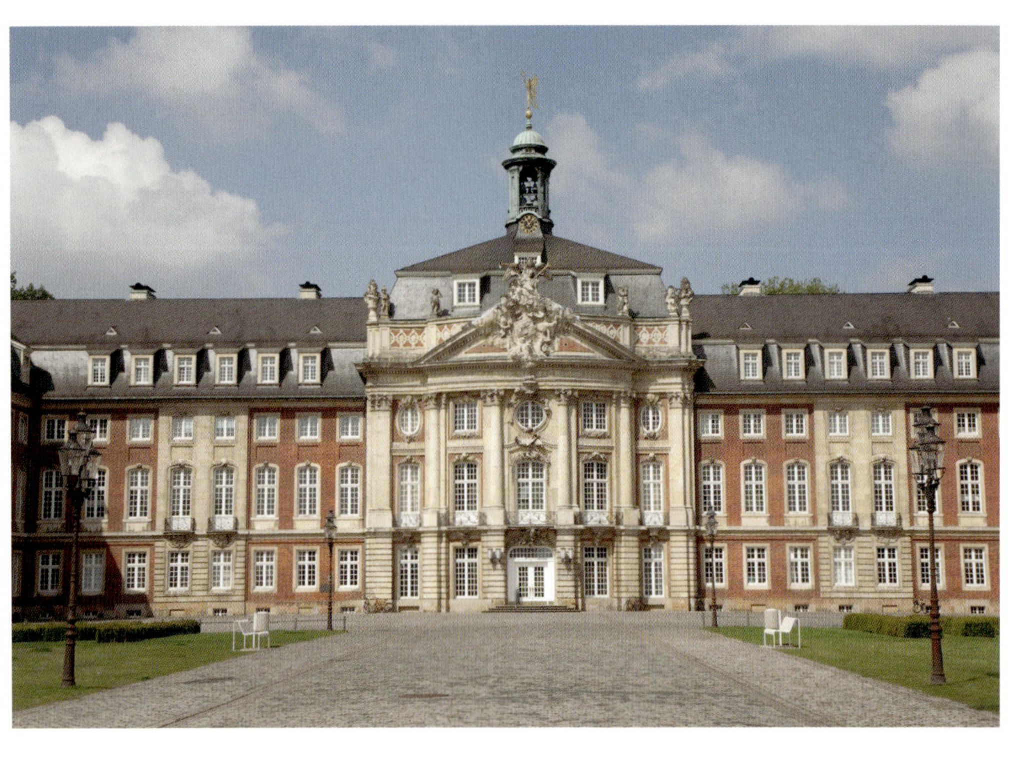

It is a commonplace in the survey literature on the arts of the eighteenth
century that owing to its frivolity, decadence and association with an
increasingly irrelevant aristocracy the Rococo was swept away by the fresh
breeze of Enlightenment thought, secularism and the championing of
Reason and Revolution. Most accounts sound Rococo's death knell in the
middle of the century, as if Neoclassicism's march across Europe was swift
and uncompromising. However as we have seen, the golden age of central
European Rococo abbeys extended well into the next two decades and artists
such as Josef Anton Mesmer were painting illusionistic ceilings in rural
Switzerland as late as 1815 (see Chapter Three). Some of the most important
figures in Rococo art and architecture flourished long after the style's purported
death. Johann Conrad Schlaun (1695–1773), court architect to the Prince-
Bishop of Münster and favourite of patrons throughout staunchly Catholic
Münsterland, completed the opulent Prince-Bishop's Palace with its swelling
façade and oversized cloudburst relief, in 1773 (235). *The Prophets of Bom Jesus
do Matozinhos*, one of the most important suites of late Rococo sculpture –
their dance-like poses and faceted, painterly drapery share the lightness of
Asam's stuccowork – was carved by mulatto artist Antônio Francisco Lisboa
(1730/8–1814), better known as 'Aleijadinho', in Brazil between 1800 and
1803 (236). In more remote parts of Latin America like Guatemala or the
Colca Canyon in Peru, where non-white artists who were kept out of the
metropolitan academies found enthusiastic patrons among Amerindians,
Baroque and Rococo churches were still being built in the 1850s.

Scholars are now questioning the supposed dichotomy between Rococo
and Enlightenment ideals, observing in the works of Antoine Watteau
the same intellectual freedom, direct engagement with nature, and spirit
of inventiveness that fuelled the speculations of Jean-Jacques Rousseau
(1712–1778) and Voltaire (1694–1778; see 76), and pointing out that Rococo
continued to appeal to key proponents of the Enlightenment: Rousseau was
a patron of François Boucher; Frederick the Great of Prussia (r. 1740–1786)

**235.
Johann
Conrad
Schlaun,**
Prince-Bishop's
Palace,
1767–73.
Münster
(Germany)

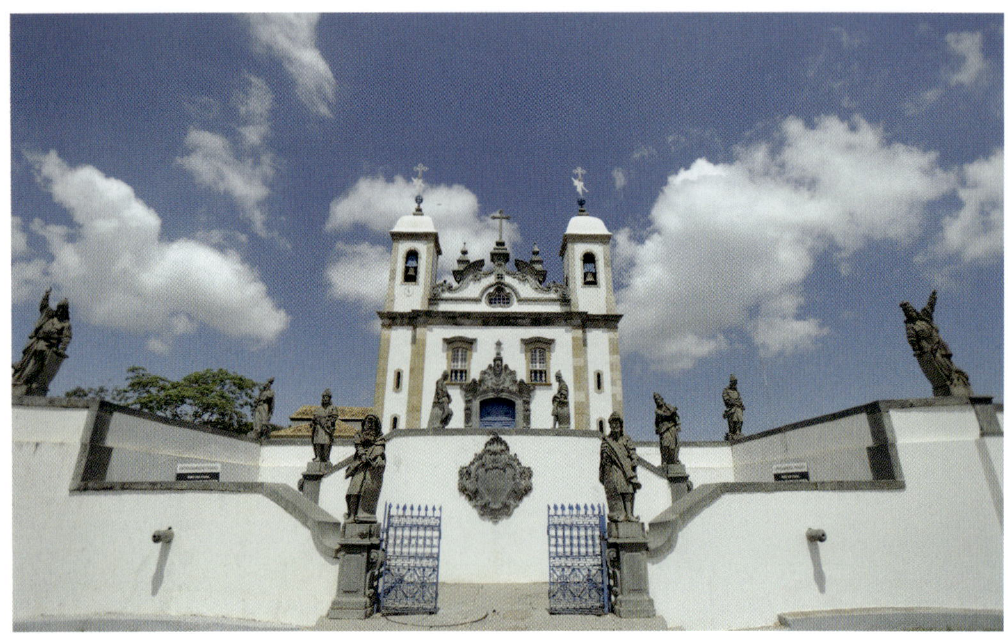

was a keen collector of Watteau (and his garden palace at Sanssouci is one of the most fanciful Rococo architectural confections anywhere) (237); and even the Rococo's fiercest critics had praise for the paintings of Boucher. Such were the philosopher and encyclopedist Denis Diderot (1713–1784), who acknowledged grudgingly that Boucher was one of the 'glories of our school' and had a 'particular talent' for painting women, and the engraver Charles-Nicolas Cochin (1715–1790) – his 1754–5 articles in the journal *Mercure de France* were a manifesto against Rococo decor – who defended Boucher as 'a very great painter in the genre [of history].' By the same token leading figures of Rococo culture commissioned Neoclassical works. Madame de Pompadour, Boucher's champion and the woman considered to be the epitome of Rococo frivolity, commissioned the Petit Trianon at Versailles, a monument of such staid and modest classicism that it has been compared to the Queen's House in Greenwich (238; see 141), and as we will soon see the Panthéon, Neoclassicism's signature monument, was founded by Louis XV (241). Even artistic developments that are repeatedly presented as quintessentially Neoclassical – the English 'natural garden' being one of the most prominent – are heavily indebted to Baroque and Rococo culture as I have discussed in Chapter Seven.

**236.
Antônio Francisco Lisboa,** Prophets of Bom Jesus do Matozinhos, Congonhas do Campo, 1800–3 (Brazil)

**237.
Georg Wenzeslaus von Knobelsdorf:** Sanssouci, 1745–7. Potsdam (Germany)

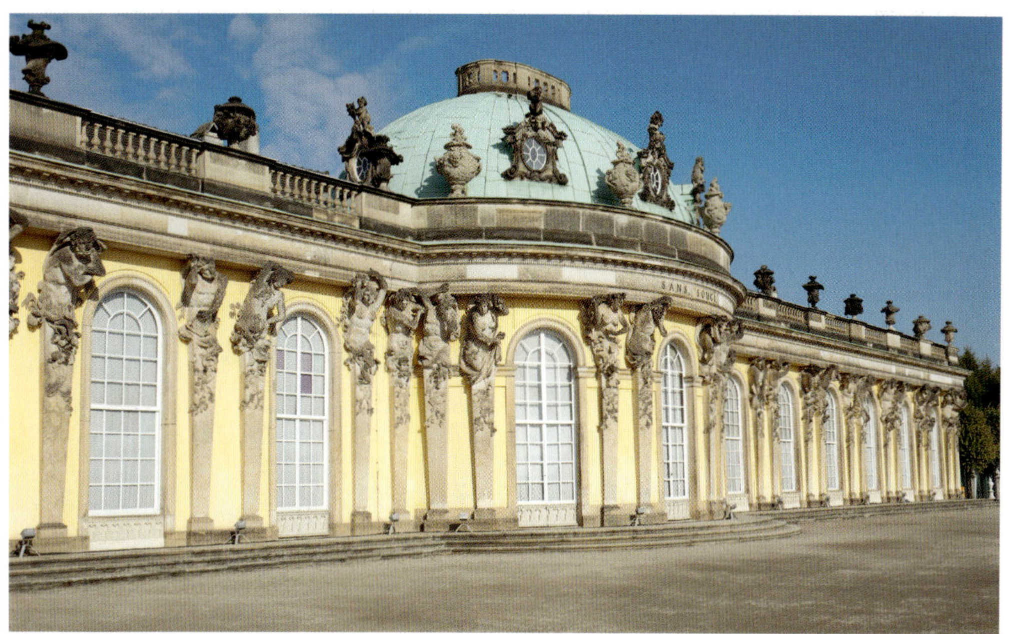

Going back to Diderot, it is his remarks (usually about Boucher) in his famous *Salons* of the 1760s that have been cited by so many as proof that French society in the second half of the eighteenth century was tired or even shocked by the Rococo. Certainly they are full of delectable quotations such as famous quip about Boucher that 'when he paints a naked woman her buttocks are as heavily rouged as her face', and his dismissal of Boucher's paintings of the Virgin Mary as 'cute little strumpets' (85). He did have a point: works like his *Birth of Venus* – an essay in blushing pinks under a thin veneer of mythology that recalls his detractors' remarks that Boucher's palette was inspired by ladies' cosmetics – are hard to take seriously, even if few paintings equalled its tonal luminosity or calligraphic curves (239). Yet recent scholarship has pointed out that the *Salons* did not reflect the taste of most art patrons of the time.

Certainly few artistic movements would seem to contrast as bluntly with Baroque and Rococo as Neoclassicism, an academic reclamation of the Graeco-Roman tradition that began in Rome and Paris in the 1750s – it was a more stringent manifestation of the academic theories of Félibien and his ilk a century earlier (see Chapter Two). In many ways Neoclassicism was

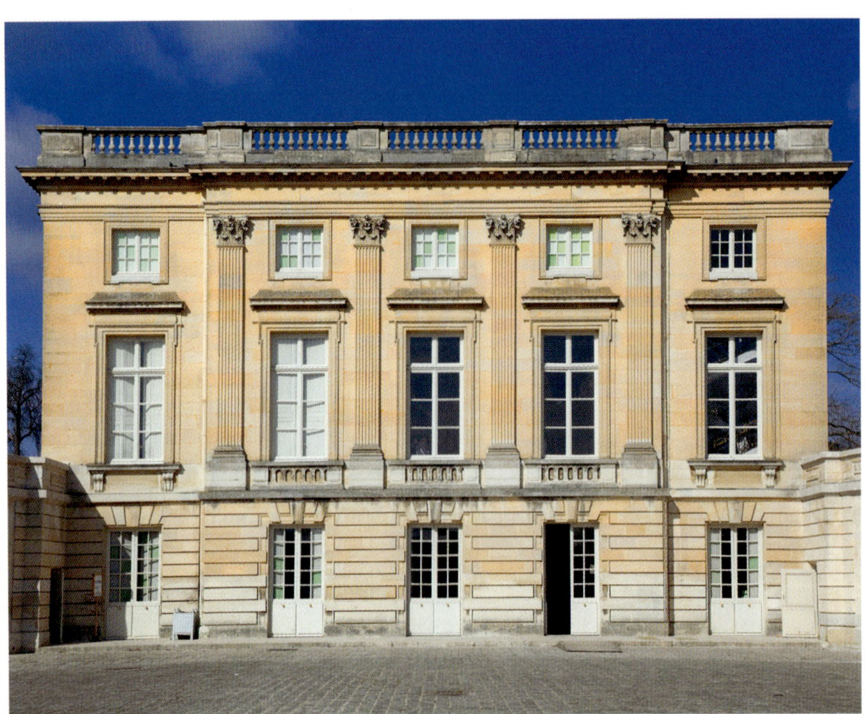

238.
Ange-Jacques Gabriel. The Petit Trianon, 1762–8. Versailles (France)

rigid where Baroque and Rococo were flexible, austere where they were exuberant and elitist where they were inclusive. Even though the Academy was born during the Baroque and Rococo, these styles emerged from a culture of personal apprenticeship and traditional workshop training in which people of humble backgrounds could rise to the top of their profession. The Incamminati were a family atelier rather than a formal academy, Borromini began as a stonemason, Cuvilliés was a court dwarf, and Melchor Pérez Holguín, born of a Native American mother, became the greatest painter of Potosí, one of the richest and largest cities in the world. Neoclassicism abandoned many traditional methods of instruction in favour of a strictly regulated academic program involving study of the liberal arts as well as more systematic copying of classical models. In fact, published books on art theory – such as Marc-Antoine Laugier's *Essai sur l'architecture* (1753) with its emphasis on rationality and functionality – dominated the arts in a way that even the treatise writers of the Catholic Reformation did not in their day (see Chapter One). Institutions such as the Royal Academy of Saint Ferdinand

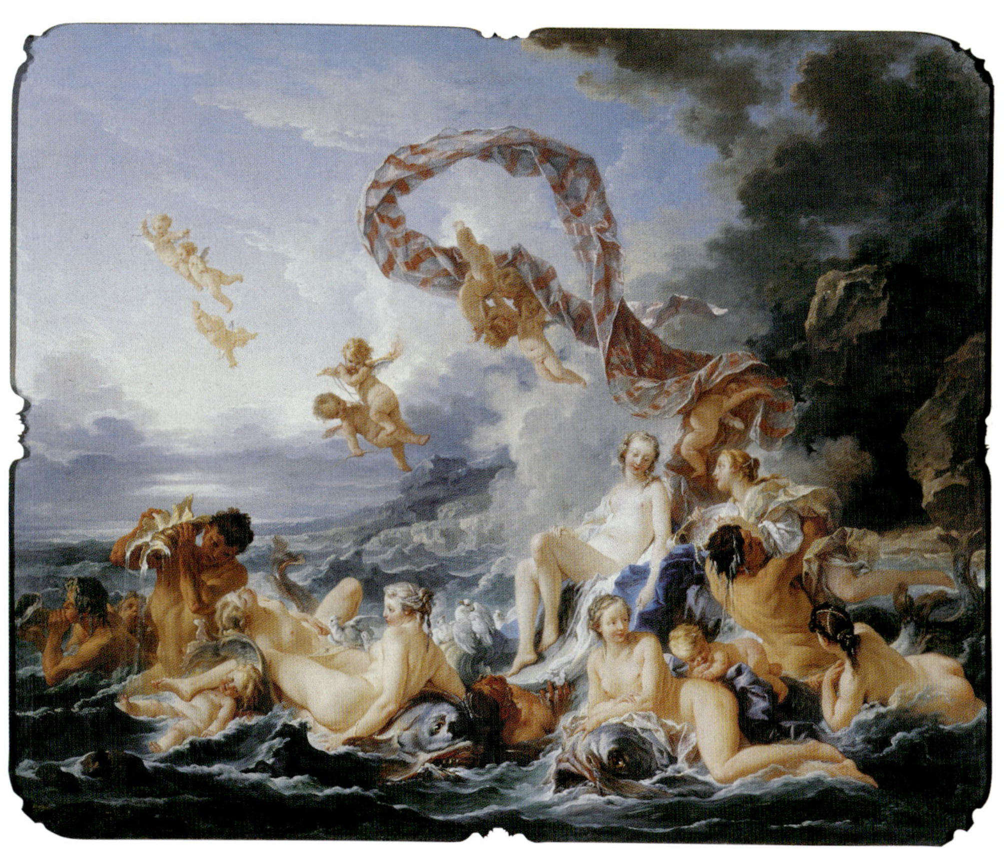

239.
François
Boucher, *The*
Birth of Venus,
1740. Oil on
canvas; 130 ×
162 cm (51¼
× 63¾ in).
National-
museum,
Stockholm

in Madrid (founded 1744), the Royal Academy of Arts in London (founded 1768), and the Royal Academy of San Carlos in Mexico City (founded 1785) were more centralized than traditional workshops and they were harder to get into. Students tended to be educated and socially advantaged – an expensive Grand Tour of the classical world was de rigueur – and competition for the coveted entrance scholarships, such as the *Prix de Rome* of the French Academy in Rome (founded 1666), was fierce. Perhaps most significantly, Neoclassicism is seen as curbing Rococo's inventiveness and experimentation with an archaeological insistence on authenticity.

Certainly the worst Neoclassical art and architecture is dryly derivative in its desire to get classical models 'just right' and even the best can seem constrained and cold when compared to the Rococo, but the movement's aim was not to become frozen in the past but to use Antiquity and its ideals in a way that was relevant to contemporary society. Despite its often turgid morality and its academic earnestness Neoclassicism did not discourage lightness and elegance – the very qualities that make so much of it pleasing to the public today. One would have to be very churlish indeed not to be delighted by the delicacy of the stucco and painted Greek-inspired ornament that graced Robert Adam's (1728–92) interiors in Osterley Park, near London, a building that is blessed with having nearly all of its original furnishings intact, unlike any of the interiors discussed in this book (240). Although derived from Greek pottery, Adam's stucco lacework of leafy spirals, vases, garlands, trophies and sphinxes exhibited in the Eating Room still echoes a profoundly Rococo aesthetic, with its division of the wall into panels, its pastel colour scheme and its integration into stucco panels of small painted roundels (by Antonio Zucchi; 1726–1795). Adams commented about the room that it 'is desirable to have [it] fitted up with elegance and splendour', a sentiment with which Germain Boffrand would have entirely been in agreement (see 163).

Although best known for its ties to revolution and Protestantism, Neoclassicism was born in the waning years of the Bourbon Dynasty in France. We have already witnessed a powerful classical strain in French Baroque from the beginning, as epitomized by the architecture of Jules

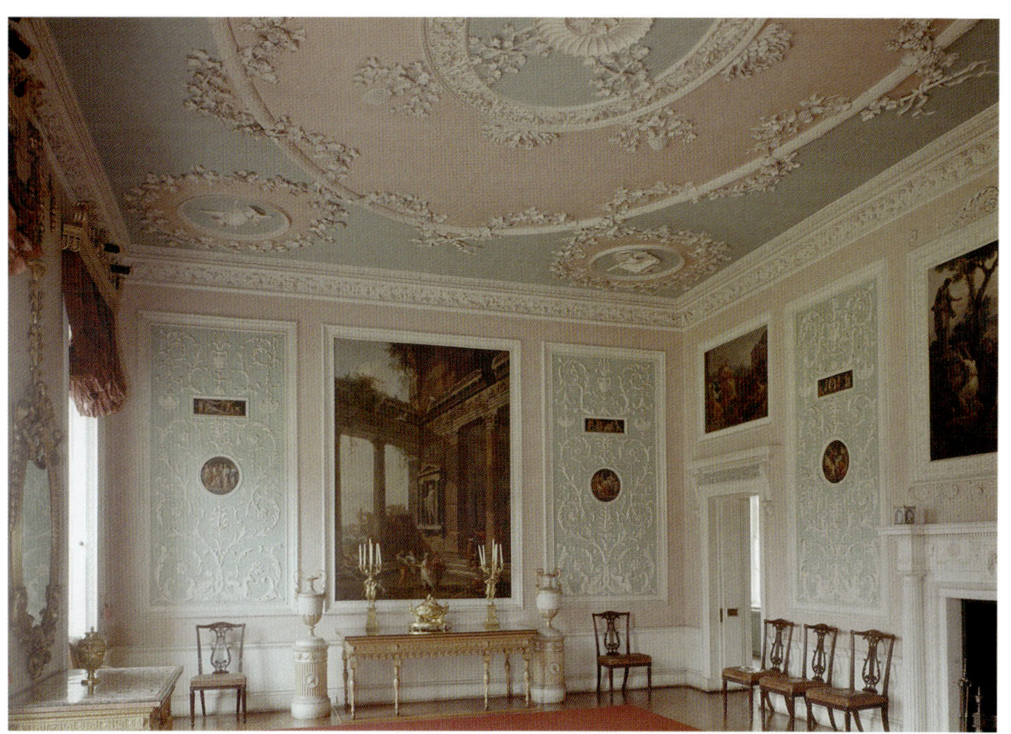

240.
Robert Adam,
Eating Room,
Osterley Park,
begun 1761.
Hounslow
(England)

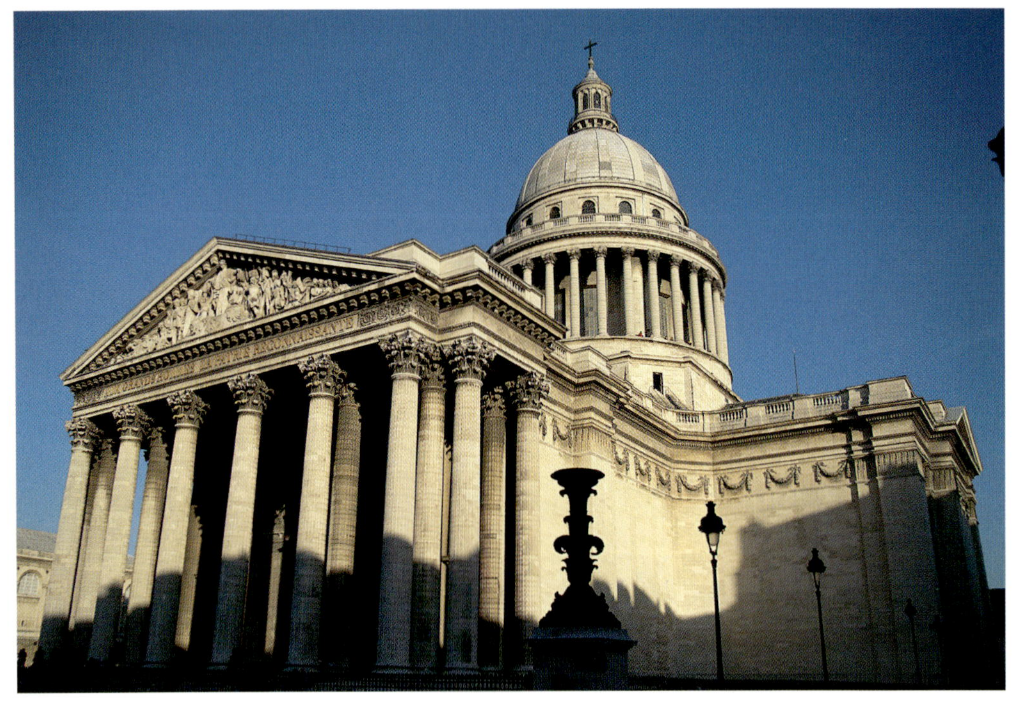

**241.
Jacques-
Germain
Soufflot,**
Sainte-
Geneviève
(Pantheon),
1758–89. Paris

Hardouin-Mansart (see 145) and the paintings of Poussin (see 52), but it was redoubled upon the discovery of new archaeological remains, particularly the ancient Roman cities of Pompeii and Herculaneum in the 1730s and 1740s, but also with a new enthusiasm for the arts of classical Greece, ancient Egypt and the Etruscans. Neoclassicism in France was stimulated by the French Academy in Rome, where students religiously copied original or reproduction Graeco-Roman sculpture and architecture – the painting by Giovanni Paolo Panini showing pupils sketching paintings of Roman monuments gives an idealized glimpse into the workings of an Academy (see 73) – as well as the works of Raphael and Poussin. Neoclassical paintings tended to be populated with figures posed and attired like specific classical statues or reliefs, set against a background of meticulously rendered archaeological details. Neoclassicism favoured Greek style over Roman, considering it purer and more authentically classical in its aesthetic goals.

One of the grandest Neoclassical buildings was built as a votive church for Louis XV but was recycled after 1789 as the paradigmatic monument to revolutionary secularism. Sainte-Geneviève, now known as the Panthéon and a mausoleum for the most prominent citizens of France, was designed by Jacques-Germain Soufflot (1713–1780), an alumnus of the French Academy in Rome (241). Conceived on a Greek-cross plan, it projects a solid, austere and stringently classical image, even though its combination of structures – a dome on top of a Greek temple – never existed in antiquity and was inspired by Baroque models such as St Peter's in Rome or the Dôme des Invalides (see 145). In fact, a comparison between the Panthéon and the classicizing Dôme isolates the more subtle distinctions between the two styles since the two buildings look similar at first glance. Both incorporate Corinthian porticoes into the façade but the one on the Panthéon – a single straight colonnade surmounted by a triangular pediment – is academically correct while the Dôme takes liberties by doubling the colonnades (one on each storey) and having them advance from the sides towards the centre to emphasize the entrance. The walls of the Panthéon are plain like a Greek temple, adorned only with restrained garland friezes at the top (the original windows were blocked in at the last moment in response to academic criticism), whereas those at the Pantheon are pierced by generously proportioned windows.

The figural decoration on the Panthéon is limited to the Greek-style reliefs on the pediment whereas the Dôme has statues of saints in niches on the ground floor and free-standing saints on the upper level (here the pediments are adorned with a heraldic crest). The domes of the two structures are also radically different: the Dôme's two drums are enlivened by shifting wall planes below and volutes above whereas the Panthéon, inspired by circular Roman temples, has a single drum surrounded by a colonnade and no transition between drum and dome. The surface of the Panthéon's dome features unobtrusive ribs – again not strictly correct since ribs are a Gothic feature – while that of its Baroque counterpart is richly decorated with gilded garlands and panels and is punctuated by round windows. Both churches dominate their surroundings, but whereas the Dôme manipulates the classical idiom the Panthéon is manipulated by it. This contrast between testing the boundaries and working within them is the essential difference between the two styles.

We can witness an even more dramatic contrast in a single building, Haus Stapel near Münster (242, 243). German Neoclassicism, as promoted by architects like the Prussian Karl Friedrich Schinkel (1781–1841), was exceptionally severe, favouring minimal decoration, austere Doric columns and plain piers – a reaction, no doubt, to the exceptional popularity of Rococo style in central Europe. Recent studies are demonstrating that Neoclassicism enjoyed more patronage in German-speaking areas than anywhere else in Europe, particularly in metropolitan centres like Berlin. Haus Stapel, a grand country seat fronting onto the River Aa, combines a Rococo entrance gate begun in 1719 with a Neoclassical country house started exactly a century later. The entrance gate, designed by Schlaun's teacher Maximilian von Welsch (1671–1745), is the model of Rococo elegance: diminutive and delicate, it features a trio of slender towers capped with gambrelled cupolas and finials that fine-tune perspective to make them seem taller than they are. By comparison, the block-like house by August Reinking (1776–1819) is ponderous and dull. Its rectangular windows are undressed, its walls are relentlessly plain and even its pediment is free of carving. The only respite is a plain Ionic colonnade in front of the main doorway on the courtyard side of the building.

242. Maximilian von Welsch, main gateway of Haus Stapel, begun 1819. Havixbeck (Germany)

243. August Reinking, Haus Stapel, begun 1819. Havixbeck (Germany)

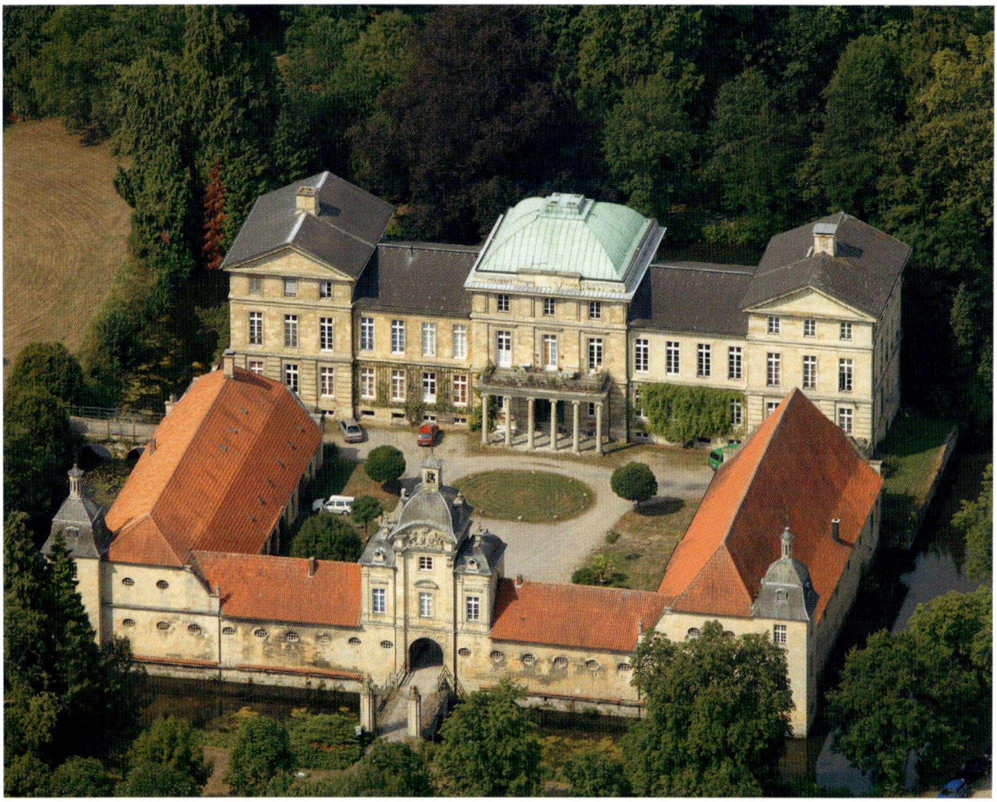

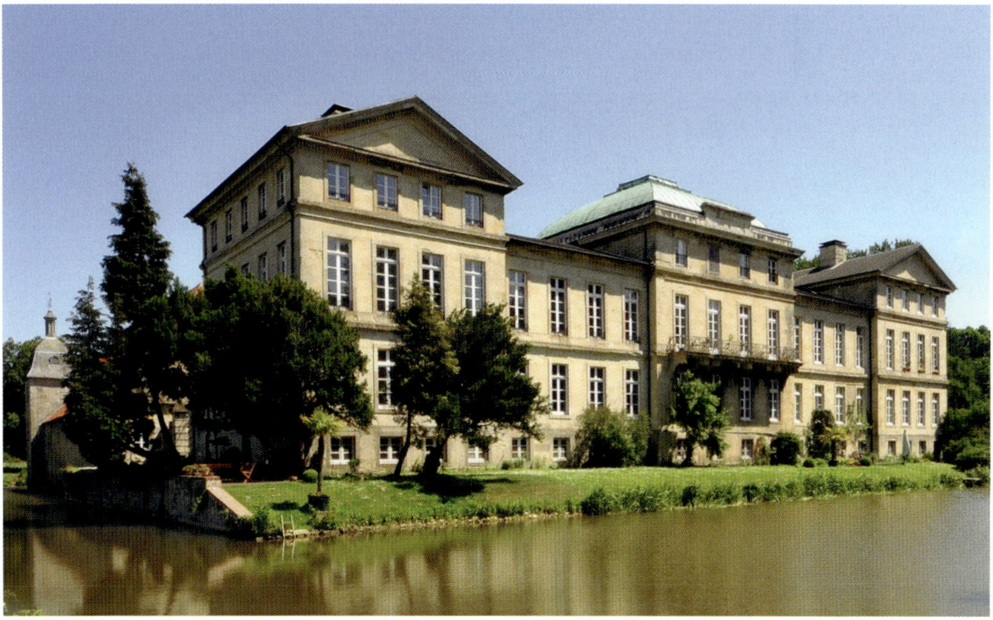

Neoclassical painting was profoundly influenced by the German writer Johann Joachim Winckelmann (1717–1768), who resurrected the idea of 'nature perfected' (see Chapter One) but more rigorously than his Baroque predecessors. Singling out Greek art as his ideal, he declared that ancient art was superior to nature and exhorted artists to create idealized physiognomies and gestures based on harmonious syntheses of form. Most importantly, individual traits and blemishes were to be avoided. These principles underlay the work of the prototypical Neoclassical painter of the next generation, Jacques-Louis David (1748–1825). Winner of the *Prix de Rome* in 1774 and the most recognized painter of the French Revolution and Napoleonic era, David expressed his partisanship with the revolutionary cause through works like his *Death of Socrates*, a paean to self-sacrifice that celebrated stoicism, civic responsibility and steadfastness (244).

In *Death of Socrates* the Greek philosopher coolly holds forth on the immortality of the soul as he reaches with his left hand for the deadly hemlock jar, choosing death over the abandonment of his principles. A comparison with Rubens' *Miracles of Ignatius of Loyola* (see 46) shows how far David's style diverges from the Baroque. Both paintings focus on male protagonists – one a saint and the other saintly – preaching before crowds of rapt supporters, and both contrast the impassiveness of the principal figures with the emotional frailty of their audiences. But here the similarities end. Rubens electrifies his scene with dramatic diagonals, dancing brushwork, turbulent cloudbursts and writhing bodies. He expresses grandeur through lofty architecture and brilliant, rich colours. The viewer clearly sees the actions of God through blasts of divine light, whirling angels and fleeing devils, and the reactions of his figures are exaggerated and theatrical. David avoids overt reference to the Divine – this he shares with Caravaggio, although he flattens the Roman painter's light contrasts – setting the episode in a darkened chamber. His figures' emotions are congealed and have studied and generic facial responses (compare with the Apostles' outpouring of grief in the high altar at Rohr; see 103). In fact, David's figures look more like sculptures than living entities, an effect he heightens by arranging them into a frieze and downplaying brushwork in favour of burnished surfaces and sharply defined contours. The figure of Socrates quotes a Roman relief

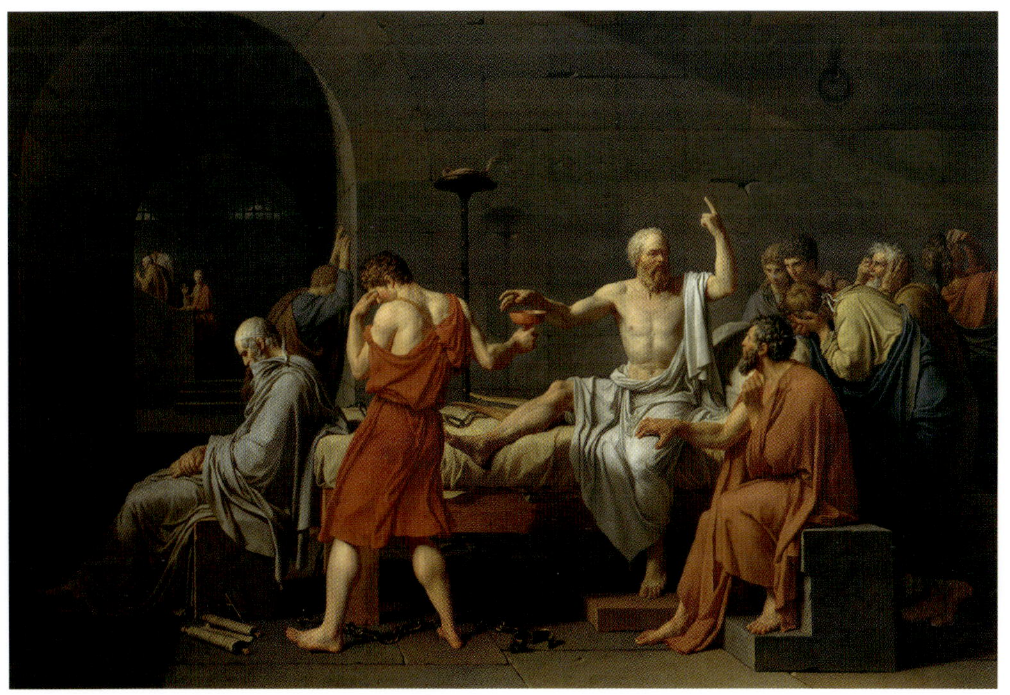

**244.
Jacques-Louis
David,** *Death
of Socrates,*
1787. Oil on
canvas; 129.5
× 196.2 cm
(51 × 77¼ in).
Metropolitan
Museum of
Art, New York

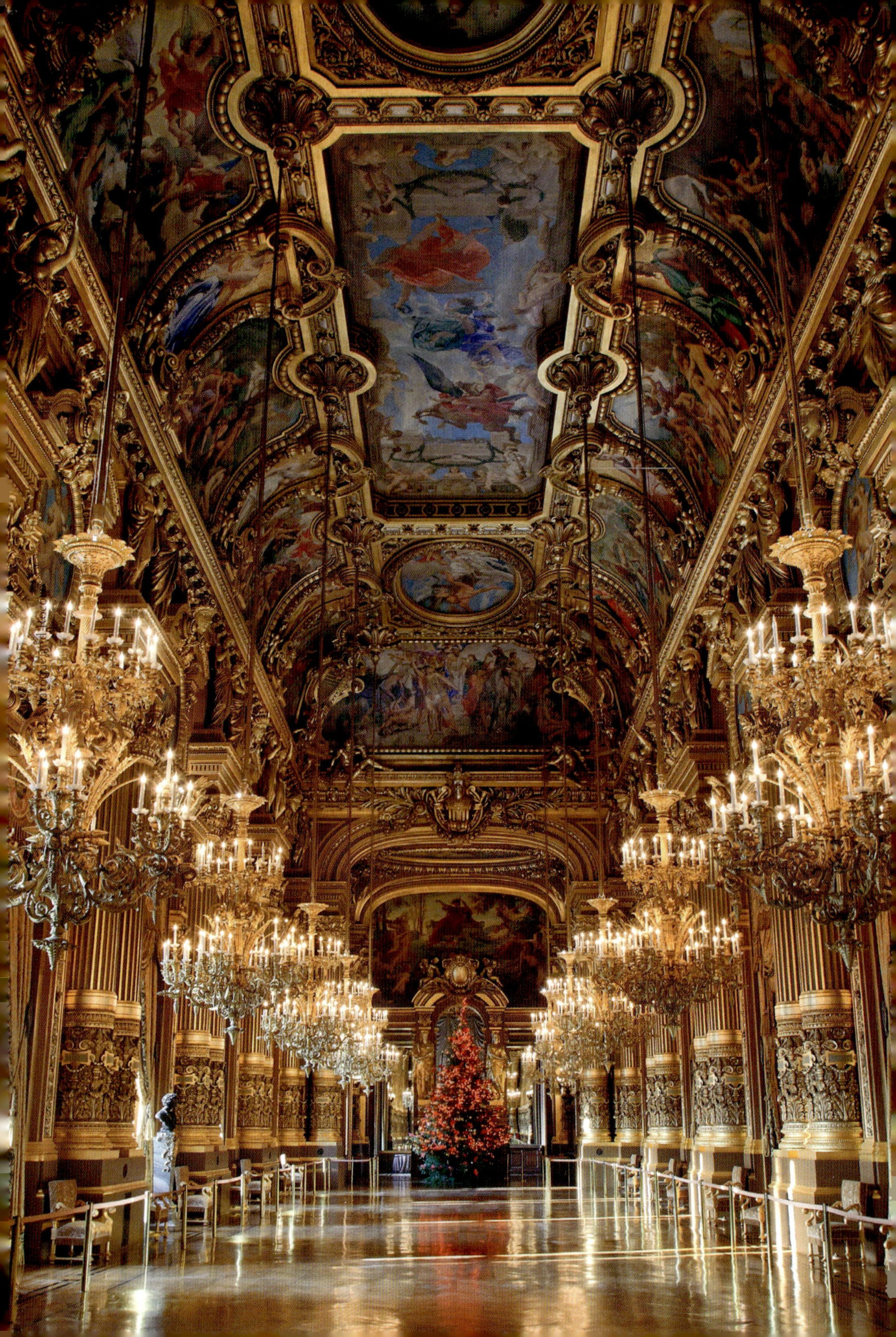

carving in the Vatican Museum and the heads of his disciples are based on other sculptural models. David's use of a limited range of carefully balanced colours – the four main figures wear alternately light (grey/white) and dark (red/brown) robes and the juxtaposition of hues in the grieving figures to the right pay homage to Raphael – add to the stateliness and sobriety of the scene. Both paintings purport to show a protagonist caught in mid-action, but where Rubens captures time David offers timelessness.

Although Baroque and Rococo suffered from unusually harsh criticism in subsequent centuries – scholarly appreciation began only in the late 1940s – aspects of the styles have been adopted by artists and art movements from the late nineteenth century to the present, either by mimicking their appearance and techniques or by reviving their compositions, illusionistic tricks, or their rebellious and energetic spirit. Two in particular stand out. The most wholehearted Baroque revival began in the 1850s in France, in the same decade that the last glimmer of true Rococo died away in secluded villages in Peru and Guatemala. The Beaux Arts movement, named after the school in Paris where it developed, aimed for a Baroque opulence through lavishly decorated monumental structures that evoked Louis XIV's Versailles. The premier Beaux Arts monument is the Paris Opéra by Charles Garnier, a structure that dominates an entire neighbourhood and still astonishes visitors with its majestic staircase and reception halls: the Grand Foyer immediately recalls the Hall of Mirrors at Versailles (245; see 157) with its illusionistic ceiling frescos, heavy gilded frames, caryatids and broken pediments. Yet the Beaux-Arts movement was no mere Baroque revival but sought a synthesis of styles, here seen in Renaissance elements such as the grotesque decoration around the lower part of the columns. At the end of the century Art Nouveau, or *Jugendstil* as it was known in German, also reached out to the Baroque in its attempt to rescue the arts from academicism and mass production. Like the Baroque, Art Nouveau aimed at a fusion of the media (they called it a 'total work of art') and it was characterized in particular by sinewy, plant-like designs. The two styles had a natural affinity – we have already seen Baroque works that anticipate Art Nouveau's organic nature (see 10, 178) – and nowhere was this connection explored more fully than in Bohemia and Moravia (present-day Czech Republic), where Baroque and Art Nouveau

245.
Charles Garnier,
Grand Foyer,
Paris Opéra,
1857–74. Paris

alike were claimed by nationalists as manifestations of the Czech spirit. Some of the most successful fusions of the two styles occurred in Olomouc, where renovations of existing Baroque churches provided an ideal opportunity for experimentation. When the organ loft of the church of St Michael was rebuilt at the turn of the century, the building's Dominican patrons replaced the Baroque original with a bold essay in Art Nouveau style, complete with a horseshoe entryway, curving vines and giant female angels who sweep up from the sides to support the balustrade (246). It is a much more satisfactory integration into the older building than the Toledo Transparente's setting in a plain Gothic ambulatory (104).

More recently, the fall of the Iron Curtain and consequent rise of Catholicism and Orthodoxy in central and eastern Europe has given the Baroque an unexpected role as a symbol of religious and intellectual freedom. Lithuania and the Czech Republic have resurrected their Baroque identities by restoring seventeenth- and eighteenth-century churches and palaces from Vilnius to Brno, and their tourist boards promote Baroque–themed travel, often combined with religious pilgrimage. This revival is keenly felt in arts scholarship as the masterpieces of eastern European art and architecture are increasingly brought to the attention of Western audiences (indeed this has been one of the goals of this book). Painters such as the Bohemian Karel Škréta (1610–1674) – his *St Barbara and St Catherine with the Holy Family*, with its balance of warm colours heightened by deep chiaroscuro, is a profoundly moving study of rapture – were championed by dissidents during the Communist regime as the very personification of Czech identity and are once again the subject of a groundswell of scholarship (247). In Ukraine and Russia municipalities and church groups have rebuilt or restored Baroque and Rococo monuments destroyed or neglected by the Soviets, such as St Michael in Kiev (see 208) and the interior of the Peter and Paul Cathedral in St Petersburg, refurbished in the late 1990s as the mausoleum of the newly exhumed Tsar Nicholas II and his family. A brochure published by St Michael's – the Soviets demolished the church to make way for a car park – could not be clearer about the significance of these restorations: 'St Michael's Monastery's revival, renovation, and restoration in Kiev is a real miracle for those who have endured the difficult time of the communist regime.'

246.
Organ loft, late 19th century. Church of St Michael, Olomouc (Czech Republic)

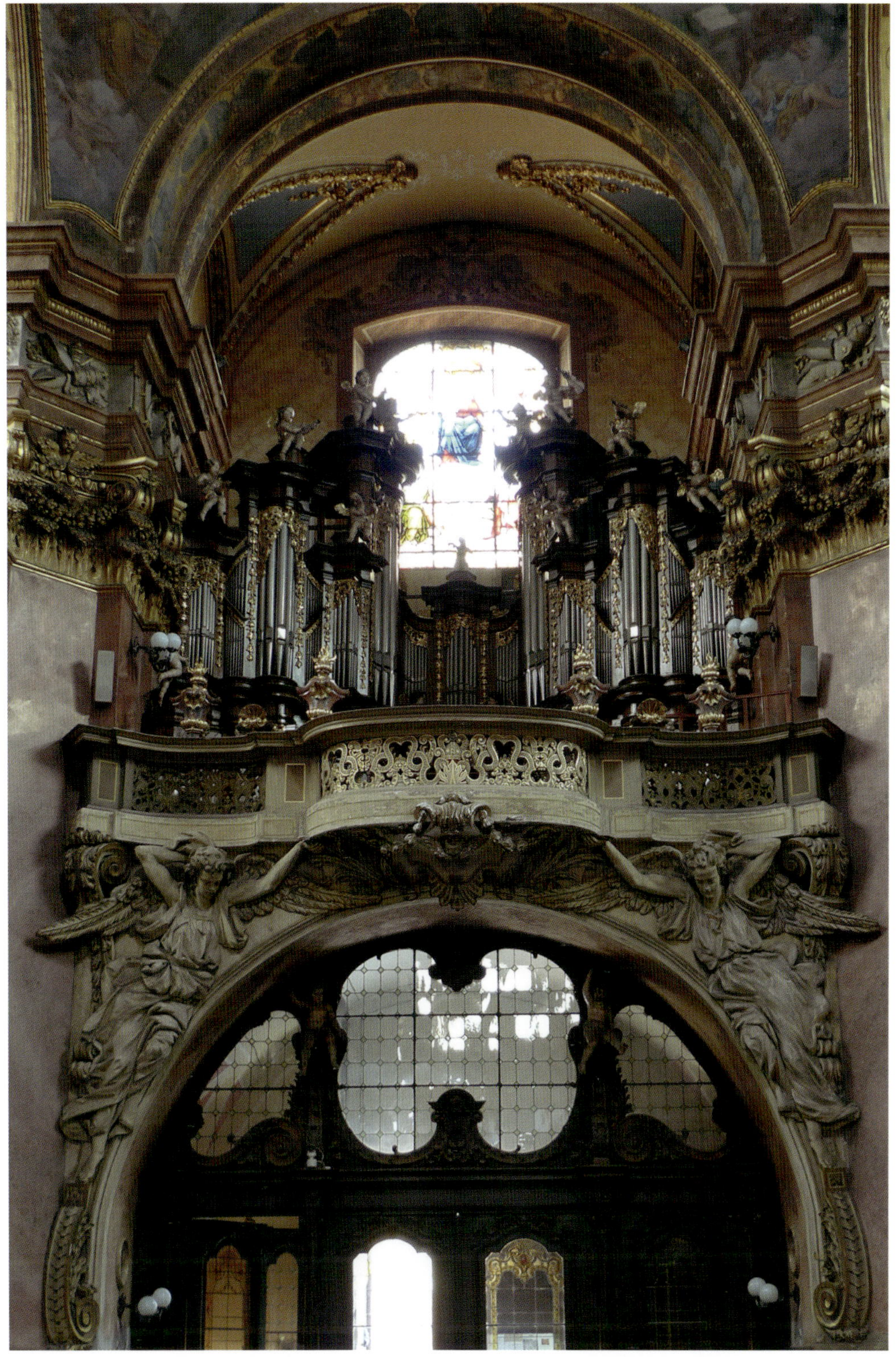

But the most emblematic Baroque symbol of renewal – and a fitting way to end this book – is the Dresden Frauenkirche, a Lutheran cathedral built for the Prince-Elector of Saxony by Georg Bähr (1666–1738) in 1726–43 and obliterated between 13 and 15 February 1945 by one of the most horrific aerial bombardments of the Second World War, one that cost 40,000 lives (248). The pathetic heap of rubble that was Dresden's greatest monument – it was left untouched for forty-four years by the East German government as a memorial to Communist victory over Nazism – was incorporated in 2004–5 into a complete reconstruction in which a handful of original stones, carefully preserved and inventoried by Dresden citizens over the decades, stand out in scorched black against the golden hue of new masonry erected on the basis of

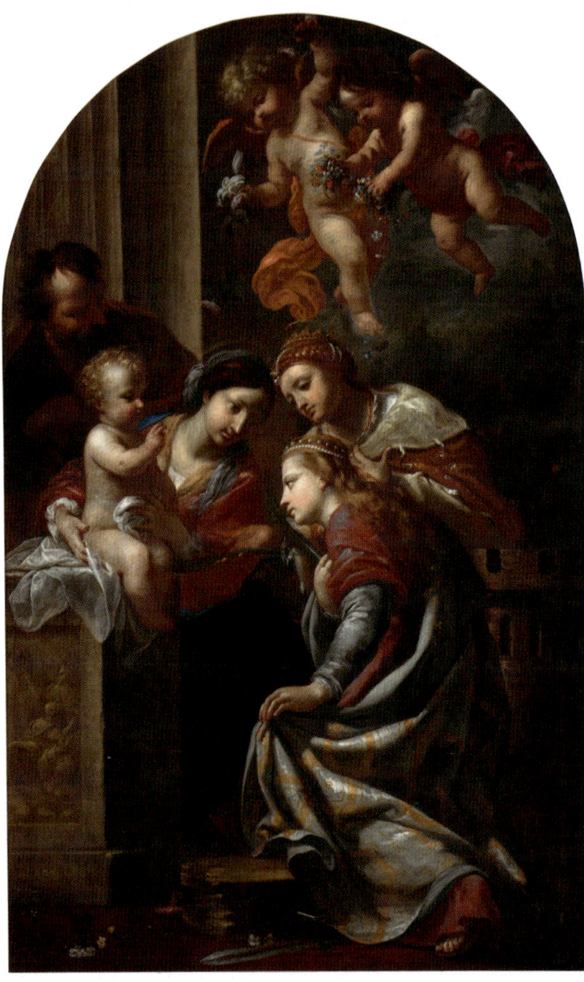

247.
Karel Škréta,
St Barbara and St Catherine with the Holy Family. Early 1660s. Oil on canvas; 24.5 × 14 m (8 ft × 4 ft 7 in). National Gallery, Prague

248.
Georg Bähr,
Frauenkirche, 1726–43; destroyed 1945; rebuilt 2004–5. Dresden

detailed paintings by Canaletto's nephew Bernardo Bellotto (1720–80) and computer imaging. Rising like a phoenix from the ashes – the cliché may be tired, but nowhere more appropriate – this magnificent church is a symbol of the enduring power of Baroque and Rococo art, with its astonishing grandiosity, popular allure, and perhaps also its sense of hope, comfort and order.

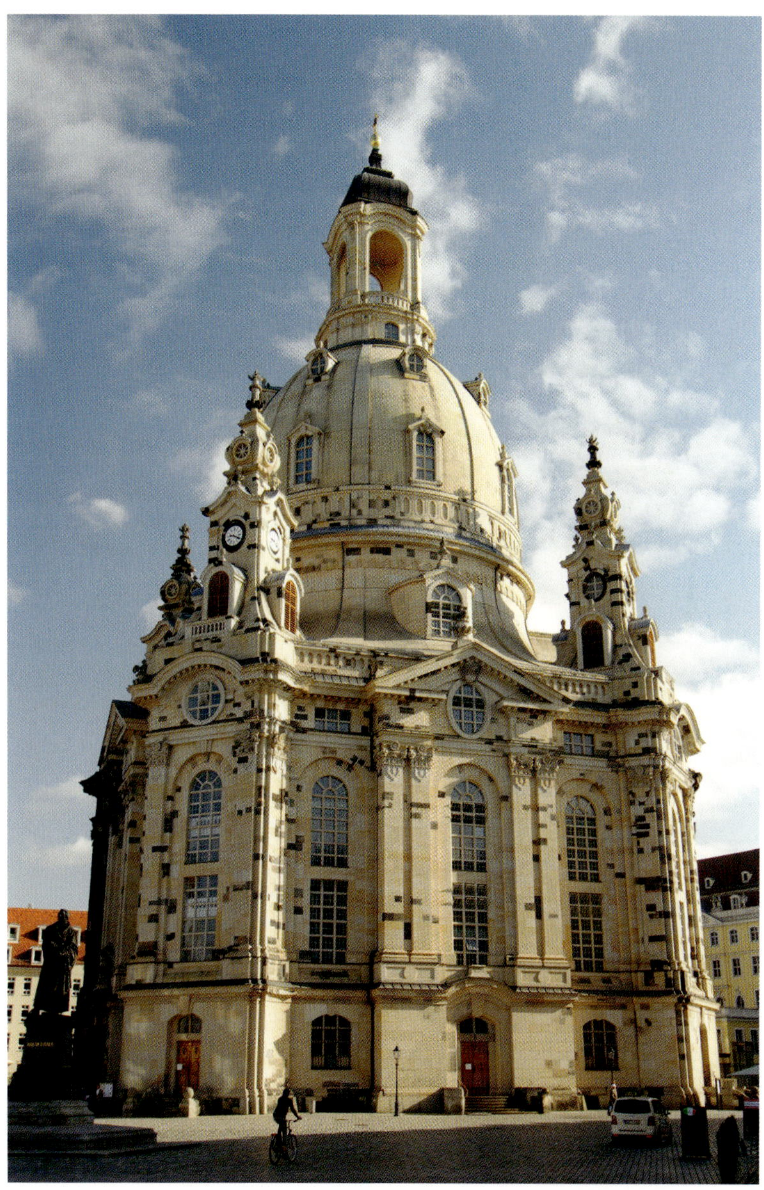

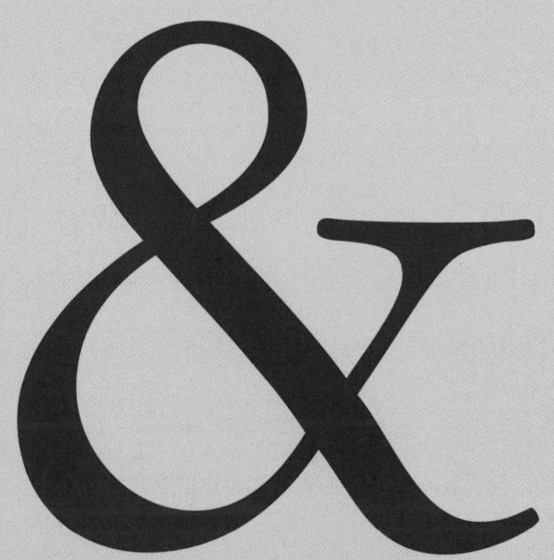

Academies Professional organizations that train artists and maintain artistic standards; an artist's entry into the academy was very significant for his or her career, although many prominent artists did not join academies.

apparato A temporary plaster and wood backdrop, often with false clouds and candles, used in Italy to display the Eucharist, especially during a Lenten vigil called a Forty Hours Devotion.

bel composto Coined by Bernini's biographer Filippo Baldinucci, it means a 'beautiful whole' and refers to the Baroque unity of the arts media.

cartouche A small panel, originally like a heraldic shield, with an elaborately decorated, usually curvilinear and asymmetrical frame.

cheminée Literally 'chimney', in Rococo decor it refers to a wall panel with a mantle-piece that reflects the style of an entire room. Engravings of cheminées were published in Rococo design manuals as guides for decorators.

chiaroscuro Literally 'light and dark', the term denotes the effects created by shading in paintings or drawings.

chinoiserie Rococo style of décor and architecture that imitates Chinese and Japanese art, although usually not very accurately.

concetto Literally 'conceit' but in the context of Baroque art the term denotes a theme or idea behind a work of art. A concetto often has a humorous aspect and usually challenges convention, often through a visual or thematic trick.

disegno Literally 'drawing' but in the Renaissance and Baroque the term also relates to the genius of the artist and the first realization of the concetto. In central Italy drawing was also the necessary beginning of the artistic process.

doelenstuk In Dutch painting a corporate group portrait in which individual likenesses are combined into a single painting so that the sitters seem to interact naturally and participate in a single activity.

enfilade A row of apartments in a palace organized along a single axis separated by open doorways.

entablature The horizontal element in a work of architecture, in classical tradition it sometimes carries the frieze and is usually directly on top of the columns. It also separates storeys in a building even where there are no columns.

etching A printing process in which a design is scratched onto a plate covered with acid-proof resin and then bathed in acid to bore it deeper into the metal.

fête champêtre A country outing, often with entertainment, or a romantic tryst in a wooded setting, both popularized in the paintings of French Rococo artists such as Antoine Watteau.

Flügelaltar A German winged altarpiece and ancestor of the Spanish retablo that combines a wooden framework with sculpture and paintings.

genre A category of painting defined by the academies, it is subdivided into major and minor genres. The principal major genre is history painting, while the minor genres include landscape, portraiture and still-life. The term 'genre painting' also refers to paintings of everyday life usually without a distinct narrative – themselves a minor genre.

genre pittoresque Rococo décor which is asymmetrical with natural elements (flora, fauna) and exotica, especially the styles of India and East Asia.

giant order Columns or pilasters that rise through two or more storeys; the concept was devised by Michelangelo.

gloria, or heavenly glory In architectural sculpture it is circular sunburst, usually of gilt bronze sunrays, with an empty centre lit from a window behind. The most famous is the Gloria at St Peter's in Rome by Bernini.

history painting Considered the noblest of the genres as defined by the academies, it involves scenes with multiple figures depicting historical, mythological or religious subjects.

impasto Heavy, three-dimensional laying-on of paint, sometimes with a painter's knife.

memento mori Literally 'reminder of death', it usually takes the form of a skull or corpse in a painting to remind the viewer of the corruptibility of the flesh.

natural garden Also known as the 'English garden', an informal garden that attempts to replicate a natural setting but often does so artificially.

novità Literally 'novelty' the term refers to an intellectual game in which an artist refers to and improves upon the work of a well-known old master.

order, architectural Classical architecture divides into styles or 'orders' that derive from Graeco-Roman temple design. These are Doric, Ionic and Corinthian in the Greek tradition, to which the Romans added Tuscan and Composite. They form the building blocks of Renaissance and Baroque architecture.

Palladian Motif An arch between two trabeated rectangular openings originating in the architecture of Sebastiano Serlio and Palladio; also popularly called a 'Palladian Window' it was especially widespread in England.

paragone A Renaissance literary debate in which painting and sculpture (and to a degree architecture) were each championed as superior, and therefore distinct, from the others.

parterre In a formal French garden, parterres are raised plantings near the house with patterns made of flowers, shrubs and gravel so that when viewed from above they resemble tapestries.

pendentive A trapezoidal curving section at the junction of two walls that serves as a transition between a square space below and a dome above.

putto (pl. putti) A cherub, usually taking the form of a nude baby with wings; one of the most common decorative motifs of the Baroque and Rococo.

quadratura Literally 'squaring', it refers to a framework of feigned architecture, usually in a fresco, that in turn serves as a setting for figures and scenery.

quadro riportato Literally 'a relocated painting' it is similar to quadratura but instead of feigned architecture it creates a grid of false picture frames that make whatever is painted inside them look like easel paintings.

retablo Spanish term for retable, or altarpiece. In Spanish and Latin American architecture they take the form of an architectural, usually wooden, framework enclosing paintings and sculptures and can occupy the entire apse of a church or end wall of a chapel.

rocaille Origin of the term 'Rococo': a kind of decorative shellwork.

rustication Usually on the exterior of the ground floor of a building, it refers to large masonry blocks with rough exterior faces that recall fortification architecture; in the Renaissance rustication originally served a defensive purpose but during the course of the sixteenth century and in the Baroque and Rococo it became purely decorative.

servitù particolare Literally 'private service', it refers to a professional relationship in which an artist is taken on as a member of staff by a wealthy patron, lives in his house, produces artworks and entertainments primarily for that patron and has access to his or her art collection.

speaking likeness Developed by Bernini, the term refers to a portrait in which the sitter is depicted just before or after talking, as if engaging the viewer or someone else in the room directly.

sprezzatura Studied nonchalance; the depiction of an important person in a very informal way to communicate superiority or even aristocratic disdain.

tenebrism Characteristic of Caravaggio, it is a more intense form of chiaroscuro in which the bright sections seem spotlighted and darkest shadows are impossible or nearly impossible to penetrate.

triumphal arch In Roman tradition triumphal arches are single or triple-arched structures built over the route taken by triumphant armies returning to the city. In the Baroque context temporary triumphal arches of wood, canvas and plaster were constructed at ephemeral events – also often triumphal entries into cities.

Aleijadinho (Antônio Francisco Lisboa) (1730/8–1814) South America's most celebrated sculptor and one of the last practitioners of the Rococo in the world, Aleijadinho was born to an architect father and black slave mother. He succumbed to leprosy or syphilis at the age of 39, lost his fingers and was reduced to working with tools strapped to his arms. Nevertheless, assisted by stone cutters, carpenters and wood carvers – not to mention his own slaves – Aleijadinho produced the most important monuments of the Brazilian rococo, including the façade of the Church of the Third Order of St Francis in Ouro Prêto and above all the Twelve Prophets at Congonhas do Campo.

Sofonisba Anguissola (c.1535–1625) The most prominent woman painter of her age, Anguissola was sent by her father to study with Bernardino Campi. She is known for her keen observation of physiognomy, which was typical of her native Lombardy. Her best known works are portraits and self-portraits that celebrated her cultured background. Her fame was such that she served as court painter to Queen Isabella of Spain. Although most of her work predates the Baroque, she lived long enough to witness the new style and at the age of 89 she gave artistic advice to a young Anthony van Dyck.

Egid Quirin Asam (c.1692–1750) Together with his brother the painter Cosmas Damian (1686–1739), sculptor Egid Quirin was the premier interior decorator of Rococo Central Europe. The Asam brothers created an ideal synthesis between stucco and painting that was imitated throughout the region and they enjoyed a wealth of important commissions, including the interiors of the abbeys at Rohr and Weingarten and above all the church of St John Nepomuk in Munich, popularly known as the Asamkirche (Asam Church).

Gianlorenzo Bernini (1598–1680) The single most important artist of the Baroque, Bernini invented Baroque sculpture and the idea of the *bel composto* (unity of the arts) and, together with Francesco Borromini and Pietro da Cortona, was responsible for the first monuments of Baroque architecture.

His influence inside and outside Rome is incalculable and he is responsible for such world-famous monuments as *Apollo and Daphne*, the *Ecstasy of Saint Teresa*, and the Baldacchino and Gloria in St Peter's Basilica in Rome. A cultured socialite, Bernini was favoured by successive papal courts and that of Louis XIV of France.

Germain Boffrand (1667–1754) Boffrand was to Rococo architecture what Bernini was to the Baroque, having designed the most celebrated Rococo interior at the suite of apartments at the Hôtel de Soubise in Paris. He planned some of the most important town and country houses of his age as well as public works projects such as hospitals and bridges. Boffrand's fame spread throughout Europe thanks to his architectural manual the *Livre d'Architecture* (*Book of Architecture*, 1745), a work that had a particularly profound impact on British architects.

Francesco Borromini (1599–1667) Popularly depicted as Bernini's arch rival, Francesco Borromini was jointly responsible for the creation of Baroque architecture. Borromini fused techniques and styles of Hellenistic, Late Roman and Gothic traditions to create structures of geometric and symbolic complexity that went against the grain of the more Classical Baroque favoured by Roman critics. Like Bernini he sought a unity of the arts but one in which architecture dominated, sculpture appearing as mere accents to structures that, through their undulating walls and unorthodox details, are treated like sculptures themselves. Borromini was particularly influential in the north of Italy and in Central Europe.

Michelangelo Merisi da Caravaggio (1571–1610) Today considered the superstar of Roman Baroque painting, Caravaggio was widely criticized during his short career and had a greater impact in southern Italy, the Netherlands, Spain and France than in Rome itself. Born in Lombardy where keen naturalism was already a tradition, Caravaggio brought pictorial realism to a new height, discarding the kind of Classically inspired idealism practised by rivals such as Annibale Carracci and intensifying shading to increase drama. He enjoyed significant private and public patronage before fleeing Rome after killing a man in 1606. Caravaggio spent the remaining four years of his life in southern Italy and Malta.

Annibale Carracci (1560–1609) Arguably the founder of the Baroque style, Annibale introduced an earthy realism into painting in his native Bologna in the 1580s at a time when central Italian painting was dominated by artifice and virtuosity. An extraordinary draughtsman and observer of everyday life he caught the attention of Roman patrons and moved to the city in 1595 where he executed the *Loves of the Gods* at the Palazzo Farnese – the first major ceiling fresco of the Baroque. Annibale's idealized, cooler late style was promoted for decades in the work of his mostly Bolognese pupils and followers (Domenichino, Guido Reni).

Pietro da Cortona (Pietro Berrettini) (1596–16 May 1669) Considered the third of the triumvirate of Roman Baroque architects (after Bernini and Borromini), Cortona was equally important as a painter. His renovation of the façade of the church of S. Maria della Pace and its square, both inspired by theatrical structures, is one of the most ingenious illusionistic spaces in the early Baroque. Cortona also executed the second great ceiling fresco of the Baroque in the Palazzo Barberini and his stucco and frescoes in the Pitti Palace in Florence were of fundamental importance for the development of French palace decoration under Louis XIV.

François de Cuvilliés (1695–1768) The man who brought the Rococo to Central Europe was once a court dwarf to Elector Max Emanuel of Bavaria. The Elector soon recognized Cuvilliés' capabilities as a designer and sent him in the 1720s to Paris to study with Rococo pioneer Jean-François Blondel. Upon his return to Central Europe Cuvilliés designed some of the most spectacular Rococo interiors yet devised, including the apartments at the Munich Residenz, Schloß Brühl and his masterpiece, the Amalienburg pavilion in Nymphenburg Park. His influence spread far and wide thanks to volumes of engravings of his works.

Johann Bernhard Fischer von Erlach (1656–1723) Fischer von Erlach was more responsible than any other architect for bringing the Italian Baroque to Central Europe. The son of a sculptor in Graz, Fischer von Erlach spent his formative years as an artist in Venice and Rome, where he trained as a sculptor with Bernini and Johann Paul Schor. Deeply impressed with the architecture of Bernini and Borromini, as well as the ceiling frescoes of Baciccio, Fischer von Erlach introduced a monumental and classicizing late Baroque style to the Imperial court in Vienna with buildings like the Schönbrunn Palace, Imperial Library and the Karlskirche, his greatest work.

Artemisia Gentileschi (1593–c.1656) The first woman artist to enter an art academy (the Accademia del Disegno in Florence), Artemisia brought the professionalism of her father Orazio and a deep immersion in the style of Caravaggio to bear in her work. Artemisia was one of the few women to specialize in history painting, particularly mythological or religious subjects featuring powerful or sympathetic female protagonists. A shrewd businesswoman, Artemisia appealed in particular to a male clientele fascinated (or titillated) by female nudes painted by a woman, but she also painted altarpiece commissions and maintained a correspondence with leading intellectuals of her time.

Jan Josephsz van Goyen (1596–1656) Together with Jacob van Ruisdael, van Goyen created the quintessential Dutch Golden Age landscape style. He was well travelled, both at home and outside Holland, training in Leiden and then in Haarlem, the historic center of landscape painting, where he worked with Esaias van de Velde. Van Goyen soon developed a style of landscape known as the monochrome landscape: landscapes that use a very limited palette, in his case emphasizing greys and greens. An artist of extraordinary productivity, he left about 1,200 paintings and 800 drawings at the time of his death. Van Goyen's most famous pupil was Jan Steen, who married his daughter in 1649.

Guarino Guarini (1624–1683) Like Borromini, Guarini had a profound interest in Gothicism that manifested itself in complex domes with interlacing ribs and centralized plans based on stars and triangles. A Theatine priest, Guarini left his most important work in Turin, but he travelled to Paris, Lisbon and Prague, and his skeletal structures with their mystical manipulation of light appealed in particular to architects and patrons in Central Europe. He assured a lasting legacy through nine academic treatises, particularly *Disegni d'architettura civile ed* *ecclesiastica* (1686) and *Architettura civile* (1737), which served as practical design manuals for decades.

Guercino (Giovanni Francesco Barbieri) (1591–1666) Guercino (or 'squint-eye') was one of the most accomplished central Italian artists of the generation after Annibale. Born in Cento (between Bologna and Ferrara), where he kept his workshop until moving to Bologna in 1642, Guercino was essentially a self-taught artist, too young to have studied with the Carracci yet deeply influenced by them, particularly Ludovico Carracci, whom he knew. His early style combines the classicism of the Bolognese school with powerful drama and the heightened shading of Caravaggio, but his mature work features brighter, richer tones, particularly a stunning deep blue. His greatest patron was Pope Gregory XV.

Frans Hals (c.1580–1666) The master of the staccato brushstroke, Antwerp-born Hals (he worked in Haarlem) is one of the greatest portrait painters of the Dutch tradition. Through his signature choppy brushwork that animated his sitters, he became the darling of Haarlem society. Together with Rembrandt he was also a master of the *doelenstuk*, or group-portrait, in which he combined individual likenesses into a single scene united through animated expressions and gestures, and he also painted genre pictures. Hals studied with Karel van Mander, the poet and art biographer, and may have met Peter Paul Rubens. Judith Leyster was one of his pupils.

Nicholas Hawksmoor (c.1661–1736) Hawskmoor was arguably the most Baroque architect in Britain. Born in lowly circumstances in Nottinghamshire, he studied and collaborated with Christopher Wren, at the time the Surveyor of the King's Works. He caught the attention of architect Sir John Vanbrugh, who employed him in the building of Castle Howard and later collaborated with him at Blenheim Palace. Hawksmoor is perhaps best known for his six London churches, built after the 1711 act of parliament requiring the construction of fifty new religious structures. Hawksmoor's forte is his treatment of the towers which, like Borromini, combined Late Classical, Hellenistic and Gothic elements.

Melchor Pérez Holguín (1660/5–1732) One of the greatest painters of colonial Peru, Melchor Pérez (called Holguín), was active both in Potosí and nearby Charcas (Sucre). Born into a prominent mestizo family in Cochabamba, Holguín at first specialized in austere portraits of Franciscan saints with carefully observed costume textures. Yet one of his most memorable early canvases was for a secular patron: *The Entry of the Viceroy Archbishop Morcillo into Potosí*. Holguín's genius is in his landscapes, with verdant plants, splashing waterfalls, and dramatic, faceted mountains. Holguín adds Andean touches to give his paintings local colour, including indigenous costume and native flora and fauna.

William Kent (1685–1748) William Kent was the inventor of the English 'natural' garden. Although he trained as a painter in Italy under Carlo Maratta and won second prize at the Roman Accademia di S. Luca in 1713, Kent became a garden designer upon his return to England, collaborating with Richard Boyle, Lord Burlington on the garden at Chiswick Park, the first 'natural' garden. Kent and Boyle's design deliberately eschewed the symmetry and formality of André Le Nôtre, but the informal 'naturalism' they created was just as contrived, involving artificial hillocks, carefully planned lawns, and excavated ponds and canals.

Jan Kupecký (1667–1740) Often called the Rembrandt of Central Europe, Kupecký was an enormously successful portraitist in Vienna, Bohemia and Nuremberg, working for such luminaries as Charles VI of Austria, the Elector of Saxony, Augustus III the King of Poland, and Peter the Great of Russia. Trained in Italy but influenced by Dutch masters, his style was very precise with a smooth finish, which suited his keen eye for naturalism and facilitated his uncanny ability to evoke the individual character of his sitters.

Charles Le Brun (1619–1690) No one was more responsible for the creation of the Louis XIV style than his indefatigable artistic impresario, Charles Le Brun. Not only was he one of the founders of the Royal Academy of Painting and Sculpture, but he oversaw the manufacture of all the King's art projects, palace decor, garden sculpture, furnishings, and tapestries – the latter two through the industrial-scale Gobelins manufactory, of which he was director. As the First Painter to the King, Le Brun also produced massive canvases to promote the King's self-image as a conqueror and divinely-guided monarch. The interiors at Versailles are his most celebrated legacy.

André Le Nôtre (1613–1700) The Bernini

of landscape design, Le Nôtre invented the French Baroque garden, designing not only the parks at Vaux-le-Vicomte and Versailles, but also at Clagny, Maintenon, Saint-Cyr and possibly Marly. His combination of *parterres*, *allées*, *bosquets*, and sculpture groups became the standard for Baroque gardens throughout Europe. Although he only came to the King's attention in his forties, he became General Controller of the King's Buildings and received an aristocratic title. He worked at the Vatican gardens and elsewhere in Rome, and although he never visited England he designed royal gardens at Greenwich and Hampton Court.

Claude Lorrain (1600–1682) Born Claude Gellée and first trained as a pastry chef, Claude left his native Lorraine for Central Europe and Rome, where he studied with perspective painter Agostino Tassi. Claude settled in Rome for good in the late 1620s and became a friend of Poussin. His method of sketching the Roman countryside and then finishing it in his studio was influenced by Annibale, Domenichino and German emigré Adam Elsheimer, but he perfected his own balance between classicism and naturalism that was widely imitated throughout Europe. He was so popular that he copied his compositions into a 'Book of Truth' to keep imitators from stealing his inventions.

Balthasar Neumann (1687–1753) Although born into a family of clothiers and apprenticed as a bell-founder, Balthasar Neumann quickly impressed patrons with his engineering and geometrical skills, and by the end of the 1720s he was already one of Central Europe's most celebrated architects. His early style was muted and classical in a period when Rococo was ascendant and is best seen in the Würzburg Residenz. Later he adopted a lighter style with curvilinear walls and large windows as Vierzehnheiligen, which was nevertheless much altered from his original design.

Nicolas Poussin (1594–1665) Although arguably the most important French painter of the Baroque, Poussin worked almost his entire life in Rome. Although his early work was in the tempestuous style of the early Baroque, after a disastrous rejection of his only large scale altarpiece he moved to smaller easel paintings and an increasingly classical and cool style. An enthusiastic student of the Antique, he sketched Roman ruins and sculptures and used classical themes from sources such as Ovid in his work. Like Claude, and with him, he sketched the Roman countryside and then 'corrected' it in his studio in his quest for greater sobriety and compositional rigour.

Andrea Pozzo (1642–1709) A Jesuit lay brother from Trent Pozzo won the most important Jesuit commissions, not only because he worked for free but because his skill at perspective geometry allowed him to paint artificial architecture that was much cheaper than the real thing. But his triumphal style – his perspective made his ceilings seem to open up into the sky and he populated them with cloudbursts, saints and angels – also appealed to a resurgent Catholic Church and to private patrons. His technique was of fundamental importance in northern Italy and in Central Europe, partly because of the popularity of his manual on perspective architecture.

Francesco Bartolomeo Rastrelli (1700–1771) Born in Florence and raised in Paris, Rastrelli became the most important Rococo architect of Russia, thanks to the patronage of Tsarina Elizabeth. The Empress was struck by his ability to synthesize traditional Russian forms, such as the centralized multi-domed Russian church, with the latest European styles. His output was prodigious in both ecclesiastical and palace architecture and his most notable monuments are the Summer Palace at Tsarskoe Selo, the Winter Palace at the Hermitage, and the Smolny Convent (all in St Petersburg) and his masterpiece the diminutive St Andrew's Church in Kiev.

Rembrandt Harmensz van Rijn (1606–1669) The premier painter of the Dutch Baroque, Rembrandt combined extraordinary innovation with an ability to play the art market, at times living richly and at others suffering from bankruptcy. He worked most of his life in Amsterdam painting whatever his patrons wanted: history paintings, religious paintings, portraits (including group portraits such as the *Night Watch*), and most famously his nearly a hundred self-portraits. From the 1630s he adopted the deep shading of Caravaggio (but second hand, via other Dutch artists), and his style developed from precise brushwork with a smooth finish to heavy, loose handling and coarse impasto. He is equally known for his etchings and drawings.

Peter Paul Rubens (1577–1640) Rembrandt was a recluse who mostly stayed in his studio but Rubens was the consummate socialite and statesman, travelling across Europe and turning his studio into combination workshop and reception area for important visitors – based on an Italian palace it even had a sculpture hall designed after the Pantheon. After an early stay in Italy he based himself in Antwerp but travelled constantly, serving the Kings of Spain and England and the Queen of France, and combining artistic endeavours with diplomacy and even espionage. Unlike Holland, the Catholic Netherlands still gave artists the opportunity to paint major altarpiece commissions, at which Rubens excelled.

Jacob Isaackszoon van Ruisdael (c.1628–1682) Considered Holland's greatest landscape painter, van Ruisdael began painting at an early age in his birthplace of Haarlem. He was the nephew of Salomon van Ruysdael (they spelled their last name differently), another celebrated landscapist who was likely an early teacher. Although Ruisdael recorded nature in its wild state he always altered what he saw in the studio, giving trees or windmills a monumental scale that they lacked in reality. He also painted townscapes and the sea, although he is best known for his heroic interpretations of the natural world.

Giovanni Santini (Jan Blažej Santini Aichel) (1677–1723) The unrecognized genius of Baroque architecture, Santini is as original as Borromini or Guarini, both of whom were influential in his work. Although the latter were both influenced by Gothic forms, Santini created a true synthesis between Baroque and Gothic, as seen at the abbey church at Kladruby and the pilgrimage church at Žd'ár nad Sazavou. Born in Prague to an Italian family of masons, Santini trained instead as a painter and architectural designer. The turning point in his career was a trip to Rome in 1696 when he witnessed the architecture of Borromini. Santini's hybrid architecture is one of the most creative architectural innovations of the Central European Baroque.

Johann Paul Schor (Giovanni Paolo Tedesco) (1615–1674) The leading designer of the Italian Baroque, Schor was championed by his sometime collaborator Gianlorenzo Bernini, who shocked the French court by claiming that he was better than Charles Le Brun. Much more than a furniture designer, Schor combined the sculptural, stucco and architectural innovations of Bernini and Pietro da Cortona to create everything from side tables and silver sconces to coaches and stage sets. Schor was born into a family of painters in Innsbruck, and made his fortune after working for the popes in Rome from 1656 until his death. Schor was known in Italian as Giovanni Paolo Tedesco ('The German').

Giacomo Serpotta (1652–1732) Sicilian Giacomo Serpotta was the greatest stucco sculptor of the southern Italian Baroque. Working primarily for small confraternity chapels in Palermo he created an idiosyncratic version of the *bel composto* using stucco alone. He unified his interiors through a tapestry of high-relief stucco carving that he spread out over the walls like a fresco yet painted entirely in milky white. One of his innovations was the *teatrino*, a small shadow box set into the wall with tiny stucco figurines representing everything from battle scenes to religious subjects.

Karel Škréta (1610–1674) Long unfamiliar to Western art history Prague painter Škréta is now receiving his due as one of the most original followers of the Bolognese tradition outside Italy. A long and formative stay in Italy during his youth exposed him to the leading artists of Central Italy at a time when Annibale's followers were enjoying their apex. Back in Prague in 1630 he was showered with commissions for grand altarpieces. In his greatest works, such as the *St Martin Sharing his Cloak with a Begger* (1645) Škréta equals Guercino's figural monumentality, dramatic shading and manipulations of emotion.

Jan Steen (1626–1679) A Catholic genre painter working in Calvinist Holland, Steen became famous for his scenes of topsy-turvy households and taverns that combined humour with gentle moralizing, although he also produced religious paintings and mythological history paintings. Like Rembrandt he studied at Leiden University, although unlike Rembrandt he actually graduated and his literary credentials show up in the erudition behind much of his work. He worked primarily in Leiden with short spells in Haarlem, Utrecht and The Hague. Steen had the distinction of being the only painter of tavern scenes who was actually a tavern-keeper: born into a family of brewers he kept a bar in Leiden.

Anthony van Dyck (1599–1641) Rubens's junior associate Anthony van Dyck enjoyed a life of nearly equal repute, wealth, and travel, including time in Italy when he almost caught the plague while quarantined in Palermo in 1624. The loose brushwork that gave his portraits such electricity was derived from a close study of the work of Titian. Born in Antwerp, van Dyck is best known for the work he did in England, where he became the chief portraitist of Charles I and his court. His elongated figures with their studied disdain and shimmering garb encapsulated aristocratic pretention and were imitated for centuries by artists from Thomas Gainsborough to John Singer Sargent.

Diego Velázquez (1599–1660) Velázquez reinvented Spanish Baroque painting at a time when it had not yet found its voice. Born in Seville, a flourishing centre for painting, he apprenticed with Francisco Pacheco, best known for his moralistic manual for painters. Velázquez combined striking realism with mysticism and dramatic shading effects adopted indirectly from Caravaggio. His greatest works are also enlivened by a sense of enigma and expectation. Velázquez became the King's chief painter at an early age and the resulting exposure to the royal collection, particularly the Titians, had a great impact on his later work. He knew Rubens personally and later made his first of two trips to Italy.

Johannes Vermeer (1632–1675) Rivalling Rembrandt as Holland's best-known artist, Johannes Vermeer is considerably more mysterious. Virtually unknown for hundreds of years, this painter of a mere thirty-five known works kept to himself in his native Delft and left few records of his life, influences or patrons. Although his early work shows the influence of Caravaggio (second hand) he came to specialize in simple genre scenes, mostly in interiors and usually depicting one or two women. His greatest achievement is his use of light, which is not merely naturalistic but has an intimacy and mystical quality that make his canvases much more than mere depictions of everyday life.

Marie-Louise-Élisabeth Vigée-Lebrun (1755–1842) The most celebrated woman artist of the Rococo, Vigée-Lebrun was favoured by a daunting number of high-level patrons, including Queen Marie-Antoinette of France, Empress Maria Theresa of Austria, Tsarina Catherine the Great of Russia, Queen Elizabeth of Prussia, and the Prince Regent (future George IV) of England. She also had more academic credentials than most male painters of her time: she enjoyed memberships in the Académie de Saint-Luc and Académie Royale in Paris, the Roman Accademia di San Luca, the Imperial Academy of Saint Petersburg and the Berlin Academy of Painting. Her *Souvenirs de ma vie* (1835–7) was the first autobiography of a woman artist.

Jean-Antoine Watteau (1684–1721) Quintessentially Rococo yet more introspective than many of his contemporaries, Antoine Watteau was one of the most important painters of the eighteenth century. He is best known for his *fêtes galantes* (scenes of people dispersed in a landscape, usually eating, dancing or simply in conversation), and figures from the theatre, particularly the Italian *Commedia dell'Arte* who had been banned under Louis XIV. His characters have an enigmatic quality as they engage themselves in conversations, often with rapt expressions on their faces. While there is an undeniable sensuality to some of his pictures, there is none of the overt sexuality of a Boucher or Natoire.

Numbers in square brackets refer
to illustrations

Baroque & Rococo

1580 Ideal city of Zamość founded in
Poland [122]

1583 Annibale Carracci unveils his
altarpiece *Crucifixion with Saints* in
Bologna [26]

1584–1608 The first cycle of paintings
executed in the Jesuit church of Il Gesù in
Rome [88]

1597–1602 Annibale Carracci frescoes the
Farnese ceiling in Rome [13]

1599 First public commission of Caravaggio
at the Contarelli Chapel.
S. Luigi dei Francesi (Rome) [33]

1601 Jesuits build churches of São Paulo
in Diu (India) and São Paulo in Macao
(China) [225]

1605 Construction begins on the Place
Royale (Place des Vosgues) in Paris [124]

1606 After murdering Ranuccio Tomassoni,
Caravaggio flees Rome

1608 Peter Paul Rubens returns from eight
year sojourn in Italy

1609 Death of Annibale Carracci

1610 Death of Caravaggio

1611–12 Claes Jansz Visscher popularizes
the Dutch landscape with his series of
prints called '*plaisante plaetsen*' (pleasant
places)

1612 Rape trial of Artemisia Gentileschi

1613 Paulus van Vianen executes his 'Diana
Plate' [177]

1615 St Peter's Basilica completed in Rome
by Carlo Maderno and others [126]

1617–18 Rubens executes monumental
pair of altarpieces for Jesuit church in
Antwerp [46]

c.1621 Gregorio Fernández completes his
Ecce Homo [94]

1621 Philippe de Champaigne arrives in
Paris from Flanders

1622 Gianlorenzo Bernini begins *Apollo and
Daphne* for Scipione Borghese [2]

1623 Diego Velázquez appointed Royal
Painter to the Spanish King

1630 Rubens marries sixteen-year old
second wife Hélène Fourment

1632 Rembrandt paints the *Anatomy Lecture
of Dr. Nicolaes Tulp* [65]
Gianlorenzo Bernini creates his first
'speaking portrait' with *Portrait of Scipione
Borghese* [55]

1633–9 Pietro da Cortona revolutionizes
fresco painting with his *Glorification of the
Reign of Urban VIII* at the Barberini Palace
in Rome [51]

c.1635 Van Dyck paints *Portrait of Charles I
at the Hunt* [58]

1635 Rubens designs the Arch of the Mint,
a temporary triumphal arch celebrating
Spanish sovereignty over Peru [191]

1638 Nicolas Poussin begins painting *The
Arcadian Shepherds* [52]

1639 Georges de La Tour named 'Painter
to the King' of France

1640 Niklaus Geissler begins the *Dormition
Altar* at the Hofkirche in Lucerne
(Switzerland) [93]

1642 Francesco Borromini begins S. Ivo
alla Sapienza, Rome [108]

1647 Poussin develops his system
of 'modes'
Bernini begins the Cornaro Chapel in S.
Maria della Vittoria, Rome [95]

1649 Francesco Pacheco publishes *The Art
of Painting* in Seville

1650 Bernini begins the Palazzo
Montecitorio, Rome [132]

1651 Jean-Baptiste Gilles and Martínez de Oviedo begin reconstruction of the Church of the Transfiguration, Cuzco (Peru) [214]

1652 Girolamo and Carlo Rainaldi begin S. Agnese in Agone, Rome [143]

1654 Hans Ulrich Räber begins the pilgrimage church at Hergiswald (Switzerland) [90]

1656 Bernini begins St Peter's Square, Rome [125]
Pietro da Cortona, begins façade of S. Maria della Pace, Rome [142]

1657 Louis Le Vau and his team begin the Château and gardens of Vaux-le-Vicomte (France) [134]
Bernini begins the Cathedra Petri at St Peter's Basilica, Rome [102]

c.1657 Jan Vermeer paints *Girl Reading a Letter at an Open Window* [75]

1658 Bernini, Sant'Andrea al Qurinale, Rome, plan, 1658–61 [100]

1662 Jean-Baptiste Colbert founds the Gobelins Manufactory in Paris
Fireworks Display at Trinità de' Monti to celebrate birth of French Dauphin [186]

1663 Jan Steen paints *The World Upside Down* [74]

1665 Louis XIV invites Gianlorenzo Bernini to Paris to complete the Louvre
Christopher Wren visits Paris, meets Bernini

1665–8 Charles Le Brun paints the Alexander series for Louis XIV and establishes his primacy in France [53]

1668 Louis Le Vau and his team begin massive renovations of the Château of Versailles (France) [135]
Louis Le Vau and François d'Orbay begin the Collège des Quatre Nations, Paris [140]
Guarino Guarini begins S. Lorenzo, Turin (Italy) [110–11]

c.1669 Rembrandt van Rijn paints *The Return of the Prodigal Son* [49]

1670 Juan de Valdés Leal paints *In Ictu Oculi* and its pendant for the Hospital de la Caridad, Seville (Spain) [78]
Jules Hardouin-Mansart begins the Dôme des Invalides, Paris [145]

1671 Académie royale d'architecture founded in Paris

1676–85 Baciccio frescoes *The Triumph of the Name of Jesus* at the Gesù, Rome [117]

1678 Hardouin Mansart and Charles Le Brun begin the Hall of Mirrors at Versailles [157]

1685 Giacomo Serpotta begins stuccoing the Oratorio del Rosario di S. Cita, Palermo (Italy) [106]

1686 Posthumous publication of Guarino Guarini's *Disegni d'architettura civile*

1688 John Stalker and George Parker publish *A Treatise on Japanning and Varnishing*

1691 Andrea Pozzo begins frescoing the *Allegory of the Missionary Work of the Society of Jesus* at S. Ignazio, Rome [118]

1693, 1698 Pozzo publishes the two volume *Perspectiva pictorum et architectorum*

1693 Angelo Italia and others begin the ideal city of Noto (Italy) [123]

1694 Foundation of the Augustinian church at Paoay, Luzon (Philippines) [227]

1695 Wren begins reconstruction of the Royal Naval Hospital, Greenwich, London [141]

1698 Diego de Adrián completes the façade of the Compañía, Arequipa (Peru) [215]

1702 Jacob Prandtauer begins work on the Abbey of Melk (Austria) [147]

1703 Christoph Dientzenhofer begins work on Sv. Mikuláš, Prague (Czech Republic) [113]

1709 Matthäus Daniel Pöppelmann and Bathasar Permoser begin the Zwinger in Dresden (Germany) [137]
First European recipe for porcelain achieved in Saxony

1710 Foundation of the S. Michele Manufactory Rome

1715–17 Antoine Watteau paints *The Pleasures of the Ball* [76]

1716 Gaspar Ferreira begins construction of the University Library, Coimbra (Portugal) [161]

c.1716 The Oceans' Coach is assembled in Rome [185]

1717 King João V orders Johann Friedrich Ludwig to begin construction of Palace-Abbey of Mafra (Portugal) [148]

1717 or 1721 Egid Quirin and Cosmas Damian Asam begin the apse of the Abbey church at Rohr (Germany) [103]

c.1719 Brother Caspar Moosbrugger begins Einsiedeln Monastery (Switzerland) [6]

1719 Giovanni Santini begins Pilgrimage chapel of St John Nepomuk, Žd'ár nad Sazavou (Czech Republic) [115]

1721 Narciso and Diego Tomé design the Transparente in Toledo Cathedral [104]

1724 François de Cuvilliés returns from Paris, bringing Rococo to Germany

1729 Nicholas Hawksmoor completes Christ Church Spitalfields, London [146]
William Kent and Richard Boyle design the Gardens at Chiswick House (England) [203]
Pozzo's *Perspectiva pictorum et architectorum* translated into Chinese
Filippo Juvarra begins construction of Stupinigi Hunting Lodge (Italy) [136]

c.1732 William Kent takes charge of the gardens at Stowe (England) [204]

1734 François de Cuvilliés begins work on the Amalienburg Pavilion (Germany) [165–6]

1737 Guarini's *Architettura civile* is published posthumously [112]
Johann Christoph Glaubitz begins University Church of St John, Vilnius (Lithuania) [120]

1738 High Rococo style inaugurated at Germain Boffrand's Salon de la Princesse in the Hôtel Soubise, Paris [163]
Fernando de Casos y Novoa begins new façade of the Cathedral of Santiago de Compostela (Spain) [8]

1740 Hipólito Rovira y Brocandel begins work on the doorway of the Palace of the Marquis de Dos Aguas in Valencia (Spain) [10]

1741 Lancelot 'Capability' Brown takes charge of the gardens at Stowe [204]

1743 Empress Maria Theresia of Austria begins modernisation of the Schönbrunn Palace, Vienna [167]
François Boucher paints the *Brunette Odalisque* [85]
Johann Balthasar Neumann begins work on the Pilgrimage Church of Vierzehnheiligen (Germany) [150]

1745 Georg Wenzeslaus von Knobelsdorf builds the Sanssouci pavilion at Potsdam (Germany) for Frederick the Great of Prussia [236]

1747 Bartolomeo Rastrelli begins construction of St Andrew's Cathedral in Kiev (Ukraine) [210]

1749 Bartolomeo Rastrelli begins construction of the Imperial palace at Tsarskoe Selo, Puskin (Russia) [211]

1751 Franz Joseph Spiegler frescoes the nave ceiling of the Abbey church at Zwiefalten (Germany) [121]

1752–5 Barthélémy Guibal constructs the Fountains of Neptune and Amphitrite, Nancy (France) [128]

1752 Luigi Vanvitelli begins work on the Palace at Caserta (Italy) [16]

1753 The Treppenhaus at the Würzburg Residenz (Germany) completed by Bathasar Neumann and others [162]

1755 Posthumous publication of Borromini's *Opus Architectonicum*

c.1782 Marie-Louise-Élisabeth Vigée-Lebrun paints *Self-Portrait in a Straw Hat* [62]

1783 Rococo Garden of Perfect Clarity completed at the Imperial summer residence of Yuanmingyuan (China) [232]
Work begins on the Capela-Mor in the Benedictine Monastery of São Bento, Olinda (Brazil) [217]

c.1784 Carlos Luís Ferreira Amarante and others begin the Grand Staircase at the Pilgrimage Church of Bom Jesus do Monte, Braga (Portugal) [149]

1800 Antônio Francisco Lisboa begins his prophet sculptures at the pilgrimage church of Bom Jesus do Matozinhos, Congonhas do Campo (Brazil) [235]

1517 Martin Luther begins Reformation at Wittenberg (Germany)

1519 Michelangelo Buonarroti begins the New Sacristy at S. Lorenzo, Florence. Charles V becomes King of Spain and Holy Roman Emperor. Death of Leonardo da Vinci in Blois, France

1520 Death of Raphael

1526–30 Antonio da Correggio paints the *Assumption of the Virgin* in Parma Cathedral

1527 Sack of Rome by troops of the Holy Roman Empire

1531 Henry VIII proclaimed Head of the Church of England

1540 Paul III approves foundation of Society of Jesus (Jesuits)

1543 Publication of Copernicus' *On the Revolution of Heavenly Orbs*

1545 Council of Trent begins

1547 Death of Sebastiano del Piombo

1556 Charles V abdicates

1559 Scottish iconoclasm begins after inflammatory sermon by John Knox in Perth

1560 Jesuits found College of São Paulo in Goa (India)

1563 Final session of the Council of Trent, on relics and imagery

1564 Death of Michelangelo

1566 The Beeldenstorm brings religious struggle and iconoclasm to the Low Countries

1568 The Eighty Years War begins in the Low Countries between Spain and Dutch insurgents

1569 Union of Lublin creates Polish-Lithuanian Commonwealth

1571 Spanish Conquest of the Philippines

1572 St Bartholomew's Day massacre in Paris

1574 Foundation of Oratorian order in Rome

1581 Protestant Netherlands declares independence

c.1581 Final collapse of Inca Empire in Peru

1582 Gabriele Paleotti publishes *On Sacred and Profane Art*

1585 Sixtus V begins giant urban renewal project in Rome

1593 Foundation of Accademia di S. Luca, Rome

1598 Edict of Nantes, Huguenots granted freedom of religion in France

1600 English East India Company founded

1601 Clement VIII reaffirms Litany of Loreto

1602 Dutch East India Company founded

1607 Claudio Monteverdi, creator of the opera, premieres *L'Orfeo* in Mantua

1608 Foundation of Quebec City in Nouvelle-France

1609 Twelve-year truce declared between Spain and Dutch Republic

1613 Galileo publishes his study of sunspots

1614 Settlement of the Dutch colony of New Amsterdam, later renamed New York

1618 Beginning of Thirty Years War

1621 End of the Twelve Year Truce.

1622 Henry Peacham publishes *The Compleat Gentleman*

1623–44 Reign of Pope Urban VIII Barberini

1624 Great plague of Palermo

1630–54 Northeastern Brazil under Dutch governorship

1631 Mount Vesuvius erupts

1633 Galileo placed under house arrest

1640 Death of Peter Paul Rubens

1641 Death of Anthony van Dyck

1642–8 English civil war

1643–1715 Reign of Louis XIV of France

1644–55 Reign of Pope Innocent X Pamphilj

1645 Foundation of French Académie Royale de Peinture et de Sculpture

1645–69 Ottoman war with Venice

1647 Revolt of Masaniello in Naples

1648 Peace of Westphalia, end of Thirty Years War

1649 Charles I of England executed

1650 Cuzco Earthquake

1651 André Mollet publishes *Le jardin de plaisir*

1652 Dutch colony founded at Cape of Good Hope, Africa

1653 Innocent X condemns Jansenism

1660 Antonio Stradivari makes his first violins under his own name

1661 August Fouquet invites Louis XIV to Vaux-le-Vicomte

1661 Death of Cardinal Mazarin, Chief Minister of France

1663 Robert Hooke discovers cells, through a microscope

1664 Molière premieres his play *Tartuffe*

1665 Jean-Baptiste Colbert takes office as French Finance Minister

1666 Great Fire of London

1667 André Félibien publishes Conférences de l'Academie royale de peinture et de sculpture

1672–6 Polish–Ottoman war

1672–8 Franco–Dutch war

1680 The Pueblo Revolt drives the Spanish from Mexico

1685 Louis XIV revokes Edict of Nantes

1687 Isaac Newton defines the Law of Gravity

1688 William of Orange gains throne of England

1689 Nearly bankrupted by war, Louis XIV begins melting down the silver furniture of Versailles

1692–4 Famine in France kills 2 million

1693 Discovery of gold in Minas Gerais (Brazil), flooding Portugal's coffers

1694–1733 Reign of Augustus the Strong of Saxony and Poland

1696 Peter the Great becomes Tsar of Russia

1701–14 War of the Spanish Succession

1703 Peter the Great founds St Petersburg in Russia

1711 English parliament releases coal tax to finance fifty new churches for London

1715–22 French court briefly moves back to Paris from Versailles during regency

1715–74 Reign of Louis XV of France

1721 Ottoman Turkish embassy to France

1723 Antonio Vivaldi premieres his *Four Seasons*

1727 Johann Sebastian Bach premieres his *St Matthew's Passion*

1740–8 War of the Austrian Succession

1748 Discovery of the ruins of Pompeii

1751 *Encyclopédie* begun by D'Alembert and Diderot

1753 Founding of The British Museum

1755 Lisbon Earthquake

1756–63 Seven years war between Britain, Prussia and Hanover, and France, Austria, Russia, Saxony, and Sweden

1759 Voltaire publishes *Candide*

1762 Death of Tsarina Elizabeth, the greatest patron of Rococo in Russia

1764 Johann Joachim Winckelmann publishes *The History of Ancient Art*

1770 Cook lands at Botany Bay and claims east coast of Australia for Britain

1774–92 Reign of Louis XVI

1776 American War of Independence

1782 James Watt develops first rotary steam engine

1788 First steam-boat built

1789 French Revolution

1791 Mozart premieres his opera *The Magic Flute*

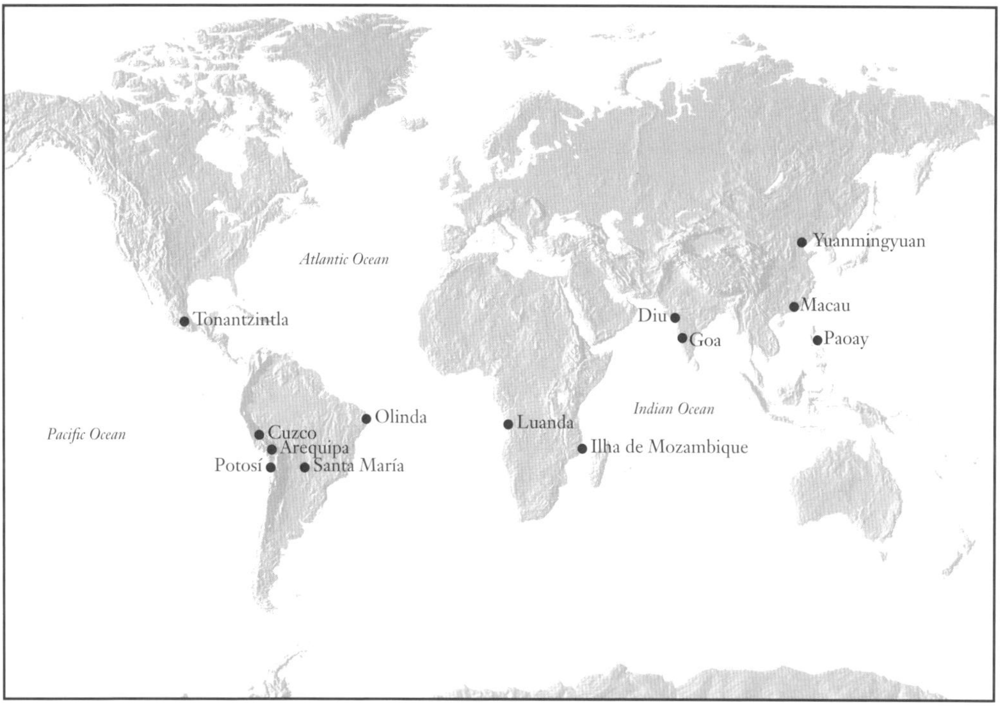

Atlantic Ocean
Pacific Ocean
Indian Ocean
Tonantzintla
Olinda
Cuzco
Arequipa
Potosí
Santa María
Luanda
Ilha de Mozambique
Diu
Goa
Yuanmingyuan
Macau
Paoay

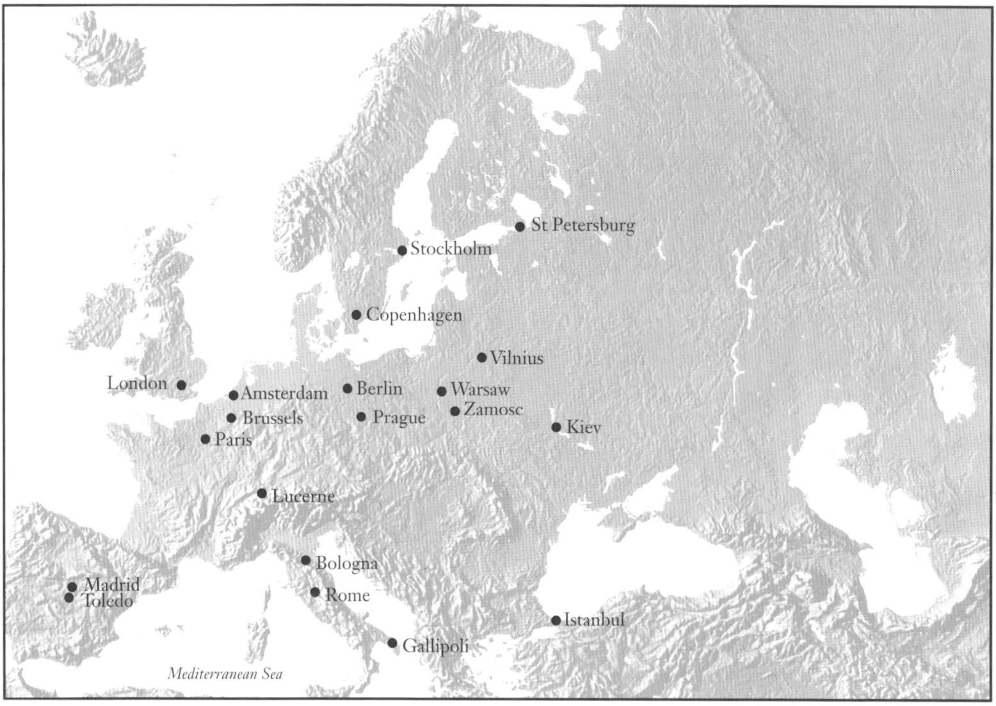

St Petersburg
Stockholm
Copenhagen
Vilnius
London
Amsterdam
Berlin
Warsaw
Brussels
Prague
Zamosc
Kiev
Paris
Lucerne
Bologna
Madrid
Toledo
Rome
Istanbul
Gallipoli
Mediterranean Sea

A daunting amount of literature exists on the Baroque and Rococo and its exploration would take many years. What follows is a very selective bibliography intended to indicate the crucial sources for each chapter and some studies that augment the arguments presented. For more comprehensive readings on Baroque and Rococo in Latin America see my *Art of Colonial Latin America* (Phaidon, 2005).

Early Sources

Giovanni Baglione, *Le vite de' pittori, scultori, et architetti*, ed. by Jacob Hess and Herwarth Röttgen, 3 vols. (Vatican City, 1995)

Filippo Baldinucci, *Notizie de' professori del disegno* (Florence, 1702)

Paola Barocchi, ed., *Trattati d'arte del Cinquecento fra manierismo e controriforma*, 2 vols. (Bari, 1960–2)

Giovanni Battista Bellori, *Le vite de' pittori, scultori et architetti moderni* (Rome, 1672)

Anthony Blunt, *Artistic Theory in Italy 1450–1600* (London, 1940)

Jonathan Brown, *Images & Ideas in Seventeenth-Century Spanish Painting* (Princeton, 1978)

Jean Chaufourier, *Les jardins de Louis XIV à Versailles*, ed. Pierre Arizzoli-Clémentel (Montreuil, 2009)

Antoine de Courtin, *Nouveau traité de la civilité qui se pratique en France parmi les honnête gens*, Marie-Claire Grassi, ed. (Clermont-Ferrand, 1998)

Denis Diderot, *Diderot on Art*, ed. and trans. by John Goodman (New Haven, 1995)

Robert Enggass and Jonathan Brown, eds., *Italian and Spanish Art 1600–1750: Sources and Documents* (Evanston, 1992)

André Félibien, *Conférences de l'Académie Royale de Peinture et de Sculpture* (Paris, 1668)

Sydney Freedberg, 'Johannes Molanus on Provocative Paintings,' in *Journal of the Warburg and Courtauld Institutes* 34 (1971), pp.229–36

Barbara Ghelfi, ed., *Il libro dei conti del Guercino, 1629–1666* (Venice, 1997)

Pamela Jones, *Federico Borromeo and the Ambrosiana* (Cambridge, 1993)

Merit Laine and Börje Magnusson, eds., *Travel Notes, 1673–77 and 1687–88: Nicodemus Tessin the Younger* (Stockholm, 2002)

Ignatius of Loyola, *The Spiritual Exercises*, ed. and trans. by Louis J. Puhl, S.J. (Chicago, 1951)

Giulio Mancini, *Considerazioni sulla pittura* (Rome, 1956)

Walter S. Melion, *Shaping the Canon: Karel van Mander's Schilder-boeck* (Chicago, 1991)

Cesare Ripa, *Iconologia*, ed. by Erna Mandowsky (Hildesheim and New York, 1970)

Louis de Rouvroy, duc de Saint-Simon, *Memoirs of Duc de Saint-Simon*, ed. and trans. by Lucy Norton (Warwick, 2007)

Peter Paul Rubens, *The Letters of Peter Paul Rubens*, ed. by Ruth Saunders Magurn (Evanston, 1955)

Filippo Titi, *Descrizione delle pitture, sculture e architetture esposte al pubblico in Roma* (Florence, 1987)

Elisabeth Vigée-Lebrun, *Memoires of Madame Vigée-Lebrun*, ed. Lionel Strachey (Gloucester, 2010)

Evelyn Carole Voelker, 'Charles Borromeo's Instructiones Fabricae et Supellectilis Ecclesiasticae, 1577. A Translation with Commentary and Analysis' (Ph.D. dissertation, University of Syracuse)

J. Waterworth, ed., *The Council of Trent Canons and Decrees* (Chicago, 1848)

Basic Studies

Germain Bazin, *Baroque and Rococo* (London, 1985)

Anthony Blunt, ed., *Baroque and Rococo: Architecture and Decoration* (New York, 1978)

Bruce Boucher, *Italian Baroque Sculpture* (London, 1998)

Beverly Louise Brown, *The Genius of Rome* (London, 2001)

Jonathan Brown, *Painting in Spain 1500–1700* (New Haven and London, 1998)

Giovanni Careri, *Giovanni, Baroques* (Princeton and Oxford, 2003)

André Chastel, *L'art français: ancien régime 1620–1775* (Paris, 2000)

Sydney Freedberg, *Circa 1600: A Revolution of Style in Italian Painting* (Cambridge MA and London, 1994)

Robert Harbison, *Reflections on Baroque* (Chicago, 2001)

Francis Haskell, *Patrons and Painters: A Study in the Relations between Italian Art and Society in the Age of the Baroque* (New York, 1963)

Julius Held and Donald Posner, *17th and 18th Century Art: Baroque painting, sculpture, Architecture* (New York, 1971)

Eberhard Hempel, *Baroque Art and Architecture in Central Europe* (Harmondsworth, 1965)

Michael Kitson, *The Age of Baroque* (London, 1966)

George Kubler and Martin Soria, *Art and Architecture in Spain and Portugal and their American Dominions, 1500–1800* (Harmondsworth, 1959)

Michael Levey, *Rococo to Revolution: Major Trends in Eighteenth-century Painting* (New York, 1966)

Denis Mahon, *Studies in Seicento Art and Theory* (Westport, 1971)

Emile Mâle, *L'art religieux après le Concile de Trente* (Paris, 1932)

John Rupert Martin, *Baroque* (New York, 1977)

Vernon Hyde Minor, *Baroque & Rococo Art & Culture* (New York, 1999)

Christian Norberg-Schulz, *Baroque Architecture* (New York, 1971)

Christian Norberg-Schulz, *Late Baroque and Rococo Architecture* (New York, 1985)

John W O'Malley and Gauvin Alexander Bailey, eds., *The Jesuits and the Arts 1540–1773* (Philadelphia, 2005)

Giuseppe Pacciarotti, *La pittura del seicento* (Torino, 1997)

Laurie Schneider-Adams, *Key Monuments of the Baroque* (New York, 2000)

Sacheverell Sitwell, *Baroque and Rococo* (New York, 1967)

Sacheverell Sitwell, *Southern Baroque Art* (New York, 1924)

Michael Snodin and Nigel Llewellyn, eds., *Baroque: Style in the Age of Magnificence* (London, 2009)

The Age of Rococo (Munich, 1958)

Rolf Toman, ed. *Baroque and Rococo* (Berlin, 2003)

Varriano, John, *Italian Baroque and Rococo Architecture* (New York and Oxford, 1986)

Hans Vlieghe, *Flemish Art and Architecture 1585–1700* (New Haven and London, 1999)

Rudolf Wittkower, Joseph Connors and Jennifer Montagu, *Art and Architecture in Italy: 1600–1750*, 3 vols (London, 1999)

Introduction

Matthew Smith Anderson, *Europe in the Eighteenth Century, 1713–1783* (London and New York, 1987)

Ronald Asch, *The Thirty Years War* (New York, 1997)

Maurice Ashley, *The Golden Century: Europe 1598–1715* (New York, 1969)

Nigel Aston, *Art and Religion in Eighteenth-Century Europe* (London, 2009)

Gauvin Alexander Bailey et al., *Hope and Healing: Painting in Italy in a Time of Plague 1500–1800* (Worcester and Chicago, 2005)

Ann Bermingham and John Brewer, eds., *The Consumption of Culture 1600–1800* (London and New York, 1995)

Jeremy Black, *Eighteenth-century Europe, 1700–1789* (New York, 1990)

James B. Collins, *The State in Early Modern France* (Cambridge, 1995)

Thomas James Dandelet, *Spanish Rome: 1500–1700* (New Haven and London, 2001)

Willam Doyle, *The Old European Order, 1660–1800* (Oxford and New York, 1978)

J. H. Elliott, *Spain and its World 1500–1700* (London and New Haven, 1990)

Marc Forster, *Catholic Revival in the Age of the Baroque* (Cambridge, 2001)

Ronnie Po-Chia Hsia, *The World of Catholic Renewal, 1540–1770* (Cambridge and New York, 1998)

Hubert Jedin, *Katholische Reformation oder Gegenreformation?* (Lucerno, 1946)

Frederick J. McGinness, *Right Thinking and Sacred Oratory in Counter-Reformation Rome* (Princeton, 1995)

David Maland, *Europe in the Seventeenth Century* (New York, 1966)

José Antonio Maravall, *Culture of the Baroque*, trans. Terry Cochran (Minneapolis, 1986)

Colin Mooers, *The Making of Bourgeois Europe* (London and New York, 1991)

Thomas Munck, *Seventeenth-century Europe: State, Conflict and the Social Order in Europe, 1598–1700* (New York, 1990)

Edward Norman, *The Roman Catholic Church: An Illustrated History* (London, 2007)

John W O'Malley, *John, The First Jesuits* (Cambridge MA, 1993)

Geoffrey Parker and Lesley M. Smith, eds, *The General Crisis of the Seventeenth Century* (London and New York, 1978)

Ludwig von Pastor, *The History of the Popes from the Close of the Middle Ages*, multiple vols. (London, 1924–53)

Theodore K Rabb, *The Struggle for Stability in Early Modern Europe* (New York, 1975)

Simon Schama, *The Embarrassment of Riches: Dutch Culture in the Golden Age* (New York, 1987)

Mariët Westermann, *A Worldly Art: The Dutch Republic, 1585–1718* (London and New York, 1996)

Chapter 1

Pamela Askew, 'Caravaggio: Outward Action, Inward Vision,' in (ed.) Stefania Macioce, *Michelangelo Merisi da Caravaggio: La vita e le opere attraverso i documenti* (Rome, 1996), pp.248–69

Gauvin Alexander Bailey, *Between Renaissance and Baroque: Jesuit Art in Rome, 1560–1610* (Toronto, 2003)

Andrea Bayer, *Painters of Reality: The Legacy of Leonardo and Caravaggio in Lombardy* (New York, 2004)

Daniele Benati et al., *The Drawings of Annibale Carracci* (Washington, 1999)

Jonathan Brown, *Velázquez* (New Haven and London, 1988)

Charles Dempsey, *Annibale Carracci and the Beginnings of Baroque Style* (Florence, 1977)

Charles Dempsey, *Annibale Carracci: the Farnese Gallery, Rome* (New York, 1995)

David Franklin and Sebastian Schütze, *Caravaggio & his Followers in Rome* (Ottawa, 2011)

Jack Freiburg, *The Lateran in 1600: Christian Concord in Counter-Reformation Rome* (Cambridge, 1995)

Walter Friedlaender, *Caravaggio Studies* (New York, 1969)

John Gash, *Caravaggio* (London, 2003)

Marcia Hall, *After Raphael: Painting in Central Italy in the Sixteenth Century* (Cambridge, 1999)

Pamela Jones, *Altarpieces and Their Viewers in the Churches of Rome from Caravaggio to Guido Reni* (Aldershot, 2008)

Pamela Jones and Thomas Worcester, eds. *From Rome to Eternity: Catholicism and the Arts in Italy, ca. 1550–1650* (Leiden, Boston, Cologne, 2002)

Helen Langdon, *Caravaggio: A Life* (New York, 2000)

Erik Larsen, *Seventeenth Century Flemish Painting* (Freren, 1985)

Metropolitan Museum of Art, *The Age of Caravaggio* (New York and Milan, 1985)

Franco Mormando, ed., *Saints & Sinners: Caravaggio & the Baroque Image* (Boston, 1999)

Benedict Nicholson and Christopher Wright, *Georges de la Tour* (London, 1974)

Catherine Puglisi, *Caravaggio* (London, 1998)

Giuseppe Scandiani, ed., *Sebastiano del Piombo* (Rome, 2008)

Otto von Simson, *Peter Paul Rubens (1577–1640)* (Mainz, 1996)

John Spike, *Caravaggio* (New York and London, 2001)

David Stone, *Guercino: Catalogo completo* (Florence, 1991)

David Stone, *Guercino: Master Draftsman* (Padua, 1991)

Claudio Strinati, ed., *Caravaggio* (Rome, 2010)

Claudio Strinati and Alessandro Zuccari, *I Caravaggeschi: percorsi e protagonisti* (Rome, 2010)

Arthur J. Wheelock, *Rembrandt's Late Religious Portraits* (Washington and Chicago, 2005)

Rudolf Wittkower and Irma B. Jaffe, eds. *Baroque Art: The Jesuit Contribution* (NewYork, 1972)

Zell, Michael, *Reframing Rembrandt: Jews and the Christian Image in Seventeenth-century Amsterdam* (Berkeley, 2002)

Federico Zeri, *Pittura e controriforma* (Vicenza, 1997)

Alessandro Zuccari, *Arte e committenza nella Roma di Caravaggio* (Torino, 1984)

Chapter 2

Svetlana Alpers, *The Art of Describing: Dutch Art in the Seventeenth Century* (Chicago, 1983)

Svetlana Alpers, *Rembrandt's Enterprise: The Studio and the Market* (Chicago, 1988)

Charles Avery, *Bernini: Genius of the Baroque* (Boston, 1997)

Susan Barnes, ed., *Van Dyck, A Complete Catalogue of the Paintings* (New Haven and London, 2004)

Oskar Bätschmann, *Nicolas Poussin: Dialectics of Painting* (London, 1990)

Maria Grazia Bernardini and Maurizio Fagiolo dell'Arco, *Gian Lorenzo Bernini: regista del barocco* (Milan, 1999)

R. Ward Bissell, *Artemisia Gentileschi and the Authority of Art* (University Park, 1999)

Per Bjurströöm, 'The Carracci Brothers and Landscape Drawing', *Konsthistorisk tidskrift/Journal of Art History*, 71:4 (2002), pp.204–17

Anthony Blunt, *Nicholas Poussin* (London, 1995)

Christopher Brown, *Images of a Golden Past: Dutch Genre Painting of the 17th Century* (New York, 1984)

H. Perry Chapman et al., *Jan Steen: Painter and Storyteller* (Washington, 1996)

H. Perry Chapman, *Rembrandt's Self-Portraits: A Study in Seventeenth-century Identity* (Princeton, 1990)

Keith Christiansen and Judith W. Mann, *Orazio and Artemisia Gentileschi* (New Haven and London, 2001)

Max Friedländer, *Landscape, Portrait, Still-Life* (New York, 1963)

Rudy Fuchs, *Dutch Painting* (London, 1984)

Mary D. Garrard, *Artemisia Gentileschi* (Princeton, 1989)

Ivan Gaskell and Michiel Jonker, eds., *Vermeer Studies* (Washington, 1998)

Walter S. Gibson, *Pleasant Places: the Rustic Landscape from Breughel to Ruisdael* (Berkeley and Los Angeles, 2000)

Carl Goldstein, *Visual Fact over Verbal Fiction* (Cambridge, 1988)

Carl Goldstein, *Teaching Art: Academies and Schools from Vasari to Albers* (Cambridge, 1996)

Lawrence Gowing, *Vermeer* (Berkeley, 1997)

Klaus Grimm, *Stilleben: Die niederländischen und deutschen Meister* (Stuttgart and Zürich, 1988)

Howard Hibbard, *Bernini* (Harmondsworth, 1982)

Howard Hibbard, *Caravaggio* (New York, 1985)

Margaretha Rossholm Lagerlöf, *Ideal Landscape: Annibale Carracci, Nicolas Poussin and Claude Lorrain* (New Haven and London, 1990)

Erik Larsen, *The Paintings of Anthony van Dyck* (Freren, 1988)

Catherine Levesque, *Journey through Landscape in Seventeenth-Century Holland* (University Park, 1994)

Jennifer Montagu, *Roman Baroque Sculpture: The Industry of Art* (New Haven and London, 1989)

National Gallery of Art, *The Age of Correggio and the Carracci* (Washington, 1986)

National Gallery of Art, *Johannes Vermeer* (New Haven and London, 1995)

National Museum of Women in the Arts, *Italian Women Artists from Renaissance to Baroque* (Turin, 2007)

Konrad Oberhuber, *Poussin, The Early Years: The origins of French Classicism* (Fort Worth, 1988)

Nikolaus Pevsner, *Academies of Art, Past and Present* (Cambridge, 1940)

John Pope-Hennessy, *Italian High Renaissance and Baroque Sculpture* (New York, 1985)

Donald Posner, *Antoine Watteau* (Ithaca, 1984)

Jakob Rosenberg, *Rembrandt: Life and Work* (Ithaca, 1980)

Norbert Schneider, *Stilleben: Realität und Symbolik der Dinge. Die Stillebenmalerei der frühen Neuzeit* (Cologne, 1994)

Gary Schwartz, *Rembrandt: His Life, His Paintings* (London, 1991)

John Beldon Scott, *Images of Nepotism: The Painted Ceilings of Palazzo Barberini* (Princeton, 1991)

Sam Segal, *Flowers and Nature: Netherlandish Flower Painting of Four Centuries* (The Hague, 1990)

Mary D. Sheriff, *The Exceptional Woman: Elisabeth Vigée-Lebrun and the Cultural Politics of Art* (Chicago, 1996)

Seymour Slive, *Dutch Painting 1600–1800* (New Haven and London, 1995)

Seymour Slive, *Frans Hals*, 2 vols. (London, 1970)

Richard Spear et al., *Domenichino: 1581–1641* (Milan, 1996)

Wolfgang Stechow, *Dutch Landscape Painting of the Seventeenth Century* (Oxford, 1981)

Paul Taylor, *Dutch Flower Painting 1600–1720* (New Haven and London, 1995)

Janis Tomlinson, *From El Greco to Goya: Painting in Spain, 1561–1828* (New York, 1997)

Mary Vidal, *Watteau's Painted Conversations* (New Haven and London, 1992)

David Wakefield, *Boucher* (London, 2005)

E. John Walford, *Jacob van Ruisdael and the Perception of Landscape* (New Haven and London, 1991)

Genevieve Warwick, 'Speaking Statues: Bernini's *Apollo and Daphne* at the Villa Borghese', Art History 27:3 (2004), pp.353–81

Ellis Waterhouse, *Painting in Britain 1530–1790* (New Haven and London, 1993)

Ann Thomas Wilkins, 'Bernini and Ovid: Expanding the Concept of Metamorphosis', *International Journal of the Classical Tradition*, 6:3 (Winter 2000), pp.383–408

Chapter 3

Fritz Barth, *Santini 1677–1723: Ein Baumeister des Barock in Böhmen* (Ostfildern, 2004)

Alberti Battisti, ed., *Andrea Pozzo* (Milan, Trent, 1996)

Eugenio Bianchi, *Andrea Pozzo pittore e prospettico in Italia settentrionale* (Trent 2009)

Anthony Blunt, *Borromini* (Cambridge MA 1979)

Xavier Bray, *The Sacred Made Real: Spanish Painting and Sculpture 1600–1700* (London, 2009)

Giovanni Careri, *Bernini: Flights of Love, the Art of Devotion* (Chicago and London, 1995)

I colori del bianco: gli stucchi dei Serpotta a Palermo (Palermo, 1996)

Joseph Connors, *Borromini and the Roman Oratory* (Cambridge MA 1982)

Ralph Dekoninck, *Ad Imaginem: Statuts, fonctions et usages de l'image dans la literature spirituelle jésuite du XVIIe siècle* (Geneva, 2005)

Robert Enggass, *The Painting of Baciccio* (University Park, 1964)

Peter Felder, *Luzerner barockplastik* (Lucerne, 2004)

Karsten Harries, *The Bavarian Rococo Church* (New Haven and London, 1983)

Henry-Russell Hitchcock, *Rococo Architecture in Southern Germany* (London, 1968)

Pavel Kalina, 'In opere gotico unicus: the Hybrid Architectures of Jan Blažej Santini-Aichl and Patterns of Memory in Post-Reformation Bohemia,' in *Umění* LVIII (2010), pp.42–56

Anna C Knaap, 'Meditation, Ministry, and Visual Rhetoric in Peter Paul Rubens's Program for the Jesuit Church in Antwerp', in John W O'Malley et al. (eds.) *The Jesuits II* (Toronto, 2006), pp.157–81

Nanette and Raimund Kolb, *Franz Joseph Spiegler: Kostbarkeiten barocker Malerei* (Passau, 1991)

Irving Lavin, *Bernini and the Unity of Visual Arts*, 2 vols. (New York and London, 1980)

Anna Lo Bianco, *Pietro da Cortona, 1597–1669* (Milan, 1997)

Stefania Macioce, *Undique spendent: Aspetti della pittura sacra nella Roma di Clemente VIII Aldobrandini* (Rome, 1990)

Martin Mádl et al., eds., *Baroque Ceiling Painting in Central Europe* (Prague, 2001)

John Rupert Martin, *The Ceiling Paintings for the Jesuit Church in Antwerp* (London, 1968)

Harry Alan Meek, *Guarino Guarini and his Architecture* (New Haven and London, 1988)

Mindaugas Paknys, *Lietuvos Didžiosios Kunigaikštijos dailės ir architektūros istorija* (Vilnius, 2009)

Louise Rice, *The Altars and Altarpieces of New St Peter's: Outfitting the Basilica, 1621–1666* (Cambridge, 1997)

Jeffrey Chipps Smith, *Sensuous Worship: Jesuits and the Art of the Early Catholic Reformation in Germany* (Princeton, 2002)

Victor I Stoichita, *Visionary Experience in the Golden Age of Spanish Art* (London, 1995)

V. Viale, ed., *Guarino Guarini e l'internazionalità del Barocco*, 2 vols (Torino, 1970)

Mark S. Weil, 'The Devotion of the Forty Hours and Roman Baroque Illusions,' in *Journal of the Warburg and Courtauld Institutes* 37 (1974), pp.218–48

Rudolf Wittkower, *Gothic vs. Classic: Architectural Projects in Seventeenth-Century Italy* (New York, 1974)

Chapter 4

Gustav Barthel and Walter Hege, *Barockkirchen in Altbayern und Schwaben* (Munich, Berlin, 1960)

Anthony Blunt, *Art and Architecture in France 1500–1700* (New Haven and London, 1999)

Günter Brucher, ed., *Die Kunst des Barock in Österreich* (Salzburg and Vienna, 1994)

C. G. Canale, *Noto: la struttura continua della città tardo-barocca* (Palermo, 1976)

Angela Delaforce, *Art and Patronage in Eighteenth-Century Portugal* (Cambridge, 2002)

Kerry Downes, *The Architecture of Wren* (New York, 1982)

Pierre de la Ruffinière DuPrey, *Hawksmoor's London Churches* (Chicago, 2000)

Mario Manieri Elia, *Barocco leccese* (Milan, 1989)

Howard Hibbard, *Carlo Maderno and Roman Architecture, 1580–1630* (University Park, 1971)

Andrew Hopkins, *Italian Architecture from Michelangelo to Borromini* (London, 2002)

Mariusz Karpowicz, *Baroque in Poland* (Warsaw, 1991)

Jay Levenson, *The Age of the Baroque in Portugal* (Washington, 1993)

Michael Levey, *Giambattista Tiepolo: His Life and Art* (New Haven and London, 1986)

W. H. Lewis, *The Splendid Century: Life in the France of Louis XIV* (Chicago, 1997)

Norbert Lieb, *Barock Kirchen zwischen Donau und Alpen* (Munich, 1997)

Norbert Lieb, *Die Vorarlberger Barockbaumeister* (Munich and Zürich, 1976)

Tod Marder, *Bernini and the Art of Architecture* (New York, 1998)

Jaromir Neumann, *Das Bömische Barock* (Hannover, 1970)

Werner Hager, *Die Bauten des Deutschen Barocks* (Jena, 1942)

Jean-Marie Pérouse de Montclos, *Histoire de l'architecture française de la renaissance à la révolution* (Paris, 1995)

Jean-Marie Pérouse de Montclos, *Vaux-le-Vicomte* (Paris, 1997)

Friedrich Polleroß, ed., *Reiselust & Kunstgenuss: Barockes Böhmen, Mähren und Österreich* (Petersberg, 2004)

Jorg Martin Merz and Anthony Blunt, *Pietro da Cortona and Roman Baroque Architecture* (New Haven and London, 2008)

John Summerson, *Architecture in Britain 1530–1800* (New Haven and London, 1993)

Wend Von Kalnein, *Architecture in France in the 18th Century* (New Haven and London, 1995)

Vít Vlnas, ed., *The Glory of the Baroque in Bohemia* (Prague, 2001)

Giedra Zokaityt, ed., *Lietuvos bažnyčios* (Vilnius, 2009)

Chapter 5

Alvar González-Palacios, 'Bernini as a furniture designer,' in *The Burlington Magazine* 112, 812 (November 1970), pp.719–22

Philippe Béchu and Christian Taillard, *Les hôtels de Soubise et de Rohan-Strasbourg* (Paris, 2004)

Edgar Peters Bowron and Joseph J Rishel, *Art in Rome in the Eighteenth Century* (Philadelphia, 2000)

Frances Buckland, 'Silver Furnishings at the Court of France, 1643–70,' in *The Burlington Magazine* 131, 1034 (May 1989), pp.328–36

Peter Burke, *The Fabrication of Louis XIV* (New Haven and London, 1992)

Malcolm Campbell, *Pietro da Cortona at the Pitti Palace: A Study of the Planetary Rooms and Related Projects* (Princeton, 1977)

Benedetta Craveri, *The Age of Conversation* (New York, 2006)

Pearl M Ehrlich, 'Johann Paul Schor' (Ph.D. dissertation, Columbia University)

Alain Gruber, ed., *The History of the Decorative Arts: Classicism and Baroque in Europe* (New York, 1992)

Carl Hernmarck, *The Art of the European Silversmith 1430–1830* (London, 1977)

Hugh Honour, *Goldsmiths and Silversmiths* (New York, 1971)

Dawn Jacobson, *Chinoiserie* (London, 1993)

Fiske Kimball, *The Creation of the Rococo* (Philadelphia, 1943)

Philippe Minguet, *Esthétique du rococo* (Paris, 1966)

Katie Scott, *The Rococo Interior* (New Haven and London, 1995)

Rolf Sonnemann and Eberhard Wächtler, eds., *Johann Friedrich Böttger: Der Erfindung des Europäischen Porzellans* (Leipzig, 1982)

J. R. ter Molen, *Van Vianen*, 2 vols (Rotterdam, 1984)

Peter Thornton, *Form & Decoration: Innovation in the Decorative Arts 1470–1870* (London, 1998)

Marjorie Trusted, *The Arts of Spain: Iberia and Latin America 1450–1700* (London, 2007)

Stefanie Walker and Frederick Hammond, eds., *Life and the Arts in the Baroque Palaces of Rome* (New Haven and London, 1999)

Chapter 6

Richard Alewyn, *Das große Welttheater. Die Epoche der höfischen Feste* (Munich, 1989)

Robert W. Berger, *In the Garden of the Sun King: Studies on the Park of Versailles under Louis XIV* (Washington, 1985)

Per Bjurström, *Feast and Theatre in Queen Christina's Rome* (Stockholm, 1966)

Gisèle Caumont, *La main du jardinier, l'oeuvre du graveur: Le Nôtre et les jardins disparus de son temps* (Sceaux, 2000)

David Coffin, *Gardens and Gardening in Papal Rome* (Princeton, 1991)

Michael Conan, ed., *Baroque Garden Cultures: Emulation, Sublimation, Subversion* (Washington, 2005)

Marcello Fagiolo, Bruno Adorni and Maria Luisa Madonna, *Barocco romano e barocco italiano: il teatro, l'effimero, l'allegoria, numerosi documenti* (Rome, 1985)

Maurizio Fagiolo dell'Arco, *La festa barocca* (Rome, 1997)

Ernest de Ganay, *André Le Nostre 1613–1700* (Paris, 1962)

Hazlehurst Hamilton, *Gardens of Illusion: the Genius of André Le Nostre* (Nashville, 1980)

Frederick Hammond, 'The Creation of a Roman Festival: Barberini Celebrations for Christina of Sweden,' in (eds.) Maria Giulia Barberini et al., *Life and the Arts in the Baroque Palaces of Rome* (New Haven and London, 1999), pp.54–7

John Dixon Hunt, *William Kent: Landscape Garden Designer* (London, 1987)

Wilfred Hansmann, *Gartenkunst der Renaissance und des Barock* (Cologne, 1983)

John Dixon Hunt and Erik de Jong, eds., *The Anglo-Dutch Garden in the Age of William and Mary* (London, 1988)

Pierre-André Lablaude, *Les jardins de Versailles* (Paris, 1995)

J. R. Mulryne et al., *Europa Triumphans: Court and Civic Festivals in Early Modern Europe* (Aldershot, 2004)

Jan K. Ostrowski, *Land of the Winged Horseman: Art in Poland 1572–1764* (Alexandria VA, 1999)

Klaus-Dieter Reus and Markus Lerner, *Faszination der Bühne: Barockes Welttheater in Bayreuth, Barocke Bühnentechnik in Europa* (Bayreuth, 2001)

Pavel Slavko, *The Castle Theatre in Český Krumlov* (Česky Krumlov, 2001)

Mårtin Snickare, ed., *Tessin: Nicodemus the Younger, Royal Architect and Visionary* (Stockholm, 2002)

Ian H. Thompson, *The Sun King's Garden: Louis XIV, André Le Nôtre and the Creation of the Gardens of Versailles* (London, 2006)

Heinrich Tintelnot, *Barocktheater und barocke Kunst* (Berlin, 1939)

Helen Watanabe-O'Kelley, *Court Culture in Dresden* (London, 2002)

Kenneth Woodbridge, *Princely Gardens: the Origins and Development of the French Formal Style* (London, 1986)

Chapter 7

Rosa María Acosta de Arias Schreiber, *Fiestas coloniales urbanas* (Lima, 1997)

Gauvin Alexander Bailey, *The Andean Hybrid Baroque: Convergent Cultures in the Churches of Colonial Peru* (Notre Dame, 2010)

Gauvin Alexander Bailey, *Art of Colonial Latin America* (London, 2005)

Gauvin Alexander Bailey, *Art on the Jesuit Missions in Asia and Latin America* (Toronto, 1999)

Clara Bargellini and Michael K. Komanesky, *The Arts of the Missions of Northern New Spain* (Mexico City, 2009)

Norma Campos Vera, ed., *Barroco andino*, 4 vols. (La Paz, 2003–7)

James Cracraft, *The Petrine Revolution in Russian Architecture* (Chicago, 1988)

Pedro Dias, *Arte Indo-Portuguesa* (Coimbra, 2004)

Pedro Dias, *História da arte portuguesa no mundo (1415–1822)*, 2 vols, (Navarre, 1998)

Guillermo Furlong, *Misiones y sus pueblos de Guaranies* (Buenos Aires, 1962)

César Guillén Nuñez, *Macao's Church of Saint Paul: A Glimmer of the Baroque in China* (Hong Kong, 2009)

Instituto Cultural de Macau, *A Monument Towards the Future: St Paul's Ruins* (Macau, 1994)

Norma Ipac-Alarcon, *Philippine Architecture During the Pre-Spanish and Spanish Periods* (Manila 1991)

Regalado Trota José, *Simbahan: Church Art in Colonial Philippines 1565–1898* (Manila, 1991)

Alexandra Kennedy, ed. *Arte de la Real Audiencia de Quito*, (Quito, 2002)

Doğan Kuban, 'Influences sur l'art européen sur l'architecture Ottomane au XVIIIème siècle,' in *Palladio* V (1955), pp.149–57

Doğan Kuban, 'Notes on Building Technology of the 18th Century. The Building of the Mosque of Nuruosmaniye at Istanbul,' in *I. Uluslararasi Türk-Islam Bilim ve Teknoloji Tarihi Kongresi 14–18 Eylül 1981* (Istanbul, 1981), pp.271–98

Doğan Kuban, *Türk Barok Mimarisi Hakkinda bir Deneme* (Istanbul, 1954)

Jay Levenson, ed., *Encompassing the Globe: Portugal and the World in the 16th and 17th Centuries*, 3 vols (Washington, 2007)

Janna Lytvynchuk, *St Andrew's Church* (Kiev, 2006)

Macau Museum of Art, *The Golden Exile: Pictorial Expressions of the School of Western Missionaries* (Macau, 2002)

E. Mamboury, 'L'art turc du XVIIIème siècle,' in *La turquie kemaliste* 19 (1937), pp.2–11

José de Mesa and Teresa Gisbert, *La pintura en los museos de Bolivia* (La Paz and Cochabamba, 1990)

Ramón Mujica Pinilla, ed., *Barroco Peruano*, 2 vols (Lima, 2002–3)

Ramón Mujica Pinilla, *Orígines y devociones virreinales de la imaginería popular* (Lima, 2008)

Elena Phipps et al., eds., *The Colonial Andes: Tapestries and Silverwork, 1530-1830* (New York, 2004)

Josefina Plá, *El barrocco hispano-Guaraní* (Asunción, 2006)

Myriam Andrade Ribeiro de Oliveira, *O rococó religioso no Brasil e seus antecedentes Europeus* (São Paulo, 2003)

Joseph J Rishel, ed., *The Arts in Latin America 1492–1820* (Philadelphia, 2006)

Cornelia Skodock, *Barock in Russland: zum oeuvre des Hofarchitekten Francesco Bartolomeo Rastrelli* (Wiesbaden, 2006)

Epilogue

Pierre Francastel, 'L'esthétique des lumières,' in (ed.) Pierre Francastel, *Utopie et institutions au XVIIIe.siècle. Le pragmatism des lumières* (Paris, 1963), pp.335–57

Michael Fried, *Absorption and Theatricality, Painting and Beholder in the Age of Diderot* (Chicago 1980)

Dena Goodman, *The Republic of Letters: A Cultural History of the French Enlightenment* (Cornell, 1996)

Melissa Hyde, *Making up the Rococo: François Boucher and his Critics* (Los Angeles, 2006)

Melissa Hyde and Mark Ledbury, eds., *Rethinking Boucher* (Los Angeles, 2006)

David Irwin, *Neoclassicism* (London, 1997)

National Gallery in Prague, *Mannerist and Baroque in Bohemia* (Prague, 2005)

Florian Matzner, *Johann Conrad Schlaun 1695–1773: Das Gesamtwerk* (Stuttgart, 1995)

Jaromír Neumann, *Škrétove: Karel Škréta a jeho syn* (Prague, 2000)

Paula Rea Radisich, *Hubert Robert: Painted Spaces of the Enlightenment* (London, 1998)

Mary D. Sheriff, *Moved by Love, Inspired Artists and Deviant Women in Eighteenth-Century France* (Chicago, 2004)

Rémy Saisselin, *The Enlightenment against the Baroque: Economics and Aesthetics in the Eighteenth Century* (Berkeley, 1992)

Photographic credits

AA World Travel Library/Alamy: 135; AFP/Getty Images: 218; Åke E:son Lindman: 202; akg-images: 67; akg-images/Album/Oronoz: 222; akg-images/De Agostini: 28; akg-images/Erich Lessing: 166; akg-images/euroluftbild.de: 242; akg-images/Gilles Mermet: 221; akg-images/Rabatti - Domingie:158; akg-images/Schutze/Rodemann: 21; Alamy: 19; Albert Knapp/Alamy:128; Alinari Archives, Florence: 37, 66; Alinari Archives/Corbis: 39; Angelo Hornak/Alamy: frontispiece, 132, 165; Archivo General del IPCE, Madrid: 94; Aref MostafaZadeh: 230; B.O'Kane/Alamy: 113; Barry Charles Hitchcox/fotoLibra: 205; Bildarchiv Monheim GmbH/Alamy: 6, 8, 162, 199; Blauel/Gnamm/ARTOTHEK: 184; Chuck Pefley/Alamy: 9; Comune di Roma, Museo di Roma: 186; Corbis: 73; Country Life Picture Library: 159; Danita Delimont/Alamy: 224; Darko Sustersic: 220; DEA/C. SAPPA/De Agostini/Getty Images: 200; Dinodia/age Fotostock/Getty Images: 223; DK Limited/Corbis: 248; dk/Alamy: 164; Europe/Alamy: 52; Florian Monheim/Arcaid/Corbis: 150; Foto Staatsgalerie Stuttgart: 61; Frans Hals Museum, Haarlem, photo Margareta Svensson: 64; Gauvin Alexander Bailey: 93, 115, 116, 120, 131, 134, 145, 152, 203, 216, 217, 241; Gavin Hellier/Robert Harding World Imagery/Corbis: 210; Hemera/Thinkstock: 137; Herve Champollion/akg-images: 105, 163; Il Gesu, Rome, photo Gabriele Viviani: 88; Image Source/Corbis: 146; imagebroker/Alamy: 235; Images Etc Ltd/Alamy: 5; INDEX/Arusa: 35; INDEX/Giulia Cotti: 26; INDEX/Marco Ravenna: 106; INDEX/Soprintendeza PSAE, Urbino: 29; INDEX/Vasari: 22; INDEX/Zeno Colantoni: 15; INTERFOTO/Alamy: 91, 169; iStockphoto/Thinkstock: 138; Jan Wiodarczyk/Alamy: 122; Jeffrey Chipps Smith: 89; JLImages/Alamy: 126; John Heseltine/Corbis: 111; John McCabe/Getty Images: 225; Jose Elias/Lusoimages-Landmarks/Alamy: 185; JTB Photo Communications, inc./Alamy: 148; Judy de Bustamante: 219; Juraj Kaman: 246; Ken McEwen: 151; Kevin Foy/Alamy: 10; Kirchengemeinde Creglingen: 92; Lebrecht Music and Arts Photo Library/Alamy: 46; Library and Archives Canada/photo Brechin Group: 82; Lonely Planet Images/Alamy: 211; LOOK die Bildagentur der Fotografen GmbH/Alamy: 121; Lubos Paukeje/Alamy: 237; Marcello Paternostro/AFP/Getty Images: 123; mauritius images GmbH/Alamy: 101; Michael Klinec/Alamy: 212; Michael Wald/Alamy: 141; Michele Falzone/Alamy: 102, 226; Museo di Roma/Photo Scala, Florence: 189; National Gallery in Prague: 247; National Palace Museum, Taiwan, Republic of China: 232; Patrice Latron/Corbis: 124; Patrons' Permanent Fund, image courtesy of National Gallery of Art, Washington DC: 36; Paul Brown/Alamy: 213; Pediconi Barritt/Alamy: 109; Peter Barritt/Alamy: 109; Photo Scala, Florence: 1, 13, 54, 87, 103, 104, 143, 168; Photo Scala, Florence – courtesy of the Ministero Beni e Att. Culturali: 4, 18, 25, 31, 55, 60, 97, 108; Photo Scala, Florence/BPK, Bildagentur fuer Kunst, Kultur und Geschichte, Berlin: 47, 75, 80, 84; Photo Scala, Florence/Fondo Edifici di Culto – Min. dell'Interno: 96, 98, 117, 118; Photo Scala, Florence/Luciano Romano: 16; Photo Scala, Florence/Luciano Romano/Fondo Edifici di Culto - Min. dell'Interno: 119; Photo Scala, Florence/Luciano Romano/Ministero Beni e Att. Culturali: 2; Photo Scala, Florence/Mauro Ranzani: 32; Photo Scala, Florence/Ministero Beni e Attivita Culturali: 50; Rijksmuseum, Amsterdam: 20, 172, 177, 178, 181, 183; RMN (Château de Versailles)/Christian Jean/Jean Schormans: 170; RMN (Château de Versailles)/Gérard Blot/Hervé Lewandowski: 155; RMN (Domaine de Chantilly)/Franck Raux: 12; RMN (Musée du Louvre)/Gérard Blot: 43; RMN/Franck Raux: 44; RMN/Martine Beck-Coppola: 171, 176; RMN/Michele Bellot: 30; Robert Harding Picture Library/Alamy: 215; Robert Holmes/Corbis: 228; Royal Castle, Warsaw, photo Andrezej Ring: 188; Royal Library of Belgium: 187, 191; Saint Louis Art Museum, Museum Purchase and gift of Edward Mallinckrodt, Sydney M Shoenberg Sr, Horace Morison, Mrs Florence E Bing, Morton D May in honor of Perry T Rathbone, Mrs James Lee Johnson Jr, Oscar Johnson, Fredonia J Moss, Mrs Arthur Drefs, Mrs W Welles Hoyt, J Lionberger Davis, Jacob M Heimann, Virginia Linn Bullock in memory of her husband George Benbow Bullock, C Wickham Moore, Mrs Lyda D'Oench Turley and Miss Elizabeth F D'Oench, and J Harold Pettus, and bequests of Mr Alfred Keller and Cora E Ludwig, by exchange: 83; Saverio Maria Gallotti/Alamy: 130; Sekretariat Hergiswald: 90; Sergio Azenha/Alamy: 161; Sławomir Staciwa/Alamy: 139; Sotheby's Picture Library: 81; State Castle Ceský Krumlov, photo Pavel Slavko: 197; Steve Vidler/Alamy: 127; Sylvain Sonnet/Corbis:238, 245; TAO Images Limited/Alamy: 234; The Art Archive/Alamy: 56, 78, 79, 175; The British Library Board. Shelfmark 605.d.27 (9): 190; The British Library Board. Shelfmark C.33.1.2: 192; The British Library Board. Shelfmark C.33.1.2: 193; The British Library Board. Shelfmark 143.f.3: 195; The British Library Board. Shelfmark 605.e.30 (1): 194; The British Library Board. Shelfmark 813.h.17: 196; The Cleveland Museum of Art: 179; The Metropolitan Museum of Art/Art Resource/Scala, Florence: 71, 173, 244; The Museum of Fine Arts Budapest, photo Jozsa Denes/Photo Scala, Florence: 69; The Museum of Fine Arts Budapest/Scala, Florence: 42; The Museum of Fine Arts, Houston; Museum purchase with funds provided by the Agnes Cullen Arnold Endowment Fund: 45; The National Gallery, London/Photo Scala, Florence: 24, 27, 62; The National Trust Photolibrary/Alamy: 240; The Print Collector/Alamy: 17; Travel Division Images/Alamy: 125; Travel Pictures/Alamy: 213; TuttItalia/Alamy: 213; V&A Images. All Rights Reserved: 174, 180, 182, 233; Vanni Archive/Corbis: 153; Vito Arcomano/Alamy: 142; Vladimir Khirman/Alamy: 3; Vranov Castle: 160; wcities.com: 133; White Images/Photo Scala, Florence: 53, 58, 76, 140, 156; Widener Collection, Image courtesy National Gallery of Art, Washington DC: 48; Wolfgang Kaehler/Corbis: 209; Wolfgang WeinHaupl/Westend61/Corbis: 147; WoodyStock/Alamy: 129.

Index

Numbers in *bold* refer to
illustrations

Phaidon Press Limited
Regent's Wharf
All Saints Street
London N1 9PA

Phaidon Press Inc.
180 Varick Street
New York, NY 10014

www.phaidon.com

ISBN 978 0 7148 5742 8

A CIP catalogue record of this book is available from the British Library.

Text typeset in Janson

Printed in Singapore

Cover illustration Gianlorenzo Bernini, *Apollo and Daphne*, 1622–5 (2)

Frontispiece illustration François de Cuvilliés, Circular Salon (Hall of Mirrors), 1734–49. Amalienburg Pavilion (165)

The author is grateful to many people and institutions for their time, conversation, and assistance during the writing of this book. As always, I acknowledge the companionship and enthusiasm of Peta Gillyatt Bailey, who travelled with me to so many of the places in this book, from Arequipa to Kiev, Macau to Seville. Space compels me to list the rest of these generous individuals in alphabetical order: David Anfam, Jens Baumgarten, Xavier Bray, Jill Burke, Frank Büttner, Maria Conelli, Joseph Connors, Pedro Dias, Pierre DuPrey, Martin Elbel, Marc Fumaroli, John Gash, Mina Grigori, Michael Hall, Peter Hawkins, Pamela Jones, Pavel Kalina, Ebba Koch, Lubomír Konečný, Blanka Kubíková, Ivana Kyzourová, Nigel Llewellyn, Julia MacKenzie, Martin Mádl, John O'Malley, S.J., Robert Maniura, Helen Miles, Jeffrey Muller, Tiffany Racco, Myriam Ribeiro, Mary Sheriff, Jeffrey Chipps Smith, Jan Stejskal, David Stone, Claudio Strinati, Alain Tapié, Marjorie Trusted, Nuno Vassallo e Silva, Vít Vlnas, James Welu, and Ines Zupanov. I also wish to acknowledge the contribution of my students in my 'Age of Bernini' seminar and biannual London/Paris fieldtrips at the University of Aberdeen, particularly Jayne Ford, Lauren Henning, Amy O'Sullivan, Dora Rozsahegyi, and Aaron Thom.

Research travel for this book was supported by the British Academy, the Carnegie Foundation for the Universities of Scotland, the University of Aberdeen, and the Arts and Humanities Research Council (UK).

This book is dedicated to the memory of Leslie William Poe (1962–2010).